SAVING PLACE
An Ecocomposition Reader

Sidney I. Dobrin
University of Florida, Gainesville

Boston   Burr Ridge, IL   Dubuque, IA   Madison, WI   New York
San Francisco   St. Louis   Bangkok   Bogotá   Caracas   Kuala Lumpur
Lisbon   London   Madrid   Mexico City   Milan   Montreal   New Delhi
Santiago   Seoul   Singapore   Sydney   Taipei   Toronto

This one's for Maryhelen and Hugh Harmon.

Mc Graw Hill **Higher Education**

SAVING PLACE: AN ECOCOMPOSITION READER

Published by McGraw-Hill, a business unit of The McGraw-Hill Companies, Inc. 1221 Avenue of the Americas, New York, NY, 10020. Copyright © 2005 by The McGraw-Hill Companies, Inc. All rights reserved. No part of this publication may be reproduced or distributed in any form or by any means, or stored in a database or retrieval system, without the prior written consent of The McGraw-Hill Companies, Inc., including, but not limited to, in any network or other electronic storage or transmission, or broadcast for distance learning.

Some ancillaries, including electronic and print components, may not be available to customers outside the United States.

♻ This book is printed on recycled acid-free paper.

2 3 4 5 6 7 8 9 0 DOC/DOC 0 9 8 7 6 5

0-7674-1324-5

Publisher: *Lisa Moore*
Senior Sponsoring Editor: *Alexis Walker*
Editorial Assistant: *Jesse Hassenger*
Marketing Manager: *Lori DeShazo*
Senior Media Technology Producer: *Todd Vaccaro*
Project Manager: *Roger Geissler*
Senior Production Supervisor: *Richard DeVitto*
Senior Designer: *Cassandra Chu*
Interior Designer: *Linda Robertson*
Cover Designer: *Yvo Riezebos*
Art Editor: *Robin Mouat*
Permissions Editor: *Marty Granahan*
Photo Research Coordinator: *Nora Agbayani*
Compositor: *Thompson Type*
Printer: *RR Donnelly/Crawfordsville*
Cover Image: © *Ian Cartright/Getty*

Library of Congress Cataloging-in-Publication Data

Dobrin, Sidney
    Saving Place: An Ecocomposition Reader
        p. cm.
    ISBN 0-7674-1324-5
    1. English Language—Rhetoric.   2. Environmental protection.   3.   Readers—
    Environmental protection.   4. Nature Problems, exercises, etc.   5. College readers.
    6. Readers—Nature.
    II. Title
PE 1408.D57   2005
808'.0427–dc21   200439787

Contents

Preface

Saving Place is designed with the composition classroom in mind and seeks to move beyond the ways in which nature writing, environmental writing, and ecological writings have been introduced into classrooms in the past The readings found in this collection range from canonized nature writing to new-media representations of nature and address not only traditional environmental writing, but issues of recreation (kayaking, surfing, bicycling, fishing, hiking, climbing, and so on), survival, consumption, and other topics of interest to college students.

Many writing instructors believe that some of the most important recent work in composition has been the endeavor to understand the links between writing and environment. For those of us engaged in what has become known as *ecocomposition,* what is most important is not merely asking students to write about issues of environment and ecology, but helping them to see that writing and environment are deeply enmeshed. *Saving Place* is a writing textbook that encourages students to explore the ways in which the activity of writing both interacts with environments, nature, and places, and is itself ecological.

Saving Place asks students (along with their teachers) to explore the ways in which writers influence the very survival of environments. At the same time, the book examines how writing and texts must develop functional relationships in order to survive in their own environments. That is, *Saving Place* examines how writing and texts rely on relationships with other texts in order for them to be understood and useful.

Matters of Pedagogy

There are four primary reasons that I wrote *Saving Place* specifically for composition classrooms:

1. The public spaces of composition classrooms provide students with the opportunities to read and write about the environmental issues that are crucial to them and to their communities. Composition classrooms can be the sites

in which students learn not just to think critically about environment and the texts that represent those environments, but specifically about how to produce those texts.

3. *Saving Place* encourages student writing to be much more dynamic in both form and content. Without neglecting traditional academic writing, Saving Place encourages students to think more broadly about the kinds of texts they interpret and produce not just for academic audiences, but for public audiences, as well.

4. By examining texts from a range of places, locations, sources, students using *Saving Place* can begin to understand the variety of opportunities they have for producing their own texts, for writing their own spaces.

Many composition programs and teachers now design first-year writing classes to match (or come close to matching) the goals established by the "Writing Program Administration's Outcome Statement for First-Year Writing." *Saving Place* is specifically designed with these goals in mind. *Saving Place* acknowledges that learning to write and to analyze texts is a complex process, involving both individual and social contexts. To this end, the text emphasizes **rhetorical understanding** of how texts are both produced and interpreted, examining issues of **purpose, audience, rhetorical situation, conventions** applicable to that situation, and the role of various **genres** in how we read and write texts. Likewise, *Saving Place* emphasizes **critical and analytical thinking** in students' writing and reading of environment, place, ecology–and, in turn, culture in general. It provides a wealth of opportunities for students to **evaluate, analyze,** and **synthesize** texts, incorporating their own ideas in order to better understand how language, knowledge, culture, power, text, and environment interact. *Saving Place* offers numerous analytical and writing prompts that ask students to engage in critical/analytical approaches to texts, issues, and places. These assignments also stress the processes through which students produce their own texts, including attention to the social/collaborative facets of writing.

KEY FEATURES

Wide range of selections addressing various environmental/ecological issues
56 selections invite students to engage a variety of kinds of texts–including essays, poetry, film, comics, and other visual texts–and address numerous subjects, including reading, writing, and defining nature; thinking ecologically, playing and relaxing in nature; consuming nature; surviving nature; living in/with nature; and our future with nature. These readings represent a range of writers, including many recognizable names (Ralph Waldo Emerson, William Cronon, Barry Lopez, Terry Tempest Williams, Joyce Carol Oates, Ursula Le Guin, bell hooks, Alice Walker, Aldo Leopold, and Wendell Berry, to name but only a few) as well as many less-anthologized writers.

Substantial pedagogical apparatus

Each chapter begins with a detailed introduction, providing background information—historical, political, and cultural—on the issue addressed in the chapter. Preceding each reading selection, students will find a journal assignment that asks them to reflect on their preconceptions about the issue addressed in the reading. Following the journal assignment, a headnote offers basic information about the reading selection and the writer, along with some rhetorical guidance on what students may want to note about the piece as they read it.

Following each reading selection, two sets of primary questions ask students to think about the ecological issues presented in the reading (*Focus on Ecology*) and about the author's rhetorical choices, and the rhetorical context for the piece (*Focus on Writing*). Detailed prompts for classroom discussions follow these two sets of questions, and, finally, in a series of prompts, students are asked to write about the issues addressed in the reading. These writing exercises ask for a variety of genres of writing: essays, letters, research papers, and op ed pieces, for example.

At the end of each chapter, students encounter broader topics for classroom discussion and writing prompts that ask students to consider the chapter's issues in terms of their *personal experience;* its importance in a *local (regional, communal, or home) context;* and, more formally, as a topic for *research.* Many of these writing prompts ask students to consider writing for more public audiences than other students and the teacher.

At the end of each chapter, I provide a list of URLs for web sites and ten to fifteen bibliographic sources for further reading that might assist students in their research.

PRINT AND ELECTRONIC SUPPLEMENTS

Website to accompany *Saving Place* at www. mhhe.com/savingplace

Offering abundant links relevant to chapters and individual reading selections, this site provides further apparatus for each chapter, including on-line resources for student projects and research papers. A chapter not found in the print text devoted to visual representations of nature is also available on the web page.

Resources for teaching *Saving Place*

This substantial instructor's resource manual, available online, provides further background information about the reading selections, sample answers to the questions, sample syllabi for both 10- and 16- week courses, and additional activities/considerations.

Teaching Composition Faculty Listserve at www.mhhe.com/tcomp

Moderated by Chris Anson at North Carolina State University and offered by McGraw-Hill as a service to the composition community, this listserv brings together senior members of the college composition community with newer members–junior faculty, adjuncts, and teaching assistants–through an online newsletter and accompanying discussion group to address issues of pedagogy, both in theory and practice.

PageOut

McGraw-Hill's own PageOut service is available to help you get your course up and running online in a matter of hours–at no cost. Additional information about the service is available at **http://www.pageout.net.**

ACKNOWLEDGMENTS

I first had the idea for *Saving Place* in 1998; it was the first time I considered writing a textbook. At that time, Nancy Perry of Bedford/St.Martin's spent a good deal of time talking with me about the book and about how textbooks are made, particularly books that address environmental issues. I am deeply grateful for all that she and others at Bedford/St. Martin's did to encourage me with this project and for what they taught me about thinking about textbooks. Later that same year, I met Renée Deljon, then editor at Mayfield Publishing, who saw *Saving Place* for what it could be: a new approach to integrating writing instruction with environmental concern, a book that would be timely as the four or five other mainstream environmental readers began to age. For close to four years she and I wrote and re-wrote *Saving Place.* Each time she saw my latest version, she had new ideas about how to expand the book's range and agenda. I can never articulate fully enough my appreciation for what she has taught me, for what she has encouraged me to do, and for her friendship. So, while this book is dedicated to my dear friends Hugh and Maryhelen Harmon and appears under my name, it is also Renée's book.

Likewise, in the years that it took to build this book, I have had numerous conversations with friends and colleagues whose insight and work have been crucial in the development of *Saving Place.* I am indebted to Anis Bawarshi for his time in reading and commenting on drafts; to Chris Keller for his endless involvement with this project and his willingness to point out that it is just as important to watch NCAA basketball and to drink beer as it is to write textbooks (be sure to check out Chris' Instructor's Manual to *Saving Place*); to Trish Ventura and Dean Swinford for their research assistance; to Carla Blount for her never ending support and her ability to be sure I have time to write; to Kenneth Kidd for his friendship, collaboration, and advice about readings in children's literature; and to the Idyots for their never-ending encouragement and assistants: Raul Sanchez, Joe Hardin, Julie Drew, Todd Taylor, and Steve Brown.

I am also deeply grateful for the ongoing collaboration I have with Christian Weisser. There is little question, as I explain in the Introduction to *Saving Place*, that Christian's work with me in writing *Natural Discourse: Toward Ecocompsoition* and in editing *Ecocomposition: Theoretical and Pedagogical Approaches* was the primary scholarly influence in writing this textbook.

I would like to acknowledge the Department of English at the University of Florida for its support of my research and writing endeavors.

Thanks to Sheryl St. Germain, Steven Curry, Joe Balaz, and Steve Greenberg for providing me with hard-to-find biographical information.

Of course, it would be impossible for me to write books like *Saving Place* without the support of my wife, my best friend, and my adventure partner, Teresa. For her support, for her, I am deeply grateful.

I am also indebted to the reviewers who made suggestions for revisions during the many drafting stages:

Kaye Adkins, Missouri Western State College
Shawn Fullmer, Fort Lewis College
Thomas A. Goodman, University of Miami
Ginger Hurajt, Northern Essex Community College
Mary Elizabeth Lang, Southern Connecticut State University
Charles Nicol, Indiana State University
Christina Salvin, Gavilan College

Finally, I would like to thank the folks at McGraw-Hill for their support, effort, and dedication. At McGraw-Hill, I have enjoyed and appreciated the expert contributions of Lisa Moore, Publisher; Alexis Walker, Senior Sponsoring Editor; Jesse Hassenger, Editorial Assistant; and Roger Geissler, Project Manager.

Introduction

PART I

This book is about writing. More specifically, it is about the ways in which the activity of producing writing both interacts with environments, nature, and places and is itself ecological. In fact, this book borrows methodologies from the ecological sciences for better understanding how we produce writing and how that writing, in turn, affects and is affected by environments. *Saving Place,* then, is based in an area of study known as *ecocomposition*—simply, the ecological study of writing.

The science of ecology is a science of relationships. The German biologist and philosopher Ernst Haeckel first defined "oecologie" in 1866 as "the total relations of the animal both to its organic and to its inorganic environment" and as "the study of all the complex interrelationships referred to by Darwin as the conditions of the struggle for existence." It is this concept of relationships and survival that drives this book. Throughout *Saving Place* we will explore the ways in which writers influence the very survival of environments through their production of writing. At the same time, we will examine how writing and texts must develop functional relationships to survive in their own environments. That is, we explore how writing and texts rely on relationships with other texts for them to be understood and useful.

Ultimately, then, *Saving Place* will ask you to participate in two intellectual inquiries. First, we will think and write about the environments and places we live in and engage with. Second, we will look closely at the role writing plays in how we perceive places, at how places affect our writing, and at how our writing affects those places.

QUESTIONS

Our primary means for pursuing both lines of inquiry will be through reading the writers' writing and examining and responding to it in discussion and writing. We will do this by asking some rather large questions:

- How as readers and writers do we come to define what we mean by "nature," "environment," and "place"?

- What does it mean to think ecologically?

We will ask more specific questions:

- How do we engage and think about nature, environment, and places through recreation?

- How do we consume nature, environment, and place, both as resource and as food?

- How do scenarios of survival force us to contend with environments, places, or nature, and why are stories of survival so popular?

- How do we live in relationship to nature or particular environments or places, whether they are urban, rural, or natural?

- How are our relationships with nature, environments, and places reinforced and represented through religious beliefs?

- How are nature, environments, and places represented to children who are at a point in their lives when they develop most of their lifelong attitudes toward people, phenomena, and places?

- And finally, how have we begun to reconcile all of these relationships?

All of these issues will be examined ecologically; that is to say, all of these topics and the issues they raise will be examined as they relate not only to one another but to your own life and to the lives of others.

DEFINITIONS

One of the things you may have noticed about the list above is the recurring use of three words: *nature, environment,* and *place*. One of the goals of *Saving Place* is that we begin thinking about how we understand these words, these concepts. Each of these three words is difficult to define because each one carries different meanings for different people, different cultures, different contexts. As writer David Quammen has explained, "*Nature* is a dauntingly difficult word to define." One of the agendas of *Saving Place* is to encourage you to think about exactly *why* these words are so difficult to define and to consider the importance of how we define them. Likewise, *Saving Place* will ask you to consider the meanings—literal, ideological, historical, contextual—of several other related terms throughout the readings, words like *environmentalism, conservation, preservation,* and *activism*. Our definitions of these words directly affect our relationships with nature, environment, and place, and all of our understanding of nature, environment, and place.

Writing, since humans began it, has been used to express relationships with nature, with environments, with places, with other organisms. Migratory routes of prey species, for instance, were tracked and their appearances were recorded. Methods for hunting were painted on cave walls. Seasonal agricultural growing cycles were carved into stone. The earliest forms of writing—Anasazi cave paintings, for instance, or Egyptian hieroglyphs—all depict relationships between humans and nature, between humans and their environments. In fact, one may go so far as to suggest that written language evolved as a necessary means for communicating our relationships to one another and with our environment.

In time, our languages—particularly our written languages—became the very vehicles through which we created our relationships with nature. Native American cultures, for instance, did not distinguish between civilization and nature; they were all one and the same. Other cultures named places *mountains, deserts, valleys, towns, farms* to mark their differences. Some human cultures began to make distinctions between "nature" and "man-made," paved and unpaved, wild and civilized. Colonizers of the New World sought to tame wild places and animals and peoples. Landscapes were modified, and human populations grew to overtake most natural places. Now we label some environments *habitats, parks, preserves*. We establish boundaries between ourselves and wild environments. And, until recently, we believed that we could exist separately from those places, that we could fence off the world and keep nature away from us.

However, we have had to relearn what early humans knew and lived: humans are part of all natural systems. Our actions affect everything on this planet, and many of our actions are manifest in the production of writing.

Saving Place is not necessarily an "environmentalist" book in that it does not ask that you consider protecting natural places because natural places are somehow inherently good. *Saving Place* is an ecological book. It asks that you consider the relationships you have to places—individually, as a member of the human species, and as an organism living in a biosphere. *Saving Place* asks that you consider these relationships in order that human consumption does not destroy those very places on which we depend for survival.

ECOCOMPOSITION

As I mentioned earlier, ecocomposition combines the study of writing—composition—with the study of relationships between organisms and their environments—ecology. For many, this is an important area of inquiry as it recognizes the crucial role we as humans play in our world, and it recognizes the crucial role writing and the production of texts play in this same world. In other words, ecocompositionists acknowledge that humans do not exist outside of natural environments but instead are living organisms that have an important relationship with those environments. One of the first formal definitions of *ecocomposition* appeared in a book called *Natural Discourse: Toward Ecocomposition,* which I co-wrote with my friend and colleague Christian Weisser who at the time was a professor at the University of Hawaii, Hilo. I offer it here both to explain what I mean by *ecocomposition* and to offer a foundation from which *Saving Place* developed. Much of my own thinking about ecocomposition grows from this definition, and, in turn, affects what is presented in this book, both the readings and the attached apparatus:

> *Ecocomposition is the study of the relationships between environments (and by that we mean natural, constructed, and even imagined places) and discourse (speaking, writing, and thinking). Ecocomposition draws primarily from disciplines that study discourse (chiefly composition, but also including literary studies, communication, cultural studies, linguistics, and philosophy) and merges the perspectives of them with work in disciplines that examine environment (these include ecology, environmental studies, sociobiology, and other "hard" sciences). As a result, ecocomposition attempts to provide a more holistic, encompassing framework for studies of the relationship between discourse and environment.*

What makes this definition so exciting is that it opens the doors to all sorts of possibilities in studying ecocomposition. For our purposes, though, *Saving Place* focuses on two primary branches of ecocomposition: ecological literacy and discursive ecology.

Ecological Literacy

Simply put, the term *ecological literacy* refers to a conscious awareness and understanding of the relationships between people, other organisms, and the environments in which they live. The term is most frequently associated with the work of David Orr and his book *Ecological Literacy: Education and the Transition to a Postmodern World.* In this book, Orr claims that "all education is environmental education," but that most education now presents environment and nature as resources for people, as products for consumers, as things we as humans act upon rather than within. Orr says that if we talk about and teach ecology in schools, colleges, and universities in all subject areas, we might be able to change the ways we think about environment. According to Orr, ecological literacy requires three things: first, "a broad understanding of how people and societies relate to each other and to natural systems"; second, an understanding of the importance of and the speed of the environmental crisis that we face; and finally, an attentiveness to how an ecological consciousness might develop.

One of the agendas of *Saving Place* is to encourage your development in terms of ecological literacy to better understand your effect on the world and its effect on you. To do so, *Saving Place* looks specifically at how the production of writing contributes to ecological literacy. In fact, the second chapter of *Saving Place* is specifically about how we can develop our own ecological literacies.

Discursive Ecology

Earlier I said that the definition of *ecocomposition* that Christian Weisser and I developed in our book *Natural Discourse: Toward Ecocomposition* affected how I edited this book. In fact, this book is affected by all of the books I have ever read or written in some way or another, just as how you read this book is affected by other texts that you have read. (This book will also affect how you read other books.) This is an example of discursive ecology: the idea that all writing, all language, all discourse is bound together in a web. Ecologist Barry Commoner says, "Everything is connected to everything else." I believe this holds true particularly for writing. Our writing is connected to everything, and throughout this book, we will explore the possible ramifications of a discursive ecology and an ecology of writing.

You may also have noticed that I have used the plural pronoun "we" when referring to what work will be done through this book. This plural pronoun suggests that I am part of the exploration you are about to undertake and that you and I will be working together. Certainly, by the time you read this book I will have finished writing it, and it is very possible you and I will never meet in person. Yet, through writing and editing this book that you and your classmates will read, discuss, and respond to in writing, we have entered into a discursive relationship. Together, then, we will create new relationships through writing.

PART 2—CHAPTER APPARATUS

To examine the ways writing affects and is affected by environment, place, and nature, *Saving Place* offers an array of writing selections and other representations of nature, place, and environment organized into seven chapters. Each of these chapters also contains a number of different kinds of questions designed to encourage you to think about, discuss, and write about the issues addressed in the writing selections. *Saving Place*, unlike many of the textbooks with which you are likely familiar, does not ask you to produce only traditional academic essays in response. Because writing in many forms and genres affects our environments and because as writers we need to think about how different kinds of writing are produced, *Saving Place*'s writing prompts offer opportunities for a number of kinds of writing assignments, including journals, annotated lists, critical reviews, summaries, brochures, pamphlets, and letters. A full description of all the apparatus supporting the reading selections follows.

Introduction

Each chapter begins with a detailed introduction to the issues addressed in that particular chapter. These introductions introduce the readings contained in each chapter, not individually, but as the ways an array of writers approach the particular issues and subjects presented in each chapter. The introduction to each chapter provides background information, historical information, and political information about the issue addressed in the chapter. In other words, the introductions set the stage for the writing we will explore and the questions I will ask you to consider in each chapter.

Journal Assignments

Often, keeping a journal can be a great way of sorting out how we think about particular issues. For many of the subjects we will consider in the pages of *Saving Place*, you may already have opinions regarding the subject. Before you read each of the pieces of writing in each chapter, I'll ask you to consider what the writer addresses, and I'll ask you to examine in writing your preconceptions, prejudices, and assumptions about that subject. Once you have read the text, you may feel differently about the subject, or the piece may strengthen your opinion. Keeping a journal will help you make sense of your own thinking about things.

Head Notes

Prior to each reading selection, I provide a short head note with basic information about the reading selection and the writer. These head notes also offer some guidance as to what you may want to note about the piece as you read it.

Reading Selections

Each chapter contains numerous pieces of writing dealing with the subject of that chapter. Many of these selections are written by well-known writers, but many others are by writers you may not recognize or be familiar with. In many ways, much of the writing found here falls into the genre of "Nature Writing," which generally refers to a kind of writing that is produced specifically to raise awareness about nature, places, environments. The authors of these pieces have chosen the production of writing and text as their means for publicly discussing issues of place, nature, and environment, and what they write will ultimately affect how we think about such issues.

I should also note that for the most part, the writing selections gathered here address the ideas of nature, place, environment, ecology, environmentalism, conservation, sustainability, and so on primarily from a North American (U.S.) perspective. Other cultures represent and approach nature differently, and their writings and thoughts are also crucial to our ways of thinking about these issues. However, because *Saving Place* is intended to reach an audience of college students in North America, and because *Saving Place* has been written in English for a predominantly English-speaking audience, I have selected writings that most directly connect to North American cultural mythologies and understandings about natures, places, environments. I do not mean to dismiss other views in this book by not including them, and I hope you won't discount them either simply because they are not here.

It is also important to note that many of the selections found in *Saving Place* are not what we might refer to traditionally as "writing." In addition to essays, stories, poems, and articles, *Saving Place* also contains other kinds of texts: comics, pictures, advertisements, films, television programs, and web sites. My hope in including these other texts is that we start to see that all kinds of texts require "writing," require production, and that all these kinds of written texts affect and are affected by environments, by places, by ecologies. "Writing," then, should be understood as something more than the action of a single writer putting words on paper. Writing includes many forms and genres; it includes more than just words. Writing communicates through images, through language, through places. All forms of "writing" play a role in how we interact with our environments, and we must consider the role writing plays in those very relationships.

Preliminary Questions

Following each piece of writing you will find two sets of primary questions that ask you to think specifically about ecological literacy and discursive ecology issues pertaining to the piece of writing.

Focus on Ecology

The first set of preliminary questions ask you to think about ecological issues, about controversy, about preservation, about the role the piece has in how we think about what it represents. Ultimately, these questions ask you to consider what the writer is saying about the issue at hand and what you think about the issues at hand, both in terms of your own thinking and your response to the writer.

Focus on Writing

The second set of preliminary questions asks you about the discursive ecology of the reading selection. That is, these questions ask about the writing as writing—about rhetorical choices and about where the reading fits in larger conversations.

Discussion Questions

Like writing in journals, talking with others about issues can often help us to clarify our own thoughts, in addition to helping us learn how others think about subjects and helping us learn more about a subject. After each writing selection, I will ask you to consider an issue addressed by the writer through a discussion with your classmates.

Writing in Response

Following each selection, I'll provide a prompt or question that will ask you to consider the selection and to respond in writing to it. These writing exercises will ask for a variety of genres: essays, letters, research papers, and op ed pieces, for example. But all will ask you to think about and write about ecological issues.

Discussing the Issues

Once you have considered all of the selections provided in each chapter, I offer two suggestions for discussion regarding the subject of the entire chapter.

Writing About the Issues

In addition, at the end of each chapter you will find three writing prompts that ask you to write about the chapter's issues. These writing prompts require different kinds of responses: the first asks you to take into account your *personal experiences,* to write about how you feel about the subject, and to think about your relationship with the issue. The second question asks you to explore how the issue discussed in the chapter is addressed in your region, your community, your home. That is, the first writing prompt asks you to consider the issue in terms of *local context.* The third prompt asks you to do some *research,* to learn more about the subject at hand, and to write a more formal academic research paper about the subject.

Many of these writing prompts will also ask you to consider writing for a more public audience than just your classmates and teacher. Public writing is crucial when it comes to issues regarding environments and places, as writing about these issues needs to enter into public relationships to affect those very places and environments.

Research Links

At the end of each chapter I provide a list of URLs for web sites that might help you in your research and in your further exploration of the subject addressed in that chapter.

Further Readings

In addition to the *Research Links,* I also provide 10 to 15 bibliographic sources for further research and reading about the subject addressed in the chapter.

THE *SAVING PLACE* COMPANION WEB SITE

When I first designed *Saving Place,* it contained more than 180 reading selections as opposed to the more manageable 60 or so in the version you now hold. Thankfully, the editors at McGraw-Hill pointed out the difficulty in publishing a book that large, both in terms of what it would cost students and in terms of what the book would weigh—not to mention the number of trees we'd have to use to make the paper. Yet, the editors and I agreed that the material that was to be removed from the earlier version was still important in the overall agenda of *Saving Place.* Hence, we decided to make as much of this material as possible available to you and your teachers through the *Saving Place* companion web site which can be found at **www.mhhe.com/savingplace.**

The web site is organized just like the print book you hold now, divided into seven chapters, each one paralleling a chapter from the print book. Each companion chapter references several more possible readings and provides ways for you to continue your work in that particular chapter. Detailed bibliographic citations are provided, making it easy to locate these readings. In many instances, too, links are offered to take you directly to online versions of the texts or other web sites that address the text. Following the introduction to each chapter you'll find a quick reminder to check out the materials for that chapter on the *Saving Place* companion web site.

In addition, the companion web site also provides the outline of an additional chapter not found in the text version. This chapter explores the ways nature is represented visually, in print advertisements, television shows, comics, films, online images, sculpture, painting, and photography. I urge you—either with your class or individually—to spend some time thinking about how visual representations of nature, place, and environment affect our understandings of those ideas.

PART 3—GETTING STARTED

At the beginning of this introduction, I made the simple statement, "This book is about writing." This simple statement of purpose opens many doors to not-so-simple concepts, to exciting avenues of thinking, to intriguing areas of research. *Saving Place,* then, is not a simple book. It asks you to think about complex issues, to reconsider your own preconceptions and thinking. It asks you to consider the ways you live your everyday lives and the ways writing affects those lives. Ultimately, to say "this book is about writing" is to say a great deal. I hope that as we explore together the texts gathered here and your own writing, we will help establish relationships that will better protect our world and help us in the task of saving places.

Praise for *Saving Place*

"I think the possibilities presented by *Saving Place* outrun anything currently in print." Thomas A. Goodmann, University of Miami

"*Saving Place* is an excellent reader for composition classes focused on ecology, the environment, and nature. Its strengths include an emphasis on our relationship to the world, the idea that the environment is socially constructed through written and visual texts, and the tenet that we have an ethical obligation to protect where we live." Shawn Fulmer, Fort Lewis College

"What sets *Saving Place* apart from other readers is the apparatus. This collection is not just a group of essays loosely related by theme. There is a coherent vision at work in this text, and the introductory materials and assignments reinforce that vision." Kaye Adkins, Missouri Western State College

"The main strengths of the book are the *variety* of approaches to the topic of nature and the environment that are offered, and the journal topics preceding each piece (if this would convince me to have students write journals for the class, it has to be good!)." Ginger Hurajt, Northern Essex Community College

"Its sustained focus is its greatest strength. I would also recommend it for the strength of the prereading and postreading activities." Mary Elizabeth Lang, Southern Connecticut State University

CHAPTER 1

Reading, Writing, and Defining Nature

As I mentioned in the Introduction to *Saving Place*, part of the agenda of this book is to encourage you to think about how we define problematic concepts like *nature, place,* and *environment,* and to consider how the very contexts in which these terms are used affect those definitions. Throughout this chapter we will examine not only why words like *nature, environment,* and *place* are so difficult to define, but how different writers define these terms. Likewise, we will consider how your writing and reading both reflect your definitions of these terms and help you to establish more encompassing definitions.

Many writers, like Lame Deer (whose writing appears in Chapter 4), William Cronon, Ted Kerasote, and Louis Owens (all of whom have selections in this chapter), have asserted that before white settlers came to the new world, native populations did not make distinctions between what was nature and what was civilization. That is, many cultures identified themselves as part of their environments—not as residents *within* places and environments, separated from those places, but as unified with them. European colonists held a different image of their position in the world: that of a culture separate from nature, and often pitted against nature. In fact, as many of you know, one of the common themes of American literature is often described as "Man versus Nature." That is to say, American writers have traditionally situated nature as a force opposi-tional to humans. Places had to be conquered, tamed, and domesticated before they could be inhabited.

This chapter asks you to think about this traditional western view as well as other views that might be less familiar to us. It asks you to consider how tra-ditional definitions of *nature, place,* and *environment* have affected how we un-derstand and behave toward places, environments, and nature. This chapter does not try to establish any particular definition for these terms; the readings are designed to encourage you to think about how American culture has de-fined these terms and how you personally have understood these terms, while pushing you to see the difficulties that arise in creating rigid definitions. To do so, the readings in this chapter ask you to consider a range of ideas, including

- the relationship between language and nature
- the problematic definitions of *wilderness*
- the ways in which we identify nature as occupying certain places and not others
- the politics of where wilderness can be
- the role places play in how we tell stories
- the differences between what we mean when we say "nature" and when we say "wild"
- the relationship between how we view nature and how we understand the erotic
- the ways in which we exert dominance over places by naming them
- the ways Native Americans view wilderness, nature, and place
- the ways in which women have been situated in relationship to wilderness

"Nature" and "Language" From "Nature"

Ralph Waldo Emerson

Ralph Waldo Emerson is one of the most influential writers in American literary history. Born in Boston in 1803, Emerson graduated from Harvard in 1821. He was ordained as a minister of the Unitarian church in Boston in 1829, but due to his questions and mistrust of the ways Christian learning was incorporated in the Unitarian church, he left the ministry after three years. For Emerson, "to be a good minister it was necessary to leave the ministry." Emerson eventually moved to Concord, Massachusetts, where he came to know Henry David Thoreau, Nathaniel Hawthorne, and other writers and thinkers, all of whom considered themselves transcendentalists. Emerson became the chief spokesperson for American transcendentalism. For Emerson, nature was an image through which humans could glimpse the divine, could transcend the existence of human beings. In the portions of the essay "Nature" that follow,

Emerson examines both the idea of "nature" and the role language plays in understanding nature. As you read these pieces, consider in what ways Emerson's ideas are or are not still prevalent in contemporary thinking about nature.

JOURNAL ASSIGNMENT

Much of this chapter is devoted to examining how we define *nature*. It asks you to consider where nature is and where it is not. We will begin by reading selections from Ralph Waldo Emerson's essay "Nature." In the first part of this essay, also called "Nature," Emerson explains that "Nature never wears a mean appearance. Neither does the wisest man extort her secret, and lose his curiosity by finding out all her perfection. Nature never became a toy to a wise spirit." This is part of Emerson's definition. How do you define *nature*? In your journal begin to work out your definition of nature. Is nature tangible? Is it controllable? Is it identifiable?

> *A subtle chain of countless rings*
> *The next unto the farthest brings;*
> *The eye reads omens where it goes,*
> *And speaks all languages the rose;*
> *And, striving to be man, the worm*
> *Mounts through all the spires of form.*

I

NATURE

To go into solitude, a man needs to retire as much from his chamber as from society. I am not solitary whilst I read and write, though nobody is with me. But if a man would be alone, let him look at the stars. The rays that come from those heavenly worlds will separate between him and what he touches. One might think the atmosphere was made transparent with this design, to give man, in the heavenly bodies, the perpetual presence of the sublime. Seen in the streets of cities, how great they are! If the stars should appear one night in a thousand years, how would men believe and adore; and preserve for many generations the remembrance of the city of God which had been shown! But every night come out these envoys of beauty, and light the universe with their admonishing smile.

The stars awaken a certain reverence, because though always present, they are inaccessible; but all natural objects make a kindred impression, when the mind is open to their influence. Nature never wears a mean appearance. Neither does the wisest man extort her secret, and lose his curiosity by finding out all her perfection. Nature never became a toy to a wise spirit. The flowers, the animals, the mountains, reflected the wisdom of his best hour, as much as they had delighted the simplicity of his childhood.

3   When we speak of nature in this manner, we have a distinct but most poetical sense in the mind. We mean the integrity of impression made by manifold natural objects. It is this which distinguishes the stick of timber of the woodcutter from the tree of the poet. The charming landscape which I saw this morning is indubitably made up of some twenty or thirty farms. Miller owns this field, Locke that, and Manning the woodland beyond. But none of them owns the landscape. There is a property in the horizon which no man has but he whose eye can integrate all the parts, that is, the poet. This is the best part of these men's farms, yet to this their warranty-deeds give no title.

4   To speak truly, few adult persons can see nature. Most persons do not see the sun. At least they have a very superficial seeing. The sun illuminates only the eye of the man, but shines into the eye and the heart of the child. The lover of nature is he whose inward and outward senses are still truly adjusted to each other; who has retained the spirit of infancy even into the era of manhood. His intercourse with heaven and earth becomes part of his daily food. In the presence of nature a wild delight runs through the man, in spite of real sorrows. Nature says—he is my creature, and maugre all his impertinent griefs, he shall be glad with me. Not the sun or the summer alone, but every hour and season yields its tribute of delight; for every hour and change corresponds to and authorizes a different state of the mind, from breathless noon to grimmest midnight. Nature is a setting that fits equally well a comic or a mourning piece. In good health, the air is a cordial of incredible virtue. Crossing a bare common, in snow puddles, at twilight, under a clouded sky, without having in my thoughts any occurrence of special good fortune. I have enjoyed a perfect exhilaration. I am glad to the brink of fear. In the woods, too, a man casts off his years, as the snakes his slough, and at what period soever of life is always a child. In the woods is perpetual youth. Within these plantations of God, a decorum and sanctity reign, a perennial festival is dressed, and the guest sees not how he should tire of them in a thousand years. In the woods, we return to reason and faith. There I feel that nothing can befall me in life—no disgrace, no calamity (leaving me my eyes), which nature cannot repair. Standing on the bare ground—my head bathed by the blithe air and uplifted into infinite space—all mean egotism vanishes. I become a transparent eyeball; I am nothing; I see all; the currents of the Universal Being circulate through me; I am part or parcel of God. The name of the nearest friend sounds then foreign and accidental: to be brothers, to be acquaintances, master or servant, is then a trifle and a disturbance. I am the lover of uncontained and immortal beauty. In the wilderness, I find something more dear and connate than in streets or villages. In the tranquil landscape, and especially in the distant line of the horizon, man beholds somewhat as beautiful as his own nature.

5   The greatest delight which the fields and woods minister is the suggestion of an occult relation between man and the vegetable. I am not alone and unac-

knowledged. They nod to me, and I to them. The waving of the boughs in the storm is new to me and old. It takes me by surprise, and yet is not unknown. Its effect is like that of a higher thought or a better emotion coming over me, when I deemed I was thinking justly or doing right.

Yet it is certain that the power to produce this delight does not reside in nature, but in man, or in a harmony of both. It is necessary to use these pleasures with great temperance. For nature is not always tricked in holiday attire, but the same scene which yesterday breathed perfume and glittered as for the frolic of the nymphs is overspread with melancholy to-day. Nature always wears the colors of the spirit. To a man laboring under calamity, the heat of his own fire hath sadness in it. Then there is a kind of contempt of the landscape felt by him who has just lost by death a dear friend. The sky is less grand as it shuts down over less worth in the population.

IV

LANGUAGE

LANGUAGE is a third use which Nature subserves to man. Nature is the vehicle of thought, and in a simple, double, and three-fold degree.
1. Words are signs of natural facts.
2. Particular natural facts are symbols of particular spiritual facts.
3. Nature is the symbol of spirit.

1.   Words are signs of natural facts. The use of natural history is to give us aid in supernatural history; the use of the outer creation, to give us language for the beings and changes of the inward creation. Every word which is used to express a moral or intellectual fact, if traced to its root, is found to be borrowed from some material appearance. *Right* means *straight; wrong* means *twisted; Spirit* primarily means *wind; transgression,* the crossing of a *line; supercilious,* the *raising of the eyebrow.* We say the *heart* to express emotion, the *head* to denote thought; and *thought* and *emotion* are words borrowed from sensible things, and now appropriated to spiritual nature. Most of the process by which this transformation is made, is hidden from us in the remote time when language was framed; but the same tendency may be daily observed in children. Children and savages use only nouns or names of things, which they convert into verbs, and apply to analogous mental acts.

2.   But this origin of all words that convey a spiritual import—so conspicuous a fact in the history of language—is our least debt to nature. It is not words only that are emblematic; it is things which are emblematic. Every natural fact is a symbol of some spiritual fact. Every appearance in nature corresponds to some state of the mind, and that state of the mind can only be described by presenting that natural appearance as its picture. An enraged man is a lion, a cunning man is a fox, a firm man is a rock, a learned man is a torch. A lamb is innocence; a snake is subtle spite; flowers express to us the delicate affections. Light and darkness are our familiar expression for knowledge and

ignorance; and heat for love. Visible distance behind and before us, is respectively our image of memory and hope.

10   Who looks upon a river in a meditative hour and is not reminded of the flux of all things? Throw a stone into the stream, and the circles that propagate themselves are the beautiful type of all influence. Man is conscious of a universal soul within or behind his individual life, wherein, as in a firmament, the natures of Justice, Truth, Love, Freedom, arise and shine. This universal soul he calls Reason: it is not mine, or thine, or his, but we are its; we are its property and men. And the blue sky in which the private earth is buried, the sky with its eternal calm, and full of everlasting orbs, is the type of Reason. That which intellectually considered we call Reason, considered in relation to nature, we call Spirit. Spirit is the creator. Spirit hath life in itself. And man in all ages and countries embodies it in his language as the FATHER.

11   It is easily seen that there is nothing lucky or capricious in these analogies but that they are constant, and pervade nature. These are not the dreams of a few poets, here and there, but man is an analogist, and studies relations in all objects. He is placed in the centre of beings, and a ray of relation passes from every other being to him. And neither can man be understood without these objects, nor these objects without man. All the facts in natural history taken by themselves, have no value, but are barren, like a single sex. But marry it to human history, and it is full of life. Whole floras, all Linnæus' and Buffon's volumes, are dry catalogues of facts; but the most trivial of these facts, the habit of a plant, the organs, or work, or noise of an insect, applied to the illustration of a fact in intellectual philosophy, or in any way associated to human nature, affects us in the most lively and agreeable manner. The seed of a plant—to what affecting analogies in the nature of man is that little fruit made use of, in all discourse, up to the voice of Paul, who calls the human corpse a seed—"It is sown a natural body; it is raised a spiritual body." The motion of the earth round its axis and round the sun, makes the day and the year. These are certain amounts of brute light and heat. But is there no intent of an analogy between man's life and the seasons? And do the seasons gain no grandeur or pathos from that analogy? The instincts of the ant are very unimportant considered as the ant's; but the moment a ray of relation is seen to extend from it to man, and the little drudge is seen to be a monitor, a little body with a mighty heart, then all its habits, even that said to be recently observed, that it never sleeps, become sublime.

12   Because of this radical correspondence between visible things and human thoughts, savages, who have only what is necessary, converse in figures. As we go back in history, language becomes more picturesque, until its infancy, when it is all poetry; or all spiritual facts are represented by natural symbols. The same symbols are found to make the original elements of all languages. It has moreover been observed, that the idioms of all languages approach each other in passages of the greatest eloquence and power. And as this is the first language, so it is the last. This immediate dependence of language upon nature, this conver-

sion of an outward phenomenon into a type of somewhat in human life, never loses its power to affect us. It is this which gives that piquancy to the conversation of a strong-natured farmer or backwoodsman, which all men relish.

A man's power to connect his thought with its proper symbol, and so to utter it, depends on the simplicity of his character, that is, upon his love of truth and his desire to communicate it without loss. The corruption of man is followed by the corruption of language. When simplicity of character and the sovereignty of ideas is broken up by the prevalence of secondary desires—the desire of riches, of pleasure, of power, and of praise—and duplicity and falsehood take place of simplicity and truth, the power over nature as an interpreter of the will is in a degree lost; new imagery ceases to be created, and old words are perverted to stand for things which are not; a paper currency is employed, when there is no bullion in the vaults. In due time the fraud is manifest, and words lose all power to stimulate the understanding or the affections. Hundreds of writers may be found in every long-civilized nation who for a short time believe and make others believe that they see and utter truths, who do not of themselves clothe one thought in its natural garment, but who feed unconsciously on the language created by the primary writers of the country, those, namely, who hold primarily on nature.

But wise men pierce this rotten diction and fasten words again to visible things; so that picturesque language is at once a commanding certificate that he who employs it is a man in alliance with truth and God. The moment our discourse rises above the ground line of familiar facts and is inflamed with passion or exalted by thought, it clothes itself in images. A man conversing in earnest, if he watch his intellectual processes, will find that a material image more or less luminous arises in his mind, contemporaneous with every thought which furnishes the vestment of the thought. Hence, good writing and brilliant discourse are perpetual allegories. This imagery is spontaneous. It is the blending of experience with the present action of the mind. It is proper creation. It is the working of the Original Cause through the instruments he has already made.

These facts may suggest the advantage which the country-life possesses for a powerful mind, over the artificial and curtailed life of cities. We know more from nature than we can at will communicate. Its light flows into the mind evermore, and we forget its presence. The poet, the orator, bred in the woods, whose senses have been nourished by their fair and appeasing changes, year after year, without design and without heed—shall not lose their lesson altogether, in the roar of cities or the broil of politics. Long hereafter, amidst agitation and terror in national councils—in the hour of revolution—these solemn images shall reappear in their morning lustre, as fit symbols and words of the thoughts which the passing events shall awaken. At the call of a noble sentiment, again the woods wave, the pines murmur, the river rolls and shines, and the cattle low upon the mountains, as he saw and heard them in his infancy. And with these forms, the spells of persuasion, the keys of power are put into his hands.

16   3.   We are thus assisted by natural objects in the expression of particular meanings. But how great a language to convey such pepper-corn informations! Did it need such noble races of creatures, this profusion of forms, this host of orbs in heaven, to furnish man with the dictionary and grammar of his municipal speech? Whilst we use this grand cipher to expedite the affairs of our pot and kettle, we feel that we have not yet put it to its use, neither are able. We are like travellers using the cinders of a volcano to roast their eggs. Whilst we see that it always stands ready to clothe what we would say, we cannot avoid the question whether the characters are not significant of themselves. Have mountains, and waves, and skies, no significance by what we consciously give them when we employ them as emblems of our thoughts? The world is emblematic. Parts of speech are metaphors, because the whole of nature is a metaphor of the human mind. The laws of moral nature answer to those of matter as face to face in a glass. "The visible world and the relation of its parts, is the dial plate of the invisible." The axioms of physics translate the laws of ethics. Thus, "the whole is greater than its part;" "reaction is equal to action;" "the smallest weight may be made to lift the greatest, the difference of weight being compensated by time;" and many the like propositions, which have an ethical as well as physical sense. These propositions have a much more extensive and universal sense when applied to human life than when confined to technical use.

17   In like manner, the memorable words of history and the proverbs of nations consist usually of a natural fact, selected as a picture or parable of a moral truth. Thus: A rolling stone gathers no moss; A bird in the hand is worth two in the bush; A cripple in the right way will beat a racer in the wrong; Make hay while the sun shines; 'T is hard to carry a full cup even; Vinegar is the son of wine; The last ounce broke the camel's back; Long-lived trees make roots first— and the like. In their primary sense these are trivial facts, but we repeat them for the value of their analogical import. What is true of proverbs, is true of all fables, parables, and allegories.

18   This relation between the mind and matter is not fancied by some poet, but stands in the will of God, and so is free to be known by all men. It appears to men, or it does not appear. When in fortunate hours we ponder this miracle, the wise man doubts if at all other times he is not blind and deaf;

> *Can such things be,*
> *And overcome us like a summer's cloud,*
> *Without our special wonder?*

for the universe becomes transparent, and the light of higher laws than its own shines through it. It is the standing problem which has exercised the wonder and the study of every fine genius since the world began; from the era of the Egyptians and the Brahmins to that of Pythagoras, of Plato, of Bacon, of Leibnitz, of Swedenborg. There sits the Sphinx at the road-side, and from age to age, as each prophet comes by, he tries his fortune at reading her riddle. There seems to be a necessity in spirit to manifest itself in material forms; and day and night, river and storm, beast and bird, acid and alkali, preëxist in necessary Ideas in the mind of God, and are what they are by virtue of preceding affections in the world of spirit. A Fact is the end or last issue of spirit. The visible creation is the terminus or the circumference of the invisible world. "Material objects," said a French philosopher, "are necessary kinds of *scoriæ* of the substantial thoughts of the Creator, which must always preserve an exact relation to their first origin; in other words, visible nature must have a spiritual and moral side."

This doctrine is abstruse, and though the images of "garment," "scoriæ," 19 "mirror," etc., may stimulate the fancy, we must summon the aid of subtler and more vital expositors to make it plain. "Every scripture is to be interpreted by the same spirit which gave it forth," is the fundamental law of criticism. A life in harmony with Nature, the love of truth and of virtue, will purge the eyes to understand her text. By degrees we may come to know the primitive sense of the permanent objects of nature, so that the world shall be to us an open book, and every form significant of its hidden life and final cause.

A new interest surprises us, whilst, under the view now suggested, we con- 20 template the fearful extent and multitude of objects; since "every object rightly seen, unlocks a new faculty of the soul." That which was unconscious truth, becomes, when interpreted and defined in an object, a part of the domain of knowledge—a new weapon in the magazine of power.

FOCUS ON ECOLOGY

1. What does Emerson mean when he writes, "few adult persons can see nature"? How do we "see" nature?
2. One of the most famous lines from this essay, in fact from all of Emerson's writing, is "Standing on the bare ground—my head bathed by the blithe air and uplifted into infinite space—all mean egotism vanishes. I become a transparent eyeball; I am nothing; I see all." What do you suppose Emerson means by this? What does it mean to become a "transparant eyeball"?

FOCUS ON WRITING

1. Toward the beginning of "Nature," when referring to nature, Emerson writes, "Neither does the wisest man extort her secret, and lose his curiosity by finding out all her perfection." Why does Emerson assign a feminine gender to nature? Are there historical contexts for doing so? How does this affect how we read this selection?
2. When explaining the relationship between language and nature, Emerson writes, "Every appearance in nature corresponds to some state of the mind,

and that state of the mind can only be described by presenting that natural appearance as its picture." Do you agree with Emerson? How would you describe the relationship between language and nature?

3. Emerson also addresses the relationships between writers and nature, claiming that "Hundreds of writers may be found in every long-civilized nation who for a short time believe and make others believe that they see and utter truths, who do not of themselves clothe one thought in its natural garment, but who feed unconsciously on the language created by the primary writers of the country, those, namely, who hold primarily on nature." Considering that in this chapter we are exploring the ways nature and wilderness get named, defined, and described primarily by writers, how do you respond to Emerson's description of the relationship between writers and nature? How would you define such a relationship in terms of the writers with whom you are familiar and whom you like to read?

FOR DISCUSSION

Emerson writes in "Language," "Who looks upon a river in a meditative hour and is not reminded of the flux of all things?" As a class, consider first what Emerson might mean by "a meditative hour." What might he mean by saying that the flux of all things can be seen in the river? Is Emerson being literal or figurative?

WRITING IN RESPONSE

Since this chapter deals specifically with reading, writing, and defining nature, and since Emerson provides a discussion of how nature and language are linked, it might be of use for us to begin writing about nature by considering these very relationships. In a definition essay, define nature in terms of writing and explain how you view the relationship between writing and nature. Don't, however, be bound to Emerson's notion of what writing is. Don't forget that in contemporary America, the images of nature that are presented on television, in films, on bumper stickers and T-shirts, and online are as much a kind of writing and share as much a relationship with nature as do the pen and paper writing to which Emerson refers.

The Trouble with Wilderness

William Cronon

William J. Cronon is Fredrick Jackson Turner Professor of History, Geography, and Environmental Studies at the University of Wisconsin, Madison. He is the author of Uncommon Ground: Rethinking the Human Place in Nature, Changes in the Land: Indians, Colonists, and the Ecology of New England, *which won the Francis Parkman prize in 1984, and* Nature's Metropolis: Chicago and the Great West, *which won the Bancroft prize in 1992. Cronon's research and teaching interests include environmental history, history of the American West, and comparative frontier history. In the essay that follows, Cronon asks us to reconsider how we see wilderness. As you read this selection, consider Cronon's argument for defining "wilderness" as he does.*

JOURNAL ASSIGNMENT

William Cronon begins his essay "The Trouble with Wilderness" by claiming, "the time has come to rethink wilderness." Since we have just discussed issues of *nature* through reading Emerson's essay, this seems a good place also to begin to consider how you think about *wilderness.* In your journal, take the time to consider how you would define the term *wilderness.* Consider what that term embodies, how it is set in opposition to other terms like *man-made,* or what images the term conjures for you. Consider "wild" in *wilderness.* In what contexts do you use or hear the word *wilderness* used?

The time has come to rethink wilderness.   1

    This will seem a heretical claim to many environmentalists, since the idea   2
of wilderness has for decades been a fundamental tenet—indeed, a passion—of the environmental movement, especially in the United States. For many Americans wilderness stands as the last remaining place where civilization, that all too human disease, has not fully infected the earth. It is an island in the polluted sea of urban-industrial modernity, the one place we can turn for escape from our own too-muchness. Seen in this way, wilderness presents itself as the best antidote to our human selves, a refuge we must somehow recover if we hope to save the planet. As Henry David Thoreau once famously declared, "In Wildness is the preservation of the World."

3   But is it? The more one knows of its peculiar history, the more one realizes
that wilderness is not quite what it seems. Far from being the one place on earth
that stands apart from humanity, it is quite profoundly a human creation—indeed, the creation of very particular human cultures at very particular moments in human history. It is not a pristine sanctuary where the last remnant of
an untouched, endangered, but still transcendent nature can for at least a little
while longer be encountered without the contaminating taint of civilization.
Instead, it is a product of that civilization, and could hardly be contaminated
by the very stuff of which it is made. Wilderness hides it unnaturalness behind
a mask that is all the more beguiling because it seems so natural. As we gaze
into the mirror it holds up for us, we too easily imagine that what we behold is
Nature when in fact we see the reflection of our own unexamined longings and
desires. For this reason, we mistake ourselves when we suppose that wilderness can be the solution to our culture's problematic relationships with the
nonhuman world, for wilderness is itself no small part of the problem.

4   To assert the unnaturalness of so natural a place will no doubt seem absurd or even perverse to many readers, so let me hasten to add that the nonhuman world we encounter in wilderness is far from being merely our own
invention. I celebrate with others who love wilderness the beauty and power
of the things it contains. Each of us who has spent time there can conjure images and sensations that seem all the more hauntingly real for having engraved
themselves so indelibly on our memories. Such memories may be uniquely our
own, but they are also familiar enough to be instantly recognizable to others.
Remember this? The torrents of mist shoot out from the base of a great waterfall in the depths of a Sierra canyon, the tiny droplets cooling your face as you
listen to the roar of the water and gaze up toward the sky through a rainbow
that hovers just out of reach. Remember this too: looking out across a desert
canyon in the evening air, the only sound a lone raven calling in the distance,
the rock walls dropping away into a chasm so deep that its bottom all but vanishes as you squint into the amber light of the setting sun. And this: the moment beside the trail as you sit on a sandstone ledge, your boots damp with the
morning dew while you take in the rich smell of the pines, and the small red
fox—or maybe for you it was a raccoon or a coyote or a deer—that suddenly
ambles across your path, stopping for a moment to gaze in your direction with
cautious indifference before continuing on its way. Remember the feelings of
such moments, and you will know as well as I do that you were in the presence of something irreducibly nonhuman, something profoundly Other than
yourself. Wilderness is made of that too.

5   And yet: what brought each of us to the places where such memories became possible is entirely a cultural invention. Go back 250 years in American
and European history, and you do not find nearly so many people wandering
around remote corners of the planet looking for what today we would call "the
wilderness experience." As late as the eighteenth century, the most common

usage of the word "wilderness" in the English language referred to landscapes that generally carried adjectives far different from the ones they attract today. To be a wilderness then was to be "deserted," "savage," "desolate," "barren"—in short, a "waste," the word's nearest synonym. Its connotations were anything but positive, and the emotion one was most likely to feel in its presence was "bewilderment"—or terror.

Many of the word's strongest associations then were biblical, for it is used 6 over and over again in the King James Version to refer to places on the margins of civilization where it is all too easy to lose oneself in moral confusion and despair. The wilderness was where Moses had wandered with his people for forty years, and where they had nearly abandoned their God to worship a golden idol. "For Pharaoh will say of the Children of Israel," we read in Exodus, "They are entangled in the land, the wilderness hath shut them in." The wilderness was where Christ had struggled with the devil and endured his temptations: "And immediately the Spirit driveth him into the wilderness. And he was there in the wilderness for forty days tempted of Satan; and was with the wild beasts; and the angels ministered unto him." The "delicious Paradise" of John Milton's Eden was surrounded by "a steep wilderness, whose hairy sides / Access denied" to all who sought entry. When Adam and Eve were driven from that garden, the world they entered was a wilderness that only their labor and pain could redeem. Wilderness, in short, was a place to which one came only against one's will, and always in fear and trembling. Whatever value it might have arose solely from the possibility that it might be "reclaimed" and turned toward human ends—planted as a garden, say, or a city upon a hill. In its raw state, it had little or nothing to offer civilized men and women.

But by the end of the nineteenth century, all this had changed. The waste- 7 lands that had once seemed worthless had for some people come to seem almost beyond price. That Thoreau in 1862 could declare wildness to be the preservation of the world suggests the sea change that was going on. Wilderness had once been the antithesis of all that was orderly and good—it had been the darkness, one might say, on the far side of the garden wall—and yet now it was frequently likened to Eden itself. When John Muir arrived in the Sierra Nevada in 1869, he would declare, "No description of Heaven that I have ever heard or read of seems half so fine." He was hardly alone in expressing such emotions. One by one, various corners of the American map came to be designated as sites whose wild beauty was so spectacular that a growing number of citizens had to visit and see them for themselves. Niagara Falls was the first to undergo this transformation, but it was soon followed by the Catskills, the Adirondacks, Yosemite, Yellowstone, and others. Yosemite was deeded by the U.S. government to the state of California in 1864 as the nation's first wildland park, and Yellowstone became the first true national park in 1872.

By the first decade of the twentieth century, in the single most famous 8 episode in American conservation history, a national debate had exploded over whether the city of San Francisco should be permitted to augment its water supply by damming the Tuolumne River in Hetch Hetchy valley, well within the boundaries of Yosemite National Park. The dam was eventually built, but what today seems no less significant is that so many people fought to prevent its completion. Even as the fight was being lost, Hetch Hetchy became the battle cry of an emerging movement to preserve wilderness. Fifty years earlier, such opposition would have been unthinkable. Few would have questioned the merits of "reclaiming" a wasteland like this in order to put it to human use. Now the defenders of Hetch Hetchy attracted widespread national attention by portraying such an act not as improvement or progress but as desecration and vandalism. Lest one doubt that the old biblical metaphors had been turned completely on their heads, listen to John Muir attack the dam's defenders. "Their arguments," he wrote, "are curiously like those of the devil, devised for the destruction of the first garden—so much of the very best Eden fruit going to waste; so much of the best Tuolumne water and Tuolumne scenery going to waste." For Muir and the growing number of Americans who shared his views, Satan's home had become God's own temple.

9   The sources of this rather astonishing transformation were many, but for the purposes of this essay they can be gathered under two broad headings: the sublime and the frontier. Of the two, sublime is the older and more pervasive cultural construct, being one of the most important expressions of that broad transatlantic movement we today label as romanticism; the frontier is more peculiarly American, though it too had its European antecedents and parallels. The two converged to remake wilderness in their own image, freighting it with moral values and cultural symbols that it carries to this day. Indeed, it is not too much to say that the modern environmental movement is itself a grandchild of romanticism and post-frontier ideology, which is why it is no accident that so much environmentalist discourse takes its bearings from the wilderness these intellectual movements helped create. Although wilderness may today seem to be just one environmental concern among many, it in fact serves as the foundation for a long list of other such concerns that on their face seem quite remote from it. That is why its influence is so pervasive and, potentially, so insidious.

10   To gain such remarkable influence, the concept of wilderness had to become loaded with some of the deepest core values of the culture that created and idealized it: it had to become sacred. This possibility had been present in wilderness even in the days when it had been a place of spiritual danger and moral temptation. If Satan was there, then so was Christ, who had found angels as well as wild beasts during his sojourn in the desert. In the wilderness the boundaries between human and nonhuman, between natural and supernatural, had always seemed less certain than elsewhere. This was why the early Christian saints and mystics had often emulated Christ's desert retreat as they sought to experience for themselves the visions and spiritual testing he had endured. One might meet devils and run the risk of losing one's soul in such a place, but one might also meet God. For some that possibility was worth almost any price.

By the eighteenth century this sense of the wilderness as a landscape where 11
the supernatural lay just beneath the surface was expressed in the doctrine of
the *sublime,* a word whose modern usage has been so watered down by commercial hype and tourist advertising that it retains only a dim echo of its former power. In the theories of Edmund Burke, Immanuel Kant, William Gilpin,
and others, sublime landscapes were those rare places on earth where one had
more chance than elsewhere to glimpse the face of God. Romantics had a clear
notion of where one could be most sure of having this experience. Although
God might, of course, choose to show himself anywhere, he would most often
be found in those vast, powerful landscapes where one could not help feeling
insignificant and being reminded of one's own mortality. Where were these
sublime places? The eighteenth-century catalogue of their locations feels very
familiar, for we still see and value landscapes as it taught us to do. God was on
the mountaintop, in the chasm, in the waterfall, in the thundercloud, in the
rainbow, in the sunset. One has only to think of the sites that Americans chose
for their first national parks—Yellowstone, Yosemite, Grand Canyon, Rainier,
Zion—to realize that virtually all of them fit one or more of these categories.
Less sublime landscapes simply did not appear worthy of such protection; not
until the 1940s, for instance, would the first swamp be honored, in Everglades
National Park, and to this day there is no national park in the grasslands.

Among the best proofs that one had entered a sublime landscape was the 12
emotion it evoked. For the early romantic writers and artists who first began to
celebrate it, the sublime was far from being a pleasurable experience. The classic description is that of William Wordsworth as he recounted climbing the Alps
and crossing the Simplon Pass in his autobiographical poem *The Prelude.* There,
surrounded by crags and waterfalls, the poet felt himself literally to be in the
presence of the divine—and experienced an emotion remarkably close to terror:

> The immeasurable height
> Of woods decaying, never to be decayed,
> The stationary blasts of waterfalls,
> And in the narrow rent at every turn
> Winds thwarting winds, bewildered and forlorn,
> The torrents shooting from the clear blue sky,
> The rocks that muttered close upon our ears,
> Black drizzling crags that spake by the way-side
> As if a voice were in them, the sick sight
> And giddy prospect of the raving stream,
> The unfettered clouds and region of the
> Heavens,
> Tumult and peace, the darkness and the light—
> Were all like workings of one mind, the features
> Of the same face, blossoms upon one tree;
> Characters of the great Apocalypse,

The types and symbols of Eternity,
Of first, and last, and midst, and without end.

This was no casual stroll in the mountains, no simple sojourn in the gentle lap of nonhuman nature. What Wordsworth described was nothing less than a religious experience, akin to that of the Old Testament prophets as they conversed with their wrathful God. The symbols he detected in this wilderness landscape were more supernatural than natural, and they inspired more awe and dismay than joy or pleasure. No mere mortal was meant to linger long in such a place, so it was with considerable relief that Wordsworth and his companion made their way back down from the peaks to the sheltering valleys.

13   Lest you suspect that this view of the sublime was limited to timid Europeans who lacked the American know-how for feeling at home in the wilderness, remember David Henry Thoreau's 1846 climb of Mount Katahdin, in Maine. Although Thoreau is regarded by many today as one of the great American celebrators of wilderness, his emotions about Katahdin were no less ambivalent than Wordsworth's about the Alps.

> It was vast, Titanic, and such as man never inhabits. Some part of the beholder, even some vital part, seems to escape through the loose grating of his ribs as he ascends. He is more lone than you can imagine. . . . Vast, Titanic, inhuman Nature has got him at disadvantage, caught him alone, and pilfers him of some of his divine faculty. She does not smile on him as in the plains. She seems to say sternly, why came ye here before your time? This ground is not prepared for you. Is it not enough that I smile in the valleys? I have never made this soil for thy feet, this air for thy breathing, these rocks for thy neighbors. I cannot pity nor fondle thee here, but forever relentlessly drive thee hence to where I *am* kind. Why seek me where I have not called thee, and then complain because you find me but a stepmother?

This is surely not the way a modern backpacker or nature lover would describe Maine's most famous mountain, but that is because Thoreau's description owes as much to Wordsworth and other romantic contemporaries as to the rocks and clouds of Katahdin itself. His words took the physical mountain on which he stood and transmuted it into an icon of the sublime: a symbol of God's presence on earth. The power and the glory of that icon were such that only a prophet might gaze on it for long. In effect, romantics like Thoreau joined Moses and the children of Israel in Exodus when "they looked toward the wilderness, and behold, the glory of the Lord appeared in the cloud."

14   But even as it came to embody the awesome power of the sublime, wilderness was also being tamed—not just by those who were building settlements in its midst but also by those who most celebrated its inhuman beauty. By the second half of the nineteenth century, the terrible awe that Wordsworth and Thoreau regarded as the appropriately pious stance to adopt in the presence of their mountaintop God was giving way to a much more comfortable, almost sentimental demeanor. As more and more tourists sought out the wilderness as a spectacle to be looked at and enjoyed for its great beauty, the sublime in

effect became domesticated. The wilderness was still sacred, but the religious sentiments it evoked were more those of a pleasant parish church than those of a grand cathedral or a harsh desert retreat. The writer who best captures this late romantic sense of a domesticated sublime is undoubtedly John Muir, whose descriptions of Yosemite and the Sierra Nevada reflect none of the anxiety or terror one finds in earlier writers. Here he is, for instance, sketching on North Dome in Yosemite Valley:

> No pain here, no dull empty hours, no fear of the past, no fear of the future. These blessed mountains are so compactly filled with God's beauty, no petty personal hope or experience has room to be. Drinking this champagne water is pure pleasure, so is breathing the living air, and every movement of limbs is pleasure, while the body seems to feel beauty when exposed to it as it feels the campfire or sunshine, entering not by the eyes alone, but equally through all one's flesh like radiant heat, making a passionate ecstatic pleasure glow not explainable.

The emotions Muir describes in Yosemite could hardly be more different from Thoreau's on Katahdin or Wordsworth's on the Simplon Pass. Yet all three men are participating in the same cultural tradition and contributing to the same myth: the mountain as cathedral. The three may differ in the way they choose to express their piety—Wordsworth favoring an awe-filled bewilderment, Thoreau a stern loneliness, Muir a welcome ecstacy—but they agree completely about the church in which they prefer to worship. Muir's closing words on North Dome diverge from his older contemporaries only in mood, not in their ultimate content:

> Perched like a fly on this Yosemite dome, I gaze and sketch and bask, oftentimes settling down into dumb admiration without definite hope of ever learning much, yet with the longing, unresting effort that lies at the door of hope, humbly prostrate before the vast display of God's power, and eager to offer self-denial and renunciation with eternal toil to learn any lesson in the divine manuscript.

Muir's "divine manuscript" and Wordsworth's "Characters of the great Apocalypse" were in fact pages from the same holy book. The sublime wilderness had ceased to be a place of satanic temptation and become instead a sacred temple, much as it continues to be for those who love it today.

But the romantic sublime was not the only cultural movement that helped ₁₅ transform wilderness into a sacred American icon during the nineteenth century. No less important was the powerful romantic attraction of primitivism, dating back at least to Rousseau—the belief that the best antidote to the ills of an overly refined and civilized modern world was a return to simpler, more primitive living. In the United States, this was embodied most strikingly in the national myth of the frontier. The historian Frederick Jackson Turner wrote in 1893 the classic academic statement of this myth, but it had been part of American cultural traditions for well over a century. As Turner described the process, easterners and European immigrants, in moving to the wild unsettled lands of the frontier, shed the trappings of civilization, rediscovered their primitive racial energies, reinvented direct democratic institutions, and thereby rein-fused themselves with a vigor, an independence, and a creativity that were the source of American democracy and national character. Seen in this way, wild country became a place not just of religious redemption but of national re-newal, the quintessential location for experiencing what it meant to be an American.

16   One of Turner's most provocative claims was that by the 1890s the frontier was passing away. Never again would "such gifts of free land offer themselves" to the American people. "The frontier has gone," he declared, "and with its going has closed the first period of American history." Built into the frontier myth from its very beginning was the notion that this crucible of American identity was temporary and would pass away. Those who have celebrated the frontier have almost always looked backward as they did so, mourning an older, simpler, truer world that is about to disappear forever. That world and all of its attractions, Turner said, depended on free land—on wilderness. Thus, in the myth of the vanishing frontier lay the seeds of wilderness preservation in the United States, for if wild land had been so crucial in the making of the nation, then surely one must save its last remnants as monuments to the Amer-ican past—and as an insurance policy to protect its future. It is no accident that the movement to set aside national parks and wilderness areas began to gain real momentum at precisely the time that laments about the passing frontier reached their peak. To protect wilderness was in a very real sense to protect the nation's most sacred myth of origin.

17   Among the core elements of the frontier myth was the powerful sense among certain groups of Americans that wilderness was the last bastion of rugged individualism. Turner tended to stress communitarian themes when writing frontier history, asserting that Americans in primitive conditions had been forced to band together with their neighbors to form communities and democratic institutions. For other writers, however, frontier democracy for communities was less compelling than frontier freedom for individuals. By fleeing to the outer margins of settled land and society—so the story ran—an individual could escape the confining strictures of civilized life. The mood among writers who celebrated frontier individualism was almost always nos-talgic; they lamented not just a lost way of life but the passing of the heroic men who had embodied that life. Thus Owen Wister in the introduction to his classic 1902 novel *The Virginian* could write of "a vanished world" in which "the horseman, the cow-puncher, the last romantic figure upon our soil" rode only "in his historic yesterday" and would "never come again." For Wister, the cowboy was a man who gave his word and kept it ("Wall Street would have found him behind the times"), who did not talk lewdly to women ("Newport would have thought him old fashioned"), who worked and played hard, and whose "ungoverned hours did not unman him." Theodore Roosevelt wrote with much the same nostalgic fervor about the "fine, manly qualities" of the "wild rough-rider of the plains." No one could be more heroically masculine, thought Roosevelt, or more at home in the western wilderness:

There he passes his days, there he does his life-work, there, when he meets death, he faces it as he has faced many other evils, with quiet, uncomplaining fortitude. Brave, hospitable, hardy, and adventurous, he is the grim pioneer of our race; he prepares the way for the civilization from before whose face he must himself disappear. Hard and dangerous though his existence is, it has yet a wild attraction that strongly draws to it his bold, free spirit.

This nostalgia for a passing frontier way of life inevitably implied ambivalence, if not downright hostility, toward modernity and all that it represented. If one saw the wild lands of the frontier as freer, truer, and more natural than other, more modern places, then one was also inclined to see the cities and factories of urban-industrial civilization as confining, false, and artificial. Owen Wister looked at the post-frontier "transition" that had followed the "horseman of the plains," and did not like what he saw: "a shapeless state, a condition of men and manners as unlovely as is that moment in the year when winter is gone and spring not come, and the face of Nature is ugly." In the eyes of writers who shared Wister's distaste for modernity, civilization contaminated its inhabitants and absorbed them into the faceless, collective, contemptible life of the crowd. For all of its troubles and dangers, and despite the fact that it must pass away, the frontier had been a better place. If civilization was to be redeemed, it would be by men like the Virginian who could retain their frontier virtues even as they made the transition to post-frontier life.

The mythic frontier individualist was almost always masculine in gender: here, in the wilderness, a man could be a real man, the rugged individual he was meant to be before civilization sapped his energy and threatened his masculinity. Wister's contemptuous remarks about Wall Street and Newport suggest what he and many others of his generation believed—that the comforts and seductions of civilized life were especially insidious for men, who all too easily became emasculated by the feminizing tendencies, of civilization. More often than not, men who felt this way came, like Wister and Roosevelt, from elite class backgrounds. The curious result was that frontier nostalgia became an important vehicle for expressing a peculiarly bourgeois form of anti-modernism. The very men who most benefited from urban-industrial capitalism were among those who believed they must escape its debilitating effects. If the frontier was passing, then men who had the means to do so should preserve for themselves some remnant of its wild landscape so that they might enjoy the regeneration and renewal that came from sleeping under the stars, participating in blood sports, and living off the land. The frontier might be gone, but the frontier experience could still be had if only wilderness were preserved.

Thus the decades following the Civil War saw more and more of the nation's wealthiest citizens seeking out wilderness for themselves. The elite passion for wild land took many forms: enormous estates in the Adirondacks and elsewhere (disingenuously called "camps" despite their many servants and amenities), cattle ranches for would-be roughriders on the Great Plains, guided big-game hunting trips in the Rockies, and luxurious resort hotels wherever railroads pushed their way into sublime landscapes. Wilderness suddenly emerged as the landscape of choice for elite tourists who brought with them strikingly urban ideas of the countryside through which they traveled. For them, wild land was not a site for productive labor and not a permanent home; rather, it was a place of recreation. One went to the wilderness not as a producer but as a consumer, hiring guides and other backcountry residents who could serve as romantic surrogates for the rough riders and hunters of the frontier, if one was willing to overlook their new status as employees and servants of the rich.

21   In just this way, wilderness came to embody the national frontier myth, standing for the wild freedom of America's past and seeming to represent a highly attractive natural alternative to the ugly artificiality of modern civilization. The irony, of course, was that in the process wilderness came to reflect the very civilization its devotees sought to escape. Ever since the nineteenth century, celebrating wilderness has been an activity mainly for well-to-do city folks. Country people generally know far too much about working the land to regard *un*worked land as their ideal. In contrast, elite urban tourists and wealthy sportsmen projected their leisure-time frontier fantasies onto the American landscape and so created wilderness in their own image.

22   There were other ironies as well. The movement to set aside national parks and wilderness areas followed hard on the heels of the final Indian wars, in which the prior human inhabitants of these areas were rounded up and moved onto reservations. The myth of the wilderness as "virgin," uninhabited land had always been especially cruel when seen from the perspective of the Indians who had once called that land home. Now they were forced to move elsewhere, with the result that tourists could safely enjoy the illusion that they were seeing their nation in its pristine, original state, in the new morning of God's own creation. Among the things that most marked the new national parks as reflecting a post-frontier consciousness was the relative absence of human violence within their boundaries. The actual frontier had often been a place of conflict, in which invaders and invaded fought for control of land and resources. Once set aside within the fixed and carefully policed boundaries of the modern bureaucratic state, the wilderness lost its savage image and became safe: a place more of reverie than of revulsion or fear. Meanwhile, its original inhabitants were kept out by dint of force, their earlier uses of the land redefined as inappropriate or even illegal. To this day, for instance, the Blackfeet continue to be accused of "poaching" on the lands of Glacier National Park that originally belonged to them and that were ceded by treaty only with the proviso that they be permitted to hunt there.

23   The removal of Indians to create an "uninhabited wilderness"—uninhabited as never before in the human history of the place—reminds us just how invented, just how constructed, the American wilderness really is. To return to my opening argument: there is nothing natural about the concept of wilderness. It is entirely a creation of the culture that holds it dear, a product of the very history it seeks to deny. Indeed, one of the most striking proofs of the cultural invention of wilderness is its thoroughgoing erasure of the history from

which it sprang. In virtually all of its manifestations, wilderness represents a flight from history. Seen as the original garden, it is a place outside of time from which human beings had to be ejected before the fallen world of history could properly begin. Seen as the frontier, it is a savage world at the dawn of civilization, whose transformation represents the very beginning of the national historical epic. Seen as the bold landscape of frontier heroism, it is the place of youth and childhood, into which men escape by abandoning their pasts and entering a world of freedom where the constraints of civilization fade into memory. Seen as the sacred sublime, it is the home of a God who transcends history by standing as the One who remains untouched and unchanged by time's arrow. No matter what the angle from which we regard it, wilderness offers us the illusion that we can escape the cares and troubles of the world in which our past has ensnared us.

This escape from history is one reason why the language we use to talk 24 about wilderness is often permeated with spiritual and religious values that reflect human ideals far more than the material world of physical nature. Wilderness fulfills the old romantic project of secularizing Judeo-Christian values so as to make a new cathedral not in some petty human building but in God's own creation, Nature itself. Many environmentalists who reject traditional notions of the godhead and who regard themselves as agnostics or even atheists nonetheless express feelings tantamount to religious awe when in the presence of wilderness—a fact that testifies to the success of the romantic project. Those who have no difficulty seeing God as the expression of our human dreams and desires nonetheless have trouble recognizing that in a secular age Nature can offer precisely the same sort of mirror.

Thus it is that wilderness serves as the unexamined foundation on which 25 so many of the quasi-religious values of modern environmentalism rest. The critique of modernity that is one of environmentalism's most important contributions to the moral and political discourse of our time more often than not appeals, explicitly or implicitly, to wilderness as the standard against which to measure the failings of our human world. Wilderness is the natural unfallen antithesis of an unnatural civilization that has lost its soul. It is a place of freedom in which we can recover the true selves we have lost to the corrupting influences of our artificial lives. Most of all, it is the ultimate landscape of authenticity. Combining the sacred grandeur of the sublime with the primitive simplicity of the frontier, it is the place where we can see the world as it really is, and so know ourselves as we really are—or ought to be.

But the trouble with wilderness is that it quietly expresses and reproduces 26 the very values its devotees seek to reject. The flight from history that is very nearly the core of wilderness represents the false hope of an escape from responsibility, the illusion that we can somehow wipe clean the slate of our past and return to the tabula rasa that supposedly existed before we began to leave our marks on the world. The dream of an unworked natural landscape is very much the fantasy of people who have never themselves had to work the land to make a living—urban folk for whom food comes from a supermarket or a restaurant instead of a field, and for whom the wooden houses in which they live and work apparently have no meaningful connection to the forests in which trees grow and die. Only people whose relation to the land was already alienated could hold up wilderness as a model for human life in nature, for the romantic ideology of wilderness leaves precisely nowhere for human beings actually to make their living from the land.

27   This, then, is the central paradox: wilderness embodies a dualistic vision in which the human is entirely outside the natural. If we allow ourselves to believe that nature, to be true, must also be wild, then our very presence in nature represents its fall. The place where we are is the place where nature is not. If this is so—if by definition wilderness leaves no place for human beings, save perhaps as contemplative sojourners enjoying their leisurely reverie in God's natural cathedral—then also by definition it can offer no solution to the environmental and other problems that confront us. To the extent that we celebrate wilderness as the measure with which we judge civilization, we reproduce the dualism that sets humanity and nature at opposite poles. We thereby leave ourselves little hope of discovering what an ethical, sustainable, *honorable* human place in nature might actually look like.

28   Worse: to the extent that we live in an urban-industrial civilization but at the same time pretend to ourselves that our *real* home is in the wilderness, to just that extent we give ourselves permission to evade responsibility for the lives we actually lead. We inhabit civilization while holding some part of ourselves—what we imagine to be the most precious part—aloof from its entanglements. We work our nine-to-five jobs in its institutions, we eat its food, we drive its cars (not least to reach the wilderness), we benefit from the intricate and all too invisible networks with which it shelters us, all the while pretending that these things are not an essential part of who we are. By imagining that our true home is in the wilderness, we forgive ourselves the homes we actually inhabit. In its flight from history, in its siren song of escape, in its reproduction of the dangerous dualism that sets human beings outside of nature—in all of these ways, wilderness poses a serious threat to responsible environmentalism at the end of the twentieth century.

29   By now I hope it is clear that my criticism in this essay is not directed at wild nature per se, or even at efforts to set aside large tracts of wild land, but rather at the specific habits of thinking that flow from this complex cultural construction called wilderness. It is not the things we label as wilderness that are the problem—for nonhuman nature and large tracts of the natural world *do* deserve protection—but rather what we ourselves mean when we use that label. Lest one doubt how pervasive these habits of thought really are in contemporary environmentalism, let me list some of the places where wilderness serves as the ideological underpinning for environmental concerns that might otherwise seem quite remote from it. Defenders of biological diversity, for instance, although sometimes appealing to more utilitarian concerns, often point to "untouched" ecosystems as the best and richest repositories of the undiscovered species we must certainly try to protect. Although at first blush an ap-

parently more "scientific" concept than wilderness, biological diversity in fact invokes many of the same sacred values, which is why organizations like the Nature Conservancy have been so quick to employ it as an alternative to the seemingly fuzzier and more problematic concept of wilderness. There is a paradox here, of course. To the extent that biological diversity (indeed, even wilderness itself) is likely to survive in the future only by the most vigilant and self-conscious management of the ecosystems that sustain it, the ideology of wilderness is potentially in direct conflict with the very thing it encourages us to protect.

The most striking instances of this have revolved around "endangered species," which serve as vulnerable symbols of biological diversity while at the same time standing as surrogates for wilderness itself. The terms of the Endangered Species Act in the United States have often meant that those hoping to defend pristine wilderness have had to rely on a single endangered species like the spotted owl to gain legal standing for their case—thereby making the full power of sacred land inhere in a single numinous organism whose habitat then becomes the object of intense debate about appropriate management and use. The case with which anti-environmental forces like the wise-use movement have attacked such single-species preservation efforts suggests the vulnerability of strategies like these.

Perhaps partly because our own conflicts over such places and organisms have become so messy, the convergence of wilderness values with concerns about biological diversity and endangered species has helped produce a deep fascination for remote ecosystems, where it is easier to imagine that nature might somehow be "left alone" to flourish by its own pristine devices. The classic example is the tropical rain forest, which since the 1970s has become the most powerful modern icon of unfallen, sacred land—a veritable Garden of Eden—for many Americans and Europeans. And yet protecting the rain forest in the eyes of First World environmentalists all too often means protecting it from the people who live there. Those who seek to preserve such "wilderness" from the activities of native peoples run the risk of reproducing the same tragedy—being forcibly removed from an ancient home—that befell American Indians. Third World countries face massive environmental problems and deep social conflicts, but these are not likely to be solved by a cultural myth that encourages us to "preserve" peopleless landscapes that have not existed in such places for millennia. At its worst, as environmentalists are beginning to realize, exporting American notions of wilderness in this way can become an unthinking and self-defeating form of cultural imperialism.

Perhaps the most suggestive example of the way that wilderness thinking can underpin other environmental concerns has emerged in the recent debate about "global change." In 1989 the journalist Bill McKibben published a book entitled *The End of Nature*, in which he argued that the prospect of global climate change as a result of unintentional human manipulation of the atmosphere means that nature as we once knew it no longer exists. Whereas earlier generations inhabited a natural world that remained more or less unaffected by their actions, our own generation is uniquely different. We and our children will henceforth live in a biosphere completely altered by our own activity, a planet in which the human and the natural can no longer be distinguished because the one has overwhelmed the other. In McKibben's view, nature has died, and we are responsible for killing it. "The planet," he declares, "is utterly different now."

33   But such a perspective is possible only if we accept the wilderness premise that nature, to be natural, must also be pristine—remote from humanity and untouched by our common past. In fact, everything we know about environmental history suggests that people have been manipulating the natural world on various scales for as long as we have a record of their passing. Moreover, we have unassailable evidence that many of the environmental changes we now face also occurred quite apart from human intervention at one time or another in the earth's past. The point is not that our current problems are trivial, or that our devastating effects on the earth's ecosystems should be accepted as inevitable or "natural." It is rather that we seem unlikely to make much progress in solving these problems if we hold up to ourselves as the mirror of nature a wilderness we ourselves cannot inhabit.

34   To do so is merely to take to a logical extreme the paradox that was built into wilderness from the beginning: if nature dies because we enter it, then the only way to save nature is to kill ourselves. The absurdity of this proposition flows from the underlying dualism it expresses. Not only does it ascribe greater power to humanity than we in fact possess—physical and biological nature will surely survive in some form or another long after we ourselves have gone the way of all flesh—but in the end it offers us little more than a self-defeating counsel of despair. The tautology gives us no way out: if wild nature is the only thing worth saving, and if our mere presence destroys it, then the sole solution to our own unnaturalness, the only way to protect sacred wilderness from profane humanity, would seem to be suicide. It is not a proposition that seems likely to produce very positive or practical results.

35   And yet radical environmentalists and deep ecologists all too frequently come close to accepting this premise as a first principle. When they express, for instance, the popular notion that our environmental problems began with the invention of agriculture, they push the human fall from natural grace so far back into the past that all of civilized history becomes a tale of ecological declension. Earth First! founder Dave Foreman captures the familiar parable succinctly when he writes:

> Before agriculture was midwifed in the Middle East , humans were in the wilderness. We had no concept of "wilderness" because everything was wilderness and *we were a part of it*. But with irrigation ditches, crop surpluses, and permanent villages, we became *apart from* the natural world. . . . Between the wilderness that created us and the civilization created by us grew an ever-widening rift

In this view, the farm becomes the first and most important battlefield in the long war against wild nature, and all else follows in its wake. From such a starting place, it is hard not to reach the conclusion that the only way human beings can hope to live naturally on earth is to follow the hunter-gatherers back into a wilderness Eden and abandon virtually everything that civilization has given us. It may indeed turn out that civilization will end in ecological collapse or nuclear disaster, whereupon one might expect to find any human survivors returning to a way of life closer to that celebrated by Foreman and his followers. For most of us, though, such a debacle would be cause for regret, a sign that humanity had failed to fulfill its own promise and failed to honor its own highest values—including those of the deep ecologists.

In offering wilderness as the ultimate hunter-gatherer alternative to civilization, Foreman reproduces an extreme but still easily recognizable version of the myth of frontier primitivism. When he writes of his fellow Earth Firsters that "we believe we must return to being animal, to glorying in our sweat, hormones, tears, and blood" and that "we struggle against the modern compulsion to become dull, passionless androids," he is following in the footsteps of Owen Wister. Although his arguments give primacy to defending biodiversity and the autonomy of wild nature, his prose becomes most passionate when he speaks of preserving "the wilderness experience." His own ideal "Big Outside" bears an uncanny resemblance to that of the frontier myth: wide open spaces and virgin land with no trails, no signs, no facilities, no maps, no guides, no rescues, no modern equipment. Tellingly, it is a land where hardy travelers can support themselves by hunting with "primitive weapons (bow and arrow, at-latl, knife, sharp rock)." Foreman claims that "the primary value of wilderness is not as a proving ground for young Huck Finns and Annie Oakleys," but his heart is with Huck and Annie all the same. He admits that "preserving a quality wilderness experience for the human visitor, letting her or him flex Paleolithic muscles or seek visions, remains a tremendously important secondary purpose." Just so does Teddy Roosevelt's Rough Rider live on in the greener garb of a new age.

However much one may be attracted to such a vision, it entails problematic consequences. For one, it makes wilderness the locus for an epic struggle between malign civilization and benign nature, compared with which all other social, political, and moral concerns seem trivial. Foreman writes, "The preservation of wildness and native diversity is *the* most important issue. Issues directly affecting only humans pale in comparison." Presumably, so do any environmental problems whose victims are mainly people, for such problems usually surface in landscapes that have already "fallen" and are no longer wild. This would seem to exclude from the radical environmentalist agenda problems of occupational health and safety in industrial settings, problems of toxic waste exposure on "unnatural" urban and agricultural sites, problems of poor children poisoned by lead exposure in the inner city, problems of famine and poverty and human suffering in the "overpopulated" places of the earth— problems, in short, of environmental justice. If we set too high a stock on wilderness, too many other corners of the earth become less than natural and too many other people become less than human, thereby giving us permission not to care much about their suffering or their fate.

It is no accident that these supposedly inconsequential environmental problems affect mainly poor people, for the long affiliation between wilderness and wealth means that the only poor people who count when wilderness is *the* issue are hunter-gatherers, who presumably do not consider themselves to be poor in the first place. The dualism at the heart of wilderness encourages its advocates to conceive of its protection as a crude conflict between the "human" and the "nonhuman"—or, more often, between those who value the nonhuman and those who do not. This in turn tempts one to ignore crucial differences *among* humans and the complex cultural and historical reasons why different peoples may feel very differently about the meaning of wilderness.

39   Why, for instance, is the "wilderness experience" so often conceived as a form of recreation best enjoyed by those whose class privileges give them the time and resources to leave their jobs behind and "get away from it all"? Why does the protection of wilderness so often seem to pit urban recreationists against rural people who actually earn their living from the land (excepting those who sell goods and services to the tourists themselves)? Why in the debates about pristine natural areas are "primitive" peoples idealized, even sentimentalized, until the moment they do something unprimitive, modern, and unnatural, and thereby fall from environmental grace? What are the consequences of a wilderness ideology that devalues productive labor and the very concrete knowledge that comes from working the land with one's own hands? All of these questions imply conflicts among different groups of people, conflicts that are obscured behind the deceptive clarity of "human" versus "nonhuman." If in answering these knotty questions we resort to so simplistic an opposition, we are almost certain to ignore the very subtleties and complexities we need to understand.

40   But the most troubling cultural baggage that accompanies the celebration of wilderness has less to do with remote rain forests and peoples than with the ways we think about ourselves—we American environmentalists who quite rightly worry about the future of the earth and the threats we pose to the natural world. Idealizing a distant wilderness too often means not idealizing the environment in which we live, the landscape that for better or worse we call home. Most of our serious environmental problems start right here, at home, and if we are to solve those problems, we need an environmental ethic that will tell us as much about using nature as about not using it. The wilderness dualism tends to cast any use as *ab*use, and thereby denies us a middle ground in which responsible use and non-use might attain some kind of balanced, sustainable relationship. My own belief is that only by exploring this middle ground will we learn ways of imagining a better world for all of us: humans and nonhumans, rich people and poor, women and men, First Worlders and Third Worlders, white folks and people of color, consumers and producers—a world better for humanity in all of its diversity and for all the rest of nature too. The middle ground is where we actually live. It is where we—all of us, in our different places and ways—make our homes.

41   That is why, when I think of the times I myself have come closest to experiencing what I might call the sacred in nature, I often find myself remembering wild places much closer to home. I think, for instance, of a small pond near my

house where water bubbles up from limestone springs to feed a series of pools that rarely freeze in winter and so play home to waterfowl that stay here for the protective warmth even on the coldest of winter days, gliding silently through steaming mists as the snow falls from gray February skies. I think of a November evening long ago when I found myself on a Wisconsin hilltop in rain and dense fog, only to have the setting sun break through the clouds to cast an otherworldly golden light on the misty farms and woodlands below, a scene so unexpected and joyous that I lingered past dusk so as not to miss any part of the gift that had come my way. And I think perhaps most especially of the blown-out, bankrupt farm in the sand country of central Wisconsin where Aldo Leopold and his family tried one of the first American experiments in ecological restoration, turning ravaged and infertile soil into carefully tended ground where the human and the nonhuman could exist side by side in relative harmony. What I celebrate about such places is not *just* their wildness, though that certainly is among their most important qualities; what I celebrate even more is that they remind us of the wildness in our own back yards, of the nature that is all around us if only we have eyes to see it.

Indeed, my principal objection to wilderness is that it may teach us to be 42 submissive or even contemptuous of such humble places and experiences. Without our quite realizing it, wilderness tends to privilege some parts of nature at the expense of others. Most of us, I suspect, still follow the conventions of the romantic sublime in finding the mountaintop more glorious than the plains, the ancient forest nobler than the grasslands, the mighty canyon more inspiring than the humble marsh. Even John Muir, in arguing against those who sought to dam his beloved Hetch Hetchy valley in the Sierra Nevada, argued for alternative dam sites in the gentler valleys of the foothills—a preference that had nothing to do with nature and everything with the cultural traditions of the sublime. Just as problematically, our frontier traditions have encouraged Americans to define "true" wilderness as requiring very large tracts of roadless land—what Dave Foreman calls the Big Outside. Leaving aside the legitimate empirical question in conservation biology of how large a tract of land must be before a given species can reproduce on it, the emphasis on big wilderness reflects a romantic frontier belief that one hasn't really gotten away from civilization unless one can go for days at a time without encountering another human being. By teaching us to fetishize sublime places and wide open country, these peculiarly American ways of thinking about wilderness encourage us to adopt too high a standard for what counts as "natural." If it isn't hundreds of square miles big, if it doesn't give us God's-eye views or grand vistas, if it doesn't permit us the illusion that we are alone on the planet, then it really isn't natural. It's too small, too plain, or too crowded to be *authentically* wild.

In critiquing wilderness as I have done in this essay, I'm forced to confront 43 my own deep ambivalence about its meaning for modern environmentalism. On the one hand, one of my own most important environmental ethics is that people should always be conscious that they are part of the natural world, inextricably tied to the ecological systems that sustain their lives. Any way of looking at nature that encourages us to believe we are separate from nature—as wilderness tends to do—is likely to reinforce environmentally irresponsible behavior. On the other hand, I also think it no less crucial for us to recognize and honor nonhuman nature as a world we did not create, a world with its own independent, nonhuman reasons for being as it is. The autonomy of non-human nature seems to me an indispensable corrective to human arrogance. Any way of looking at nature that helps us remember—as wilderness also tends to do—that the interests of people are not necessarily identical to those of every other creature or of the earth itself is likely to foster responsible be-havior. To the extent that wilderness has served as an important vehicle for ar-ticulating deep moral values regarding our obligations and responsibilities to the nonhuman world, I would not want to jettison the contributions it has made to our culture's ways of thinking about nature.

44   If the core problem of wilderness is that it distances us too much from the very things it teaches us to value, then the question we must ask is what it can tell us about home, the place where we live. How can we take the positive val-ues we associate with wilderness and bring them closer to home? I think the answer to this question will come by broadening our sense of the otherness that wilderness seeks to define and protect. In reminding us of the world we did not make, wilderness can teach profound feelings of humility and respect as we confront our fellow beings and the earth itself. Feelings like these argue for the importance of self-awareness and self-criticism as we exercise our own ability to transform the world around us, helping us set responsible limits to human mastery—which without such limits too easily becomes human hubris. Wilderness is the place where, symbolically at least, we try to withhold our power to dominate.

45   Wallace Stegner once wrote of

> the special human mark, the special record of human passage, that distinguishes man from all other species. It is rare enough among men, impossible to any other form of life. *It is simply the deliberate and chosen refusal to make any marks at all.* . . . We are the most dangerous species of life on the planet, and every other species, even the earth itself, has cause to fear our power to exterminate. But we are also the only species which, when it chooses to do so, will go to great effort to save what it might destroy.

The myth of wilderness, which Stegner knowingly reproduces in these re-marks, is that we can somehow leave nature untouched by our passage. By now it should be clear that this for the most part is an illusion. But Stegner's deeper message then becomes all the more compelling. If living in history means that we cannot help leaving marks on a fallen world, then the dilemma we face is to decide what kinds of marks we wish to leave. It is just here that our cultural traditions of wilderness remain so important. In the broadest sense, wilderness teaches us to ask whether the Other must always bend to our will, and, if not, under what circumstances it should be allowed to flourish without our intervention. This is surely a question worth asking about every-thing we do, and not just about the natural world.

When we visit a wilderness area, we find ourselves surrounded by plants 46 and animals and physical landscapes whose otherness compels our attention. In forcing us to acknowledge that they are not of our making, that they have little or no need of our continued existence, they recall for us a creation far greater than our own. In the wilderness, we need no reminder that a tree has its own reasons for being, quite apart from us. The same is less true in the gar-dens we plant and tend ourselves: there it is far easier to forget the otherness of the tree. Indeed, one could almost measure wilderness by the extent to which our recognition of its otherness requires a conscious, willed act on our part. The romantic legacy means that wilderness is more a state of mind than a fact of nature, and the state of mind that today most defines wilderness is *wonder*. The striking power of the wild is that wonder in the face of it requires no act of will, but forces itself upon us—as an expression of the nonhuman world expe-rienced through the lens of our cultural history—as proof that ours is not the only presence in the universe.

Wilderness gets us into trouble only if we imagine that this experience of 47 wonder and otherness is limited to the remote corners of the planet, or that it somehow depends on pristine landscapes we ourselves do not inhabit. Noth-ing could be more misleading. The tree in the garden is in reality no less other, no less worthy of our wonder and respect, than the tree in an ancient forest that has never known an axe or a saw—even though the tree in the forest re-flects a more intricate web of ecological relationships. The tree in the garden could easily have sprung from the same seed as the tree in the forest, and we can claim only its location and perhaps its form as our own. Both trees stand apart from us; both share our common world. The special power of the tree in the wilderness is to remind us of this fact. It can teach us to recognize the wild-ness we did not see in the tree we planted in our own back yard. By seeing the otherness in that which is most unfamiliar, we can learn to see it too in that which at first seemed merely ordinary. If wilderness can do this—if it can help us perceive and respect a nature we had forgotten to recognize as natural—then it will become part of the solution to our environmental dilemmas rather than part of the problem.

This will happen, however, only if we abandon the dualism that sees the 48 tree in the garden as artificial—completely fallen and unnatural—and the tree in the wilderness as natural—completely pristine and wild. Both trees in some ultimate sense are wild; both in a practical sense now depend on our manage-ment and care. We are responsible for both, even though we can claim credit for neither. Our challenge is to stop thinking of such things according to a set of bipolar moral scales in which the human and the nonhuman, the unnatural and the natural, the fallen and the unfallen, serve as our conceptual map for understanding and valuing the world. Instead, we need to embrace the full continuum of a natural landscape that is also cultural, in which the city, the suburb, the pastoral, and the wild each has its proper place, which we permit ourselves to celebrate without needlessly denigrating the others. We need to honor the Other within and the Other next door as much as we do the exotic Other that lives far away—a lesson that applies as much to people as it does to (other) natural things. In particular, we need to discover a common middle ground in which all of these things, from the city to the wilderness, can somehow be encompassed in the word "home." Home, after all, is the place where finally we make our living. It is the place for which we take responsibility, the place we try to sustain so we can pass on what is best in it (and in ourselves) to our children.

49   The task of making a home in nature is what Wendell Berry has called "the forever unfinished lifework of our species." "The only thing we have to preserve nature with," he writes, "is culture; the only thing we have to preserve wildness with is domesticity." Calling a place home inevitably means that we will *use* the nature we find in it, for there can be no escape from manipulating and working and even killing some parts of nature to make our home. But if we acknowledge the autonomy and otherness of the things and creatures around us—an autonomy our culture has taught us to label with the word "wild"—then we will at least think carefully about the uses to which we put them, and even ask if we should use them at all. Just so can we still join Thoreau in declaring that "in Wildness is the preservation of the World," for *wild*ness (as opposed to wilderness) can be found anywhere: in the seemingly tame fields and woodlots of Massachusetts, in the cracks of a Manhattan sidewalk, even in the cells of our own bodies. As Gary Snyder has wisely said, "A person with a clear heart and open mind can experience the wilderness anywhere on earth. It is a quality of one's own consciousness. The planet is a wild place and always will be." To think ourselves capable of causing "the end of nature" is an act of great hubris, for it means forgetting the wildness that dwells everywhere within and around us.

50   Learning to honor the wild—learning to remember and acknowledge the autonomy of the Other—means striving for critical self-consciousness in all of our actions. It means that deep reflection and respect must accompany each act of use, and means too that we must always consider the possibility of non-use. It means looking at the part of nature we intend to turn toward our own ends and asking whether we can use it again and again and again—sustainably— without its being diminished in the process. It means never imagining that we can flee into a mythical wilderness to escape history and the obligation to take responsibility for our own actions that history inescapably entails. Most of all, it means practicing remembrance and gratitude, for thanksgiving is the simplest and most basic of ways for us to recollect the nature, the culture, and the history that have come together to make the world as we know it. If wildness can stop being (just) out there and start being (also) in here, if it can start being as humane as it is natural, then perhaps we can get on with the unending task of struggling to live rightly in the world—not just in the garden, not just in the wilderness, but in the home that encompasses them both.

FOCUS ON ECOLOGY

1. Cronon makes the claim that "the most troubling cultural baggage that accompanies the celebration of wilderness has less to do with remote rain forests and peoples than with the ways we think about ourselves." How do you see the interaction between humans and wilderness? Do your experiences with "wilderness" affect how you think about not just the wilderness you've encountered, but ones you have never seen?
2. To expand on the discussion you began in your journal, consider, after having read Cronon's essay, what your definition of wilderness excludes and what it includes. What you have learned from Cronon's essay?
3. When did wilderness begin?

FOCUS ON WRITING

1. Cronon recounts a good deal of history regarding the idea of wilderness. How would you summarize the historical definitions of wilderness? What has the relationship been between wilderness and history? What effect does Cronon's account of the history of wilderness have on how he makes his argument?
2. Part of what Cronon suggests in looking at the ways wilderness has been represented historically is that wilderness was not defined by a singular force—one book, one person, one time—but that history is continuously altering the idea of wilderness. If this is the case, *wilderness* is a term whose definition is dependent on the understanding of many texts, cultural arti facts, and histories. What kinds of texts would you suggest contribute to our understanding of wilderness? Do those texts affect how we read Cronon's essay? Did they affect how Cronon wrote this essay?
3. What does Cronon mean when he concludes the essay by saying "Learning to honor the wild—learning to remember and acknowledge the autonomy of the Other—means striving for critical self-consciousness in all of our actions"?

FOR DISCUSSION

Early in his essay, Cronon makes the claim that part of our definitions of *wilderness* come from experiences that at first seem special to us as individuals, but that we later learn are similar to experiences other individuals have had, too. As a class, discuss some of the experiences you've had in wilderness settings. As you discuss these moments, try to find similar experiences within the class population and discuss how these familiar experiences help you personally and the class as a whole to think about wilderness. Also, consider how the class's similar experiences might differ from experiences students in a different geographical, cultural, economic, or historical location may have.

WRITING IN RESPONSE

Cronon turns to journalist Bill McKibben's book *The End of Nature,* in which McKibben argues, "We and our children will henceforth live in a biosphere completely altered by our own activity." In McKibben's view, "nature has died, and we are responsible for killing it." Obviously, we cannot respond to all of McKibben's argument here, but the summary Cronon provides is already a strong argument.

Begin by considering whether you agree with McKibben's position, then consider how you would defend your own position as to the state of the planet's natural environment. In a short essay, respond to McKibben's argument and explain why you align yourself with McKibben or against him.

What We Talk About When We Talk About Wilderness

Ted Kerasote

Ted Kerasote has written for Sports Afield *for over 19 years. He is also the author of* Heart of Home: People, Wildlife, Place. *Much of his writing, like the essay found here, addresses the relationships between people and nature. Unlike many who write about such subjects, Kerasote's writing reaches a large population through the medium of an outdoor magazine.*

JOURNAL ASSIGNMENT

Consider what a reader who might purchase *Sports Afield* might look for in an article that attempts to define nature and wilderness. That is, take a few minutes to write about who you envision readers of *Sports Afield* to be.

1 Before Europeans came to the Americas the continents had no wilderness. What they did have was tens of millions of aboriginal people who—centuries before the landfalls of Columbus, Erik the Red, and probably various Chinese, Egyptian, and Celtic mariners—had already explored and named nearly every mountain range, valley, swamp, prairie, peninsula, cove and forest of the "new world." These people—Algonquin, Gros Ventre and Inca, Navajo, Carib and

Sioux—ate the two continents' fish and birds and mammals, their fruit and roots and leaves, burned their grasses, cut their trees, and hoed their soil. They traveled far, trading hides and shells and stones: Yellowstone obsidian is found in gravesites as far away as Ohio and Ontario.

These Americans had commerce and culture, waterways, roads and trails, 2 and many of them had the acute sense that the world was infused with spirit and supported them kindly. They didn't live in a wilderness—meaning what the European mind conceived of as a hostile blank stretch on the map needing to be tamed and filled in. Rather, what Europeans called wilderness, aboriginal Americans called home.

In *Wilderness and the American Mind,* the historian Roderick Nash discusses 3 how the unique circumstances of Old World geography and the tenets of Christianity gave birth to the idea of wilderness as something separate from human life. When agrarian Teutonic cultures expanded into dark, primeval and northern forests, they used the root word *will* to describe these landscapes as self-willed, or uncontrollable. From *willed* came *wild*, meaning lost or unruly, to which the Old English suffixed *déor* (animal) to denote creatures not under the control of man. Etymologically, *wild-déor-ness* means "the place of wild beasts."

When Europeans colonized North America they found forests and beasts 4 aplenty, and they inevitably colored the territory with the geography of the Near East and the parables of the Bible. These defined wilderness not merely as an inhospitable wasteland, but also as a place of testing, purification, and final redemption when God transformed the arid wilderness into a watered agrarian paradise overseen by the faithful. "In the wilderness shall waters break out," declares the prophet Isaiah, "and streams in the desert. . . . And a highway shall be there . . . called The Way of Holiness; . . . no lion shall be there, nor any ravenous beast . . . but the redeemed shall walk there." Little wonder that Puritans like Michael Wigglesworth and Cotton Mather saw the forest-choked shore of New England as "a waste and howling wilderness," "the Devils den" waiting to be cleared, plowed and filled with livestock.

Two centuries of American energy were spent on this very task. The forest 5 was cut and the prairie plowed at an astonishing rate: 25 million acres of the Mississippi Valley were deforested each year during the mid-1800s. Crossing the river, pioneers slaughtered the bison and trapped-out the beaver, exterminating wolves and grizzlies and Indians along the way. The continent was bridged by rail and telegraph. In 1893 the historian Frederick Jackson Turner declared the frontier gone; the geography, actual and imaginary, that made these new Americans American—wild country, wild beasts, wild challenges— had been "conquered," and had vanished. Today, there is no place in the lower 48 states farther than 30 miles from a road.

Fifty years before Turner penned his famous essay, some Americans had al- 6 ready begun to take stock of what was being lost. Henry David Thoreau, who lived in a cabin at Walden Pond, a mile from his nearest neighbor, from 1845 to

1847, wrote that society—urbanized, pastoral, disconnected from its roots—had become tame and insipid, and that men had "become the tools of their tools" and led "lives of quiet desperation." He wanted to live deliberately, sturdily and simply, trying to learn what the woods had to teach. Living at Walden was the seminal time of Thoreau's life, shaping not only his own credo concerning the difference between civilization and nature, but also that of generations that would follow him and whom history would call environmentalists. "Life consists with wildness," Thoreau stated boldly. "The most alive is the wildest." He concluded: "In Wildness is the preservation of the World."

7   The Civil War diverted American thought from what balance might be struck between advancing civilization and retreating nature. In the peace that followed, Congress did take action, creating Yellowstone as the world's first national park in 1872. Given the immensity of the West, and the enormity of the destruction that was taking place, the 2.2-million-acre park was a gesture of postage-stamp proportions. Few knew this more clearly than Theodore Roosevelt—hunter, Dakota cattle rancher, and well-connected New York socialite and politician. In 1887, depressed and angered by the slaughter of wildlife for market hunting, he helped form the Boone and Crockett Club. The purpose was to "promote manly sport with the rifle," to work "for the preservation of the large game of this country," and to set aside the nation's forests in protected "reserves" that would be cradles of wildlife.

8   The latter goal was implemented when Boone and Crockett, members began to lobby President Benjamin Harrison's new Secretary of the Interior, John W. Noble, who helped to tack an innocuous rider, "Section 24," onto some pending legislation. At the counseling of Noble, and using the powers granted him by the rider, Harrison proclaimed 15 forest reserves totaling 13 million acres. It set a precedent; millions of acres in forests were set aside by later presidents.

9   Opinion on what to do with these forest reserves was split, some individuals calling for their total preservation, others for their management and use. John Muir, explorer of Yosemite, mountaineer and writer, was in the former camp. Standing on the edge of Yosemite Falls as a young man, he had imagined himself a drop of water cascading in rainbows to the valley below, exulting, "You bathe in these spirit-beams, turning round and round, as if warming at a camp-fire. Presently you lose consciousness of your own separate existence: you blend with the landscape, and become part and parcel of nature." He spent his adult life expounding the message of unity between humans and nature, barnstorming for the creation of national parks and national forests as inviolable sanctuaries. "Thousands of tired, nerve-shaken, over-civilized people," he wrote in the January 1898 issue of *Atlantic*, "are beginning to find out that going to the mountains is going home; that wildness is a necessity; and that mountain parks and reservations are useful not only as fountains of timber and irrigating rivers, but as fountains of life."

10   One of his companions on an 1896 government-sponsored forest commission to decide how to manage the nation's forests, the European-trained silvi-

culturist, Gifford Pinchot, thought differently. Schooled in the tradition of sustained yield, he wrote, "Forestry is Tree Farming. Forestry is handling trees so that one crop follows another." As first head of the U.S. Forest Service under President Theodore Roosevelt, Pinchot was able to win over Roosevelt to this utilitarian ideal and began to implement it, changing forever the complexion of wild lands in America. After Pinchot, some of the national forests would be managed for multiple use, including logging, mining, grazing as well as recreation, and some set aside as roadless, de facto "wilderness," though that term was not created in the legal sense until 1964.

In the intervening six decades the nascent rift that had existed in the back-to- 11 nature movement widened into a canyon: the multiple-use conservationists on one rim, the forever-wild preservationists on the other, the question of how much wild lands should be set aside debated constantly between them. Two of the most eloquent spokesmen for more wild lands were Robert Marshall and Aldo Leopold. Marshall was a phenomenal hiker, covering 30, 40, even 60 miles a day, a man who had a hunger for living in undeveloped country. Starting in 1924, he roamed over Montana, Idaho and Alaska, seeing the remaining wild lands of the United States and beginning to formulate a plan to preserve them. In the February 1930 issue of *Scientific Monthly* he published "The Problem of Wilderness," which set down a definition of the term. "The dominant attributes of such an area," wrote Marshall, "are: first, that it requires anyone who exists in it to depend exclusively on his own effort for survival; and second, that it preserves as nearly as possible the primitive environment. This means that all roads, power transportation and settlement are barred." This language was partially incorporated into the Wilderness Act of 1964. Lest his readers be unable to grasp the need for setting aside such areas, Marshall documented the value of wilderness: It had intrinsic beauty; it allowed people space to re-create mind, heart, and inner peace; it gave urbanites the opportunity for adventure, which for Marshall meant "venturing beyond the boundary of normal aptitude, extending oneself to the limit of capacity, [and] courageously facing peril."

No Pollyanna, Marshall anticipated the counter-arguments of the motor- 12 ized vehicle industry, which would claim that wilderness would exclude the majority of recreationists. "This is almost as irrational," said Marshall, "as contending that because more people enjoy bathing than art exhibits, therefore we should change our picture galleries into swimming holes." He also noted that "there are certain things that cannot be enjoyed by everybody. If everybody tries to enjoy them, nobody gets any pleasure out of them."

As chief forester of the Bureau of Indian Affairs from 1933 to 1937, and then 13 as chief of the Division of Recreation and Lands in the Forest Service, Marshall helped set aside 18.8 million acres for study as roadless areas. He also helped inaugurate and bankroll The Wilderness Society, which proposed that roadless areas be protected from commercialization.

14   Marshall died in 1939 at the age of 38, but eventually, the country he mapped in Alaska became Gates of the Arctic National Park; the Idaho land in which he did his doctoral research was named the Selway-Bitterroot Wilderness Area; and Montana's Bob Marshall Wilderness Area of course bears his name. He also brought Aldo Leopold into The Wilderness Society.

15   Beginning his professional career as a forester in Arizona and New Mexico, Leopold was able to get the U.S. Forest Service to create its first roadless area in 1924—574,000 acres of the Gila National Forest in New Mexico. He went on to write the first game management text and eventually a slim volume of essays, *A Sand County Almanac,* in which he melded biology, ethics and politics, counseling a less domineering role for humans in nature. Published in 1949, the essays describe what Leopold called "The Land Ethic."

16   "A thing is right," he wrote, "when it preserves the integrity, stability and beauty of the biotic community. It is wrong when it tends otherwise." Such communities could not be created, said Leopold, until people changed their role "from conqueror of the land-community to plain member and citizen of it." Nothing could help reduce human conquest of land more than by setting aside big chunks of it as wilderness. How big? Leopold thought wilderness had to be "big enough to absorb a two week pack trip."

17   The problem, however, was that even when wilderness areas were set aside in national forests or parks, they were maintained by administrational fiat. They could be lost because the next administration didn't like them. A national wilderness system was needed. By 1964 supporters of such a system, spearheaded by The Wilderness Society, the Sierra Club and the National Wildlife Federation, had enough votes in Congress to pass the unprecedented legislation, which declared, "A wilderness, in contrast with those areas where man and his own works dominate the landscape, is hereby recognized as an area where the earth and its community of life are untrammeled by man, where man himself is a visitor who does not remain." Congress's definition went on to say that wilderness retained its primeval character, did not have permanent improvements or human habitation, had outstanding opportunities for solitude or a primitive and unconfined type of recreation, and must be at least 5000 acres.

18   Today the National Wilderness Preservation System consists of 104 million acres, or 4.7 percent of the United States, ranging from the 19-million-acre immensity of the Arctic National Wildlife Refuge (ANWR), 8 million acres of which is legally designated wilderness, to the 2420-acre Monomoy Wilderness at the bend of Cape Cod, Massachusetts. (The Eastern Wilderness Act of 1974 allowed areas smaller than 5000 acres to be considered.)

19   Both ANWR and Monomoy are legally designated wildernesses, yet there is a crucial difference between the two, and it isn't merely size or remoteness: it's wildlife. As iconoclastic nature writer Edward Abbey once remarked, the essential ingredient of wilderness is the presence of big, dangerous animals that can kill you.

But that only gets at half of the importance of dangerous animals. If a 20 wilderness has healthy populations of predators like grizzly bears and wolves (the latter of which virtually never eat people these days), it often means that it is big enough to support not only these wide-ranging species but also the entire food chain beneath them. Such an ecosystem has a full complement of its indigenous life: It is rich in biodiversity.

Ultimately, how we define wildness may be determined by this biological 21 definition. As Peter Steinhart explains in *The Company of Wolves*, "In the future, wildness is going to be defined by the ways the environment modifies the expression of genes."

In most civilized environments humans have drastically curtailed the ex- 22 pression of genes. Such places—farms, cities, suburbs—may be economically rich but biologically impoverished and dull. Again Thoreau was ahead of his time when he said, "Dullness is but another name for tameness."

Tameness occurs not only when we destroy habitat, causing species to go 23 extinct. It also occurs as wild places become popularized and overvisited, their likenesses copied and recopied in photographs, videos and guidebooks, destroying their firsthand, first-seen magic that an original encounter with the wild produces. Surely, much of the power of the wild lies in its unadvertised, numinous privacy. It is this very quality—sacredness—that is fast vanishing from the natural world.

The question before us now is whether we will continue to control nature, even 24 in those places we define as wild. Will we restore, for instance, predators like wolves, grizzly bears, and mountain lions, only to confine them to the narrow political boundaries of their recovery areas? Will we let wildfires rage, beaches erode, avalanches seal canyons, creating habitats, that to our eyes look ugly but are essential for the healthy function of ecosystems? Can we limit human visitation, can we leave the wild alone, or will we continue to manipulate nature in the name of preserving it, creating a miniature version that makes us feel in control?

It may continue to be easier to designate truncated, set-aside landscapes 25 called "wildernesses," and manage them for an encapsulated form of biodiversity than to let the wild out of the wilderness to circulate freely around our lives. To accomplish that we would have to change the basic paradigm of how we live: with gross human overpopulation; with unsustainable use of resources; with an almost total lack of participation in procuring our food, fuel and shelter—a lack that allows us to assume that we live here in civilization and wild nature exists *out there.*

More than trying to redefine the wild in order to preserve it, we might bet- 26 ter spend our energies redefining ourselves, creating a definition that understands nature and wildness as the stewards of humanity rather than positing humanity as the steward of nature. This will take a long time. It has taken 500 years to modify the Americas to a civilized ideal. It may take another 500 years—ecological awareness improving generation by generation—to reduce the earth's human population to a billion or so people; to develop technologies that operate as nature does, each byproduct of industry "food" for useful production rather than toxic waste; to not only preserve endangered species in national parks and reserves, but also to allow them to repopulate their vast historic ranges while simultaneously letting forests and prairies reclaim the monoculture plant communities of agribusiness.

27   Perhaps then we might have the kind of country that Columbus "discovered." Not a wilderness—a wildly alive country. Home.

FOCUS ON ECOLOGY

1. In the concluding section of Kerasote's essay, he writes, "The question before us now is whether we will continue to control nature, even in those places that we define as wild." What in your experience might suggest that we have begun to answer Kerasote's question, either positively or negatively? That is, do you see local organizations and governments wanting to extend more control over wild places or are they backing away from control? What local laws affect local wild places?
2. Kerasote introduces Aldo Leopold's "The Land Ethic" toward the end of his essay. Leopold is often credited with asking us to think about how we behave in regard to nature. That is, he added ethics to our considerations about nature. Many of the environmental arguments taking place in your home environments can be evaluated and considered from ethical positions. What are the ethical dilemmas expressed in a local environmental debate with which you are familiar? Try to define and discuss them without becoming caught up in the emotions of the debate.
3. How would you characterize the history of wilderness in America? What would you consider to be some of the most important factors in defining wilderness now that you have read Kerasote's article?

FOCUS ON WRITING

1. We noted that Kerasote's essay was published in *Sports Afield*. Might a *Sports Afield* audience define nature and wilderness differently from other audiences? Why? What assumptions do you make about that audience?
2. Why do you suppose that Kerasote, when describing the lives of America's aboriginal residents, is clear to note that they had "explored and named nearly every mountain range, valley, swamp, prairie, peninsula, cove and forest of the 'new world'"? What is gained by expanding this point?
3. Kerasote spends some time examining the meaning of the word *wilderness* not only from a historical perspective but from a linguistic perspective as well. He states, for instance, "etymologically, *wild-déor-ness* means 'the place of wild beasts.'" Why might it be important for us to know this meaning

while reading Cronon's argument? Can you find similar definitions of words like *nature* or *environment?*

FOR DISCUSSION

Kerasote begins his essay with the simple statement, "Before Europeans came to the Americas the continents had no wilderness." What Kerasote suggests is that by naming something "wilderness" we assign it a particular value. Kerasote then discusses how wilderness was viewed by [pre-European] inhabitants of the Americas. Discuss with your classmates some of these values and how we might learn from them. Consider why we split "nature" from "culture."

WRITING IN RESPONSE

Kerasote notes that "there is no place in the lower 48 states farther than 30 miles from a road." Think of place in the lower 48 states which you visited and considered, at the time, to be truly wild. Knowing what Kerasote has said about the availability of roads, does the place about which you are thinking become any "less wild"? In a personal narrative, address your perception of that place before and after reading Kerasote's essay.

Landscape and Narrative

Barry Lopez

Barry [Holstun] Lopez was born in 1945 in Port Chester, New York. He grew up in southern California and New York City and attended college in the Midwest before moving to Oregon, where he has lived since 1968. He has worked as a professional writer since 1970, publishing 18 books of fiction and nonfiction, including Of Wolves and Men, Arctic Dreams: Imagination and Desire in a Northern Landscape, Crossing Open Ground, The Rediscovery of North America, About This Life: Journeys on the Threshold of Memory, Apologia, *and* Lessons from the Wolverine. *His books have been translated into numerous languages including Chinese, Dutch, Finnish, French, German, Italian, Japanese, Norwegian, Spanish, and Swedish. Lopez's work is most frequently referred to as "nature writing" and he has earned a reputation as one of the best writers writing about natural history and environment. In "Landscape and Narrative," Lopez examines the relationship between the physical landscape of a place and the landscape of a place that is created through storytelling.*

As you read this essay, consider not only what Lopez proposes about this relationship, but also about how his essay also creates landscape in the places it describes.

JOURNAL ASSIGNMENT

In his essay "Landscape and Narrative," Lopez specifically looks at how we identify something as *landscape* and what role that landscape plays in storytelling. In your journal, address what you understand *landscape* to mean and then write what you see as the relationship—if there is one—between landscape and storytelling.

1   One summer evening in a remote village in the Brooks Range of Alaska, I sat among a group of men listening to hunting stories about the trapping and pursuit of animals. I was particularly interested in several incidents involving wolverine, in part because a friend of mine was studying wolverine in Canada, among the Cree, but, too, because I find this animal such an intense creature. To hear about its life is to learn more about fierceness.

2   Wolverines are not intentionally secretive, hiding their lives from view, but they are seldom observed. The range of their known behavior is less than that of, say, bears or wolves. Still, that evening no gratuitous details were set out. This was somewhat odd, for wolverine easily excite the imagination; they can loom suddenly in the landscape with authority, with an aura larger than their compact physical dimensions, drawing one's immediate and complete attention. Wolverine also have a deserved reputation for resoluteness in the worst winters, for ferocious strength. But neither did these attributes induce the men to embellish.

3   I listened carefully to these stories, taking pleasure in the sharply observed detail surrounding the dramatic thread of events. The story I remember most vividly was about a man hunting a wolverine from a snow machine in the spring. He followed the animal's tracks for several miles over rolling tundra in a certain valley. Soon he caught sight ahead of a dark spot on the crest of a hill—the wolverine pausing to look back. The hunter was catching up, but each time he came over a rise the wolverine was looking back from the next rise, just out of range. The hunter topped one more rise and met the wolverine bounding toward him. Before he could pull his rifle from its scabbard the wolverine flew across the engine cowl and the windshield, hitting him square in the chest. The hunter scrambled his arms wildly, trying to get the wolverine out of his lap, and fell over as he did so. The wolverine jumped clear as the snow machine rolled over, and fixed the man with a stare. He had not bitten, not even scratched the man. Then the wolverine walked away. The man thought of reaching for the gun, but no, he did not.

The other stories were like this, not so much making a point as evoking 4 something about contact with wild animals that would never be completely understood.

When the stories were over, four or five of us walked out of the home of 5 our host. The surrounding land, in the persistent light of a far northern summer, was still visible for miles—the striated, pitched massifs of the Brooks Range; the shy, willow-lined banks of the John River flowing south from Anaktuvuk Pass; and the flat tundra plain, opening with great affirmation to the north. The landscape seemed alive because of the stories. It was precisely these ocherous tones, this kind of willow, exactly this austerity that had informed the wolverine narratives. I felt exhilaration, and a deeper confirmation of the stories. The mundane tasks which awaited me I anticipated now with pleasure. The stories had renewed in me a sense of the purpose of my life.

This feeling, an inexplicable renewal of enthusiasm after storytelling, is familiar 6 to many people. It does not seem to matter greatly what the subject is, as long as the context is intimate and the story is told for its own sake, not forced to serve merely as the vehicle for an idea. The tone of the story need not be solemn. The darker aspects of life need not be ignored. But I think inti-macy is indispensable—a feeling that derives from the listener's trust and a storyteller's certain knowledge of his subject and regard for his audience. This intimacy deepens if the storyteller tempers his authority with humility, or when terms of idiomatic expression, or at least the physical setting for the story, are shared.

I think of two landscapes—one outside the self, the other within. The external landscape is the one we see—not only the line and color of the land and its 7 shading at different times of the day, but also its plants and animals in season, its weather, its geology, the record of its climate and evolution. If you walk up, say, a dry arroyo in the Sonoran Desert you will feel a mounding and rolling of sand and silt beneath your foot that is distinctive. You will anticipate the crumbling of the sedimentary earth in the arroyo bank as your hand reaches out, and in that tangible evidence you will sense a history of water in the region. Perhaps a black-throated sparrow lands in a paloverde bush—the resiliency of the twig under the bird, that precise shade of yellowish-green against the milk-blue sky, the fluttering whir of the arriving sparrow, are what I mean by "the landscape." Draw on the smell of creosote bush, or clack stones together in the dry air. Feel how light is the desiccated dropping of the kangaroo rat. Study an animal track obscured by the wind. These are all elements of the land, and what makes the landscape comprehensible are the relationships between them. One learns a landscape finally not by knowing the name or identity of everything in it, but by perceiving the relationships in it—like that between the sparrow and the twig. The difference between the relationships and the elements is the same as that between written history and a catalog of events.

The second landscape I think of is an interior one, a kind of projection 8 within a person of a part of the exterior landscape. Relationships in the exterior landscape include those that are named and discernible, such as the nitrogen cycle, or a vertical sequence of Ordovician limestone, and others that are un-codified or ineffable, such as winter light falling on a particular kind of granite, or the effect of humidity on the frequency of a blackpoll warbler's burst of song. That these relationships have purpose and order, however inscrutable they may seem to us, is a tenet of evolution. Similarly, the speculations, intu-itions, and formal ideas we refer to as "mind" are a set of relationships in the interior landscape with purpose and order; some of these are obvious, many impenetrably subtle. The shape and character of these relationships in a per-son's thinking, I believe, are deeply influenced by where on this earth one goes, what one touches, the patterns one observes in nature—the intricate history of one's life in the land, even a life in the city, where wind, the chirp of birds, the line of a falling leaf, are known. These thoughts are arranged, further, accord-ing to the thread of one's moral, intellectual, and spiritual development. The interior landscape responds to the character and subtlety of an exterior land-scape: the shape of the individual mind is affected by land as it is by genes.

9   In stories like those I heard at Anaktuvuk Pass about wolverine, the rela-tionship between separate elements in the land is set forth clearly. It is put in a simple framework of sequential incidents and apposite detail. If the exterior landscape in limned well, the listener often feels that he has heard something pleasing and authentic—trustworthy. We derive this sense of confidence I think not so much from verifiable truth as from an understanding that lying has played no role in the narrative. The storyteller is obligated to engage the reader with a precise vocabulary, to set forth a coherent and dramatic rendering of in-cidents—and to be ingenuous.

10   When one hears a story one takes pleasure in it for different reasons—for the euphony of its phrases, an aspect of the plot, or because one identifies with one of the characters. With certain stories certain individuals may experience a deeper, more profound sense of well-being. This latter phenomenon, in my un-derstanding, rests at the heart of storytelling as an elevated experience among aboriginal peoples. It results from bringing two landscapes together. The exterior landscape is organized according to principles or laws or tendencies beyond human control. It is understood to contain an integrity that is beyond human analysis and unimpeachable. Insofar as the storyteller depicts various subtle and obvious relationships in the exterior landscape accurately in his story, and inso-far as he orders them along traditional lines of meaning to create the narrative, the narrative will "ring true." The listener who "takes the story to heart" will feel a pervasive sense of congruence within himself and also with the world.

11   Among the Navajo and, as far as I know, many other native peoples, the land is thought to exhibit a sacred order. That order is the basis of ritual. The rituals themselves reveal the power in that order. Art, architecture, vocabulary, and costume, as well as ritual, are derived from the perceived natural order of the universe—from observations and meditations on the exterior landscape. An indigenous philosophy—metaphysics, ethics, epistemology, aesthetics, and logic—may also be derived from a people's continuous attentiveness to both

the obvious (scientific) and ineffable (artistic) orders of the local landscape. Each individual, further, undertakes to order his interior landscape according to the exterior landscape. To succeed in this means to achieve a balanced state of mental health.

I think of the Navajo for a specific reason. Among the various sung cere- 12 monies of this people—Enemyway, Coyoteway, Red Antway, Uglyway—is one called Beautyway. In the Navajo view, the elements of one's interior life—one's psychological makeup and moral bearing—are subject to a persistent principle of disarray. Beautyway is, in part, a spiritual invocation of the order of the exterior universe, that irreducible, holy complexity that manifests itself as all things changing through time (a Navajo definition of beauty, hózhǫ́ǫ́). The purpose of this invocation is to recreate in the individual who is the subject of the Beautyway ceremony that same order, to make the individual again a reflection of the myriad enduring relationships of the landscape.

I believe story functions in a similar way. A story draws on relationships in 13 the exterior landscape and projects them onto the interior landscape. The purpose of storytelling is to achieve harmony between the two landscapes, to use all the elements of story—syntax, mood, figures of speech—in a harmonious way to reproduce the harmony of the land in the individual's interior. Inherent in story is the power to reorder a state of psychological confusion through contact with the pervasive truth of those relationships we call "the land."

These thoughts, of course, are susceptible to interpretation. I am convinced, 14 however, that these observations can be applied to the kind of prose we call nonfiction as well as to traditional narrative forms such as the novel and the short story, and to some poems. Distinctions between fiction and nonfiction are sometimes obscured by arguments over what constitutes "the truth." In the aboriginal literature I am familiar with, the first distinction made among narratives is to separate the authentic from the inauthentic. Myth, which we tend to regard as fictitious or "merely metaphorical," is as authentic, as real, as the story of a wolverine in a man's lap. (A distinction is made, of course, about the elevated nature of myth—and frequently the circumstances of myth-telling are more rigorously prescribed than those for the telling of legends or vernacular stories—but all of these narratives are rooted in the local landscape. To violate *that* connection is to call the narrative itself into question.)

The power of narrative to nurture and heal, to repair a spirit in disarray, 15 rests on two things: the skillful invocation of unimpeachable sources and a listener's knowledge that no hypocrisy or subterfuge is involved. This last simple fact is to me one of the most imposing aspects of the Holocene history of man.

We are more accustomed now to thinking of "the truth" as something that 16 can be explicitly stated, rather than as something that can be evoked in a metaphorical way outside science and Occidental culture. Neither can truth be reduced to aphorism or formulas. It is something alive and unpronounceable. Story creates an atmosphere in which it becomes discernible as a pattern. For a storyteller to insist on relationships that do not exist is to lie. Lying is the opposite of story. (I do not mean to confuse ignorance with deception, or to imply that a storyteller can perceive all that is inherent in the land. Every storyteller falls short of a perfect limning of the landscape—perception and language both fail. But to make up something that is not there, something which can never be corroborated in the land, to knowingly set forth a false relationship, is to be lying, no longer telling a story.)

17   Because of the intricate, complex nature of the land, it is not always possible for a storyteller to grasp what is contained in a story. The intent of the storyteller, then, must be to evoke, honestly, some single aspect of all that the land contains. The storyteller knows that because different individuals grasp the story at different levels, the focus of his regard for truth must be at the primary one—with who was there, what happened, when, where, and why things occurred. The story will then possess similar truth at other levels—the integrity inherent at the primary level of meaning will be conveyed everywhere else. As long as the storyteller carefully describes the order before him, and uses his storytelling skill to heighten and emphasize certain relationships, it is even possible for the story to be more successful than the storyteller himself is able to imagine.

18 I would like to make a final point about the wolverine stories I heard at Anaktuvuk Pass. I wrote down the details afterward, concentrating especially on aspects of the biology and ecology of the animals. I sent the information on to my friend living with the Cree. When, many months later, I saw him, I asked whether the Cree had enjoyed these insights of the Nunamiut into the nature of the wolverine. What had they said?

19   "You know," he told me, "how they are. They said, 'That could happen.'"

20   In these uncomplicated words the Cree declared their own knowledge of the wolverine. They acknowledged that although they themselves had never seen the things the Nunamiut spoke of, they accepted them as accurate observations, because they did not consider story a context for misrepresentation. They also preserved their own dignity by not overstating their confidence in the Nunamiut, a distant and unknown people.

21   Whenever I think of this courtesy on the part of the Cree I think of the dignity that is ours when we cease to demand the truth and realize that the best we can have of those substantial truths that guide our lives is metaphorical—a story. And the most of it we are likely to discern comes only when we accord one another the respect the Cree showed the Nunamiut. Beyond this—that the interior landscape is a metaphorical representation of the exterior landscape, that the truth reveals itself most fully not in dogma but in the paradox, irony, and contradictions that distinguish compelling narratives—beyond this there are only failures of imagination: reductionism in science; fundamentalism in religion; fascism in politics.

22   Our national literatures should be important to us insofar as they sustain us with illumination and heal us. They can always do that so long as they are written with respect for both the source and the reader, and with an under-

standing of why the human heart and the land have been brought together so regularly in human history.

FOCUS ON ECOLOGY

1. Barry Lopez is rather deliberate in defining what he means by *landscape.* How do you define the term? What, for you, does the phrase *the land* evoke?
2. Lopez writes in "Landscape and Narrative," "the shape of the individual mind is affected by land as it is by genes." What do you suppose Lopez means when he claims that the mind is affected by land? Do you agree with his statement? Why or why not?
3. What do you suppose Lopez means when he writes, "Because of the intricate, complex nature of the land, it is not always possible for a storyteller to grasp what is contained in a story"?

FOCUS ON WRITING

1. In the context of Barry Lopez's "Landscape and Narrative," what is the purpose of the first section of this essay? Why does Lopez recount the wolverine story at the beginning of this piece? How does that story affect the rest of the essay?
2. According to Lopez, what is the relationship between vocabulary, storytelling, and landscape? Why do you suppose vocabulary is identified in terms of the landscapes Lopez is discussing? Do you agree with his assessment of the role of vocabulary in storytelling? Why or why not? How does Lopez himself use particular vocabularies?
3. Why does Lopez use the example of the Navajo ceremonies and Navajo thinking? What does it lend to his position?

FOR DISCUSSION

What are some of the best landscape stories you have heard? As a class, take turns telling stories that you see as exhibiting the links to landscape that Lopez discusses. Then, discuss the role of that landscape in the story and the relationship between the two.

WRITING IN RESPONSE

Take some time to write a landscape narrative. Consider the difference between telling such a story and writing such a story.

Cultured or Crabbed

Gary Snyder

Gary Snyder is the author of many poems, articles, and books, including Turtle Island (1975), The Practice of the Wild *(1990), and* Coming into the Watershed *(1994). He is considered one of the most important contemporary nature writers. His essay "Cultured or Crabbed" first appeared in his book* The Practices of the Wild *and was later reprinted in the collection* Deep Ecology for the Twenty-First Century. *In this essay, Snyder examines "what we know" and argues for a deeper sense of environmental politics. He contends that environmental politics have spread worldwide and that humans need to find a deeper connection with the natural world. As you read this essay, think about the organization of Snyder's essay as he moves from conversations about knowledge to conversations about politics.*

JOURNAL ASSIGNMENT

This selection addresses types of knowing; that is, Gary Snyder asks us to consider how we know nature, and how we know the difference between *nature* and *wild*. Throughout the assignments in this chapter, you have been asked to consider how you define, think about, and know wilderness and nature. In your journal, reflect upon your definitions and the definitions of the authors in this chapter. Are they flawed or accurate? Misleading or informative?

1   We still only know what we know: "The flavors of the peach and the apricot are not lost from generation to generation. Neither are they transmitted by book-learning" (Ezra Pound). The rest is hearsay. There is strength, freedom, sustainability, and pride in being a practiced dweller in your own surroundings, knowing what you know. There are two kinds of knowing.

2   One is that which grounds and places you in your actual condition. You know north from south, pine from fir, in which direction the new moon might be found, where the water comes from, where the garbage goes, how to shake hands, how to sharpen a knife, how the interest rates work. This sort of knowledge itself can enhance public life and save endangered species. We learn it by revivifying culture, which is like reinhabitation: moving back into a terrain that has been abused and half-forgotten—and then replanting trees, dechannelizing streambeds, breaking up asphalt. What—some would say—if there's no

"culture" left? There always is—just as much as there's always (no matter where) place and language. One's culture is in the family and the community, and it lights up when you start to do some real work together, or play, tell stories, act up—or when someone gets sick, or dies, or is born—or at a gathering like Thanksgiving. A culture is a network of neighborhoods or communities that is rooted and tended. It has limits, it is ordinary. "She's very cultured" shouldn't mean elite, but more like "well-fertilized."

(The term *culture* goes back to Latin meanings, via *colere*, such as "worship, ₃ attend to, cultivate, respect, till, take care of." The root *kwel* basically means to revolve around a center—cognate with *wheel* and Greek *telos*, "completion of a cycle," hence *teleology*. In Sanskrit this is *chakra*, "spinning wheel"—or "great wheel of the universe." The modern Hindu word is *charkha*, "spinning wheel"—with which Gandhi meditated the freedom of India while in prison.)

The other kind of knowledge comes from straying outside. Thoreau writes of ₄ the crab apple, "*Our* wild apple is wild only like myself, perchance, who belong not to the aboriginal race here, but have strayed into the woods from cultivated stock." John Muir carries these thoughts along. In *Wild Wool* he quotes a farmer friend who tells him, "Culture is an orchard apple; Nature is a crab." (To go back to the wild is to become sour, astringent, crabbed. Unfertilized, unpruned, tough, resilient, and every spring *shockingly* beautiful in bloom.) Virtually all contemporary people are cultivated stock, but we can stray back to the woods.

One departs the home to embark on a quest into an archetypal wilderness ₅ that is dangerous, threatening, and full of beasts and hostile aliens. This sort of encounter with the other—both the inner and the outer—requires giving up comfort and safety, accepting cold and hunger, and being willing to eat anything. You may never see home again. Loneliness is your bread. Your bones may turn up someday in some riverbank mud. It grants freedom, expansion, and release. Untied. Unstuck. Crazy for a while. It breaks taboo, it verges on transgression, it teaches humility. Going out—fasting—singing alone—talking across the species boundaries—praying—giving thanks—coming back.

On the mythical plane this is the source of the worldwide hero narratives. ₆ On the spiritual plane it requires embracing the other as oneself and stepping across the line—not "becoming one" or mixing things up but holding the sameness and difference delicately in mind. It can mean seeing the houses, roads, people of your old place as for the first time. It can mean every word heard to its deepest echo. It can mean mysterious tears of gratitude. Our "soul" is our dream of the other.

There is a movement toward creating a "culture of the wilderness" from ₇ within contemporary civilization. The Deep Ecology philosophers and the struggles and arguments which have taken place between them and the Green movement, the Social Ecologists, and the Ecofeminists are all part of the emerging realization that this could be tried. Deep Ecology thinkers insist that the natural world has value in its own right, that the health of natural systems should be our first concern, and that this best serves the interests of humans as well. They are well aware that primary people everywhere are our teachers in these values. The emergence of Earth First! brings a new level of urgency, boldness, and humor into environmentalism. Direct-action techniques that go back to the civil rights and labor movement days are employed in ecological issues. With Earth First!, the Great Basin finally steps onto the stage of world politics. The established environmental organizations are forced by these mavericks to become more activist. At the same time there is a rapidly growing grassroots movement in Asia, Borneo, Brazil, Siberia. It is a cause for hope that so many people worldwide—from Czech intellectuals to rainforest-dwelling mothers in Sarawak—are awakening to their power.

8   The original American environmental tradition came out of the politics of public lands and wildlife (geese, fish, ducks—hence the Audubon Society, the Izaak Walton League, and Ducks Unlimited). For decades a narrow but essential agenda of wilderness preservation took up everyone's volunteer time. With the 1970s, "conservation" became "environmentalism" as concerns extended out of the wilderness areas to broader matters of forest management, agriculture, water and air pollution, nuclear power, and all the other issues we know so well.

9   Environmental concerns and politics have spread worldwide. In some countries the focus is almost entirely on human health and welfare issues. It is proper that the range of the movement should run from wildlife to urban health. But there can be no health for humans and cities that bypasses the rest of nature. A properly radical environmentalist position is in no way antihuman. We grasp the pain of the human condition in its full complexity, and add the awareness of how desperately endangered certain key species and habitats have become. We get a lot of information—paradoxically—from deep inside civilization, from the biological and social sciences. The critical argument now within environmental circles is between those who operate from a human-centered resource management mentality and those whose values reflect an awareness of the integrity of the whole of nature. The latter position, that of Deep Ecology, is politically livelier, more courageous, more convivial, riskier, and more scientific.

10   It comes again to an understanding of the subtle but critical difference of meaning between the terms *nature* and *wild*. Nature is the subject, they say, of science. Nature can be deeply probed, as in microbiology. The wild is not to be made subject or object in this manner; to be approached it must be admitted from within, as a quality intrinsic to who we are. Nature is ultimately in no way endangered; wilderness is. The wild is indestructible, but we might not *see* the wild.

11   A culture of wilderness starts somewhere in this terrain. Civilization is part of nature—our egos play in the fields of the unconscious—history takes place in the Holocene—human culture is rooted in the primitive and the paleolithic—our body is a vertebrate mammal being—and our souls are out in the wilderness.

FOCUS ON ECOLOGY

1. Considering Snyder's claim about the spread of environmental politics, think about the ways in which you have seen environmental politics publicized in your daily life. Think, for example, about advertisements you see on television or in magazines. Consider the ways product labels draw your attention to "environmentally sound" aspects of the product. Where do you stand on the issue of using environmentalism in product advertising?
2. Snyder claims that "Environmental concerns and politics have spread worldwide." Yet, for many of us, contemplating worldwide issues is overwhelming; exploring local issues can seem a much more manageable task. Take some time to consider a local environmental issue and what the outcome might mean for local understanding of what is nature or what is wilderness. For instance, a city ordinance that permits or denies certain activities in city parks may also suggest what types of behaviors or what types of activities are appropriate in nature (camping, building fires, drinking alcoholic beverages, hunting, etc.). In what ways does your community define nature?
3. What are the two kinds of knowledge according to Snyder? What kinds of things have you come to learn through these two kinds of knowledge? Are there other kinds of knowledge as well? How might other kinds of knowledge affect how cultures view and define nature?

FOCUS ON WRITING

1. Snyder says that "there's always (no matter where) place and language." What might he mean by this? How might language be present in the middle of a wilderness? How does place appear in the middle of a conversation? Does place appear in Snyder's essay?
2. Why is it important—or is it important—that Snyder defines *culture* in the ways that he does? Does accepting his definition affect how we read his argument?
3. How does Snyder define *Deep Ecology?* What role do other schools of thought—ecofeminism, philosophy, and so on—play in Deep Ecology? How do conversations in these other areas affect the thinking and language of Deep Ecology?

FOR DISCUSSION

In "Cultured or Crabbed," Gary Snyder writes that "Civilization is part of nature." In many other definitions of nature, perhaps even in your own definitions of *nature* and *wilderness,* we often see civilization as a thing that is opposed to nature, such as R. Edward Grumbine's notion that "culture can only be opposed to wilderness." As a group, discuss the implications of Snyder's claim.

WRITING IN RESPONSE

One of the things that Snyder's essay does indirectly is to ask us to consider our own politics. In a personal narrative, explain where you stand regarding the larger, more global notions of environmental politics that Snyder addresses. That is, think about how you align yourself politically with environmental issues. Do you consider yourself an activist? Do you stay informed about issues? What issues are important to you and why? Are you more apt to be concerned about local or global issues? What do you do to show your political affiliations? Remember, by thinking of yourself as not affiliated with a particular position, you necessarily affiliate yourself with another position.

Film: *The Mosquito Coast*

The Mosquito Coast *was released by Warner Brothers in 1986. The film stars Harrison Ford as Allie Fox, an inventor who has become disgusted with American materialism. Convincing his family that America is headed to a cataclysmic war, he moves them to a South American jungle where they can start a new life. Fox hopes that the natural world of the South American jungles will provide the ideal location to introduce civilization to a culture not yet jaded by American materialism. His family—Mother (played by Helen Mirren), Charlie (played by River Phoenix), Jerry (played by Jadrien Steele), and the twins (played by Hilary and Rebecca Gordon)—faithfully follow Fox into the wilds. Their respect and devotion to Fox is ultimately questioned as his apparent madness drives him to greater extremes, imperiling his family. As you watch this film, pay close attention to how the filmmakers have chosen to visually depict different places: the jungle, urban America, a missionary post. Compare these images with the ways in which these places are discussed in the dialogue.*

JOURNAL ASSIGNMENT

The film, at its core, is not just a study of one man's mental and emotional failing, but a critique of how Americans tend to view the relationships between nature and civilization. In your journal, consider the difference between culture and nature, but address specifically why someone might want to abandon one of these situations (nature or civilization) in favor of the other.

FOCUS ON ECOLOGY

1. Why does Allie Fox choose the jungles of South America as the location for his experiment?
2. Is ice as important an invention as Fox makes it out to be? What effect do you see ice as having had in world history?
3. How does *The Mosquito Coast* depict agriculture?

FOCUS ON WRITING

1. To what specific geographical region does the title of this film refer? What role does the title play in how we watch or "read" this film?
2. The film *The Mosquito Coast* is based on a novel by Paul Theroux. In what ways do you suppose a film might depict places like those shown in the film differently from the way a novel might?
3. What role does language play in this film?

FOR DISCUSSION

As a class, discuss initial reactions to *The Mosquito Coast*. Then, consider the film for its ecological text. Does it paint a particular picture about places and the people who inhabit those places? If so, how do you respond to that image?

WRITING IN RESPONSE

From the standpoint of someone interested in issues of ecology, ecological literacy, nature, environment, write a review of *The Mosquito Coast*.

Nature

Luther Standing Bear

Luther Standing Bear was born in December 1868 on the Pine Ridge Reservation in South Dakota. His given Sioux (Lakota) name was Ota Kte, or Plenty Kill. His father was Chief Standing Bear. Luther Standing Bear was in the first class to graduate from Carlisle Indian School in Carlisle, Pennsylvania, but when he returned home, he found his people had been forced onto reservations and persecuted by the American government. Standing Bear became an activist for Indian rights. He also worked in Buffalo Bill Cody's Wild West Show, and upon returning from traveling with the show, he was made chief of the Oglala Sioux. After seven years of being chief, Luther Standing Bear left the reservation, primarily because of ongoing conflicts with the American government. He then went to Hollywood where he became president of the Indian Actor's Association and a member of the Actor's Guild of Hollywood. Standing Bear wrote several books, including his autobiography, My People the Sioux, *which was translated into both French and German;* My Indian Boyhood, *a children's book;* Land of the Spotted Eagle, *a cultural study; and a book of folktales called* Stories of the Sioux. *His writings also appeared in* American Mercury, Game and Gossip, Boy's Life, *and the* Sunday Times Magazine. *He died on February 19, 1939.*

JOURNAL ASSIGNMENT

In this selection, Luther Standing Bear, writes, "Kinship with all creatures of the earth, sky, and water was a real and active principle." Consider what it means to have not only a real principle but an active one when it comes to defining your relationship with nature. In your journal write about your current principles toward nature. What parts of your principles toward nature are principles you live by on a daily basis, and which are more idealistic?

The Lakota was a true naturist—a lover of Nature. He loved the earth and all 1 things of the earth, the attachment growing with age. The old people came literally to love the soil and they sat or reclined on the ground with a feeling of being close to a mothering power. It was good for the skin to touch the earth and the old people liked to remove their moccasins and walk with bare feet on the sacred earth. Their tipis were built upon the earth and their altars were made of earth. The birds that flew in the air came to rest upon the earth and it was the final abiding place of all things that lived and grew. The soil was soothing, strengthening, cleansing, and healing.

This is why the old Indian still sits upon the earth instead of propping him- 2 self up and away from its life-giving forces. For him, to sit or lie upon the ground is to be able to think more deeply and to feel more keenly; he can see more clearly into the mysteries of life and come closer in kinship to other lives about him.

The earth was full of sounds which the old-time Indian could hear, some- 3 times putting his ear to it so as to hear more clearly. The forefathers of the Lakotas had done this for long ages until there had come to them real understanding of earth ways. It was almost as if the man were still a part of the earth as he was in the beginning, according to the legend of the tribe. This beautiful story of the genesis of the Lakota people furnished the foundation for the love they bore for earth and all things of the earth. Wherever the Lakota went, he was with Mother Earth. No matter where he roamed by day or slept by night, he was safe with her. This thought comforted and sustained the Lakota and he was eternally filled with gratitude.

From Wakan Tanka there came a great unifying life force that flowed in 4 and through all things—the flowers of the plains, blowing winds, rocks, trees, birds, animals—and was the same force that had been breathed into the first man. Thus all things were kindred and brought together by the same Great Mystery.

Kinship with all creatures of the earth, sky, and water was a real and active 5 principle. For the animal and bird world there existed a brotherly feeling that kept the Lakota safe among them. And so close did some of the Lakotas come to their feathered and furred friends that in true brotherhood they spoke a common tongue.

The animal had rights—the right of man's protection, the right to live, the 6 right to multiply, the right to freedom, and the right to man's indebtedness—

and in recognition of these rights the Lakota never enslaved the animal, and spared all life that was not needed for food and clothing.

7   This concept of life and its relations was humanizing and gave to the Lakota an abiding love. It filled his being with the joy and mystery of living; it gave him reverence for all life; it made a place for all things in the scheme of existence with equal importance to all. The Lakota could despise no creature, for all were of one blood, made by the same hand, and filled with the essence of the Great Mystery. In spirit the Lakota was humble and meek. 'Blessed are the meek; for they shall inherit the earth' was true for the Lakota, and from the earth he inherited secrets long since forgotten. His religion was sane, normal, and human.

8   Reflection upon life and its meaning, consideration of its wonders, and observation of the world of creatures, began with childhood. The earth, which was called *Maka,* and the sun, called *Anpetuwi,* represented two functions somewhat analogous to those of male and female. The earth brought forth life, but the warming, enticing rays of the sun coaxed it into being. The earth yielded, the sun engendered.

9   In talking to children, the old Lakota would place a hand on the ground and explain: 'We sit in the lap of our Mother. From her we, and all other living things, come. We shall soon pass, but the place where we now rest will last forever.' So we, too, learned to sit or lie on the ground and become conscious of life about us in its multitude of forms. Sometimes we boys would sit motionless and watch the swallow, the tiny ants, or perhaps some small animal at its work and ponder on its industry and ingenuity; or we lay on our backs and looked long at the sky and when the stars came out made shapes from the various groups. The morning and evening star always attracted attention, and the Milky Way was a path which was traveled by the ghosts. The old people told us to heed *wa maka skan,* which were the 'moving things of earth.' This meant, of course, the animals that lived and moved about, and the stories they told of *wa maka skan* increased our interest and delight. The wolf, duck, eagle, hawk, spider, bear, and other creatures, had marvelous powers, and each one was useful and helpful to us. Then there were the warriors the who lived in the sky and dashed about on their spirited horses during a thunder storm, their lances clashing with the thunder and glittering with the lightning. There was *wiwila,* the living spirit of the spring, and the stones that flew like a bird and talked like a man. Everything was possessed of personality, only differing with us in form. Knowledge was inherent in all things. The world was a library and its books were the stones, leaves, grass, brooks, and the birds and animals that shared, alike with us, the storms and blessings of earth. We learned to do what only the student of nature ever learns, and that was to feel beauty. We never railed at the storms, the furious winds, and the biting frosts and snows. To do so intensified human futility, so whatever came we adjusted ourselves, by more effort and energy if necessary, but without complaint. Even the lightning did us no harm, for whenever it came too close, mothers and grandmothers in every tipi put cedar leaves on the coals and their magic kept danger away.

Bright days and dark nights were both expressions of the Great Mystery, and the Indian reveled in being close to the Big Holy. His worship was unalloyed, free from the fears of civilization.

I have come to know that the white mind does not feel toward nature as 10 does the Indian mind, and it is because, I believe, of the difference in childhood instruction. I have often noticed white boys gathered in a city by-street or alley jostling and pushing one another in a foolish manner. They spend much time in this aimless fashion, their natural faculties neither seeing, hearing, nor feeling the varied life that surrounds them. There is about them no awareness, no acuteness, and it is this dullness that gives ugly mannerisms full play; it takes from them natural poise and stimulation. In contrast, Indian boys, who are naturally reared, are alert to their surroundings; their senses are not narrowed to observing only one another, and they cannot spend hours seeing nothing, hearing nothing, and thinking nothing in particular. Observation was certain in its rewards; interest, wonder, admiration grew, and the fact was appreciated that life was more than mere human manifestation; that it was expressed in a multitude of forms. This appreciation enriched Lakota existence. Life was vivid and pulsing; nothing was casual and commonplace. The Indian lived—lived in every sense of the word—from his first to his last breath.

The character of the Indian's emotion left little room in his heart for antag- 11 onism toward his fellow creatures, this attitude giving him what is sometimes referred to as 'the Indian point of view.' Every true student, every lover of nature has 'the Indian point of view,' but there are few such students, for few white men approach nature in the Indian manner. The Indian and the white man sense things differently because the white man has put distance between himself and nature; and assuming a lofty place in the scheme of order of things has lost for him both reverence and understanding. Consequently the white man finds Indian philosophy obscure—wrapped, as he says, in a maze of ideas and symbols which he does not understand. A writer friend, a white man whose knowledge of 'Injuns' is far more profound and sympathetic than the average, once said that he had been privileged, on two occasions, to see the contents of an Indian medicine-man's bag in which were bits of earth, feathers, stones, and various other articles of symbolic nature; that a 'collector' showed him one and laughed, but a great and world-famous archeologist showed him the other with admiration and wonder. Many times the Indian is embarrassed and baffled by the white man's allusions to nature in such terms as crude, primitive, wild, rude, untamed, and savage. For the Lakota, mountains, lakes, rivers, springs, valleys, and woods were all finished beauty; winds, rain, snow, sunshine, day, night, and change of seasons brought interest; birds, insects, and animals filled the world with knowledge that defied the discernment of man.

But nothing the Great Mystery placed in the land of the Indian pleased the 12 white man, and nothing escaped his transforming hand. Wherever forests have not been mowed down; wherever the animal is recessed in their quiet protection; wherever the earth is not bereft of four-footed life—that to him is an 'unbroken wilderness.' But since for the Lakota there was no wilderness; since nature was not dangerous but hospitable; not forbidding but friendly, Lakota philosophy was healthy—free from fear and dogmatism. And here I find the great distinction between the faith of the Indian and the white man. Indian faith sought the harmony of man with his surroundings; the other sought the dominance of surroundings. In sharing, in loving all and everything, one people naturally found a measure of the thing they sought; while, in fearing, the other found need of conquest. For one man the world was full of beauty; for the other it was a place of sin and ugliness to be endured until he went to another world, there to become a creature of wings, half-man and half-bird. Forever one man directed his Mystery to change the world He had made; forever this man pleaded with Him to chastise His wicked ones; and forever he implored his Wakan Tanka to send His light to earth. Small wonder this man could not understand the other.

13   But the old Lakota was wise. He knew that man's heart, away from nature, becomes hard; he knew that lack of respect for growing, living things soon led to lack of respect for humans too. So he kept his youth close to its softening influence.

—1933

FOCUS ON ECOLOGY

1. *The Land of the Spotted Eagle,* from which this selection was taken, was published in 1933. In this selection, Luther Standing Bear writes, "The animals had rights." This seems a familiar phrase and idea to us now as animal rights debates and animal rights activists are a predominant part of contemporary environmental conversations. [But how new was the idea of animal rights in 1933? Consider Luther Standing Bear's use of this phrase, and then track the history of animal rights movements. Was this a new idea in 1933?] How might his words have been received in 1933?
2. Immediately after explaining that animals had rights in the Lakota way of thinking, Luther Standing Bear also says that "this concept of life and its relations was humanizing and gave to the Lakota an abiding love." What do you suppose Standing Bear means by saying it was "humanizing"? What are the implications of Standing Bear's use of this word in this way in this piece?
3. "Knowledge was inherent in all things," writes Luther Standing Bear. What do you suppose he means by this? What knowledge have you gained from natural things?

FOCUS ON WRITING

1. At a few points in this piece, Luther Standing Bear provides the Lakota names for things: *Mako, Anpetuwi,* and *maka skan.* Why might Standing Bear

have decided to provide these names? How do you react to seeing, reading these words?

2. What does Luther Standing Bear mean by discussing Indian philosophy? Why do you suppose he identifies the white man as having difficulty grasping Indian philosophy? What exactly is meant by *philosophy*?

3. How would you describe the writing in "Nature"?

FOR DISCUSSION

Considering that this piece was written in 1933, how applicable is it today, 70 years later? As a class, discuss what you can glean from Luther Standing Bear's words to develop a contemporary vision of nature. Ask how Luther Standing Bear might write this piece today; what other things might he want to say?

WRITING IN RESPONSE

Luther Standing Bear makes the interesting point that he sees the difference between the whites' feelings toward nature and Indians' feelings toward nature as being an issue of childhood education. Consider how and what you learned about nature as a child. First, in a personal narrative, recount your educational experiences regarding nature. Don't limit your understanding of education simply to what you were taught in school or by your parents; consider what you learned on your own, in books you read, movies you saw, television you watched. Once you have written the narrative, speculate as to what might have made your childhood environmental education more enlightening.

Against Nature

Joyce Carol Oates

*To say that **Joyce Carol Oates** is a prolific author is an understatement. She has written more than 45 novels (sometimes under her pseudonym Rosemond Smith), more than 20 collections of stories, more than a dozen collections of poetry, more than 10 books of nonfiction, and more than 20 plays; she has edited or co-edited more than 18 collections. Since 1959, her writing has been honored with awards at least 28 times; she has twice been a Pulitzer Prize finalist and has won the National Book Award. Her writing is often described as suspenseful and uses elements of terror. As she explains in a* Chicago Tribune Book World *interview, "I am concerned with only one thing: the*

moral and social conditions of my generation." Often, that concern is expressed in sto-
ries that examine a creepy side of American life. Born June 16, 1938, in Lockport, New
York, Oates graduated from Syracuse University in 1960 and earned her master's de-
gree from the University of Wisconsin in 1961. She is currently the Roger S. Berlind
Distinguished Professor in the Department of Creative Writing at Princeton Univer-
sity. In this piece, "Against Nature," Oates offers a vision of nature a bit different from
others we have looked at. As you read this piece, consider the many different claims
about nature Oates makes. Consider too the style and language she uses to do so.

JOURNAL ASSIGNMENT

In "Against Nature," Joyce Carol Oates asks a simple question of nature: "why
glamorize it, romanticize it"? In your journal, consider the ways contemporary
American culture romanticizes and glamorizes nature. Write about what effect
such glamorization has on our definitions of nature.

We soon get through with Nature. She excites an expectation
which she cannot satisfy.
                              —THOREAU, Journal, *1854*

Sir, if a man has experienced the inexpressible, he is under no
obligation to attempt to express it.
                              —SAMUEL JOHNSON

1   *The writer's resistance to Nature.*
2   It has no sense of humor: in its beauty, as in its ugliness, or its neutrality,
    there is no laughter.
3   It lacks a moral purpose.
4   It lacks a satiric dimension, registers no irony.
5   Its pleasures lack resonance, being accidental; its horrors, even when pre-
    meditated, are equally perfunctory, "red in tooth and claw" et cetera.
6   It lacks a symbolic subtext—excepting that provided by man.
7   It has no (verbal) language.
8   It has no interest in ours.
9   It inspires a painfully limited set of responses in "nature-writers"
    —REVERENCE, AWE, PIETY, MYSTICAL ONENESS.
10   It eludes us even as it prepares to swallow us up, books and all.

11 I was lying on my back in the dirt-gravel of the towpath beside the Delaware-
    Raritan Canal, Titusville, New Jersey, staring up at the sky and trying, with no
    success, to overcome a sudden attack of tachycardia that had come upon me

out of nowhere—such attacks are always "out of nowhere," that's their charm—and all around me Nature thrummed with life, the air smelling of moisture and sunlight, the canal reflecting the sky, red-winged blackbirds testing their spring calls—the usual. I'd become the jar in Tennessee, a fictitious center, or parenthesis, aware beyond my erratic heartbeat of the numberless heartbeats of the earth, its pulsing pumping life, sheer life, incalculable. Struck down in the midst of motion—I'd been jogging a minute before—I was "out of time" like a fallen, stunned boxer, privileged (in an abstract manner of speaking) to be an involuntary witness to the random, wayward, nameless motion on all sides of me.

Paroxysmal tachycardia is rarely fatal, but if the heartbeat accelerates to 12 250–270 beats a minute you're in trouble. The average attack is about 100–150 beats and mine seemed so far to be about average; the trick now was to prevent it from getting worse. Brainy people try brainy strategies, such as thinking calming thoughts, pseudo-mystic thoughts, *If I die now it's a good death,* that sort of thing, *if I die this is a good place and a good time,* the idea is to deceive the frenzied heartbeat that, really, you don't care: you hadn't any other plans for the afternoon. The important thing with tachycardia is to prevent panic! you must prevent panic! otherwise you'll have to be taken by ambulance to the closest emergency room, which is not so very nice a way to spend the afternoon, really. So I contemplated the blue sky overhead. The earth beneath my head. Nature surrounding me on all sides, I couldn't quite see it but I could hear it, smell it, sense it—there is something *there,* no mistake about it. Completely oblivious to the predicament of the individual but that's only "natural" after all, one hardly expects otherwise.

When you discover yourself lying on the ground, limp and unresisting, 13 head in the dirt, and helpless, the earth seems to shift forward as a presence; hard, emphatic, not mere surface but a genuine force—there is no other word for it but *presence.* To keep in motion is to keep in time and to be stopped, stilled, is to be abruptly out of time, in another time-dimension perhaps, an alien one, where human language has no resonance. Nothing to be said about it expresses it, nothing touches it, it's an absolute against which nothing human can be measured. . . . Moving through space and time by way of your own volition you inhabit an interior consciousness, a hallucinatory consciousness, it might be said, so long as breath, heartbeat, the body's autonomy hold; when motion is stopped you are jarred out of it. The interior is invaded by the exterior. The outside wants to come in, and only the self's fragile membrane prevents it.

The fly buzzing at Emily's death.   14

Still, the earth *is* your place. A tidy grave-site measured to your size. Or, 15 from another angle of vision, one vast democratic grave.

Let's contemplate the sky. Forget the crazy hammering heartbeat, don't lis- 16 ten to it, don't start counting, remember that there is a clever way of breathing that conserves oxygen as if you're lying below the surface of a body of water breathing through a very thin straw but you *can* breathe through it if you're careful, if you don't panic, one breath and then another and then another, isn't that the story of all lives? careers? Just a matter of breathing. Of course it is. But contemplate the sky, it's there to be contemplated. A mild shock to see it so blank, blue, a thin airy ghostly blue, no clouds to disguise its emptiness. You are beginning to feel not only weightless but near-bodiless, lying on the earth like a scrap of paper about to be blown off. Two dimensions and you'd imagined you were three! And there's the sky rolling away forever, into infinity—if "infinity" can be "rolled into"—and the forlorn truth is, that's where you're going too. And the lovely blue isn't even blue, is it? isn't even there, is it? a mere optical illusion, isn't it? no matter what art has urged you to believe.

17 Early Nature memories. Which it's best not to suppress.

18   . . . Wading, as a small child, in Tonawanda Creek near our house, and afterward trying to tear off, in a frenzy of terror and revulsion, the sticky fat black bloodsuckers that had attached themselves to my feet, particularly between my toes.

19   . . . Coming upon a friend's dog in a drainage ditch, dead for several days, evidently the poor creature had been shot by a hunter and left to die, bleeding to death, and we're stupefied with grief and horror but can't resist sliding down to where he's lying on his belly, and we can't resist squatting over him, turning the body over . . .

20   . . . The raccoon, mad with rabies, frothing at the mouth and tearing at his own belly with his teeth, so that his intestines spilled out onto the ground . . . a sight I seem to remember though in fact I did not see. I've been told I did not see.

21 Consequently, my chronic uneasiness with Nature-mysticism; Nature-adoration; Nature-as-(moral)-instruction-for-mankind. My doubt that one can, with philosophical validity, address "Nature" as a single coherent noun, anything other than a Platonic, hence discredited, is-ness. My resistance to "Nature-writing" as a genre, except when it is brilliantly fictionalized in the service of a writer's individual vision—Throeau's books and *Journal,* of course—but also, less known in this country, the miniaturist prose-poems of Colette (*Flowers and Fruit*) and Ponge (*Taking the Side of Things*)—in which case it becomes yet another, and ingenious, form of storytelling. The subject is *there* only by the grace of the author's language.

22   Nature has no instructions for mankind except that our poor beleaguered humanist-democratic way of life, our fantasies of the individual's high worth, our sense that the weak, no less than the strong, have a right to survive, are absurd.

23   In any case, where *is* Nature? one might (skeptically) inquire. Who has looked upon her/its face and survived?

24 But isn't this all exaggeration, in the spirit of rhetorical contentiousness? Surely Nature is, for you, as for most reasonably intelligent people, a "perennial" source of beauty, comfort, peace, escape from the delirium of civilized life; a

respite from the ego's ever-frantic strategies of self-promotion, as a way of insuring (at least in fantasy) some small measure of immortality? Surely Nature, as it is understood in the usual slapdash way, as human, if not dilettante, *experience* (hiking in a national park, jogging on the beach at dawn, even tending, with the usual comical frustrations, a suburban garden), is wonderfully consoling; a place where, when you go there, it has to take you in?—a palimpsest of sorts you choose to read, layer by layer, always with care, always cautiously, in proportion to your psychological strength?

Nature: as in Thoreau's upbeat Transcendentalist mode ("The indescribable 25 innocence and beneficence of Nature,—such health, such cheer, they afford forever! and such sympathy have they ever with our race, that all Nature would be affected . . . if any man should ever for a just cause grieve"), and not in Thoreau's grim mode ("Nature is hard to be overcome but she must be overcome").

Another way of saying, not *Nature-in-itself* but *Nature-as-experience*. 26

The former, Nature-in-itself, is, to allude slantwise to Melville, a blankness 27 ten times blank; the latter is what we commonly, or perhaps always, mean when we speak of Nature as a noun, a single entity—something of *ours*. Most of the time it's just an activity, a sort of hobby, a weekend, a few days, perhaps a few hours, staring out the window at the mind-dazzling autumn foliage of, say, Northern Michigan, being rendered speechless—temporarily—at the sight of Mt. Shasta, the Grand Canyon, Ansel Adams's West. Or Nature writ small, contained in the back yard. Nature filtered through our optical nerves, our "senses," our fiercely romantic expectations. Nature that pleases us because it mirrors our souls, or gives the comforting illusion of doing so. As in our first mother's awakening to the self's fatal beauty—

> I thither went
> With unexperienc't thought, and laid me down
> On the green bank, to look into the clear
> Smooth Lake, that to me seem'd another Sky.
> As I bent down to look, just opposite,
> A Shape within the watr'y gleam appear'd
> Bending to look on me, I started back,
> It started back, but pleas'd I soon return'd,
> Pleas'd it return'd as soon with answering looks
> Of sympathy and love; there I had fixt
> Mine eyes till now, and pin'd with vain desire.

in these surpassingly beautiful lines from Book IV of Milton's *Paradise Lost*.

Nature as the self's (flattering) mirror, but not ever, no, never, Nature-in- 28 itself.

Nature is mouths, or maybe a single mouth. Why glamorize it, romanticize it, 29 well yes but we must, we're writers, poets, mystics (of a sort) aren't we, precisely what else are we to do but glamorize and romanticize and generally

exaggerate the significance of anything we focus the white heat of our "creativity" upon . . . ? And why not Nature, since it's there, common property, mute,
can't talk back, allows us the possibility of transcending the human condition
for a while, writing prettily of mountain ranges, white-tailed deer, the purple
crocuses outside this very window, the thrumming dazzling "life-force" we
imagine we all support. Why not.

30   Nature *is* more than a mouth—it's a dazzling variety of mouths. And it
pleases the senses, in any case, as the physicists' chill universe of numbers certainly does not.

31 Oscar Wilde, on our subject: "Nature is no great mother who has borne us. She
is our creation. It is in our brain that she quickens to life. Things are because
we see them, and what we see, and how we see it, depends on the Arts that
have influenced us. To look at a thing is very different from seeing a thing. . . .
At present, people see fogs, not because there are fogs, but because poets and
painters have taught them the mysterious loveliness of such effects. There may
have been fogs for centuries in London. I dare say there were. But no one saw
them. They did not exist until Art had invented them. . . . Yesterday evening
Mrs. Arundel insisted on my going to the window and looking at the glorious
sky, as she called it. And so I had to look at it. . . . And what was it? It was simply a very second-rate Turner, a Turner of a bad period, with all the painter's
worst faults exaggerated and over-emphasized."

32   (If we were to put it to Oscar Wilde that he exaggerates, his reply might
well be: "Exaggeration? I don't know the meaning of the word.")

33 *Walden,* that most artfully composed of prose fictions, concludes, in the rhapsodic chapter "Spring," with Henry David Thoreau's contemplation of death,
decay, and regeneration as it is suggested to him, or to his protagonist, by the
spectacle of vultures feeding off carrion. There is a dead horse close by his cabin
and the stench of its decomposition, in certain winds, is daunting. Yet: ". . . the
assurance it gave me of the strong appetite and inviolable health of Nature was
my compensation. I love to see that Nature is so rife with life that myriads can
be afforded to be sacrificed and suffered to prey upon one another; that tender
organizations can be so serenely squashed out of existence like pulp,—tadpoles
which herons gobble up, and tortoises and toads run over in the road; and that
sometimes it has rained flesh and blood! . . . The impression made on a wise
man is that of universal innocence."

34   Come off it, Henry David. You've grieved these many years for your elder
brother John, who died a ghastly death of lockjaw; you've never wholly recovered from the experience of watching him die. And you know, or must know,
that you're fated too to die young of consumption. . . . But this doctrinaire Transcendentalist passage ends *Walden* on just the right note. It's as impersonal, as
coolly detached, as the Oversoul itself: a "wise man" filters his emotions
through his brain.

Or through his prose.   35

Nietzsche: "We all pretend to ourselves that we are more simple-minded than   36
we are: that is how we get a rest from our fellow men."

> Once out of nature I shall never take
> My bodily form from any natural thing,
> But such a form as Grecian goldsmiths make
> Of hammered gold and gold enamelling
> To keep a drowsy Emperor awake;
> Or set upon a golden bough to sing
> To lords and ladies of Byzantium
> Of what is past, passing, or to come.
>
> —William Butler Yeats, "Sailing to
> Byzantium"

Yet even the golden bird is a "bodily form taken from (a) natural thing." No,
it's impossible to escape!

The writer's resistance to Nature.   37
    Wallace Stevens: "In the presence of extraordinary actuality, consciousness   38
takes the place of imagination."

Once, years ago, in 1972 to be precise, when I seemed to have been another per-   39
son, related to the person I am now as one is related, tangentially, sometimes
embarrassingly, to cousins not seen for decades, —once, when we were living
in London, and I was very sick, I had a mystical vision. That is, I "had" a "mystical vision"—the heart sinks: such pretension—or something resembling one.
A fever-dream, let's call it. It impressed me enormously and impresses me still,
though I've long since lost the capacity to see it with my mind's eye, or even, I
suppose, to believe in it. There is a statute of limitations on "mystical visions"
as on romantic love.
    I was very sick, and I imagined my life as a thread, a thread of breath, or   40
heartbeat, or pulse, or light, yes it was light, radiant light, I was burning with
fever and I ascended to that plane of serenity that might be mistaken for (or *is*,
in fact) Nirvana, where I had a waking dream of uncanny lucidity—
    My body is a tall column of light and heat.   41
    My body is not "I" but "it."   42
    My body is not one but many.   43
    My body, which "I" inhabit, is inhabited as well by other creatures, un-   44
known to me, imperceptible—the smallest of them mere sparks of light.
    My body, which I perceive as substance, is in fact an organization of infinitely   45
complex, overlapping, imbricated structures, radiant light their manifestation,

the "body" a tall column of light and blood-heat, a temporary agreement among atoms, like a high-rise building with numberless rooms, corridors, corners, elevator shafts, windows. . . . In this fantastical structure the "I" is deluded as to its sovereignty, let alone its autonomy in the (outside) world; the most astonishing secret is that the "I" doesn't exist!—but it behaves as if it does, as if it were one and not many.

46   In any case, without the "I" the tall column of light and heat would die, and the microscopic life-particles would die with it . . . will die with it. The "I," which doesn't exist, is everything.

> But Dr. Johnson is right, the inexpressible need not be expressed.
> And what resistance, finally? There is none.

47 This morning, an invasion of tiny black ants. One by one they appear, out of nowhere—that's their charm too!—moving single file across the white Parsons table where I am sitting, trying without much success to write a poem. A poem of only three or four lines is what I want, something short, tight, mean, I want it to hurt like a white-hot wire up the nostrils, small and compact and turned in upon itself with the density of a hunk of rock from the planet Jupiter. . . .

48   But here come the black ants: harbingers, you might say, of spring. One by one by one they appear on the dazzling white table and one by one I kill them with a forefinger, my deft right forefinger, mashing each against the surface of the table and then dropping it into a wastebasket at my side. Idle labor, mesmerizing, effortless, and I'm curious as to how long I can do it, sit here in the brilliant March sunshine killing ants with my right forefinger, how long I, and the ants, can keep it up.

49   After a while I realize that I can do it a long time. And that I've written my poem.

FOCUS ON ECOLOGY

1. What might Oates be suggesting when she writes that nature is "completely oblivious to the predicament of the individual"?
2. How does Oates distinguish between "nature-in-itself" and "nature-as-experience"? Does this distinction affect your definition of nature? Why or why not?
3. What point is Oates trying to make by referring to nature as a mouth? Could this metaphor be constructed in another way? How?

FOCUS ON WRITING

1. This essay, if it can be called that, takes on a rather fragmented form: it is divided into short sections; some sections are simply short descriptions, others more narrative in form; some are seemingly incomplete. Why

might Oates have written in this form? What does she accomplish or lose by doing so?

2. To what does Oates refer when she writes "red in tooth and claw"? To what does she refer when she writes "The fly buzzing at Emily's death"? Oates makes many references throughout the piece. Do you recognize these references? Does it matter if you do?

3. Do you agree with Oates when she writes of nature, "it has no (verbal) language"? Why or why not? What does she gain or lose by making this argument in this essay?

FOR DISCUSSION

This piece contains a tremendous number of position statements. It leaves much to be considered, discussed. Rather than trying to tackle all of the issues as a class, consider what Oates means when she writes, "Nature has no instruction for mankind except that our poor beleaguered humanist-democratic way of life, our fantasies of the individual's high worth, our sense that the weak, no less than the strong, have a right to survive, are absurd." What are the ramifications of making such a claim? How do you feel about such a claim?

WRITING IN RESPONSE

Part of what "inspires" the narrator in this piece to consider nature is an attack of tachycardia. In a personal narrative, consider the kind of event that might trigger your own contemplation of nature. Would it need to be as frightening as the one described in "Against Nature"? If you have had such an event, write about how you began to consider or reconsider your understanding of nature during and since the event.

Calvin and Hobbes

Bill Watterson

William B. Watterson II was born July 5, 1958, in Washington, D.C. He graduated from Kenyon College in Ohio in 1980 with a degree in political science. Watterson was nominated for the Ruben Award for Outstanding Cartoonist of the Year three times—in 1986 (the youngest cartoonist to have been so honored) and again in 1988 and 1992. Watterson's "Calvin and Hobbes" proved to be one of the most popular comic strips of all times. Depicting the antics of the overly intelligent eight-year-old Calvin and his best friend, stuffed tiger Hobbes, the strip is known for its ability to wrap humor around crucial issues, often environmental and ecological issues, such as the one depicted in the strip reprinted here. As you read this strip, consider the commentary Watterson is offering regarding the importance of naming.

JOURNAL ASSIGNMENT

In the "Calvin and Hobbes" comic strip printed here, Calvin and Hobbes have a dispute over the right to name a creek. In your journal, consider the importance of naming places and make a list of place names that you have always wondered why such a place was named as it is. Then, write what those names suggest about the place.

CALVIN AND HOBBES © 1986 Watterson. Reprinted with permission of Universal Press Syndicate. All rights reserved.

FOCUS ON ECOLOGY

1. In the second frame of this comic strip, Calvin says, "When you discover something, you're allowed to name it and put up a sign." Think, for a moment, about how powerful a statement this is. What does it mean to "discover" something? Can you "discover" something like a creek? Consider whom Calvin refers to when he says "you're allowed." Who is the authority that grants such an allowance? Why would Calvin want to "name it"? What does the symbol of putting up a sign indicate? Could he have named the creek and kept the name secret, or does the sign signify something beyond his declaration of a name?

2. Some people argue that knowing the names of places and things helps you really "know" those places or things more intimately. Consider the place names in your community and region. Who named your town or city? What

does that name mean? Were there other names of that place before the one with which you are familiar? Who "discovered" your town or region? When?

3. Is calling the thing both Calvin and Hobbes wish to name a "creek" also an act of naming? What does it indicate about a place?

FOCUS ON WRITING

1. What power and value does Calvin stake in the placement of signs? What value and power do we as a culture stake in signs? How are signs "written" and "read"?
2. Why doesn't the final frame of this strip need dialogue?
3. Why do Calvin and Hobbes each want to name the creek after themselves? What happens when we place our own names on something else?

FOR DISCUSSION

This "Calvin and Hobbes" strip is an excellent beginning point for discussing the act of naming. As a class, consider what power there is in naming things. Why do people name places? After what do they generally name them? What happens to a place when it is named? Does the naming of a place affect how that place is defined? As a class, discuss the names of places in your town and consider what those names mean and how the act of naming those places affects those places. Think also beyond just the proper nouns we attribute to a place. We may name a place Seattle or Atlanta, but we also name it a city; we may name a place Mt. McKinley, but we also name it a park; we may name a place a farm or a plain, a valley or a mountain. What happens when we name?

WRITING IN RESPONSE

Select the name of a place that has been important to you—this may be a town, a city, a region, a geographical area, a field, a building, and so on. Do a bit of research to find out where the name of that place originated. Was the place called something else before it was given its current name? In a short historical essay, trace the history of the name of the place you have selected. Be sure to consider not only why the place was named as it was, but also what effect that name had on the place.

The American Indian Wilderness

Louis Owens

Louis Owens has said in Contemporary Authors, *"I write, in part, to explore my own identity as a mixed-blood American of Choctaw, Cherokee, and Irish-American heritage. And I write to explore the dilemmas of all mixed-bloods in America. And I write to illuminate our relationships with the natural world. And I write because it is the greatest pleasure." Owens was born on July 18, 1948, in Lompoc, California, as one of nine children. He got his first job at the age of nine as a bean picker and later worked as a forest ranger for the U.S. Forest Service at Glacier Peak Wilderness in northern Washington. He earned a bachelor's degree and master's degree from the University of California, Santa Barbara, and a Ph.D. from the University of California, Davis. He has taught at a number of universities and was honored with the Outstanding Teacher of the Year Award by the International Steinbeck Society for the teaching year 1985–86. Owens has written a number of books including several novels and several books of criticism:* Wolfsong *(1991),* The Sharpest Sight *(1992),* Bone Game *(1994),* Nightland *(1996),* Dark River *(1999),* John Steinbeck's Re-Vision of America *(1985),* American Indian Novelists: An Annotated Critical Biography *(with Tom Colonnese, 1985),* The Grapes of Wrath: Trouble in the Promised Land *(1989),* Other Destinies: Understanding the American Indian Novel *(1992), and* Mixedblood Messages: Literature, Film, Family, Place *(1998). His writing is often described both as eerie and as having an environmental agenda. In the piece found here, "The American Indian Wilderness," Owens reflects on how American culture has come to define wilderness and how his own thinking shifted following an encounter in Washington's Cascade mountains. As you read this short piece, consider not only the way Owens discusses the definitions of wilderness, but the way he makes use of his narrative to depict the shift in his thinking about wilderness.*

JOURNAL ASSIGNMENT

Louis Owens writes in "The American Indian Wilderness" about an old, three-sided, log shelter that the U.S. Forest Service had him burn down in the mountains of northern Washington. The shelter, he later learns, had been used by Native Americans during berry picking season. As he contemplates the destruction of the shelter, Owens writes, "Those human-made structures were as natural a part of the Cascade ecosystem as the burrows of marmots in the steep scree slopes." In your journal, consider the ways in which humans are natural, are part of ecosystems. Try to formulate an image of a local ecosystem and the role humans play in it.

In the center of the Glacier Peak Wilderness in northern Washington, a magnif- 1
icent, fully glaciated white volcano rises over a stunningly beautiful region of
the North Cascades. On maps, the mountain is called Glacier Peak. To the Salishan people who have always lived in this part of the Cascades, however, the
mountain is *Dakobed,* or the Great Mother, the place of emergence. For more
than eighty years, a small, three-sided log shelter stood in a place called White
Pass just below one shoulder of the great mountain, tucked securely into a
meadow between thick stands of mountain hemlock and alpine fir.

In the early fall of seventy-six, while working as a seasonal ranger for the 2
U.S. Forest Service, I drew the task of burning the White Pass shelter. After all
those years, the shelter roof had collapsed like a broken bird wing under the
weight of winter snow, and the time was right for fire and replanting. It was
part of a Forest Service plan to remove all human-made objects from wilderness areas, a plan of which I heartily approved. So I backpacked eleven miles
to the pass and set up camp, and for five days, while a bitter early storm sent
snow driving horizontally out of the north, I dismantled the shelter and burned
the old logs, piling and burning and piling and burning until nothing remained. The antique, hand-forged spikes that had held the shelter together I
put into gunny sacks and cached to be packed out later by mule. I spaded up
the earth beaten hard for nearly a century by boot and hoof, and transplanted
plugs of vegetation from hidden spots on the nearby ridge.

At the end of those five days, not a trace of the shelter remained, and I felt 3
good, very smug in fact, about returning the White Pass meadow to its "original" state. As I packed up my camp, the snowstorm had subsided to a few flur-
ries and a chill that felt bone-deep with the promise of winter. My season was
almost over, and as I started the steep hike down to the trailhead my mind was
on the winter I was going to spend in sunny Arizona.

A half-mile from the pass I saw the two old women. At first they were dark, 4
hunched forms far down on the last long switchback up the snowy ridge. But
as we drew closer to one another, I began to feel a growing amazement that, by
the time we were face-to-face, had become awe. Almost swallowed up in their
baggy wool pants, heavy sweaters and parkas, silver braids hanging below
thick wool caps, they seemed ancient, each weighted with at least seventy years
as well as a small backpack. They paused every few steps to lean on their staffs
and look out over the North Fork drainage below, a deep, heavily forested river
valley that rose on the far side of the glaciers and sawtoothed black granite of
the Monte Cristo Range. And they smiled hugely upon seeing me, clearly surprised and delighted to find another person in the mountains at such a time.

We stood and chatted for a moment, and as I did with all backpackers, I re- 5
luctantly asked them where they were going. The snow quickened a little, ob-
scuring the view, as they told me that they were going to White Pass.

6   "Our father built a little house up here," one of them said, "when he worked the Forest Service like you. Way back before we was born, before this century."

7   "We been coming up here each year since we was little," the other added. "Except last year when Sarah was not well enough."

8   "A long time ago, this was all our land," the one called Sarah said. "All Indi'n land everywhere you can see. Our people had houses up in the mountains, for gathering berries each year."

9   As they took turns speaking, the smiles never leaving their faces, I wanted to excuse myself, to edge around these elders and flee to the trailhead and my car, drive back to the district station and keep going south. I wanted to say, "I'm Indian too. Choctaw from Mississippi; Cherokee from Oklahoma"—as if mixed blood could pardon me for what I had done. Instead, I said, "The shelter is gone." Cravenly I added, "It was crushed by snow, so I was sent up to burn it. It's gone now."

10   I expected outrage, anger, sadness, but instead the sisters continued to smile at me, their smiles changing only slightly. They had a plastic tarp and would stay dry, they said, because a person always had to be prepared in the mountains. They would put up their tarp inside the hemlock grove above the meadow, and the scaly hemlock branches would turn back the snow. They forgave me without saying it—my ignorance and my part in the long pattern of loss which they knew so well.

11   Hiking out those eleven miles, as the snow of the high country became a drumming rain in the forests below, I had long hours to ponder my encounter with the sisters. Gradually, almost painfully, I began to understand that what I called "wilderness" was an absurdity, nothing more than a figment of the European imagination. Before the European invasion, there was no wilderness in North America; there was only the fertile continent where people lived in a hard-learned balance with the natural world. In embracing a philosophy that saw the White Pass shelter—and all traces of humanity—as a shameful stain upon the "pure" wilderness, I had succumbed to a five-hundred-year-old pattern of deadly thinking that separates us from the natural world. This is not to say that what we call wilderness today does not need careful safeguarding. I believe that White Pass really is better off now that the shelter doesn't serve as a magnet to backpackers and horsepackers who compact the soil, disturb and kill the wildlife, cut down centuries-old trees for firewood, and leave their litter strewn about. And I believe the man who built the shelter would agree. But despite this unfortunate reality, the global environmental crisis that sends species into extinction daily and threatens to destroy all life surely has its roots in the Western pattern of thought that sees humanity and "wilderness" as mutually exclusive.

12   In old-growth forests in the North Cascades, deep inside the official Wilderness Area, I have come upon faint traces of log shelters built by Suiattle and Upper Skagit people for berry harvesting a century or more ago—just as the sisters said. Those human-made structures were as natural a part of the

Cascade ecosystem as the burrows of marmots in the steep scree slopes. Our Native ancestors all over this continent lived within a complex web of relations with the natural world, and in doing so they assumed a responsibility for their world that contemporary Americans cannot even imagine. Unless Americans, and all human beings, can learn to imagine themselves as intimately and inextricably related to every aspect of the world they inhabit, with the extraordinary responsibilities such relationship entails—unless they can learn what the indigenous peoples of the Americas knew and often still know—the earth simply will not survive. A few square miles of something called wilderness will become the sign of failure everywhere.

–1994

FOCUS ON ECOLOGY

1. Louis Owens writes, "Our Native ancestors all over this continent lived within a complex web of relations with the natural world, and in doing so they assumed a responsibility for their world that contemporary Americans cannot even imagine. Unless Americans, and all human beings, can learn to imagine themselves as intimately and inextricably related to every aspect of the world they inhabit, with the extraordinary responsibilities such relationship entails—unless they can learn what the indigenous peoples of the Americas knew and often still know—the earth simply will not survive." This is a fairly powerful statement, not only regarding what Americans must learn and do, but also regarding the power of what indigenous populations already knew. Respond to Owens's statement, Do you think that indigenous peoples had a "better" way of understanding their relationship with the earth?

2. What does Owens mean when he says, "gradually, almost painfully, I began to understand that what I called "wilderness" was an absurdity, nothing more than a figment of the European imagination." What do you think he means by this? Do you agree?

3. Owens also makes the powerful statement, "there was no wilderness in North America." What does he mean by this? What role does the act of naming and defining play in Owens's statement? Could Owens just as likely have said "there was no North America"?

FOCUS ON WRITING

1. For you, what is the most powerful moment of Owens's narrative? Why?

2. The argument that Owens makes here is similar to arguments found in several other pieces included in *Saving Place*. Yet, Owens's essay is considerably

shorter. Is Owens's essay successful? If so, what makes it work? If not, what does it lack?

3. Why do you suppose that Owens, at the beginning of "The American Indian Wilderness," distinguishes between the naming of Glacier Peak and the Salishan name *Dakobed?* Does this maneuver play any role in the larger argument that Owens makes?

FOR DISCUSSION

Owens's essay "The American Indian Wilderness" brings up a number of important points to consider: the relationship of Americans to the wilderness, American definitions of wilderness, Native American definitions of wilderness, the ways in which cultures name, Owens's search for his own Native American identity and his realization about his own Americanized thinking, and even the disappearance of indigenous artifacts and customs that remind us of another way of thinking about the land. As a class, discuss the ways that Owens addresses these issues and respond to them.

WRITING IN RESPONSE

Owens's essay "The American Indian Wilderness" asks us to reconsider our relationships with wilderness. Owens accomplishes this by providing a narrative that shows how he came to question his own thinking. During the course of this narrative, Owens compares what he learned about native thinking versus American thinking about wilderness. In a comparison and contrast paper, examine a pervasive local attitude toward wilderness—where wilderness can be, what wilderness is, what can be done in wilderness areas, how people enter into wilderness—and compare and contrast that view with a Native American view. Keep in mind that if you are not Native American, you cannot simply assume what the Native American attitude or philosophy might be. Instead, do a little research and explore what Native Americans have written about the attitudes you are addressing in your writing.

Woman/Wilderness

Ursula Le Guin

Ursula Le Guin is most often referred to as a science fiction or fantasy writer, but her work breaks through the barriers of these labels. Born on October 21, 1929, in Berkeley, California, Le Guin writes in a variety of genres including novels, short stories, essays, poetry, and children's books. Her writing has been recognized through many awards including the Nebula Award and Hugo Awards for work in science fiction, the Newbery Award for work in children's literature, and the National Book Award for children's literature, to name but a few. Her writing is often characterized by a sense of relationship, ecology. That is, much of her writing emphasizes the need for humans to acknowledge and live in relationship to environments and to each other. For Le Guin, these relationships are forged in individual responsibility, a theme that appears in much of her work. The essay that follows, "Woman/Wilderness," is a version of a talk Le Guin gave to a class in wilderness offered by Gary Snyder at the University of California, Davis, in 1986. Le Guin writes that when invited by Snyder to speak to the class, "I told him I would like to say a little about woman and wilderness and read some poetry, mostly from my book Always Coming Home. *What follows is what I said before getting into the reading. Highly tendentious, it was meant to, and did, provoke lively discussion." As you read this piece, consider Le Guin's comments here and think about why she intended this piece to provoke discussion and why it might do just that.*

JOURNAL ASSIGNMENT

In her essay, a print version of a talk she delivered, Ursula Le Guin writes, "All children are wild." What do you suppose she means by this? In your journal, respond to Le Guin's statement and consider how children may or not be wild.

Civilized Man says: I am Self, I am Master, all the rest is Other—outside, below,   1 underneath, subservient. I own, I use, I explore, I exploit, I control. What I do is what matters. What I want is what matter is for. I am that I am, and the rest is women and the wilderness, to be used as I see fit.

2   To this, Civilized Woman, in the voice of Susan Griffin, replies as follows:

> We say there is no way to see his dying as separate from her living, or what he had
> done to her, or what part of her he had used. We say if you change the course of
> this river you change the shape of the whole place. And we say that what she did
> then could not be separated from what she held sacred in herself, what she had felt
> when he did that to her, what we hold sacred to ourselves, what we feel we could
> not go on without, and we say if this river leaves this place, nothing will grow and
> the mountain will crumble away, and we say what he did to her could not be sepa-
> rated from the way that he looked at her, and what he felt was right to do to her, and
> what they do to us, we say, shapes how they see us. That once the trees are cut down,
> the water will wash the mountain away and the river be heavy with mud, and there
> will be a flood. And we say that what he did to her he did to all of us. And that one
> fact cannot be separated from another. And had he seen more clearly, we say, he
> might have predicted his own death. How if the trees grew on that hillside there
> would be no flood. And you cannot divert this river. We say look how the water
> flows from this place and returns as rainfall, everything returns, we say, and one
> thing follows another, there are limits, we say, on what can be done and everything
> moves. We are all a part of this motion, we say, and the way of the river is sacred,
> and this grove of trees is sacred, and we ourselves, we tell you, are sacred.[1]

3   What is happening here is that the wilderness is answering. This has never
happened before. We who live at this time are hearing news that has never been
heard before. A new thing is happening.

> Daughters, the women are speaking.
> They arrive
> over the wise distances
> on perfect feet.

The women are speaking: so says Linda Hogan of the Chickasaw people.[2] The
women are speaking. Those who were identified as having nothing to say, as
sweet silence or monkey-chatterers, those who were identified with Nature,
which listens, as against Man, who speaks—those people are speaking. They
speak for themselves and for the other people, the animals, the trees, the rivers,
the rocks. And what they say is: We are sacred.

4   Listen: they do not say, "Nature is sacred." Because they distrust that word,
Nature. Nature as not including humanity, Nature as what is not human, that
Nature is a construct made by Man, not a real thing; just as most of what Man
says and knows about women is mere myth and construct. Where I live as
woman is to men a wilderness. But to me it is home.

5   The anthropologists Shirley and Edwin Ardener, talking about an African
village culture, made a useful and interesting mental shape. They laid down
two circles largely but not completely overlapping, so that the center of the figure is the tall oval of interlap, and on each side of it are facing crescents of non-
overlap. One of the two circles is the Dominant element of the culture, that is,

Men. The other is the Muted element of the culture, that is, Women. As Elaine Showalter explains the figure, "All of male consciousness is within the circle of the Dominant structure and thus accessible to or structured by language." Both the crescent that belongs to men only and the crescent that belongs to women only, outside the shared, central, civilized area of overlap, may be called "the wilderness." The men's wilderness is real; it is where men can go hunting and exploring and having all-male adventures away from the village, the shared center, and it is accessible to and structured by language. "In terms of cultural anthropology, women know what the male crescent is like, even if they have never seen it, because it becomes the subject of legend. . . . But men do not know what is in the wild,"[3] that is, the no-man's-land, the crescent that belongs to the Muted group, the silent group, the group within the culture that *is not spoken,* whose experience is not considered to be part of human experience, that is, the women.

Men live their whole lives within the Dominant area. When they go off hunting bears, they come back with bear stories, and these are listened to by all, they become the history or the mythology of that culture. So the men's "wilderness" becomes Nature, considered as the property of Man.

But the experience of women as women, their experience unshared with men, that experience is the wilderness or the wildness that is utterly other— that is in fact, to Man, unnatural. That is what civilization has left out, what culture excludes, what the Dominants call animal, bestial, primitive, undeveloped, unauthentic—what has not been spoken, and when spoken, has not been heard—what we are just beginning to find words for, our words not their words: the experience of women. For dominance-identified men and women both, that is true wildness. Their fear of it is ancient, profound, and violent. The misogyny that shapes every aspect of our civilization is the institutionalized form of male fear and hatred of what they have denied and therefore cannot know, cannot share: that wild country, the being of women.

All we can do is try to speak it, try to say it, try to save it. Look, we say, this land is where your mother lived and where your daughter will live. This is your sister's country. You lived there as a child, boy or girl, you lived there— have you forgotten? All children are wild. You lived in the wild country. Why are you afraid of it?

NOTES

1. Susan Griffin, *Woman and Nature* (New York: Harper & Row, Colophon Books, 1978), p. 186.
2. Linda Hogan, "The Women Speaking," in *That's What She Said: Contemporary Poetry and Fiction by Native American Women,* ed. Rayna Green (Bloomington: Indiana University Press, 1984), p. 72
3. Elaine Showalter, "Feminist Criticism in the Wilderness," in *The New Feminist Criticism,* ed. Elaine Showalter (New York: Pantheon Books, 1985),

p. 262. See also Shirley Ardener, ed., *Perceiving Women* (New York: Halsted Press, 1978).

FOCUS ON ECOLOGY

1. Le Guin writes, "Listen: they do not say 'Nature is sacred.' Because they distrust that word Nature." What do you suppose she means by this? Is nature sacred? How is it treated as sacred or treated as not sacred?
2. Le Guin also writes, "Where I live as woman is to men a wilderness. But to me it is home." What do you understand Le Guin to mean by this?
3. How do you suppose Le Guin would define *nature, wilderness,* and *environment*?

FOCUS ON WRITING

1. According to Le Guin, what is the relationship between language and nature? How does she make this point? Do you agree with her? Has Le Guin's claim shifted your understanding of this relationship? If so, in what way?
2. Le Guin writes, "'But men do not know what is in the wild,' that is, the no-man's-land, the crescent that belongs to the Muted group, the silent group, the group within the culture that *is not spoken,* whose experience is not considered to be part of human experience, that is, the women." What does Le Guin mean by a culture that "is not spoken"? What do you see as the relationship between culture, that which is spoken, that which is not spoken, and nature?
3. What kind of fear is Le Guin addressing at the end of this essay? What might she be implying by asking the questions she asks at the end of this piece? What effect do these questions have on the conclusion of the piece?

FOR DISCUSSION

Le Guin makes some exciting claims in "Woman/Wilderness" not only about the relationships between men and nature, women and nature, and nature and language, but about how we culturally construct those relationships and how we culturally define what is nature. Considering the position she takes in regard to women's position in relation to nature, how do you respond to this piece? Remember, Le Guin specifically says that this piece was intended to spark lively discussion. What about this piece might spark lively discussion? Why? As a class, discuss your responses to Le Guin's argument.

WRITING IN RESPONSE

That is, Do men and women see their relationships with nature, wilderness, and environment as different specifically because of gender? In an essay, consider how you have defined nature, environment, and wilderness thus far and consider how your definition is specifically gendered. Are there characteristics of your definition that might be seen as male and others seen as female?

DISCUSSING THE ISSUES

1. Throughout this chapter you have been asked to think about how we define *wilderness, nature, environment,* and even *wildness.* Early in the chapter you and your class discussed your conceptions of wilderness. Given what you have read in this chapter, return to those comments and discuss whether your own definitions have changed. Have the definitions of others in the class shifted? Why? What led you to reconsider your definitions if you have?
2. One of the things that many of the authors in this chapter allude to is Western culture's assessment of the value of wilderness. Edward Grumbine, for instance, writes, "The radical Western split between nature and culture allows us to presume that ecological sources may be transformed into natural resources for human use only, and that a mountain lion's home range is immaterial to the dedication of wildlands." Owens, Standing Bear, Williams, and Le Guin also make specific claims about this cultural split. Discuss with your class what values contemporary American culture assigns to nature and wilderness. Consider how these values are taught: schools, religion, family, popular media, literature, and so on. Can such values be changed? Should they be changed?

WRITING ABOUT THE ISSUES

1. *Personal Experience:* Now that you have read a variety of approaches to thinking about wilderness, nature, and environment, you probably have a better grasp of your own thoughts about these ideas. Writing often provides us the opportunity to weed through our ideas, to synthesize what we are thinking with what we have read, and to organize our thoughts into more coherent formulations. Drawing on your own experiences and observations as well as the selections from this chapter, write an essay that details your definitions of wilderness, nature, and environment.
2. *Local Context:* Many of the authors whose work is included in this chapter have examined the relationships between nature and culture. One of the things that such a comparison might lend itself to is the consideration of how our own hometowns make a distinction between nature and culture, or between wild places and civilized places. Begin by thinking about the boundaries between nature and civilization in your hometown. Are there designated parks? Farm land? Forests? Beaches? Mountains? Rivers? Preserves? Conservation areas? Are there rules, regulations, laws, and ordinances designed to delegate what's nature and what is not? Are there laws designed to protect? How does the community treat those natural places? What are the conventional wisdoms about natural settings in your community?

In a well-developed descriptive essay, describe a particular place in your community that seems typical of how nature is or is not part of your hometown. Describe the boundaries that do or do not exist between nature and human-made environments. Give details that show how and why such boundaries exist and how people in the community respect or ignore those boundaries. Consider how an urban population versus a rural population might create these boundaries within communities.

3. *Research:* The perspectives regarding definitions of nature and environment presented by the authors in this chapter are exciting and engaging, but many other authors have addressed similar issues. Take some time to research other perspectives about the definitions of wilderness and environment. Look for articles and books that address issues similar to those discussed in this chapter. Talk with your classmates about the selections they have found, but try to write about readings other than those about which your classmates are writing. Select five or so of the readings you find in your research and write brief summaries and assessments of each. Once you and your classmates have completed your individual bibliographies, merge them into one large resource file, perhaps placing this larger annotated bibliography online. This resource file will be of great benefit should you wish to pursue further reading, and if you publish it online it will be a wonderful resource for others exploring these subject areas. The articles, books, and World Wide Web URLs listed at the end of this chapter may be of use as you look for other resources to include in your bibliography.

RESEARCH PATHS

The Association for the Study of Literature and Environment (ASLE) (www.asle.umn.edu/)

National Wilderness Perservation System (www.wilderness.net/nwps/legis/nwps_act.cfm)

Bureau of Land Management (www.blm.gov/nhp/Preservation/wilderness/wild22.html)

Wilderness and Arctic Cultures (arcticcircle.uconn.edu/HistoryCulture/wilderness.html)

Wildernet (pantheon.cis.yale.edu/~thomast/names.html)

FURTHER READINGS

Bill McKibben, *The End of Nature*
Aldo Leopold, "Wildlife and American Culture"
Aldo Leopold, "Wilderness"
John Elders, *Family of Earth and Sky: Indigenous Tales of Nature from Around the World*
Annie Dillard, "Seeing"

Lewis Thomas, "The Tucson Zoo"

Barry Commoner, "At War with the Planet"

Wendell Berry, "Mayhem in the Industrial Paradise"

Martin Lewis, "On Human Connectedness with Nature"

Terry Tempest Williams, "To Be Taken"

David Abram, "Scattered Notes on the Relation between Language and the Land"

Max Oelschlager, "The Idea of Wilderness as Deep Ecological Ethic"

Mark Daniel Barringer, *Selling Yellowstone: Capitalism and the Construction of Nature, Development of Western Resources*

Bruce Braun and Noel Castree, *Remaking Reality: Nature at the Millennium*

William Cronon, *Changes in the Land: Indians, Colonists, and the Ecology of New England*

William Cronon, Uncommon Ground: Rethinking the Human Place in Nature

Roderick Nash, *Wilderness and the American Mind*

David T. Suzuki and Peter Knudtson, *Wisdom of the Elders: Sacred Native Stories of Nature*

CHAPTER **2**

Thinking Ecologically

What does it mean to "think ecologically"? That is, how do we think about our relationships to the world in which we live? Why might it be important for us to think about such relationships? In what ways does what we read and see affect how we might think ecologically? How might our own writing be affected by our ecological thinking? This chapter of *Saving Place* initiates our investigation into our relationships with the places where we live, work, and play through a series of readings, questions, and writing prompts about relationships. This chapter provides readings and questions that ask us to consider both our *thinking* and our *ecology*.

The reading selections reprinted in this chapter do not establish a single approach to thinking ecologically but rather offer a variety of approaches for inquiring about our ecological positions both globally and locally. The writers in this chapter ask us to consider an array of topics:

- the role of ethics in our relationships to the world

- how we live our daily lives in relation to the places in which we live

- how through aggression we might protect places, environments, and nature

- why we might seek to defend and protect places, environments, and nature

- why we might label some places as *wilderness* and not others

- how places, environments, and nature can be seen as parts of a larger ecological system

- how Native Americans have identified with places, environments, and nature

- how humor might play a role in the way we address our relationships with places, environments, and nature

- how we might think metaphorically about our relationships with the world

- how personal experiences affect how we think about these relationships

- how issues of race and culture affect these relationships

- how science informs our ecological literacy and our thinking about nature, places, and environments

From *The Web of Life*

Fritjof Capra

In the epilogue to The Web of Life, ***Fritjof Capra*** *brings together a range of scientific theories to help readers develop a better understanding of ecological thinking. Capra defines the concept of ecological literacy and the ways in which human societies must become more ecologically literate to survive. As you read this selection, think not only about the dynamics between human society and ecosystems that Capra sets up, but consider also the language he uses to describe these uniquely linked systems.*

JOURNAL ASSIGNMENT

Before reading Capra's essay here, take a few minutes to write in your journal what you believe *ecological literacy* to be. How does one become ecologically literate? What does the term mean? Are you ecologically literate, and if so, in what ways?

Reconnecting with the web of life means building and nurturing sustainable   1
communities in which we can satisfy our needs and aspirations without diminishing the chances of future generations. For this task we can learn valuable lessons from the study of ecosystems, which *are* sustainable communities of plants, animals, and microorganisms. To understand these lessons, we need to learn the basic principles of ecology. We need to become, as it were, ecologically literate. Being ecologically literate, or "ecoliterate," means understanding the principles of organization of ecological communities (ecosystems) and using those principles for creating sustainable human communities. We need to revitalize our communities—including our educational communities, business communities, and political communities—so that the principles of ecology become manifest in them as principles of education, management, and politics.

The theory of living systems discussed in *The Web of Life* provides a con-   2
ceptual framework for the link between ecological communities and human

communities. Both are living systems that exhibit the same basic principles of organization. They are networks that are organizationally closed, but open to the flows of energy and resources; their structures are determined by their histories of structural changes; they are intelligent because of the cognitive dimensions inherent in the processes of life.

3   Of course, there are many differences between ecosystems and human communities. There is no self-awareness in ecosystems, no language, no consciousness, and no culture; and therefore no justice or democracy; but also no greed or dishonesty. We cannot learn anything about those human values and shortcomings from ecosystems. But what we *can* learn and must learn from them is how to live sustainably. During more than three billion years of evolution the planet's ecosystems have organized themselves in subtle and complex ways so as to maximize sustainability. This wisdom of nature is the essence of ecoliteracy.

4   Based on the understanding of ecosystems as autopoietic networks and dissipative structures, we can formulate a set of principles of organization that may be identified as the basic principles of ecology and use them as guidelines to build sustainable human communities.

5   The first of those principles is interdependence. All members of an ecological community are interconnected in a vast and intricate network of relationships, the web of life. They derive their essential properties and, in fact, their very existence from their relationships to other things. Interdependence—the mutual dependence of all life processes on one another—is the nature of all ecological relationships. The behavior of every living member of the ecosystem depends on the behavior of many others. The success of the whole community depends on the success of its individual members, while the success of each member depends on the success of the community as a whole.

6   Understanding ecological interdependence means understanding relationships. It requires the shifts of perception that are characteristic of systems thinking—from the parts to the whole, from objects to relationships, from contents to patterns. A sustainable human community is aware of the multiple relationships among its members. Nourishing the community means nourishing those relationships.

7   The fact that the basic pattern of life is a network pattern means that the relationships among the members of an ecological community are nonlinear, involving multiple feedback loops. Linear chains of cause and effect exist very rarely in ecosystems. Thus a disturbance will not be limited to a single effect but is likely to spread out in ever-widening patterns. It may even be amplified by interdependent feedback loops, which may completely obscure the original source of the disturbance.

8   The cyclical nature of ecological processes is an important principle of ecology. The ecosystem's feedback loops are the pathways along which nutrients are continually recycled. Being open systems, all organisms in an ecosystem produce wastes, but what is waste for one species is food for another, so that

the ecosystem as a whole remains without waste. Communities of organisms have evolved in this way over billions of years, continually using and recycling the same molecules of minerals, water, and air.

The lesson for human communities here is obvious. A major clash between 9 economics and ecology derives from the fact that nature is cyclical, whereas our industrial systems are linear. Our businesses take resources, transform them into products plus waste, and sell the products to consumers, who discard more waste when they have consumed the products. Sustainable patterns of production and consumption need to be cyclical, imitating the cyclical processes in nature. To achieve such cyclical patterns we need to fundamentally redesign our businesses and our economy.

Ecosystems differ from individual organisms in that they are largely (but 10 not completely) closed systems with respect to the flow of matter, while being open with respect to the flow of energy. The primary source of that flow of energy is the sun. Solar energy, transformed into chemical energy by the photosynthesis of green plants, drives most ecological cycles.

The implications for maintaining sustainable human communities are 11 again obvious. Solar energy in its many forms—sunlight for solar heating and photovoltaic electricity, wind and hydro-power, biomass, and so on—is the only kind of energy that is renewable, economically efficient, and environmentally benign. By disregarding this ecological fact, our political and corporate leaders again and again endanger the health and well-being of millions around the world. The 1991 war in the Persian Gulf, for example, which killed hundreds of thousands, impoverished millions, and caused unprecedented environmental disasters, had its roots to a large extent in the misguided energy policies of the Reagan and Bush administrations.

To describe solar energy as economically efficient assumes that the costs of 12 energy production are counted honestly. This is not the case in most of today's market economies. The so-called free market does not provide consumers with proper information, because the social and environmental costs of production are not part of current economic models. These costs are labeled "external" variables by corporate and government economists, because they do not fit into their theoretical framework.

Corporate economists treat as free commodities not only the air, water, and 13 soil, but also the delicate web of social relations, which is severely affected by continuing economic expansion. Private profits are being made at public costs in the deterioration of the environment and the general quality of life, and at the expense of future generations. The marketplace simply gives us the wrong information. There is a lack of feedback, and basic ecological literacy tells us that such a system is not sustainable.

One of the most effective ways to change the situation would be an ecolog- 14 ical tax reform. Such a tax reform would be strictly revenue neutral, shifting the tax burden from income taxes to "eco-taxes." This means that taxes would be added to existing products, forms of energy, services, and materials, so that prices would better reflect the true costs. In order to be successful, an ecological tax reform needs to be a slow and long-term process to give new technologies and consumption patterns sufficient time to adapt, and the eco-taxes need to be applied predictably to encourage industrial innovation.

15   Such a long-term and slow ecological tax reform would gradually drive wasteful and harmful technologies and consumption patterns out of the market. As energy prices go up, with corresponding income tax reductions to offset the increase, people will increasingly switch from cars to bicycles, use public transportation, and carpool on their way to work. As taxes on petrochemicals and fuel go up, again with offsetting reductions in income taxes, organic farming will become not only the healthiest but also the cheapest means of producing food.

16   Eco-taxes are now under serious discussion in several European countries and are likely to be introduced in all countries sooner or later. To remain competitive under such a new system, managers and entrepreneurs will need to become ecologically literate. In particular, detailed knowledge of the flow of energy and matter through a company will be essential, and this is why the newly developed practice of "eco-auditing" will be of paramount importance. An eco-audit is concerned with the environmental consequences of the flows of material, energy, and people through a company and therefore with the true costs of production.

17   Partnership is an essential characteristic of sustainable communities. The cyclical exchanges of energy and resources in an ecosystem are sustained by pervasive cooperation. Indeed, we have seen that since the creation of the first nucleated cells over two billion years ago, life on Earth has proceeded through ever more intricate arrangements of cooperation and coevolution. Partnership— the tendency to associate, establish links, live inside one another, and cooperate— is one of the hallmarks of life.

18   In human communities partnership means democracy and personal empowerment, because each member of the community plays an important role. Combining the principle of partnership with the dynamic of change and development, we may also use the term "coevolution" metaphorically in human communities. As a partnership proceeds, each partner better understands the needs of the other. In a true, committed partnership both partners learn and change—they coevolve. Here again we notice the basic tension between the challenge of ecological sustainability and the way in which our present societies are structured, between economics and ecology. Economics emphasizes competition, expansion, and domination; ecology emphasizes cooperation, conservation, and partnership.

19   The principle of ecology mentioned so far—interdependence, the cyclical flow of resources, cooperation, and partnership—are all different aspects of the same pattern of organization. This is how ecosystems organize themselves to maximize sustainability. Once we have understood this pattern, we can ask more detailed questions. For example, what is the resilience of these ecological

communities? How do they react to outside disturbances? These questions lead us to further principles of ecology—flexibility and diversity—that enable ecosystems to survive disturbances and adapt to changing conditions.

The flexibility of an ecosystem is a consequence of its multiple feedback 20 loops, which tend to bring the system back into balance whenever there is a deviation from the norm, due to changing environmental conditions. For example, if an unusually warm summer results in increased growth of algae in a lake, some species of fish feeding on the algae may flourish and breed more, so that their numbers increase and they begin to deplete the algae. Once their major source of food is reduced, the fish will begin to die out. As the fish population drops, the algae will recover and expand again. In this way the original disturbance generates a fluctuation around a feedback loop, which eventually brings the fish/algae system back into balance.

Disturbances of that kind happen all the time, because things in the envi- 21 ronment change all the time, and thus the net effect is continual fluctuation. All the variables we can observe in an ecosystem—population densities, availability of nutrients, weather patterns, and so forth—always fluctuate. This is how ecosystems maintain themselves in a flexible state, ready to adapt to changing conditions. The web of life is a flexible, ever-fluctuating network. The more variables are kept fluctuating, the more dynamic is the system; the greater is its flexibility; and the greater is its ability to adapt to changing conditions.

All ecological fluctuations take place between tolerance limits. There is al- 22 ways the danger that the whole system will collapse when a fluctuation goes beyond those limits and the system can no longer compensate for it. The same is true of human communities. Lack of flexibility manifests itself as stress. In particular, stress will occur when one or more variables of the system are pushed to their extreme values, which induces increased rigidity throughout the system. Temporary stress is an essential aspect of life, but prolonged stress is harmful and destructive to the system. These considerations lead to the important realization that managing a social system—a company, a city, or an economy—means finding the *optimal* values for the system's variables. If one tries to maximize any single variable instead of optimizing it, this will invariably lead to the destruction of the system as a whole.

The principle of flexibility also suggests a corresponding strategy of conflict 23 resolution. In every community there will invariably be contradictions and conflicts, which cannot be resolved in favor of one or the other side. For example, the community will need stability *and* change, order *and* freedom, tradition *and* innovation. Rather than by rigid decisions, these unavoidable conflicts are much better resolved by establishing a dynamic balance. Ecological literacy includes the knowledge that both sides of a conflict can be important, depending on the context, and that the contradictions within a community are signs of its diversity and vitality and thus contribute to the system's viability.

In ecosystems the role of diversity is closely connected with the system's net- 24 work structure. A diverse ecosystem will also be resilient, because it contains many species with overlapping ecological functions that can partially replace one another. When a particular species is destroyed by a severe disturbance so that a link in the network is broken, a diverse community will be able to survive and reorganize itself, because other links in the network can at least partially fulfill the function of the destroyed species. In other words, the more complex the network is, the more complex its pattern of interconnections, the more resilient it will be.

25   In ecosystems the complexity of the network is a consequence of its biodiversity, and thus a diverse ecological community is a resilient community. In human communities ethnic and cultural diversity may play the same role. Diversity means many different relationships, many different approaches to the same problem. A diverse community is a resilient community, capable of adapting to changing situations.

26   However, diversity is a strategic advantage only if there is a truly vibrant community, sustained by a web of relationships. If the community is fragmented into isolated groups and individuals, diversity can easily become a source of prejudice and friction. But if the community is aware of the interdependence of all its members, diversity will enrich all the relationships and thus enrich the community as a whole, as well as each individual member. In such a community information and ideas flow freely through the entire network, and the diversity of interpretations and learning styles—even the diversity of mistakes—will enrich the entire community.

27   These, then, are some of the basic principles of ecology—interdependence, recycling, partnership, flexibility, diversity, and, as a consequence of all those, sustainability. As our century comes to a close and we go toward the beginning of a new millennium, the survival of humanity will depend on our ecological literacy, on our ability to understand these principles of ecology and live accordingly.

FOCUS ON ECOLOGY

1. How does Capra define *interdependence?* What role does this concept play in his argument?
2. Generally speaking, what is the relationship between human society and natural ecosystems, according to Capra? Can you identify in your community any sites in which these relationships are apparent?
3. What does Capra mean by *diversity?* Why, according to Capra, is diversity important?

FOCUS ON WRITING

1. Whom might Fritjof Capra be addressing in this essay? What action might he hope that his audience will take upon reading this essay? Is this essay an effective approach to promoting such action?
2. About midway through this essay, Capra makes reference to the 1991 war in the Persian Gulf and links the results of that war to the environmental poli-

cies of the Reagan and Bush administrations. Other than offering an example of how environment and economy are linked, Capra uses this example to suggest other kinds of connections. What are they? Can you think of other such connections?

3. Capra provides the example of taxes to show how human culture and ecosystems are linked. Do you recognize other ways in which writing (such as tax laws or other legislation) might be directly linked to human interaction with natural ecosystems?

FOR DISCUSSION

In "Ecological Literacy" Capra calls for us to become aware of principles of ecology in order to help develop a more sustainable society: "the survival of humanity," he writes, "will depend on our ecological literacy, on our ability to understand these principles of ecology and live accordingly." Consider how we as individuals might be able to live well, more ecologically literate lives. As a group, talk about strategies for better understanding principles of ecology and develop some methods for how we might each live more sustainable lives.

WRITING IN RESPONSE

Once you have discussed Capra's essay and considered as a group how each of us might live a more sustainable life, develop a series of suggestions for how we might become more ecologically literate. As a class, think in particular about how your campus might better interact with its local ecosystems. As you develop this list, expand your ideas into a short pamphlet, brochure, or booklet that might be printed and distributed around campus to promote ecological literacy among the campus community. Consider contacting student government or other organizations that might sponsor such a project.

"Thinking Like a Mountain" from *A Sand County Almanac*

Aldo Leopold

Aldo Leopold is considered to have been one of the most influential and important conservationist thinkers and his writings and are often reprinted in collections of nature writing and ecology, though he never thought of himself as a nature writer. Leopold was born in Burlington, Iowa in 1887, and he died in 1947, a year before his award-winning book A Sand County Almanac *was published. In 1978, Leopold was posthumously awarded the John Burroughs Medal for* A Sand County Almanac. *This book, from which the selection below is taken, is often spoken of as comparable to the work of Henry David Thoreau. In the foreword to* A Sand County Almanac, *Leopold explains, "Conservation is getting nowhere because it is incompatible with our Abrahamic concept of land. We abuse land because we see it as a commodity belonging to us. When we see land as a community to which we belong, we may begin to use it with love and respect." As you read this famous selection, "Thinking Like a Mountain," consider the ways Leopold encourages us to see land as a "community to which we belong."*

JOURNAL ASSIGNMENT

Early in this essay, Leopold writes, "Only the mountain has lived long enough to listen objectively to the howl of a wolf." In your journal, take a few minutes to write about what Leopold might mean by this sentence. Think (and write) specifically about what this sentence might mean in the context of a piece called "Thinking Like a Mountain."

1   A deep chesty bawl echoes from rimrock to rimrock, rolls down the mountain, and fades into the far blackness of the night. It is an outburst of wild defiant sorrow, and of contempt for all the adversities of the world.

2   Every living thing (and perhaps many a dead one as well) pays heed to that call. To the deer it is a reminder of the way of all flesh, to the pine a forecast of midnight scuffles and of blood upon the snow, to the coyote a promise of gleanings to come, to the cowman a threat of red ink at the bank, to the hunter a challenge of fang against bullet. Yet behind these obvious and immediate hopes and fears there lies a deeper meaning, known only to the mountain itself. *Only the mountain has lived long enough to listen objectively to the howl of a wolf.*

3   Those unable to decipher the hidden meaning know nevertheless that it is there, for it is felt in all wolf country, and distinguishes that country from all other land. It tingles in the spine of all who hear wolves by night, or who scan their tracks by day. Even without sight or sound of wolf, it is implicit in a hundred small events: The midnight whinny of a pack horse, the rattle of rolling rocks, the bound of a fleeing deer, the way shadows lie under the spruces. Only the ineducable tyro can fail to sense the presence or absence of wolves, or the fact that mountains have a secret opinion about them.

4   My own conviction on this score dates from the day I saw a wolf die. We were eating lunch on a high rimrock, at the foot of which a turbulent river elbowed its way. We saw what we thought was a doe fording the torrent, her breast awash in white water. When she climbed the bank toward us and shook out her tail, we realized our error: it was a wolf. A half-dozen others, evidently grown pups, sprang from the willows and all joined in a welcoming mêlée of

wagging tails and playful maulings. What was literally a pile of wolves writhed and tumbled in the center of an open flat at the foot of our rimrock.

In those days we had never heard of passing up a chance to kill a wolf. In a 5 second we were pumping lead into the pack, but with more excitement than accuracy: how to aim a steep downhill shot is always confusing. When our rifles were empty, the old wolf was down, and a pup was dragging a leg into impassable slide rocks.

We reached the old wolf in time to watch a fierce green fire dying in her 6 eyes. I realized then, and have known ever since, that there was something new to me in those eyes— something known only to her and to the mountain. I was young then, and full of trigger-itch; I thought that because fewer wolves meant more deer, that no wolves would mean hunters' paradise. But after seeing the green fire die, I sensed that neither the wolf nor the mountain agreed with such a view.

• • •

Since then I have lived to see state after state extirpate its wolves. I have watched 7 the face of many a newly wolfless mountain, and seen the south-facing slopes wrinkle with a maze of new deer trails. I have seen every edible bush and seedling browsed, first to anaemic desuetude, and then to death. I have seen every edible tree defoliated to the height of a saddlehorn. Such a mountain looks as if someone had given God a new pruning shears, and forbidden Him all other exercise. In the end the starved bones of the hoped-for deer herd, dead of its own too-much, bleach with the bones of the dead sage, or molder under the high-lined junipers.

I now suspect that just as a deer herd lives in mortal fear of its wolves, so 8 does a mountain live in mortal fear of its deer. And perhaps with better cause, for while a buck pulled down by wolves can be replaced in two or three years, a range pulled down by too many deer may fail of replacement in as many decades.

So also with cows. The cowman who cleans his range of wolves does not 9 realize that he is taking over the wolf's job of trimming the herd to fit the range. He has not learned to think like a mountain. Hence we have dustbowls, and rivers washing the future into the sea.

• • •

We all strive for safety, prosperity, comfort, long life, and dullness. The deer 10 strives with his supple legs, the cowman with trap and poison, the statesman with pen, the most of us with machines, votes, and dollars, but it all comes to the same thing: peace in our time. A measure of success in this is all well enough, and perhaps is a requisite to objective thinking, but too much safety seems to yield only danger in the long run. Perhaps this is behind Thoreau's dictum: In wildness is the salvation of the world. Perhaps this is the hidden meaning in the howl of the wolf, long known among mountains, but seldom perceived among men.

FOCUS ON ECOLOGY

1. In the second paragraph of "Thinking Like a Mountain," Leopold lists the ways both animals and humans respond to the echoing cry. What might Leopold's agenda be in placing both humans and animals in this list of responses?
2. What does Leopold learn from shooting the wolf? Have you ever had an experience that changed the way you think about animals?
3. At the end of this piece, Leopold repeats Henry David Thoreau's idea that "In wildness is the salvation of the world." What might Leopold mean by this?

FOCUS ON WRITING

1. At the end of this piece, when Leopold invokes the name of Thoreau, he does so not only to quote Thoreau's dictum but to acknowledge the influence Thoreau had on Leopold's thinking. Since Leopold ends his piece with this reference to Thoreau. How can we see Thoreau's work (particularly the dictum he mentions) influencing Leopold throughout this piece?
2. Why do you suppose Leopold decided to divide this piece into sections? Are there distinctions between the sections? If so, do they affect how you read and understand this piece?
3. Twice in this essay Leopold suggests that the wolf's howl has "meaning." Can a wolf's howl mean things the same way the statesman's pen writes things with "meaning"? Does this essay give meaning to the howl in any way?

FOR DISCUSSION

Now that you have read Leopold's essay consider what he suggests in his title. As a group, talk about the ways we might think differently about the roles of nature and our interactions with them.

WRITING IN RESPONSE

In an essay modeling Leopold's strategies, write about how we might think like another natural formation from an environment familiar to you. For instance, you may want to write an essay called "Thinking Like a Valley," "Thinking Like an Island," "Thinking Like an Isthmus," or "Thinking Like a Plain." Use this as an opportunity not to mimic Leopold but to consider how you can think about your own local environment from a perspective and strategy similar to Leopold's.

Eco-Defense

Edward Abbey

Edward Abbey is perhaps best known for his novel The Monkey Wrench Gang, *which introduces his famous character Hayduke. Hayduke and his friends are eco-terrorists, who destroy the property of companies that endanger natural environments. Abbey also wrote a good deal about protecting wilderness. His landmark book* Desert Solitaire *recounts his time spent as a park ranger at Arches National Monument in Moab, Utah. As you read "Eco-Defense" think about the role Abbey asks us to take in relationship to nature. Consider what his unorthodox call for protection might suggest regarding the ecological relationship between people and nature.*

JOURNAL ASSIGNMENT

Before reading this essay, consider carefully what the/of "eco-defense" concept might mean. In your journal, write what you think the term means and explain how we each might be eco-defensive.

If a stranger batters your door down with an axe, threatens your family and 1 yourself with deadly weapons, and proceeds to loot your home of whatever he wants, he is committing what is universally recognized—by law and in common morality—as a crime. In such a situation the householder has both the right and the obligation to defend himself, his family, and his property by whatever means are necessary. This right and this obligation is universally recognized, justified, and praised by all civilized human communities. Self-defense against attack is one of the basic laws not only of human society but of life itself, not only of human life but of all life.

The American wilderness, what little remains, is now undergoing exactly 2 such an assault. With bulldozer, earth mover, chainsaw, and dynamite the international timber, mining, and beef industries are invading our public lands—property of all Americans—bashing their way into our forests, mountains, and rangelands and looting them for everything they can get away with. This for the sake of short-term profits in the corporate sector and multimillion-dollar annual salaries for the three-piece-suited gangsters (MBA—Harvard, Yale, University of Tokyo, et alia) who control and manage these bandit enterprises. Cheered on, naturally, by *Time, Newsweek,* and *The Wall Street Journal,* actively encouraged, inevitably, by those jellyfish government agencies that are supposed to *protect* the public lands, and as always aided and abetted in every way possible by the compliant politicians of our Western states, such as Babbitt, DeConcini, Goldwater, McCain, Hatch, Garn, Simms, Hansen, Andrus, Wallop, Domenici and Co. Inc.—who would sell the graves of their mothers if there's a quick buck in the deal, over or under the table, what do they care.

3   Representative government in the United States has broken down. Our legislators do not represent the public, the voters, or even those who voted for them but rather the commercial industrial interests that finance their political campaigns and control the organs of communication—the TV, the newspapers, the billboards, the radio. Politics is a game for the rich only. Representative government in the USA represents money, not people, and therefore has forfeited our allegiance and moral support. We owe it nothing but the taxation it extorts from us under threats of seizure of property, imprisonment, or in some cases already, when resisted, a violent death by gunfire.

4   Such is the nature and structure of the industrial megamachine (in Lewis Mumford's term) which is now attacking the American wilderness. That wilderness is our ancestral home, the primordial homeland of all living creatures including the human, and the present final dwelling place of such noble beings as the grizzly bear, the mountain lion, the eagle and the condor, the moose and the elk and the pronghorn antelope, the redwood tree, the yellow pine, the bristlecone pine, and yes, why not say it?—the streams, waterfalls, rivers, the very bedrock itself of our hills, canyons, deserts, mountains. For many of us, perhaps for most of us, the wilderness is more our home than the little stucco boxes, wallboard apartments, plywood trailer-houses, and cinderblock condominiums in which the majority are now confined by the poverty of an overcrowded industrial culture.

5   And if the wilderness is our true home, and if it is threatened with invasion, pillage, and destruction—as it certainly is—then we have the right to defend that home, as we would our private quarters, by whatever means are necessary. (An Englishman's home is his castle; the American's home is his favorite forest, river, fishing stream, her favorite mountain or desert canyon, his favorite swamp or woods or lake.) We have the right to resist and we have the obligation; not to defend that which we love would be dishonorable. The majority of the American people have demonstrated on every possible occasion that they support the ideal of wilderness preservation; even our politicians are forced by popular opinion to *pretend* to support the idea; as they have learned, a vote against wilderness is a vote against their own reelection. We are justified then in defending our homes—our private home and our public home—not only by common law and common morality but also by common belief. We are the majority; they—the powerful—are in the minority.

6   How best defend our homes? Well, that is a matter of the strategy, tactics, and technique which eco-defense is all about.

7   What is eco-defense? Eco-defense means fighting back. Eco-defense means sabotage. Eco-defense is risky but sporting; unauthorized but fun; illegal but

ethically imperative. Next time you enter a public forest scheduled for chain-saw massacre by some timber corporation and its flunkies in the US Forest Service, carry a hammer and a few pounds of 60-penny nails in your creel, saddlebag, game bag, backpack, or picnic basket. Spike those trees; you won't hurt them; they'll be grateful for the protection; and you may save the forest. Loggers hate nails. My Aunt Emma back in West Virginia has been enjoying this pleasant exercise for years. She swears by it. It's good for the trees, it's good for the woods, and it's good for the human soul. Spread the word.

FOCUS ON ECOLOGY

1. What does Abbey accomplish by equating protecting the wilderness with protecting one's home and family?
2. Do you agree with Abbey's positions, which some consider extreme? Why or why not?
3. What might Abbey be suggesting when he writes, "For many of us, perhaps for most of us, the wilderness is more our home than the little stucco boxes, wallboard apartments, plywood trailer-houses, and cinderblock condominiums in which the majority are now confined by the poverty of an overcrowded industrial culture"?

FOCUS ON WRITING

1. Toward the middle of this essay, Abbey makes reference to "the compliant politicians of our Western states" and then lists 11 politicians by name. First, do you recognize any of the names on Abbey's list? If so, what have they done to earn their place on this list? Is it necessary to know who these people are to understand Abbey's argument?
2. The title of this essay is "Eco-Defense," yet Abbey does not mention or define the term *eco-defense* until the last two paragraphs. Why might he have chosen to do this? Would the essay be more or less effective had he written these last two paragraphs as the introduction to the essay?

FOR DISCUSSION

Edward Abbey's call for eco-defense may seem extreme to some. Many of us would be hesitant to commit acts that could be considered violent or might put other people at risk or damage the property of a business or individual. Yet Abbey suggests that it is our duty to engage in such activities to protect our wildernesses. As a class, consider Abbey's proposal. Is Abbey out of line? Is his call to arms justified? Do you know of cases that could be seen as an answer to Abbey's call? How were they received publicly? How did you respond to them?

WRITING IN RESPONSE

Abbey's essay, whether you agree with it or not, certainly evokes some kind of response from most readers. Many find Abbey's criticism of how we treat wilderness accurate but are put off by his violent response. Others find Abbey's position to misunderstand the needs and wants of the very majority he claims to be speaking for. In a letter written to Abbey in response to his essay, explain why you agree with or disagree with him.

The American Wilderness: Why It Matters

Robert F. Kennedy, Jr.

Robert F. Kennedy, Jr., is an attorney for the Natural Resources Defense. "The American Wilderness: Why It Matters" was originally published in the August 1998 issue of Sports Afield, *a magazine devoted to outdoor sports like hunting, fishing, kayaking, climbing, and camping. In this essay, Kennedy explains why protecting wildernesses is a crucial part of American culture. In making his argument, he refers to historical figures, authors and books, and historical events. As you read this essay, consider how and why Kennedy makes so many references to other texts, people, and events in developing his argument.*

JOURNAL ASSIGNMENT

How do you imagine "wilderness" to be used in this title? What is the American wilderness? Where is the American wilderness? Who is responsible for the care of the American wilderness? Address these questions in your journal.

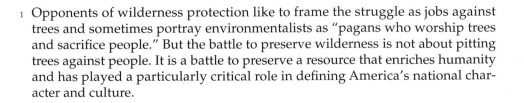

1   Opponents of wilderness protection like to frame the struggle as jobs against trees and sometimes portray environmentalists as "pagans who worship trees and sacrifice people." But the battle to preserve wilderness is not about pitting trees against people. It is a battle to preserve a resource that enriches humanity and has played a particularly critical role in defining America's national character and culture.

The Europeans destroyed the last of their wilderness 1000 years ago. In   2
North America, we have managed to preserve great vestiges, thanks to the fore-
sight of leaders who recognized our nation's strong cultural and historical
connections to wilderness: It is the centerpiece of American culture. Our nation's first great historian, Frederick Jackson Turner, argued that American
democracy was rooted in the wilderness and that our political institutions
could not have evolved in its absence. Whether Turner's frontier hypothesis is
true, it is a theme that has been persistently echoed by our most visionary political leadership. Jefferson and most of the other founding fathers were deists
who believed God's will and appropriate mechanisms for governing people
could be discerned through the observation of undisturbed nature.

One of my favorite passages in Alexis de Tocqueville's *Journey to America* is   3
the description of a Pontiac innkeeper in the tractless forests of the Michigan
frontier responding to a question posed by the French adventurer. De Tocqueville asked why all frontiersmen were American-born rather than evenly
representing the cacophony of immigrant races then found in the continent's
tamer regions. A smile of condescension and satisfied pride spread over the
host's face as he heard the question: "It is only Americans," he answered emphatically, "who could have the courage to submit to such trials and who know
how to purchase comfort at such a price."

Americans have prided themselves on their toughness and stoicism and,   4
like de Tocqueville, have long assumed that such character traits emerged from
the wilderness experience. America's favorite native heroes—from Abe Lincoln
to Andrew Jackson, Sergeant York, Will Rogers and Chuck Yeager, Daniel Boone,
Davey Crockett, Geronimo, Ethan Allen and Swamp Fox, and the cowboys and
Indians of the American West—annealed their heroic qualities of self-reliance,
physical courage and perseverance in the American wilderness. Following the
close of the frontier, it was the fear that Americans would lose these traits and
become sissified that prompted progressives at the turn of the century to found
the Boy Scouts; led Teddy Roosevelt to recreate himself as a frontiersman; drove
President Kennedy to begin his national campaign for physical fitness. The same
impulse caused my father to climb Mount Kennedy, the tallest unclimbed peak
in the Canadian Rockies, and drag me and eight or nine brothers and sisters
hiking in our national parks and paddling on most of the major whitewater
rivers. He saw these adventures as frontier metaphors that allowed us to struggle with nature without destroying it.

And the woods, it was thought, would instill us with character beyond beef-   5
jerky toughness. Virtually every classic American writer, including Hawthorne,
Irving, Twain, Faulkner, London and Melville, celebrated wilderness as the
source of a range of national virtues. Europeans made James Fenimore Cooper's
Leather-stocking Tales our first international best-sellers. Cooper's hero, Natty
Bumppo, has all the virtues that European Romantics associated with the American woods—self-reliance, courage, stoicism, humility, wisdom, craftiness, fortitude, humor, kindness and generosity—as well as a special spiritual depth.

6   Since the advent of language, the poetry, art and religious hymns of every culture celebrated wild nature as the clearest way to talk about God. So it was natural that, from the early settlement of the American wilderness, our cultural and political leaders were telling our people that wilderness would imbue Americans with a special spiritual dimension. A generation after Cooper, Emerson and Thoreau led American writers in embracing nature as the undiluted source of divine wisdom and grace uniquely available to Americans. If, they suggested, an American wanted to hear the voice of God, he must venture into the wilderness and listen to the bird songs and rustle of leaves; to see the American soul, one might look into the mirror of Walden Pond.

7   I don't believe nature is God or that we ought to be worshiping it as such. But I do believe that wilderness and nature are the places where God communicates to human beings most forcefully. Destroying these last wild places—the last spots where we can view creation undiluted by the mark of man—is the moral equivalent of tearing the last pages from the last Bible, Talmud, Upanishad or Koran on earth.

8   The experience of wilderness links Americans to a unique spiritual legacy, with 300 years of American colonial history and the 12,000-year history of pre-Columbian America. It links us to the season and tides and the 10,000 generations of human beings that lived before laptops. Recognizing these connections, environmentalists fight to preserve wilderness not for its own sake but because it enriches us culturally, spiritually, aesthetically and historically. Human beings have appetites for these things and if we don't feed them, we will never grow up or fulfill ourselves. Environmentalists are not fighting for the ancient forests of the Pacific Northwest for the sake of the spotted owl (as Rush Limbaugh likes to say) but because we believe that those trees are more valuable to humanity standing than they would be if we cut them down. If we allow the last of these wild areas to be destroyed, we diminish ourselves and impoverish our children.

FOCUS ON ECOLOGY

1. Why, according to Kennedy, do we need to protect the American wilderness? Is this reason a good one? Do you agree with him?
2. What, according to Kennedy, is the relationship between wilderness and religion? What do you see as the relationship (if any) between religion and God (if any)?

FOCUS ON WRITING

1. Kennedy writes, "Virtually every classic American writer, including Hawthorne, Irving, Twain, Faulkner, London and Melville, celebrated wilderness as the source of a range of national virtues." He also writes about Alexis

de Tocqueville, Abe Lincoln, Andrew Jackson, Sergeant York, Will Rogers, Chuck Yeager, Daniel Boone, Davey Crockett, Geronimo, Ethan Allen, Emerson, Thoreau, President Kennedy, and Teddy Roosevelt. Why do you suppose Kennedy doesn't mention any women in this article? What does this suggest not only about Kennedy's writing, but of the very "American history" he tries to depict?

2. This essay was initially published in *Sports Afield.* What kinds of assumptions might Kennedy have made about his audience? That is, who do you imagine reads *Sports Afield* and why would Kennedy direct such an essay toward them?

3. What effect do you think other texts have had on Kennedy's thinking about wilderness? Consider the ways his experiences with these books may have affected how he thinks about wilderness and ultimately how they affected his writing of this piece.

FOR DISCUSSION

Think about the images you picture when you read the term *American wilderness*. First, as a class, discuss those images, allowing everyone an opportunity to describe places that the term evokes. Then, consider how you as a class might define that term. Once you have reached agreement on a possible definition, develop a list of characteristics a place must have to be considered an American wilderness according to your definition.

WRITING IN RESPONSE

Kennedy links his conception of American wilderness to his conception of an American history. Think about the places you consider to be wilderness and write an essay explaining what role those places had in history (American or otherwise). Be sure to explain how that history affects not only your thinking about that place, but also how that history impacts the reasons the place is thought of as wilderness.

The Words of Chief Seattle

The two readings found here are generally attributed to Chief Seattle *of the Skokomish (Suquamish) Indians, a tribe native to the Northwest of the United States, now known as Washington state. There has been a good deal of controversy and disagreement regarding the two selections found here, most of which surrounds the question of whether Chief Seattle actually wrote or spoke these words. The first selection is generally thought to be either a speech or a letter written by Chief Seattle in 1851 in response to the U.S. government's bid to purchase Native American land and move Native Americans onto reservations. However, there has also been some speculation that this speech (or letter) may have been written in 1972 by a television scriptwriter named Ted Perry. The second selection is attributed to Chief Seattle as a speech given in 1854, but there is question too about the authorship of this selection as the speech first appeared in print in the* Seattle Sunday Star *on October 29, 1887, in a column by Henry A. Smith.*

JOURNAL ASSIGNMENT

In these selections, we encounter the famous statement, "We are part of the Earth and it is part of us." Before reading these pieces, think about the implications of this statement and what it suggests about the relationship between people and earth. Write the words across the top of a blank page in your journal. In a column on the left side of your page, make a list of the ways that we are part of the earth. On the right side of the page make a list of the ways that the earth is part of us.

1   How can you buy or sell the sky, the warmth of the land? The idea is strange to us. If we do not own the freshness of the air and the sparkle of the water, how can you buy them?

2   Every part of this Earth is sacred to my people. Every shining pine needle, every sandy shore, every mist in the dark woods, every clearing, and every humming insect is holy in the memory and experience of my people. The sap which courses through the trees carries the memory of the red man.

3   The white man's dead forget the country of their birth when they go to walk among the stars. Our dead never forget this beautiful Earth, for it is the mother of the red man. We are part of the Earth and it is part of us. The perfumed flowers are our sisters; the deer, the horse, the great eagle, these are our brothers. The rocky crests, the juices in the meadows, the body heat of the pony, and man—all belong to the same family.

4   So, when the Great Chief in Washington sends word that he wishes to buy our land, he asks much of us. The Great Chief sends word that he will reserve us a place so that we can live comfortably to ourselves. He will be our father and we will be his children.

5   So we will consider your offer to buy our land. But it will not be easy.

6   For this land is sacred to us. This shining water that moves in the streams and rivers is not just water but the blood of our ancestors. If we sell you land, you must remember that it is sacred, and you must teach your children that it is sacred, and that each ghostly reflection in the clear water of the lakes tells of

events and memories in the life of my people. The water's murmur is the voice of my father's father.

The rivers are our brothers; they quench our thirst. The rivers carry our ca- 7 noes and feed our children. If we sell you our land, you must remember, and teach your children, that the rivers are our brothers and yours, and you must henceforth give the rivers the kindness you would give any brother.

We know that the white man does not understand our ways. One portion 8 of land is the same to him as the next. For he is a stranger who comes in the night and takes from the land whatever he needs. The Earth is not his brother, but his enemy, and when he has conquered it, he moves on. He leaves his father's grave behind, and he does not care. He kidnaps the Earth from his children, and he does not care. His father's grave and his children's birthright are forgotten. He treats his mother, the Earth, and his brother, the sky, as things to be bought, plundered, sold like sheep or bright beads. His appetite will devour the Earth and leave behind only a desert.

I do not know. Our ways are different from your ways. The sight of your 9 cities pains the eyes of the red man. There is no quiet place in the white man's cities. No place to hear the unfurling of leaves in spring or the rustle of the insect's wings. The clatter only seems to insult the ears. And what is there to life if a man cannot hear the lonely cry of the whippoorwill or the arguments of the frogs around the pond at night? I am a red man and I do not understand. The Indian prefers the soft sound of the wind darting over the face of a pond and the smell of the wind itself, cleansed by a midday rain, or scented with piñon pine. The air is precious to the red man, for all things share the same breath, the beast, the tree, the man, they all share the same breath. The white man does not seem to notice the air he breathes. Like a man dying for many days he is numb to the stench. But if we sell you our land, you must remember that the air is precious to us, that the air shares its spirit with all the life it supports.

The wind that gave our grandfather his first breath also receives his last 10 sigh. And if we sell you our land, you must keep it apart and sacred as a place where even the white man can go to taste the wind that is sweetened by the meadow's flowers.

You must teach your children that the ground beneath their feet is the ashes 11 of our grandfathers. So that they will respect the land, tell your children that the Earth is rich with the lives of our kin. Teach your children that we have taught our children that the Earth is our mother. Whatever befalls the Earth befalls the sons of the Earth. If men spit upon the ground, they spit upon themselves.

This we know: the Earth does not belong to man; man belongs to the Earth. 12 All things are connected. We may be brothers after all. We shall see.

One thing we know which the white man may one day discover: our God is 13 the same God. You may think now that you own Him as you wish to own our land; but you cannot. This Earth is precious to Him, and to harm the Earth is to heap contempt on its creator. The whites too shall pass; perhaps sooner than all other tribes. Contaminate your bed and you will one night suffocate in your own waste.

14   But in your perishing you will shine brightly, fired by the strength of the God who brought you to this land and for some special purpose gave you dominion over this land and over the red man.

15   That destiny is a mystery to us, for we do not understand when the buffalo are all slaughtered, the wild horses all tame, the street corners of the forest heavy with the scent of many men, and the ripe hills blotted by talking wires.

16   Where is the thicket? Gone. Where is the eagle? Gone.

17   The end of living and the beginning of survival.

1   Yonder sky that has wept tears of compassion upon my people for centuries untold, and which to us appears changeless and eternal, may change. Today is fair. Tomorrow it may be overcast with clouds. My words are like the stars that never change. Whatever Seattle says, the great chief at Washington can rely upon with as much certainty as he can upon the return of the sun or the seasons. The white chief says that Big Chief at Washington sends us greetings of friendship and goodwill. This is kind of him for we know he has little need of our friendship in return. His people are many. They are like the grass that covers vast prairies. My people are few. They resemble the scattering trees of a storm-swept plain. The great, and I presume—good, White Chief sends us word that he wishes to buy our land but is willing to allow us enough to live comfortably. This indeed appears just, even generous, for the Red Man no longer has rights that he need respect, and the offer may be wise, also, as we are no longer in need of an extensive country.

2   There was a time when our people covered the land as the waves of a wind-ruffled sea cover its shell-paved floor, but that time long since passed away with the greatness of tribes that are now but a mournful memory. I will not dwell on, nor mourn over, our untimely decay, nor reproach my paleface brothers with hastening it, as we too may have been somewhat to blame.

3   Youth is impulsive. When our young men grow angry at some real or imaginary wrong, and disfigure their faces with black paint, it denotes that their hearts are black, and that they are often cruel and relentless, and our old men and old women are unable to restrain them. Thus it has ever been. Thus it was when the white man began to push our forefathers ever westward. But let us hope that the hostilities between us may never return. We would have everything to lose and nothing to gain. Revenge by young men is considered gain, even at the cost of their own lives, but old men who stay at home in times of war, and mothers who have sons to lose, know better.

4   Our good father in Washington—for I presume he is now our father as well as yours, since King George has moved his boundaries further north—our great and good father, I say, sends us word that if we do as desires he will protect us. His brave warriors will be to us a bristling wall of strength, and his wonderful ships of war will fill our harbors, so that our ancient enemies far to

the northward—the Haidas and Tsimshians—will cease to frighten our women, children, and old men. Then in reality he will be our father and we his children. But can that ever be? Your God is not our God! Your God loves your people and hates mine! He folds his strong protecting arms lovingly about the paleface and leads him by the hand as a father leads an infant son. But, He has forsaken His Red children, if they really are His. Our God, the Great Spirit, seems also to have forsaken us. Your God makes your people wax stronger every day. Soon they will fill all the land. Our people are ebbing away like a rapidly receding tide that will never return. The white man's God cannot love our people or He would protect them. They seem to be orphans who can look nowhere for help. How then can we be brothers? How can your God become our God and renew our prosperity and awaken in us dreams of returning greatness? If we have a common Heavenly Father He must be partial, for He came to His paleface children. We never saw Him. He gave you laws but had no word for His red children whose teeming multitudes once filled this vast continent as stars fill the firmament. No; we are two distinct races with separate origins and separate destinies. There is little in common between us.

To us the ashes of our ancestors are sacred and their resting place is hal- 5 lowed ground. You wander far from the graves of your ancestors and seemingly without regret. Your religion was written upon tablets of stone by the iron finger of your God so that you could not forget. The Red Man could never comprehend or remember it. Our religion is the traditions of our ancestors—the dreams of our old men, given them in solemn hours of the night by the Great Spirit; and the visions of our sachems, and is written in the hearts of our people.

Your dead cease to love you and the land of their nativity as soon as they 6 pass the portals of the tomb and wander away beyond the stars. They are soon forgotten and never return. Our dead never forget this beautiful world that gave them being. They still love its verdant valleys, its murmuring rivers, its magnificent mountains, sequestered vales and verdant lined lakes and bays, and ever yearn in tender fond affection over the lonely hearted living, and often return from the happy hunting ground to visit, guide, console, and comfort them.

Day and night cannot dwell together. The Red Man has ever fled the ap- 7 proach of the White Man, as the morning mist flees before the morning sun. However, your proposition seems fair and I think that my people will accept it and will retire to the reservation you offer them. Then we will dwell apart in peace, for the words of the Great White Chief seem to be the words of nature speaking to my people out of dense darkness.

It matters little where we pass the remnant of our days. They will not be 8 many. The Indian's night promises to be dark. Not a single star of hope hovers above his horizon. Sad-voiced winds moan in the distance. Grim fate seems to be on the Red Man's trail, and wherever he will hear the approaching footsteps of his fell destroyer and prepare stolidly to meet his doom, as does the wounded doe that hears approaching footsteps of the hunter.

A few more moons, a few more winters, and not one of the descendants of 9 the mighty hosts that once moved over this broad land or lived in happy homes, protected by the Great Spirit, will remain to mourn over the graves of a people once more powerful and hopeful than yours. But why should I mourn at the untimely fate of my people? Tribe follows tribe, and nation follows nation, like the waves of the sea. It is the order of nature, and regret is useless. Your time of decay may be distant, but it will surely come, for even the White Man whose God walked and talked with him as friend to friend, cannot be exempt from the common destiny. We may be brothers after all. We will see.

10   We will ponder your proposition and when we decide we will let you know. But should we accept it, I here and now make this condition that we will not be denied the privilege without molestation of visiting at any time the tombs of our ancestors, friends, and children. Every part of this soil is sacred in the estimation of my people. Every hillside, every valley, every plain and grove, has been hallowed by some sad or happy event in days long vanished. Even the rocks, which seem to be dumb and dead as the swelter in the sun along the silent shore, thrill with memories of stirring events connected with the lives of my people, and the very dust upon which you now stand responds more lovingly to their footsteps than yours, because it is rich with the blood of our ancestors, and our bare feet are conscious of the sympathetic touch. Our departed braves, fond mothers, glad, happy hearted maidens, and even the little children who lived here and rejoiced here for a brief season, will love these somber solitudes and at eventide they greet shadowy returning spirits. And when the last Red Man shall have perished, and the memory of my tribe shall have become a myth among the White Men, these shores will swarm with the invisible dead of my tribe, and when your children's children think themselves alone in the field, the store, the shop, upon the highway, or in the silence of the pathless woods they will not be alone. In all the earth there is no place dedicated to solitude. At night when the streets of your cities and villages are silent and you think them deserted, they will throng with the returning hosts that once filled them and still love this beautiful land. The White Man will never be alone.

11   Let him be just and deal kindly with my people, for the dead are not powerless. Dead, did I say? There is no death, only a change of worlds.

FOCUS ON ECOLOGY

1. How does Chief Seattle describe the relationship between Native Americans and nature? How does he describe the relationship between White Men and nature?
2. What does Chief Seattle see as the future of Native Americans? Of the white people? Has his prediction been accurate?

FOCUS ON WRITING

1. Compare these two pieces. Do they "sound" as though they were written by the same person? What characteristics about the writing lead you to your answer?

2. Consider what characteristics of each selection might lead one to read it as a speech intended for spoken delivery rather than as a text written as a letter, or vice versa.

3. Would it matter if the first selection had been written by a television scriptwriter in 1972 or if the second piece had been fabricated by a newspaper writer rather than actually spoken by Chief Seattle? In what ways would or wouldn't this knowledge affect your understanding of each piece?

FOR DISCUSSION

Assume both selections *were* composed nearly 200 years ago. Did anyone pay heed to their words? What evidence do you have in support of your response?

WRITING IN RESPONSE

Remembering that each of these pieces may have originally been presented as either a speech or a written text, think about how one writes each kind of text differently. Next, compose a short response to Chief Seattle. First, write your response as a speech, as though you would deliver it in a short talk to an audience in which Chief Seattle was present. Then, re-compose the piece as a letter to Chief Seattle.

Touching the Earth

bell hooks

Gloria Jean Watkins was born on September 25, 1952, in Hopkinsville, Kentucky, to Veodis Watkins, a custodian, and Rosa Bell, a homemaker. Watkins writes under the name bell hooks, which was the name of her grandmother. As she has explained many times, she chose this name not only as a tribute to her grandmother but to "honor the unlettered wisdom of her foremothers." hooks also writes her name with all lower-case letters as a sign that writing, language, discourse need not always comply with traditional, male doctrines of correctness. The name bell hooks, then, serves to remind readers of the often unheard voices of black women, and hooks uses the name to disrupt the traditional conventions that have enforced that silence. bell hooks is known as a public intellectual—one who works to bring intellectual work to larger audiences than just the university community. For hooks, writing has to reach more than just an audience of college professors and students. Hence, a good deal of hooks's writing appears in popular magazines and journals, and her books address issues that are important

*to many people: race, feminism, culture. In the piece that follows, hooks writes specifi-
cally about the relationship between black people and the land.*

JOURNAL ASSIGNMENT

In the piece you are about to read, hooks writes, "Living close to nature, black
folks were able to cultivate a spirit of wonder and reverence for life," and later
"living in modern society, without a sense of history, it has been easy for folks
to forget that black people were first and foremost a people of the land, farmers."
Think about this statement and write about how and why living close to nature
might be of particular importance to African-Americans, particularly in light
of what you know of the history of blacks in America.

*I wish to live because life has within it that which is good, that which is beautiful,
and that which is love. Therefore, since I have known all these things, I have found them
to be reason enough and —I wish to live. Moreover, because this is so, I wish others to
live for generations and generations and generations and generations.*
       —Lorraine Hansberry, *To Be Young, Gifted, and Black*

1   When we love the earth, we are able to love ourselves more fully. I believe
this. The ancestors taught me it was so. As a child I loved playing in dirt, in
that rich Kentucky soil, that was a source of life. Before I understood anything
about the pain and exploitation of the southern system of sharecropping, I understood that grown-up black folks loved the land. I could stand with my
grandfather Daddy Jerry and look out at fields of growing vegetables, tomatoes, corn, collards, and know that this was his handiwork. I could see the look
of pride on his face as I expressed wonder and awe at the magic of growing
things. I knew that my grandmother Baba's backyard garden would yield
beans, sweet potatoes, cabbage, and yellow squash, that she would walk with
pride among the rows and rows of growing vegetables showing us what the
earth will give when tended lovingly.

2   From the moment of their first meeting, Native American and African people shared with one another a respect for the life-giving forces of nature, of the
earth. African settlers in Florida taught the Creek Nation runaways, the "Seminoles," methods for rice cultivation. Native peoples taught recently arrived
black folks all about the many uses of corn. (The hotwater cornbread we grew
up eating came to our black southern diet from the world of the Indian.) Sharing the reverence for the earth, black and red people helped one another remember that, despite the white man's ways, the land belonged to everyone.
Listen to these words attributed to Chief Seattle in 1854:

> How can you buy or sell the sky, the warmth of the land? The idea is strange to us.
> If we do not own the freshness of the air and the sparkle of the water, how can you

buy them? Every part of this earth is sacred to my people. Every shining pine needle, every sandy shore, every mist in the dark woods, every clearing and humming insect is holy in the memory and experience of my people . . . We are part of the earth and it is part of us. The perfumed flowers are our sisters; the deer, the horse, the great eagle, these are our brothers. The rocky crests, the juices in the meadows, the body heat of the pony, and man—all belong to the same family.

The sense of union and harmony with nature expressed here is echoed in testimony by black people who found that even though life in the new world was "harsh, harsh," in relationship to the earth one could be at peace. In the oral autobiography of granny midwife Onnie Lee Logan, who lived all her life in Alabama, she talks about the richness of farm life—growing vegetables, raising chickens, and smoking meat. She reports:

> We lived a happy, comfortable life to be right outa slavery times. I didn't know nothin else but the farm so it was happy and we was happy . . . We couldn't do anything else but be happy. We accept the days as they come and as they were. Day by day until you couldn't say there was any great hard time. We overlooked it. We didn't think nothin about it. We just went along. We had what it takes to make a good livin and go about it.

Living in modern society, without a sense of history, it has been easy for folks to forget that black people were first and foremost a people of the land, farmers. It is easy for folks to forget that at the first part of the 20th century, the vast majority of black folks in the United States lived in the agrarian south.

Living close to nature, black folks were able to cultivate a spirit of wonder and reverence for life. Growing food to sustain life and flowers to please the soul, they were able to make a connection with the earth that was ongoing and life-affirming. They were witnesses to beauty. In Wendell Berry's important discussion of the relationship between agriculture and human spiritual well-being, *The Unsettling of America*, he reminds us that working the land provides a location where folks can experience a sense of personal power and well-being:

> We are working well when we use ourselves as the fellow creature of the plants, animals, material, and other people we are working with. Such work is unifying, healing. It brings us home from pride and despair, and places us responsibly within the human estate. It defines us as we are: not too good to work without our bodies, but too good to work poorly or joylessly or selfishly or alone.

There has been little or no work done on the psychological impact of the "great migration" of black people from the agrarian south to the industrialized north. Toni Morrison's novel *The Bluest Eye* attempts to fictively document the way moving from the agrarian south to the industrialized north wounded the psyches of black folk. Estranged from a natural world, where there was time for silence and contemplation, one of the "displaced" black folks in Morrison's novel, Miss Pauline, loses her capacity to experience the sensual world around her when she leaves southern soil to live in a northern city. The south is associated in her mind with a world of sensual beauty most deeply expressed in the world of nature. Indeed, when she falls in love for the first time she can name that experience only by evoking images from nature, from an agrarian world and near wilderness of natural splendor:

> When I first seed Cholly, I want you to know it was like all the bits of color from that time down home when all us chil'ren went berry picking after a funeral and I put some in the pocket of my Sunday dress, and they mashed up and stained my hips. My whole dress was messed with purple, and it never did wash out. Not the dress nor me. I could feel that purple deep inside me. And that lemonade Mama used to make when Pap came out of the fields. It be cool and yellowish, with seeds floating near the bottom. And that streak of green them june bugs made on the tress that night we left from down home. All of them colors was in me. Just sitting there.

Certainly, it must have been a profound blow to the collective psyche of black people to find themselves struggling to make a living in the industrial north away from the land. Industrial capitalism was not simply changing the nature of black work life, it altered the communal practices that were so central to survival in the agrarian south. And it fundamentally altered black people's relationship to the body. It is the loss of any capacity to appreciate her body, despite its flaws, Miss Pauline suffers when she moves north.

6   The motivation for black folks to leave the south and move north was both material and psychological. Black folks wanted to be free of the overt racial harassment that was a constant in southern life and they wanted access to material goods—to a level of material well-being that was not available in the agrarian south where white folks limited access to the spheres of economic power. Of course, they found that life in the north had its own perverse hardships, that racism was just as virulent there, that it was much harder for black people to become landowners. Without the space to grow food, to commune with nature, or to mediate the starkness of poverty with the splendor of nature, black people experienced profound depression. Working in conditions where the body was regarded solely as a tool (as in slavery), a profound estrangement occurred between mind and body. The way the body was represented became more important than the body itself. It did not matter if the body was well, only that it appeared well.

7   Estrangement from nature and engagement in mind/body splits made it all the more possible for black people to internalize white-supremacist assumptions about black identity. Learning contempt for blackness, southerners transplanted in the north suffered both culture shock and soul loss. Contrasting the harshness of city life with an agrarian world, the poet Waring Cuney wrote this popular poem in the 1920s, testifying to lost connection:

> *She does not know her beauty*
> *She thinks her brown body*
> *has no glory.*
> *If she could dance naked,*
> *Under palm trees*

And see her image in the river
She would know.
But there are no palm trees on the street,
And dishwater gives back no images.

For many years, and even now, generations of black folks who migrated 8
north to escape life in the south, returned down home in search of a spiritual
nourishment, a healing, that was fundamentally connected to reaffirming one's
connection to nature, to a contemplative life where one could take time, sit on
the porch, walk, fish, and catch lightning bugs. If we think of urban life as a location where black folks learned to accept a mind/body split that made it possible
to abuse the body, we can better understand the growth of nihilism and despair
in the black psyche. And we can know that when we talk about healing that psyche we must also speak about restoring our connection to the natural world.

Wherever black folks live we can restore our relationship to the natural 9
world by taking the time to commune with nature, to appreciate the other creatures who share this planet with humans. Even in my small New York City
apartment I can pause to listen to birds sing, find a tree and watch it. We can
grow plants—herbs, flowers, vegetables. Those novels by African-American
writers (women and men) that talk about black migration from the agrarian
south to the industrialized north describe in detail the way folks created space
to grow flowers and vegetables. Although I come from country people with serious green thumbs, I have always felt that I could not garden. In the past few
years, I have found that I can do it—that many gardens will grow, that I feel
connected to my ancestors when I can put a meal on the table of food I grew. I
especially love to plant collard greens. They are hardy, and easy to grow.

In modern society, there is also a tendency to see no correlation between 10
the struggle for collective black self-recovery and ecological movements that
seek to restore balance to the planet by changing our relationship to nature and
to natural resources. Unmindful of our history of living harmoniously on the
land, many contemporary black folks see no value in supporting ecological
movements, or see ecology and the struggle to end racism as competing concerns. Recalling the legacy of our ancestors who knew that the way we regard
land and nature will determine the level of our self-regard, black people must
reclaim a spiritual legacy where we connect our well-being to the well-being of
the earth. This is a necessary dimension of healing. As Berry reminds us:

> Only by restoring the broken connections can we be healed. Connection is health.
> And what our society does its best to disguise from us is how ordinary, how com-
> monly attainable, health is. We lose our health—and create profitable diseases and
> dependencies—by failing to see the direct connections between living and eating,
> eating and working, working and loving. In gardening, for instance, one works
> with the body to feed the body. The work, if it is knowledgeable, makes for excel-
> lent food. And it makes one hungry. The work thus makes eating both nourishing
> and joyful, not consumptive, and keeps the eater from getting fat and weak. This
> health, wholeness, is a source of delight.

Collective black self-recovery takes place when we begin to renew our relationship to the earth, when we remember the way of our ancestors. When the earth is sacred to us, our bodies can also be sacred to us.

FOCUS ON ECOLOGY

1. In what ways does hooks identify connections between African-Americans and the land? What historical contexts does hooks use to discuss these connections? Is there a general relationship between history and a people's relationship with the land?
2. According to hooks, why were black people motivated to leave the agrarian life they found in the South and migrate to the North? What does she suggest was lost in this migration? Do you agree with her?
3. Toward the end of this essay, hooks makes the connection between black self-discovery and ecological movements. Many writers, particularly ecofeminists, have noted that there is a correlation between the oppression of different groups of people and the oppression of nature. Do you see a correlation between environmental degradation and oppressions like sexism, racism, anti-Semitism, homophobia, and so on?

FOCUS ON WRITING

1. Early in this piece, hooks draws some parallels between black people's relationships with the land and Native Americans' relationship with the land. She turns to a quote from Chief Seattle (the full selection of the reading is found in this chapter) to expand on how the land was viewed by Indians and blacks. Why do you suppose she chooses this text to draw from? What effect does it have on her position?
2. In addition to the quote from Chief Seattle, hooks turns to a number of other textual references (Toni Morrison, Wendell Berry, Onnie Lee Logan) in this short piece. Where does hooks position her own argument in relation to these other texts? Could hooks take the stand she takes without linking it to works by others?
3. To whom might hooks be writing in this selection? What might she hope to accomplish in writing this essay?

FOR DISCUSSION

In this essay, hooks makes a strong argument that reconsidering relationships with the land may ultimately lead to a fight against racism and other forms of oppression. She also argues that reconsidering connections to land may help in the search for black self-recovery. As a class, discuss the relationships between land use and racism. How might a better understanding of environment and connections to the land be connected to racism or other oppression?

WRITING IN RESPONSE

In a short research paper, explore the tradition of the relationships between African-Americans and the environment. Consider examining work being done that questions the relationship between predominantly black residential areas and hazardous waste disposal. Consider the social history of African-Americans in both the agrarian South and the industrial North. Be sure to identify how these relationships have evolved historically.

DISCUSSING THE ISSUES

1. Now that you have considered the pieces in this chapter, how would you define *ecology*? What does it mean to "think ecologically"? In what ways do the readings in this chapter help you think ecologically? As a class, discuss thinking ecologically in relation to the selections you have read from this chapter. As a class, develop a notion of ecological literacy on your campus. What must one know to be ecologically literate on your campus? How is that information conveyed to members of your campus community?
2. Each of the pieces in this chapter adds a different dimension to how we might think ecologically: Leopold offers us ethics, hooks and Chief Seattle bring race to the conversation, and Abbey notes the use of violence. Yet each of these writers addresses ideas about ecological literacy. Consider the variety of ways we might address ecological literacy, and then, as a class, discuss what each of these approaches brings to such a discussion. Which approaches do you see as most valuable, or as most contributing to our understanding of what it means to think ecologically?

WRITING ABOUT THE ISSUES

1. *Personal Experience:* Many of the writers whose work is represented here turn to their personal experiences to address their own ecological literacies. Personal experiences are crucial to how we think about ecological issues. Many of your responses to the questions found in this chapter and the rest of *Saving Place* grow directly from your personal experiences: from what you have seen, what you have done, what you have read. In a nonfiction, personal essay, describe an experience or series of experiences (think about discussions you've had, books or articles you've read, places you've been, television shows or movies you've seen) that have had a direct impact on how you think about a particular ecological issue.
2. *Local Context:* Identify one of the primary ecological issues facing your community. Spend some time learning as much about that issue as you can from a variety of sources: learn about how the media are addressing the issue, learn about how the local governing bodies are addressing the issue, learn about how the issues are discussed in general (if, for instance, landfill issues are your focus, learn about how landfills function ecologically). Then, write

an analysis of the ways in which local debates address the issue at hand and what might be done in the future in addressing these issues.

3. *Research:* The study of ecology is a fairly recent development in the history of science, yet within this field a number of varying subfields have evolved. Thinking about the variety of subjects the writers in this chapter have addressed, consider what kinds of subjects housed under the umbrella term *ecology* might be of interest to you. Then, spend some time reading about your chosen subject and considering how one might become ecologically literate about a specific subject within the large expanse of ecological literacy. Write an informative paper that describes the area you have studied and how one might become more ecologically aware of that subject.

RESEARCH PATHS

Thinking Ecologically (www.yale.edu/nextgen/book.html)
Ecology (www.ecology.com)
Audubon Magazine (magazine.audubon.org/)
Greenpeace http:(www.greenpeace.org/)
The Sierra Club http:(www.sierraclub.org/)
The Population Institute http:(www.populationinstitute.org/)
Environmental Organizations (www.webdirectory.com/Pollution/)

FURTHER READINGS

David Abram, "The Ecology of Magic: A Personal Introduction into the Inquiry"
Fritjof Capra, *The Web of Life*
Robert Bullard, "Dumping in Dixie"
Janisse Ray, *Ecology of a Cracker Childhood*
Daniel B. Botkin, *Discordant Harmonies: A New Ecology for the Twenty-first Century*
Donald Worster, *Nature's Economy: A History of Ecological Ideas*

CHAPTER **3**

Playing and Relaxing in Nature

For many Americans, wilderness and nature are places into which we venture for recreational purposes. That is, nature and wilderness are sites we visit and interact in, not sites where we live our daily lives. This distinction can be attributed to the ways we have come to define what is and what is not wilderness and nature, what places and environments are for daily life and what places are sites of tourism, places to go play and relax. Quite frequently, we think about protecting places not because of their ecological value but because of their recreational value. When we think about nature and wilderness, many Americans think about places like national parks, national forests, and national seashores, places that have been set aside and named as preserves, habitats, conservation areas. We tend to think of these as places we can go to and leave; places that somebody else will maintain and that will be available to us when we want to go back to them.

In contemporary American culture, outdoor recreation has become popular. Traditional activities like hunting and fishing, which began as activities necessary for survival but are now primarily as recreational, are joined by other activities such as kayaking, canoeing, mountain climbing, surfing, skiing, archery, hiking, camping, and scuba diving. Each of these activities requires an environment conducive to the activity. Most frequently, this means going to places we have identified as wilderness or nature: oceans and beaches, mountains, forests, rivers, and so on. Hence, for many, how we think about such places is directly related to how we think about the activities in which we engage while in those places.

The readings in this chapter are anthologized to encourage you to think not only about the variety of ways in which Americans turn to wilderness and nature as sites of recreation, but to encourage you to consider how outdoor activity influences the ways we think about places, environments, and nature. For instance, issues of conquest become apparent in fishing and hunting as well as in mountain climbing and other sports. Such thinking often positions nature or places or environments as oppositional forces, as entities in need of conquering. Such thinking might, for example, lead one to see a place as an enemy force. More often, however, people who engage in recreational activities outdoors are interested in protecting those places so that they remain available for recreation.

The readings in this chapter address a wide range of recreational activities such as hunting, fishing, boating, mountain climbing, surfing, hiking, paddling, and biking. In addition, the readings also address the formation of the United States' National Parks the role of zoos and wildlife parks in how we learn about nature and wildlife, the ways women come to learn about traditionally male outdoor activities like hunting and fishing, and the ways ethics affect our outdoor recreation.

As you read the pieces found in this chapter, consider the outdoor activities in which you engage. Are they part of your daily life, like walking through a field to get home, or are they activities in which you participate as escape from your daily routine? How does your participation in such activities affect how you think about the places and environments in which you engage in those activities? How does reading and writing about outdoor activities affect how you think about the places and environments in which outdoor recreations take place?

Features of the Proposed Yosemite National Park

John Muir

John Muir is perhaps one of the most important thinkers and writers in the American conservation movement. Many—including Muir himself—identify the importance of his writing not in its literary quality but in the messages Muir conveyed through it. Born in Dunbar, Scotland, on April 21, 1838, Muir immigrated to the United States in 1849 and attended the University of Wisconsin from 1860 until 1863. He spent a good deal of his life exploring the West, particularly the Sierra Nevada. Muir did not begin writing until late in his life, but he was quite prolific and produced more than a dozen books. Though Muir was often asked to write about his travel and exploration experiences, he found writing to be a difficult task. Often, however, he wrote in response to requests because he said he was obligated "to entice people to look at nature's loveliness." Muir became most active in his push toward conservationism late in his life; he

*was a founding member of the Sierra Club and served as its first president from 1892
until 1914. Much of his writing encouraged Americans to set aside lands for public
use, and many consider his writing to be responsible for the development of the United
States' National Parks. The essay found here, "Features of the Proposed Yosemite National Park," makes such an argument, describing the beauty of the Yosemite region
and calling for its protection. "Features of the Proposed Yosemite National Park" was
published in* The Century Magazine *(volume 40) in September 1890, before Yosemite
National Park had been dedicated.*

JOURNAL ASSIGNMENT

For millions of Americans, parks provide access to wild environments as locations for recreation. Think about your own outdoor recreational experiences.
Have you visited any of America's national parks? In your journal write about
your impressions of your visit to a national park. If you haven't been to one,
write about why national parks haven't been accessible to you or why the
parks have not been part of your experiences.

The upper Tuolumne Valley is the widest, smoothest, most serenely spacious,   1
and in every way the most delightful summer pleasure park in all the high
Sierra. And since it is connected with Yosemite by two good trails, and with the
levels of civilization by a broad, well-graded carriage-road that passes between
Yosemite and Mount Hoffman, it is also the most accessible. It lies in the heart
of the high Sierra at a height of from 8500 to 9000 feet above the level of the sea,
at a distance of less than ten miles from the northeastern boundary of the
Yosemite reservation. It is bounded on the southwest by the gray, jagged, picturesque Cathedral range, which extends in a south-easterly direction from
Cathedral Peak to Mount Lyell and Mount Ritter, the culminating peaks of the
grand mass of icy mountains that form the "crown of the Sierra"; on the northeast, by a similar range or spur, the highest peak of which is Mount Conness; on
the east, by the smooth, majestic masses of Mount Dana, Mount Gibbs, Mount
Ord, and others, nameless as yet, on the axis of the main range; and on the west
by a heaving, billowy mass of glacier-polished rocks, over which the towering
masses of Mount Hoffman are seen. Down through the open sunny levels of the
valley flows the bright Tuolumne River, fresh from many a glacial fountain in
the wild recesses of the peaks, the highest of which are the glaciers that lie on
the north sides of Mount Lyell and Mount McClure. Along the river are a series
of beautiful glacier meadows stretching, with but little interruption, from the
lower end of the valley to its head, a distance of about twelve miles. These form
charming sauntering grounds from which the glorious mountains may be enjoyed as they look down in divine serenity over the majestic swaths of forest

that clothe their bases. Narrow strips of pine woods cross the meadow-carpet from side to side, and it is somewhat roughened here and there by groves, moraine boulders, and dead trees brought down from the heights by avalanches; but for miles and miles it is so smooth and level that a hundred horsemen may ride abreast over it.

2   The main lower portion of the meadow is about four miles long and from a quarter to half a mile wide; but the width of the valley is, on an average, about eight miles. Tracing the river we find that it forks a mile above the Soda Springs, which are situated on the north bank opposite the point where the Cathedral trail comes in—the main fork turning southward to Mount Lyell, the other eastward to Mount Dana and Mount Gibbs. Along both forks strips of meadow extend almost to their heads. The most beautiful portions of the meadows are spread over lake basins, which have been filled up by deposits from the river. A few of these river-lakes still exist, but they are now shallow and are rapidly approaching extinction. The sod in most places is exceedingly fine and silky and free from rough weeds and bushes; while charming flowers abound, especially gentians, dwarf daisies, ivesias, and the pink bells of dwarf vaccinium. On the banks of the river and its tributaries Cassiope and Bryanthus may be found where the sod curls over in bosses, and about piles of boulders. The principal grass of these meadows is a delicate Calamagrostis with very slender leaves, and when it is in flower the ground seems to be covered with a faint purple mist, the stems of the spikelets being so fine that they are almost invisible, and offer no appreciable resistance in walking through them. Along the edges of the meadows beneath the pines and throughout the greater part of the valley tall ribbon-leaved grasses grow in abundance, chiefly Bromus, Triticum, and Agrostis.

3   In October the nights are frosty, and then the meadows at sunrise, when every leaf is laden with crystals, are a fine sight. The days are warm and calm, and bees and butterflies continue to waver and hum about the late-blooming flowers until the coming of the snow, usually late in November. Storm then follows storm in close succession, burying the meadows to a depth of from ten to twenty feet, while magnificent avalanches descend through the forests from the laden heights, depositing huge piles of snow mixed with uprooted trees and boulders. In the open sunshine the snow lasts until June, but the new season's vegetation is not generally in bloom until late in July. Perhaps the best time to visit this valley is in August. The snow is then melted from the woods, and then the meadows are dry and warm, while the weather is mostly sunshine, reviving and exhilarating in quality; and the few clouds that rise and the showers they yield are only enough for freshness, fragrance, and beauty.

4   The groves about the Soda Springs are favorite camping-grounds on account of the pleasant-tasting, ice-cold water of the springs, charged with carbonic acid, and because of the fine views of the mountains across the meadow—the Glacier Monument, Cathedral Peak, Cathedral Spires, Unicorn Peak, and their many nameless companions rising in grand beauty above a noble swath of forest that is growing on the left lateral moraine of the ancient Tuolumne

Glacier, which, broad and deep and far-reaching, exerted vast influence on the scenery of this portion of the Sierra. But there are fine camping-grounds all along the meadows, and one may move from grove to grove every day all summer enjoying a fresh home and finding enough to satisfy every roving desire for change.

There are four capital excursions to be made from here—to the summits of 5 Mounts Dana and Lyell; to Mono Lake and the volcanoes, through Bloody Cañon; and to the great Tuolumne Cañon as far as the foot of the main cascades. All of these are glorious, and sure to be crowded with joyful and exciting experiences; but perhaps none of them will be remembered with keener delight than the days spent in sauntering in the broad velvet lawns by the river, sharing the pure air and light with the trees and mountains, and gaining something of the peace of nature in the majestic solitude.

The excursion to the top of Mount Dana is a very easy one; for though the 6 mountain is 13,000 feet high, the ascent from the west side is so gentle and smooth that one may ride a mule to the very summit. Across many a busy stream, from meadow to meadow, lies your flowery way, the views all sublime; and they are seldom hidden by irregular foregrounds. As you gradually ascend, new mountains come into sight, enriching the landscape; peak rising above peak with its individual architecture, and its masses of fountain snow in endless variety of position and light and shade. Now your attention is turned to the moraines, sweeping in beautiful curves from the hollows and cañons of the mountains, regular in form as railroad embankments, or to the glossy waves and pavements of granite rising here and there from the flowery sod, polished a thousand years ago and still shining. Towards the base of the mountain you note the dwarfing of the trees, until at a height of about 11,000 feet you find patches of the tough white-barked pine pressed so flat by the ten or twenty feet of snow piled upon them every winter for centuries that you may walk over them as if walking on a shaggy rug. And, if curious about such things, you may discover specimens of this hardy mountaineer of a tree, not more than four feet high and about as many inches in diameter at the ground, that are from two hundred to four hundred years old, and are still holding on bravely to life, making the most of their short summers, shaking their tasseled needles in the breeze right cheerily, drinking the thin sunshine, and maturing their fine purple cones as if they meant to live forever. The general view from the summit is one of the most extensive and sublime to be found in all the range. To the eastward you gaze far out over the hot desert plains and mountains of the "Great Basin," range beyond range extending with soft outlines blue and purple in the distance. More than six thousand feet below you lies Lake Mono, overshadowed by the mountain on which you stand. It is ten miles in diameter from north to south and fourteen from east to west, but appears nearly circular, lying bare in the treeless desert like a disk of burnished metal, though at times it is swept by storm-winds from the mountains and streaked with foam. To the south of the lake there is a range of pale-gray volcanoes, now extinct, and though the highest of them rise nearly two thousand feet above the lake, you can look down into their well-defined circular, cup-like craters, from which, a comparatively short time ago, ashes and cinders were showered over the surrounding plains and glacier-laden mountains.

7   To the westward the landscape is made up of gray glaciated rocks and ridges, separated by a labyrinth of cañons and darkened with lines and broad fields of forest, while small lakes and meadows dot the foreground. Northward and southward the jagged peaks and towers that are marshaled along the axis of the range are seen in all their glory, crowded together in some places like trees in groves, making landscapes of wild, extravagant, bewildering magnificence, yet calm and silent as the scenery of the sky.

8   Some eight glaciers are in sight. One of these is the Dana Glacier on the northeast side of the mountain, lying at the foot of a precipice about a thousand feet high, with a lovely pale-green lake in the general basin a little below the glacier. This is one of the many small shrunken remnants of the vast glacial system of the Sierra that once filled all the hollows and valleys of the mountains and covered all the lower ridges below the immediate summit fountains, flowing to right and left away from the axis of the range, lavishly fed by the snows of the glacial period.

9   In the excursion to Mount Lyell the immediate base of the mountain is easily reached on horseback by following the meadows along the river. Turning to the southward above the forks of the river you enter the Lyell branch of the valley, which is narrow enough and deep enough to be called a cañon. It is about eight miles long and from 2000 to 3000 feet deep. The flat meadow bottom is from about 300 to 200 yards wide, with gently curved margins about 50 yards wide, from which rise the simple massive walls of gray granite at an angle of about thirty-three degrees, mostly timbered with a light growth of pine and streaked in many places with avalanche channels. Towards the upper end of the cañon the grand Sierra crown comes into sight, forming a sublime and finely balanced picture, framed by the massive cañon walls. In the foreground you have the purple meadow fringed with willows; in the middle distance, huge swelling bosses of granite that form the base of the general mass of the mountain, with fringing lines of dark woods marking the lower curves, but smoothly snow-clad except in the autumn.

10   There is a good camping-ground on the east side of the river about a mile above. A fine cascade comes down over the cañon wall in telling style and makes fine camp music. At one place near the top careful climbing is necessary, but it is not so dangerous or difficult as to deter any climber of ordinary strength and skill, while the views from the summit are glorious. To the northward are Mammoth Mountain, Mounts Gibbs, Dana, Warren, Conness, and many others unnumbered and unnamed; to the southeast the indescribably wild and jagged range of Mount Ritter and the Minarets; southwestward stretches the dividing ridge between the North Fork of the San Joaquin and the Merced, uniting with the Obelisk or Merced group of peaks that form the main fountains of the Illilouette branch of the Merced River; and to the northwest-

ward extends the Cathedral spur. All these spurs, like distinct ranges, meet at your feet. Therefore you look over them mostly in the direction of their extension and their peaks seem to be massed and crowded together in bewildering combinations; while immense amphitheaters, cañons and subordinate masses, with their wealth of lakes, glaciers, and snow-fields, maze and cluster between them. In making the ascent in June or October the glacier is easily crossed, for then its snow mantle is smooth or mostly melted off. But in midsummer the climbing is exceedingly tedious, because the snow is then weathered into curious and beautiful blades, sharp and slender, and set on edge in a leaning position. They lean towards the head of the glacier, and extend across from side to side in regular order in a direction at right angles to the direction of greatest declivity, the distance between the crests being about two or three feet, and the depth of the troughs between them about three feet. No more interesting problem is ever presented to the mountaineer than a walk over a glacier thus sculptured and adorned.

The Lyell Glacier is about a mile wide and less than a mile long, but presents, 11 nevertheless, all the more characteristic features of large, river-like glaciers—moraines, earth-bands, blue-veins, crevasses etc., while the streams that issue from it are turbid with rock-mud, showing its grinding action on its bed. And it is all the more interesting since it is the highest and most enduring remnant of the great Tuolumne Glacier, whose traces are still distinct fifty miles away, and whose influence on the landscape was so profound. The McClure Glacier, once a tributary of the Lyell, is much smaller. Eighteen years ago I set a series of stakes in it to determine its rate of motion which towards the end summer, in the middle of the glacier, I found to be a little over an inch in twenty-four hours. The trip to Mono from the Soda Springs can be made in a day, but Bloody Cañon will be found rough for animals. The scenery of the cañon, however, is wild and rich, and many days may profitably be spent around the shores of the lake and out on its islands and about the volcanoes.

In making the trip down the Big Tuolumne Cañon animals may be led as far 12 as a small, grassy, forested lake basin that lies below the crossing of the Virginia Creek trail. And from this point any one accustomed to walk on earthquake boulders carpeted with cañon chaparral, can easily go down the cañon as far as the big cascades and return to camp in one day. Many, however, are not able to do this, and it is far better to go leisurely, prepared to camp anywhere, and enjoy the marvelous grandeur of the place.

The cañon begins near the lower end of the meadows and extends to the 13 Hetch Hetchy Valley, a distance of about eighteen miles, though it will seem much longer to any one who scrambles through it. It is from 1200 to about 5000 feet deep, and is comparatively narrow, but there are several fine, roomy, park-like openings in it, and throughout its whole extent Yosemite features are displayed on a grand scale—domes, El Capitan rocks, gables, Sentinels, Royal Arches, glacier points, Cathedral Spires, etc. There is even a Half Dome among its wealth of rock forms, though less sublime and beautiful than the Yosemite

Half Dome. It also contains falls and cascades innumerable. The sheer falls, except when the snow is melting in early spring, are quite small in volume as compared with those of Yosemite and Hetch Hetchy, but many of them are very beautiful, and in any other country would be regarded as great wonders. But it is the cascades or sloping falls on the main river that are the crowning glory of the cañon, and these in volume, extent, and variety surpass those of any other cañon in the Sierra. The most showy and interesting of the cascades are mostly in the upper part of the cañon, above the point where Cathedral Creek and Hoffman Creek enter. For miles the river is one wild, exulting, on-rushing mass of snowy purple bloom, spreading over glacial waves of granite without any definite channel, and through avalanche taluses, gliding in silver plumes, dashing and foaming through huge boulder-dams, leaping high into the air in glorious wheel-like whirls, tossing from side to side, doubling, glinting, singing in glorious exuberance of mountain energy. Every one who is anything of a mountaineer should go on through the entire length of the cañon, coming out by Hetch Hetchy. There is not a dull step all the way. With wide variations it is a Yosemite Valley from end to end.

14   Most people who visit Yosemite are apt to regard it as an exceptional creation, the only valley of its kind in the world. But nothing in Nature stands alone. She is not so poor as to have only one of anything. The explorer in the Sierra and elsewhere finds many Yosemites that differ not more than one tree differs from another of the same species. They occupy the same relative positions on the mountain flanks, were formed by the same forces in the same kind of granite, and have similar sculpture, waterfalls, and vegetation. The Hetch Hetchy Valley has long been known as the Tuolumne Yosemite. It is said to have been discovered by Joseph Screech, a hunter, in 1850, a year before the discovery of the great Merced Yosemite. It lies in a northwesterly direction from Yosemite, at a distance of about twenty miles, and is easily accessible to mounted travelers by a trail that leaves the Big Oak Flat road at Bronson's Meadows, a few miles below Crane Flat. But by far the best way to it for those who have useful limbs is across the divide direct from Yosemite. Leaving the valley by Indian Cañon or Fall Cañon, you cross the dome-paved basin of Yosemite Creek, then bear to the left around the head fountains of the South Fork of the Tuolumne to the summit of the Big Tuolumne Cañon, a few miles above the head of Hetch Hetchy. Here you will find a glorious view. Immediately beneath you, at a depth of more than 4000 feet, you see a beautiful ribbon of level ground, with a silver thread in the middle of it, and green or yellow according to the time of year. That ribbon is a strip of meadow, and the silver thread is the main Tuolumne River. The opposite wall of the cañon rises in precipices, steep and angular, or with rounded brows like those of Yosemite, and from this wall as a base extends a fine wilderness of mountains, rising dome above dome, ridge above ridge, to a group of snowy peaks on the summit of the range. Of all this sublime congregation of mountains Castle Peak is king: robed with snow and light, dipping unnumbered points and spires into the thin blue sky, it maintains amid noble companions a perfect and commanding individuality.

You will not encounter much difficulty in getting down into the cañon, for bear trails may readily be found leading from the upper feeding-grounds to the berry gardens and acorn orchards of Hetch Hetchy, and when you reach the river you have only to saunter by its side a mile or two down the cañon before you find yourself in the open valley. Looking about you, you cannot fail to discover that you are in a Yosemite valley. As the Merced flows through Yosemite, so does the Tuolumne through Hetch Hetchy. The bottom of Yosemite is about 4000 feet above sea level, the bottom of Hetch Hetchy is about 3800 feet, and in both the walls are of gray granite and rise abruptly in precipices from a level bottom, with but little debris along their bases. Furthermore it was a home and stronghold of the Tuolumne Indians, as Ahwahne was of the grizzlies. Standing boldly forward from the south wall near the lower end of the valley is the rock Kolána, the outermost of a picturesque group corresponding to the Cathedral Rocks of Yosemite, and about the same height. Facing Kolána on the north side of the valley is a rock about 1800 feet in height, which presents a bare, sheer front like El Capitan, and over its massive brow flows a stream that makes the most graceful fall I have ever seen. Its Indian name is Tu-ee-u-la-la, and no other, so far as I have heard, has yet been given it. From the brow of the cliff it makes a free descent of a thousand feet and then breaks up into ragged, foaming web of cascades among the boulders of an earthquake talus. Towards the end of summer it vanishes, because its head streams do not reach back to the lasting snows of the summits of the range, but in May and June it is indescribably lovely. The only fall that I know with which it may fairly be compared is the Bridal Veil, but it excels even that fall in peaceful, floating, swaying gracefulness. For when we attentively observe the Bridal Veil, even towards the middle of summer when its waters begin to fail, we may discover, when the winds blow aside the outer folds of spray, dense comet-shaped masses shooting through the air with terrible energy; but from the top of the cliff, where the Hetch Hetchy veil first floats free, all the way to the bottom it is in perfect repose. Again, the Bridal Veil is in a shadow-haunted nook inaccessible to the main wind currents of the valley, and has to depend for many of its gestures on irregular, teasing side currents and whirls, while Tu-ee-u-la-la, being fully exposed on the open cliff, is sun drenched all day, and is ever ready to yield graceful compliance to every wind that blows. Most people unacquainted with the behavior of mountain streams fancy that when they escape the bounds of their rocky channels and launch into the air they at once lose all self-control and tumble in confusion. On the contrary, on no part of their travels do they manifest more calm self-possession. Imagine yourself in Hetch Hetchy. It is a sunny day in June, the pines sway dreamily, and you are shoulder-deep in grass and flowers. Looking across the valley through beautiful open groves you see a bare granite wall 1800 feet high rising abruptly out of the green and yellow vegetation and glowing with sunshine, and in front of it the fall, waving like a downy scarf, silver bright, burning with white sun-fire in every fiber. In coming forward to the edge of the tremendous precipice and taking flight a little hasty eagerness appears, but this is speedily hushed in divine repose. Now observe the marvelous distinctness and delicacy of the various kinds of sun-filled tissue into which the waters are woven. They fly and float and drowse down the face of that grand gray rock in so leisurely and unconfused a manner that you may examine their texture and patterns as you would a piece of embroidery held in the hand. It is a flood of singing air, water, and sunlight woven into cloth that spirits might wear.

16   The great Hetch Hetchy Fall, called Wa-páma by the Tuolumnes, is on the same side of the valley as the Veil, and so near it that both may be seen in one view. It is about 1800 feet in height, and seems to be nearly vertical when one is standing in front of it, though it is considerably inclined. Its location is similar to that of the Yosemite Fall, but the volume of water is much greater. No two falls could be more unlike than Wa-páma and Tu-ee-u-la-la, the one thundering and beating in a shadowy gorge, the other chanting in deep, low tones and with no other shadows about it than those of its own waters, pale-gray mostly, and violet and pink delicately graded. One whispers, "He dwells in peace," the other is the thunder of his chariot wheels in power. This noble pair are the main falls of the valley, though there are many small ones essential to the perfection of the general harmony.

17   The wall above Wa-páma corresponds, both in outlines and in details of sculpture, with the same relative portion of the Yosemite wall. Near the Yosemite Fall the cliff has two conspicuous benches extending in a horizontal direction 500 and 1500 feet above the valley. Two benches similarly situated, and timbered in the same way, occur on the same relative position on the Hetch Hetchy wall, and on no other portion. The upper end of Yosemite is closed by the great Half Dome, and the upper end of Hetch Hetchy is closed in the same way by a mountain rock. Both occupy angles formed by the confluence of two large glaciers that have long since vanished. In front of this head rock the river forks like the Merced in Yosemite. The right fork as you ascend is the main Tuolumne, which takes its rise in a glacier on the north side of Mount Lyell and flows through the Big Cañon. I have not traced the left fork to its highest source, but, judging from the general trend of the ridges, it must be near Castle Peak. Upon this left or North Fork there is a remarkably interesting series of cascades, five in number, ranged along a picturesque gorge, on the edges of which we may saunter safely and gain fine views of the dancing spray below. The first is a wide-spreading fan of white, crystal-covered water, half leaping half sliding over a steep polished pavement, at the foot of which it rests and sets forth clear and shining on its final flow to the main river. A short distance above the head of this cascade you discover the second, which is as impressively wild and beautiful as the first, and makes you sing with it as though you were a part of it. It is framed in deep rock walls that are colored yellow and red with lichens, and fringed on the jagged edges by live-oaks and sabine pines, and at the bottom in damp nooks you may see ferns, lilies, and azaleas.

18   Three or four hundred yards higher you come to the third of the choir, the largest of the five. It is formed of three smaller ones inseparably combined,

which sing divinely, and make spray of the best quality for rainbows. A short distance beyond this the gorge comes to an end, and the bare stream, without any definite channel, spreads out in a thin, silvery sheet about 150 feet wide. Its waters are, throughout almost its whole extent, drawn out in overlapping folds of lace, thick sown with diamond jets and sparks that give an exceedingly rich appearance. Still advancing, you hear a deep muffled booming, and you push eagerly on through flowery thickets until the last of the five appears through the foliage. The precipice down which it thunders is fretted with projecting knobs, forming polished keys upon which the wild waters play.

The bottom of the valley is divided by a low, glacier-polished bar of granite, the lower portion being mostly meadow land, the upper dry and sandy, planted with fine Kellogg oaks, which frequently attain a diameter of six or seven feet. On the talus slopes the pines give place to the mountain live-oak, which forms the shadiest groves in the valley and the greatest in extent. Their glossy foliage, warm yellow-green and closely pressed, makes a kind of ceiling, supported by bare gray trunks and branches gnarled and picturesque. A few specimens of the sugar pine and tamarack pine are found in the valley, also the two silver firs. The Douglas spruce and the libocedrus attain noble dimensions in certain favorable spots, and few specimens of the interesting Torreya Californica may be found on the south side. The brier-rose occurs in large patches, with tall, spiky mints and arching grasses. On the meadows lilies, larkspurs and lupines of several species are abundant, and in some places reach above one's head. Rock-ferns of rare beauty fringe and rosette the walls from top to bottom—Pellaea densa, P. mucronata and P. Bridgesii, Cheilanthes gracillima, Allosorus, etc. Adiantum pedatum occurs in a few mossy corners that get spray from the falls. Woodwardia radicans and Asplenium felix-faemina are the tallest ferns of the valley—six feet high, some of them. The whole valley was a charming garden when I last saw it, and the huts of the Indians and a one cabin were the only improvements. [19]

As will be seen by the map, I have thus briefly touched upon a number of the chief features of a region which it is proposed to reserve out of the public domain for the use and recreation of the people. A bill has already been introduced in Congress by Mr. Vandever creating a national park about the reservation which the State now holds in trust for the people. It is very desirable that the new reservation should at least extend to the limits indicated by the map, and the bill cannot too quickly become a law. Unless reserved or protected the whole region will soon or late be devastated by lumbermen and sheepmen, and so, of course be made unfit for use as a pleasure ground. Already it is with great difficulty that campers, even in the most remote parts of the proposed reservation and in those difficult of access, can find grass enough to keep their animals from starving; the ground is already being gnawed and trampled into a desert condition, and when the region shall be stripped of its forests the ruin will be complete. Even the Yosemite will then suffer in the disturbance effected on the water-shed, the clear streams becoming muddy and much less regular [20] in their flow. It is also devoutly to be hoped that the Hetch Hetchy will escape such ravages of man as one sees in Yosemite. Ax and plow, hogs and horses, have long been and are still busy in Yosemite's gardens and groves. All that is accessible and destructible is being rapidly destroyed—more rapidly than in any other Yosemite in the Sierra, though this is the only one that is under the special protection of the Government. And by far the greater part of this destruction of the fineness of wildness is of a kind that can claim no right relationship with that which necessarily follows use.

FOCUS ON ECOLOGY

1. Years ago, most park rangers were experts in natural history, ecology, local environments, and were assigned to work in parks to both provide information to visitors and to work to protect the park environment; however, more recently, most park rangers are trained as officers of the law and are assigned to parks to help police the large numbers of people who visit them. How do you feel about access to America's parks? Are we "loving the parks to death," as is often said?
2. Do you agree with the idea of setting aside land like Yosemite for recreational use? Would you prefer to see some wilderness areas preserved by closing them to the public altogether? Explain.

FOCUS ON WRITING

1. What does the word *park* mean? Where did the idea for parks come from? Do a bit of research and see how the idea of parks has evolved and when humans began to see a need for parks. How does Muir use the word in this selection?
2. Considering that Muir published this piece in *The Century Magazine* in September 1890, what were some of the historical contexts and conditions under which he wrote this piece? That is, what was happening historically that would allow for the publication of an essay that calls for the protection of American lands?
3. What role does description play in this essay?

FOR DISCUSSION

Consider the parks you have visited or heard about or read about. As a class, discuss what parks are easily accessible to you locally. How do they compare to other parks with which you are familiar? Which parks do you like best? What makes a good park? Are there parks you would like to visit that you haven't? Have others in your class been there? What did you notice about the way parks were used for recreation? Were there things about the use of the park that bothered you?

WRITING IN RESPONSE

Much of Muir's essay describes the natural features of Yosemite. It is evident from the writing that Muir spent a good deal of time exploring and observing the features he describes. He provides his readers with not just one glimpse of Yosemite, but with many, detailed descriptions to provide a larger landscape view of the soon-to-be park. While Muir spent years observing Yosemite before writing these descriptions, often our first observations can also lead to captivating descriptions. Visit a local park for a morning or afternoon or longer. You don't need to trek into a large national park such a Yosemite (though you may choose to); a small city park, county park, or state park is just fine. Select an area of the park and spend some time observing. If there is information about the history of the park, read a bit about the area you are observing. Talk to rangers or other park officials about the park. In a descriptive essay, describe the park you visited. Take into account not just the natural environment you observe, but think and write about the way that park is used by its visitors. What impact do you see the visitors having on the park? What does the park provide to its visitors?

Wilderness Reserves:
Yellowstone Park

Theodore Roosevelt

Theordore Roosevelt was inaugurated as the twenty-sixth president of the United States on September 14, 1901, following the assassination of President McKinley. Roosevelt, who had earned a reputation as a rough and brash politician, had become well known in 1898, when the United States declared war on Spain. While fighting in Cuba with the U.S. First Volunteer Cavalry, which became known as the Rough Riders, Roosevelt led the charge to take Kettle Hill on July 1, 1898. Roosevelt lost a quarter of his men during that encounter, but won the battle. He was later awarded the Congressional Medal of Honor for his action during the battle. Roosevelt was also a devout lover of the outdoors. In his younger years, he spent a good deal of time studying ornithology. He wrote more than 50 books during his life time, most addressing either his experiences outdoors studying wildlife and hunting or his experiences in the military. It was under Roosevelt that many of the United States' national parks were dedicated. In 1908 he helped create both the Grand Canyon National Monument and the Muir Woods National Monument (named for John Muir and his work in protecting America's wild places). In the essay found here, "Wilderness Reserves: Yellowstone Park," Roosevelt not only discusses the importance of the conservation and protection of wilderness and wild animals but also makes important connections between those acts of conservation and political legislation and economics. As you read this essay, think about how Roosevelt situates conservation in the realm of the political.

JOURNAL ASSIGNMENT

Theodore Roosevelt's essay "Wilderness Reserves: Yellowstone Park" deals with the protection of game species that attract hunters. He writes not only of the importance of protection and conservation for the sake of natural protection, but also from an economic standpoint. For instance, he writes, "the live deer is worth far more than the dead deer, because of the way in which it brings money into the wilderness." Does this argument make sense to you? In your journal, consider the implied connection between conservation, hunting, and economics.

1 The most striking and melancholy feature in connection with American big game is the rapidity with which it has vanished. When, just before the outbreak of the Revolutionary War, the rifle-bearing hunters of the backwoods first pene-trated the great forests west of the [Alleghanies,] deer, elk, black bear, and even buffalo, swarmed in what are now the States of Kentucky and Tennessee and the country north of the Ohio was a great and almost virgin hunting-ground. From that day to this the shrinkage has gone on, only partially checked here and there, and never arrested as a whole. As a matter of historical accuracy, however, it is well to bear in mind that many writers, in lamenting this extinc-tion of the game, have from time to time anticipated or overstated the facts. Thus as good an author as Colonel Richard Irving Dodge spoke of the buffalo as practically extinct, while the great Northern herd still existed in countless thousands. As early as 1880 sporting authorities spoke not only of the buffalo but of the elk, deer, and antelope as no longer to be found in plenty; and re-cently one of the greatest of living hunters has stated that it is no longer possi-ble to find any American wapiti bearing heads comparable with the red deer of Hungary. As a matter of fact, in the early eighties there were still large regions where every species of game that had ever been known within historic times on our continent was still to be found as plentifully as ever. In the early nineties there were still big tracts of wilderness in which this was true of all game except the buffalo; for instance, it was true of the elk in portions of northwestern Wyoming, of the blacktail in northwestern Colorado, of the whitetail here and

there in the Indian Territory, and of the antelope in parts of New Mexico. Even at the present day there are smaller, but still considerable, regions where these four animals are yet found in abundance; and I have seen antlers of wapiti shot since 1900 far surpassing any of which there is record from Hungary. In New England and New York, as well as New Brunswick and Nova Scotia, the white-tail deer is more plentiful than it was thirty years ago, and in Maine (and to an even greater extent in New Brunswick) the moose, and here and there the caribou, have, on the whole, increased during the same period. There is yet ample opportunity for the big-game hunter in the United States, Canada, and Alaska.

While it is necessary to give this word of warning to those who, in praising time past, always forget the opportunities of the present, it is a thousandfold more necessary to remember that these opportunities are, nevertheless, vanishing; and if we are a sensible people, we will make it our business to see that the process of extinction is arrested. At the present moment the great herds of caribou are being butchered, as in the past the great herds of bison and wapiti have been butchered. Every believer in manliness and therefore in manly sport, and every lover of nature, every man who appreciates the majesty and beauty of the wilderness and of wild life, should strike hands with the farsighted men who wish to preserve our material resources, in the effort to keep our forests and our game beasts, game-birds, and game-fish,—indeed, all the living creatures of prairie and woodland and seashore—from wanton destruction.

Above all, we should realize that the effort toward this end is essentially a democratic movement. It is entirely in our power as a nation to preserve large tracts of wilderness, which are valueless for agricultural purposes and unfit for settlement, as playgrounds for rich and poor alike, and to preserve the game so that it shall continue to exist for the benefit of all lovers of nature, and to give reasonable opportunities for the exercise of the skill of the hunter, whether he is or is not a man of means. But this end can only be achieved by wise laws and by a resolute enforcement of the laws. Lack of such legislation and administration will result in harm to all of us, but most of all in harm to the nature-lover who does not possess vast wealth. Already there have sprung up here and there through the country, as in New Hampshire and the Adirondacks, large, private preserves. These preserves often serve a useful purpose, and should be encouraged within reasonable limits; but it would be a misfortune if they increased beyond a certain extent or if they took the place of great tracts of wild land, which continue as such either because of their very nature, or because of the protection of the State exerted in the form of making them State or national parks or reserves. It is foolish to regard proper game-laws as undemocratic, unrepublican. On the contrary, they are essentially in the interests of the people as a whole, because it is only through their enactment and enforcement that the people as a whole can preserve the game and can prevent its becoming purely the property of the rich, who are able to create and maintain extensive private preserves. The wealthy man can get hunting anyhow, but the man of small means is dependent solely upon wise and well-executed game-laws for his enjoyment of the sturdy pleasure of the chase. In Maine, in Vermont, in the

Adirondacks, even in parts of Massachusetts and on Long Island, people have waked up to this fact, particularly so far as the common whitetail deer is concerned, and in Maine also as regards the moose and caribou. The effect is shown in the increase in these animals. Such game protection results, in the first place, in securing to the people who live in the neighborhood permanent opportunities for hunting; and in the next place, it provides no small source of wealth to the locality because of the visitors which it attracts. A deer wild in the woods is worth to the people of the neighborhood many times the value of its carcass, because of the way it attracts sportsmen, who give employment and leave money behind them.

4   True sportsmen, worthy of the name, men who shoot only in season and in moderation, do no harm whatever to game. The most objectionable of all game-destroyers is, of course, the kind of game-butcher who simply kills for the sake of the record of slaughter, who leaves deer and ducks and prairie-chickens to rot after he has slain them. Such a man is wholly obnoxious; and, indeed, so is any man who shoots for the purpose of establishing a record of the amount of game killed. To my mind this is one very unfortunate feature of what is otherwise the admirably sportsmanlike English spirit in these matters. The custom of shooting great bags of deer, grouse, partridges, and pheasants, the keen rivalry in making such bags, and their publication in sporting journals, are symptoms of a spirit which is most unhealthy from every standpoint. It is to be earnestly hoped that every American hunting or fishing club will strive to inculcate among its own members, and in the minds of the general public, that anything like an excessive bag, any destruction for the sake of making a record, is to be severely reprobated.

5   But, after all, this kind of perverted sportsman, unworthy though he be, is not the chief actor in the destruction of our game. The professional skin or market hunter is the real offender. Yet he is of all others the man who would ultimately be most benefited by the preservation of the game. The frontier settler, in a thoroughly wild country, is certain to kill game for his own use. As long as he does no more than this, it is hard to blame him; although if he is awake to his own interests he will soon realize that to him, too, the live deer is worth far more than the dead deer, because of the way in which it brings money into the wilderness. The professional market-hunter who kills game for the hide or for the feathers or for the meat or to sell antlers and other trophies; the marketmen who put game in cold storage; and the rich people, who are content to buy what they have not the skill to get by their own exertions—these are the men who are the real enemies of game. Where there is no law which checks the market-hunters, the inevitable result of their butchery is that the game is completely destroyed, and with it their own means of livelihood. If, on the other hand, they were willing to preserve it, they could make much more money by acting as guides. In northwestern Colorado, at the present moment, there are still blacktail deer in abundance, and some elk are left. Colorado has fairly good game-laws, but they are indifferently enforced. The country in which the game

is found can probably never support any but a very sparse population, and a large portion of the summer range is practically useless for settlement. If the people of Colorado generally, and above all the people of the counties in which the game is located, would resolutely co-operate with those of their own number who are already alive to the importance of preserving the game, it could, without difficulty, be kept always as abundant as it now is, and this beautiful region would be a permanent health resort and playground for the people of a large part of the Union. Such action would be a benefit to every one, but it would be a benefit most of all to the people of the immediate locality.

The practical common sense of the American people has been in no way 6 made more evident during the last few years than by the creation and use of a series of large land reserves—situated for the most part on great plains and among the mountains of the West—intended to keep the forests from destruction, and therefore to conserve the water-supply. These reserves are, and should be, created primarily for economic purposes. The semiarid regions can only support a reasonable population under conditions of the strictest economy and wisdom in the use of the water-supply, and in addition to their other economic uses the forests are indispensably necessary for the preservation of the water-supply and for rendering possible its useful distribution throughout the proper seasons. In addition, however, to this economic use of the wilderness, selected portions of it have been kept here and there in a state of nature, not merely for the sake of preserving the forests and the water but for the sake of preserving all of its beauties and wonders unspoiled by greedy and shirt-sighted vandalism. What has been actually accomplished in the Yellowstone Park affords the best possible object-lesson as to the desirability and practicability of establishing such wilderness reserves. This reserve is a natural breeding-ground and nursery for those stately and beautiful haunters of the wilds which have now vanished from so many of the great forests, the vast lonely plains, and the high mountain ranges, where they once abounded.

On April 8, 1903, John Burroughs and I reached the Yellowstone Park, and 7 were met by Major John Pitcher of the regular army, the superintendent of the Park. The major and I forthwith took horses; he telling me that he could show me a good deal of game while riding up to his house at the Mammoth Hot Springs. Hardly had we left the little town of Gardiner and gotten within the limits of the Park before we saw prongbuck. There was a band of at least a hundred feeding some distance from the road. We rode leisurely toward them. They were tame compared to their kindred in unprotected places; that is, it was easy to ride within fair rifle-range of them; and though they were not familiar in the sense that we afterward found the bighorn and the deer to be familiar, it was extraordinary to find them showing such familiarity almost literally in the streets of a frontier town. It spoke volumes for the good sense and law-abiding spirit of the people of the town. During the two hours following my entry into the Park we rode around the plains and lower slopes of the foot-hills in the neighborhood of the mouth of the Gardiner and we saw several hundred—probably a thousand all told—of these antelopes. Major Pitcher informed me that all the pronghorns in the Park wintered in this neighborhood. Toward the end of April or the first of May they migrate back to their summering homes in the open valleys along the Yellowstone and in the plains south of the Golden Gate. While migrating they go over the mountains through forests if occasion demands. Although there are plenty of coyotes in the Park, there are no big wolves, and save for very infrequent poachers, the only enemy of the antelope, as indeed the only enemy of all the game, is the cougar.

8   Cougars, known in the Park, as elsewhere through the West, as "mountain-lions," are plentiful, having increased in numbers of recent years. Except in the neighborhood of the Gardiner River—that is within a few miles of Mammoth Hot Springs—I found them feeding on elk, which in the Park far outnumber all other game put together, being so numerous that the ravages of the cougars are of no real damage to the herds. But in the neighborhood of the Mammoth Hot Springs the cougars are noxious because of the antelope, mountain-sheep, and deer which they kill; and the superintendent has imported some hounds with which to hunt them. These hounds are managed by Buffalo Jones, a famous old plainsman, who is now in the Park taking care of the buffalo. On this first day of my visit to the Park I came across the carcass of a deer and of an antelope which the cougars had killed. On the great plains cougars rarely get antelope, but here the country is broken so that the big cats can make their stalks under favorable circumstances. To deer and mountain-sheep the cougar is a most dangerous enemy—much more so than the wolf.

9   The antelope we saw were usually in bands of from twenty to one hundred and fifty, and they traveled strung out almost in single file, though those in the rear would sometimes bunch up. I did not try to stalk them, but got as near them as I could on horseback. The closest approach I was able to make was to within about eighty yards of two which were by themselves—I think, a doe and a last year's fawn. As I was riding up to them, although they looked suspiciously at me, one actually lay down. When I was passing them at about eighty yards' distance the big one became nervous, gave a sudden jump, and away the two went at full speed.

10   Why the prongbacks were so comparatively shy I do not know, for right on the ground with them we came upon deer, and, in the immediate neighborhood, mountain-sheep, which were absurdly tame. The mountain-sheep were nineteen in number—for the most part does and yearlings with a couple of three-year-old rams—but not a single big fellow, for the big fellows at this season are off by themselves, singly or in little bunches, high up in the mountains. The band I saw was tame to a degree matched by but few domestic animals.

11   They were feeding on the brink of a steep washout at the upper edge of one of the benches on the mountainside just below where the abrupt slope began. They were alongside a little gully with sheer walls. I rode my horse to within forty yards of them, one of them occasionally looking up and at once continuing to feed. Then they moved slowly off, and leisurely crossed the gully to the other side. I dismounted, walked around the head of the gully, and moving

cautiously, but in plain sight, came closer and closer until I was within twenty yards, when I sat down on a stone and spent certainly twenty minutes looking at them. They paid hardly any attention to my presence—certainly no more than well-treated domestic creatures would pay.

• • •

On the last day of my stay it was arranged that I should ride down from Mammoth Hot Springs to the town of Gardiner, just outside the Park limits, and there make an address at the laying of the corner-stone of the arch by which the main road is to enter the Park. Some three thousand people had gathered to attend the ceremonies. A little over a mile from Gardiner we came down out of the hills to the flat plain; from the hills we could see the crowd gathered around the arch, waiting for me to come. We put spurs to our horses and cantered rapidly toward the appointed place, and on the way we passed within forty yards of a score of blacktails, which merely moved to one side and looked at us, and within almost as short a distance of half a dozen antelope. To any lover of nature it could not help being a delightful thing to see the wild and timid creatures of the wilderness rendered so tame; and their tameness in the immediate neighborhood of Gardiner, on the very edge of the Park, spoke volumes for the patriotic good sense of the citizens of Montana. At times the antelope actually cross the Park line to Gardiner, which is just outside, and feed unmolested in the very streets of the town; a fact which shows how very far advanced the citizens of Gardiner are in right feeling on this subject; for of course the Federal laws cease to protect the antelope as soon as they are out of the Park. Major Pitcher informed me that both the Montana and Wyoming people were co-operating with him in zealous fashion to preserve the game and put a stop to poaching. For their attitude in this regard they deserve the cordial thanks of all Americans interested in these great popular playgrounds, where bits of the old wilderness scenery and old wilderness life are to be kept unspoiled for the benefit of our children's children. Eastern people and especially Eastern sportsmen, need to keep steadily in mind the fact that the Westerners who live in the neighborhood of the forest preserves are the men who in the last resort will determine whether or not these preserves are to be permanent. They cannot in the long run be kept as forest and game reservations unless the settlers round about believe in them and heartily support them; and the rights of these settlers must be carefully safeguarded, and they must be shown that the movement is really in their interest. The Eastern sportsman who fails to recognize these facts can do little but harm by advocacy of forest reserves.

It was in the interior of the Park, at the hotels beside the lake, the falls, and the various geyser basins, that we would have seen the bears had the season been late enough; but unfortunately the bears were still for the most part hibernating. We saw two or three tracks, but the animals themselves had not yet begun to come about the hotels. Nor were the hotels open. No visitors had previously entered the Park in the winter or early spring, the scouts and other employees being the only ones who occasionally traverse it. I was sorry not to see the bears, for the effect of protection upon bear life in the Yellowstone has been one of the phenomena of natural history. Not only have they grown to realize that they are safe, but, being natural scavengers and foul feeders, they have come to recognize the garbage heaps of the hotels as their special sources of food-supply. Throughout the summer months they come to all the hotels in numbers, usually appearing in the late afternoon or evening, and they have become as indifferent to the presence of men as the deer themselves—some of them very much more indifferent. They have now taken their place among the recognized sights of the Park, and the tourists are nearly as much interested in them as in the geysers. In mussing over the garbage heaps they sometimes get tin cans stuck on their paws, and the result is painful. Buffalo Jones and some of the other scouts in extreme cases rope the bear, tie him up, cut the tin can off his paw, and let him go again. It is not an easy feat, but the astonishing thing is that it should be performed at all.

14   It was amusing to read the proclamations addressed to the tourists by the Park management, in which they were solemnly warned that the bears were really wild animals, and that they must on no account be either fed or teased. It is curious to think that the descendants of the great grizzlies which were the dread of the early explorers and hunters should now be semidomesticated creatures, boldly hanging around crowded hotels for the sake of what they can pick up, and quite harmless so long as any reasonable precaution is exercised, They are much safer, for instance, than any ordinary bull or stallion, or even ram, and, in fact, there is no danger from them at all unless they are encouraged to grow too familiar or are in some way molested. Of course among the thousands of tourists there is a percentage of fools; and when fools go out in the afternoon to look at the bears feeding they occasionally bring themselves into jeopardy by some senseless act. The black bears and the cubs of the bigger bears can readily be driven up trees, and some of the tourists occasionally do this. Most of the animals never think of resenting it; but now and then one is run across which has its feelings ruffled by the performance. In the summer of 1902 the result proved disastrous to a too inquisitive tourist. He was traveling with his wife, and at one of the hotels they went out toward the garbage pile to see the bears feeding. The only bear in sight was a large she, which, as it turned out, was in a bad temper because another party of tourists a few minutes before had been chasing her cubs up a tree. The man left his wife and walked toward the bear to see how close he could get. When he was some distance off she charged him, whereupon he bolted back toward his wife. The bear overtook him, knocked him down, and bit him severely. But the man's wife, without hesitation, attacked the bear with her thoroughly feminine weapon, an umbrella, and frightened her off. The man spent several weeks in the Park hospital before he recovered. Perhaps the following telegram sent by the manager of the Lake Hotel to Major Pitcher illustrates with sufficient clearness the mutual relations of the bears, the tourists, the guardians of the public weal in the Park. The original was sent me by Major Pitcher. It runs:

15   "Lake. 7–27–'03. Major Pitcher, Yellowstone: As many as seventeen bears in an evening appear on my garbage dump. To-night eight or ten. Campers and

people not of my hotel throw things at them to make them run away. I cannot, unless there personally, control this. Do you think you could detail a trooper to be there every evening from say six o'clock until dark and make people remain behind danger line laid out by Warden Jones? Otherwise I fear some accident. The arrest of one or two of these campers might help. My own guests do pretty well as they are told. James Barton Key. 9 A. M."

Major Pitcher issued the order as requested.

At times the bears get so bold that they take to making inroads on the kitchen. One completely terrorized a Chinese cook. It would drive him off and then feast upon whatever was left behind. When a bear begins to act in this way or to show surliness it is sometimes necessary to shoot it. Other bears are tamed until they will feed out of the hand, and will come at once if called. Not only have some of the soldiers and scouts tamed bears in this fashion, but occasionally a chambermaid or waiter girl at one of the hotels has thus developed a bear as a pet.

This whole episode of bear life in the Yellowstone is so extraordinary that it will be well worth while for any man who has the right powers and enough time to make a complete study of the life and history of the Yellowstone bears. Indeed, nothing better could be done by some of our outdoor faunal naturalists than to spend at least a year in the Yellowstone, and to study the life habits of all the wild creatures therein. A man able to do this, and to write down accurately and interestingly what he has seen, would make a contribution of permanent value to our nature literature.

FOCUS ON ECOLOGY

1. Roosevelt writes about protecting game populations: "Above all, we should realize that the effort toward this end is essentially a democratic movement." He goes on to say that "this end can only be achieved by wise laws and by a resolute enforcement of the laws. Lack of such legislation and administration will result in harm to all of us, but most of all in harm to the nature-lover who does not possess vast wealth." In these few sentences, Roosevelt makes some interesting links: between politics and conservation, between politics and the lives of the wild animals, between money and the protection of wild species, between wealthy and nonwealthy nature lovers. How would you describe the relationship between politics, money, and nature?
2. According to Roosevelt, who is responsible for the process of extinction? Do you agree with him? Have you witnessed any action in your local community that could be considered part of the process of extinction under Roosevelt's definition?
3. This chapter of *Saving Place* deals specifically with recreation and the ways humans turn to nature as a site for recreation. In what ways might Roosevelt's argument regarding conservation of wild game species be seen as an argument about recreation? What is the relationship between recreation and conservation as you see it?

FOCUS ON WRITING

1. Roosevelt writes that "the practical common sense of the American people has been in no way made more evident during the last few years than by the creation and use of a series of large land reserves—situated for the most part on great plains and among the mountains of the West—intended to keep the forests from destruction, and therefore to conserve the water-supply. These reserves are, and should be, created primarily for economic purposes." What is Roosevelt trying to accomplish in connecting economics and protection with common sense in this selection?

2. About midway through this essay, Roosevelt tells us that "On April 8, 1903, John Burroughs and I reached the Yellowstone Park," yet he does not tell us who John Burroughs is. Are we to assume that we should know who Burroughs is? Do you know who Burroughs is? Why might Roosevelt want us to know he went to Yellowstone Park with him? Is there a significance in the fact that they were there together? Take a moment to find out who Burroughs was in order to understand why Roosevelt acknowledges his presence. What does this reference add to this essay?

3. Notice the ways in which Roosevelt makes gender distinctions in this essay. For instance, he refers to "the true sportsmen," and to "that thoroughly feminine weapon, an umbrella." What role does gender play in this essay? What role does gender play in your envisioning of "the hunter"? In Roosevelt's?

FOR DISCUSSION

Hunting, also addressed in several other essays in this chapter, is often seen as an important recreation, one having deep roots in native traditions. Roosevelt's essay also argues for a view of the hunter as conservationist. He writes, for instance, "True sportsmen, worthy of the name, men who shoot only in season and in moderation, do no harm whatever to game." As a class discuss Roosevelt's claim. Do you agree with him? Are hunters "sportsmen"?

WRITING IN RESPONSE

Roosevelt concludes "Wilderness Reserves: Yellowstone Park" by saying that if "a man" was able to observe the bears of Yellowstone for at least a year and "to write down accurately and interestingly what he has seen, [he] would make a contribution of permanent value to our nature literature." Since Roosevelt wrote this, many naturalists have conducted detailed studies not only of the lives of the bears of Yellowstone but of many species around the world and have written remarkable books about their findings. These books have not only helped convey information about different species, but have, as Roosevelt predicted, contributed to the literature of nature. For this writing assignment, select a species of animal that you would like to learn more about and find a book about that species. Once you have read that book, write an essay explaining what you learned specifically about that species. Pay close attention to how the role of human recreation or other human activity has affected that species.

Why I Hunt

Rick Bass

Rick Bass, born in 1958 in Fort Worth, Texas, now makes his home on an isolated ranch in Montana in an area known as the Yaak Valley, an area about which he often writes. His writing, whether nonfiction or fiction, is most frequently about environmental protection. His The Book of the Yaak *makes a strong plea for protecting the unique ecosystems of the Yaak Valley. Bass also frequently writes of his relationships with the places he lives. His first book,* The Deer Pasture, *for instance, recounts his childhood in Texas and what he learned hunting with his family on their land. Likewise,* Winter: Notes from Montana *describes his first winter in the Yaak Valley "Why I Hunt," which was published in* Sierra Magazine *in 2001, explores Bass's understanding of hunting as a necessary part of his life.*

JOURNAL ASSIGNMENT

Bass writes that when he thinks about his hunting, he thinks not only about the animals he has pursued but about all that he has harvested from nature: wood for fires, berries, fruits, vegetables, and so on. Consider this idea that hunting is more than just pursuing animals—that is, in fact, also gathering. In your journal, write about the relationship between hunting and gathering. Is what Bass identifies as part of his hunting really hunting? Why or why not?

I was a hunter before I came far up into northwest Montana, but not to the degree I am now. It astounds me sometimes to step back, particularly at the end of autumn, the end of the hunting season, and take both mental and physical inventory of all that was hunted and all that was gathered from this life in the mountains. The woodshed groaning tight, full of firewood. The fruits and herbs and vegetables from the garden, canned or dried or frozen; the wild mushrooms, huckleberries, thimbleberries, and strawberries. And most precious of all, the flesh of the wild things that share with us these mountains and the plains to the east—the elk, the whitetail and mule deer; the ducks and geese, grouse and pheasant and Hungarian partridge and dove and chukar and wild

1

turkey; the trout and whitefish. Each year the cumulative bounty seems unbelievable. What heaven is this into which we've fallen?

2   How my wife and I got to this valley—the Yaak—15 years ago is a mystery, a move that I've only recently come to accept as having been inevitable. We got in the truck one day feeling strangely restless in Mississippi, and we drove. What did I know? Only that I missed the West's terrain of space. Young and healthy, and not coincidentally new-in-love, we hit that huge and rugged landscape in full stride. We drove north until we ran out of country—until the road ended, and we reached Canada's thick blue woods—and then we turned west and traveled until we ran almost out of mountains: the backside of the Rockies, to the wet, west-slope rainforest.

3   We came over a little mountain pass—it was August and winter was already fast approaching—and looked down on the soft hills, the dense purples of the spruce and fir forests, the ivory crests of the ice-capped peaks, and the slender ribbons of gray thread rising from the chimneys of the few cabins nudged close to the winding river below, and we fell in love with the Yaak Valley and the hard-logged Kootenai National Forest—the way people in movies fall with each other, star and starlet, as if a trap door has been pulled out beneath them: tumbling through the air, arms windmilling furiously, and suddenly no other world but each other, no other world but this one, and eyes for no one, or no place, else.

4   Right from the beginning, I could see that there was extraordinary bounty in this low-elevation forest, resting as it does in a magical seam between the Pacific Northwest and the northern Rockies. Some landscapes these days have been reduced to nothing but dandelions and fire ants, knapweed and thistle, where the only remaining wildlife are sparrows, squirrels, and starlings. In the blessed Yaak, however, not a single mammal has gone extinct since the end of the Ice Age. This forest sustains more types of hunters—carnivores—than any valley in North America. It is a predator's showcase, home not just to wolves and grizzlies, but wolverines, lynx, bobcat, marten, fisher, black bear, mountain lion, golden eagle, bald eagle, coyote, fox, weasel. In the Yaak, everything is in motion, either seeking its quarry, or seeking to avoid becoming quarry.

5   The people who have chosen to live in this remote valley—few phones, very little electricity, and long, dark winters—possess a hardness and dreaminess both. They—we—can live a life of deprivation, and yet are willing to enter the comfort of daydreams and imagination. There is something mysterious happening here between the landscape and the people, a thing that stimulates our imagination, and causes many of us to set off deep into the woods in search of the unknown, and sustenance—not just metaphorical or spiritual sustenance, but the real thing.

6   Only about 5 percent of the nation and 15 to 20 percent of Montanans are hunters. But in this one valley, almost everyone is a hunter. It is not the peer pressure of the local culture that recruits us into hunting, nor even necessarily the economic boon of a few hundred pounds of meat in a cash-poor society. Rather, it is the terrain itself, and one's gradual integration into it, that summons the hunter. Nearly everyone who has lived here for any length of time has ended up—sometimes almost against one's conscious wishes—becoming a hunter. This wild and powerful landscape sculpts us like clay. I don't find such

sculpting an affront to the human spirit, but instead, wonderful testimony to our pliability, our ability to adapt to a place.

I myself love to hunt the deer, the elk, and the grouse—to follow them into 7 the mouth of the forest, to disappear in their pursuit—to get lost following their snowy tracks up one mountain and down the next. One sets out after one's quarry with senses fully engaged, wildly alert: entranced, nearly hypnotized. The tiniest of factors can possess the largest significance—the crack of a twig, the shift of a breeze, a single stray hair caught on a piece of bark, a fresh-bent blade of grass.

Each year during such pursuits, I am struck more and more by the conceit that people in a hunter-gatherer culture might have richer imaginations than those who dwell more fully in an agricultural or even post-agricultural environment. What else is the hunt but a stirring of the imagination, with the quarry, or goal, or treasure lying just around the corner or over the next rise? A hunter's imagination has no choice but to become deeply engaged, for it is never the hunter who is in control, but always the hunted, in that the prey directs the predator's movements.

The hunted shapes the hunter; the pursuit and evasion of predator and 8 prey are but shadows of the same desire. The thrush wants to remain a thrush. The goshawk wants to consume the thrush and in doing so, partly become the thrush—to take its flesh into its flesh. They weave through the tangled branches of the forest, zigging and zagging, the goshawk right on the thrush's tail, like a shadow. Or perhaps it is the thrush that is the shadow thrown by the light of the goshawk's fiery desire.

Either way the escape maneuvers of the thrush help carve and shape and 9 direct the muscles of the goshawk. Even when you are walking through the woods seeing nothing but trees, you can feel the unseen passage of pursuits that might have occurred earlier that morning, precisely where you are standing— pursuits that will doubtless, after you are gone, sweep right back across that same spot again and again.

As does the goshawk, so too do human hunters imagine where their prey 10 might be, or where it might go. They follow tracks hinting at not only distance and direction traveled, but also pace and gait and the general state of mind of the animal that is evading them. They plead to the mountain to deliver to them a deer, an elk. They imagine and hope that they are moving toward their goal of obtaining game.

When you plant a row of corn, there is not so much unknown. You can be 11 fairly sure that, if the rains come, the corn is going to sprout. The corn is not seeking to elude you. But when you step into the woods, looking for a deer—well, there's nothing in your mind, or in your blood, or in the world, but imagination.

Most Americans neither hunt nor gather nor even grow their own food, 12 nor make, with their own hands, any of their other necessities. In this post-agricultural society, too often we confuse anticipation with imagination. When we wander down the aisle of the supermarket searching for a chunk of frozen chicken, or cruise into Dillard's department store looking for a sweater, we can be fairly confident that grayish wad of chicken or that sweater is going to be there, thanks to the vigor and efficiency of a supply-and-demand marketplace.

The imagination never quite hits second gear. Does the imagination atrophy, from such chronic inactivity? I suspect that it does.

14   All I know is that hunting—beyond being a thing I like to do—helps keep my imagination vital. I would hope never to be so blind as to offer it as prescription; I offer it only as testimony to my love of the landscape where I live— a place that is still, against all odds, its own place, quite unlike any other. I don't think I would be able to sustain myself as a dreamer in this strange landscape if I did not take off three months each year to wander the mountains in search of game; to hunt, stretching and exercising not just my imagination, but my spirit. And to wander the mountains, too, in all other seasons. And to be nourished by the river of spirit that flows, shifting and winding, between me and the land.

FOCUS ON ECOLOGY

1. After reading Bass's "Why I Hunt," how do you respond to his understanding of the role of hunting?
2. How do you respond to Bass's identification of carnivores as "hunters." Why might he align human hunting with the activity of animals eating by naming those animals hunters? What does he accomplish in doing so?
3. How do you respond to the image Bass depicts of the people who live in the Yaak valley?

FOCUS ON WRITING

1. Several times in this essay, Bass uses the word *bounty* to describe the amount of game available to him. What does this word mean to you? In what other contexts is it most frequently used?
2. What role do description and narrative play in this essay?
3. To whom do you suppose Bass is writing this essay? What about the text leads you to this conclusion?

FOR DISCUSSION

Bass's "Why I Hunt" offers a rather personal approach to thinking about hunting. Often the personal argument is more appealing than is the scientific or statistical approach to the same argument. As a class, discuss how you respond both to Bass's argument and to his approach to his argument.

WRITING IN RESPONSE

"Why I Hunt" was first published in *Sierra* magazine in 2001, but it was not the first essay by this title that Rick Bass had published. In 1990, *Esquire* magazine featured an essay by Rick Bass also titled "Why I Hunt." Go to your library and find a copy of Bass's 1990 "Why I Hunt" essay. (*Esquire* is a popular magazine and most libraries will have bound volumes or archived volumes on microfiche or microfilm). Once you have read the earlier essay, consider its similarities to and differences from the Bass essay published here. Has Bass's explanation for why he hunts changed in the 11 years between publications? In what ways? Are there similarities or differences in how Bass has written these two essays? Write an essay of your own that compares and contrasts these two essays and addresses why you think Bass may have written a second "Why I Hunt" essay 11 years after writing the first.

Anyting You Kill, You Gada Eat

Joe Balaz

Joe Balaz is a writer of Slovakian, Irish, and Hawaiian ancestry who was born and raised in Hawaii. He writes in American English and Hawaii Creole English, also known as pidgin. His work has been published nationally and internationally. Balaz is the editor of Hoomanoa: An Anthology of Contemporary Hawaiian Literature, *which includes only writers of Hawaiian ancestry who create works predominantly in English. He has also served as editor of the* Ohahu Review, *a literary and art journal that published contemporary multiethnic writing of Hawaii. Balaz is the author of* Electric Laulau, *an experimental CD of Hawaii Creole English. The poem reprinted here, "Anyting You Kill, You Gada Eat," appears on* Electric Laulau *under the title* "Gottah Eat 'Um" *and is listed in the collection of satirical works. The poem was originally published in 1988 in the* Hawaii Review. *As you read this poem, consider specifically how Balaz uses pidgin to give it context.*

JOURNAL ASSIGNMENT

The title "Anyting You Kill, You Gada Eat" suggests a kind of hunter ethic. Why might such an ethic be taken up by those who hunt? In your journal, consider Balaz's title and what it suggests to a hunter.

ANYTING YOU KILL, YOU GADA EAT

Wen I wuz wun small kid
My fadah told me
anyting you kill, you gada eat

You shoot da dove
wit da BB gun—
you gada eat 'um

You speah da small manini
at da beach—
you gada eat 'um

You help your madah
kill da chicken in da backyard—
you gada eat 'um

Whoa brah—
tinking back to small kid time
and da small kid games I used to play
aftah I heard dat
no moa I kill flies wit wun rubbahband.

FOCUS ON ECOLOGY

1. How do you respond to this poem, both in terms of how it reads and in terms of what it suggests about ethics and hunting?
2. Why do you suppose this poem points out that the lesson "Anyting you kill, you gada eat" was passed down from "my fadah"? What do you understand the role of fathers and sons to be in discussing hunting and hunting ethics?
3. Though this poem certainly addresses hunting through shooting and spearing, it also addresses the domestic killing of a chicken. In what ways is the slaughter of a chicken related to hunting?

FOCUS ON WRITING

1. Why do you suppose Joe Balaz chose to write this poem using pidgin?
2. What role does the final stanza of this poem play in the argument of this poem?
3. How does Joe Balaz incorporate issues of family and of place into this poem?

DISCUSSION

Chances are, most of us have killed an animal at some point in our lives, either through hunting or fishing, or accident, or by swatting a fly, stepping on a roach, swatting a mosquito, or other similar action. As a class, consider what it means to kill something and to hunt for something. Is there a difference? Does our thinking about actions like swatting a fly or setting a mouse trap differ from our thinking about hunting? Why or why not?

WRITING IN RESPONSE

Try to state your position on hunting in a poem. (Style and form are up to you.) After you're done, consider: How effectively do you think you made your case? How is writing an argument in a poem different from writing an arugument in an essay?

The Company of Men

Pam Houston

Pam Houston *was born in New Jersey in 1962. In addition to being a best-selling author, she is a river guide and hunting guide and has worked an array of interesting jobs: as a bartender, as a flag person on a highway repair crew, as a horse trainer, as a ski instructor, and as a university creative writing instructor. Houston's writing has been recognized for its rugged, humorous traits and is often noted for its ability to stand solidly in a genre most frequently associated with male writers: depicting the rugged individual in the outdoors. Her first book,* Cowboys Are My Weakness *is a collection of 12 short stories that was awarded the 1993 Western States Book Award. The stories, often narrated in the first person by a woman who has given up much to pursue a rugged man earned critical acclaim, and the book became a best-seller. She is also the editor of the collection* Women on Hunting *and her fiction and nonfiction have appeared in a variety of publications such as* Mademoiselle, New York Times, The Mississippi Review, Outside, Elle, *and* House and Garden. *The essay here exemplifies Houston's ability as a nonfiction writer but does not abandon her often-used theme of women negotiating territories traditionally defined and claimed by men. In "The Company of Men," Houston writes of her fishing adventures with three men. As you read this essay consider not just how Houston enters into a decidedly male situation, but how she narrates the events as opposed to how she sees her male companions experiencing the same events.*

JOURNAL ASSIGNMENT

In "The Company of Men," Houston, writes about how she carves space in a rather male-dominated scenario, she also talks about fishing as an activity, the comradery shared among the males on the trip, and their efforts to include her. In your journal, respond to a simple question: what does it mean "to go fishing"?

1   I can't remember the last time I envied a man, or, in fact, if I ever have. I have loved men, hated them, befriended them, taken care of them, and all too often compromised my sense of self for them, but I don't think I have ever looked at a man and actually coveted something his maleness gave him. And yet envy was at least one of the surprising things I felt last spring when I found myself standing armpit-deep in a freshwater stream at 2:00 A.M., near Interlochen, Michigan, fly casting for steelhead with a bunch of male poets.

2   Winters are long in northern Michigan, and dark and frozen. Spring is late and wet and full of spirit-breaking storms. The landscape is primarily forest and water and has not been tamed like most of the Midwest. Both the wildness and the hardship show on the faces of the people who choose to live there.

3   When a man named Jack Driscoll first calls and invites me to Interlochen, he tells me about the Academy, a place where talented high-school students from forty-one states and fifteen countries are given a lot of time to develop their art. Although he makes it clear that I will be expected to read from my fiction and talk to the students about craft, every other time we speak on the phone, all he really wants to talk about is fishing.

4   For all the time I spend outdoors, I am not much of a fisherman. And fly fishing, like all religions, is something I respect but don't particularly understand. If Jack bothers to ask me if I want to go fishing, I will say yes. I have always said yes, and as a result the shape of my life has been a long series of man-inspired adventures, and I have gone tripping along behind those men, full of strength and will and only a half-baked kind of competence, my goal being not to excel, but to simply keep up with them, to not become a problem, to be a good sport. It is a childhood thing (I was my father's only son), and I laugh at all the places this particular insecurity has taken me: sheep hunting in Alaska, helicopter skiing in Montana, cliff diving in the Bahamas, ice climbing in the Yukon territory. Mostly, I have outgrown the need to impress men in this fashion; in the adventures I take these days, I make the rules. But, as my trip to Michigan draws nearer, I feel a familiar and demented excitement to be back at the mercy of a bunch of lunatic outdoorsmen, a stubborn novice with something intangible to prove.

5   I fly up to Traverse City on what the woman at the United Express counter calls the "big" plane, a twin-engine that bumps between thunderstorms and patches of dense fog for an hour before skidding to a stop on a bleak and rainy runway surrounded by a leafless April woods.

6   I am greeted by what looks like a small committee of fit and weathered middle-aged men. Their names are Jack Driscoll, Mike Delp, Nick Bozanic and

Doug Stanton. Their books are titled after the landscape that dominates their lives, collections of poetry called *Under the Influence of Water, The Long Drive Home* and *Over the Graves of Horses,* and Jack's award-winning collection of stories titled *Wanting Only to Be Heard.* They fight over my luggage, hand me snacks and sodas and beers, and all but carry me to the car on the wave of their enthusiasm.

"Weather's been good," Mike says, by way of a greeting. "The lake ice is 7 breaking."

"It's a real late run for the steelhead," Doug says. "You're just in time." 8

"Any minute now, any minute now," Jack says, his mind full of the long, 9 dark bodies of fish in the river, and then, "You've got a reading in forty-five minutes, then a dinner that should be over by ten, the president of the local community college wants to meet you. At midnight, we fish."

By 12:25 A.M. I am dressed in my long underwear, Jack's camouflage sweat 10 clothes, Mike's neoprene liners, Doug's waders and Nick's hat. I look like the Michelin tire man, the waders so big and stiff I can barely put one foot in front of the other. We pile into Mike's Montero, rods and reels jangling in the back. Jack and Mike and Doug and I. Nick, each man has told me (privately, in a quiet, apprehensive voice), is recovering from bursitis and a divorce, and for one or the other of these reasons, he will not fish this year.

No one asks me if I'm tired, nor do I ask them. These men have had nine 11 months of winter to catch up on their sleep, cabin fever reflecting in their eyes like exclamations. The steelhead will start running soon, maybe tonight, and there is no question about where they should be.

It takes almost an hour to get to the river with what I quickly understand 12 is an obligatory stop at the Sunoco in the tiny town called Honor for day-old doughnuts and Coca-Cola and banter with the cashier. Along the way we listen to what Mike and Jack say is their latest road tape, three Greg Brown songs recorder over and over to fill a ninety-minute drive. "Gonna meet you after midnight," say the lyrics repeatedly, "at the Dream Cafe."

The rotating sign on the Honor State Bank says 1:51 A.M. and twenty-two 13 degrees. The men have bet on what the temperature will be. They have also bet on how many cars we will pass on the two-lane highway, how many deer we will see in the woods between Mike's house and the bridge, if it will snow or rain and, if so, how hard (hardness gauged by comparison with other nights' fishing). Doug wins the temperature bet, closest without going over, at twenty-one degrees.

The betting is all part of a long, conversational rap among them, a rap that 14 moves from Mike's last fish to Jack's latest fiction to concern for Nick and his lost house to the girl at the Sunoco to an in-unison sing-along to their favorite Greg Brown lyrics. The whole conversation is less like speaking, really, and more like singing, a song they've spent years and years of these cold spring nights together learning, nights anybody anywhere else in the world would call winter, nights filled with an expectation that can only be called boyish and shadowed by too much of the grown-up knowledge that can ultimately defeat men.

Sometimes they remember I am there, sometimes they forget I am a woman. 15

16   I feel, in those moments, like I've gone undercover, like I've been granted security clearance to a rare and private work of art. And though I have always believed that women bond faster, tighter, deeper than men could ever dream of, there is something simple and pure between these men, a connection so thick and dense and timeless that I am fascinated, and jealous, and humbled, all at the same time.

17   "Shit," Jack says, "Look at 'em all." We have come finally out of the woods and to a bridge no longer than the width of the two-lane roadway. As impossible as it is for me to believe, at two A.M. the gravel areas on both sides of the bridge are lined with pickups, a counterculture of night stalkers, two and three trucks deep.

18   I can see by the posture of the men who line the bridge and look gloomily over the edge that they do not teach poetry at Interlochen Arts Academy. One of them staggers toward the truck, reeling drunk. A boy of nine or ten, dressed all in camouflage, tries to steady him from behind.

19   "They ain't here yet," the old man says, an edge in his voice like desperation. "It may be they just aren't coming."

20   "They'll be here," Jack says, easing himself out of the Montero and steering the man away from the broken piece of bridge railing. "It's been a long winter for everybody," Jack says, almost cooing, and the old man drunkenly, solemnly, nods.

21   Mike pulls me out of the truck and hands me a flashlight. We creep to the edge of the bridge and peer over. "Just on for a second and off," he whispers. Even to me it is unmistakable; the flashlight illuminates a long, dark shape already half under the pylon. "Don't say anything," Mike mouths to me soundlessly. Jack leaves the old-timer to sleep in his car and joins us. Mike holds up one finger, and Jack nods. "We'll go downstream," Jack says, after some consideration. "Nobody's gonna do any good here."

22   We drive downriver while Mike points out all the sights as if we can see them—a place called the toilet hole, where Doug and Nick got lucky, the place Mike got his car stuck so bad four-wheel drive couldn't help him, the place Jack caught last year's biggest fish. We can see the headlights of people who are smelt-dipping out where the river empties into the lake, and a red and white channel marker lit up and looming in the darkness, its base still caked with lake ice and snow.

23   We drop Doug off at his favorite hole near the mouth of the river, drive back upstream a few hundred yards, park the Montero and step out into the night.

24   "It's a little bit of a walk from here," Mike says, "and the mud's pretty deep." It is impossible for me to imagine how I will move my stiff and padded legs through deep mud, how, at twenty-two degrees, I will step into that swift and icy river, much less stand in it for a couple of hours. I can't imagine how, with all these clothes and pitch dark around me, I'll be able to cast my fly with anything resembling grace.

25   Two steps away from the truck and already I feel the suction. The mud we are walking in ranges from mid-calf to mid-thigh deep. I'm following Jack like

a puppy, trying to walk where he walks, step where he steps. I get warm with the effort, and a little careless, and suddenly there's nothing beneath me and I'm in watery mud up to my waist. Mike and Jack, each on one arm, pull me out of the hole so fast it seems like part of the choreography.

"Let's try to cross the river," says Jack, and before I can even brace for the 26 cold, we are in it, thigh . . . hip . . . waist . . . deep, and I feel the rush of the current tug me toward Lake Michigan. "One foot in front of the other," Jack says. "The hole's right in front of you; when you're ready, go ahead and cast."

I lift the rod uneasily into the night, close my eyes and try to remember how 27 they did it in *A River Runs Through It,* and then bring it down too fast and too hard with an ungraceful splat. "Let out a little more line," Jack says, so gently it's as if he is talking to himself. A few more splats, a little more line, and I am making casts that aren't embarrassing. Jack moves without speaking to help Mike with a snarl in his line. "This is your night, Delp," Jack says, his shadowy form floating away from me, a dark and legless ghost.

What in the world are you doing here? a voice giggles up from inside me, 28 and the answers sweep past me, too fast to catch: because I can't turn down a challenge, because my father wanted a boy, because touching this wildness is the best way I know to undermine sadness, because of the thin shimmery line I am seeing between the dark river and the even darker sky.

Soon I stop thinking about being washed to Lake Michigan. I marvel at how 29 warm I am in the waders, so warm and buoyant that I forget myself from time to time and dip some unprotected part of me, my hand or my elbow, into the icy water. A deer crackles sticks in the forest across the river; an angry beaver slaps his tail. In whispers we take turns identifying planets and constellations— Ursa Major, Draco, Cassiopeia, Mars and Jupiter—and murmur at the infrequent but lovely falling stars.

When we are quiet I can hear a faint crashing—constant, reverberant— 30 sounding in the dark for all the world like the heartbeat of the Earth. "Lake Michigan coming over the breakwater," Jack says to my unasked question. "There must be a big wind on the other side."

My fishing is steadily improving: every fifth or seventh cast hangs a long 31 time in the air and falls lightly, almost without sound.

"You know," Jack says, "there aren't too many people who could come out 32 here like this and not hook themselves or me or the shoreline . . . isn't that right, Delp?" Mike murmurs in agreement, and my head swells with ridiculously disproportionate pride.

The constellations disappear, and a light snow begins falling. "God, I love 33 the weather," Mike says, his voice a mixture of sarcasm and sincerity, and for a while there is only the whisper of the line and the flies.

"Fish!" Jack shouts suddenly. "Fish on the line!" I am startled almost out of 34 my footing, as if I've forgotten what we've come for, as if the silence and the night and the rhythm of the flies hitting the water have become reason enough. We reel in our lines and watch Jack land his fish. It is long and thin, and its speckled belly gleams silver as it thrashes in the tiny beam of the flashlight. Jack looks at us helplessly, delighted by his luck and skill and yet wishing, simultaneously, that it had been me who caught the fish, wishing even harder, I can see, that it had been Mike.

35   We fish a little longer, but now there's no need to stay. The spell has been broken; the first steelhead has been caught in its journey up the Platte.

36   "Let's wade downriver a little," Jack says, when we've reeled in our lines, "to try and avoid the mud." I take short rapid breaths as we move through the water. "This part is deep," Jack says. "Take it slow."

37   The water creeps up my chest and into my armpits; I'm walking, weightless, through a dark and watery dream. For a moment there is nothing but my forward momentum and the lift of water under the soles of my boots that keep me from going under. Then I feel the bank rise suddenly beneath my feet.

38   "No problem," I say, just before my foot slips and I do go under, head and all into the icy current. I thrash my arms toward shore, and Jack grabs me. "Better get you home," he says, as the cold I've ignored for hours moves through my body with logarithmic speed. "You've gotta meet students in a couple hours." Back at the truck Doug is curled under a blanket like a dog.

39   The next day Jack sleeps while Mike makes sure I meet my classes. The students are bright, skeptical, interested. My head buzzes with the heat of the all-nighter, a darkness, like the river dark, threatening to close in. Mike and I drink bad machine coffee in one of the tunnels that connects the English department to the other school buildings, tunnels to keep the students from getting lost in the storms that bring the blowing snow.

40   "It's hard to explain how much I love these guys," Mike says suddenly, as if I've asked him. "I don't know what I'd do without what we have."

41   The cement walls of this poor excuse for a lounge move in on us like the weather, and this poet who more resembles a wrestler looks for a moment as if he might cry.

42   It is late in the evening. I have met three classes, talked to at least thirty students, given another reading, signed books in Traverse City, and as part of an orgy of a potluck, cooked elk steaks, rare, on the grill. Mike, in his other favorite role of DJ, plays one moody song after another on the stereo: John Prine, John Gorka and early Bonnie Raitt. We are all a little high from the good food and tequila. Mike's ten-year-old daughter Jaime and Jack dance cheek to cheek in their socks on the living room floor.

43   "So are we gonna do it?" Jack says when the song ends, a sparkle in his eyes that says the river is always in him, whether he's standing in it or not. This fish and fiction marathon is in its thirty-eighth hour, and I am beyond tired now to some new level of consciousness.

44   I have spent too much of my life proving I can be one of the guys, never saying uncle, never admitting I'm tired, or hurting or cold. Tonight I am all three, but the thing that makes me nod my head and say yes I want to go back

again and stand in that icy river has nothing, for a change, to do with my father, or my childhood, or all the things in the world that I need to prove. It is the potent and honest feeling between these men that I covet, that I can't miss an opportunity to be close to. I have stumbled, somehow, onto this rare pack of animals who know I am there and have decided, anyway, to let me watch them at their dance. I want to memorize their movements. I want to take these river nights home with me for the times when the darkness is even heavier than it is in this Michigan sky.

A flurry of rubber and neoprene, and we're back inside the Montero. Greg   45
Brown is singing the song about the laughing river. "This is your night, Delp," Jack says, "I can feel it." Around the next bend will be Honor's scattered lights.

FOCUS ON ECOLOGY

1. Does Pam Houston's fishing adventure sound inviting to you? Is it the kind of recreational activity you'd like to participate in? Why or why not?
2. In several of the essays in this chapter, we looked at the role of hunting as recreation and as a site for environmental/natural engagement. Often, hunting and fishing are seen as similar activities. Yet, fishing is more apt to be seen as a contemplative recreation. Many Americans are more sympathetic to fishing than to hunting. How do you think about of fishing? Do you fish? Do you know people who fish?
3. When questioning her own motivation for being out fishing in the middle of a cold night, Houston concludes that "touching this wildness is the best way I know to undermine sadness." What do you suppose Houston means by this? What might she be suggesting about the connection she (and perhaps others) make with wilderness?

FOCUS ON WRITING

1. At the opening of this essay, Pam Houston is clear that she does not envy men. In doing so, and in the first paragraph, in general, she establishes a feminine identity. Yet a few paragraphs later, she writes, "I am not much of a fisherman." Notice that she uses this gendered word rather than a gender-neutral word like *angler*. What role does gender play in Houston's writing beyond her acknowledgment that she is a woman in the company of men?
2. Houston's essay contributes to a vast genre of fishing literature with a history as long as the history of literature itself. Why do you suppose fishing is such a prominent subject about which to write?
3. Why do you suppose Houston makes reference to *A River Runs Through It?* What does this reference elicit from an audience, particularly an audience

who may not be familiar with fly fishing? What effect do you suppose the film might have had on Houston's view of what fly fishing should be like?

FOR DISCUSSION

In this writing, Houston opens the door to a number of important questions not just about male/female relationships outdoors, but to male/female participation in outdoor activities in general. As a class, consider whether women's inclusion in traditionally male outdoor activities has helped to change how we envision and understand those outdoor activities. You may also want to consider the effect women have had on the industries that surround activities like fishing.

WRITING IN RESPONSE

Fishing has been a favored topic for as long as writers have been producing written work. In contemporary America, the literature of fishing is one of the most popular kinds of sports writing; there is a demand not only for huge numbers of books published on the subject, but also essays and stories about fishing that appear in countless local and national magazines each month. Locate a work on fishing, either a fictional or a nonfictional piece. Read the selection and write an essay in which you compare and contrast how Pam Houston depicts the activity of fishing in "The Company of Men" and how your selected work depicts fishing.

The Young Woman and the Sea

Lorian Hemingway

The title of this essay by Lorian Hemingway, forces us to connect the author with her grandfather Ernest Hemingway. Yet, Lorian Hemingway has rightfully earned respect as a writer independent of the Hemingway name. Her books Walking into the River: A Novel *and* Walk on Water: A Memoir *have earned her critical acclaim. Hemingway often writes about fishing, and her work on the subject has appeared in* Horizon Magazine, Pacific Northwest, Sports Afield *and the* New York Times. *"The Young Woman and the Sea" was published in a collection called* Uncommon Waters: Women Write about Fishing, *edited by Holly Morris. As you read this essay, consider the relationship between sport and economics in the author's depictions of marlin fishing.*

JOURNAL ASSIGNMENT

In this essay, Hemingway discusses the legacy of the name Hemingway as it pertains specifically to fishing. In your journal make a list of what you know already about Ernest Hemingway and his work. Then, make a list of why you might connect the Hemingway name with fishing.

The name is a joke to those too smug to believe in the enduring power of a heritage. Others see it as an accident, a casual gift that allows Hemingway family members to walk the world with their heads high, never quite knowing why they do. And I have heard some say that the name is a curse, something made volatile by the memory of the despairs and exhilarations of a fine writer too long dead.

It has been all things to me: self-doubt, strength, justice and abomination. *It has been a wish to drink hard and relentlessly, to paper myself with the guilt that is the other legacy Papa's name bestows.* But for all the fine and the sinister gifts my grandfather's name has given to three generations of his family, there is one we all embrace without question. The belief in luck that Papa lived by makes the name worthwhile; a legacy of luck for the proud, confused children on whom Ernest was such an influence.

I'm glad we do not have to try to kill the stars. Imagine if a man each day must try to kill the moon. The moon runs away. But imagine if a man each day should have to try to kill the sun. We are born lucky. Yes, we are born lucky.

> —The Old Man and the Sea

There was a cocktail party the night before. It was the second night of the third annual Hemingway Billfishing Tournament, and many participants had been working on a decent, stabilizing drunk for several days. I had had my share of beer. Enough to float one of the sunken sailboats in Bimini's harbor.

Had I been sober, I would have looked less kindly upon the scene before me. The rich yachting types who courted Papa, and whom Papa swore he never liked, were all around. They were perfect-looking men and women, dressed in perfect sports clothes, and were standing around the pool at the Blue Water Marina, talking of marlin fishing and Ernest Hemingway and their suntans. I had a good suntan, but my clothes weren't perfect and there was a Band-Aid over my right eye (a testimonial to the rough and clumsy night before). But I made many friends and was jealous of them because they would be fishing the next day for something my grandfather had loved—something I had wanted for years, and had actually fished for several times, but had never caught.

"You want to catch a marlin, don't you?" asked Dr. Howard Engle, an old friend of Papa's and a new friend of mine. "I can tell by your eyes," he said.

Dr. Engle was right. I had wanted to fight a marlin for three years, ever since I had come upon that wondrous yearly event my great-uncle Leicester, Ernest's brother, had decided to call the Hemingway Billfishing Tournament. There are four kinds of marlin—blue, black, white and striped. Of these, the blue is most prized on Bimini because it is the largest and fights hardest.

But I wasn't entered in the tournament. I didn't own a boat, and if I had wished to charter one, I would have been milked for $650 for a day's fishing.

"The very rich are different from you and me," F. Scott Fitzgerald said.

"Yes," Ernest told the world. "They have more money."

It's a good thing they do, because if Dr. Engle hadn't befriended Capt. Marion Merritt, a fugitive from the Mau Mau rebellion in Kenya some thirty years ago, then I would have been left behind, sipping beer on the dock for the remaining three days of the tournament.

I had met Captain Marion the year before and had a healthy respect for his Georgia accent and his stories about the ruthlessness of the Mau Mau. He had bought a boat and named it Kembé in honor of the Watusi tribal chief who had helped him escape from Africa.

"Young lady," Captain Marion told me, after Dr. Engle had spent two hours at the party helping to convince him of my desperate need to fish, "you are gonna catch a marlin your granddaddy would be proud of. But you're gonna do every damn bit of work yourself."

Melodrama, perhaps. But those were the words I had wanted to hear.

"You be down here at 9 a.m. We'll catch us a fish. Where'd you get all those gray hairs?"

"Too much beer, I guess," I said.

"On you it looks good," he told me. "You need another beer, doncha?"

I told him that I didn't really.

"Yes you do, by God. You wait here while I get you one."

Captain Marion brought me a Budweiser, and, as Papa would say, "it tasted good."

I tried saying, "It tastes good," under my breath just to see if I could make it sound right. I wanted to walk up to everyone at the party, hold out my bottle of beer and say, "It tastes good." Or even "real well." But I wasn't quite ready to start talking like Jake Barnes in *The Sun Also Rises.*

I was, however, ready to fish my heart out as soon as Bimini's dead-heat sun broke the horizon the next morning. It was a good day for fishing. I could tell by the way I felt as I hurried to make it down to the boat. I didn't feel the usual beery stupor too much, but I drank one while I was getting dressed just to make sure the night before wouldn't catch up with me.

"Nothing like a cold beer in the morning," Dr. Engle shouted as he left Les Hemingway's houseboat, on which he was staying. He was heading down to the Kembé to chat with Captain Marion and make everything as right as he could. He had been acting as patriarch of the clan since Leicester had been hospitalized for a blood clot five days before. He had fixed fine meals for my husband, Douglas, and me and Les's daughter Hilary (my cousin), and he had made our stay in Bimini a good one.

Dr. Engle, with his salt-and-pepper beard and suntanned face, is often mistaken for a Hemingway. We don't all have beards, but there's something about the jaw structure that suggests a need for one. Dr. Engle wears his well. And happily. He was our alarm clock the entire time we were in Bimini, so eager was he to be up and to scout the island for a new adventure. This day he had fixed it so that I could chase one of Papa's perfect fantasies, one which might become real.

Bimini's summer is a great furnace. It must be avoided and resisted. And as I walked to Captain Marion's boat that morning, the heat was nearly suffocating. "Eight-thirty in the morning and it's hotter than hell," someone said. There was a little breeze that would wilt before the day was over.

"Ready to catch a big one?" Captain Marion bellowed from the bobbing stern as we approached. It was a beautiful boat, a forty-seven-foot custom job with impressive woodwork and a flying bridge designed only for those sure-footed enough to walk a plank in thirty-foot seas. Hilary, Douglas and I went on board. I said good morning to Tommy Sewell, a young man who has the reputation on the island as one of the best mates around.

Captain Marion took me into the cabin and pulled a monstrous rod and reel from one of the overhead supports. Dr. Engle was on the sofa, having his fifth cup of coffee. He watched as Captain Marion began to drill me on the fishing equipment.

"You'll be usin' a rod like this. Fifty-pound test line, so it'll be a little easier on your arms. It's harder to catch a big marlin on 50 pounds because you have to be aware of what you're feeling when he pulls. Too much and it'll break." He handed the rod to me.

The weight of the rod was enough to send me off balance. I supported the butt in my right hand and kept my left on the grip.

"How's it feel?" Captain Marion asked.

"Fine," I lied.

"Now you're gonna be the only one that knows what's going on with that fish. I can only *guess.* Tommy can only guess. You gotta tell us so I know what the hell to do with that boat. We never want the fish to get under the boat."

Captain Marion seemed to know everything. With his white beard and perfectly round red cheeks, he looked like Santa Claus. And there was that certain integrity in his face that children appreciate: an almost sad willingness to give a part of himself that will later prove valuable to the recipient. But his voice was all business. He was being rough so he could prepare me for what might be ahead.

He taught me all about the rod and reel. And how to set the drag, which controls the amount of pressure a hooked fish has to exert to take out line. "Don't set the thing all the way up," he told me. "If you do, you'll break the line. If you got a five-hundred-pound marlin on the end of this thing, it'll snap like a toothpick unless you do everything right. You gotta let him run once you hook in. Just keep enough pressure on the line so you know he's there. You'll know it when you feel it."

I wasn't sure I would. I had read all of Papa's books, had been told how stupid men lose fish through carelessness, had tried to tell myself that if I ever hooked such a grand thing I would be able to handle it. I was thinking about what I knew about marlin. Not much, but more than the average novice. I heard stories about them from Les Hemingway, Dr. Engle and many experienced captains and mates. One man lost an eye to the needle-sharp bill of a marlin brought alongside the boat before the fight was out of it. Another man was gouged in the side as the marlin took a final leap before the gaff reached it.

I had seen marlin dead on the docks and had seen them thrown, uncut and wasted, into the harbor for the barracuda to feed on. I had seen them mounted, one on the north wall of the Compleat Angler Hotel, where Papa used to stay when he was on Bimini. And I had seen films of them jumping majestically, trying to throw their hooks while great ribbons of scarlet streamed from their intestines.

Papa boated over one hundred marlin in his time. And once they were boated, he either released them or kept them for food and an occasional trophy. He never let them rot as they do on Bimini now, nor did he turn is back on them once they were dead. He kept the memory of the fight and wrote of it so someday a scared kid like me would halfway get over her nerves as she listened to these precise instructions from rough and bearded Captain Marion.

"Look outside there," Captain Marion demanded. "There's two flat lines, girl. There's a left rigger and a right rigger hooked up to them clothespin-lookin' things. When I yell, 'Flat line!' you go to that flat line and take the pole. When I yell right or left rigger, you take that pole and knock the line out of the pin if it's not knocked out already. Get in the chair then, and Tommy will strap you down. *You* set the drag. *You* do it, girl. When I say, 'Let him go,' let him go, then you let the drag run. When I say, 'Hit him,' then set the drag. Here, put this belt on, because if you get a hit on a flat line, you'll need it before you can get to the chair."

He handed me a wide rubber belt that hooked in back and had a cuplike gimbaled socket in front to hold the pole. It was too wide and too loose for someone as small as I am. The doctor helped me adjust it.

"You've got to rest it on the pubic bone," he said. "Otherwise you'll have internal injuries." What have I gotten myself into, I thought. I grabbed a beer from the cooler. We were headed out of the harbor now, and Tommy was setting the baits.

"OK," Captain Marion yelled from the bridge a few minutes later as we were heading at half-speed toward the Gulf-Stream. "This is gonna be your drill. The next time you hear it, it'll be for real. Get used to the pull of the bait on the rigger. It pulls hard, girl. But when you get a marlin on, you damn well better know the difference."

"Flat line! Flat line!" Captain Marion yelled.

I ran to the right side of the stern. I grabbed the pole from its grip and tried to work it into the belt strapped around my waist.

"Let him go! Let him go!"

I set the drag down as low as it would go.

"Hit him!" Captain Marion bellowed.

I set the drag up and pulled on the bait, a mullet as large as a good-sized trout.

"See how it feels, girl?" Captain Marion asked. I told him I did. It took a lot of muscle just to pull the bait out of the wake.

We weren't in the Gulf Stream yet, but there was a light chop, and the sun, at 10 a.m., was as high as it ever seems to get in a northern city like Seattle, where I live. The bank of black clouds in the distance, which had threatened rain the night before, was the backdrop for a sight I had never seen. The waves were green and aqua peaks, as if painted by a seaworthy Van Gogh, with all their madness and tranquility taken into account. There were fish swimming along the corridors of reefs, their heads and tails flashing colors more brilliant than the light of the water.

"Right rigger. Right rigger!" Captain Marion yelled now. I stumbled toward the right rigger and grabbed the rod.

"Knock it out!" he demanded. I slapped the pole to my left with all my weight, grinding the butt of the pole against my right ribs, and managed to knock the line out of the pin. Then I jumped into the chair, set the drag, moved it to strike and gave a big tug.

I was feeling proud of myself. A few calisthenics in the morning never hurt.

"The next time," Captain Marion reminded me, "it'll be for real."

Dr. Engle helped me adjust my belt again, and I headed to the cooler for another beer. We were at sea now. Bimini's pastel waters and the shadowy symmetry of the coral reefs were lost to the purple shadow of the Gulf Stream passing just east of us.

I sat beside Dr. Engle near the fighting chair. He was waiting as patiently and as nervously as I. "You're going to have to do the whole damn thing yourself, Lorian," he told me. "Your grandfather's looking down on you."

"Up at you," my husband corrected.

This wasn't the easy time on a boat I had known before. Sure, I had gotten my sea legs, learned how to climb the ladder to the bridge during a storm without falling into the Gulf Stream's warm, almost thick-looking waters. I knew how to tell a bad squall from an inconsequential one, and I knew where the flying fish would settle. But I never knew, nor had ever conceived, the power and the unalterable beauty that a marlin at its fiercest and most loyal to its element would offer.

I was standing by the cabin door, smoking a cigarette, when the yell came. I thought Captain Marion and Dr. Engle might be teasing me.

"RI-ITE REE-GUH! Rrriii-iite ree-guh!"

Go to hell, I thought.

"Right rigger!" Dr. Engle yelled with comparative calm.

I ran to the rod, clawed my way into the chair and was strapped in by Tommy and Douglas. The boat came to a rocking halt in the water. Everyone except Captain Marion, who was piloting the boat, rushed toward the stern.

"Let him go! Let him go!" Captain Marion yelled.

"He's five-hundred pounds, boss," Tommy said.

"Hit him!" I heard Captain Marion scream. I pulled back and felt the monster take hold.

"Jesus Christ," I whispered.

I could feel the pain in my back as soon as I hooked into him. Tommy had taken off my waist belt and was adjusting the straps on the harness. But it did not fit. I was pulling with all my weight just to keep myself in the chair. My muscles were cramping, and I knew that I had to distribute my weight better or else lose a kidney or have my arm yanked off by this unseen great fish.

I started the business of pulling back on the rod to get some slack and then slowly reeling in as I leaned forward.

"You tell us how it feels," I heard Captain Marion say. "You tell us how it damn well feels. Lorian! Where's he goin' now?"

"Take up the slack," Tommy said. Tommy was at my left, ready to shout at me and keep up my spirit as long as the fish stayed with me. I could feel the brutal pull on my left arm as the fish jerked the line out.

"He's taking out, Tommy," I screamed.

"Slow the boat, boss. He's taking too much." Captain Marion inched the boat back, and I felt a bit of slack on the line and began to take some of it in.

Thirty minutes passed. I knew because, after each ten minutes, Dr. Engle would boom out the length of my fight.

A wet towel had been put on my head. Then a bucket of sea water.

"Give him hell, Lorian," came the rough voice from the bridge.

Douglas kept rubbing my cramped back. My head ached. I dearly wanted to see the thing that was sharing so much pain with me.

"Where the hell is he?" I asked.

The blue marlin brought himself out of the water with a muscular leap. His colors were a deep blur of blues, greens and purples. His bright mouth, open to cast off the hook, was like a red gash.

I let out a yell that made no sense. I screamed and pounded my right fist against my leg and heard all the other screams coming into chorus around me. Then I took up the slack on the line.

I fought him for fifty-seven minutes, the doctor told me, before the line broke. I had watched the weak section of line rushing out as the fish sounded. But I hoped to God that it would hold.

Luck, luck, luck, Papa.

I felt the weight of the fish release as quickly as I felt it take hold.

I cried.

"That's one big baby you just labored over," I heard Dr. Engle say.
"I never cry," I told them all.

I sat and brooded in the cool of the cabin.

"You didn't do a damn thing wrong," the doctor told me. "You handled the rig like a pro. Papa would be proud of you."

And I felt proud. The fight had been enough for me. I couldn't imagine holding onto a fish like that for twelve hours. And I couldn't imagine losing him either. But I began to hope that the whole day was over and that Captain Marion would decide to head back to the dock.

No chance.

"The next one's going to be a tough one," the doctor told me, "so get your strength back and be ready."

I laughed to myself and thought never again would I put myself through so much pain. I remembered a man I had met several years before who had fought a marlin for just thirty minutes before his arm cramped into an indefinable shape. My left arm was still shaking, and my mouth was still dry after two more beers. I needed to take a nap, to lose my consciousness to the slow rock of the boat.

But I kept myself awake just to wait for what I might possibly see. I felt my work was over, but I wanted to wait for another unimaginable delight that might tear itself from the ocean, which now looked like a mirror under the high sun.

"You don't need any more beer," my husband told me when I suggested what my lunch would be.

"I sweated it all off out there," I told him.

"It'll make you weak if you drink any more."

"*You* go out and try to fight the fish." I was getting a little testy. "Beer won't hurt me. Pour it over my head. I'll take a sip when it runs into my mouth."

I was feeling rather tough now. The true fisherwoman. Out at sea. Never seasick. I was hard and tough and a lot of fun, just like Papa. Or so I thought. I had to think that way to keep myself ready for what everyone on the boat considered the true test. I hoped it would not come. At 104 pounds, my body was not ready for another beating.

"Ri-ite rigger. Damnit, Tommy. Ri-ite rigger!" Tommy, Douglas and I fought our way out of the cabin. Tommy let out a scream that shocked even him. Hilary crashed down from the tower to take a place near the chair.

I grabbed the rod in a panic, and Tommy and Douglas strapped me in again. I felt the same pull when I hooked in as I had the last time. I listened to Captain Marion's directions and did exactly as he said until I was sure the fish was solid.

"He's hooked in the jaw, girl. He's hooked solid."

Then the work was mine. Bloody, wrenching, brutal work. I commended Papa for his courage. My hands were blistered from the previous fight. I could see the pink skin on my hands bubbling into some gelatinous shape I had seen only in science-fiction movies.

"Get the gloves on her," Tommy yelled.

The rod was set securely in the gimbals, and I was hooked to it. I could feel the unerring strength of the fish as he took out the line, steadily, against my own weight.

"What is it?" I hollered to no one in particular.

"It's a blue, baby," Dr. Engle called back.

Whatever was said after that bit of news I only vaguely remember. There was Tommy's steady talk at my left. A litany: "Reel. Pull. Just take an inch, no more. Save your strength. Half an inch is good. Get the belt under you. Don't give him any slack. She needs water. Doug! Pour some water over her. Keep the tip up! Keep the tip *UP!* Take up the drag."

"There is no drag, Tommy," I would hear myself mumble. "He's pulling me in."

"Back her up, boss. Back her up. He's taking too much. Put that towel on her head. More water! She'll die out here in this calm if she don't have water. Get it in her eyes. Don't matter."

And so on. The talk was constant and beautiful. Everyone was with me. Captain Marion and Dr. Engle called me names to make me mad enough to hold on to the monster that was tearing at my muscles. And I called them names back, just to please them and also because I was overflowing with anger.

"Reel, you dummy," Captain Marion yelled.

"REEL, damn it!" came Dr. Engle's voice.

"I am reeling!"

"Lorian, are you OK?" I heard Hilary, Les's, daughter, ask.

Then the violins came up, and I grimaced at the idea of being such a sentimental kid.

You are killing me, fish, the old man thought. But you have a right to. Never have I seen a greater, or more beautiful or a calmer or more noble thing than you, brother. Come on and kill me. I do not care who kills who.

—The Old Man and the Sea

The fish had sounded four times. I had got him in to the leader wire, which connects with the hook, three times, thinking that the unconquerable pain in my arms and back was over. But as soon as I'd get him close enough, he'd take off like a madman, sounding the line until I thought there would be none left. I was using eighty-pound test line this time, which allowed this marlin to pull harder than the first one without the line breaking. Hilary and Douglas held me down in the chair at one point. My back was bowed against the unpredictable leaps and dives the marlin was taking under the water.

All the things Papa wrote about the fight are true. There is not another strength as holy and unrestrained as the strength of that one beautifully mad fish. Once it is hooked, it will seek its freedom a thousand times before it gives up.

Before, I had thought it was all foolishness, this man's business of fighting a fish. But it is not. There is luck involved in the testing of one life against another. And you *do* begin to love the fish because all the pain you are going through just to keep him on the line is equal to the pain he feels in his attempts to lose the thing that has gripped him.

I became nearly delirious after an hour and a half in the chair. The sun was high and there were no clouds or even a faint breeze. The wet towel was still on my head and countless buckets of sea water from the Gulf Stream had been poured over me. The salt had dried on my arms and I could taste the brine running down the parched back of my throat. I had a few sips of beer, a drag off a cigarette and a Fig Newton that Hilary crammed into my mouth. My feet were cramping because I had to strain to reach the footplates on the fighting chair.

I kept trying desperately to find the horizon and some sign of the blue marlin that Tommy said weighed four hundred pounds and that was feeling heavier by the minute. But I wasn't seeing too well. There were silver spots floating before me and my heart was skipping beats.

Heatstroke. Sunstroke, I thought. Maybe just a good, old-fashioned stroke. I'll fall off this chair and never be able to walk again and then they'll be sorry for what they've put me through.

But please know I would have stopped this long ago except that I know that if David catches this fish he'll have something inside him for all his life and it will make everything else easier.

—*Islands in the Stream*

I was stretched flat-out in the chair. The back was down and I was holding onto the fish with everything I had left. And I was cursing Papa in my head. Just a good-luck curse is all.

Hilary looked worried. She poured another bucket of water over me.

"He's comin'! He's comin', boss. Comin' up!"

"Reel! Damn it, Lorian, REEL!"

"I can't reel."

"YES, YOU CAN!"

If the screams hadn't been so loud, I would have passed into the perfectly peaceful unconsciousness I had already begun to dream about. I took up the slack, sitting forward in that huge chair built for a man or a large woman. I am neither.

And I saw my friend standing on his tail in the water, moving that body that was all muscle and the same amount of fury. His colors could never be duplicated, not even in the memory of Papa. He was shot with purple streaks, and his body threw off sparks of green and spinning marbles of sea water. He was as blue as the finest robe of the finest silk worn by the grandest Emperor of China. He stood in twisting power on the water as if he could walk, and he threw his head furiously. His open mouth was that brilliant red seldom seen anywhere but in the most perfect of tropical flowers.

"Lorian!" Hilary screamed. "Do you see him!"

"I see him Hilary!"

He was going down again, but everyone knew it was almost over. I wasn't betting on it, though, because he was one hell of a fine fish.

The cries grew around me, louder than any amplified rock band. And they were full of so much love and excitement that I could do nothing but respond to them with what was left of my arms. My muscles were torn, but there was enough strength left for the thing I had not finished.

"REEL! PULL! REEL! PULL!"

"You come down and fight him," I screamed. "I AM REELING!"

I watched the line grow fatter on the reel. I had watched it run out five times and had lost my heart each time. Now I was gaining on him, and I could feel that he was tired.

When Hilary asked if I wanted to bring him on board or let him go, I told her I did not care. But when I reeled him in to the leader wire with the last of my strength (it *always* seemed like the last of my strength), I knew what I would do.

Someone helped me out of the chair. I think it was Douglas. I staggered over to the side where Tommy was holding onto the wire. Three feet from his hand, just breaking the surface of the purple water, was the marlin, belly up, silver and huge, His length dissolved into shadows, and I could not see where he began or ended. Unbelievable, perfect of form, definite and true, he had run himself to the pure edge of death, and in that honored state had surrendered. Only two confused fins on his belly twitched in the air to declare he was still alive.

"Will he live?" I asked.

"I think he's dead," Hilary said.

Captain Marion and Tommy pulled the body back and forth in the water to resuscitate him, and I watched as he gave a half-turn.

"He's alive," Captain Marion said.

"Let him go," I said. "Let him go."

"That marlin's got your name on him, girl. He's gonna give somebody else hell one of these days," Captain Marion told me. Tommy reached over the side and separated the leader wire from the hook. The hook was left in the marlin's jaw, where it would dissolve in time.

The fish pushed his bill down with what instinct was left to him and paddled slowly away. Dr. Engle presented me with the wire that had held him for two hours.

It wasn't the longest fight on record. But it was the one I had wanted. Papa would have pounded me on the back and given me a shot of the best whiskey for my effort. Captain Marion pulled the cork on some champagne, and we all cavorted in a mad sequence of hugging. And we all praised the damnable spirit of the fish that had fought its imprisonment so spectacularly.

I see now that what I felt during the marlin fight sounds like the makings of tall and foolish stories. But it is not. Papa had it right all along in *The Old Man and the Sea:* "But who knows. Maybe when luck comes your way you are ready."

Captain Marion flew the "Fish Caught — Released" flag when we headed into Bimini's harbor. He broadcast our day at sea over the radio to anyone who would listen.

"An average of eighteen days' fishing it takes to get a look at a marlin, and you hook two in one day," Dr. Engle applauded. "And then you let it go. Papa was smiling on you today."

Someone threw me in the drink because it was the thing to do. Time-honored on Bimini, I was told. My bruised and swollen hands were grabbed by everyone who passed me.

And as I remembered the slow and perfect agony of the fight, even days later when my right arm swelled to the size of my thigh, I believed that Papa had conned someone into testing me. It could have been Captain Marion. It could have been Dr. Engle. It could have been the fish itself. And wouldn't it be fine to think so?

ADDENDUM

I have always believed a writer grows in response to demands made on her character. New ways of looking at past experiences occur during this growth process, and one day the writer will pick up an old piece of writing—her own—read it, and wonder who the hell the person was who wrote it. It was this way when I reread my marlin story. I know the woman in this story as I know friends from years past, vaguely, their faces lacking definition, their antics legendary.

At the time I wrote "The Young Woman and the Sea," I was very studiously trying to be enamored of my grandfather's legend. It was something that did not come naturally. From the time I was a kid, I resented his unseen influence on my life; the funny way people would act when they knew my last name; the way teachers expected me, by sheer right of this last name, to be brilliant; his suicide, kept from me as if it were a shameful thing, until I read of it in a magazine. I winced when I read the endearment "Papa" throughout my story. I never called him Papa, as the world did, nor did I identify with his writings. Until the age of twenty, I refused to read his work. Yet in this story I have recreated a Hemingway world in which the granddaughter embraces some of her grandfather's most sacred territory. Why? Because I wanted to belong, somehow, to a sense of family. All my life I had been told I had certain characteristics because I was a Hemingway. It was time for proof, for a birthright to be recognized, and I believed this proof existed in trying my damndest to be like the man: fishing, drinking, living on an adventurous edge that grew more precarious as the years passed. For a time I believed it was real, even praying to my grandfather's spirit when something went wrong, as if prayer to a dead man could fix my life.

When I reread the actual marlin fights, I recalled—I hope accurately—the actual pain and exhilaration of the experience. It *was* fun. It *was* a test of strength. And I still believe that on some ultraconscious level I did communicate with the fish. But what it was not was an experience manipulated by the ghost of Ernest Hemingway. If anything it was a generous gift from Dr. Engle and Captain Marion. I see this now, no longer clouded by alcohol as I was both the day I fished *and* wrote the story.

What stands out in this piece now, for me stronger than the determination of the fight, is the drinking. The article is, as one *New York Times* editor put it, "afloat in beer." Even so, it was accepted by my editors and by those who read it as part of the day's adventure. I look back to that day off Bimini and see that the drinking ritual I kept then—all day long, starting in the morning—was one I would perfect over the years until I ended up in a detox ward vomiting blood, a peculiar sort of landsickness common to chronic alcoholics. I was alcoholic then. I am now. But then I drank and called it heritage. Now I do not and call it grace.

What I did not understand back in 1980, when I was nobly trying to keep up the Hemingway drinking image, was that my grandfather was debilitated by drinking and that it was indeed the major contributing factor to his suicide. Hemingway scholars argue with me over this, believing in the superhuman myth and the man. But I understand the pain and degradation my grandfather endured when his drinking began to destroy his talent, his health. It is the one thing we truly had in common, and not one I need pretend to. And this understanding allows me compassion for a man who bore the necessary cross of being human and for the young woman in the story who had not yet recognized the dimensions of her own cross.

There have been changes, too, in my views of big game fishing. All too often it is wholesale slaughter, fish taken for prize money in big game tournaments, and I cannot participate in the slow and certain decimation of these fish populations. As a woman who fishes, I have forsaken this arena of big game fish, partly because having caught and released marlin, tarpon, shark and barracuda, I find it more enjoyable to spend time on a lake or in a trout stream. The physical energy required is not as great, and the conscience rests easier.

And there is also nothing left to prove. Maybe there never was. If I proved anything it was that ghosts and legends can grow beyond their boundaries into powers great enough to consume those who take them on. But I have a freedom now from this business of legends. Caught and released, in a way.

FOCUS ON ECOLOGY

1. Unlike the depictions of fishing presented in Pam Houston's "The Company of Men," the view that Lorian Hemingway offers us is one of big game fishing. After reading the essay, how did you envision this kind of fishing? Would you call it "recreation"? How would you describe tournament fishing in relation to the environment in which it takes place?
2. Hemingway writes, "There is luck involved in the testing of one life against another." As Hemingway describes her battle with the fish, how do you feel

about the activity? Is there a challenge in recreational activities such as fishing?

3. Why do you suppose Hemingway discusses what becomes of marlin after they are caught? Why do you suppose she is careful to explain what her grandfather Ernest Hemingway did with his fish? What is her ecological or environmental goal in this section of the essay?

FOCUS ON WRITING

1. What does Lorian Hemingway gain or lose in beginning her essay with the discussion of her name and its significance?

2. What effect does Hemingway gain in including dialogue in this essay? Could Hemingway have written this same essay with the same effectiveness by dropping the dialogue and simply summarizing what was said?

3. This essay seems to have a strong element of adventure. In what ways does Hemingway create that sense of adventure?

FOR DISCUSSION

Much of Lorian Hemingway's essay is about struggle: the struggle between her and the fish that becomes representative of the struggle she has with her name and heritage. George Orwell writes in his book *Coming Up for Air* that "fishing is the opposite of war" referring to its peaceful, contemplative nature; yet as Lorian Hemingway describes it, it seems more like war: the intrusion of one population into another, the struggle of members of one population against another, and often death. How do you as a class see the various kinds of struggles between humans and nature in recreational activities like fishing? What role does an archetype like "man versus nature" play in our telling of stories like Hemingway's, as well as in our desire to participate in outdoor activities like fishing?

WRITING IN RESPONSE

In a personal narrative, recount an adventurous encounter you have had during outdoor recreation. Consider the role the environment or a specific animal had in that incident.

Calvin and Hobbes

Bill Watterson

For biographical information, see page 65.

JOURNAL ASSIGNMENT

Is fishing funny? According to Bill Watterson it certainly has some funny facets. In your journal write about what you see as funny about fishing. You may want to write about a funny thing that happened while you were fishing, or if you do not fish, you may want to write about what you see as funny about others fishing or how the activity in general seems funny. If you can't think of anything funny about fishing you can and draw pictures of fishing in your journal.

CALVIN AND HOBBES © 1986 Watterson. Reprinted with permission of Universal Press Syndicate. All rights reserved.

CALVIN AND HOBBES © 1987 Watterson. Reprinted with permission of Universal Press Syndicate. All rights reserved.

CALVIN AND HOBBES © 1986 Watterson. Reprinted with permission of Universal Press Syndicate. All rights reserved.

FOCUS ON ECOLOGY

1. George Orwell writes, in *Coming Up for Air*, "Is it any use talking about it, I wonder—the sort of fairy light that fish and fishing tackle have in a kid's eyes? Some kids feel the same about guns and shooting, some feel it about motor-bikes or aeroplanes or horses. It's not a thing you can explain

or rationalize, it's merely magic." Why do you suppose fishing has this kind of attraction for some kids? Does Calvin share this attraction?

2. How do you respond to Calvin and Hobbes's reactions to putting worms on hooks? To not wanting to eat things that eat worms? To challenging cheeseburgers instead of fish? What might Watterson be suggesting in the final frame of the first strip?

3. Does it matter in any of these strips where Calvin is fishing? Why or why not?

FOCUS ON WRITING

1. At the beginning of the first strip, Calvin asks Hobbes, "wanna catch some fish?" In the next frame, Watterson shows Calvin and Hobbes playing "catch" baseball style–with a fish. What role do these frames have within the strip as a whole?

2. Calvin and Hobbes's expressions are rather detailed, not only in the strips found here but throughout all of "Calvin and Hobbes." What visual effect do the characters' expressions have in conveying meaning in these strips? Look, for instance, at the second frame of the second strip. Could Watterson have simply written the speech caption ". . . Besides the obvious, I mean" and not shown us Calvin's face? Would the strip have been as effective if we had not seen Calvin in this frame? What about the final frame of the second strip: what effect does the image have on our reading of the strip? Or the third strip in which no words are offered in the final two frames?

3. In what ways does Calvin describe wilderness? That is, how does this comic strip, through the character of Calvin, present a young boy's view of what wilderness is? What words specifically offer clues to this representation?

FOR DISCUSSION

In the strips found here, Calvin is bored with the slow pace and lack of activity and excitement in fishing. Is the representation of his impatience to be read as the impatience of youth or as understandable impatience with a boring activity? Is fishing a good way to introduce children to outdoor activities?

WRITING IN RESPONSE

In the third strip found here, Calvin says "Fishing is the most boring sport in the world." Is Calvin right? Is fishing a sport? Is it boring? What makes something boring? In a definition paper, define the differences between boring and exciting outdoor recreations and discuss what constitutes "sport" in these activities.

Kilimanjaro

Jimmy Carter

Jimmy Carter, the thirty-ninth president of the United States, was born October 1, 1924 in Plains, Georgia. He graduated from the United States Naval Academy in 1946 and served in the Navy until 1953. In 1970, Carter was elected governor of Georgia, and as a young new governor he earned recognition for emphasizing ecology among his political concerns. Much of Carter's ecological and environmental understanding came from his childhood experiences of growing up on a farm. In his book An Outdoor Journal, *Carter recounts not only his childhood connections with nature but the ways those experiences affected his political policies and work in environmental politics. Since his tenure as president, Carter has remained an important and respected political figure. He continues to represent the United States in affairs of state, in peacekeeping missions, and as an observer of elections in other democratic nations. In 1984 Carter, along with his wife Rosalynn, became involved with Habitat for Humanity International, a nonprofit, nondenominational Christian housing organization that works to provide housing around the world to those in need. Carter has also been a successful author, writing critically acclaimed books like* An Outdoor Journal, *from which "Kilimanjaro" is taken;* Always a Reckoning And Other Poems, *Carter's first book of poetry;* Atlanta: The Right Kind of Courage; The Blood of Abraham; Keeping Faith: Memoirs of a President; Living Faith *and* The Little Baby Snoogle-Fleejer, *a children's book which Carter's daughter Amy illustrated. In the essay found here, "Kilimanjaro," Carter narrates a trip he and his family took to Tanzania in 1988 and their attempt to climb Mt. Kilimanjaro, the tallest mountain in Africa. As you read this essay, pay close attention to the relationship Carter describes between the mountain and the people climbing the mountain.*

JOURNAL ASSIGNMENT

In your journal, consider why the activity of writing one's name in a book atop the tallest mountain in Africa might be important to those who make the climb. What does such an act signify?

The Carter Center has health, agriculture, or peacekeeping projects in more than two dozen African nations. One of our most successful, the production of food grain, took us to Tanzania in 1986. During this visit we signed an accord with President Ali Hassan Mwinyi, agreeing to provide an expert agronomist, access to superior varieties of maize, and modest amounts of fertilizer. The government would furnish a number of agricultural extension workers and transportation for farm supplies, and it would pay most of the costs of the project.

2   Over the next five-year period, beginning in 1987, we worked with fifty thousand Tanzanian families who had small farms, each of which cultivated about two acres. Very few of the farmers had any oxen, and most used only hand tools, planting with pointed sticks and cultivating with hoes. Their average yields tripled, and during this time seven hundred extension workers were trained.

3   President Mwinyi had urged us to bring other members of our family to his country, visit some of the game parks, and perhaps attempt to climb Mount Kilimanjaro. I was the only one who had a favorable memory of our earlier Himalaya trek, so Rosalynn and I were reluctant to accept his invitation. However, when some of our children and grandchildren heard about the opportunity, there was a rapid kindling of interest in the excursion.

4   On one of our regular visits to East Africa in the summer of 1988 to assess our projects, we decided to set aside nine days to enjoy the hospitality of Tanzania. Our two oldest sons, Jack and Chip, Jack's wife, Judy, and our three oldest grandchildren, Jason, thirteen, James, eleven, and Sarah, nine, went with me and Rosalynn. A young staff assistant, Chris Mitchell, also joined our party. In addition to sleeping bags, binoculars, an altimeter, and guidebooks, we took our Frisbees. This was a favorite source of exercise and pleasure that was easy to carry, sailed beautifully at high altitudes, and had been a curiosity among the Sherpas in the Himalayas and the Tibetans at Lhasa, whom we had visited on one of our trips to China.

5   As we crossed the equator and headed south to Tanzania from Cairo, Egypt, we sighted Kilimanjaro in the distance, 180 miles away. A few minutes later, we circled the mountain and the adjacent Mount Mawenzi, flying at an altitude of twenty thousand feet, almost level with the mountain top. We were sobered by the snow, ice, small glaciers, and the steep approach to the crater that soared more than three and a half miles above the nearby sea. We were met at the Kilimanjaro International Airport by ministers of lands, natural resources, and tourism and driven to the Kibo Hotel in Moshi, near the base of the mountain. I noticed that the farm families along the way were producing thatching straw, coffee, bananas, papayas, and corn (most of which would not yield any more than five bushels per acre).

6   After supper with the officials and Maj. Gen. Mirisho Sarakikya, our expedition leader, we went to bed early, having flown almost twenty-four hours through eight time zones. The last thing we heard before retiring was a report to the minister of tourism that the porters had just arrived with the body of a Yugoslavian who had died of a heart attack while attempting to reach the top of the mountain.

Hours later, I heard Rosalynn's clock go off, and after a while she came out 7 of the bathroom, fully dressed, to waken me. "It's time to get up. Breakfast is scheduled for eight o'clock," she said. I looked at my watch and saw that it was only 1:30 A.M. She was delighted to realize that her clock, still on Georgia time, thought it was 7:00 P.M., which she read as A.M., and that now she could sleep six more hours.

We learned at a briefing the next morning that, along with two adjacent 8 volcanoes, Kilimanjaro had reached its maximum height about five hundred thousand years ago, during a time of intense volcanic activity in the region. Ever since its existence was first reported in Europe in 1849, more than two dozen expeditions had failed to reach the rim of the crater, with many climbers dying in the attempt. Malaria, attacks by natives, exposure, or the then-mysterious altitude sickness had all claimed victims. The first successful effort to reach the peak was in 1889 by a German explorer, Dr. Hans Meyer, who had to devote three full years to meet his great challenge. Our hosts were already planning for a ceremonial climb the following year to celebrate the hundredth anniversary of this achievement.

We were surprised to learn that the standard charge to a trekker for a guide 9 and three porters for five days was only $270, about the cost of a New York hotel room for one night. Each of us was issued a walking staff with a steel tip. When Rosalynn handed hers back, saying "I don't like to walk with a stick," the chief guide replied, "When you get near the top and sit down to rest, you may not be able to get back up without a staff." We were taught a few Kiswahili words: "haraka" means "speed up"; "asante" means "thank you"; "simama" means "stop"; "jambo" means "hello"—and the most important, "poli poli," means "very slow." This last phrase was to become a constant warning message when we were fresh and full of energy on the lowest slopes.

After driving a short distance to the park entrance, where the altitude is 10 about six thousand feet, we prepared to hike five hours to the Mandara huts, to an elevation of twenty-seven hundred meters (nine thousand feet). I taught the grandchildren to shift from meters to feet, dividing meters by three and adding a zero.

Each day after that, our plan was to hike six or seven hours, gaining about 11 three thousand feet in altitude. After Mandara, we would spend the next two nights at Horombo and Kibo. Then, if things went well, shortly after midnight we would leave this last rest stop and climb six hours to Gillman's Point on the crater's edge. After that it would take us a day and a half to descend from the peak, with an overnight stay in the Horombo huts.

Someone counted thirty-five people in our party, including our family, 12 some Tanzanian news reporters and photographers, government ministers and their aides, and our guides. In addition, a group of porters, whom we seldom saw except in camp, carried more than a ton of food, fuel, sleeping bags, photographic equipment, and other necessities. Tanzanian Elizabeth Charles would be Rosalynn's personal guide, and Abdallah Kondo would be mine. Both of them were also trained as security agents. They and the other guides stayed close to us, giving us a constant stream of advice and information about Kilimanjaro and its history.

13   The first day we wore boots while walking through a rain forest, where frequent afternoon showers sent mud and streams of water down the narrow trail. This day we were lucky, blessed with hot sun and sweat instead of rain and cold. During the rest stops throughout our climb, I dictated reports of events and observations into a small tape recorder. Listening to them now, the most impressive sound is my gasping for breath.

14   Even on the wide and only slightly inclined trail, we heard a regular chant of "poli poli." The guides were determined that we get into the habit of poking along, to conserve our energy for the coming four more days and the twelve-thousand-foot climb. One couple we met on their way down said they went up with three other groups, and every day the couple left first in the morning and arrived last at the next hut, while the others seemed to be in much better shape and moved more rapidly. This slow couple was the only one who made it to the crater. Chip expressed it well with a little song: "Go fast and you won't last; Go slow and you'll see snow."

15   After a couple of hours the path narrowed and steepened, and we had to use slick tree roots as handholds and steps. Rosalynn particularly enjoyed the brilliant wild sultana and begonia blossoms on vines, James and Sarah counted the blue monkeys, and Chip said it was like being in a Tarzan movie. Even at this low altitude, about seventy-five hundred feet, Judy and Jason were not feeling well. When asked, Jason said, "I'm not having a very good time."

16   After a little more then seven miles of steady uphill walking, we arrived at Mandara Camp. Most of our group wanted only to rest, but James and Sarah joined me on a thirty-minute climb to Maundi Crater, a beautiful little round volcanic cone. We walked all the way around its rim, from which we had a breathtaking panoramic view, including far into Kenya toward the north and east. Back in camp, there were pads for about sixty trekkers to sleep on in A-frame huts that were built by the Norwegian mountain climbers and Tanzanians in 1975. There was one dribbling faucet that provided enough water for brushing teeth and washing hands, which was about all the bathing we wanted to do in the cold weather. We had a good night's sleep and two adequate meals. Already, though, at only nine thousand feet, the food didn't taste quite right.

17   The next morning, Judy and Jason seriously considered turning back, but Jack finally persuaded them to try going on with us for a while. After a little exercise, they were soon feeling better. We had changed from boots to running shoes, since the climb would likely be dry and at a steady upward slope. The first hour was quite steep, up through the highest rain forest. Then, at about ten thousand feet, we had our first view of Mount Kilimanjaro, with its top hidden in clouds. We were surrounded by many different flowers in a lovely

meadowland, similar to scenes in the movie *Sound of Music*. Our guides knew both the common and Latin names of the flowers, pointing out gentians, buttercups, wild iris, gladiolus, a "red hot poker" (*Kniphofia thomsonii*), heather, and a species of protea that was especially beautiful. Everywhere, there was a strong smell of sage.

For most of the day, Judy walked behind me and held one end of my climbing stick. All of us welcomed our frequent rest stops, where we ate orange slices and trail mix and drank a lot of water. Rarely was it necessary during that afternoon for the guides to shout "poli poli." Beginning at 11,500 feet we began to pass giant lobelias (*Lobelia deckenii*), some nine feet high, which were endemic to this alpine slope. The only ones we saw blooming were in a burned-off area. There were a few bunches of yellow flowers at the ends of limbs and on the tops of the plants. Some of the porters gathered wood along the way for the supper fires, adding the sticks to the thirty-five-pound loads already on their heads or backs. The stronger ones carried more than twice this load. 18

After seven hours, eleven miles, and 3500 feet more altitude, we arrived at the Horombo huts, similar to those at Mandara but somewhat larger and twice as many, with sleeping pads for 120 people. We were now at 12,500 feet, about 3000 feet above cloud cover. A sparse forest of what the guides called giant senecios (*Senecio cottoni* and *S. kilimanjari*), some almost twenty feet high, stretched out to the east. Nearby was a small stream, the last source of clean water on the upward hike. We had a quick supper of oatmeal, dry cereal, fruits, boiled eggs, cheese, bread, and hot tea or bottled soft drinks and were in bed soon after dark, at seven o'clock. 19

This is where all of us should have rested for an extra day and become acclimated to the altitude. A break would have made the rest of the climb much easier. Everyone slept fairly well that night, though, except Judy, who decided not to go any farther. Instead, she would stay here, rest, read, explore a little, and wait for us to descend after our attempt to reach the top. This was August 7, Jason's birthday, and I realized that we were scheduled to reach the crater rim on a numerically special date: 8-8-88. At breakfast, we had a birthday party, with an inflatable plastic cake and thirteen candles. We had fun, but it was obvious to our chief guide that our celebration was rather forced and that none of us was particularly lively. He gave us a somewhat counterproductive pep talk, attempting to emphasize how well we had done. He said that only one in eight who begin the hike ever reach the crater rim at Gillman's Point, and most never even get to the Horombo huts; that Sir Edmund Hillary, the first man who climbed Mount Everest, was one of those who had to turn back on Kilimanjaro. Having noticed several indications of sickness, he said it was perfectly normal to have headaches, to be very tired, and to "throw out" every now and then. We thought his expression was more accurate than ours. 20

Typically, we would begin each cold morning by clutching and sipping a mug of hot coffee or tea, perhaps gathering around the small stove in the dining 21 area. Although even the best appetites faded away at higher altitudes, breakfast was the best meal of the day, with papaya, bananas, corn porridge (similar to grits), eggs, bread and jelly, and always either hot tea or coffee. We would then start hiking at eight o'clock, stopping every hour or so for a few slices of orange, dried fruits and nuts, and small candies. At all stops, we were urged to drink a lot of water or tea—more than we wanted—to avoid dehydration at the high altitude. At noon we had lunch on the trail: an orange, two small bananas, a hard-boiled egg, a meat sandwich with too much butter, and fresh tomatoes. We usually arrived at our destination in mid-afternoon, had a light snack, and slept for a couple of hours. Then we got up and ate supper, which was usually soup, a beef stew or some other kind of meat, boiled potatoes, and vegetables. After eating we would go to bed, sleep for about eleven hours, then start out again.

22   Each small hut at Mandara and Horombo was divided into two rooms, consisting of a small open space bordered by wooden pads that accommodated four sleeping bags. For the entire five days we never took off our clothes and only bathed in spots, sharing each morning a small pan of warm water brought by the porter who woke us. Toilets in most places were just slots in the ground, as they were in Nepal. Once we had the luxury of wooden seats like those in our outdoor privies. The waste from a row of them was carried away by water from a stream that came down from the mountain above us. On the trail, we soon became less sensitive about urinating, with men just turning away from the trail and women squatting behind a nearby rock, even when only small ones were available. After consuming maximum quantities of fluids all day, all of us had to get up some at night. No matter how cold it was, we soon decided wisely that it was best not to lie awake resisting the call of nature, but to go out in the cold, get it done, and quickly go back to sleep.

23   The heroes of our party were the three grandchildren. They led the group most of the time, after learning to walk slowly enough to accommodate the slowest adult. They never complained or fussed, but helped to keep everyone's spirits up. Even when the adults were lethargic, the young ones were still looking for games to play or questions to ask. We learned that no one under eleven years old had ever made it to Gillman's Point. We thought about Sarah and James holding a record.

24   After being dismayed by all the trash and garbage in the Mount Everest region in Nepal, it was a pleasant surprise to see how perfectly clean the trails were on Kilimanjaro. The guides and porters policed the area thoroughly, and all of us were instructed to use the round holes that were dug each day in the ground at halfway points for a small amount of degradable lunch trash, such as egg shells and fruit peelings. Other waste was carried away by the porters.

25   Despite the relatively steady slope, the climb was never easy. The third morning, as we paused to rest at Maua Mto (Flower River) not far above the Horombo huts, we all agreed that the ascent was much more difficult than we had anticipated. Jack was sure he couldn't make it beyond the highest huts at Kibo, still 3,000 feet above us, at 15,600 feet. As we plodded along, using our

walking staffs, most of what we saw were just the heels of the person ahead. Now when we stopped, there was little talking. We would urinate behind a nearby rock, find another one to sit on or lean against, take a drink, eat a handful of snacks, and try to relax all our muscles until the time came to shuffle on upward. At times we took some photographs, and I also accepted suggestions about what to dictate.

This day, the first five groups we met coming down had all failed to make it to Gillman's Point, on the crater's edge. Next came two experienced Japanese mountaineers, who said they had been successful. Most of the hikers had turned around at Kibo hut, but the next couple said they had climbed three more hours and had reached Han Meyer cave, halfway between Kibo and the crater. This was very discouraging. My guide told me that only ten out of one hundred received a certificate, signed by an official guide, for a successful climb to the crater's edge. Chris Mitchell had a terrible headache, but insisted on pressing upward. We put him in front, as the slowest one. When we stopped to rest, he said he couldn't sit down and then hope to get up again. Like an automaton, he lurched forward, carefully planting one foot in front of the other, barely moving his head, body, or arms, just clutching the neck of a water flask in his left hand. Slowly, inexorably, he never stopped until he got to Kibo hut, where he sat on his bunk, not able to put his head down.

When we first sighted Kibo's two rock buildings, all of us guessed how long it would take to reach them, and our estimates ranged from thirty minutes to an hour. It took seventy-five minutes. Approaching Kibo, Rosalynn said, "My muscles hurt, my knees are weak, my nose is bleeding, my head aches, but I'm still walking and feeling better this afternoon than this morning. I've been taking one thousand milligrams of diamox a day, and it must be working."

There was no vegetation at this altitude, above fifteen thousand feet, except a few lichens. At Kibo, in each of the large bunkrooms, there were thin mattresses under our bedrolls. As we prepared for a nap, I polled the crowd. Jason: "I feel wonderful!" James: "Wonderful!" Sarah: "Great!" Chip: "I feel good." Jack: "I have a headache, my feet hurt, my hands are cold, I have to get up at midnight, and I know I can't sleep." I was tired, sleepy, and not at all hungry. We had climbed for ten miles, up thirty-three hundred feet, and were now at the same altitude as Mount Blanc, the highest mountain in the European Alps.

That night General Sarakikya surprised us by announcing that we would have to divide into three groups for the climb to the top, depending on our speed. It was something like triage. He had been watching us closely, and he suggested that Chip and I be in group one, Jack and Chris in the second, and Rosalynn and the grandchildren in group three. Everyone finally agreed, but this later turned out to be a mistake because Rosalynn could have done much better if she had been with me.

Up at midnight, we tried to eat something, and then began climbing at 1:00 A.M. It was already snowing. Our pace seemed very slow, and I encouraged Jack and Chris to stay in the front group with us. Coming behind us with Rosalynn, the children had to stop and "throw out" every hundred yards or so—after two hours they went back to Kibo. Rosalynn pressed forward, but it took her four hours to reach Hans Meyer cave, at seventeen thousand feet. Moving comparatively fast, our group had stopped there for a brief rest after not much more than half that time.

31   The trail was too steep and the footing too loose for us to go anywhere near straight upward. Instead, we zigzagged slowly across the face of the loose pumice, or scree. The only trail was the slightly indented bed of small, flat, slippery rocks, which were somewhat discolored by previous footprints. This morning we all walked like zombies, taking small steps in the tracks of the person ahead, then sliding backward several inches. It was debilitating, both physically and psychologically—like walking up a slippery treadmill.

32   For the first time, the guides seemed to be pushing us to maintain speed. (Later, they told us that they knew worse weather was coming.) Our stops were extremely brief, and we never sat down, except for about ten minutes in Hans Meyer cave, which was just an overhanging rock. By 3:30 A.M., the accumulated snow made it difficult to see any path. General Sarakikya was in the lead, with me just behind. We stopped frequently, usually when someone had to throw up. I shone my small two-cell flashlight ahead, but it soon seemed to be made of lead. I became ever more thankful for the steadying effect of my walking stick with its steel point. It was a great relief to us when we eventually reached an altitude where there was enough permanent freezing to hold some of the scree together and permit longer zigzags.

33   Every so often, the general would give a high-pitched yell and then listen for a response from Rosalynn's guide. I couldn't hear anything, but he would say, "They're still coming." Finally, after a yell, he said, "They've turned back."

34   When we reached the rocks above the scree area, approaching eighteen thousand feet, the trail was much steeper and the stops were more frequent. It was snowing harder, with a strong wind blowing from the west. I felt weak and somewhat dizzy, but I was the only member of our party who never had headaches or nausea. Chris had made a miraculous recovery during the previous night and now plodded on with the rest of us. He said later that he didn't remember much of the climb. Several people turned back or stopped to await our return, including one of the government ministers and all the reporters and photographers except one.

35   When we began asking how much farther it was to the top, we became confused and somewhat aggravated. The first reply was "two hundred more meters." After climbing fifteen more minutes, the distance was still "one hundred and fifty meters." Finally, I asked the guide how far it was from Kibo hut to Gillman's Point, and he said, "one thousand meters." We finally realized that their measurements were the changes in altitude. Now that the path was nearly vertical, at least our total travel and the distance straight up were becoming almost the same.

Nearing the top, we stopped every (vertical) thirty feet or so. The rocks were 36
slippery with ice, and the snow concealed their exact shape. It was difficult to
know where to step or grasp a hold. I slipped once or twice, and bruised my left
hip. Our heavy mittens and Arctic parkas were good protection, though, both
from the cold and the sharp rocks.

Finally, I glimpsed the rod sticking up on Gillman's Point, with a piece of 37
flapping rag tied on it. After two more stops, we reached the top, sat down,
and looked for the sun, which at that time should have been just rising in the
east. We could only see the snow, clouds, and nearby rocks. There was a sign
that said "Gillman's Point, Altitude 18,640 feet." The swirling wind made the
snow intermittent, and once we glimpsed the moon.

We wanted to walk around the crater to Uhuru, the highest point, but the 38
general and our guides said that it would be too dangerous in the bad weather.
We couldn't see anything; the trails were covered with ice and new-fallen snow;
and even if we made it safely, it would take too long, perhaps four more hours
for the round trip. There was not much argument. We were dismayed to find
that our cameras were inoperative, but after warming them inside our parkas,
we finally got two of them to function and took some close-up photos in the
early morning light. Once, just for a few seconds, the snow and clouds blew
away enough for us to see down into the crater. After our fingers thawed out,
we scrawled our names in the logbook inside a waterproof metal box, dating
them 8-8-88. The pen beside the book was frozen, so we used mine, and I left it
in the box. Since leaving Kibo we had traveled about seven miles and climbed
thirty-three hundred feet. After fifteen minutes or so, we started back down.

Descending, we found the trail to be even more dangerous. When we had 39
climbed upward, our eyes could observe at close range where our next
footholds would be. Now it was difficult to see where our feet would be going,
and each fall we took was downhill, with much more momentum. The chief
guide and Abdallah Kondo stayed close to me. While still on the rocks, I threw
my Frisbee as far as I could, straight down the mountain. It sliced badly to the
right, leveled off, sailed over some rocks high above the trail, then curved left
and landed less than a foot from the main path, traveling an incredible distance. On the way down, Jack and I tried several more throws, then turned our
attention toward the Kibo huts.

When we got to the scree, we found that it was better to avoid the paths 40
we had made coming up so that our feet would not sink so deeply in the loose
footing. Chip and his guide began to lead the way, moving rapidly almost
straight down the mountain, and were soon out of sight. It was now bright
daylight, and less snow was falling. When we arrived at Kibo at 8:30, all the
porters, cooks, and guides were lined up to congratulate us, clapping their
hands and singing a song about Kilimanjaro.

Rosalynn had not returned to Kibo until 8:10, shortly before Chip got there. 41
She was already in her bunk asleep, but I woke her up to congratulate her and

to exchange reports on what we had done. She had reached 17,500 feet after an extremely slow climb for the first two hours, having to stay with the children, all of whom climbed above 16,000 feet. She explained that the two younger children had been nauseated and had thrown up every few steps, so after an hour she sent them back with a guide. Jason lasted for another half hour or so, then became too sick to continue. Rosalynn was also sick, but couldn't "throw out." Her ultimate goal became Hans Meyer cave, halfway up. After resting there, her group had a long discussion about what to do. With the guide urging her on and the security agent wanting to go back, she decided to continue upward. At first, she felt good and climbed for an hour or more. Then she could only go five or six steps without stopping to lean on her stick, nauseated. When she finally turned back, she said, it was "like sliding down a sawdust pile."

42   We slept for a couple of hours, then began to pack. Rosalynn asked what to do with the leftover diamox tablets. I said, "Throw them away. I've climbed my last mountain." She said, "Thank God." We then descended to the Horombo huts. It was easy and pleasant to walk through the saddle between Kilimanjaro and Mount Mawenzi, and it reminded us of the Yellow Brick Road in the *Wizard of Oz*. Everyone was in a great mood. Rosalynn and I began to talk about a return trip to Kilimanjaro with the younger grandchildren; we planned to go all the way to the highest point at Uhuru, or trek in the Annapurna region in Nepal. We decided to keep the diamox after all. Judy was feeling all right, and she was eager to hear what Sarah and Jason had done. We slept again, then had supper in the dining area with several other trekkers.

43   One businessman from New Jersey had gotten to Hans Meyer cave last year and was back to try for Gillman's Point again. He was spending an extra day at 12,500 feet to become better acclimated. Another, a college president with his bride, had lost his left leg and had severe curvature of the spine. He was determined to get to Kibo hut and to attempt to reach the crater.

44   While at Horombo, we received a radio message from Tanzanian President Mwinyi congratulating us and requesting that we come to Dar es Salaam so he could present certificates in person to those of us who had reached the top.

45   Even though we had really come down the mountain in a hurry, all of us realized now how tired we were. Rosalynn said, "I've still got on my same clothes and I haven't had a bath for five days. But I feel so bad, I don't even care. I just want to survive and move one foot at a time."

46   We had a hard job keeping up with the children, who led the way down. We walked eighteen miles the last day to the entry point, before lunch. It had rained, and the lower forest trail was difficult, muddy, and slick. We all agreed that the secret to success in climbing the mountain was "poli poli" the first two days. The last two days there was no temptation to move fast. Going from 5,000 to 18,600 feet in four days was much more rapid climbing than we had ever experienced in the Himilayas. We walked for twenty-seven hours going up Kilimanjaro, and it took us eleven more to come down. The entire round trip was sixty miles.

There was a throng to meet us at the entrance gate, with singing, hand-shakes, garlands of flowers for me and the boys, and bouquets for Sarah and the women. After driving to the nearby Kibo Hotel, we only had ten minutes before a late lunch, with all the dignitaries waiting. During this time I quickly washed my hair in the sink. After almost a week under the same hat, my hair felt like strings soaked in stale butter.

At lunch, I mentioned to Chip that I had left my pen on the mountaintop, and immediately the chief guide, who was sitting across the table, offered to send a porter up to retrieve it! Embarrassed by his offer, I replied that it was an honor for my pen to be used as long as it might last. Certificates were presented by our guides to all those who had climbed the mountain, with special ones to the small group who had reached the crater. We also received some gifts from the hotel manager, including our hiking sticks as souvenirs.

After lunch and the ceremony, we drove two hours to Mount Maru Hotel in Arusha, where we finally had a good bath and some rest. It was a very nice hotel, managed by a Tanzanian trained in Switzerland. The hotel staff offered us a fancy menu, but we voted unanimously for hamburgers. The rolls were tiny, the burgers huge, and each person was served a full bottle of catsup and chili sauce. It was a fine banquet!

The next morning, before leaving Tanzania, we began a journey on some of the worst roads I have ever seen. In just a few days, we visited Tarangire Lodge, Ngorongoro Crater, Olduvai Gorge, and Manyara Lodge, stopped at Masai vil-lages, and learned a lot about geology and paleontology. The adults and grand-children began counting the elephant, giraffe, gazelle, cape buffalo, baboons, and lions, but soon we were in a hot competition to sight new species, either birds or animals. A new sunbird became much more important than another ostrich or oryx. Since that time, six years ago, Rosalynn and I have become avid birdwatchers.

When our safari travels were over, we flew to Dar as Salaam, where Presi-dent Mwinyi presented our Kilimanjaro diplomas. He even stated, before the television cameras, that he planned to climb the mountain within the next year or two. Quickly, we taught him the important words, "poli poli."

FOCUS ON ECOLOGY

1. It is probably safe to say that the recreational activity of climbing Kiliman-jaro, is not an activity most American families would experience. Do we all have equal access to wilderness areas for purposes of recreation? Does it matter?
2. Did you notice, while reading "Kilimanjaro," how Carter points out not only the changes that they felt physically as the altitude increased but the way the topography and environment changed? What is the relationship between alti-tude and environment? What effect does the environment have on Carter and his family physically? How does altitude affect their bodies?

3. Why do you suppose Carter pays such close attention to the food that was consumed on this trip? Is food an important part of our outdoor recreation?

FOCUS ON WRITING

1. One of the characteristics of Carter's narrative is that it maintains a strict chronology. He starts at the beginning of the trip at the bottom of the mountain, marches us up the mountain, and then takes us back down again. There are no flashbacks, no predictions of what's to come. He does not set us up for surprise endings or twists. Why do you suppose Carter chose to depict the trip in such a way?
2. Is Carter a good storyteller? If so, what makes it a good story? If not, why isn't it a good story?
3. How much research do you suppose Carter had to do to write this essay? Is there information conveyed in this essay that he could not have learned simply by climbing Kilimanjaro with his family? If so, what effect does including information have on the essay? If not, are there points in the essay that might have been more interesting had more information been included?

FOR DISCUSSION

When you read "Kilimanjaro," a narrative about a famous, powerful man climbing a famous, powerful mountain, how do you respond to the drama of it all? Is this a story for a movie, something more than real, something grand? Or is this a story of a family on an outdoor adventure? As a class, consider what happens when we tell the stories of our outdoor experiences. De we aggrandize stories of wilderness activity more than other kinds of stories? Do we offer more description?

WRITING IN RESPONSE

Much of "Kilimanjaro" describes the trip as difficult, exhausting, and uncomfortable. While some people seek out these characteristics in their outdoor recreations and adventures, many more do not. In an argumentative essay, promote climbing Kilimanjaro as a family adventure.

Occurrence at Waimea Bay

Mark Foo

*As a young surfer, **Mark Foo** struggled to be recognized in the North Shore tournament series, but he had a difficult time breaking into the ranks of the top 50 surfers. Foo decided to set himself apart from other surfers by devoting his time specifically to big-wave surfing. He was also the first to promote himself as a surfer; that is, Mark Foo began to market himself and the surf industry. He earned a reputation as one of the premiere big-wave surfers for his surfing at Waimea Bay, but his fame grew when he became one of the first to conquer the massive waves at Maverick's on the California coast. Because of Foo's innovations, the annual big-wave tournament at Maverick's has become the premiere surfing event of the world. In 1994, Foo died while surfing the waves of Maverick's. "Occurrence at Waimea Bay" recounts the events of January 18, 1985, when a rapidly building surf at Waimea Bay put several surfers in danger.*

JOURNAL ASSIGNMENT

Surfers maintain a culture all their own with their own jargon, music, and philosophies. Many books have been written on surf culture, and it is often portrayed in contemporary movies like *Point Break* or *Fast Times at Ridgemont High*. In the past, surfing was culturally depicted in the songs of the Beach Boys or Jan and Dean or even in films like the Gidget movies as being the sport of good wholesome kids. In your journal, describe what you envision when you think of surfers, or the activity of surfing.

I awoke early on January 18, 1985, unaware that I had a date with destiny. My wake-up surf check revealed 12- to 15-foot waves, too big for anywhere except Waimea (which had been cooking consistently since the beginning of the year) but still not quite large enough to make the Bay break in traditional big wave form. The amazing thing about the Bay is it takes so much energy to make it show. Places like Sunset, Pipe, and Haleiwa will all be nothing but maxed-out, second-reef sets—and Waimea hardly dribbles. 1

By midday the surf met the 18- to 20-foot requirement to become "real" Waimea, and over the next two hours the swell continued to build into 25-foot sets firing at 20-minute intervals. Naturally, guys started to venture out: Ken Bradshaw (of course), Dick Asmus, and a couple of others paddled out in hopes 2 of riding traditional frill-size Bay, but the waves were breaking in an untraditional pattern. Due to the extreme west direction of the swell and the inordinate amount of sand in the Bay from a recent onshore storm, the waves were sucking and pitching like a shallow sandbar. It looked more like Inside Sunset or low-tide Backdoor, except it was massive Waimea—and the riptide was getting serious, too.

3   The surf continued to increase in both size and viciousness, intimidating everybody until they paddled to shore—all except Bradshaw, who got caught inside on a 30-foot set. He swam for his board but couldn't get to it before the rip pulled him into the danger zone. Knowing what to do, he swam back out all the way into the lineup and tried to stroke it in again; but again the rip pulled him toward the killer shorebreak and again Ken had to swim back out and around. It took three full cycles before he made it to safety. It was an impressive display of water knowledge and stamina—the kind necessary just to survive here. After seeing Bradshaw's ordeal, everyone thought thrice about going out except for James Jones, who paddled out just as Ken reached the beach.

4   At that point I was unaware of how serious the surf had become. I was on my way back from errands in Haleiwa and I saw there was no one out. I was just shaking the flu and had been in the water only once in the last ten days. I was far from being in the most prepared state, but Waimea was doing its thing and there was only one guy in the lineup. I wanted to get out there.

5   By the time I got down to the beach, James was already out and had been joined by bodyboarder J. P. Patterson. I finished my stretch just in time for a lull and hit it through the shorebreak without ever getting a good look at it—when there is an opening at big Waimea you have to make your move. Alec Cooke was right behind me. You usually feel a bit apprehensive paddling out at the Bay, so I always take a slow, extra-wide course to properly prepare myself for what's to come. Alec and I were both almost all the way out, but very much in the middle of the Bay when a wave came out of nowhere and cleaned us up. Leashes prevented both of us from swimming, and we soon joined J. P. and James in the lineup.

6   We all quickly realized that this was no ordinary big day. Most of the waves were too edgy to even consider. All four of us were sitting really wide in the channel, yet waves were jacking up and pitching in a place that normally would be considered the safety zone. Twenty-five-foot waves were breaking where 12-footers normally would and were unbelievably hollow and way too gnarly to ride. I picked up a couple of stock sets and started getting my sea legs back.

7   The interval between big sets lessened to under 10 minutes. Another set appeared, and one wave was a full-on 30 feet and had us all scratching up the face and looking into the pit of the beast. It was a moment I will never forget. The monster pitched up and out and turned into the biggest tube you could ever imagine. On other days at Waimea, Sunset, Pipeline, or Honolua, I've seen some big holes but nothing like this. It looked like a huge cavern with half the

ocean as its roof and sides. With so much power, the water no longer seemed liquid, rather solid and hard, like concrete. At that instant I came to realize that there was no way to ride such a wave, no matter how long a board, no matter how early you got in. There was just too much energy and moving water. The proportions were just far too large. We all made it over that mountainous wave stoked and awed. James told me how he took off on one like that on the morning of the '74 Smirnoff, got pitched, and almost died—and that he'd never do it again. He only half jokingly yelled, "Hey, Alec, if you had caught that one you would have had the record."

The set interval lessened to about five minutes, which meant the 25- to 8 30-foot waves were only the average ones and the big set waves would show up around every 20 minutes. I didn't know if it was that long, but another set popped up way outside and we headed out over a 20-footer.

Suddenly I could hear screaming from people on the point, but I still couldn't 9 see the next wave. I was the farthest over and inside and I just made it over the last wall to see this beast of a wave fill the entire horizon. I had been looking at waves in the 25- to 30-foot range, which were as big as I'd ever seen, but this thing or wave or tsunami was clearly twice as big as anything I had ever encountered. It was standing and feathering a good 200 yards outside, but the only thing I could see was a towering wall of water. No sky; nothing but this massive, angry wave. James, who saw it first, was already digging for the horizon, but there was no way he or any of us would be able to get far enough out, so I decided to bolt for the other side of the Bay, as far into the channel as possible. Of course, I didn't think that this wave would turn out to be a monstrous left that started peeling far, far outside and ended up breaking top to bottom all the way across the Bay. So there I was, having paddled right into the worst place possible. All the other guys were already diving for the bottom as the wave transformed into a thundering avalanche of whitewater—truly awesome. James later called it 48 feet. As far as I'm concerned you could have called it 50 or 60 or anything you wanted.

Bradshaw, who was standing on the beach with Waimea greats Gary 10 Spence, Owl Chapman, Charlie Walker, and Peter Cole, later said, "They're paddling over sets, like 25 to 30 feet, and then this rogue set comes in. And I'm just, 'Wow . . . look at this thing! It's giant!' We were calling this wave 45 feet, conservative. It could have been over 50—who knows. [Bradshaw later called it "the biggest wave surfers had ever encountered."] I'm jumping up and down on the beach, going, 'These guys are history!'"

As destiny or miracles would have it, my leash held. We all surfaced and 11 the other three started swimming. J. P., whose bodyboard leash snapped, asked me, "What kind of leash you got on, a chain?" I was too busy thinking about the next wave to respond.

The lifeguards called in the helicopter as soon as they saw this rogue wave 12 close out the bay. At this stage it was no longer possible to swim in through the rip or the shorebreak. James, with 15 years of big wave experience, didn't hesitate: The moment the chopper was overhead with its dangling basket, James was in it. Alec had just swum into serious trouble and was getting pulverized by the shorebreak. He was in the worst place on earth at that moment and looking like a goner. They kept dropping the basket for him, but there was too much turmoil and roiling water for him to reach it and more close-out sets kept rolling through. As Alec put it, "I was about to become hamburger on the rocks."

13   At last Alec was able to reach up and grab the bottom of the basket, which was all the pounding sets would allow. As they started pulling him out, another wave smashed into him, rocking the basket and the entire chopper. Heavy drama!

14   Meanwhile, J. P. had retrieved his board, but he still couldn't beat the rip. He lost his board again as more close-outs poured through and then got plucked out just after Alec.

15   They left me out there alone, surfing in closed-out Waimea. I realized the seriousness of the situation and my main objective was to get in. The sets just kept coming. I knew that the only way for me to get out of there was to ride a wave into the keyhole in the corner of the beach, and that was what I intended to do. I figured to try and paddle over the huge close-out sets and then try and shoot back into the normal lineup, trying to pick up a 20- or 25-foot in-betweener. The problem was that I couldn't get far enough in before another big set would show and I'd have to hightail it back out. This went on for two or three sets before the helicopter guys came to get me. I waved them off because I still figured I could ride one in.

16   With the helicopter hovering overhead and another big set approaching, I decided to stay inside and position myself to catch one of the set waves. I was way, way outside and in the middle of the bay as the first wave neared. It looked like a left and I made a serious effort to catch it. I changed my mind because it started sucking out and there was just too much water drawing off the bottom. I knew there was another one behind it, and I figured it would be breaking in deeper water after this first wave and give me a better shot at entry. My theory was correct. It backed off momentarily, long enough to take off and start driving. Then, again, the whole thing started sucking and turning concave. I was already at full speed, but I felt like I was going backward. I saw the free fall coming, but having made a couple free-fall takeoffs earlier in the month, I had the confidence to launch myself over the ledge of what looked like a moving cliff. Technically and mentally I kept it together as I feel-fell vertically a good 25 feet on my board. But the flight was too long and the wave too concave and I crashed upon contact with the wave face. The thing about Waimea is that you're going so fast with so much momentum and power that it's not like landing on water; it feels more like pavement. The worst part is, you bounce and skip, instead of penetrating the surface, leaving your body at the mercy of the wave, which usually results in a journey over the falls. This time I hit so hard I saw stars, then I started bouncing down the face as a good portion of the Pacific started to collapse on top of me. I felt the explosion of the lip; I heard my board snap like kindling; I felt my watch break away from my wrist and then felt my-

self get sucked up and over for another thrashing. Things turned pretty gray for the rest, and when I resurfaced the helicopter was waiting. I had given it my best shot. The bay was whitewater from end to end. I jumped into the basket for the ride home.

For all of us who lived through the experience, life and waves took on a   17
new perspective. I will never forget that monster tube or that monster closeout and especially that takeoff. I believe much more in destiny now. The series of timing, circumstance, and events that resulted in me being out there with the others, and then alone and surviving, makes me know it was meant to be for me, and telling the story is part of that fate. Thank God we're all still alive.

EPILOGUE

In the aftermath there has been much hoopla and controversy surrounding the question of who has ridden the largest wave ever. The answer? Nobody. Several men hold the record and have successfully made truly huge waves, the type you could safely call 30 or 35 feet. Now that I have seen even larger waves first-hand, I do not believe it is possible to ride them. There have only been rare times when such waves, the ones above all the rest, have even been seen, let alone at-tempted. Those waves remain in another realm . . . the Unridden Realm.

FOCUS ON ECOLOGY

1. Though this essay is primarily about the adventure of surfing at Waimea Bay, Foo also describes some important environmental characteristics of Waimea and the physics of waves. How do these descriptions play into his narrative? What do his descriptions of the waves suggest about his knowl-edge of the environment he enters as a surfer?
2. Foo writes, "For all of us who lived through the experience, life and waves took on a new perspective." Have you had a harrowing experience while participating in an outdoor activity? How did it change your perspective?
3. Why do people like Mark Foo and the others he mentions ride big waves?

FOCUS ON WRITING

1. Throughout this essay, Foo refers to traditional surf locations as though they should be familiar to all readers. Yet for many of us, these names are not fa-miliar. As you read this essay, how did you respond to reading these names? What is Foo conveying about places by naming them as places with which he expects his readers to be familiar?
2. Notice that Foo has included an epilogue in his essay that does not deal specifically with the occurrence at Waimea Bay. Why do you suppose Foo includes this epilogue? How does it affect the essay?

3. How did you respond to Foo's descriptions? Would you consider this a descriptive essay? Why or why not?

FOR DISCUSSION

As a class, discuss your responses to Foo's essay. Consider how he represents the relationship between the participants in the activity of surfing during this rather frightening day and the environment they enter to surf.

WRITING IN RESPONSE

In a research report, discuss the history of surfing. Consider not only the culture of surfing, its music, literature, and customs, but also look at the ways surfers talk and write about the very waters in which they surf. If you surf, you may want to use this short research paper to teach others about your sport/hobby/way of life.

From *Caught Inside*

Daniel Duane

Daniel Duane is known as a "Generation X" writer and has even been called a spokesperson for that group. He writes most about surfing and mountain climbing, and his writing describes those activities in exciting detail. Duane, who was born in Berkeley, California, in 1967, attended Cornell University, but upon graduating, he resisted cultural pressures to join the typical 9-to-5 workforce and instead took a job in his hometown in an outdoor outfitters store. Together with his father and uncle, Duane climbed one of the most challenging mountains in the Sierra Nevadas: El Capitan. Drawing on his experiences while training for and making this climb, Duane wrote his first book, Lighting Out: A Vision of California and the Mountains. *For a while, Duane attended graduate school at the University of California, Santa Cruz. While in California, Duane immersed himself in local surfing culture and wrote a magnificent book called* Caught Inside: A Surfer's Year on the California Coast, *the source of the selection reprinted here. He has written several other books, including one he co-authored with Matt Warshaw called* Maverick's: The Story of Big-Wave Surfing. *In the selection found here, taken from* Caught Inside, *Duane describes a day's surfing with his friend Skinny.*

JOURNAL ASSIGNMENT

In this selection from Duane's *Caught Inside,* the narrator (Duane) and his buddy Skinny spend a good deal of time searching for the right waves. In many ways this quest is a search to match the waves with their mood of the day. That is, they want to surf the way they feel. In your journal, write about this relationship between feelings, mood, and outdoor recreation. How do the two affect one another?

The wave, ruler-edged in the bright winter dawn, feathered ahead as I flew; cold, wet speed as the lip thinned to ten yards of spray, ready to break. Two toes off the tip trimming toward that shaking fringe, then carving high and, just as the whole wave leapt forward, soaring along the breaking back. And, in that instant's tableau—a telescopic view down a glimmering glass wall below a snowcapped green mountain and a morning rainbow—I became airborne just as a truly enormous dolphin (perhaps nine feet long) exploded from the wave ahead, its shining gray body for a moment in flight. We both hung in the rising sun long enough for me to shout out loud in astonishment and lose all balance, tumble into the foam as the dolphin speared the surface and vanished. I bobbed about on my back, stared at the dark blue sky and tried to think of a God to whom I might say thanks.

But such moments are a dime a dozen in a life by the water, and serve mostly to deflate the day's anxieties. Which was just as well, because as I stripped off the rubber at this secluded longboarding break, Skinny pulled his truck over for a chat, smiled, shook hands, and we swapped details about where we'd been surfing. We made plans for the next morning that led to yet another hello from the man in the gray fish-leather suit. Skinny certainly shuffled through the seasonal shift in surf spots, and since I hadn't seen him since the muddy-socks debacle, I was happy to catch up. He'd absolutely sworn off the Point, but was happy to take me on a search farther afield; and he made good company, with just the right irony around his relentless surfer chatter to make it more pleasant than ridiculous. I'd finally improved sufficiently to avoid embarrassing either of us—all that time at the Point without competition for resources. The next morning, the air fifty-five degrees in predawn light, Skinny worked through a power breakfast of four Advil, a cup of coffee, and an Indica bong hit while that feline grin of his split his tanned face under black sunglasses.

"Sooooo," he said, exhaling, "good morning, my son. Where we go?"

Sun not yet up, high clouds in the eastern sky reddening with the dawn, he sat in the open door of his tiny trailer and cracked his knuckles. Slipped his toes into worn-out flip-flops. Sipped at the coffee.

"Sharkenport?" he asked. "Shark's creek? Lane? Oooooooh. Indicator's, ya?" I finally got a glimpse inside that trailer, saw more or less what you'd expect:

clothes everywhere, a mattress filling most of it, walls papered with cutouts from surf magazines, particularly the ubiquitous islander-woman-in-thong-bikini. We drove fifteen miles north to check his favorite spot—a remote beach also favored for male-male trysts-in-the-trees.

"No good," Skinny said. "Seen it better. See that little morning sickness bump?"

Didn't, but didn't argue. Where to? Ortegas?

"The Lane could be sick." So, about-face and back to town, sun now rising over the Gabilan Mountains, two women in black tights jogging the side-walk . . .

"Dude," Skinny said suddenly.

Yeah?

"If we're surfing the Lane together, you gotta be cool."

Howzat?

"You just get aggro. Like, I don't want to be associated with you, necessarily. I mean, just don't hoot and shit, all right? Don't hoot at me."

Ever? Why the hell not? Had he heard about my day with the kayaker? My explosion at Apollo?

"It's just," he said, "you got to keep a low profile. I don't think you realize." Skinny surfed crowded breaks, generally speaking, which means he surfed breaks with well-established local pecking orders. And as a guy who spent much of his energy dodging the world's imaginary blows and avoiding per-ceived grudges, he'd never fought his way into those pecking orders—just accepted his peripheral caste in the surf world.

A little rubber shark lay on the dashboard. Its mouth was all teeth. While he rattled off the breaks we were passing—Chicos, Fresnos, Gas Chambers, Electric Chairs—I staged upward surges on my finger from the deep, imagined the angle of approach that would get that mouth high enough to hit a surfer. The little rubber toy dangled tenaciously off my finger.

At Steamer Lane, cars and trucks already gathering: carpenters, roofers and painters, doctors, lawyers and professors, all having a look before work, sipping coffee, windows up against the cold. A railing separated the sidewalk from the cliff along which the waves peeled. In the diffuse light, sun still behind clouds, someone tore along a clean green wall, breezing along in the dawn—looked great.

"Don't think so."

Huh?

"It's lost the sand it had over the reef last spring, racetrack's not lining. I want zip today. High performance. Something I can slam."

Wherezit?

"Ooooooh, don't know. Need something I can shrack, you know? Like that feeling when you just blow, like the whole . . ."—he gritted his teeth, looked tense—"the whole, fucking lip off the entire, just, you know, separate . . . like remove . . . literally, the whole top of the wave?

How about surfing Cowdoodies? A ripping left beach-break that required a hike over pasture.

"Local scene's too heavy."

"Nobody's ever there."

"But you still don't want them to catch you out there—those guys took a dump in my buddy's pack."

Protected plover habitat anyway—little sand-nesting birds.

Skinny, Skinny, Skinny. He'd been at Berkeley High School just before me, in the late seventies and early eighties. Basketball, weight lifting, petty theft, and green buds. Lots of black speech inflections—the hometown idiom. Dad a poverty lawyer, brothers going the same route. Skinny was hiding out. Even Berkeley'd gotten too heavy: no waves, for one thing, but also too many enemies. With a fierce little-guy complex, he'd fought his way through twelve grades. Still did a hundred daily push-ups and sit-ups.

"To stay in shape for surfing?" I'd asked.

"Nah," he'd said with admirable irony. "I figured out early I was a shrimp, so I figured I'd be a huge shrimp." And he was.

"Look, let's just rush it," I said, looking down at Steamer Lane, hoping Apollo had an early math class. "Looks killer! Totally surfable. Little inside nuggets doing the shuffle, maybe a big drop or two outside."

"Dude, look how many guys are out. Fuckin', probably be all the local heavies: Floater Brothers, Slacker Brothers, Peepee, Batboy . . . " Two guys with wafer-thin boards scrambled down a concrete stairway to the water.

"Don't let 'em faze you, dude," I said. "Just do your thing."

"It ain't like that." He looked pained by my ignorance. "But where're we going to surf?"

"The Point?"

"Read my lips. I DO NOT SURF THE POINT. Boring and lame. HP. High Performance. That's what's needed."

The Steamer Lane lifers were starting to show up, guys with reputations for spending their disability checks on beer and whole days screaming obscenities at the action in the water. They'd obviously known each other much of their lives, gathered daily on that cliff like farmers coming in to market—mostly for the joy of bullshitting in a pretty place.

Then it struck Skinny.

"Ooooooh," he said, "see way in the middle of the bay? The Dunes, buya! See those two smokestacks?"

Against the agricultural haze of the Salinas Valley hung two thin lines of smoke.

"Which way's the smoke going?" He asked this quickly, quizzing.

Uuuuuh . . .

"Offshore. Let's go. It'll be shacking."

"Shacking?"

"Green rooms, shelter sheds," he said with a smile, loving the talk. "You know, tubulation."

But . . . but . . . we'd already wasted an hour and a half . . . tide coming up . . . the Dunes a solid forty minutes away.

"You want speed or not?"

Unbelievable. I really took that shark at my finger while we tore south through the beach towns of Capitola, Aptos, then Salinas Valley farmland, Steinbeck country—surfer as existential wanderer consumed by angst. I mean, life on the road, following the waves—it's all a load of fun, but this driving and indecision and compromising, not to mention this dereliction of worldly obligation . . . although, if there were indeed barrels, I mean, I'd been *dreaming* of tubes lately. Usually, my dreams were collages of anxieties and memories, but surfing inspired wish-fulfillment fantasies in which I launched aerials at will, took off on gargantuan, open-ocean monsters with ease. And the night before, in fact, the shimmering blue sheet of the wave's lip started to throw over me and, instead of straightening out and fleeing, I ducked under. Suddenly, I was in a sparkling, roaring cave, a palimpsest of all the tube-ride photos I'd ever seen. As I shot out unhurt, a Hawaiian surfer in a yellow neoprene tank top—and he was an important part of the dream—made smiling eye contact with me; I stuck out my tongue in stoke and thought, in the dream, "That guy has no idea what just happened to me. He doesn't realize that was my first legitimate tube ride." Tube riding is counterintuitive, except on the most perfect of waves. You're shooting along, you see the wave "go square"—lurching over to break so hard the lip throws out well past the bottom of the wave—and instinct demands getting the hell out of the way. In photographs it always looks like that most peaceful of places, the ultimate mellow; but really, it's the eye of the storm.

Small highway, farms, somebody's kooky castle with a fake train engine in the front yard. Skinny said the Dunes faced due west toward this gargantuan underwater canyon, so northwest swell got less watering down by continental shelf than outside the bay. Then he brought up our mutual acquaintance Orin—now rumored to have a hundred thousand dollars in the bank from those three years in New York.

"I'm not sure I'd trade for a hundred gees," Skinny said. "I don't know. Maybe I would. But . . . ten years of surfing? Nah. No way. Yeah. No way would I trade." Skinny's girlfriend had been worried about him, thought he ought to get a life. His guru at the local baseball-card store told him just to let her know he was capable of physical violence—solve everything. Hadn't worked. Parents? Simpatico: Oregon Summer Trail crew didn't wash.

"I told them I'd *love* to get a career going," he said, "and I really would, but the problem is, and I told them, I'm really busy surfing. I don't have time. And, anyway, I told them, like, I've accomplished a lot. I mean, shit, I can surf! That ain't easy. People don't realize that." Making the summer's earnings stretch, he never ate out, ever. Not even a bagel. Never a burrito. A true ascetic, though a patently unspiritual one. He'd even salvaged his TV from a friend's garbage pile. "And my girlfriend's moving to Hawaii to teach," Skinny said. "It'd be so killer to get back over there. She'd have like her own place where I could stay, probably no rent. I think she wants to get married, but shit, she says I'd have to get a job. I've got the money to go and everything, and it sounds killer to be in the islands with her, but I'm thinking, damn, for the same amount I could get a new board and wetsuit."

Past beautiful farms in the alluvial plains of the inner bay, Skinny talked recession, how the guys in the high-school class before us got in on the economy before it soured. "After our year," he said, "I swear it all dried up—no jobs." Affirmative action, he explained, kept the Forest Service from hiring white men more than part-time. They laid him off each fall, rehired him each summer. "And that's my chosen career," he said, shaking his head and watching a semi pass on the right, "so I'm screwed. That's it. Twenty-eight years old, and it's over. There's honestly nothing for me to do nine months out of the year but surf and collect unemployment."

When we got to the Dunes, a harbor seal splashed in the lagoon, and broad Ekhorn Slough—a sort of swampy river of lush bottom land—wound back inland with its rusty grasses now turning quite green. A few pickups were parked where a trail led up the dunes. Skinny parked about fifty yards away.

"Why the hike?" I asked.

"Locals Only parking up there. Trust me. And don't go dropping in on anybody."

The sand path was riprapped with dowels; about twenty yards up, we got a view: from a harbor jetty, the beach stretched clear north to Santa Cruz and there were peaks everywhere, shoulder to head-high and peeling very, very quickly. Just offshore bobbed a ring of white buoys marking the border of the Monterey Bay Canyon, a colossal, submerged rift every bit as big as the Grand and of unclear origin. (Three rivers emptying into the bay—and more or less matching arms of the canyon—suggested old river gorges, like the Colorado's. But lately the theory had been that it was cataclysmic in origin, a function of shifting tectonic plates.) Regardless, deep water unsettles, and the proximity of profoundly deep water unsettles more—one heard of enormous, amorphous life forms populating its lightless depths, vast, drifting jellyfish. We jogged up the beach, boards in arms, and swarms of little sanderlings scurried in and out with the ebbing and flowing foam, legs too skinny to be visible, their bodies appearing to float about like fish. Farther along, near the peak we'd chosen, another swarm flew in the breeze—dark on top, white below, and flying in such tight formation that when they banked as a group, their white underfeathers flashed like a school of tropical fish catching the sun. As we paddled out, three seals took a good long look from about ten feet away. Then one went under and swam right toward us. A creepy feeling: you realize your mobility is in two dimensions, a slug in a field of snakes.

Beach-break peaks shift as sandbars flow with swell and tide; very unlike a reef break, where you always wait over the same submerged stone. We paddled left, then right, then outside, and the waves had an exquisite uniformity to their peel—also unlike reef waves, since even the most symmetrical of local rock reefs suck out here or mush there as the depth changes. But sand under water settles into smooth, organized form, like a denser liquid within a liquid. Skinny kept hooting at me to "pull in," to duck under the heaving sections and go for coverage. At first I just couldn't find the tube, or bring myself to get in its way. But then Skinny screamed at me to go late on an overhead peak, to stand up just as it broke. I took off at an angle, and as the wave screamed right, I got the oddest feeling that the light around me had changed, perhaps even that time had slowed, and then I'd been double-flipped and body-slammed onto the sand bottom. Came up coughing, but thrilled—tried again and again and started to understand; I never made it out of a tube, but each time I ducked under, I got that same peculiar phase-shift sensation. Waves are, after all, forms moving through mass, bundles of energy expressed as curves: when a curve can't maintain shape because of a shoaling sandbar, its energy bunches higher and tighter until it reaches up over itself, remaking the wave form by pushing water out to close the curve; expressing the original arc, but with a hollow, spinning core. In which the surfer stands. The climber never quite penetrates the mountain, the hiker remains trapped in the visual prison, but the surfer physically penetrates the heart of the ocean's energy—and this is in *no sense* sentimentality—stands wet in its substance, pushed by its drive inside the kinetic vortex. Even riding a river, one rides a medium itself moved by gravity, likewise with a sailboard or on skis. Until someone figures out how to ride sound or light, surfing will remain the only way to ride energy.

Then a very big guy—he looked like James Dean on steroids—paddled near and, with great effort not to sound patronizing, asked if I'd like a tube-riding tip.

"Absolutely," I answered.

"Keep your eyes open." He laughed out loud with me, then introduced himself in a warm, vulnerable way quite at odds with his commandolike appearance. He explained that he'd just moved to the area from down south. "You know what?" he said, smiling again.

"What?"

"I'm so stoked, dude." He had a square-cut jaw and perfect teeth.

"Why?"

"Dude. I'm stoked. Because, just being here in Santa Cruz, I can tell I'm turning a corner. I can tell it's going to change."

"What is?" We'd drifted closer together, both sitting on our boards.

"Just the whole way I've been living."

"How you been living?" I asked.

"Oh dude. Just not dealing. Not doing school. I was really good in school, too. I'm going to be a doctor."

"An M.D.?"

"Yeah. I'm really good at that stuff. I'm going to go to Community College for a couple of years, then to UC and get my shit together. Then go to medical school. Five years and I'll be done and I'll be stoked!" He giggled at the thought as though it were a dead certainty, as though saying it could make it true, in advance. And perhaps it could. He told me his sister had inspired him to come up here. She just had her shit together, that's all. A geography teacher in Florida now, she'd gotten the hell out of southern California. He said it was going to be *so* great supporting just himself.

"How do you mean?"

"My dad's just like lost everything," he said, lying down on his board to paddle toward a set. His arms were comically muscular, with bricklike triceps. The waves didn't materialize, and he sat up again. "Dad's just a mess," he said. "It's like all he does is watch TV and sit on the couch. He freaks me out. It like kind of grosses me out how he just like gave up on everything. He doesn't even go looking for a job and I've been paying his rent. That's why I had to drop out of junior college down south. So I could do construction full-time to pay for my dad's life too." Then his face turned from upbeat denial to a downcast admission of his own role in it all; he said he hadn't been doing all that well in school anyway—got real distracted. "I'd go to the library to study," he said. "Honestly, but then I'd get into studying my own thing and spend *five hours* in the library just reading. Reading whatever books looked cool. But I did pretty badly in my classes."

He spun and took off on a hollow, spinning right, ducked into its tube with fearless poise, and then I saw a big fin surface directly before me, held up by a long gray body. Even as I converted the sight into terror, three more fins appeared and they all turned enough for their raked curves to be visible: dolphins. Then three more, and two more after that—a parade left and right, behind and before, watery-slick and so humanoid in size. A small wave rolled toward me with three warping dark forms submerged inside it, dolphins giving us all a show by riding the constant pressure surfaces deep inside. And one shot along a perfect wall (dolphins, by the way, *only* ride the good set waves) toward the crowd, only high enough for the top inch of its dorsal fin to break the surface and draw a speeding, razorlike line across the wave. Then wave and rider passed under me; I turned to watch the rolling water's back, and suddenly that six-foot body erupted into the air above, scattering golden drops before the sun . . . Showing off? Oblivious?

"Dude," Skinny said, paddling near, "be cool, all right?"

Huh?

"Those guys are giving you stink-eye."

Who?

"Locals over there. Talking a little shit about you."

Four more dolphins, with something even and paced about their fins arcing into the air and down again, like the inexorable sine curve of the swell.

"Dude," Skinny said, intent, looking furtively over his shoulder, "remember as long as we live, we're kooks 'cause we're not really from here."

FOCUS ON ECOLOGY

1. In this selection, Skinny doesn't want to surf at several locations because of the crowds at those places. Often, other people at a location affect how we interact with that place. When engaging in outdoor recreation, do you like crowds or solitude? Do you avoid places because of crowds? Why or why not?
2. How do you respond when Skinny explains that he can't get a career going because he's "really busy surfing"? How do you respond to people in general who have given their lives over to surfing, rock climbing, river rafting, fishing, or any other of the many outdoor recreations that seem to have followers who do nothing but pursue those activities? Would you like to devote your life to any one particular outdoor recreation? If so, which one? If not, why not?
3. What is the role of the "local" in this selection? Do locals have particular rights to places that visitors do not? How do locals in your area or in places you visit seem to view others who visit places local to them?

FOCUS ON WRITING

1. To what does Duane refer when he talks about part of the California coast as "Steinbeck country"?
2. Looking at the moments when Duane is describing the natural environment versus the moments when he is describing Skinny, how would you characterize Duane's use of description? Do you "see" the environment more than you "see" Skinny?
3. Look back at the language Duane uses to recount the dialogue of Skinny and others in this selection. Do you "hear" their voices? How does the written word convey these voices?

FOR DISCUSSION

Is Skinny's devotion to surfing a good thing or a bad thing? Do you know anyone like Skinny? As a class, consider how we as a culture view people like Skinny, people who have refused to "play by the rules" and get a job, but instead have devoted their lives to their passions.

WRITING IN RESPONSE

In one of the most beautiful passages of this selection, Duane writes: "Waves are, after all, forms moving through mass, bundles of energy expressed as curves: when a curve can't maintain shape because of a shoaling sandbar, its energy bunches higher and tighter until it reaches up over itself, remaking the wave form by pushing water out to close the curve; expressing the original arc, but with a hollow, spinning core. In which the surfer stands." Short descriptions like this one can sometimes more vividly describe an event, a moment, a phenomenon, a wave better than pages and pages of description. Select a particular activity, a particular natural event, place, moment, and in a short descriptive paragraph, describe in detail that place or event.

Trekking Tropical Trails

Stephen Gorman

Paddling a Watery Wilderness

James Campbell

Gliding through the Glades

Don Stap

These three selections are about recreational activity in Florida's Everglades, one of the most unique ecosystems on the planet. I have grouped these three readings together because they address a singular setting but discuss three different ways to engage that same place through recreation: hiking, canoeing, and biking. The three articles were originally published, as they are here, together in the July–August 2001 issue of Audubon Magazine, *which caters to environmentally conscious readers who often seek out encounters in wilderness areas. As you read these three short pieces, consider why* Audubon *might publish articles like these about hiking, canoeing, and biking rather than three articles about say, fishing, hunting, and air-boating.*

JOURNAL ASSIGNMENT

The three short pieces found here address what we might call "low-impact" activities, activities that don't have much of an effect on the environments in which they take place. In your journal, create lists of activities that might be considered low-impact and activities that might be considered higher impact.

Then write about what differences you see in these two lists. Which activities would you rather participate in? Why?

TREKKING TROPICAL TRAILS

1   Just beyond the northern boundary of Everglades National Park lies a vast, primordial swamp of dwarf pond cypresses and slash pine islands, of hardwood hammocks and wet prairies, of sawgrass marshes and mangrove forests. Here, in Big Cypress National Preserve, 700-year-old great cypresses somehow escaped the loggers' blades; blooming air plants perch on tropical hardwoods like flocks of strange birds at rest; and alligators slip into the dark pools of backwater sloughs.

2   These sights await the adventurous hikers who set out on the Florida Trail—a national scenic trail that will eventually stretch 1,300 miles to Gulf Islands National Seashore, on the western edge of Florida. Thirty-eight miles of the trail are in the preserve, and hiking this singular footpath is a chance to immerse yourself in the splendor of the tropical wilderness.

3   Once home to the Seminole Indians, whose reservation lies just to the north, Big Cypress National Preserve acts as a buffer between the fragile ecosystem of Everglades National Park and the land development sweeping unchecked across South Florida. But the preserve, which was established in 1974, not only protects the park from human sprawl, it provides the Everglades with its lifeblood. With a gradient of a scant two inches per mile all the way to the Gulf of Mexico, the vast sheet of water spreading through the preserve releases a gradual flow of nutrient-rich fresh water into the national park.

4   Today both ecologists and recreationists acclaim Big Cypress as a natural gem in its own right. The preserve's vast, swampy reaches are critical habitat for a rich and diverse wildlife community that includes alligators, black bears, white-tailed deer, and West Indian manatees. The endangered wood stork, the snail kite, and the red-cockaded woodpecker also find sanctuary in these 729,000 protected acres. Several Florida panthers, which now number fewer than 50, prowl behind the preserve's veil of Spanish moss and saw palmettos.

5   After a long day on the trail, you set up camp among the live oaks on a small hump of land, change into dry footwear, and relax. Stars glitter through the tangled branches overhead. Somewhere nearby, a bobcat's scream tears through the night, and you sit bolt upright. But when your heartbeat returns to normal, you smile, flushed with exhilaration—the lifting of the spirit that is the true gift of this wild and ancient place.

PADDLING A WATERY WILDERNESS

1   The sun is bright and warm, and I'm floating in my canoe a few hours into the first of eight blissful days on the Everglades' Wilderness Waterway. Two voracious mosquitoes are filling up on my left forearm, but when I think about the

cold, gray skies of Chicago back home, I don't even care. I'm here to fish, loaf, and linger. In my backpack is Peter Matthiessen's evocative *Killing Mister Watson,* which is set in this tropical maze of mangrove islands and murky, tannin-stained waters. No less important is my supply of fresh water—enough, it would seem, to hydrate the entire Florida Coast Guard—and, for when the thrill of being in Florida in January wears off, bug spray.

Despite my charts and the occasional trail marker, narrow channels wander 2 off in every direction, and I'm left guessing at my route. There are no landmarks to assist me, so I keep the sun to my left and hope for the best. The Wilderness Waterway is a wild, 99-mile route that winds along the western edge of Everglades National Park, from Everglades City in the north to Flamingo at Florida's southern tip. It is neither ocean nor river but a hybrid of the two. Here, salt water from the Gulf of Mexico melds with the sweet-water sheet that flows southwest through Everglades National Park from Lake Okeechobee.

To early European explorers, this land was so formidable that they told 3 fantastical tales of prowling saber-toothed tigers. Today, looking around, it appears that little has changed in the intervening years. *Prehistoric* is the word that comes to mind. Through much of South Florida has been dammed, diked, drained, and diverted, I am in a postdiluvian world of water and wildlife. I round a bend and snowy egrets and white ibis erupt from the branches of a tree in the kind of sky-darkening flock that isn't supposed to exist anymore. An alligator slithers by a little too close for comfort. And high-flying ospreys catch waves of wind and wait for lunch.

Four days into my trip, I hit high tide between the Lostman's River and the 4 Shark River, and I'm spared the cruelties of a section called "the Nightmare." Had it been low tide, I might have been stranded here, run aground among muck and mosquitoes. But luck is with me, as it has been the entire trip. Now, halfway through my adventure, I've encountered only a lone fisherman, casting for redfish. I wanted wilderness, and the waterway obliged.

GLIDING THROUGH THE GLADES

Shortly before dawn I set out, heading west down a woodland trail. Within 1 moments, the pine forest fills with birdsong and the first light of day. This is Everglades National Park, and I am not exploring on foot. I'm riding a bike.

Biking can be an intimate way to experience the landscape and wildlife of 2 the nation's most famous wetlands. It's also a good way to escape the crowds. Several areas of the park are open to bicycles, including 14 miles of nature trails on Long Pine Key, the site of my own early-morning jaunt.

This area's main trail, approximately five miles west of the Ernest F. Coe 3 Visitor Center, is two wheel ruts cut into the limestone bedrock—an old access road created before the national park was established, in 1947. It winds through the shady pinewoods and intersects several paths that can be explored on foot. Dominated by slash pines and with an understory of more than 200 species of subtropical plants, the uplands habitat is the most diverse in the park. The scenery is wonderfully strange. Florida's limestone bedrock is exposed throughout much of the area, and the forest appears to be growing out of the floor of an ancient ocean—which is exactly the case.

4   To experience the essence of the Everglades, visitors can also ride a 15-mile paved loop road that starts at the Shark Valley Visitor Center, or explore the Old Ingraham Highway near the Royal Palm Visitor Center, a 22-mile round-trip ride. Both go through a freshwater marsh whose expanse of sawgrass stretches for miles in every direction. The Shark Valley loop offers easy riding, an observation tower at its midpoint, and the possibility of seeing alligators—oblivious to bikers—basking within feet of the path. It also attracts more people than the other bike trails, and many of them take the two-hour narrated tram ride that uses the same road.

5   On the Old Ingraham Highway, I was met with only the soughing of the wind through the sawgrass and the cries of red-shouldered hawks. From time to time I would pause to walk, but whenever I climbed back on my bike I realized once more the beauty of traveling this way: The pure, physical sensation of gliding forward gracefully through the landscape brought me ever closer to what that red-shouldered hawk must have felt as it soared above.

FOCUS ON ECOLOGY

1. In "Trekking Tropical Trails," Stephen Gorman writes, "Hiking this singular footpath is a chance to immerse yourself in the splendor of the tropical wilderness." How does hiking allow for immersion in wilderness in ways other recreations do not? Does hiking limit you in any way?

2. In "Paddling a Watery Wilderness," James Campbell not only describes his canoe trip through the Everglades and the Wilderness Waterway, but he does so making reference to specific geographical locations: the Gulf of Mexico, Flamingo, Everglades City, Lake Okeechobee, Lostman's River, Shark River. Do you know where these places are? Do you need to know to understand Campbell's trip? What role do specific places play in an essay like this, in our reading of an essay like this?

3. Don Stap writes in "Gliding through the Glades," "Biking can be an intimate way to experience the landscape and wildlife of the nation's most famous wetlands." What do you suppose Stap means by intimate? Have you ever had an intimate view of landscape or other facet of nature or environment? How would you describe that experience?

FOCUS ON WRITING

1. Each of these three pieces makes use of alliteration—the same initial sound in two or more words in a given phrase—in their titles: "Trekking Tropic

Trails," "Paddling a Watery Wilderness," and "Gliding through the Glades." Keeping in mind that these three essays were originally published together, why do you suppose they were titled this way?

2. In "Paddling a Watery Wilderness," James Campbell writes, "*Prehistoric* is the word that comes to mind" in describing the Everglades. Why might he have selected it as the single word with which to sum up his description? Would other words have worked as well? Pick a local area where you have spent time and try to find a single word that describes that place.

3. Why might the editors have chosen to publish these three independent pieces rather than a single piece on several outdoor recreational activities in the Everglades?

FOR DISCUSSION

As a class consider the three activities described in these essays. What do you see as the benefits and/or limits of these activities? Are these the kinds of activities in which you would like to engage? What opportunities for these activities are there locally? As a class, consider asking your teacher to take you for a hike right now to explore your campus. If he or she says "no," keep asking.

WRITING IN RESPONSE

These short essays provide details not only about three trips, but about what the writers saw and how they felt. In a short essay, describe a hike, a bike ride, or a canoe trip you have recently taken. If you haven't hiked, biked, or canoed before, take an afternoon to go for a walk or a bike ride.

DISCUSSING THE ISSUES

1. The readings in this chapter of *Saving Place* give us only a glimpse of the ways people think about nature and wilderness as sites for outdoor recreation. There are countless other activities that can be situated outdoors or that require outdoor settings. Think for instance about skiing, hang gliding, scuba diving, wake boarding, snow boarding, archery, base jumping, trap and skeet, running, sky diving, rock and mountain climbing, spelunking, horseback riding, mountain biking and so on. Think also about the popularity of ESPN's Great Outdoor Games and X-Games. As a class, consider the numerous types of outdoor activities that are not discussed in this chapter. What role does wilderness play in each of those? How do those activities affect wilderness and nature?

2. Part of our conversation regarding outdoor recreation has to consider not only the activities themselves, but the places in which those activities take place. Considering the readings found in this chapter and your own classroom

discussions and ideas, think about how we decide what places can and should be used for recreation.

WRITING ABOUT THE ISSUES

1. *Personal Experience:* What is your favorite outdoor activity? What is an outdoor activity with which you would like to become involved or in which you are simply interested and would like to learn more? In a personal narrative, discuss how you view the activity, the people who engage in activity, and the role that activity has in the place in which it occurs.
2. *Local Context:* Chances are that wherever you live, there are organized groups of people engaging in outdoor activities. Quite frequently, these organizations and clubs provide not only an outlet for people who share similar interests but also training and instruction for those people new to an activity. These same groups also may provide justification and rationale for the role of the activity in local environments. Take some time to check out such a local organization. Learn what you can about that group. Then, write an informative essay that explains both the activity and the ways in which the group discusses its own impact on local environments.
3. *Research:* Think about the variety of subjects the writers in this chapter have addressed, of interest to you. Then, spend some time reading about your chosen subject and write an informative paper on it.

RESEARCH PATHS (WEB LINKS, ETC.)

U.S. National Parks (www.us-national-parks.net/)
Yosemite National Park (www.nps.gov/yose/home.htm)
A Guide to Yosemite National Park (www.jrabold.net/yosemite/)
Exploring America's National Parks (www.americanparks.com/)
National Recreation and Park Association (www.nrpa.org/)
Recreational Boating and Fishing Foundation (www.WaterWorksWonders.org)
Kilimanjaro National Park (www.gorp.com/gorp/location/africa/tanzania/
    home_kil.htm)
Kilimanjaro Expedition (www.tusker.com/Kilimanjaro.htm)
Climbing Kilimanjaro (www.climbingkilimanjaro.com/)
American Camping Association (www.acacamps.org/)
Camping (www.camping.about.com/)
Climbing Magazine Online (www.climbing.com/)
Surfrider Foundation (www.surfrider.org/)
Everglades Area Parks (everglades.areaparks.com/)
Florida Everglades (www.florida-everglades.com/)
Becoming an Outdoors-Woman (www.uwsp.edu/cnr/bow/)
Florida Fish and Wildlife Conservation Commission
    (www.floridaconservation.org)

Appalachian Trail Conference (www.atconf.org/)
Outside Magazine (www.outsidemag.com/index.html)
Sports Afield (www.sportsafield.com/)
Field and Stream (www.fieldandstream.com/)
The In-Fisherman (www.in-fisherman.com/)
Florida Sportsman (www.floridasportsman.com/)

FURTHER READINGS

Carl Hiaasen, *Team Rodent: How Disney Devours the World*
James A. Swan, *In Defense of Hunting*
Holly Morris, *Uncommon Waters: Women Write about Fishing*
Holly Morris, *A Different Angle*
Pam Houston, *Women on Hunting*
Matt Warshaw, "Death of a Legend" (recounts the death of Mark Foo at Maverick's)
Daniel Duane and Matt Warshaw, *Maverick's: The Story of Big-Wave Surfing.*
Marjorie Stoneman Douglas, *Everglades: River of Grass*
Jan D. Curran, *The Appalachian Trail: A Journey of Discovery*
Jan D. Curran, *The Appalachian Trail: How to Prepare for and Hike It*
Jan D. Curran, *The Appalachian Trail: Onward to Katahdin*
David Emblidge, ed., *The Appalachian Trail Reader*
Frank Logue, *The Best of the Appalachian Trail: Day Hikes*
Mary L. Twitty, *The Dream Trail*
Herbert F. Eye, *An Eye on the Horizon: An Appalachian Trail Odyssey*

CHAPTER 4

Consuming Nature

You've probably heard the phrase *consumer culture* used in reference to the ways Americans live their lives. But have you ever thought about what this term means? Often the term *consumer* is used in an economic sense to mean a person who purchases goods or services. But it is also important to understand that the term *consumer* refers to one who consumes. This idea is borrowed from ecology and refers specifically to the idea of burning energy and fuel. A consumer in ecological thinking is an organism in a food chain that ingests other organisms and other organic matter. To consume also carries the implication of waste, of destruction; for instance, we are likely to hear that a fire "consumed 12 acres." In economic theories of consumerism greater consumption of goods is economically beneficial. In ecology, greater consumption can prove wasteful, even destructive.

In terms of ecological thinking, we must consider the ways we consume and the effects consumption has on the things we consume. The readings found here ask you to think about how you function as an ecological consumer. Think, for instance, about the consumption of electricity you require; think about the power used to light the room you are in right now, to heat or cool that room. Think about the materials needed to build that room, to paint its walls, to insulate it, to make the carpeting or tile on the floor, and to make the furniture on which you sit. Think about all of the energy devoted to gathering the food you will eat today: the clearing of farm land, the water for irrigation, the fuel for transporting the food, the energy for preparing the food, the materials for packing the food, and so on. What this chapter addresses is not just the many ways that we as Americans consume, but the ways we think about consumption and how consumption affects the places, environments, and resources that are consumed.

The readings in this chapter ask you to consider a range of subjects pertaining to consumption:

- the idea of thinking about nature as a commodity

- the recognition of all that we consume daily, annually

- the problem of wanting to consume one population while saving another

- the role food plays as a resource

- the ways we have constructed eating as a consumer activity

- the ways we think about the foods we eat

- the ways we think about nature as a resource

- the ways we assign value to some resources and not others

- the way we overuse some resources

As you read these selections, you should begin to consider how your own consumption affects your relationships—your ecology—with the places, environments, and nature where you live. You should also note specifically the ways that writing and reading about consumption affect how we think about consumption. Are writing and reading themselves acts of production and consumption?

The Conundrum of Consumption

Alan Thein Durning

Alan Thein Durning served as a senior researcher for the Worldwatch Institute, an organization whose mission is devoted to "fostering the evolution of an environmentally sustainable society—one in which human needs are met in ways that do not threaten the health of the natural environment or the prospects of future generations. The Institute seeks to achieve this goal through the conduct of inter-disciplinary non-partisan research on emerging global environmental issues, the results of which are widely disseminated throughout the world." Durning has published a number of articles, for both Worldwatch and other national publications. He is also the author of This Place on Earth: Home and the Practice of Permanence *and* How Much Is Enough? The Consumer Society and the Future of the Earth, *from which "The Conundrum of Consumption" is taken. As you read this selection, pay close attention to the relationships Durning sets up between consumer societies and the natural environment, and consider how you fit into the dynamic Durning defines.*

JOURNAL ASSIGNMENT

What do you suppose is meant by the word *consumption* that Durning uses in his title? What does it mean to consume? In your journal, work out a definition of consumption and answer the question, In what ways do I consume?"

1   For Sidney Quarrier of Essex, Connecticut, Earth Day 1990 was Judgment Day—the day of ecological reckoning. While tens of millions of people around the world were marching and celebrating in the streets, Sidney was sitting at his kitchen table with a yellow legal pad and a pocket calculator. The task he set himself was to tally up the burden he and his family had placed on the planet since Earth Day 1970.

2   Early that spring morning he began tabulating everything that had gone into their house—oil for heating, nuclear-generated electricity, water for show-ers and watering the lawn, cans of paint, appliances, square footage of carpet, furniture, clothes, food, and thousands of other things—and everything that had come out—garbage pails of junk mail and packaging, newspapers and magazines by the cubic meter, polluted water, and smoke from the furnace. He listed the resources they had tapped to move them around by car and airplane, form fuel and lubricants to tires and replacement parts. "I worked on that list most of the day," Sid remembers. "I dug out wads of old receipts, weighed trash cans and the daily mail, excavated the basement and shed, and used tri-angulation techniques I hadn't practiced since graduate school to estimate the materials we used in the roofing job."

3   Manufacturing and delivering each of the objects on his list, Sid knew, had required additional resources he was unable to count. National statistics sug-gested, for example, that he should double the energy he used in his house and car to allow for what businesses and government used to provide him with goods and services. He visualized a global industrial network of factories mak-ing things for him, freighters and trucks transporting them, stores selling them, and office buildings supervising the process. He wondered how much steel and concrete his state needed for the roads, bridges, and parking garages he used. He wondered about resources used by the hospital that cared for him, the air force jets and police cars that protected him, the television stations that entertained him, and the veterinary office that cured his dog.

4   As his list grew, Sid was haunted by an imaginary mountain of discarded televisions, car parts, and barrels of oil—all piling up toward the sky on his lot. "It was a sober revisiting of that period. . . . It's only when you put together all the years of incremental consumption that you realize the totality." That totality hit him like the ton of paper packaging he had hauled out with the trash over the years: "The question is," Sid said, "Can the earth survive the impact of Sid, and can the Sids of the future change?"

That *is* the question. Sidney Quarrier and his family are no gluttons. "Dur- 5 ing those years, we lived in a three bedroom house on two-and-a-half acres in the country, about 35 miles from my job in Hartford," Sidney recounts. "But we have never been rich," he insists. "What frightened me was that our consumption was typical of the people here in Connecticut."

Sid's class—the American middle class—is the group that, more than any 6 other, defines and embodies the contemporary international vision of the good life. Yet the way the Quarriers lived for those 20 years is among the world's premier environmental problems, and may be the most difficult to solve.

Only population growth rivals high consumption as a cause of ecological 7 decline, and at least population growth is now viewed as a problem by many governments and citizens of the world. Consumption, in contrast, is almost universally seen as good—indeed, increasing it is the primary goal of national economic policy. The consumption levels exemplified in the two decades Sid Quarrier reviewed are the highest achieved by any civilization in human history. They manifest the full flowering of a new form of human society: the consumer society.

This new manner of living was born in the United States, and the words of 8 an American best capture its spirit. In the age of U.S. affluence that began after World War II, retailing analyst Victor Lebow declared: "Our enormously productive economy . . . demands that we make consumption our way of life, that we convert the buying and use of goods into rituals, that we seek our spiritual satisfaction, our ego satisfaction, in consumption . . . We need things consumed, burned up, worn out, replaced, and discarded at an ever increasing rate." Most citizens of western nations have responded to Lebow's call, and the rest of the world appears intent on following.

In industrial lands, consumption now permeates social values. Opinion 9 surveys in the world's two largest economies—Japan and the United States—show that people increasingly measure success by the amount they consume. The Japanese speak of the "new three sacred treasures": color televisions, air conditioning, and the automobile. One fourth of Poles deem "Dynasty," which portrays the life-style of the richest Americans, their favorite television program, and villagers in the heart of Africa follow "Dallas," the television series that portrays American oil tycoons. In Taiwan, a billboard demands "Why Aren't You a Millionaire Yet?" A *Business Week* correspondent beams: "The American Dream is alive and well . . . in Mexico." Indeed, the words "consumer" and "person" have become virtual synonyms.

The life-style made in the United States is emulated by those who can af- 10 ford it around the world, but many cannot. The economic fault lines that fracture the globe defy comprehension. The world has 202 billionaires and more than 3 million millionaires. It also has 100 million homeless people who live on roadsides, in garbage dumps, and under bridges. The value of luxury goods sales worldwide—high-fashion clothing, top-of-the-line autos, and the other trappings of wealth—exceeds the gross national products of two thirds of the world's countries. Indeed, the world's average income, about $5,000 a year, is below the U.S. poverty line.

11   The gaping divide in material consumption between the fortunate and unfortunate stands out starkly in their impacts on the natural world. The soaring consumption lines that track the rise of the consumer society are, from another perspective, surging indicators of environmental harm. The consumer society's exploitation of resources threatens to exhaust, poison, or unalterably disfigure forests, soils, water, and air. We, its members, are responsible for a disproportionate share of all the global environmental challenges facing humanity.

12   Ironically, high consumption is a mixed blessing in human terms too. People living in the nineties are on average four-and-a-half times richer than their great grandparents were at the turn of the century, but they are not four-and-a-half times happier. Psychological evidence shows that the relationship between consumption and personal happiness is weak. Worse, two primary sources of human fullfillment—social relations and leisure—appear to have withered or stagnated in the rush to riches. Thus many of us in the consumer society have a sense that our world of plenty is somehow hollow—that, hoodwinked by a consumerist culture, we have been fruitlessly attempting to satisfy with material things what are essentially social, psychological, and spiritual needs.

13   Of course, the opposite of overconsumption—destitution—is no solution to either environmental or human problems. It is infinitely worse for people and bad for the natural world too. Dispossessed peasants slash-and-burn their way into the rain forests of Latin America, hungry nomads turn their herds out onto fragile African rangeland, reducing it to desert, and small farmers in India and the Philippines cultivate steep slopes, exposing them to the erosive powers of rain. Perhaps half the world's billion-plus absolute poor are caught in a downward spiral of ecological and economic impoverishment. In desperation, they knowingly abuse the land, salvaging the present by savaging the future.

14   If environmental destruction results when people have either too little or too much, we are left to wonder, How much is enough? What level of consumption can the earth support? When does having more cease to add appreciably to human satisfaction? Is it possible for all the world's people to live comfortably without bringing on the decline of the planet's natural health? Is there a level of living above poverty and subsistence but below the consumer life-style—a level of sufficiency? Could all the world's people have central heating? Refrigerators? Clothes dryers? Automobiles? Air conditioning? Heated swimming pools? Airplanes? Second homes?

15   Many of these questions cannot be answered definitively, but for each of us in the consumer society, asking is essential nonetheless. Unless we see that more is not always better, our efforts to forestall ecological decline will be overwhelmed by our appetites. Unless we ask we will likely fail to see the forces around us that stimulate those appetites, such as relentless advertising, proliferating shopping centers, and social pressures to "keep up with the Joneses." We may overlook forces that make consumption more destructive than it need

be, such as subsidies to mines, paper mills, and other industries with high environmental impacts. And we may not act on opportunities to improve our lives while consuming less, such as working fewer hours to spend more time with family and friends.

Still, the difficulty of transforming the consumer society into a sustainable 16 one can scarcely be overestimated. We consumers enjoy a life-style that almost everybody else aspires to, and why shouldn't they? Who would just as soon *not* have an automobile, a big house on a big lot, and complete control over indoor temperature throughout the year? The momentum of centuries of economic history and the material cravings of 5.5 billion people lie on the side of increasing consumption.

We may be, therefore, in a conundrum—a problem admitting of no satisfac- 17 tory solution. Limiting the consumer life-style to those who have already attained it is not politically possible, morally defensible, or ecologically sufficient. And extending that life-style to all would simply hasten the ruin of the biosphere. The global environment cannot support 1.1 billion of us living like American consumers, much less 5.5 billion people, or a future population of at least 8 billion. On the other hand, reducing the consumption levels of the consumer society, and tempering material aspirations elsewhere, though morally acceptable, is a quixotic proposal. It bucks the trend of centuries. Yet it may be the only option.

If the life-supporting ecosystems of the planet are to survive for future gen- 18 erations, the consumer society will have to dramatically curtail its use of resources—partly by shifting to high-quality, low-input durable goods and partly by seeking fulfillment through leisure, human relationships, and other nonmaterial avenues. We in the consumer society will have to live a technologically sophisticated version of the life-style currently practiced lower on the economic ladder. Scientific advances, better laws, restructured industries, new treaties, environmental taxes, grassroots campaigns—all can help us get there. But ultimately, sustaining the environment that sustains humanity will require that we change our values.

FOCUS ON ECOLOGY

1. In this essay, Sid Quarrier asks the pointed question, "Can the earth survive the impact of Sid, and can the Sids of the future change?" (Being another Sid—perhaps one of the Sids of the future to which Quarrier refers—I find this question extremely poignant.) How do you respond to Quarrier's question?
2. If, as Durning writes, "The consumption levels exemplified in the two decades Sid Quarrier reviewed are the highest achieved by any civilization in human history," referring to 1970–1990, then what would you assume has happened to the consumption levels since 1990? What evidence can you provide to support your answer?
3. What is the relationship between a consumer culture and the natural environment?

FOCUS ON WRITING

1. To whom do you suppose Durning is writing? What choices in his writing has he made to address this audience? Why might he have chosen this specific audience?
2. Toward the end of this selection, Durning begins to ask a series of questions. Why do you suppose Durning has decided to ask questions here of his audience rather than address these issues directly?
3. What does the word *conundrum* mean? Why might we be in a conundrum of consumption? Why might Durning have selected this title?

FOR DISCUSSION

As a class, consider all of the kinds of consumption that take place during a single class period in a college classroom. Think about the construction of the building where the class is located, the furniture and other items housed in the classroom, the textbooks used (yes, including this one), the pens and pencils, the clothes you wear, the method of transportation that brought you to campus, the fliers and newspapers that are on the walls and floors, the chemicals used to clean the room each day, the electricity used to light the room and power any technological devices that may be in the room (computers, projectors, televisions, etc.), and the climate control devices used (heat and air conditioning). How does it make you feel? Do you see any need for change? Is change *possible?*

WRITING IN RESPONSE

At the start of Durning's selection, he recounts the list that Sidney Quarrier creates on Earth Day 1990. This list tallied "the burden he and his family had placed on the planet since Earth Day 1970," a period of 20 years. For this writing assignment, create a similar tally for yourself for the past week. How much of a burden have you been on the planet for the past week? Consider all aspects of your life: the food you eat, the trash you produce, the fuel you use, the water you require, the electricity used everywhere you go, the clothes you wear and how they were produced, and so on. Does your list surprise you? Upset you? Explain your thoughts and emotions on reflection.

Save the Whales, Screw the Shrimp

Joy Williams

Joy Williams was born in 1944 in Chelmsford, Massachusetts. Though known mostly for her novels and short stories—State of Grace, The Changeling, Taking Care, Breaking and Entering, Escapes, The Quick and the Dead—*her nonfiction writing has also earned high critical acclaim. Her books* D. H. Lawrence on Education, The Florida Keys: A History and Guide, Ill Nature: Rants and Reflections on Humanity and Other Animals, *as well as her many essays have earned her the reputation as one of the most important of today's writers. In addition to writing, Williams has taught at a number of universities and has also worked at a marine laboratory in Florida. The essay "Save the Whales, Screw the Shrimp" was first published in* Esquire Magazine *in 1990. As you read this essay, pay particular attention to the tone of the essay.*

JOURNAL ASSIGNMENT

In this essay, Joy Williams writes about how we interact on a daily basis with nature and how we consume nature every day. In your journal, begin to think about and write about how your daily life interacts with nature and how you personally consume nature.

I don't want to talk about *me*, of course, but it seems as though far too much at- 1 tention has been lavished on *you* lately—that your greed and vanities and quest for self-fulfillment have been catered to far too much. You just want and want and want. You haven't had a mandala dream since the eighties began. To have a mandala dream you'd have to instinctively know that it was an attempt at self-healing on the part of Nature, and you don't believe in Nature anymore. It's too isolated from you. You've abstracted it. It's so messy and damaged and sad. Your eyes glaze as you travel life's highway past all the crushed animals and the Big Gulp cups. You don't even take pleasure in looking at nature photographs these days. Oh, they can be just as pretty, as always, but don't they make you feel increasingly . . . anxious? Filled with more trepidation than peace? So what's the point? You see the picture of the baby condor or the panda munching on a bamboo shoot, and your heart just sinks, doesn't it? A picture of a poor old sea turtle with barnacles on her back, all ancient and exhausted, depositing her five gallons of doomed eggs in the sand hardly fills you with joy, because you realize, quite rightly, that just outside the frame falls the shadow of the condo. What's cropped from the shot of ocean waves crashing on a pristine shore is the plastics plant, and just beyond the dunes lies a parking lot. Hidden from immediate view in the butterfly-bright meadow, in the dusky thicket, in the oak and holly wood, are the surveyors' stakes, for someone wants to build a mall exactly there—some gas stations and supermarkets, some pizza and video shops, a health club, maybe a bulimia treatment center. Those lovely pictures of leopards and herons and wild rivers, well, you just know they're going to be accompanied by a text that will serve only to bring you down. You don't want to think about it! It's all so uncool. And you don't want to feel guilty either. Guilt is uncool. Regret maybe you'll consider. *Maybe.* Regret is a possibility, but don't push me, you say. Nature photographs have become something of a problem, along with almost everything else. Even though they leave the bad stuff out—maybe because you *know* they're leaving all the bad stuff out—such pictures are making you increasingly aware that you're a little too late for Nature. Do you feel that? Twenty years too late, maybe only ten? Not *way* too late, just a little too late? Well, it appears that you are. And since you are, you've decided you're just not going to attend this particular party.

2 Pascal said that it is easier to endure death without thinking about it than to endure the thought of death without dying. This is how you manage to dance the strange dance with that grim partner, nuclear annihilation. When the U.S. Army notified Winston Churchill that the first atom bomb had been detonated in New Mexico, it chose the code phrase BABIES SATISFACTORILY BORN. So you entered the age of irony, and the strange double life you've been leading with the world ever since. Joyce Carol Oates suggests that the reason writers—*real* writers, one assumes—don't write about Nature is that it lacks a sense of humor and registers no irony. It just doesn't seem to be of the times—these slick, sleek, knowing, objective, indulgent times. And the word *Environment.* Such a bloodless word. A flat-footed word with a shrunken heart. A word increasingly disengaged from its association with the natural world. Urban planners, industrialists, economists, and developers use it. It's a lost word, really. A cold word, mechanistic, suited strangely to the coldness generally felt toward Nature. It's their word now. You don't mind giving it up. As for *Environmentalist,* that's one that can really bring on the yawns, for you've tamed and tidied it, neutered it quite nicely. An environmentalist must be calm, rational, reasonable, and willing to compromise, otherwise you won't listen to him. Still, his beliefs are *opinions* only, for this is the age of radical subjectivism. Not long ago, Barry Commoner spoke to the Environmental Protection Agency. He scolded them. They loved it. The way they protect the environment these days is apparently to find an "acceptable level of harm from a pollutant and then issue rules allowing industry to pollute to that level." Commoner suggested that this was inappropriate. An EPA employee suggested that any other approach would

place limits on economic growth and implied that Commoner was advocating this. Limits on economic growth! Commoner vigorously denied this. Oh, it was a healthy exchange of ideas, healthier certainly than our air and water. We needed that little spanking, the EPA felt. It was refreshing. The agency has recently lumbered into action in its campaign to ban dinoseb. You seem to have liked your dinoseb. It's been a popular weed killer, even though it has been directly linked with birth defects. You must hate weeds a lot. Although the EPA appears successful in banning the poison, it will still have to pay the disposal costs and compensate the manufacturers for the market value of the chemicals they still have in stock.

That's ironic, you say, but farmers will suffer losses, too, oh dreadful financial losses, if herbicide and pesticide use is restricted.   3

Farmers grow way too much stuff anyway. They grow surplus crops with   4
subsidized water created by turning rivers great and small into a plumbing system of dams and canals. Rivers have become *systems*. Wetlands are increasingly being referred to as *filtering systems*—things deigned *useful* because of their ability to absorb urban run-off, oil from roads, et cetera.

We know that. We've known that for years about farmers. We know a lot   5
these days. We're very well informed. If farmers aren't allowed to make a profit by growing surplus crops, they'll have to sell their land to developers, who'll turn all that *arable land* into office parks. Arable land isn't Nature anyway, and besides, we like those office parks and shopping plazas, with their monster supermarkets open twenty-four hours a day with aisle after aisle after aisle of *products*. It's fun. Products are fun.

Farmers like their poisons, but ranchers like them even more. There are well-   6
funded predominantly federal and cooperative programs like the Agriculture Department's Animal Damage Control Unit that poison, shoot, and trap several thousand animals each year. This unit loves to kill things. It was created to kill things—bobcats, foxes, black bears, mountain lions, rabbits, badgers, countless birds—all to make this great land safe for the string bean and the corn, the sheep and the cow, even though you're not consuming as much cow these days. A burger now and then, but burgers are hardly cows at all, you feel. They're not all *our* cows in any case, for some burger matter is imported. There's a bit of Central American burger matter in your bun. Which is contributing to the conversion of tropical rain forest into cow pasture. Even so, you're getting away from meat these days. You're eschewing cow. It's seafood you love, shrimp most of all. And when you love something, it had better watch out, because you have a tendency to love it to death. Shrimp, shrimp, shrimp. It's more common on menus than chicken. In the wilds of Ohio, far, far from watery shores, four out of the six entrées on a menu will be shrimp, for some modest sum. Everywhere, it's all the shrimp you can eat or all you *care* to eat, for sometimes you just don't feel like eating all you *can*. You are intensively *harvesting* shrimp. Soon there won't be any left and then you can stop. It takes that, often,

to make you stop. Shrimpers shrimp, of course. That's their *business*. They put out these big nets and in these nets, for each pound of shrimp, they catch more than ten times that amount of fish, turtles, and dolphins. These, quite the worse for wear, they dump back in. There is an object called TED (Turtle Excluder Device), which would save thousands of turtles and some dolphins from dying in the nets, but the shrimpers are loath to use TEDs, as they say it would cut the size of their shrimp catch.

7   We've heard about TED, you say.

8   They want you, all of you, to have all the shrimp you can eat and more. At Kiawah Island, off the coast of South Carolina, visitors go out on Jeep "safaris" through the part of the island that hasn't been developed yet. ("Wherever you see trees," the guide says, "really, that's a lot.") The safari comprises six Jeeps, and these days they go out at least four times a day, with more trips promised soon. The tourists drive their own Jeeps and the guide talks to them by radio. Kiawah has nice beaches, and the guide talks about turtles. When he mentions the shrimpers' role in the decline of the turtle, the shrimpers, who share the same frequency, scream at him. Shrimpers and most commercial fishermen (many of them working with drift and gill nets anywhere from six to thirty miles long) think of themselves as an *endangered species*. A recent newspaper headline said, "Shrimpers Spared Anti-Turtle Devices." Even so with the continuing wanton depletion of shrimp beds, they will undoubtedly have to find some other means of employment soon. They might, for instance, become part of that vast throng laboring in the *tourist industry.*

9   Tourism has become an industry as destructive as any other. You are no longer benign in your traveling somewhere to look at the scenery. You never thought there was much gain in just looking anyway, you've always preferred to *use* the scenery in some manner. In your desire to get away from what you've got, you've caused there to be no place to get away *to*. You're just all bumpered up out there. Sewage and dumps have become prime indicators of America's lifestyle. In resort towns in New England and the Adirondacks, measuring the flow into the sewage plant serves as a business barometer. Tourism is a growth industry. You believe in growth. *Controlled* growth, of course. Controlled exponential growth is what you'd really like to see. You certainly don't want to put a moratorium or a cap on anything. That's illegal, isn't it? Retro you're not. You don't want to go back or anything. Forward. Maybe ask directions later. Growth is *desirable* as well as being *inevitable*. Growth is the one thing you seem to be powerless before, so you try to be realistic about it. Growth is—it's weird—it's like cancer or something.

10   Recently you, as tourist, have discovered your national parks and are quickly *overburdening* them. Spare land and it belong to you! It's exotic land too, not looking like all the stuff around it that looks like everything else. You want to take advantage of this land, of course, and use it in every way you can. Thus the managers—or *stewards*, as they like to be called—have developed *wise* and *multiple-use* plans, keeping in mind exploiters' interests (for they have their

needs, too) as well as the desires of the backpackers. Thus mining, timbering, and ranching activities take place in the national forests, where the Forest Service maintains a system of logging roads eight times larger than the interstate highway system. The national parks are more of a public playground and are becoming increasingly Europeanized in their look and management. Lots of concessions and motels. You deserve a clean bed and a hot meal when you go into the wilderness. At least your stewards think that you do. You keep your stewards busy. Not only must they cater to your multiple and conflicting desires, they have to manage your wildlife *resources.* They have managed wildfowl to such an extent that the reasoning has become, If it weren't for hunters, ducks would disappear. Duck stamps and licensing fees support the whole rickety duck-management system. Yes! If it weren't for the people who killed them, wild ducks wouldn't exist! Managers are managing all wild creatures, not just those that fly. They track and tape and tag and band. They relocate, restock, and reintroduce. They cull and control. It's hard to keep it all straight. Protect or poison? Extirpate or just mostly eliminate? Sometimes even the stewards get mixed up.

This is the time of machines and models, hands-on management and master 11
plans. Don't you ever wonder as you pass that billboard advertising another MASTER-PLANNED COMMUNITY just what master they are actually talking about? Not the Big Master, certainly. Something brought to you by one of the tiny masters, of which there are many. But you like these tiny masters and have even come to expect and require them. In Florida they've just started a ten-thousand-acre city in the Everglades. It's a *megaproject*, one of the largest ever in the state. Yes, they must have thought you wanted it. No, what you thought of as the Everglades, the Park, is only a little bitty part of the Everglades. Developers have been gnawing at this irreplaceable, strange land for years. It's like they just *hate* this ancient sea of grass. Maybe you could ask them about this sometime. Roy Rogers is the senior vice president of strategic planning, and the old cowboy says that every tree and bush and inch of sidewalk in the project has been planned. Nevertheless, because the whole thing will take twenty-five years to complete, the plan is going to be constantly changed. You can understand this. The important thing is that there be a blueprint. You trust a blueprint. The tiny masters know what you like. You like *a secure landscape* and *access to services.* You like grass—that is, lawns. The ultimate lawn is the golf course, which you've been told has "some ecological value." You believe this! Not that it really matters, you just like to play golf. These golf courses require a lot of watering. So much that the more inspired of the masters have taken to watering them with effluent, *treated* effluent, but yours, from all the condos and villas built around the stocked artificial lakes you fancy.

I really don't want to think about sewage, you say, but it sounds like 12
progress.

It is true that the masters are struggling with the problems of your inces- 13
sant flushing. Cuisine is also one of their concerns. Advances in sorbets—sorbet

intermezzos—in their clubs and fine restaurants. They know what you want. You want A HAVEN FROM THE ORDINARY WORLD. If you're A NATURE LOVER in the West you want to live in a $200,000 home in A WILD ANIMAL HABITAT. If you're eastern and consider yourself more hip, you want to live in new towns— brand-new reconstructed-from-scratch towns—in a house of NINETEENTH-CENTURY DESIGN. But in these new towns the masters are building, getting around can be confusing. There is an abundance of curves and an infrequency of through streets. It's the new wilderness without any trees. You can get lost, even with all the "mental bread crumbs" the masters scatter about as visual landmarks—the windmill, the water views, the various groupings of landscape "material." You *are* lost, you know. But you trust a Realtor will show you the way. There are many more Realtors than tiny masters, and many of them have to make do with less than a loaf—that is, trying to sell stuff that's already been built in an environment already "enhanced" rather than something being planned—but they're everywhere, willing to show you the path. If Dante re-turned to Hell today, he'd probably be escorted down by a Realtor, talking all the while about how it was just another level of Paradise.

14 *When have you last watched a sunset? Do you remember where you were? With whom? At Loews Ventana Canyon Resort, the Grand Foyer will provide you with that opportunity through lighting which is computerized to diminish with the approaching sunset!*

15 The tiny masters are willing to arrange Nature for you. They will compose it into a picture that you can look at at your leisure, when you're not doing work or something like that. Nature becomes scenery, a prop. At some golf courses in the Southwest, the saguaro cacti are reported to be repaired with green paste when balls blast into their skin. The saguaro can attempt to heal themselves by growing over the balls, but this takes time, and the effect can be somewhat . . . baroque. It's better to get out the pastepot. Nature has become simply a visual form of entertainment, and it had better look snappy.

16   Listen, you say, we've been at Ventana Canyon. It's in the desert, right? It's very, very nice, a world-class resort. A totally self-contained environment with everything that a person could possibly want, on more than a thousand acres in the middle of zip. It sprawls but nestles, like. And they've maintained the integrity of as much of the desert ecosystem as possible. Give them credit for that. *Great* restaurant, too. We had baby bay scallops there. Coming into the lobby there are these two big hand-carved coyotes, mutely howling. And that's the way we like them, *mute*. God, why do those things howl like that?

17 Wildlife is a personal matter, you think. The attitude is up to you. You can prefer to see it dead or not dead. You might want to let it mosey about its business or blow it away. Wild things exist only if you have the graciousness to allow them to. Just outside Tucson, Arizona, there is a brand-new structure modeled after a

French foreign legion outpost. It's the *International Wildlife Museum,* and it's full of dead animals. Three hundred species are there, at least a third of them—the rarest ones—killed and collected by one C. J. McElroy, who enjoyed doing it and now shares what's left with you. The museum claims to be educational because you can watch a taxidermist at work or touch a lion's tooth. You can get real close to these dead animals, closer than you can in a zoo. Some of you prefer zoos, however, which are becoming bigger, better, and bioclimatic. New-age zoo designers want the animals to *flow right out into your space.* In Dallas there will soon be a Wilds of Africa exhibit; in San Diego there's a simulated rain forest, where you can thread your way "down the side of a lush canyon, the air filled with a fine mist from 300 high-pressure nozzles"; in New Orleans you've constructed a swamp, the real swamp not far away on the verge of disappearing. Animals in these places are abstractions—wandering relics of their true selves, but that doesn't matter. Animal behavior in a zoo is nothing like natural behavior, but that doesn't really matter, either. Zoos are pretty, contained, and accessible. These new habitats can contain one hundred different species—not more than one or two of each thing, of course—on seven acres, three, one. You don't want to see *too much* of anything, certainly. An *example* will suffice. Sort of like a biological Crabtree & Evelyn basket selected with *you* in mind. You like things reduced, simplified. It's easier to take it all in, park it in your mind. You like things inside better than outside anyway. You are increasingly looking at and living in proxy environments created by substitution and simulation. *Resource economists* are a wee branch in the tree of tiny masters, and one, Martin Krieger, wrote, "Artificial prairies and wildernesses have been created, and there is no reason to believe that these artificial environments need be unsatisfactory for those who experience them. . . . We will have to realize that the way in which we experience nature is conditioned by our society—which more and more is seen to be receptive to responsible intervention."

Nature has become a world of appearances, a mere source of materials. 18 You've been editing it for quite some time; now you're in the process of deleting it. Earth is beginning to look like not much more than a launching pad. Back near Tucson, on the opposite side of the mountain from the dead-animal habitat, you're building Biosphere II (as compared with or opposed to Biosphere I, more commonly known as Earth)—a $2^1/2$-acre terrarium, an artificial ecosystem that will include a rain forest, a desert, a thirty-five-foot ocean, and several thousand species of life (lots of microbes), including eight human beings, who will cultivate a bit of farmland. You think it would be nice to colonize other worlds after you've made it necessary to leave this one.

Hey, that's pretty good, you say, all that stuff packed into just $2^1/2$ acres. 19 That's only about three times bigger than my entire *house.*

It's small all right, but still not small enough to be, apparently, useful. For 20 the purposes of NASA, say, it would have to be smaller, oh much smaller, and energy-efficient too. Fiddle, fiddle, fiddle. You support fiddling, as well as meddling. This is how you learn. Though it's quite apparent the environment has been grossly polluted and the natural world abused and defiled, you seem to prefer to continue pondering effects rather than preventing causes. You want proof, you insist on proof. A Dr. Lave from Carnegie-Mellon—and he's an expert, an economist, and an environmental *expert*—says that scientists will have to prove to you that you will suffer if you don't become less of a "throw-away society." *If you really want me to give up my car or my air conditioner, you'd better prove to me first that the earth would otherwise be uninhabitable,* Dr Lave says. *Me* is *you,* I presume, whereas *you* refers to them. You as in me—that is, *me, me, me*—certainly strike a hard bargain. Uninhabitable the world has to get before you rein in your requirements. You're a consumer after all, *the* consumer upon whom so much attention is lavished, the ultimate user of a commodity that has become, these days, everything. To try to appease your appetite for proof, for example, scientists have been leasing for experimentation forty-six pristine lakes in Canada.

21   They don't want to *keep* them, they just want to *borrow* them.

22   They've been intentionally contaminating many of the lakes with a variety of pollutants dribbled into the propeller wash of research boats. It's *one of the boldest experiments in lake ecology ever conducted.* They've turned these remote lakes into huge *real-world test tubes.* They've been doing this since 1976! And what they've found so far in these *preliminary* studies is that pollutants are really destructive. The lakes get gross. Life in them ceases. It took about eight years to make this happen in one of them, everything carefully measured and controlled all the while. Now the scientists are slowly reversing the process. But it will take hundreds of years for the lakes to recover. They think.

23 Remember when you used to like rain, the sound of it, the feel of it, the way it made the plants and trees all glisten. We needed that rain, you would say. It looked pretty too, you thought, particularly in the movies. Now it rains and you go, Oh-oh. A nice walloping rain these days means *overtaxing our sewage treatment plants.* It means *untreated waste discharged directly into our waterways.* It means . . .

24   Okay. Okay.

25   *Acid rain!* And we all know what this is. Or most of us do. People of power in government and industry still don't seem to know what it is. Whatever it is, they say, they don't want to curb it, but they're willing to study it some more. Economists call air and water pollution "externalities" anyway. Oh, acid rain. You do get so sick of hearing about it. The words have already become a white-noise kind of thing. But you think in terms of *mitigating* it maybe. As for *the greenhouse effect,* you think in terms of *countering* that. One way that's been discussed recently is the planting of new forests, not for the sake of the forests alone, oh my heavens, no. Not for the sake of majesty and mystery or of Thumper and Bambi, are you kidding me, but because, as every schoolchild knows, trees absorb carbon dioxide. They just soak it up and store it. They just love it. So this is the plan: you plant millions of acres of trees, and you can go

on doing pretty much whatever you're doing—driving around, using staggering amounts of energy, keeping those power plants fired to the max. Isn't Nature remarkable? So willing to serve? You wouldn't think it had anything more
to offer, but it seems it does. Of course these "forests" wouldn't exactly be
forests. They would be more like trees. *Managed* trees. The Forest Service, which
now manages our forests by cutting them down, might be called upon to
evolve in their thinking and allow these trees to grow. They would probably be
patented trees after a time. Fast-growing, uniform, genetically-created-to-be-
toxin-eating *machines*. They would be *new-age* trees, because the problem with
planting the old-fashioned variety to *combat* the greenhouse effect, which is
caused by pollution, is that they're already dying from it. All along the crest of
the Appalachians from Maine to Georgia, forests struggle to survive in a toxic
soup of poisons. They can't *help* us if we've killed them, now can they?

All right, you say, wow, lighten up will you? Relax. Tell about yourself.   26

    Well, I say, I live in Florida . . .   27

    Oh my God, you say. Florida! Florida is a joke! How do you expect us to   28
take you seriously if you still live there! Florida is crazy, it's pink concrete. It's
paved, it's over. And a little girl just got eaten by an alligator down there. It
came out of some swamp next to a subdivision and just carried her off. That set
your Endangered Species Act back fifty years, you can bet.

    I . . .   29

    Listen, we don't want to hear any more about Florida. We don't want to hear   30
about Phoenix or Hilton Head or California's Central Valley. If our wetlands—
our *vanishing* wetlands—are mentioned one more time, we'll scream. And the
talk about condors and grizzlies and wolves is becoming too de trop. We had
just managed to get whales out of our minds when those three showed up under
the ice in Alaska. They even had *names*. Bone is the dead one, right? It's almost
the twenty-first century! Those last condors are *pathetic*. Can't we just get this
over with?

    Aristotle said that all living beings are ensouled and striving to participate   31
in eternity.

    Oh, I just bet he said that, you say. That doesn't sound like Aristotle. He   32
was a humanist. We're all humanists here. This is the age of humanism. And it
has been for a long time.

You are driving with a stranger in the car, and it is the stranger behind the   33
wheel. In the back seat are your pals for many years now—DO WHAT YOU LIKE
and his swilling sidekick, WHY NOT. A deer, or some emblematic animal, something from that myriad natural world you've come from that you treat with
such indifference and scorn—steps from the dimming woods and tentatively
upon the highway. The stranger does not decelerate or brake, not yet, maybe
not at all. The feeling is that whatever it is *will get out of the way*. Oh, it's a fine

car you've got, a fine machine, and oddly you don't mind the stranger driving it, because in a way, everything has gotten too complicated, way, way out of your control. You've given the wheel to the masters, the managers, the comptrollers. Something is wrong, *maybe*, you feel a little sick, *actually*, but the car is luxurious and fast and you're *moving*, which is the most important thing by far.

34   Why make a fuss when you're so comfortable? Don't make a fuss, make a baby. Go out and get something to eat, build something. Make *another* baby. Babies are cute. Babies show you have faith in the future. Although faith is perhaps too strong a word. They're everywhere these days, in all the crowds and traffic jams, there are the babies too. You don't seem to associate them with the problems of population increase. They're just babies! And you've come to believe in them again. They're a lot more tangible than the afterlife, which, of course, you haven't believed in in ages. At least not for yourself. The afterlife now belongs to plastics and poisons. Yes, plastics and poisons will have a far more extensive afterlife than you, that's known. A disposable diaper, for example, which is all plastic and wood pulp—you like them for all those babies, so easy to use and toss—will take around four centuries to degrade. Almost all plastics do, centuries and centuries. In the sea, many marine animals die from ingesting or being entangled in discarded plastic. In the dumps, plastic squats on more than 25 percent of dump space. But your heart is disposed toward plastic. Someone, no doubt the plastics industry, told you it was convenient. This same industry is now looking into recycling in an attempt to get the critics of their nefarious, multifarious products off their backs. That should make you feel better, because *recycling* has become an honorable word, no longer merely the hobby of Volvo owners. The fact is that people in plastics are born obscurants. Recycling (practically impossible) won't solve the plastic glut, only reduction of production will, and the plastics industry isn't looking into that, you can be sure. Waste is not just the stuff you throw away, of course, it's the stuff you use to excess. With the exception of *hazardous waste*, which you do worry about from time to time, it's even thought you have a declining sense of emergency about the problem. Builders are building bigger houses because you want bigger. You're trading up. Utility companies are beginning to worry about your constantly rising consumption. Utility companies! You haven't entered a new age at all but one of upscale nihilism, deluxe nihilism.

35   In the summer, particularly in *the industrial Northeast*, you did get a little excited. The filth cut into your fun time. Dead stuff floating around. Sludge and bloody vials. Hygienic devices—appearing not quite so hygienic out of context—all coming in on the tide. The air smelled funny, too. You tolerate a great deal, but the summer of '88 was truly creepy. It was even thought for a moment that the environment would become a political issue. But it didn't. You didn't want it to be, preferring instead to continue in your politics of subsidizing and advancing avarice. The issues were the same as always—jobs, defense, the econ-

omy, maintaining and improving the standard of living in this greedy, selfish, expansionistic, industrialized society.

You're getting a little shrill here, you say.   36

You're pretty well off. You expect to be better off soon. You do. What does   37
this mean? More software, more scampi, more square footage? You have created an ecological crisis. The earth is infinitely variable and alive, and you are
killing it. It seems safer this way. But you are not safe. You want to find whole-
ness and happiness in a land increasingly damaged and betrayed, and you
never will. More than material matters. You must change your ways.

What is this? *Sinners in the Hands of an Angry God?*   38

The ecological crisis cannot be resolved by politics. It cannot be solved by   39
science or technology. It is a crisis caused by culture and character, and a deep
change in personal consciousness is needed. Your fundamental attitudes toward
the earth have become twisted. You have made only brutal contact with Nature,
you cannot comprehend its grace. You must change. Have few desires and simple pleasures. Honor nonhuman life. Control yourself, become more authentic.
Live lightly upon the earth and treat it with respect. Redefine the word *progress*
and dismiss the managers and masters. Grow inwardly and with knowledge
become truly wiser. Make connections. Think differently, behave differently. For
this is essentially a moral issue we face and moral decisions must be made.

A *moral issue!* Okay, this discussion is now toast. A *moral* issue . . . And who's   40
this *we* now? Who are *you* is what I'd like to know. You're not me, anyway. I
admit, someone's to blame and something should be done. But I've got to go.
It's getting late. That's dusk out there. That is dusk, isn't it? It certainly doesn't
look like any dawn I've ever seen. Well, take care.

FOCUS ON ECOLOGY

1. Joy Williams makes some clear distinctions as to what is and is not nature.
   According to Williams, why isn't arable land nature? What is arable land?
2. What does it mean to "harvest" something?
3. What is the relationship of the consumer to nature? How does Williams describe that relationship?

FOCUS ON WRITING

1. How would you describe the tone of this essay? What parts of the essay contribute to and create this tone? Does the tone of Williams's essay affect her
   argument?
2. Who is Williams addressing in "Save the Whales, Screw the Shrimp"? How
   do you know?
3. How does Williams intend us to understand with the final dusk/dawn
   metaphor? What role does this metaphor play in the essay?

FOR DISCUSSION

Joy Williams writes that "Nature has become simply a visual form of entertainment, and it had better look snappy." Think about your community, about your campus. In what ways is nature used as a visual on your campus? In your community? As a class, develop a list of local sites that can be identified as "Nature as visual entertainment."

WRITING IN RESPONSE

In an essay, describe the way in which your daily life consumes nature. Consider how you answered this question in your journal before reading Williams's essay. Did her piece change how you see consumption? In the essay you write, take your audience through your typical day and describe your role as consumer in that day.

"Food: The Ultimate Resource" from *The Population Explosion*

Paul R. Ehrlich and Anne H. Ehrlich

Anne Howland was born in 1933 in Des Moines, Iowa. She attended the University of Kansas. Paul R. Ehrlich was born in Philadelphia in 1932. He attended the University of Pennsylvania and did his graduate work at the University of Kansas. In 1954 Howland and Ehrlich married, and together they have become two of the most important scientists and science writers in the country. As co-authors, they have written more than seven books about environment, ecology, and the future of the earth. Individually they have each written, co-authored, and edited numerous books and collections, including The Population Bomb, *which Paul Ehrlich wrote and which won the Bestseller's Paperback of the Year Award in 1970. The selection here, "Food: The Ultimate Resource," is taken from their book* The Population Explosion. *As you read this piece, consider how the Ehrlichs present the numerous statistics and facts that they offer, and consider how these facts enhance their argument.*

JOURNAL ASSIGNMENT

In your journal, write about why food might be called "the ultimate resource," as Paul R. Ehrlich and Anne H. Ehrlich's title suggests.

To ecologists who study animals, food and population often seem like two 1
sides of the same coin. If too many animals are devouring it, the food supply
declines; too little food, and the supply of animals declines. When thinking
about population problems, ecologists quite properly focus much of their attention on food. The amount of food available restrains the size of any animal
population, unless space, disease, predators, or some other factor sets lower
limits. *Homo sapiens* is no exception to that rule, and at the moment it seems
likely that food will be our limiting resource.

Compassionate people, especially those who are offended by the notion 2
that there may be too many people, often subscribe to a pernicious fallacy about
the human food supply. They are convinced that there is no "population problem," only a problem of maldistribution of food. If only food production were
better attuned to the nutritional needs of people and shared more equally, they
say, no one would go hungry.

The fallacy is seductive, because in the short term and in a limited sense 3
this is correct. [In Chapter 1 we mentioned] a recent study showing that the 1985
food supply could provide an adequate basic diet, primarily vegetarian, to
about 6 billion people. The same food supply could provide a modestly improved diet, with about 15 percent of its calories from animal products (about
what people in South America have available today), to 4 billion people. Some
1.3 billion people in the present population would get nothing at all to eat if
that level of nutrition were given to the rest. A "full-but-healthy" diet, with approximately 35 percent of its calories from animal sources, could be fed to
roughly 2.5 billion people, less than half the 1990 population.

With the present unequal distribution of food, a billion or so people are, if 4
anything, too well fed. Most of them, of course, are in rich countries. About a
third of the world's grain harvest is fed to livestock so that the diets of the well-
to-do can be enriched with meat, eggs, and dairy products. Perhaps 3 billion
other people get enough to eat, although meat may not often grace their dinner
tables.

Nearly a billion of the world's poorest people, mostly in poor countries, 5
are hungry. An estimated 950 million people were getting deficient diets in
1988—roughly one out of three people living in developing nations outside
China. About two out of five of those (almost 400 million people) were so un-
dernourished that their health was threatened or their growth was stunted.

The great majority of the hungriest, of course, are infants and small children, 6
whose parents are themselves living on the edge of survival. This daily food deprivation is a major factor behind the high infant mortalities in poor countries.
One in ten babies born in these countries will not make it to its first birthday;
two of the surviving nine can look forward to a lifetime of chronic hunger.

If the excess food of the rich were somehow made available to the poor, the 7
poor would be better fed; but there wouldn't be much left to accommodate a

population increase. Of course, food production worldwide has continued to increase somewhat faster than the population for the last four decades, and many agricultural experts expect that yearly rise to keep on materializing—despite setbacks increasingly encountered in the 1970s and 1980s.

8   What about the assertion of the Catholic bishops that "theoretically" enough food could be produced to feed 40 billion people? The original estimate on which the bishops based their statement was made two decades ago and has long since been discredited. It was reached by assuming that all more or less flat land in the world could be farmed and would be as productive as the land on an experimental farm in Iowa. This condition can't even be met by the rest of Iowa!

9   In reality, all signs point in the opposite direction. In Africa south of the Sahara, food production has fallen far behind population growth. Grain production per person has fallen by about 20 percent since 1970, and the average diet there was already woefully inadequate then. Rising imports of food have compensated in part for the shortfalls, but most of these very poor nations cannot afford to import all that is needed. The amount of food set aside for emergency donations is a pittance compared to the need in Africa alone.

10   Since 1981, per-capita food production has also been lagging in Latin America, where population growth rates are not too far below those in Africa. In short, population growth is already outstripping food production in two major regions of the world, in which live nearly a billion people. Could this alarming trend soon spread to encompass the entire globe?

11   Between 1950 and 1984, there was an unprecedented upward trend in *global* grain production, sufficient to stay ahead of population increase (in spite of the reverse trend in Africa south of the Sahara after 1970). There were only slight fluctuations, and until 1972 no actual declines in world production from one year to the next (local or regional declines were offset by bumper crops elsewhere). Before 1987, two consecutive years of substantial global declines were unheard of. Then, after a record grain harvest in 1986, *absolute* grain production worldwide dropped by 5 percent in 1987 and fell again in 1988 another 5 percent back to the level of the early 1980s. Meanwhile the population grew by 3.6 percent in those two years.

12   Part of the 1987 decline was "planned," as a result of conservation measures in the United States and as a strategy to reduce an accumulated grain glut, and part was due to a monsoon failure in India. But the 1988 drop was the unexpected result of severe drought and crop failure in such supposedly secure granaries as the United States and Canada, as well as the Soviet Union and China. That took care of the grain glut.

13   Preliminary 1989 estimates indicate a return of production to the 1986 level, but a continuing drawdown of food reserves. It is especially ominous that population growth makes it difficult to replenish stocks even in "good" years. Unlike the gradual slippage of food production behind population growth in some less-developed regions over decades, the 1988 event signaled a different kind of vulnerability—one all but forgotten in the post–World War II era of "dependable" global food-production increases: *agricultural success still requires favorable weather and a stable climate.*

The tricks of modern agriculture (especially the adoption of high-yielding 14
crop strains in Asia and parts of Latin America, known as the Green Revolution)
that have more or less steadily resulted in ever bigger harvests for four or five
decades may now be playing out for developed nations and are proving to be less
readily transferred to poor countries than was hoped. They undeniably achieve
substantial short-term gains, but possibly for too high a price—and the bill is coming due, in terms of depleted soils, salted fields, drained aquifers, and the like.

In the rest of this chapter, we summarize the current food situation in vari- 15
ous regions of the world, focusing first on the developing nations, where the
population–food ratio seems to be worsening.

ASIA'S FOOD PRODUCTION: SO FAR, SO GOOD

Grain production in Asia continues to increase faster than the population, partly 16
because population growth rates in many Asian countries are lower than in other
developing regions and partly because of greater success with Green Revolution
technologies. Even so, signs that food production may fall behind population
growth have begun to appear in some of the world's most populous nations.

China's grain production peaked in 1984 at a level roughly three times that 17
of 1950; since then, production has fallen. After the drought-reduced 1988 harvest, China had to import about 15 million tons, some 5 percent of its domestic
grain consumption that year. In part, the decline in grain production reflects
improvements in diets, as some land formerly planted in grain now produces a
variety of other foods.

The development of nonagricultural sectors of China's economy, however, 18
is also partly responsible for reduced grain harvests. Industry is diverting
water from agriculture, and homes and factories are being built on scarce arable
land. Each year some 4,000 square miles of farmland are taken out of production, three quarters of it for construction. This is an alarming trend for a nation
that has 7 percent of Earth's farmland but is trying to feed 21 percent of the
human population.

Although China has been very successful in reducing its birthrate, housing 19
and employment still must be provided for about 15 million more people each
year. Unless the trend in land conversion can be reversed and steady growth in
grain production restored, China will become a major food importer by the
mid-1990s—if sufficient foreign exchange can be earned through industrial exports and *if* enough grain is available for sale on the world market. The latter,
of course, will depend on production elsewhere.

India, the nation that in the next century may challenge China as the most 20
populous on Earth, made dramatic increases in wheat production between 1965
and 1983, thanks to its Green Revolution. Since 1983, India's rising grain production has lost momentum, for reasons that aren't hard to find. About 40 percent of
India's land is degraded from overuse. Soil erosion is rampant, with an estimated
annual loss of 6 billion tons of topsoil—the equivalent of 8,000 square miles of
arable land (an area the size of Massachusetts) disappearing from India *each year.*

21   In addition, 40,000 square miles of the nation's irrigated land is suffering from waterlogging and salinization, reducing its average productivity by about a fifth. And water levels in aquifers are dropping rapidly in some areas. In the south in Tamil Nadu, water tables fell 80 to 100 feet between 1975 and 1985, and overdrafts of aquifers through tube wells may threaten India's breadbasket in Haryana and the Punjab. The reduced water-holding capacity of eroded lands leads to more runoff and less recharge of aquifers. On the positive side, considerable potential remains for expanding irrigated land on the plain of the Ganges River.

22   The recharge of aquifers now being drained is also hindered by deforestation, which also leads to accelerated soil loss and more rapid runoff in watersheds. Between 1960 and 1980, over 16,000 square miles of the Indian subcontinent's forests (twice the area of Massachusetts) were destroyed, leaving less than 15 percent of the land forest-covered—an area about the size of California. Rates of destruction have been accelerating, though, and if current ones continue, those forests will effectively be gone by early in the next century. Once-dependable springs in the increasingly denuded mountains are becoming seasonal or drying up entirely. Dust blown from the Rajasthan desert is loading the atmosphere, possibly adding to regional climate change.

23   That the entire subcontinent is being deforested is of great concern to Indians. As environmentalist Mohan Dharia said in a report to the Indian government: "At the rate we are destroying our forests we will not have to wait for long to see India becoming the biggest desert in the world." Roughly four fifths of India's land area is now subject to repeated droughts, often on a two- to five-year time scale.

24   India suffered greatly from hunger in the early 1970s. Following the Soviet Union's decision to buy millions of tons of grain on the world market after a disastrous crop failure in 1972, India could not buy enough to make up for its own poor harvest caused by inadequate monsoon rains. In Uttar Pradesh, Bihar, and Orissa, the nations's poorest states, there were over 800,000 hunger-related deaths above the chronic level of child mortality. Since then, observers who don't understand that India has increased grain production by "mining" its soils and underground water have been impressed by that nation's improved food security. But in fact, short-term security has been brought by risking medium-term disaster.

25   In 1987, environmental analyst R. N. Roy of the Catalyst Group in Madras described the outlook succinctly: "With two-thirds of India's land threatened by erosion, water shortages and salinity, and with the added threat of pollution and increasing urban industrial demand, the country appears to be facing a catastrophic problem in the 1990s, if not earlier." And don't forget: with an annual population growth rate of 2.2 percent, India must somehow feed an additional 16 million people each year.

26   India is certainly not the only nation in trouble on the Indian subcontinent. The region is one of the two poorest in the world (Africa south of the Sahara being the other). Its population of more than a billion is also one of the most un-

derfed, with about half of the people lacking sufficient food to carry on an active working life and one in five so deprived as to threaten health and (in children) growth. The majority of the world's hungry "absolute poor" live in South Asia.

Bangladesh is much poorer than India, even more crowded, and more vul- 27 nerable, and has a population one-seventh as large but growing one-third faster. In the 1970s, Bangladesh suffered two sharp rises in death rates due to starvation, and more of the same can be expected in the decades to come. Every year, there are 3 million more hungry mouths in Bangladesh.

Pakistan, the third major nation in the Indian subcontinent, is not signifi- 28 cantly better off than its neighbors. With a land area six times that of Bangladesh and about the same number of people, Pakistan's greatest agricultural problem is lack of water. More than three fourths of its arable land is irrigated, with all the difficulties that implies. Much formerly irrigated land has gone out of production as salts have accumulated in the soil. Lester Brown has noted "glistening white expanses of salt-covered cropland . . . now abandoned" seen from an airplane flying over Pakistan and other Middle Eastern countries. Population growth in Pakistan is also on a par with that of Bangladesh, and per-capita grain production has dropped significantly in the 1980s.

Western Asia, more familiarly known as the Middle East, has seen remark- 29 ably large increases in grain production in recent years, largely as a result of agricultural inputs purchased by oil proceeds. Through extensive irrigation, fertilizers, and planting of high-yield grain varieties, production has leaped forward. But in a region of scant rainfall and restricted irrigation opportunities, there are clearly limits to this expansion—even with unlimited budgets. The current production glut of oil, with the low prices it commands, should have underlined the problem. Some Middle Eastern nations are modernizing rapidly, while others seem to be retreating full tilt to the seventh century; but all have very high population growth rates. The oil-producing nations now can afford to drill for water everywhere and import as much food as they wish, but problems will reappear if the quantities of food available for purchase diminish—or the oil runs out.

Southeast Asia, once a rich food-exporting region, has suffered destruction 30 (including ecological destruction) as a result of the Vietnam War. Subsequent political turmoil in Kampuchea (Cambodia) has kept that nation from resuming its former role as an Asian breadbasket. Only Thailand has continued to export rice and maize; and that nation, despite a relatively successful family-planning effort, is beginning to have trouble, probably largely because of increasing deforestation in the northern part of the country.

The story in the Southeast Asian giant, Indonesia, is not much cheerier. The 31 nation had become self-sufficient in rice and had large stored reserves in 1984. Since then production has not kept up with population growth, partly because of diminishing returns to fertilizer application. Indonesia already has 185 million people, and the population is projected to increase by over 100 million by 2020, despite a birthrate considerably lower than that of India or Bangladesh. If that projection, which assumes a further decline in the birthrate, is realized, in

2020 Indonesia will have a population density of almost 400 people per square mile. That is about the density of Switzerland or New York State—and more than five times that of the United States as a whole.

32   Some two thirds of those people are now crammed onto the island of Java, which has only about 7 percent of the nation's land area. Java therefore is one of the world's most densely populated areas (now about 2,400 per square mile, more crowded than Bangladesh). In response to that crowding, Indonesia launched an ambitious program of transplanting people from Java to the relatively sparsely occupied outer islands. Between 1985 and 2005, some 65 million people, somewhat more than the projected population growth during the period, were to be sent to agricultural settlements on Kalimantan, Sumatra, Sulawesi, and Irian Jaya.

33   But the program is failing; unlike the rich volcanic soils of Java, the rainforest soils on the other islands are largely unsuitable for agriculture. Transported people often find themselves unable to make a living; many soon make their way back to Java. The program also has been enormously destructive ecologically, resulting in heavy deforestation, soil erosion, and stream siltation. And one of the most unfortunate side effects has been to divert the Indonesian government's attention away from the critical need for population control.

34   The Philippines, with a population of 65 million, has enough land theoretically to feed twice that number of people under intensive irrigation for paddy rice. But the water to supply the irrigation for those paddies is disappearing, because the islands are being rapidly deforested—interfering with a crucial ecosystem service supplied by forest ecosystems: assurance of steady, dependable flows of water in streams. Only two thirds of the Philippines' original forest cover remains, and a third of that is severely degraded. Much of the denuded land is in critical watershed areas, and the watershed areas will suffer further as the rape of the forests continues. Lowland agriculture is being subjected to floods, siltation of irrigation canals, and dry-season water shortages, all related to deforestation, and the damage is bound to increase.

35   Furthermore, the hybrid rice varieties that form the basis of the Philippines' Green Revolution have proven vulnerable to pests, which has led to an escalated use of pesticides. For instance, between 1966 and 1979 the amount spent on insecticides climbed from 2 to 90 pesos per hectare. Not only does such an increase in chemical control represent a heavy financial burden on a poor nation, it also creates nasty environmental problems. One of the most serious consequences in the Philippines, as elsewhere in Asia, is the poisoning of fishes that are raised in farm ponds and flooded rice paddies—denying some of the poorest people a key source of protein for their diets.

36   At its current growth rate, the population will double in twenty-five years. Agricultural production in the Philippines is not likely to double in the foreseeable future; indeed, it may even decline. Conservative Catholic factions, whose views are shared by President Corazón Aquino, have effectively gutted the once-active family-planning program in the Philippines. This action has set the Philippines on a sure road to famine unless that nation somehow finds the

means to buy food in the future and other nations have it to sell. In 1990, there were almost 2 million more Filipino mouths to feed than in 1989.

The industrial nations of the Far East—Japan, Korea, and Taiwan—have 37 had declining grain harvests for over a decade. Industrialization itself is partly responsible. In these already crowded nations, industrialization pulls both land and labor out of agriculture. So far, the losses have been eased by reduced population growth and compensated by a rising ability to pay for imported food. All three countries can attribute much of their industrial success to having first developed and maintained sound agricultural sectors—a lesson unfortunately too seldom pointed out.

The previous pages have portrayed a troubled continent. Still, Asia is really 38 the bright spot in the food picture among developing regions; in most countries, increases in food production have so far kept ahead of population growth. The portents for the future, however, are much less cheery.

LATIN AMERICA: FALLING BEHIND

The food situation in Latin America, especially in the tropical regions, is quite 39 different from that in Asia. Recent trends have not been encouraging, yet the outlook could be much brighter if available resources were used more rationally. It should be remembered also that the average nutritional level of Latin Americans is considerably better that that of Asians, although great variation exists in both regions. Brazil, the largest nation in the region, illustrates the problems and the variations—all too well.

At first glance, it is hard to imagine that a nation with three times the agri- 40 cultural area of China and less than one-seventh of its population could have difficulty feeding its people adequately. But the combination of an inequitable social system (which also generates faulty government policies) and the intrinsic problems of tropical agriculture has produced exactly that situation.

Brazil's problems are rooted in history. The colonial economy was based 41 on plantations growing crops for export. Rich people ran the plantations; poor people and slaves worked on them. Producing food for the poor or slaves was never a high priority—just as food for the masses isn't today. Indeed, a lack of adequate diets for a major portion of the population has plagued Brazil since the seventeenth century. A disorganized economy and chronic shortages allowed the development of a class of *atravessadores*, dishonest middlemen, who managed to keep food prices low for farmers and high for consumers, and fattened themselves on the difference.

Despite wide recognition of the problem for a long time, and sporadic at- 42 tempts at reform, curing it has proven extremely difficult. Labor unions are weak, which keeps both wages and thus effective demand for food low. This situation has been exacerbated recently by industrialization of the agriculture system for growing crops for export at the expense of home consumption, especially in the subtropical and temperate south.

43   Between 1967 and 1979, the percentage of farmland dedicated to growing food for Brazilian consumption dropped from 63 to 55, as agriculture became a major source of foreign exchange to pay for imports and help to pay off the huge foreign debt. Industrial agriculture takes place on large holdings and is energy-intensive, not labor-intensive. Small farmers have been driven off their land, many into the cities. There they have swollen the urban labor pool and helped keep wages and food demand low. Success in producing export crops— soybeans, coffee, oranges, sugarcane, cacao (cocoa), and cotton—has resulted in production of less food for Brazilians. Indeed, as production of export crops has risen, so has importation of staples to feed the poor.

44   The running of Brazil's agricultural system for the financial benefit of a few rather than the feeding of the many is not the only agricultural problem the nation faces. Brazil has "modernized" its agriculture, using techniques developed for temperate climates. The result, especially when these methods are attempted in the tropics, often is an unsustainable system.

45   For example, plowing benefits the soil in temperate regions by raising its temperature in the spring and increasing the activity of beneficial soil organisms, but has the opposite effect in the tropics and subtropics. Rather, the soil is heated enough to kill bacteria, earthworms, insects, and mites that are essential for maintaining soil fertility. Furthermore, heavy mechanical working of the soil and planting in neat rows lead to serious erosion problems in the wake of tropical cloudbursts.

46   Soil loss in Brazilian soybean-growing regions has been estimated at about 100 tons per hectare per year, while soil conservationists believe that the "limits of tolerance" (*not* the replacement rate) are in the vicinity of 15 tons at most. The entire state of Paraná (which is in temperate southern Brazil) is eroding away at a rate of almost a half inch a year—soil that would take some four hundred years to regenerate.

47   Brazilian farmers have attempted to compensate for the horrendous erosion rate by escalating their fertilizer applications. These were increased *fivefold* between 1966 and 1977, while yields (production per hectare) increased only 5–15 percent. Fertilizers can partially compensate for and mask nutrient losses from erosion for a while, but sooner or later the piper must be paid, and yields will tumble. In short, "modernization" of agriculture in Brazil is a stark case of living on capital—using up a key renewable resource (topsoil) so fast as to make it nonrenewable.

48   Similarly, the adoption of temperate-zone chemical-control systems for pests has led to worsening pest problems in Brazil. Tropical and subtropical agricultural systems do not benefit from the natural "pest control" of a winter season; instead, tropical agricultural ecosystems must depend on the natural pest controls derived from the complexity of natural tropical ecosystems. Birds, predatory insects, fungi, and other enemies of crop pests normally help limit pest outbreaks, but these natural controls are seriously disrupted by routine pesticide applications.

Further problems in Brazil have been caused by the use of much potentially 49 productive cropland as pasture for cattle—a result in part of Brazil's inequitable land-ownership patterns and outdated notions of appropriate land use. This pattern has been especially destructive when extended to the Amazon, where rainforest soils are often thin and unsuited to permanent agriculture or even pasture. Stripped of forest, the soil is eroded rapidly, and nutrients are leached by heavy tropical downpours.

In Brazil, moreover, the Amazonian "ranchers" include the Volkswagen 50 and Ford companies, which have established gigantic ranches of low productivity that soon turn into wasteland. These enterprises have been subsidized by the Brazilian people as a whole through tax exemptions granted for the purpose of "opening" the Amazon frontier. Unfortunately, while using productive land for pasture in the subtropical and temperate parts of the country is wasteful (and morally dubious when millions of Brazilians are hungry and jobless), the application of such a policy to the rainforest region is a travesty, denying present and future generations any benefit from the forest's resources.

In short, Brazil's agriculture is being pushed toward social and ecological 51 failure, in part to satisfy the demand for export crops generated in the overpopulated developed world. In the absence of a drastic overhaul of its agricultural system, the country has scant prospect of being able to maintain its export potential in the long run, or to provide adequate diets for a population "scheduled" to double in thirty-five years or so. Each year, almost 3 million more Brazilians must be carried by the staggering food-supply system.

The reasons for a 10 percent decline in per-capita food production in Latin 52 America since 1981 vary among the different nations, but some factors are common to many. Maldistribution of land ownership, irrational land-use patterns, ecological degradation, the debt crisis (which prevents capital from flowing into agricultural sectors), and rapid population growth (over 2 percent per year on average for Latin America) all contribute to the failure of agricultural production to keep up.

In the tropical Andes, particularly in present-day Peru and Ecuador, defor- 53 estation of the mountain ranges above the fertile valleys was well under way before the Spanish arrived in the sixteenth century. What the Incas had begun the Spanish colonial authorities continued, and today much of the land's productive capacity has eroded away with the soil. Stunted growth from malnutrition is obvious in the native Andeans, who live in what should be a healthy environment (compared with the disease-ridden lowland forests).

Argentina and Chile seem to have everything going for them: fertile lands, 54 a temperate climate, and moderate population growth (currently about 1.5 percent per year). But corrupt or repressive politics and stratified societies with skewed landholding patterns have tripped them up. Nonetheless, Argentina remains the sole significant net grain exporter in Latin America.

Central America has suffered from extensive deforestation, much of it to cre- 55 ate short-lived cattle ranches for exporting "cheap" beef for the North American fast-food market. As meat exports rose in the 1960s and 1970s, domestic meat consumption fell in several countries. For instance, in Costa Rica in those two decades, beef production quadrupled, but per-capita consumption declined by more than 40 percent (to a mere 35 pounds a year, barely one-third of U.S. consumption). In recent years, political turmoil in El Salvador and Guatemala has prevented the needed land reform that might put domestic food production on a more secure footing, while Nicaragua's progress has been disrupted by U.S. intervention.

56   Mexico was the Green Revolution's first success story and a showcase. In the 1950s, Mexico went from being an increasing wheat importer to an exporter as yields multiplied. Grain production increased fourfold by the mid-1980s. By the 1980s, Mexico's population growth, among the most rapid in the hemisphere, had overwhelmed those dazzling food-production increases, despite some progress in reducing the birthrate by a late-starting family-planning program.

57   Recently, Mexico's problems have been compounded by its crippling foreign debt (largely a result of the oil-price bust in the 1980s), loss of 10 percent of its grain-producing farmland to other uses, an unfinished land-reform program, and chronic corruption. Mexico's agricultural system is probably sounder than many in Latin America, but its productive land is limited (the northern part of the country is largely desert), and the population is still growing fast; there are over 2 million more Mexicans to feed each year.

58   It should be emphasized that, unlike most of Asia, Latin America is not yet pushing against physical or biological limits of agricultural production under available technology. The problems listed above are part of a generally inefficient use of resources, encouraged to a significant degree by demand from the overpopulated rich countries. Unfortunately, many trends (especially the destruction of rain forests and widespread unchecked soil erosion) are undermining the potential for future food production. And population growth could quickly close the gap between food needs and the capacity to produce it.

AFRICA: FALLING BEHIND

59 Africa is the world's nutritional "basket case." While deaths related to inadequate diets occur in poor nations everywhere, only in Africa have there been widespread famines in the last two decades. In the 1980s, more than 5 million infants—one of every five or six children born—have died each year in Africa from causes related to hunger.

60   Periodically, the severity of African famines has been brought home to citizens of the rich nations through television programs showing starving children in hideous refugee camps. The coverage usually brings outpourings of empathy and donations, often generated with the help of celebrities and rock-music groups. Unfortunately, the acute situations publicized represent the iceberg tip of a continentwide tragedy: chronic hunger, spreading and intensifying year by year.

In the short term, donated food often does not reach the people it was 61
meant for. In the Ethiopian famines of the mid-1980s, both sides in a ferocious
civil war often used donated food as a weapon, preventing it from reaching
starving people in territory controlled by "the other side." Similar tactics
played a large role in the 1988 famine in Sudan, where some 100,000 perished.

Even in peacetime, food aid doesn't always reach its intended recipients. For 62
food donations to reach the neediest famine victims, many things have to work
right. Port facilities must be adequate, warehousing must be sufficient to store
the food safely until it can be distributed, trucks and railroads capable of moving the food to the hinterland must be in working condition (along with their
roads and railbeds). At the end of the line, there often must be four-wheel-drive
vehicles available to take food to the more remote parts of the countryside where
hunger may be most acute. The entire system must function smoothly in a time
of stress, often in the face of massive corruption in the distribution system.

The magnitude of the problems that can plague a relief effort are exempli- 63
fied by the Ethiopian situation in the mid-1980s. There were lots of television
pictures of Hercules transports flying in much-needed food. Unfortunately,
however, a Hercules can carry only 21 tons of grain, whereas Ethiopia needed
1.5 *million* tons. Such mountains of grain can be carried only on ships, which
take months to reach Ethiopia from donor countries. Furthermore, at maximum capacity, Ethiopia's ports can handle only 3,500 tons per day; so even if
the ships were perfectly lined up so that they never had to wait for space, and
port facilities were never broken down or left idle, it would take fourteen
months to unload that much grain. Meanwhile about 1.5 million Ethiopians
are added each year to the ranks of those to be fed.

The barriers to distributing food aid to starving refugees only highlight 64
problems of resource distribution and development that are endemic in Africa
and other poor regions. While the starving victims of war and revolution have
captured global attention, several hundred million victims of chronic rather
than acute food shortages continue to be overlooked, and inefficient and impoverished agricultural systems fall ever farther behind in the race to stay
ahead of population growth.

Since 1968, food production per person in Africa south of the Sahara has 65
declined by some 20 percent. Tropical African nations are too poor and debt-
burdened to make up all of the deficit with imports, and far too little food has
been made available for donation. The result has been a continuous erosion of
the nutritional status of Africans and in some areas a stagnation of progress in,
among other things, reducing infant mortalities—a necessary prerequisite to
reducing birthrates.

One example is Kenya, a country in some ways fortunate: it has a reason- 66
ably stable government, a well-established and remunerative tourist industry,
and one of the better agricultural systems on the continent. Yet Kenya can't feed
its people now, and population growth is so fast that, if it continues, there will
be twice as many Kenyans in fewer than twenty years. Per-capita water supplies in that semiarid nation will be reduced by half soon after the turn of the

century, and, despite a model soil-conservation program, erosion is unlikely to be brought under control before Kenya's population has doubled. By then, it may be too late for a nation with limited arable land and so many people that a major preoccupation of men even today is squabbling over ever tinier, subdivided landholding while the women do most of the farm and domestic work. Every year, Kenya must find food for a million more people.

67   Overall, the numbers for tropical Africa are grim. An estimated 44 percent of the region's people were inadequately fed in 1980, one in every four dangerously so. Since 1980, the situation has become, if anything, worse, as per-capita food production has continued to slip and populations have continued to expand by an average of 3 percent per year.

68   Nigeria's population, 115 million in 1989, is projected to reach 160 million in 2000, some 270 million in 2020, and over 530 million before growth ceases sometime after 2050. This is as many people as lived in all of Africa in 1984. We don't take such projections very seriously, since they *ignore nearly certain rises in death rates* resulting from the manifold consequences of overpopulation.

69   Crop yields in Nigeria in the 1980s were lower than they had been thirty years earlier, in part because of soil erosion. Corruption in government, mismanagement of resources (including revenues from oil), and failure to attend to agriculture have also contributed to Nigeria's problems. Imagine what they will be like if the Nigerian population doubles and redoubles in two generations, as projected!

70   The Sahel, a swath across Africa along the southern fringe of the Sahara cutting through a dozen countries, has been plagued with recurrent drought for nearly twenty years. The resultant, almost continuous famine has ceased to be "news" for the media, but is a prime example of the consequences of overpopulation. Overgrazing and overcultivation of the region's fragile lands have led to severe desertification. The effects of a naturally occurring drought were greatly intensified because so little vegetation remained to recycle the scant rainfall. Moreover, the denuded landscape's reflectivity had changed, leading to reduced cloud formation and thus still less rain. Even with the return of more normal rains in the late 1980s, the rapidly growing Sahel populations remained dependent on imported food to meet their needs.

71   North of the Sahara, the picture is not much better. The five nations of Africa's northern coast now import half their grain. Oil revenues in some cases have helped to finance the imports, and nutritional levels have improved during the 1980s. But the region's population is growing at an average annual rate of 2.8 percent, which does not bode well for future food self-sufficiency in those desert lands.

72   Temperate South Africa is the continent's breadbasket—to the extent that there is one. South Africa sells grain to its neighbors, and sustained some of them when drought afflicted the southern part of the continent earlier in the decade. But South Africa's black and "colored" populations are increasing rapidly (a further source of tension between the races), and the country's agricultural resources are already under stress. Given the disastrous government

policies and uncertain future of the country, we can't hold out much hope for the long-term wise use of agricultural resources.

In sum, there are few nutritional bright spots in the Dark Continent.   73

THE OVERFED DEVELOPED WORLD

We have until now concentrated on the food situation in the developing world,   74
because that is where the biggest problems are—problems that are tightly tied
to population growth. But in the modern world, food production is less and
less matched to the distribution of people. Before World War II, international
food trade was modest compared to the total amount produced. And the only
region that imported substantial amounts of grain was Europe. Then, Asia,
Latin America, and Africa were all net food-exporting regions, along with
North America. Today the situation has almost completely reversed. As developing nations have lost ground in food production, they have become increasingly dependent on the world grain market to supply their needs.

Some industrialized nations are also food-deficit nations, heavily depen-   75
dent on imports to feed their populations. Japan is an outstanding example,
importing over two thirds of its grain. The Soviet Union and several Eastern
European nations in recent years also have imported substantial portions of
their grain supplies. But all these countries can comparatively easily afford the
imports, and their populations are approaching ZPG. Hunger in these nations,
where it occurs, is due to maldistribution, misallocation of resources (as in the
USSR), and callousness about the plight of the poor. Many citizens of rich nations eat too much food for good health and waste too much of it.

Only a handful of nations today are reliable food exporters, nearly all of   76
them developed nations: the United States, Canada, the European Common
Market, Australia, New Zealand, Argentina, and Thailand. Americans, fond of
viewing their country as a leading industrial power, are largely unaware that it
also is by far the world's leading grain exporter and is economically dependent on those exports to keep its balance of trade from deteriorating even further. Three fourths of the world's grain shipments are from the North American
granary; over a hundred nations around the world depend at some level on
those resources. This goes far to explain why the 1988 drought that hit the
North American grain belt was a matter for global concern.

VACUUMING THE SEA

Now we turn to another important component of the world food system—   77
fisheries. Two decades ago, it was fashionable among population optimists to
say that the hungry millions could be fed by the boundless riches of the sea.
But the boundless riches of the seas have been measured and the bounds found
to be only too real.

78   In 1970 Peru harvested almost 13 million tons of anchovetas, which provided a large amount of cheap protein for animal feed, mainly to rich nations.
In 1972, the Peruvian anchoveta fishery collapsed. A combination of overfishing
and an El Niño, the warming of the normally cool waters of the Humboldt Current, caused a drop of the fishery's harvest to just over 2 million tons in 1973.
This launched a decade in which increases in global commercial-fishery harvest
lagged behind world population growth, with catches remaining below 70 million tons per year. Then, in the mid-1980s, there was a sharp upturn to about
84 million tons of fishes extracted from the oceans, plus another 7 million tons
provided by fish-farming in 1986. The increase was due largely to the recovery,
after almost two decades, of the Peruvian anchoveta fishery, combined with an
expansion of the take of pollack, a codlike fish, in the northeastern Pacific.

79   Cheer at this news has to be tempered by the realization that many fish
stocks are already overfished. An ecologist in Alaska recently told us that the
pollack fishery in the Bering Sea was being "strip-mined" and was expected to
decline soon.

80   Extraction of fishes from the oceans overall is approaching the maximum
sustainable yield, thought to be in the vicinity of 100 million tons of conventional fishes (that is, not including such potential seafood sources as octopus
and antarctic krill). Although 100 million tons of seafood seems small when
contrasted with a global grain harvest some seventeen times bigger, fishes supply a critical protein supplement to many people who otherwise would have
much less nutritious diets. Seafood is thus a vital element in the world food
picture.

81   If the approximately 24 million tons of fish caught each year in sports and
subsistence fishing, in addition to the commercial fisheries, are counted, the
100-million-ton estimate has been exceeded. Suppose, though, that estimate
were low, and the maximum sustainable yield were actually 150 million tons.
Suppose also that a miracle happened, and each stock was carefully harvested
so as to maintain its maximum sustainable yield. Even under those circumstances, per-capita yields would fall again within a few decades as population
growth overwhelmed those miracles.

82   Unfortunately, instead of miracles, fisheries are facing disasters. Demand
for fish is climbing steadily, encouraging the destructive harvesting of stocks.
Long before eastern-Pacific pollack became the fishermen's target, many stocks
in the North Atlantic were seriously depleted; competition for the dwindling
catches even led to a shooting war between the United Kingdom and Iceland
during the 1970s. The United Nations Food and Agriculture Organization recently estimated that, of 280 fisheries it monitors, only 25 could be considered
underexploited or moderately exploited. The only underexploited fishing regions left are in the Southern Hemisphere.

83   Meanwhile, ocean pollution is rising steadily, doubtless reducing the maximum sustainable yields for some stocks and contaminating many harvested
fishes. Coastal waters are not only the sites of greatest marine pollution (being
adjacent to the sources on land), they are also where most commercial fisheries
are located—an unfortunate combination. Oil, sewage, and medical wastes

washing up on American beaches tell us something about what's happening in the oceans.

Similar problems are occurring around the world. Off the coast of China, 84 the total seawater fishing area has been reduced by a third as a result of the annual discharge of 400 billion gallons of domestic and 1200 billion gallons of industrial sewage. According to Professor He Bochuan, whitebait, yellow croaker, prawns, and river crab are almost gone from the Bohai Sea (the northwestern corner of the Yellow Sea, the closest ocean to Beijing) and its estuaries.

Fisheries productivity has also been indirectly threatened by pollution of 85 estuaries and damage or destruction of coastal wetlands, which serve as important nursery areas and sources of food for numerous oceanic fish stocks. An even greater threat to estuaries and wetlands is posed by the prospect of global warming, which will cause the sea level to rise and flood them.

It seems the riches of the sea may not save us, after all. If humanity is lucky 86 (or careful), it may be possible to maintain the present level of production in the face of the human assault on the oceans and associated wetlands. If not, seafood may increasingly become a luxury food as dwindling catches and rising prices put it beyond the reach of people of modest means.

FOCUS ON ECOLOGY

1. Which of the many statistics provided by Paul R. Ehrlich and Anne H. Ehrlich were most interesting to you? Why? Were these numbers that you knew about or were they new to you? Is it important to know about the figures that Ehrlich and Ehrlich provide? How?
2. How do you respond to this essay? What does it make you feel?
3. What, according to Ehrlich and Ehrlich, is the role of developing countries in the food situation? Why is this?

FOCUS ON WRITING

1. Ehrlich and Ehrlich use quite a few statistics in this piece. What effect do these numbers have on their argument?
2. This selection reads much like a report—that is, it provides a good deal of information, much of which may be unfamiliar to you. Yet Ehrlich and Ehrlich also make an argument here. What is their argument?
3. Ehrlich and Ehrlich name many places in this piece. Are you familiar with the geographic locations of these places? Is it necessary to be familiar with them to fully understand what Ehrlich and Ehrlich are writing about?

FOR DISCUSSION

Ehrlich and Ehrlich discuss the world's food problems on a global scale. Reading this piece is informative and interesting, but where does it leave us individually? As a class, develop an "individual's approach to the food problem."

WRITING IN RESPONSE

Ehrlich and Ehrlich's "Food: The Ultimate Resource" was published in 1990, more than 13 years ago. As they note in this piece, things change in the food situation in short periods of time. Select one of the countries or regions Ehrlich and Ehrlich address. Then, do a bit of research and see how or if the food situation and population/food issues have changed since Ehrlich and Ehrlich first wrote about them here. Write your own report documenting the changes that have occurred since 1990. Be sure to cite the sources of your information.

The Pleasures of Eating

Wendell Berry

Wendell Berry is a farmer, a teacher, and a writer. He has earned critical acclaim for his nonfiction essays, his fiction, and his poetry. Berry's writing, no matter the genre, most frequently addresses the relationship between humans and nature, and his message, as Contemporary Authors *reports it, is always clear: "Humans must learn to live in harmony with the natural rhythms of the earth or perish." Berry has said, "We must support what supports local life, which means community, family, household life—the moral capital our larger institutions have to come to rest upon. If the larger institutions undermine the local life, they destroy that moral capital just exactly as the industrial economy has destroyed the natural capital of localities—soil fertility and so on. Essential wisdom accumulates in the community much as fertility builds in the soil." Born in 1934 in Henry County, Kentucky, Berry has written more than 25 books of poetry, 20 collections of essays, 6 novels, and 3 collections of short stories. The essay here, "The Pleasures of Eating," is taken from his collection* What People Are For. *The essay addresses the ways Americans have lost touch with the production and history of their food. Berry argues that American culture distances people from the land where their food is produced. As you read this essay, think carefully about your own life and the foods you eat. How connected to your food are you?*

JOURNAL ASSIGNMENT

In your journal, make a list of everything you have eaten today. Then, next to each item, list the ingredients it took to make that item. Then, next to each item list where each of those ingredients comes from. Then make a list of what it takes to bring all of those ingredients together to provide you with food: the act of growing and what is needed for growing, transporting the food, processing the food, preparing the food, packaging the food, advertising the food, selling the food, transporting the food to your home, and so on. In making these lists, think about what you really know about your food.

Many times, after I have finished a lecture on the decline of American farming 1 and rural life, someone in the audience has asked, "What can city people do?"

"Eat responsibly," I have usually answered. Of course, I have tried to ex- 2 plain what I meant by that, but afterwards I have invariably felt that there was more to be said than I had been able to say. Now I would like to attempt a better explanation.

I begin with the proposition that eating is an agricultural act. Eating ends 3 the annual drama of the food economy that begins with planting and birth. Most eaters, however, are no longer aware that this is true. They think of food as an agricultural product, perhaps, but they do not think of themselves as participants in agriculture. They think of themselves as "consumers." If they think beyond that, they recognize that they are passive consumers. They buy what they want—or what they have been persuaded to want—within the limits of what they can get. They pay, mostly without protest, what they are charged. And they mostly ignore certain critical questions about the quality and the cost of what they are sold: How fresh is it? How pure or clean is it, how free of dangerous chemicals? How far was it transported, and what did transportation add to the cost? How much did manufacturing or packaging or advertising add to the cost? When the food product has been manufactured or "processed" or "precooked," how has that affected its quality or price or nutritional value?

Most urban shoppers would tell you that food is produced on farms. But 4 most of them do not know what farms, or what kinds of farms, or where the farms are, or what knowledge or skills are involved in farming. They apparently have little doubt that farms will continue to produce, but they do not know how or over what obstacles. For them, then, food is pretty much an abstract idea—something they do not know or imagine—until it appears on the grocery shelf or on the table.

The specialization of production induces specialization of consumption. Pa- 5 trons of the entertainment industry, for example, entertain themselves less and less and have become more and more passively dependent on commercial suppliers. This is certainly true also of patrons of the food industry, who have tended more and more to be *mere* consumers—passive, uncritical, and dependent. Indeed, this sort of consumption may be said to be one of the chief goals of industrial production. The food industrialists have by now persuaded millions of consumers to prefer food that is already prepared. They will grow, deliver, and cook your food for you and (just like your mother) beg you to eat it. That they do not yet offer to insert it, prechewed, into your mouth is only because they have found no profitable way to do so. We may rest assured that they would be glad to find such a way. The ideal industrial food consumer would be strapped to a table with a tube running from the food factory directly into his or her stomach.

6   Perhaps I exaggerate, but not by much. The industrial eater is, in fact, one who does not know that eating is an agricultural act, who no longer knows or imagines the connections between eating and the land, and who is therefore necessarily passive and uncritical—in short, a victim. When food, in the minds of eaters, is no longer associated with farming and with the land, then the eaters are suffering a kind of cultural amnesia that is misleading and dangerous. The current version of the "dream home" of the future involves "effortless" shopping from a list of available goods on a television monitor and heating precooked food by remote control. Of course, this implies and depends on, a perfect ignorance of the history of the food that is consumed. It requires that the citizenry should give up their hereditary and sensible aversion to buying a pig in a poke. It wishes to make the selling of pigs in pokes an honorable and glamorous activity. The dreamer in this dream home will perforce know nothing about the kind or quality of this food, or where it came from, or how it was produced and prepared, or what ingredients, additives, and residues it contains—unless, that is, the dreamer undertakes a close and constant study of the food industry, in which case he or she might as well wake up and play an active and responsible part in the economy of food.

7   There is, then, a politics of food that, like any politics, involves our freedom. We still (sometimes) remember that we cannot be free if our minds and voices are controlled by someone else. But we have neglected to understand that we cannot be free if our food and its sources are controlled by someone else. The condition of the passive consumer of food is not a democratic condition. One reason to eat responsibly is to live free.

8   But if there is a food politics, there are also a food esthetics and a food ethics, neither of which is dissociated from politics. Like industrial sex, industrial eating has become a degraded, poor, and paltry thing. Our kitchens and other eating places more and more resemble filling stations, as our homes more and more resemble motels. "Life is not very interesting," we seem to have decided. "Let its satisfactions be minimal, perfunctory, and fast." We hurry through our meals to go to work and hurry through our work in order to "recreate" ourselves in the evenings and on weekends and vacations. And then we hurry, with the greatest possible speed and noise and violence, through our recreation—for what? To eat the billionth hamburger at some fast-food joint hellbent on increasing the "quality" of our life? And all this is carried out in a remarkable obliviousness to the causes and effects, the possibilities and the purposes, of the life of the body in this world.

9   One will find this obliviousness represented in virgin purity in the advertisements of the food industry, in which food wears as much makeup as the actors. If one gained one's whole knowledge of food from these advertisements (as some presumably do), one would not know that the various edibles were ever living creatures, or that they all come from the soil, or that they were pro-

duced by work. The passive American consumer, sitting down to a meal of pre-prepared or fast food, confronts a platter covered with inert, anonymous sub-stances that have been processed, dyed, breaded, sauced, gravied, ground, pulped, strained, blended, prettified, and sanitized beyond resemblance to any part of any creature that ever lived. The products of nature and agriculture have been made, to all appearances, the products of industry. Both eater and eaten are thus in exile from biological reality. And the result is a kind of soli-tude, unprecedented in human experience, in which the eater may think of eat-ing as, first, a purely commercial transaction between him and a supplier and then as a purely appetitive transaction between him and his food.

And this peculiar specialization of the act of eating is, again, of obvious 10 benefit to the food industry, which has good reasons to obscure the connection between food and farming. It would not do for the consumer to know that the hamburger she is eating came from a steer who spent much of his life standing deep in his own excrement in a feedlot, helping to pollute the local streams, or that the calf that yielded the veal cutlet on her plate spent its life in a box in which it did not have room to turn around. And, though her sympathy for the slaw might be less tender, she should not be encouraged to meditate on the hy-gienic and biological implications of mile-square fields of cabbage, for vegeta-bles grown in huge monocultures are dependent on toxic chemicals—just as animals in close confinement are dependent on antibiotics and other drugs.

The consumer, that is to say, must be kept from discovering that, in the 11 food industry—as in any other industry—the overriding concerns are not qual-ity and health, but volume and price. For decades now the entire industrial food economy, from the large farms and feedlots to the chains of supermarkets and fast-food restaurants, has been obsessed with volume. It has relentlessly increased scale in order to increase volume in order (presumably) to reduce costs. But as scale increases, diversity declines; as diversity declines, so does health; as health declines, the dependence on drugs and chemicals necessarily increases. As capital replaces labor, it does so by substituting machines, drugs, and chemicals for human workers and for the natural health and fertility of the soil. The food is produced by any means or any shortcut that will increase prof-its. And the business of the cosmeticians of advertising is to persuade the con-sumer that food so produced is good, tasty, healthful, and a guarantee of marital fidelity and long life.

It is possible, then, to be liberated from the husbandry and wifery of the 12 old household food economy. But one can be thus liberated only by entering a trap (unless one sees ignorance and helplessness as the signs of privilege, as many people apparently do). The trap is the ideal of industrialism: a walled city surrounded by valves that let merchandise in but no consciousness out. How does one escape this trap? Only voluntarily, the same way that one went in: by restoring one's consciousness of what is involved in eating; by reclaiming responsibility for one's own part in the food economy. One might begin with the illuminating principal of Sir Albert Howard's *The Soil and Health,* that we should understand "the whole problem of health in soil, plant, animal, and man as one great subject." Eaters, that is, must understand that eating takes place inescapably in the world, that it is inescapably an agricultural act, and that how we eat determines, to a considerable extent, how the world is used. This is a simple way of describing a relationship that is inexpressibly complex. To eat responsibly is to understand and enact, so far as one can, this complex relationship. What can one do? Here is a list, probably not definitive:

13   1.   Participate in food production to the extent that you can. If you have a yard or even just a porch box or a pot in a sunny window, grow something to eat in it. Make a little compost of your kitchen scraps and use it for fertilizer. Only by growing some food for yourself can you become acquainted with the beautiful energy cycle that revolves from soil to seed to flower to fruit to food to offal to decay, and around again. You will be fully responsible for any food that you grow for yourself, and you will know all about it. You will appreciate it fully, having known it all its life.

14   2.   Prepare your own food. This means reviving in your own mind and life the arts of kitchen and household. This should enable you to eat more cheaply, and it will give you a measure of "quality control": you will have some reliable knowledge of what has been added to the food you eat.

15   3.   Learn the origins of the food you buy, and buy the food that is produced closest to your home. The idea that every locality should be, as much as possible, the source of its own food makes several kinds of sense. The locally produced food supply is the most secure, the freshest, and the easiest for local consumers to know about and to influence.

16   4.   Whenever possible, deal directly with a local farmer, gardener, or orchardist. All the reasons listed for the previous suggestion apply here. In addition, by such dealing you eliminate the whole pack of merchants, transporters, processors, packagers, and advertisers who thrive at the expense of both producers and consumers.

17   5.   Learn, in self-defense, as much as you can of the economy and technology of industrial food production. What is added to food that is not food, and what do you pay for these additions?

18   6.   Learn what is involved in the *best* farming and gardening.

19   7.   Learn as much as you can, by direct observation and experience if possible, of the life histories of the food species.

20   The last suggestion seems particularly important to me. Many people are now as much estranged from the lives of domestic plants and animals (except for flowers and dogs and cats) as they are from the lives of the wild ones. This is regrettable, for these domestic creatures are in diverse ways attractive; there is much pleasure in knowing them. And farming, animal husbandry, horticulture, and gardening, at their best, are complex and comely arts; there is much pleasure in knowing them, too.

21   It follows that there is great *displeasure* in knowing about a food economy that degrades and abuses those arts and those plants and animals and the soil

from which they come. For anyone who does know something of the modern history of food, eating away from home can be a chore. My own inclination is to eat seafood instead of red meat or poultry when I am traveling. Though I am by no means a vegetarian, I dislike the thought that some animal has been made miserable in order to feed me. If I am going to eat meat, I want it to be from an animal that has lived a pleasant, uncrowded life outdoors, on bountiful pasture, with good water nearby and trees for shade. And I am getting almost as fussy about food plants. I like to eat vegetables and fruits that I know have lived happily and healthily in good soil, not the products of the huge, bechemicaled factory-fields that I have seen, for example, in the Central Valley of California. The industrial farm is said to have been patterned on the factory production line. In practice, it looks more like a concentration camp.

The pleasure of eating should be an *extensive* pleasure, not that of the mere 22 gourmet. People who know the garden in which their vegetables have grown and know that the garden is healthy will remember the beauty of the growing plants, perhaps in the dewy first light of morning when gardens are at their best. Such a memory involves itself with the food and is one of the pleasures of eating. The knowledge of the good health of the garden relieves and frees and comforts the eater. The same goes for eating meat. The thought of the good pasture and of the calf contentedly grazing flavors the steak. Some, I know, will think it bloodthirsty or worse to eat a fellow creature you have known all its life. On the contrary, I think it means that you eat with understanding and with gratitude. A significant part of the pleasure of eating is in one's accurate consciousness of the lives and the world from which food comes. The pleasure of eating, then, may be the best available standard of our health. And this pleasure, I think, is pretty fully available to the urban consumer who will make the necessary effort.

I mentioned earlier the politics, esthetics, and ethics of food. But to speak 23 of the pleasure of eating is to go beyond those categories. Eating with the fullest pleasure—pleasure, that is, that does not depend on ignorance—is perhaps the profoundest enactment of our connection with the world. In this pleasure we experience and celebrate our dependence and our gratitude, for we are living from mystery, from creatures we did not make and powers we cannot comprehend. When I think of the meaning of food, I always remember these lines by the poet William Carlos Williams, which seem to be merely honest:

> There is nothing to eat,
>   seek it where you will,
>   but the body of the Lord.
> The blessed plants
>   and the sea, yield it
>   to the imagination
> intact.

1989

FOCUS ON ECOLOGY

1. In what ways, according to Berry, are eaters participants in agriculture? Does this participation vary depending on where you live?
2. Why, according to Berry, is knowing a history of your food important? Along those same lines, what does Berry mean when he writes, "Both eater and eaten are thus in exile from biological reality"?
3. What does Berry mean by a "politics of food"?

FOCUS ON WRITING

1. Is this essay more a critique of the food industry or of the eating habits of Americans? What in the essay leads you to your response?
2. Why does Berry conclude his essay with the words of another writer: William Carlos Williams? Who is William Carlos Williams? For what is he known?
3. Why do you suppose Berry decided to title this essay "The Pleasures of Eating" when the essay is primarily about how Americans have lost touch with their food? To what does he refer through this title?

FOR DISCUSSION

As a class discuss the cultural role of food in America. How do we think of food? What role does it play in our daily lives? Where does our food come from? How do other cultures think of food?

WRITING IN RESPONSE

What is your all-time favorite food? What is the thing you love to eat most? In an essay, trace the steps it takes to put that item of food on your plate. Consider what goes into making that food item, where it comes from, how it is prepared, transported, and so on. You may have to do a bit of research, as many of us don't really pay attention to what is actually in our food. For instance, how many times have you considered the energy and cost of producing the piece of parsley with which a restaurant garnishes your plate? Or do you know and understand the process for producing the cheese slice on your cheeseburger? You should find that writing this piece will help you better understand not just what it is you like to eat, but what it takes for you to eat that food.

We Alone

Alice Walker

Alice Walker was born in 1944 in Eatonton, Georgia. She is the author of seven collections of poetry, more than a dozen works of fiction, three children's books, and seven works of nonfiction, though she is perhaps best known for her third novel, The Color Purple, *for which she was awarded the Pulitzer Prize. Much of her writing recounts the life and labors of African-Americans living in the South, material she most gleaned in part from her own life in Georgia. In addition to her writing about African-American life, Walker is also known for her coining of the term womanist, which, different from feminist, evokes an interest and focus on understanding women's culture, character, and emotions. Combining her work in womanism and in African-American writing, Walker has become one of the most important and prominent voices on African-American woman's experiences. Yet despite her focus on these issues, her writing reaches broader audiences, speaking to human experience in general. In the poem here, "We Alone," Walker writes about why humans have come to place value on particular items, such as gold. She claims that we can overturn these traditional values by not accepting them. As you read this poem, think about the kind of ethical, philosophical approach Walker is advancing. Consider also why you have come to value certain things in your own life and how others value those same things.*

JOURNAL ASSIGNMENT

In your journal, make a list of those material, physical things that we as a culture find valuable and those things we do not value as much. Then, make another list of the kinds of things you personally find valuable. Compare these lists. How much of what you value are also the things that we value culturally?

We alone can devalue gold
by not caring
if it falls or rises
in the marketplace.
Wherever there is gold
there is a chain, you know,

and if your chain
is gold
so much the worse
for you.

Feathers, shells
and sea-shaped stones
are all as rare.

This could be our revolution:
To love what is plentiful
as much as
what is scarce.

FOCUS ON ECOLOGY

1. What is Alice Walker arguing for in "We Alone"? Why might she make such an argument?
2. What might be accomplished in the kind of revolution to which Walker refers? What might she mean by "revolution"?
3. What might Walker mean when she writes, "and if your chain / is gold / so much the worse / for you"? Is she being literal?

FOCUS ON WRITING

1. What do we generally mean by the word *value?* How is value generally ascribed? Is value individually or culturally determined? In either case, why might Walker have titled this poem "We Alone"?
2. What is "the marketplace" to which Walker refers? Why might she have selected this word to make her point?
3. Look back at the three stanzas (parts) of this poem. What are Walker's agendas in each of these sections? Is there a relationship between these agendas and the length of each one? Explain.

FOR DISCUSSION

Walker brings up the interesting point that value is not something that is inherent to any particular item. Gold, for instance, is valuable only because we ascribe value to it. Likewise, as Walker explains, if we were to ascribe value to things now considered less valuable or not valuable at all, we could change our overall view of what is and isn't important. As a class, discuss what might happen to our cultural vision of things like sea shells and feathers and other items of nature if such a shift were made. What kinds of things do we value, and what kinds of things don't we value? In this discussion consider what kinds of things we could/should value more highly.

WRITING IN RESPONSE

Think about one particular thing to which we ascribe value and in turn use or guard because of that value; trace the history of that thing and learn why people find it valuable. What value used to be ascribed to that thing? How is it valued now? How is that value manifested? Who is able to control or access that thing? Do many have it? Can many get it?

"The Deer at Providencia" from *Teaching a Stone to Talk*

Annie Dillard

Annie Dillard wrote her first book, Pilgrim at Tinker Creek, *in 1974. The book, which won the Pulitzer Prize, is a revision of journal notes made while she was living in a cabin in the Blue Ridge Mountains on Tinker Creek; it explores her thoughts about God and nature. Dillard has since published a novel and several volumes of poetry and essays, including* Teaching a Stone to Talk, *from which this essay is taken. Her writing has been nominated for several awards since she won the Pulitzer Prize and has been awarded several prizes of recognition. Quite often Dillard's writing is categorized as "nature writing," but often, because of its breadth, it defies such a categorization. In "The Deer at Providencia," Dillard describes what happens when she and some male companions witness the struggles of a deer that has been tied down and will later be slaughtered and eaten. Her reaction bothers the men in her group as not being the anticipated response of a woman witnessing such suffering. As you read this intriguing piece, consider not only the ramifications of the narrator's response to the events and why it disturbed her companions, but consider the way Dillard presents the different parts of her narrative.*

JOURNAL ASSIGNMENT

Before reading this essay, write in your journal about how you would expect an American woman to react to witnessing a suffering deer struggle to free itself from ropes that hold it down. Why do you have expectations of such a reaction?

1   There were four of us North Americans in the jungle, in the Ecuadorian jungle on the banks of the Napo River in the Amazon watershed. The other three North Americans were metropolitan men. We stayed in tents in one riverside village, and visited others. At the village called Providencia we saw a sight which moved us, and which shocked the men.

2   The first thing we saw when we climbed the riverbank to the village of Providencia was the deer. It was roped to a tree on the grass clearing near the thatch shelter where we would eat lunch.

3   The deer was small, about the size of a whitetail fawn, but apparently full-grown. It had a rope around its neck and three feet caught in the rope. Someone said that the dogs had caught it that morning and the villagers were going to cook and eat it that night.

4   This clearing lay at the edge of the little thatched-hut village. We could see the villagers going about their business, scattering feed corn for hens about their houses, and wandering down paths to the river to bathe. The village head-man was our host; he stood beside us as we watched the deer struggle. Several village boys were interested in the deer; they formed part of the circle we made around it in the clearing. So also did four businessmen from Quito who were attempting to guide us around the jungle. Few of the very different people standing in this circle had a common language. We watched the deer, and no one said much.

5   The deer lay on its side at the rope's very end, so the rope lacked slack to let it rest its head in the dust. It was "pretty," delicate of bone like all deer, and thin-skinned for the tropics. Its skin looked virtually hairless, in fact, and almost translucent, like a membrane. Its neck was no thicker than my wrist; it was rubbed open on the rope, and gashed. Trying to paw itself free of the rope, the deer had scratched its own neck with its hooves. The raw underside of its neck showed red stripes and some bruises bleeding inside the muscles. Now three of its feet were hooked in the rope under its jaw. It could not stand, of course, on one leg, so it could not move to slacken the rope and ease the pull on its throat and enable it to rest its head.

6   Repeatedly the deer paused, motionless, its eyes veiled, with only its rib cage in motion, and its breaths the only sound. Then, after I would think, "It has given up; now it will die," it would heave. The rope twanged; the tree leaves clattered; the deer's free foot beat the ground. We stepped back and held our breaths. It thrashed, kicking, but only one leg moved; the other three legs tightened inside the rope's loop. Its hip jerked; its spine shook. Its eyes rolled; its tongue, thick with spittle, pushed in and out. Then it would rest again. We watched this for fifteen minutes.

Once three young native boys charged in, released its trapped legs, and 7
jumped back to the circle of people. But instantly the deer scratched up its neck
with its hooves and snared its forelegs in the rope again. It was easy to imagine
a third and then a fourth leg soon stuck, like Brer Rabbit and the Tar Baby.

We watched the deer from the circle, and then we drifted on to lunch. Our 8
palm-roofed shelter stood on a grassy promontory from which we could see
the deer tied to the tree, pigs and hens walking under village houses, and black-
and-white cattle standing in the river. There was even a breeze.

Lunch, which was the second and better lunch we had that day, was hot 9
and fried. There was a big fish called *doncella,* a kind of catfish, dipped whole
in corn flour and beaten egg, then deep fried. With our fingers we pulled soft
fragments of it from its sides to our plates, and ate; it was delicate fish-flesh,
fresh and mild. Someone found the roe, and I ate of that too—it was fat and
stronger, like egg yolk, naturally enough, and warm.

There was also a stew of meat in shreds with rice and pale brown gravy. I 10
had asked what kind of deer it was tied to the tree; Pepe had answered in Spanish, *"Gama."* Now they told us this was *gama* too, stewed. I suspect the word
means merely game or venison. At any rate, I heard that the village dogs had
cornered another deer just yesterday, and it was this deer which we were now
eating in full sight of the whole article. It was good. I was surprised at its ten-
derness. But it is a fact that high levels of lactic acid, which builds up in muscle
tissues during exertion, tenderizes.

After the fish and meat we ate bananas fried in chunks and served on a 11
tray; they were sweet and full of flavor. I felt terrific. My shirt was wet and cool
from swimming; I had had a night's sleep, two decent walks, three meals, and
a swim—everything tasted good. From time to time each one of us, separately,
would look beyond our shaded roof to the sunny spot where the deer was still
convulsing in the dust. Our meal completed, we walked around the deer and
back to the boats.

That night I learned that while we were watching the deer, the others were 12
watching me.

We four North Americans grew close in the jungle in a way that was not 13
the usual artificial intimacy of travelers. We liked each other. We stayed up all
that night talking, murmuring, as though we rocked on hammocks slung above
time. The others were from big cities: New York, Washington, Boston. They all
said that I had no expression on my face when I was watching the deer—or at
any rate, not the expression they expected.

They had looked to see how I, the only woman, and the youngest, was tak- 14
ing the sight of the deer's struggles. I looked detached, apparently, or hard, or
calm, or focused, still. I don't know. I was thinking. I remember feeling very
old and energetic. I could say like Thoreau that I have traveled widely in

Roanoke, Virginia. I have thought a great deal about carnivorousness; I eat meat. These things are not issues; they are mysteries.

15   Gentlemen of the city, what surprises you? That there is suffering here, or that I know it?

16   We lay in the tent and talked. "If it had been my wife," one man said with special vigor, amazed, "she wouldn't have cared *what* was going on; she would have dropped *everything* right at that moment and gone in the village from here to there to there, she would not have *stopped* until that animal was out of its suffering one way or another. She couldn't *bear* to see a creature in agony like that."

17   I nodded.

18   Now I am home. When I wake I comb my hair before the mirror above my dresser. Every morning for the past two years I have seen in that mirror, beside my sleep-softened face, the blackened face of a burnt man. It is a wire-service photograph clipped from a newspaper and taped to my mirror. The caption reads: "Alan McDonald in Miami hospital bed." All you can see in the photograph is a smudged triangle of face from his eyelids to his lower lip; the rest is bandages. You cannot see the expression in his eyes; the bandages shade them.

19   The story, headed MAN BURNED FOR SECOND TIME, begins:

> "Why does God hate me?" Alan McDonald asked from his hospital bed.
> "When the gunpowder went off, I couldn't believe it," he said. "I just couldn't believe it. I said, 'No, God couldn't do this to me again.'"

He was in a burn ward in Miami, in serious condition. I do not even know if he lived. I wrote him a letter at the time, cringing.

20   He had been burned before, thirteen years previously, by flaming gasoline. For years he had been having his body restored and his face remade in dozens of operations. He had been a boy, and then a burnt boy. He had already been stunned by what could happen, by how life could veer.

21   Once I read that people who survive bad burns tend to go crazy; they have a very high suicide rate. Medicine cannot ease their pain; drugs just leak away, soaking the sheets, because there is no skin to hold them in. The people just lie there and weep. Later they kill themselves. They had not known, before they were burned, that the world included such suffering, that life could permit them personally such pain.

22   This time a bowl of gunpowder had exploded on McDonald.

> I didn't realize what had happened at first," he recounted. "And then I heard that sound from 13 years ago. I was burning. I rolled to put the fire out and I thought, 'Oh God, not again.'
> "If my friend hadn't been there, I would have jumped into a canal with a rock around my neck."

23 His wife concludes the piece, "Man, it just isn't fair."

I read the whole clipping again every morning. This is the Big Time here, 24
every minute of it. Will someone please explain to Alan McDonald in his dignity, to the deer at Providencia in his dignity, what is going on? And mail me
the carbon.

When we walked by the deer at Providencia for the last time, I said to Pepe, 25
with a pitying glance at the deer, *"Pobrecito"*—"poor little thing." But I was trying out Spanish. I knew at the time it was a ridiculous thing to say.

FOCUS ON ECOLOGY

1. What is the relationship between the first section of this essay in which Dillard describes the struggle of the deer tied to the tree and the second section
   that details the lunch she and her companions ate? What is the relevance of
   this relationship?
2. What might Dillard mean when she writes, "I have thought a great deal about
   carnivorousness; I eat meat. These things are not issues; they are mysteries"?
3. In this essay, Dillard describes the reactions of her male companions to her
   own response at seeing the deer. One of the men comments that his wife
   would have ended the suffering of the animal. Look back at this short section
   in the essay. What is Dillard suggesting about reactions to the suffering of an
   animal meant to be food? What does her own reaction to the man's comments
   suggest?

FOCUS ON WRITING

1. To what does Annie Dillard refer when she describes the deer tangling its
   legs in the rope as being "like Brer Rabbit and the Tar Baby"? Do we need to
   know this reference to understand her simile?
2. This essay has four primary parts: the story of the deer tied to the tree, the
   description of the lunch, the reaction of the men, and the details of the picture of the burned man that hangs on Dillard's mirror. There is little transition between these sections, which are, in fact, set apart by breaks in the essay
   rather than linked together as a single flowing narrative. How do these four
   parts interact with one another in this essay? Why do you suppose Dillard
   chose to break this essay into parts like this? Is it an effective strategy?
3. Is it important to know where the first part of this essay took place? What
   role does geography play in addressing issues such as those about which
   Dillard writes?

FOR DISCUSSION

Imagine being among Dillard's companions as they witnessed the struggles of
the deer and then went in to lunch. How would you react? Why? As a class,

consider the different reactions from different members of the class. Think about why you might react the way you think you would. Has anyone in the class had an experience similar to the one discussed here?

WRITING IN RESPONSE

Annie Dillard makes several important points in "The Deer at Providencia." Of these, the idea that she, a woman, reacted differently from what was expected certainly merits consideration. In addition, her acknowledgment that animals suffer when we kill them to eat them, but that eating meat is all right also warrants consideration. And her comparison between the suffering of animals and the suffering of humans also makes us think about her position. Take up any one of these three ideas in an essay and explore that idea in detail. Be sure to consider not just how you feel about the subject, but also the importance of how others have discussed such issues and how we are taught (and who teaches us) to think about such things.

Talking to the Owls and Butterflies

Lame Deer

Lame Deer, a medicine man and Sioux chief, lived from 1895 until 1976. His leadership and spiritual guidance to both the Sioux people and Native Americans in general was crucial. His only book, Lame Deer, Seeker of Visions, *from which "Talking to the Owls and Butterflies" is taken, was translated into more than 10 languages. This book, which addresses a variety of subjects concerning the lives of Native Americans, offers important commentary on the role white people have played in Native American lives and the relationships between Native Americans and nature. Lame Deer makes it clear that whites and Indians see nature differently, and in "Talking to the Owls and Butterflies" he addresses the differences in how whites have consumed nature versus how Indians see food and consumption. As you read this intriguing piece, pay attention to how Lame Deer establishes voice and uses the power of that voice to convey his message.*

JOURNAL ASSIGNMENT

Think about how you gather your food and from where your food comes. Think, then, about how cultures like Native American tribes gathered their food before white influences. In your journal, write about the differences in consumption and food gathering.

Let's sit down here, all of us, on the open prairie, where we can't see a high- 1
way or a fence. Let's have no blankets to sit on, but feel the ground with our
bodies, the earth, the yielding shrubs. Let's have the grass for a mattress, experiencing its sharpness and its softness. Let us become like stones, plants, and
trees. Let us be animals, think and feel like animals.

Listen to the air. You can hear it, feel it, smell it, taste it. *Woniya wakan*—the 2
holy air—which renews all by its breath. *Woniya, woniya wakan*—spirit, life,
breath, renewal—it means all that. *Woniya*—we sit together, don't touch, but
something is there; we feel it between us, as a presence. A good way to start
thinking about nature, talk about it. Rather talk to it, talk to the rivers, to the
lakes, to the winds as to our relatives.

You have made it hard for us to experience nature in the good way by being 3
part of it. Even here we are conscious that somewhere out in those hills there
are missile silos and radar stations. White men always pick the few unspoiled,
beautiful, awesome spots for the sites of these abominations. You have raped
and violated these lands, always saying, "Gimme, gimme, gimme," and never
giving anything back. You have taken 200,000 acres of our Pine Ridge reservation and made them into a bombing range. This land is so beautiful and strange
that now some of you want to make it into a national park. The only use you
have made of this land since you took it from us was to blow it up. You have
not only despoiled the earth, the rocks, the minerals, all of which you call
"dead" but which are very much alive; you have even changed the animals,
which are part of us, part of the Great Spirit, changed them in a horrible way,
so no one can recognize them. There is power in a buffalo—spiritual, magic
power—but there is no power in an Angus, in a Hereford.

There is power in an antelope, but not in a goat or in a sheep, which holds 4
still while you butcher it, which will eat your newspaper if you let it. There
was great power in a wolf, even in a coyote. You have made him into a freak—
a toy poodle, a Pekingese, a lap dog. You can't do much with a cat, which is
like an Indian, unchangeable. So you fix it, alter it, declaw it, even cut its vocal
cords so you can experiment on it in a laboratory without being disturbed by
its cries.

A partridge, a grouse, a quail, a pheasant, you have made them into chick- 5
ens, creatures that can't fly, that wear a kind of sunglasses so that they won't
peck each other's eyes out, "birds" with a "pecking order." There are some
farms where they breed chickens for breast meat. Those birds are kept in low
cages, forced to be hunched over all the time, which makes the breast muscles
very big. Soothing sounds, Muzak, are piped into these chicken hutches. One
loud noise and the chickens go haywire, killing themselves by flying against the
mesh of their cages. Having to spend all their lives stooped over makes an unnatural, crazy, no-good bird. It also makes unnatural, no-good human beings.

That's where you fooled yourselves. You have not only altered, declawed 6
and malformed your winged and four-legged cousins; you have done it to

yourselves. You have changed men into chairmen of boards, into office work-ers, into time-clock punchers. You have changed women into housewives, truly fearful creatures. I was once invited into the home of such a one.

7   "Watch the ashes, don't smoke, you stain the curtains. Watch the goldfish bowl, don't breathe on the parakeet, don't lean your head against the wallpaper; your hair may be greasy. Don't spill your liquor on that table; it has a delicate finish. You should have wiped your boots; the floor was just varnished. Don't, don't, don't . . ." That is crazy. We weren't made to endure this. You live in pris-ons which you have built for yourselves, calling them "homes," offices, facto-ries. We have a new joke on the reservation: "What is cultural deprivation?" Answer: "Being an upper-middle-class white kid living in a split-level subur-ban home with a color TV."

8   Sometimes I think that even our pitiful tar-paper shacks are better than your luxury homes. Walking a hundred feet to the outhouse on a clear wintry night, through mud or snow, that's one small link with nature. Or in the sum-mer, in the back country, leaving the door of the privy open, taking your time, listening to the humming of the insects, the sun warming your bones through the thin planks of wood; you don't even have that pleasure anymore.

9   Americans want to have everything sanitized. No smells! Not even the good, natural man and woman smell. Take away the smell from under the armpits, from your skin. Rub it out, and then spray or dab some nonhuman odor on yourself, stuff you can spend a lot of money on, ten dollars an ounce, so you know this has to smell good. "B.O.," bad breath, "Intimate Female Odor Spray"—I see it all on TV. Soon you'll breed people without body openings.

10   I think white people are so afraid of the world they created that they don't want to see, feel, smell or hear it. The feeling of rain and snow on your face, being numbed by an icy wind and thawing out before a smoking fire, coming out of a hot sweat bath and plunging into a cold stream, these things make you feel alive, but you don't want them anymore. Living in boxes which shut out the heat of the summer and the chill of winter, living inside a body that no longer has a scent, hearing the noise from the hi-fi instead of listening to the sounds of nature, watching some actor on TV having a make-believe experience when you no longer experience anything for yourself, eating food without taste—that's your way. It's no good.

11   The food you eat, you treat it like your bodies, take out all the nature part, the taste, the smell, the roughness, then put the artificial color, the artificial flavor in. Raw liver, raw kidney—that's what we old-fashioned full-bloods like to get our teeth into. In the old days we used to eat the guts of the buffalo, making a contest of it, two fellows getting hold of a long piece of intestines from opposite ends, starting chewing toward the middle, seeing who can get there first; that's eating. Those buffalo guts, full of half-fermented, half-digested grass and herbs, you didn't need any pills and vitamins when you swallowed those. Use the bitterness of gall for flavoring, not refined salt or sugar. *Wasna*—meat, kidney fat and berries all pounded together—a lump of that sweet *wasna* kept a man going for a whole day. That was food, that had the power. Not the stuff you

give us today: powdered milk, dehydrated eggs, pasteurized butter, chickens that are all drumsticks or all breast; there's no bird left there.

You don't want the bird. You don't have the courage to kill honestly—cut 12 off the chicken's head, pluck it and gut it—no, you don't want this anymore. So it all comes in a neat plastic bag, all cut up, ready to eat, with no taste and no guilt. Your mink and seal coats, you don't want to know about the blood and pain which went into making them. Your idea of war—sit in an airplane, way above the clouds, press a button, drop the bombs, and never look below the clouds—that's the odorless, guiltless, sanitized way.

When we killed a buffalo, we knew what we were doing. We apologized to 13 his spirit, tried to make him understand why we did it, honoring with a prayer the bones of those who gave their flesh to keep us alive, praying for their return, praying for the life of our brothers, the buffalo nation, as well as for our own people. You wouldn't understand this and that's why we had the Washita Massacre, the Sand Creek Massacre, the dead women and babies at Wounded Knee. That's why we have Song My and My Lai now.

To us life, all life, is sacred. The state of South Dakota has pest-control of- 14 ficers. They go up in a plane and shoot coyotes from the air. They keep track of their kills, put them all down in their little books. The stockmen and sheep-owners pay them. Coyotes eat mostly rodents, field mice and such. Only once in a while will they go after a stray lamb. They are our natural garbage men cleaning up the rotten and stinking things. They make good pets if you give them a chance. But their living could lose some man a few cents, and so the coyotes are killed from the air. They were here before the sheep, but they are in the way; you can't make a profit out of them. More and more animals are dying out. The animals which the Great Spirit put here, they must go. The man-made animals are allowed to stay—at least until they are shipped out to be butchered. That terrible arrogance of the white man, making himself something more than God, more than nature, saying, "I will let this animal live, because it makes money"; saying, "This animal must go, it brings no income, the space it occupies can be used in a better way. The only good coyote is a dead coyote." They are treating coyotes almost as badly as they used to treat Indians.

You are spreading death, buying and selling death. With all your deodor- 15 ants, you smell of it, but you are afraid of its reality; you don't want to face up to it. You have sanitized death, put it under the rug, robbed it of its honor. But we Indians think a lot about death. I do. Today would be a perfect day to die—not too hot, not too cool. A day to leave something of yourself behind, to let it linger. A day for a lucky man to come to the end of his trail. A happy man with many friends. Other days are not so good. They are for selfish, lonesome men, having a hard time leaving this earth. But for whites every day would be considered a bad one, I guess.

Eighty years ago our people danced the Ghost Dance, singing and dancing 16 until they dropped from exhaustion, swooning, fainting, seeing visions. They danced in this way to bring back their dead, to bring back the buffalo. A prophet had told them that through the power of the Ghost Dance the earth would roll up like a carpet, with all the white man's works—the fences and the mining towns with their whorehouses, the factories and the farms with their stinking, unnatural animals, the railroads and the telegraph poles, the whole works. And underneath this rolled-up white man's world we would find again the flowering prairie, unspoiled, with its herds of buffalo and antelope, its clouds of birds, belonging to everyone, enjoyed by all.

17   I guess it was not time then for this to happen, but it is coming back, I feel it warming my bones. Not the old Ghost Dance, not the rolling-up—but a new-old spirit, not only among Indians but among whites and blacks, too, especially among young people. It is like raindrops making a tiny brook, many brooks making a stream, many streams making one big river bursting all dams. Us making this book, talking like this—these are some of the raindrops.

18   Listen, I saw this in my mind not long ago: In my vision the electric light will stop sometime. It is used too much for TV and going to the moon. The day is coming when nature will stop the electricity. Police without flashlights, beer getting hot in the refrigerators, planes dropping from the sky, even the President can't call up somebody on the phone. A young man will come, or men, who'll know how to shut off all electricity. It will be painful, like giving birth. Rapings in the dark, winos breaking into the liquor stores, a lot of destruction. People are being too smart, too clever; the machine stops and they are helpless, because they have forgotten how to make do without the machine. There is a Light Man coming, bringing a new light. It will happen before this century is over. The man who has this power will do good things, too—stop all atomic power, stop wars, just by shutting the white electro-power off. I hope to see this, but then I'm also afraid. What will be will be.

19   I think we are moving in a circle, or maybe a spiral, going a little higher every time, but still returning to the same point. We are moving closer to nature again. I feel it, you feel it, your two boys here feel it. It won't be bad, doing without many things you are now used to, things taken out of the earth and wasted foolishly. You can't replace them and they won't last forever. Then you'll have to live more according to the Indian way. People won't like that, but their children will. The machine will stop, I hope, before they make electric corncobs for poor Indians' privies.

20   We'll come out of our boxes and rediscover the weather. In the old days you took your weather as it came, following the cranes, moving south with the herds. Here, in South Dakota, they say, "If you don't like the weather, wait five minutes." It can be 100 degrees in the shade one afternoon and suddenly there comes a storm with hailstones as big as golf balls, the prairie is all white and your teeth chatter. That's good—a reminder that you are just a small particle of nature, not so powerful as you think.

21   You people try to escape the weather, fly to Miami where it's summer all the time, miss the rains, miss the snow. That's pitiful. Up to 1925 we had some old men who had a sort of a club where they could get together. Somehow they could tell what the weather would be. They needed no forecaster with all those gimmicks, satellites and what have you. They just had their wisdom, something which told them what nature was up to.

Some medicine men have the power to influence the weather. One does 22 not use it lightly, only when it is absolutely necessary. When we hold our sun dance, we always try to have perfect weather. When we had a wedding ceremony in Winner, last spring, you saw me draw a design in the earth, the figure of a turtle. I picked this up from the old people. When I was a little boy I had a party where we played games. It was drizzling and I was mad. We wanted to play and the weather wouldn't let us. My grandma said, "Why don't you make the picture of a turtle?" Before we were through making it, the rain stopped. I could dry the country up, or make a special upside-down turtle and flood everything. You have to know the right prayer with it, the right words. I won't tell what they are. That's too dangerous. You don't fool around with it. I see that white man's look on your face. You don't believe this. Ask my friend Pete Catches here, a brother medicine man.

PETE CATCHES: "John is right. That sun dance he was referring to, when 23 we chopped down the sun-dance pole, we had to catch the tree. It is not supposed to touch the ground. We stood in line and I was close to the trunk of the tree, and when it fell it hit me right above the knee. I went through the sun dance with that suffering in me. And I really liked it. My sun dance was as near close to authentic as I could make it. I pierced my flesh in the morning and broke loose around three o'clock in the afternoon, the longest piercing since we revived this sacred dance. And after I broke loose, there was a big thundercloud forming in the west. A lot of people wanted to get away, to go home before the storm broke. And it was nearing, coming on fast. So, during the course of the dance, they handed me my pipe, the pipe that I always use. I call it my chief pipe. So I took that and asked the Great Spirit to part that thunder, part it in half, so we can finish our ceremony. Before all the people that great storm parted, right before their eyes. The one part went to the north, wrought havoc in the White River country, clear on in, tore off the roofs, destroyed gardens and acted like that. The part of the storm which went south, toward Pine Ridge, covered everything with hail, but on the dance ground the sun kept shining. So, to me, that sun dance in 1964 was the best one I ever did.

"And the power of the turtle design, what John told you about it, we know 24 this to be true. The heart of Keha, the turtle, is about the strongest thing there is. It keeps on beating and beating for two days after you kill the turtle. There is so much strength and endurance in it. To eat such a heart makes you tough. It imparts its power to whoever has eaten it. My sister ate that turtle heart. They had to cut it in half for her to make it possible to swallow it. This made her into a strong woman, stouthearted like a warrior. She had a growth on her breast. The doctors said it was cancer. She lit five cigarettes. She told the children to puff on them, to keep those cigarettes glowing. Then she took the lighted cigarettes, one after the other, and burned this evil thing out of her. On and on she went, deep into her breast, and her face remained calm all the while; not one muscle twitched. She is cured now. A turtle heart will do this for you.

"But all animals have power, because the Great Spirit dwells in all of them, 25 even a tiny ant, a butterfly, a tree, a flower, a rock. The modern, white man's way keeps that power from us, dilutes it. To come to nature, feel its power, let it help you, one needs time and patience for that. Time to think, to figure it all out. You have so little time for contemplation; it's always rush, rush, rush with you. It lessens a person's life, all that grind, that hurrying and scurrying about. Our old people say that the Indians of long ago didn't have heart trouble. They didn't have that cancer. The illnesses they had they knew how to cure. But between 1890 and 1920 most of the medicines, the animal bundles, the pipes, the ancient, secret things which we had treasured for centuries, were lost and destroyed by the B.I.A., by the Government police. They went about tearing down sweat lodges, went into our homes, broke the pipes, tore up the medicine bags, threw them into the fire, burned them up, completely wiped out the wisdom of generations. But the Indian, you take away everything from him, he still has his mouth to pray, to sing the ancient songs. He can still do his *yuwipi* ceremony in a darkened room, beat his small drum, make the power come back, make the wisdom return. He did, but not all of it. The elk medicines are gone. The bear medicine, too. We had a medicine man here, up the creek, who died about fifteen years ago. He was the last bear medicine man that I knew about. And he was good, too. He was really good."

26   But it is coming again, the bear power. We make bear sounds, talk bear language when we are in a fighting mood. "Harrnh"—and you are as good as gone. A bear claw, properly treated, you pierce a man for the sun dance with it, he won't feel the pain. Let me tell you about the power of the bear, natural animal power when it comes up against one of those artificial, non-animals.

27   When I was a boy, a long time ago, I was traveling with my father. We were on our way back to Standing Rock. It happened on the road. My dad stopped for a poker game at a saloon. In the next room a young bear was sitting on the counter, hardly more than a cub. He was chained down, really pitiful. They teased him, made him stand up on two legs.

28   The card players paid it no mind. They had big stacks of silver dollars before each player. I was sitting under the table. I liked those big, round, shiny silver pieces. I reached up and helped myself to some. Nobody noticed, or maybe they didn't mind. A big white man in a shaggy black coat and a derby walked into the place and sat down at the counter. With him he had a huge bulldog, really huge.

29   "You have a nice pet here," said the big man, chomping on a big cigar, to the bartender. "But you'd better watch him. If my dog gets loose, your bear will be all chewed up."

30   "That bulldog is good for nothing. He can't lick my pet!"

31   "I bet you fifty bucks he can. I give you odds—five to one—my bulldog will tear up this pet. Let's have a big fight!"

32   They put all this money up, the gamblers tripping over each other to get into the action. They took the bulldog and the bear outside. There was a big brown tent there where they used to hold revival meetings. There were four or five big cowboy hats full of betting money for the dog and for the bear. The

news of the fight spread like wildfire, with more and more people coming all the time.

My dad had sold some cattle and had money on him. He told me, "Son, 33 I'm going to bet a hundred dollars on that little pet bear." The big white man with the derby was so sure of his huge brute that he put up fistfuls of money against my dad—those big old twenty-dollar bills, gold and silver coins. They drew a circle inside the tent. Nobody was supposed to step in there. Those who had bet money could sit up front. They knelt or sat down so that the others could see what was going on. There were no bleachers. They put up some blankets, like a fence, to keep the two animals in the circle. The dog owner and the saloon keeper sat inside the circle together with the man who held the bank. I never again saw such a big heap of money all in one place. They were all puffing on their big cheroots, filling the tent with smoke. At last the big man with the dog said, "Five minutes more, after that no more bets!"

That caused a big commotion. Everybody tried to get into the act then. 34 People got so heated up arguing about who was going to win, they started fist fights all over the place, the money rolling on the ground. Those were the old gambling days!

"Quit fussing and bet!" said the big man. Then he pulled out his watch. 35 "Time's up. No more." He turned to his dog and pulled his ears a little. "Okay, get that bear, kill the little bastard. Tear him apart!"

That poor thing of a bear was sitting up like a baby, as if the whole show 36 was no concern of his. "One round, that's all," said the bartender, "one round to the finish." Still a few ranchers and cowhands came running, money in their hands. They were out of luck, or maybe lucky, depending on what they had in mind, because the dog owner pulled a gun and fired it as a starter.

The poor little bear was still sitting up there when they sicked the dog on 37 him. Boy, that bear came on slow. Under the old gas lamps his eyes looked blue. The dog was growling, snarling, his nose more wrinkled than my face is now. The bear just moved a foot closer and sat down again. He looked at that growling thing, all full of white teeth. The little bear just rubbed his paw on the earth, put some dirt on his head. That bulldog, maybe he was smarter than his owner. May he know something. He snarled, growled, made a big racket, but kept his distance. The big man in the derby got annoyed. "Come on, get on with it," he said and kicked the dog in the backside. The dog gathered himself up for the charge and finally here he comes.

The bear just reached out with his paw, the claws shooting out like so many 38 knives, and made one swipe at the dog, just one swipe, and that old bulldog is out and cold, throat ripped out, dead and gone. And the little bear made the killing sound, "harrrnh," like a Sioux Indian.

My dad won over 700 dollars on that little bear. Most of the whites had bet 39 on the bulldog; all the Indians had put their money on that puny bear. They knew he had the power.

It is the same with the buffalo. They have the power and the wisdom. We 40 Sioux have a close relationship to the buffalo. He is our brother. We have many legends of buffalo changing themselves into men. And the Indians are built like buffalo, too—big shoulders, narrow hips. According to our belief, the Buffalo Woman who brought us the peace pipe, which is at the center of our religion, was a beautiful maiden, and after she had taught our tribes how to worship with the pipe, she changed herself into a white buffalo calf. So the buffalo is very sacred to us. You can't understand about nature, about the feeling we have toward it, unless you understand how close we were to the buffalo. That animal was almost like a part of ourselves, part of our souls.

41   The buffalo gave us everything we needed. Without it we were nothing. Our tipis were made of his skin. His hide was our bed, our blanket, our winter coat. It was our drum, throbbing through the night, alive, holy. Out of his skin we made our water bags. His flesh strengthened us, became flesh of our flesh. Not the smallest part of it was wasted. His stomach, a red-hot stone dropped into it, became our soup kettle. His horns were our spoons, the bones our knives, our women's awls and needles. Out of his sinews we made our bowstrings and thread. His ribs were fashioned into sleds for our children, his hoofs became rattles. His mighty skull, with the pipe leaning against it, was our scared altar. The name of the greatest of all Sioux was Tatanka Iyotake—Sitting Bull. When you killed off the buffalo, you also killed the Indian—the real, natural, "wild" Indian.

42   The buffalo has wisdom, but man-bred cattle—that's just a factory-made thing. They have no sense. Those Mexican fighting bulls get fooled by the cape every time. They are brave, yes, but not very smart. Imagine those bullfighters taking on a buffalo. They'd all get killed. The man-bred bull, he keeps looking at the cape. But a buffalo wouldn't be horn-swoggled by a red piece of cloth. He'd be looking for the man behind the cape, and his horns would find him. Buffalo are smart. They also have a sense of humor. Remember when we were together last in the Black Hills? When it suddenly snowed after a very hot day? Those six big black bulls we saw near Blue Bell, just like six large pick-up trucks. They were so happy over that snow. Gamboling, racing around, playing like kittens. And afterward we came across the tame cattle, hunched over, miserable, pitiful. "Moo, moo, moo—I'm cold." The real, natural animals don't mind the cold; they are happy with the kind of fur coat and galoshes the Great Spirit gave them. White hunters used to call the buffalo stupid because they were easy to shoot, weren't afraid of a gun. But the buffalo was not designed to cope with modern weapons. He was designed to deal with an Indian's arrows.

43   I told you about the little bear and the bulldog. Let me tell you about the buffalo and the bull. Word got around that some ranchers were staging a fight between a buffalo and a bull at the Philips ranch. We Sioux are all natural gamblers. We used to have many betting games long before the white man came. Betting was something you didn't have to teach us. We could have taught you. My dad knew how to judge things. This happened in 1919 or 1920. We had one of those funny old Fords. It took three dollars to get from Fort Pierre to the Philips ranch. On three bucks you could go, maybe, a hundred miles. I was about sixteen years old. Dad was still taking care of me. Well, we got to that

ranch. The corral was loaded, black with people. They had two roosters fighting each other first, to warm up the crowd, get the money moving. My dad wouldn't bet on a chicken. Two poor chickens, scratching and pecking at each other, who could get excited about such a thing?

At last they drove the buffalo into the trap. The bull was already waiting in 44 a chute. It was owned by a man from Wyoming. It had a short name, but I don't remember it. You hear me, the buffalo is a "he" always, unless we are talking about a cow. But a man-bred bull, that's an "it." It was big all right, a real Bull Durham bull, the meanest bull in the country. Its balls dangled so low it almost tripped over them. They opened the chute. Boy, I've seen lots of bulls in my days, but wow—those horns! They were huge, light with black tips.

The old buffler was blowing dirt this way and that, pawing the ground, 45 looking at the crowd. Some men were sitting on top of the corral, some ladies too, I noticed. They had long skirts in those days, but I saw some nice legs. That was some crowd! They were hollering like at Billy Graham's. All that commotion stirred up the buffalo, made him excited.

My dad picked up many two-to-one and three-to-one bets. He bet the buf- 46 falo to win, but this I don't have to tell you. I thought there would be a hundred-miles-an-hour collision. The bull was about ready to charge. Its tail was sticking up in the air. I was scared it might break through the corral. My dad said, "Stay behind that big post just in case. Something could go wrong." My dad talked only when it was necessary. For a moment I was afraid that the buffalo would chicken out, because he ignored the bull. They had only about twenty yards to make their charge. The whole corral was maybe a little over a hundred feet across. At last here they came. They missed each other, horns straight up, like two passing trains coming from opposite directions. There was a big, disappointed "oh" from the crowd. But then we saw that the buffalo had ripped the side of the bull open as if with a razor blade. The ribs of the bull were cut. Two cowboys were yelling, "That bull is dead!" It still kicked a few times, but it was deader than hell. Those tame animals don't have the power.

A *hoka*—a badger—now there's a real animal. One day my uncle was on his 47 gray horse, the one he uses to round up his other ponies with. He was riding bareback, just with a rope, a hitch around the gray's nozzle. Then he saw the badger. Once a badger is in his hole, not three or four men can drag him out. My uncle roped that *hoka*, but he couldn't pull it out. The badger was going into his hole; the rope was going in, too. Pretty soon there was the horse coming on. My uncle tried to unhitch it around the nose, but the horse's head was already too close to the hole. My uncle had to shoot the rope in two. Once a badger digs in, there isn't much you can do about it.

With the body of a dead badger, you can foretell how long you are going to 48 live. There's a gift of prophecy in it. I knew a man called Night Chaser. He cut a dead badger open and let the blood stand there. You are supposed to see a vision in it. It's like a red looking glass, like seeing yourself in a mirror. Only you see yourself in that badger's blood as you will look when you are about to die.

Three or four men were looking inside that *hoka*. I was there, too. We were all young. The first man to look said, "Boy, I'm an old man, wrinkled and white-haired, stooped, no teeth left." He was happy about it. He knew he'd live to be an old granddaddy. The second one was not so happy. "I think I'm about through," he said. "I'm looking as you see me now. I die before one of my hairs get gray!" Then it was my turn, but I didn't see anything, just the dark blood. But the two others were right. The one who had seen himself as an old man is still around. The other one died long ago, only a few months after he had looked inside that badger, just as he said, before his hair turned gray.

49   We use a badger's bone pizzle, his penis, for sewing, or as an awl. You polish it, make it shiny. It lasts forever. This is a good tool, so valuable that you get a good horse in exchange for it.

50   There are some animals, a kind of gopher, very fast, with a black line down their faces. They got a lot of power; they can hypnotize you, even kill you. The power is in their eyes. They live with the prairie dogs. They are real subway users, traveling underground. They are so fast, your eyes can hardly follow them. Your eye is still here, he's already over there. They tell a funny story about a man who wanted to get one of these creatures. He was told to be fast. Shoot it and then run like hell, grab it before it disappears into its hole. The man made up his mind to be real quick about it. He shot and ran like the dickens. Something hit him in the seat of his pants—his own bullet! The earth from a gopher hole is also very powerful. It can protect you in war, make you bulletproof. I use it for curing certain illnesses.

51   An animal doesn't have to be big to be powerful. There's an ant power. Some ants have no eyes, but they can feel their way. They go out and bring back those rocks, called *yuwipi*, to put on their anthills. Tiny rocks, the size of seed beads, shiny, agate-like, little stones as clear as snow. Sometimes instead of these they bring tiny fossils. It takes two ants to get one of those rocks. One might be stepped upon and die. The ants take no chances.

52   We medicine men go out to look for anthills and get these tiny rocks. They are sacred. We put 405 of them into our gourds and rattles which we use in our ceremonies. They represent the 405 trees which grow in our land. *Tašuśka śaśa*—the red ants—we mash them up and put them in our medicine. If somebody gets shot we give this to him to drink. This ant medicine makes the wound heal faster. As to what you people call fossils, these too are used by us. Deep in the Badlands we find the bones of *unktegila*, the giant, the water monster, which lived long before human beings appeared. On a hill there lies the backbone of one of them, right along the spine of that mound. I have been up there, riding the ridge like a horse; that's the only way you can move on it. It's spooky, like riding the monster. At night there are spirit lights flitting about on that hill. I find things there which I use in my doctoring.

53   *Iktomé*—the spider—has a power, too, but it is evil. His body is short, and everything is in one place, in the center, with its legs spread out. It's sitting in

its web, waiting for a fly. Iktomé is really a man. He's a foolish guy, a smart-ass; he wants to trick everybody, wants to tantalize people, make them miserable. But he is easy to outwit.

You have to listen to all these creatures, listen with your mind. They have 54 secrets to tell. Even a kind of cricket, called *ptewoyake,* a wingless hopper, it used to tell us where to find buffalo. It has nothing to tell us now.

Butterflies talk to the women. A spirit will get into a beautiful butterfly, fly 55 over to a young squaw, sit on her shoulder. The spirit will talk through that butterfly to the young squaw and tell her to become a medicine woman. We still have a couple of these ladies. I helped one, taught her what she must know, and she is doing a good job on the reservation. She is honest, so honest that the very poor, the down-and-out winos, really believe in her. She doesn't take any money from them, just does her best for the sake of helping them.

I have a nephew, Joe Thunderhawk, who is a healer. He has the coyote 56 power. On his drum is painted the picture of a coyote, showing Joe's vision. This coyote power has been in the Thunderhawk family for a long time. Many years ago Joe's grandfather traveled in the wintertime. The snows were deep and darkness surprised him in a canyon. He had to hole up in there, trying to keep from freezing to death. In the middle of the night something came up to him, settling down by his legs. He saw that it was a coyote. They gave each other warmth, keeping each other alive, until the next morning. When that man got up to travel again, the coyote followed him.

After that, Joe's grandfather would hear the coyote bark at night, near his 57 home. It would bark in two ways—one bark sounding like a dog, the other like a little boy. One barking meant that something good was about to happen, the other foreshadowed misfortune. Joe's grandfather became a medicine man and a prophet. The coyote told him of things to come. When the old man died, his knowledge died with him. He had not been able to pass it on.

One day Joe Thunderhawk passed through that same canyon where his 58 grandfather and the coyote had warmed each other long ago. My nephew was in a wagon. Suddenly he had a feeling that someone was following him. He looked back and there was a coyote, right behind him. It was kind of lame and very thin. It started to bark in two ways—like a dog and like a child.

That night Joe Thunderhawk dreamed about this coyote and understood 59 that he was meant to be a medicine man, that he would carry on his grand-father's work. He is working now in the Indian way, with his own medicines, curing sick people who would have to undergo surgery otherwise. Thus the coyote power has returned to the Thunderhawk family.

As for myself, the birds have something to tell me. The eagle, the owl. In 60 an eagle there is all the wisdom of the world; that's why we have an eagle feather at the top of the pole during a *yuwipi* ceremony. If you are planning to kill an eagle, the minute you think of that he knows it, knows what you are planning. The black-tailed deer has this wisdom, too. That's why its tail is tied farther down at the *yuwipi* pole. This deer, if you shoot at him, you won't hit him. He just stands right there and the bullet comes right back and hits you. It is like somebody saying bad things about you and they come back at him.

61   In one of my great visions I was talking to the birds, the winged creatures. I was saddened by the death of my mother. She had held my hand and said just one word: "pitiful." I don't think she grieved for herself; she was sorry for me, a poor Indian she would leave in a white man's world. I cried up on that vision hill, cried for help, stretched out my hands toward the sky and then put the blanket over myself—that's all I had, the blanket and the pipe, and a little tobacco for an offering. I didn't know what to expect. I wanted to touch the power, feel it. I had the thought to give myself up, even if it would kill me. So I just gave myself to the winds, to nature, not giving a damn about what could happen to me.

62   All of a sudden I hear a big bird crying, and then quickly he hit me on the back, touched me with his spread wings. I heard the cry of an eagle, loud above the voices of many other birds. It seemed to say, "We have been waiting for you. We knew you would come. Now you are here. Your trail leads from here. Let our voices guide you. We are your friends, the feathered people, the two-legged, the four-legged, we are your friends, the creatures, little tiny ones, eight legs, twelve legs—all those who crawl on the earth. All the little creatures which fly, all those under water. The powers of each one of us we will share with you and you will have a ghost with you always—another self."

63   That's me, I thought, no other thing than myself, different, but me all the same, unseen, yet very real. I was frightened. I didn't understand it then. It took me a lifetime to find out.

64   And again I heard the voice amid the bird sounds, the clicking of beaks, the squeaking and chirping. "You have love for all that has been placed on this earth, not like the love of a mother for her son, or of a son for his mother, but a bigger love which encompasses the whole earth. You are just a human being, afraid, weeping under that blanket, but there is a great space within you to be filled with that love. All of nature can fit in there." I was shivering, pulling the blanket tighter around myself, but the voices repeated themselves over and over again, calling me "Brother, brother, brother." So this is how it is with me. Sometimes I feel like the first being in one of our Indian legends. This was a giant made of earth, water, the moon and the winds. He had timber instead of hair, a whole forest of trees. He had a huge lake in his stomach and a waterfall in his crotch. I feel like this giant. All of nature is in me, and a bit of myself is in all of nature.

65   PETE CATCHES: "I too feel this way. I live in an age which has passed. I live like fifty years ago, a hundred years ago. I like it that way. I want to live as humbly, as close to the earth as I can. Close to the plants, the weeds, the flowers that I use for medicine. The Great Spirit has seen to it that man can survive in this way, can live as he is meant to live. So I and my wife are dwelling in a little cabin—no electricity, no tap water, no plumbing, no road. This is what we

want. This simple log cabin knows peace. That's how we want to be for the rest of our lives. I want to exist apart from the modern world, get out, way out, in the sticks, and live much closer to nature, even, than I am doing now. I don't even want to be called a medicine man, just a healing man, because this is what I am made for. I don't ask for anything. A white doctor has a fee, a priest has a fee. I have no fee. A man goes away from me healed. That is my reward. Sometimes I do not have the power—it makes me sad. When I have the power, then I am happy. Some men think of money, how to get it. That never comes into my mind. We live off nature, my wife and I; we hardly need anything. We will somehow live. The Great Spirit made the flowers, the streams, the pines, the cedars—takes care of them. He lets a breeze go through there, makes them breathe it, waters them, makes them grow. Even the one that is down in the crags, in the rocks. He tends to that, too. He takes care of me, waters me, feeds me, makes me live with the plants and animals as one of them. This is how I wish to remain, an Indian, all the days of my life. This does not mean that I want to shut myself off. Somehow many people find their way to my cabin. I like this. I want to be in communication, reach out to people everywhere, impart a little of our Indian way, the spirit's way, to them.

"At the same time, I want to withdraw further and further away from 66 everything, to live like the ancient ones. On the highway you sometimes see a full-blood Indian thumbing a ride. I never do that. When I walk the road, I expect to walk the whole way. That is deep down in me, a kind of pride. Someday I'll still move my cabin still farther into the hills, maybe do without a cabin altogether, become a part of the woods. There the spirit still has something for us to discover—a herb, a sprig, a flower—a very small flower, maybe, and you can spend a long time in its contemplation, thinking about it. Not a rose—yellow, white, artificial, big. I hear they are breeding black roses. That's not natural. These things are against nature. They make us weak. I abhor them.

"So as I get older, I burrow more and more into the hills. The Great Spirit 67 made them for us, for me. I want to blend with them, shrink into them, and finally disappear in them. As my brother Lame Deer has said, all of nature is in us, all of us is in nature. That is as it should be. Tell me, what are you going to call the chapter of your book in which you put the things we have talked about today? I know you will call it 'Talking to the Owls and the Butterflies.'"

FOCUS ON ECOLOGY

1. What does Lame Deer mean when he writes, "You live in prisons which you have built for yourselves, calling them 'homes,' offices, factories"?
2. How do you respond to Lame Deer's description of the eating of buffalo guts? How do you react to hearing about people eating foods that you (or American culture) don't always consider food: whale meat, dog meat, insects, chicken feet, sea cucumber? How do we determine what is food and what isn't?

3. How does Lame Deer address the idea of consumption? How do you respond to his argument about consumption and connection?

FOCUS ON WRITING

1. Why does Lame Deer interject the words of Pete Catches in his narrative? What effect does this insertion have on the rest of the piece?
2. What is the B.I.A. to which Lame Deer refers? What was the B.I.A.'s job? Why might Lame Deer have chosen not to explain what these initials stand for? What effect is gained (or lost) by not doing so?
3. A few times in this piece, Lame Deer provides us with the Lakota words for what he talks about: *Woaniya wakan, wasna, yuwipi, hoka, Tašuśka śasá, unktegila, Iktomé,* and *ptewoyake,* for instance. Why do you suppose he has decided to include these words? Why might he have decided to include these words and not others? As a reader, how do you respond to seeing these words in the piece?

FOR DISCUSSION

This piece discusses a remarkable range of issues: consumption, thinking ecologically, environmental destruction, spirituality, sustainability, and Indian oppression, to name but a few. Because this essay covers so much territory, we can assume that for Lame Deer there is a connection between consumption and other aspects of thinking about the environment. As a class, consider, first, how Lame Deer makes these connections. Then, consider how or if these connections are also manifest in your local community and campus.

WRITING IN RESPONSE

In a narrative of your own, describe the traditions of food consumption that surround your family, your life. How is food understood? Does your family link spirituality with food in any way? How do you get your daily food? What connections do you find, if any, in that daily ritual of food gathering?

DISCUSSING THE ISSUES

1. Several of the pieces in this chapter address the relationships between the things we value culturally and personally and the ways we consume those things. Durning, Walker, and Lame Deer each ask us to consider the relationship between value and consumption. Now that you have looked at these pieces and have begun to consider the role value plays in consumption, take some time as a class to further your discussion about value and

consumption. Look explicitly at the ways your campus consumes and the values that are placed on those things most obviously consumed: power, water, food, paper, and so on.

2. One of the primary and ongoing debates about the world's resources is whether the world is to serve as a resource for human consumption or whether humans need to be conservative in their use of natural resources. Issues regarding oil drilling and fuel consumption, water resources, land depletion and overuse, to name but a few, fall within the rubric of this conversation. Rarely do different people agree on a single solution to problems of consumption and overuse. As a class, consider first what consumptive acts might be considered overuse on your campus. Then, try to formulate some solution to alleviate the pressure on the overused resource. Are you able, as a class, to agree on a feasible solution? If not what kinds of things prevent such consensus? Needs? Demands? Scientific data? Emotional response? What are the values of these kinds of points in such debates?

WRITING ABOUT THE ISSUES

1. *Personal Experience:* What do you consume? In the series of questions following the Durning essay, "The Conundrum of Consumption," I asked you to think about the burden of consumption you place on the planet each week. Now, I would like for you to consider in what ways are you a consumer, not in the economic sense of the word but in the ecological sense of the word. That is, write a narrative that takes your audience through a typical day in your life and that highlights your consumptions. Your essay should not necessarily critique those consumptions but should identify your feelings about and understanding of the role of those consumptive acts in your daily life and in the expanse of resources needed to provide you with those things you consume.

2. *Local Context:* One of the main focuses of this chapter is the ways we know about our foods and the ways our demands for food put pressure on particular resources. Earlier in this chapter, I asked you to consider your favorite food and all the resources needed to place that food in front of you. I'd like for you now to consider the resources necessary to produce an entire meal in the local dining hall. Take a trip to a campus food court or dining hall or some other local restaurant that serves near your campus. Make a list of the kinds of food served during a single meal period. Then, in great detail, list all the resources and energy used to prepare food for that serving.

3. *Research:* We each have specific demands on specific resources that we would consider irreplaceable. Some of us might be adamant that cutting electrical use would cause too great an inconvenience in our lives, others may contend that no expenditure is too great when it comes to having access to our favorite foods, and others still may argue that we should be able to use as

much water as we desire whenever we want it. Select the resource that you feel you need abundantly every day and are not willing to give up. Then, take some time to learn what is required to provide you with that resource every day. Learn where that resource comes from in your community—how it is produced, mined, drained, and so on. Learn how much of the resource is used in your community each day. How much do consumers spend on that resource? How much tax money is required to supply the resource? Once you have learned about the resource in your community, write an argumentative essay that justifies your position that you should not be limited in your use of such a resource and that the required costs (both financial and otherwise) you discovered in your research are justifiable.

RESEARCH PATHS

Ethical Consumption: For People, Animals, and Planet (homepage.powerup
    .com.au/~kkaos/)
Worldwatch Institute (www.worldwatch.org/)
Sustainable Consumption and Production (www.iisd.ca/linkages/consume/
    consume.html)
National Fish and Wildlife Contamination Program (www.epa.gov/ost/fish/)
National Resources Defense Council (www.nrdc.org/)
United Farm Workers (www.ufw.org/)

FURTHER READINGS

Linda Greenlaw, *The Hungry Ocean*
Sebastian Junger, *The Perfect Storm*
Alan Thein Durning, *This Place on Earth: Home and the Practice of Permanence*
Shel Silverstein, *Where the Sidewalk Ends: The Poems and Drawings of Shel Silverstein*

CHAPTER 5

Surviving Nature

Harry Crews has written that "survival is the greatest triumph." These words suggest that surviving is a sort of victory, a triumph over forces that seek our demise.

For much of the history of human beings and particularly their history as writers and readers, we have been fascinated by stories of survival, stories of people who take on nature and live. Hercules battled great beasts, Ulysses fought raging storms, Ishmael survived the Pequod's adventures, Robinson Crusoe and the Robinsons survived being stranded on desert islands. Now television programs, films, and other media aggrandize our contest with nature. Books like Sebastian Junger's *The Perfect Storm,* television shows like *When Animals Attack,* films like *Cast Away* and *Six Days and Seven Nights,* and magazines like *Outside* and *Reader's Digest* all capitalize on our fascination with survival stories. Real–life survival stories also occupy a good deal of our attention. Think, for instance, about how Miami and Homestead, Florida, survived hurricane Andrew, or how Albany survives a blizzard. Think too about how fascinated the country was with the story of the nine miners trapped for 77 hours in a mine near Somerset, Pennsylvania, in July 2002. A made-for-television movie dramatizing the incident was released by ABC on November 24, 2002, only four months after the event. Survival, it seems, sells.

Survival is the central theme in each of the selections found here. Yet, as we read the selections, we need to consider not just how and why survival fascinates us, but how such stories, whether fiction or "real-life" stories, depict nature, places, and environments and how those depictions affect how we understand and react to those same places, environments, and nature. Think for a moment about the classic movie *Jaws.* This film depicts a killer shark, one that hunts people. This film helped create an image of sharks as animals determined to kill humans. At least partly as a result, television stations like the Discovery Channel frequently air shows about shark attacks. (Peter Benchley, author of

Jaws, has said that he regrets the effect his book and film had on our perception of sharks and on how we treat sharks.) In other words, in many ways our fascination with stories of survival help construct how we understand the places, environments, and organisms that appear in those stories.

The selections in this chapter are all about survival in nature. I chose the pieces to provide a range of survival stories:

- mountain climbing survival
- surviving shipwrecks
- surviving weather events like tornados and hurricanes
- surviving in the woods after a plane crash
- subfreezing temperatures and survival
- solitude and survival
- surviving monster waves
- animal attacks

I think each of these pieces is exciting, worth reading no matter the goal of the chapter. But this chapter does have a particular goal: to ask you to consider how reading and writing stories of survival affect our understanding of our relationship with places, environments, and nature.

The Devil's Thumb

Jon Krakauer

Jon Krakauer is a contributing editor for Outside *magazine and is considered one of today's most important adventure writers. Though he writes about many outdoor sports and adventures, he is best known for his writing about mountain climbing. His first book,* Eiger Dreams: Ventures among Men and Mountains, *is a collection of essays about climbing. Krakauer was nominated for the National Magazine Award for an article he wrote about the fatal adventure of Christopher McCandless in the Alaskan wilderness, after which Krakauer wrote a more detailed account of McCandless's fatal trip in a book called* Into the Wild. *Krakauer has written, edited, and contributed to more than a dozen books, primarily about mountain climbing. In this essay, "The Devil's Thumb," Krakauer recounts his own life-threatening attempt to climb the*

infamous Devil's Thumb in Alaska. As you read, pay attention to Krakauer's recol-
lections of why he put himself at risk and consider why so many people make similar
choices when facing nature and danger.

JOURNAL ASSIGNMENT

In this essay, Krakauer recounts his attempt to climb Devil's Thumb in 1977
when he was 23. The solo adventure puts Krakauer at great risk on an isolated
mountain peak. In your journal, consider why someone might deliberately undertake an adventure that would place himself or herself at serious risk of
dying. Would you engage in a wilderness activity that put your life at risk?
Would you do so alone? Have you done so?

By the time I reached the interstate I was having trouble keeping my eyes open. 1
I'd been okay on the two lane twisting blacktop between Fort Collins and
Laramie, but when the Pontiac eased onto the smooth, unswerving pavement
of I-80, the soporific hiss of the tires began to gnaw at my wakefulness like ants
in a dead tree.

That afternoon, after nine hours of humping 2x10s and pounding recalci- 2
trant nails, I'd told my boss I was quitting: "No, not in a couple of weeks, Steve;
right now was more like what I had in mind." It took me three more hours to
clear my tools and other belongings out of the rust-stained construction trailer
that served as my home in Boulder. I loaded everything into the car, drove up
Pearl Street to Tom's Tavern and downed a ceremonial beer. Then I was gone.

At 1 am, 30 miles east of Rawlins, the strain of the day caught up to me. 3
The euphoria that had flowed so freely in the wake of my quick escape gave
way to overpowering fatigue; suddenly I felt tired to the bone. The highway
stretched straight and empty to the horizon and beyond. Outside the car the
night air was cold, and the stark Wyoming plains glowed in the moonlight like
Rousseau's painting of the sleeping gypsy. I wanted very badly just then to be
that gypsy, conked out on my back beneath the stars. I shut my eyes—just for a
second, but it was a second of bliss. It seemed to revive me, if only briefly. The
Pontiac, sturdy behemoth from the Eisenhower years, floated down the road on
its long-gone shocks like a raft on an ocean swell. The lights of an oil rig twin-
kled reassuringly in the distance. I closed my eyes a second time, and kept
them closed a few moments longer. The sensation was sweeter than sex.

A few minutes later I let my eyelids fall again. I'm not sure how long I nod- 4
ded off this time—it might have been for five seconds, it might have been for 30—
but when I awoke it was to the rude sensation of the Pontiac bucking violently
along the dirt shoulder at 70 miles per hour. By all rights, the car should have
sailed off into the rabbitbrush and rolled. The rear wheels fishtailed wildly six or

seven times, but I eventually managed to guide the unruly machine back on to the pavement without so much as blowing a tire, and let it coast gradually to a stop. I loosened my death grip on the wheel, took several deep breaths to quiet the pounding in my chest, then slipped the shifter back into drive and continued down the highway.

5   Pulling over to sleep would have been the sensible thing to do, but I was on my way to Alaska to change my life, and patience was a concept well beyond my 23-year-old ken.

6   Sixteen months earlier I'd graduated from college with little distinction and even less in the way of marketable skills. In the interim an off-again, on-again four-year relationship—the first serious romance of my life—had come to a messy, long-overdue end; nearly a year later, my love life was still zip. To support myself I worked on a house-framing crew, grunting under crippling loads of plywood, counting the minutes until the next coffee break, scratching in vain at the sawdust stuck *in perpetuum* to the sweat on the back of my neck. Somehow, blighting the Colorado landscape with condominiums and tract houses for $3.50 an hour wasn't the sort of career I'd dreamed of as a boy.

7   Late one evening I was mulling all this over on a bar stool at Tom's, picking unhappily at my existential scabs, when an idea came to me, a scheme for righting what was wrong in my life. It was wonderfully uncomplicated, and the more I thought about it, the better the plan sounded. By the bottom of the pitcher its merits seemed unassailable. The plan consisted, in its entirety, of climbing a mountain in Alaska called the Devils Thumb.

8   The Devils Thumb is a prong of exfoliated diorite that presents an imposing profile from any point of the compass, but especially so from the north: its great north wall, which had never been climbed, rises sheer and clean for six thousand vertical feet from the glacier at its base. Twice the height of Yosemite's El Capitan, the north face of the Thumb is one of the biggest granite walls on the continent; it may well be one of the biggest in the world. I would go to Alaska, ski across the Stikine Icecap to the Devils Thumb, and make the first ascent of its notorious Nordwand. It seemed, midway through the second pitcher, like a particularly good idea to do all of this solo.

9   Writing these words more than a dozen years later, it's no longer entirely clear just *how* I thought soloing the Devils Thumb would transform my life. It had something to do with the fact that climbing was the first and only thing that I'd ever been good at. My reasoning, such as it was, was fueled by the scatter-shot passions of youth, and a literary diet overly rich in the words of Nietzsche, Kerouac, and John Menlove Edwards—the latter a deeply troubled writer/psychiatrist who, before putting an end to his life with a cyanide capsule in 1958, had been one of the preeminent British rock climbers of the day.

10   Dr. Edwards regarded climbing as a "psycho-neurotic tendency" rather than sport; he climbed not for fun but to find refuge from the inner torment that characterized his existence. I remember that spring of 1977, being especially taken by a passage from an Edwards short story titled "Letter From a Man":

*So, as you would imagine, I grew up exuberant in body but with a nervy, craving
mind. It was wanting something more, something tangible. It sought for reality intensely,
always if it were not there. . . .*
But you see at once what I do. I climb.

To one enamored of this sort of prose, the Thumb beckoned like a beacon. 11
My belief in the plan became unshakable. I was dimly aware that I might be
getting in over my head, but if I could somehow get to the top of the Devils
Thumb, I was convinced, everything that followed would turn out all right.
And thus did I push the accelerator a little closer to the floor and, buoyed by
the jolt of adrenaline that followed the Pontiac's brush with destruction, speed
west into the night.

You can't actually get very close to the Devils Thumb by car. The peak 12
stands in the Boundary Ranges on the Alaska-British Columbia border, not far
from the fishing village of Petersburg, a place accessible only by boat or plane.
There is regular jet service to Petersburg, but the sum of my liquid assets
amounted to the Pontiac and $200 in cash, not even enough for one-way airfare,
so I took the car as far as Gig Harbor, Washington, then hitched a ride on a
northbound seine boat that was short on crew. Five days out, when the Ocean
Queen pulled into Petersburg to take on fuel and water, I jumped ship, shouldered my backpack, and walked down the dock in the Alaskan rain.

Back in Boulder, without exception, every person with whom I'd shared 13
my plans about the Thumb had been blunt and to the point: I'd been smoking
too much pot, they said; it was a monumentally bad idea. I was grossly overes-
timating my abilities as a climber, I'd never be able to hack a month completely
by myself, I would fall into a crevasse and die.

The residents of Petersburg reacted differently. Being Alaskans, they were 14
accustomed to people with screwball ideas; a sizeable percentage of the state's
population, after all, was sitting on half-baked schemes to mine uranium in the
Brooks Range, or sell icebergs to the Japanese, or market mail-order moose
droppings. Most of the Alaskans I met, if they reacted at all, simply asked how
much money there was in climbing a mountain like the Devils Thumb.

In any case, one of the appealing things about climbing the Thumb—and 15
one of the appealing things about the sport of mountain climbing in general—
was that it didn't matter a rat's ass what anyone else thought. Getting the
scheme off the ground didn't hinge on winning the approval of some personnel
director, admissions committee, licensing board, or panel of stern-faced judges;
if I felt like taking a shot at some unclimbed alpine wall, all I had to do was get
myself to the foot of the mountain and start swinging my ice axes.

Petersburg sits on an island, the Devils Thumb rises from the mainland. To 16
get myself to the foot of the Thumb it was first necessary to cross 25 miles of salt
water. For most of a day I walked the docks, trying without success to hire a
boat to ferry me across Frederick Sound. Then I bumped into Bart and Benjamin.

17   Bart and Benjamin were ponytailed constituents of a Woodstock Nation tree-planting collective called the Hodads. We struck up a conversation. I mentioned that I, too, had once worked as a tree planter. The Hodads allowed that they had chartered a floatplane to fly them to their camp on the mainland the next morning. "It's your lucky day, kid," Bart told me. "For 20 bucks you can ride over with us. Get to your fuckin' mountain in style." On May 3, a day and a half after arriving in Petersburg, I stepped off the Hodads' Cessna, waded onto the tidal flats at the head of Thomas Bay, and began the long trudge inland.

18   The Devils Thumb pokes up out of the Stikine Icecap, an immense, labyrinthine network of glaciers that hugs the crest of the Alaskan panhandle like an octopus, with myriad tentacles that snake down, down to the sea from the craggy uplands along the Canadian frontier. In putting ashore at Thomas Bay I was gambling that one of these frozen arms, the Baird Glacier, would lead me safely to the bottom of the Thumb, 30 miles distant.

19   An hour of gravel beach led to the tortured blue tongue of the Baird. A logger in Petersburg had suggested I keep an eye out for grizzlies along this stretch of shore. "Them bears over there is just waking up this time of year," he smiled. "Tend to be kinda cantankerous after not eatin' all winter. But you keep your gun handy, you shouldn't have no problem." Problem was, I didn't have a gun. As it turned out, my only encounter with hostile wildlife involved a flock of gulls who dive-bombed my head with Hitchcockian fury. Between the avian assault and my ursine anxiety, it was with no small amount of relief that I turned my back to the beach, donned crampons, and scrambled up on to the glacier's broad, lifeless snout.

20   After three or four miles I came to the snow line, where I exchanged crampons for skis. Putting the boards on my feet cut 15 pounds from the awful load on my back and made the going much faster besides. But now that the ice was covered with snow, many of the glacier's crevasses were hidden, making solitary travel extremely dangerous.

21   In Seattle, anticipating this hazard, I'd stopped at a hardware store and purchased a pair of stout aluminum curtain rods, each ten feet long. Upon reaching the snowline, I lashed the rods together at right angles, then strapped the arrangement to the hip belt on my backpack so the poles extended horizontally over the snow. Staggering slowly up the glacier with my overloaded backpack, bearing the queer tin cross, I felt like some kind of strange *Penitente*. Were I to break through the veneer of snow over a hidden crevasse, though, the curtain rods would—I hoped mightily—span the slot and keep me from dropping into the chilly bowels of the Baird.

22   The first climbers to venture onto the Stikine Icecap were Bestor Robinson and Fritz Wiessner, the legendary German-American alpinist, who spent a stormy month in the Boundary Ranges in 1937 but failed to reach any major summits. Wiessner returned in 1946 with Donald Brown and Fred Beckey to attempt the Devils Thumb, the nastiest-looking peak in the Stikine. On that trip Fritz mangled a knee during a fall on the hike in and limped home in

disgust, but Beckey went back that same summer with Bob Craig and Cliff Schmidtke. On August 25, after several aborted tries and some exceedingly hairy climbing on the peak's east ridge, Beckey and company sat on the Thumb's wafer-thin summit tower in a tired, giddy daze. It was far and away the most technical ascent ever done in Alaska, an important milestone in the history of American mountaineering.

In the ensuing decades three other teams also made it to the top of the 23 Thumb, but all steered clear of the big north face. Reading accounts of these expeditions, I had wondered why none of them had approached the peak by what appeared, from the map at least, to be the easiest and most logical route, the Baird. I wondered a little less after coming across an article by Beckey in which the distinguished mountaineer cautioned, "Long, steep icefalls block the route from the Baird Glacier to the icecap near Devils Thumb," but after studying aerial photographs I decided that Beckey was mistaken, that the icefalls weren't so big or so bad. The Baird, I was certain, really was the best way to reach the mountain.

For two days I slogged steadily up the glacier without incident, congratu- 24 lating myself for discovering such a clever path to the Thumb. On the third day, I arrived beneath the Stikine Icecap proper, where the long arm of the Baird joins the main body of ice. Here, the glacier spills abruptly over the edge of a high plateau, dropping seaward through the gap between two peaks in a phantasmagoria of shattered ice. Seeing the icefall in the flesh left a different impression than the photos had. As I stared at the tumult from a mile away, for the first time since leaving Colorado the thought crossed my mind that maybe this Devils Thumb trip wasn't the best idea I ever had.

The icefall was a maze of crevasses and teetering seracs. From afar it 25 brought to mind a bad train wreck, as if scores of ghostly white boxcars had derailed at the lip of the icecap and tumbled down the slope willy-nilly. The closer I got, the more unpleasant it looked. My ten-foot curtain rods seemed a poor defense against crevasses that were 40 feet across and 250 feet deep. Before I could finish figuring out a course through the icefall, the wind came up and snow began to slant hard out of the clouds, stinging my face and reducing visibility to almost nothing.

In my impetuosity, I decided to carry on anyway. For the better part of the 26 day I groped blindly through the labyrinth in the white-out, retracing my steps from one dead end to another. Time after time I'd think I'd found my way out, only to wind up in a deep blue cul-de-sac, or stranded atop a detached pillar of ice. My efforts were lent a sense of urgency by the noises emanating underfoot. A madrigal of creaks and sharp reports—the sort of protests a large fir limb makes when it's slowly bent to the breaking point—served as a reminder that it is the nature of glaciers to move, the habit of seracs to topple.

As much as I feared being flattened by a wall of collapsing ice, I was even 27 more afraid of falling into a crevasse, a fear that intensified when I put a foot through a snow bridge over a slot so deep I couldn't see the bottom of it. A little later I broke through another bridge to my waist; the poles kept me out of the hundred-foot hole, but after I extricated myself I was bent double with dry heaves thinking about what it would be like to be lying in a pile at the bottom of the crevasse, waiting for death to come, with nobody even aware of how or where I'd met my end.

28   Night had nearly fallen by the time I emerged from the top of the serac slope onto the empty, wind-scoured expanse of the high glacial plateau. In shock and chilled to the core, I skied far enough past the icefall to put its rumblings out of earshot, pitched the tent, crawled into my sleeping bag, and shivered myself to a fitful sleep.

29   Although my plan to climb the Devils Thumb wasn't fully hatched until the spring of 1977, the mountain had been lurking in the recesses of my mind for about 15 years—since April 12, 1962, to be exact. The occasion was my eighth birthday. When it came time to open birthday presents, my parents announced that they were offering me a choice of gifts: According to my wishes, they would either escort me to the new Seattle World's Fair to ride the Monorail and see the Space Needle, or give me an introductory taste of mountain climbing by taking me up the third highest peak in Oregon, a long-dormant volcano called the South Sister that, on clear days, was visible from my bedroom window. It was a tough call. I thought the matter over at length, then settled on the climb.

30   To prepare me for the rigors of the ascent, my father handed over a copy of *Mountaineering: The Freedom of the Hills*, the leading how-to manual of the day, a thick tome that weighed only slightly less than a bowling ball. Thenceforth I spent most of my waking hours poring over its pages, memorizing the intricacies of pitoncraft and bolt placement, the shoulder stand and the tension traverse. None of which, as it happened, was of any use on my inaugural ascent, for the South Sister turned out to be a decidedly less than extreme climb that demanded nothing more in the way of technical skill than energetic walking, and was in fact ascended by hundreds of farmers, house pets, and small children every summer.

31   Which is not to suggest that my parents and I conquered the mighty volcano: From the pages and pages of perilous situations depicted in *Mountaineering: The Freedom of the Hills*, I had concluded that climbing was a life-and-death matter, always. Halfway up the South Sister I suddenly remembered this. In the middle of a 20-degree snow slope that would be impossible to fall from if you tried, I decided I was in mortal jeopardy and burst into tears, bringing the ascent to halt.

32   Perversely, after the South Sister debacle my interest in climbing only intensified. I resumed my obsessive studies of *Mountaineering*. There was something about the scariness of the activities portrayed in those pages that just wouldn't leave me alone. In addition to the scores of line drawings—most of them cartoons of a little man in a jaunty Tyrolean cap—employed to illustrate arcana like the boot-axe belay and the Bilgeri rescue, the book contained 16 black-and-white plates of notable peaks in the Pacific Northwest and Alaska. All the photographs were striking, but the one on page 147 was much, much more than that: it made my skin crawl. An aerial photo by glaciologist Maynard

Miller, it showed a singularly sinister tower of ice-plastered black rock. There wasn't a place on the entire mountain that looked safe or secure; I couldn't imagine anyone climbing it. At the bottom of the page the mountain was identified as the Devils Thumb.

From the first time I saw it, the picture—a portrait of the Thumb's north 33 wall—held an almost pornographic fascination for me. On hundreds—no, make that thousands—of occasions over the decade-and-a-half that followed I took my copy of *Mountaineering* down from the shelf, opened it to page 147 and quietly stared. How would it feel, I wondered over and over, to be on that thumbnail-thin summit ridge, worrying over the storm clouds building on the horizon, hunched against the wind and dunning cold, contemplating the horrible drop on either side? How could anyone keep it together? Would I, if I found myself on the north wall, clinging to that frozen rock, even attempt to keep it together? Or would I simply decide to surrender to the inevitable straightaway, and jump?

I had planned on spending between three weeks and a month on the 34 Stikine Icecap. Not relishing the prospect of carrying a four-week load of food, heavy winter camping gear, and a small mountain of climbing hardware all the way up the Baird on my back, before leaving Petersburg I paid a bush pilot $150—the last of my cash—to have six cardboard cartons of supplies dropped from an airplane when I reached the foot of the Thumb. I showed the pilot exactly where, on his map, I intended to be, and told him to give me three days to get there; he promised to fly over and make the drop as soon thereafter as the weather permitted.

On May 6 I set up a base camp on the icecap just northeast of the Thumb 35 and waited for the airdrop. For the next four days it snowed, nixing any chance for flight. Too terrified of crevasses to wander far from camp, I occasionally went out for a short ski to kill time, but mostly I lay silently in the tent—the ceiling was too low to sit upright—with my thoughts, fighting a rising chorus of doubts.

As the days passed, I grew increasingly anxious. I had no radio, nor any 36 other means of communicating with the outside world. It had been many years since anyone had visited this part of the Stikine Icecap, and many more would likely pass before anyone did so again. I was nearly out of stove fuel, and down to a single chunk of cheese, my last package of ramen noodles, and half a box of Cocoa Puffs. This, I figured, could sustain me for three or more days if need be, but then what would I do? It would only take two days to ski back down the Baird to Thomas Bay, but then a week or more might easily pass before a fisherman happened by who could give me a lift back to Petersburg (the Hodads with whom I'd ridden over were camped 15 miles down the impassable, headland-studded coast, and could be reached only by boat or plane).

When I went to bed on the evening of May 10 it was still snowing and 37 blowing hard. I was going back and forth on whether to head for the coast in the morning or stick it out on the icecap, gambling that the pilot would show before I starved or died of thirst, when, just for a moment, I heard a faint whine, like a mosquito. I tore open the tent door. Most of the clouds had lifted, but there was no airplane in sight. The whine returned, louder this time. Then I saw it: a tiny red-and-white speck, high in the western sky, droning my way.

38 A few minutes later the plane passed directly overhead. The pilot, however, was unaccustomed to glacier flying and he'd badly misjudged the scale of the terrain. Worried about winding up too low and getting nailed by unexpected turbulence, he flew a good thousand feet above me—believing all the while that he was just off the deck—and never saw my tent in the flat evening light. My waving and screaming were to no avail; from that altitude I was indistinguishable from a pile of rocks. For the next hour he circled the icecap, scanning its barren contours without success. But the pilot, to his credit, appreciated the gravity of my predicament and didn't give up. Frantic, I tied my sleeping bag to the end of one of the crevasse poles and waived for all I was worth. When the plane banked sharply and began to fly straight at me, I felt tears of joy well in my eyes.

39 The pilot buzzed my tent three times in quick succession, dropping two boxes on each pass, then the airplane disappeared over a ridge and I was alone. As silence again settled over the glacier I felt abandoned, vulnerable, lost. I realized that I was sobbing. Embarrassed, I halted the blubbering by screaming obscenities until I grew hoarse.

40 I awoke early on May 11 to clear skies and the relatively warm temperature of 20 degrees Fahrenheit. Startled by the good weather, mentally unprepared to commence the actual climb, I hurriedly packed up a rucksack nonetheless, and began skiing towards the base of the Thumb. Two previous Alaskan expeditions had taught me that, ready or not, you simply can't afford to waste a day of perfect weather if you expect to get up anything.

41 A small hanging glacier extends out from the lip of the icecap, leading up and across the north face of the Thumb like a catwalk. My plan was to follow this catwalk to a prominent rock prow in the center of the wall, and thereby execute an end run around the ugly, avalanche-swept lower half of the face.

42 The catwalk turned out to be a series of 50-degree ice fields blanketed with knee-deep powder snow and riddled with crevasses. The depth of the snow made the going slow and exhausting; by the time I front-pointed up the overhanging wall of the uppermost bergschrund, some three or four hours after leaving camp, I was whipped. And I hadn't even gotten to the "real" climbing yet. That would begin immediately above, where the hanging glacier gave way to vertical rock.

43 The rock, exhibiting a dearth of holds and coated with six inches of crumbly rime, did not look promising, but just left of the main prow was an inside corner—what climbers call an open book—glazed with frozen melt water. This ribbon of ice led straight up for 200 or 300 feet, and if the ice proved substantial enough to support the picks of my axes, the line might go. I hacked out a small platform in the snow slope, the last flat ground I expected to feel underfoot for some time, and stopped to eat a candy bar and collect my thoughts. Fifteen minutes later I shouldered my pack and inched over to the bottom of the corner. Gingerly, I swung my right axe into the two-inch-thick ice. It was

solid, plastic—a little thinner than what I would have liked but otherwise perfect. I was on my way.

The climbing was steep and spectacular, so exposed it made my head spin. Beneath my boot soles, the wall fell away for three thousand feet to the dirty, avalanche-scarred cirque of the Witches Cauldron Glacier. Above, the prow soared with authority toward the summit ridge, a vertical half-mile above. Each time I planted one of my ice axes, that distance shrank by another 20 inches. 44

The higher I climbed the more comfortable I became. All that held me to the mountainside, all that held me to the world, were six thin spikes of chrome-molybdenum stuck half an inch into a smear of frozen water, yet I began to feel invincible, weightless, like those lizards that live on the ceilings of cheap Mexican hotels. Early on a difficult climb, especially a difficult solo climb, you're hyper-aware of the abyss pulling at your back. You constantly feel its call, its immense hunger. To resist takes a tremendous conscious effort; you don't dare let your guard down for an instant. The siren song of the void puts you on edge, it makes your movements tentative, clumsy, herky-jerky. But as the climb goes on, you grow accustomed to the exposure, you get used to rubbing shoulders with doom, you come to believe in the reliability of your hands and feet and head. You learn to trust your self-control. 45

By and by, your attention becomes so intensely focused that you no longer notice the raw knuckles, the cramping thighs, the strain of maintaining nonstop concentration. A trance-like state settles over your efforts, the climb becomes a clear-eyed dream. Hours slide by like minutes. The accrued guilt and clutter of day-to-day existence—the lapses of consciousness, the unpaid bills, the bungled opportunities, the dust under the couch, the festering familial sores, the inescapable prison of your genes—all of it is temporarily forgotten, crowded from your thoughts by an overpowering sense of purpose, and by the seriousness of the task at hand. 46

At such moments something like happiness stirs in your chest, but it isn't the sort of emotion you want to lean on very hard. In solo climbing, the whole enterprise is held together by little more than chutzpa, not the most reliable adhesive. Late in the day on the north face of the Thumb, I felt the glue disintegrate with a single swing of an ice axe. 47

I'd gained nearly 700 feet of altitude since stepping off the hanging glacier, all of it on crampon front-points and the picks of my axes. The ribbon of frozen melt water had ended 300 feet up, and was followed by a crumbly armor of frost feathers. Though just barely substantial enough to support body weight, the rime was plastered over the rock to a thickness of two or three feet, so I kept plugging upward. The wall however, had been growing imperceptibly steeper, and as it did so the frost feathers became thinner. I'd fallen into a slow, hypnotic rhythm—swing, swing; kick, kick; swing, swing; kick, kick—when my left ice axe slammed into a slab of diorite a few inches beneath the rime. 48

I tried left, then right, but kept striking rock. The frost feathers holding me up, it became apparent, were maybe five inches thick and had the structural integrity of stale cornbread. Below was 3,700 feet of air, and I was balanced atop a house of cards. Waves of panic rose in my throat. My eyesight blurred, I began to 49 hyperventilate, my calves started to vibrate. I shuffled a few feet farther to the right, hoping to find thicker ice, but managed only to bend an ice axe on the rock.

50   Awkwardly, stiff with fear, I started working my way back down. The rime gradually thickened, and after descending about 80 feet I got back on reasonably solid ground. I stopped for a long time to let my nerves settle, then leaned back from my tools and stared at the face above, searching for a hint of solid ice, for some variation in the underlying rock strata, for anything that would allow passage over the frosted slabs. I looked until my neck ached, but nothing appeared. The climb was over. The only place to go was down.

51   Heavy snow and incessant winds kept me inside the tent for most of the next three days. The hours passed slowly. In the attempt to hurry them along I chain-smoked for as long as my supply of cigarettes held out, and read. I'd made a number of bad decisions on the trip, there was no getting around it, and one of them concerned the reading matter I'd chosen to pack along: three back issues of *The Village Voice,* and Joan Didion's latest novel, *A Book of Common Prayer.* The *Voice* was amusing enough—there on the icecap, the subject matter took on an edge, a certain sense of the absurd, from which the paper (through no fault of its own) benefited greatly—but in that tent, under those circumstances, Didion's necrotic take on the world hit a little too close to home.

52   Near the end of *Common Prayer,* one of Didion's characters says to another, "You don't get any real points for staying here, Charlotte." Charlotte replies, "I can't seem to tell you what you do get real points for, so I guess I'll stick around here for a while."

53   When I ran out of things to read, I was reduced to studying the rip-stop pattern woven into the tent ceiling. This I did for hours on end, flat on my back, while engaging in an extended and very heated self-debate: Should I leave for the coast as soon as the weather broke, or stay put long enough to make another attempt on the mountain? In truth, my little escapade on the north face had left me badly shaken, and I didn't want to go up on the Thumb again at all. One the other hand, the thought of returning to Boulder in defeat—of parking the Pontiac behind the trailer, buckling on my tool belt, and going back to the same brain-dead drill I'd so triumphantly walked away from just a month before—that wasn't very appealing, either. Most of all, I couldn't stomach the thought of having to endure the smug expressions of condolence from all the chumps and nimrods who were certain I'd fail right from the get-go.

54   By the third afternoon of the storm I couldn't stand it any longer: the lumps of frozen snow poking me in my back, the clammy nylon walls brushing against my face, the incredible smell drifting up from the depths of my sleeping bag. I pawed through the mess at my feet until I located a small green stuff sack, in which there was a metal film can containing the makings of what I'd hoped would be a sort of victory cigar. I'd intended to save it for my return from the summit, but what the hey, it wasn't looking like I'd be visiting the top anytime soon. I poured most of the can's contents onto a leaf of cigarette paper, rolled it into a crooked, sorry-looking joint, and promptly smoked it down to the roach.

The reefer, of course, only made the tent seem even more cramped, more 55 suffocating, more impossible to bear. It also made me terribly hungry. I decided a little oatmeal would put things right. Making it, however, was a long, ridiculously involved process: a potful of snow had to be gathered outside in the tempest, the stove assembled and lit, the oatmeal and sugar located, the remnants of yesterday's dinner scraped from my bowl. I'd gotten the stove going and was melting the snow when I smelled something burning. A thorough check of the stove and its environs revealed nothing. Mystified, I was ready to chalk it up to my chemically enhanced imagination when I heard something crackle directly behind me.

I whirled around in time to see a bag of garbage, into which I'd tossed the 56 match I'd used to light the stove, flare up into a conflagration. Beating on the fire with my hands, I had it out in a few seconds, but not before a large section of the tent's inner wall vaporized before my eyes. The tent's built-in rainfly escaped the flames, so the shelter was still more or less waterproof; now, however, it was approximately 30 degrees cooler inside. My left palm began to sting. Examining it, I noticed the pink welt of a burn. What troubled me most, though, was that the tent wasn't even mine—I'd borrowed the shelter from my father. An expensive Early Winters Omnipo tent, it had been brand new before my trip—the hangtags were still attached—and had been loaned reluctantly. For several minutes I sat dumbstruck, staring at the wreckage of the shelter's once-graceful form amid the acrid smell of singed hair and melted nylon. You had to hand it to me, I thought: I had a real knack for living up to the old man's worst expectations.

The fire sent me into a funk that no drug known to man could have allevi- 57 ated. By the time I'd finished cooking the oatmeal my mind was made up: the moment the storm was over, I was breaking camp and booking for Thomas Bay.

Twenty-four hours later, I was huddled inside a bivouac sack under the lip 58 of the bergschrund on the Thumb's north face. The weather was as bad as I'd seen it. It was snowing hard, probably an inch every hour. Spindrift avalanches hissed down from the wall above and washed over me like surf, completely burying the sack every 20 minutes.

The day had begun well enough. When I emerged from the tent, clouds still 59 clung to the ridge tops but the wind was down and the icecap was speckled with sunbreaks. A patch of sunlight, almost blinding in its brilliance, slid lazily over the camp. I put down a foam sleeping mat and sprawled on the glacier in my long johns. Wallowing in the radiant heat, I felt the gratitude of a prisoner whose sentence has just been commuted.

As I lay there, a narrow chimney that curved up the east half of the 60 Thumb's north face, well to left of the route I'd tried before the storm, caught my eye. I twisted a telephoto lens onto my camera. Through it I could make out a smear of shiny grey ice—solid, trustworthy, hard-frozen ice—plastered to the back of the cleft. The alignment of the chimney made it impossible to discern if the ice continued in an unbroken line from top to bottom. If it did, the chimney might well provide passage over the rime-covered slabs that had foiled my first attempt. Lying there in the sun, I began to think about how much I'd hate myself a month hence if I threw in the towel after a single try, if I scrapped the whole expedition on account of a little bad weather. Within the hour I had assembled my gear and was skiing toward the base of the wall.

61   The ice in the chimney did in fact prove to be continuous, but it was very, very thin—just a gossamer film of verglas. Additionally, the cleft was a natural funnel for any debris that happened to slough off the wall; as I scratched my way up the chimney I was hosed by a continuous stream of powder snow, ice chips, and small stones, One hundred twenty feet up the groove the last remnants of my composure flaked away like old plaster, and I turned around.

62   Instead of descending all the way to base camp, I decided to spend the night in the 'schrund beneath the chimney, on the off chance that my head would be more together the next morning. The fair skies that had ushered in the day, however, turned out to be but a momentary lull in a five-day gale. By midafternoon the storm was back in all its glory, and my bivouac site became a less than pleasant place to hang around. The ledge on which I was crouched was continually swept by small spindrift avalanches. Five times my bivvy sack—a thin nylon envelope, shaped exactly like a Baggies brand sandwich bag, only bigger—was buried up to the level of the breathing slit. After digging myself out the fifth time, I decided I'd had enough. I threw all my gear in my pack and made a break for base camp.

63   The descent was terrifying. Between the clouds, the ground blizzard, and the flat, fading light, I couldn't tell snow from sky, nor whether a slope went up or down. I worried, with ample reason, that I might step blindly off the top of a serac and end up at the bottom of the Witches Cauldron, a half-mile below. When I finally arrived on the frozen plain of the icecap, I found that my tracks had long since drifted over. I didn't have a clue how to locate the tent on the featureless glacial plateau. I skied in circles for an hour or so, hoping I'd get lucky and stumble across camp, until I put a foot into a small crevasse and realized I was acting like an idiot—that I should hunker down right where I was and wait out the storm.

64   I dug a shallow hole, wrapped myself in the bivvy bag, and sat on my pack in the swirling snow. Drifts piled up around me. My feet became numb. A damp chill crept down my chest from the base of my neck, where spindrift had gotten inside my parka and soaked my shirt. If only I had a cigarette, I thought, a single cigarette, I could summon the strength of character to put a good face on this fucked-up situation, on the whole fucked-up trip. "If we had some ham, we could have ham and eggs, if we had some eggs." I remembered my friend Nate uttering that line in a similar storm, two years before, high on another Alaskan peak, the Mooses Tooth. It had struck me as hilarious at the time; I'd actually laughed out loud. Recalling the line now, it no longer seemed funny. I pulled the bivvy sack tighter around my shoulders. The wind ripped at my back. Beyond shame, I cradled my head in my arms and embarked on an orgy of self-pity.

65   I knew that people sometimes died when climbing mountains. But at the age of 23 personal mortality—the idea of my own death—was still largely out-

side my conceptual grasp; it was as abstract a notion as non-Euclidian geometry or marriage. When I decamped from Boulder in April, 1977, my head swimming with visions of glory and redemption on the Devils Thumb, it didn't occur to me that I might be bound by the same cause-effect relationships that governed the actions of others. I'd never heard of hubris. Because I wanted to climb the mountain so badly, because I had thought about the Thumb so intensely for so long, it seemed beyond the realm of possibility that some minor obstacle like the weather or crevasses or rime-covered rock might ultimately thwart my will.

At sunset the wind died and the ceiling lifted 150 feet off the glacier, enabling me to locate the base camp. I made it back to the tent intact, but it was no longer possible to ignore the fact that the Thumb had made hash of my plans. I was forced to acknowledge that volition alone, however powerful, was not going to get me up the north wall. I saw, finally, that nothing was. 66

There still existed an opportunity for salvaging the expedition, however. A week earlier I'd skied over to the southeast side of the mountain to take a look at the route Fred Beckey had pioneered in 1946—the route by which I'd intended to descend the peak after climbing the north wall. During that reconnaissance I'd noticed an obvious unclimbed line to the left of the Beckey route—a patchy network of ice angling across the southeast face—that struck me as a relatively easy way to achieve the summit. At the time, I'd considered this route unworthy of my attention. Now, on the rebound from my calamitous entanglement with the *nordwand*, I was prepared to lower my sights. 67

On the afternoon of May 15, when the blizzard finally petered out, I returned to the southeast face and climbed to the top of a slender ridge that abutted the upper peak like a flying buttress on a gothic cathedral. I decided to spend the night there, on the airy, knife-edged ridge crest, 1,600 feet below the summit. The evening sky was cold and cloudless. I could see all the way to tidewater and beyond. At dusk I watched, transfixed, as the house lights of Petersburg blinked on in the west. The closest thing I'd had to human contact since the airdrop, the distant lights set off a flood of emotion that caught me completely off guard. I imagined people watching the Red Sox on the tube, eating fried chicken in brightly lit kitchens, drinking beer, making love. When I lay down to sleep I was overcome by a soul-wrenching loneliness. I'd never felt so alone, ever. 68

That night I had troubled dreams, of cops and vampires and a gangland-style execution. I heard someone whisper, "He's in there. As soon as he comes out, waste him." I sat bolt upright and opened my eyes. The sun was about to rise. The entire sky was scarlet. It was still clear, but wisps of high cirrus were streaming in from the southwest, and a dark line was visible just above the horizon. I pulled on my boots and hurriedly strapped on my crampons. Five minutes after waking up, I was front-pointing away from the bivouac. 69

I carried no rope, no tent or bivouac gear, no hardware save my ice axes. My plan was to go ultralight and ultrafast, to hit the summit and make it back down before the weather turned. Pushing myself, continually out of breath, I scurried up and to the left across small snowfields linked by narrow tunnels of verglas and short rock bands. The climbing was almost fun—the rock was covered with large, in-cut holds, and the ice, though thin, never got steep enough 70 to feel extreme—but I was anxious about the bands of clouds racing in from the Pacific, covering the sky.

71   In what seemed like no time (I didn't have a watch on the trip) I was on the distinctive final ice fields. By now the sky was completely overcast. It looked easier to keep angling to the left, but quicker to go straight for the top. Paranoid about being caught by a storm high on the peak without any kind of shelter, I opted for the direct route. The ice steepened, then steepened some more, and as it did so it grew thin. I swung my left ice axe and struck rock. I aimed for another spot, and once again it glanced off unyielding diorite with a dull, sickening clank. And again, and again: It was a reprise on my first attempt on the north face. Looking between my legs, I stole a glance at the glacier, more than two thousand feet below. My stomach churned. I felt my poise slipping away like smoke in the wind.

72   Forty-five feet above, the wall eased back onto the sloping summit shoulder. Forty-five more feet, half the distance between third base and home plate, and the mountain would be mine. I clung stiffly to my axes, unmoving, paralyzed with fear and indecision. I looked down at the dizzying drop to the glacier again, then up, then scraped away the film of ice above my head. I hooked the pin of my left axe on a nickel-thin lip of rock, and weighted it. It held. I pulled my right axe from the ice, reached up, and twisted the crook into a half-inch crack until it jammed. Barely breathing now, I moved my feet up, scrabbling my crampon points across the verglas. Reaching as high as I could with my left arm, I swung the axe gently at the shiny, opaque surface, not knowing what I'd hit beneath it. The pick went in with a heartening THUNK! A few minutes later I was standing on a broad, rounded ledge. The summit proper, a series of slender fins sprouting a grotesque meringue of atmospheric ice, stood 20 feet directly above.

73   The insubstantial frost feathers ensured that those last 20 feet remained hard, scary, onerous. But then, suddenly, there was no place higher to go. It wasn't possible, I couldn't believe it. I felt my cracked lips stretch into a huge, painful grin. I was on top of the Devils Thumb.

74   Fittingly, the summit was a surreal, malevolent place, an improbably slender fan of rock and rime no wider than a filing cabinet. It did not encourage loitering. As I straddled the highest point, the north face fell away beneath my left boot for six thousand feet; beneath my right boot the south face dropped off for 2,500. I took some pictures to prove I'd been there and spent a few minutes trying to straighten a bent pick. Then I stood up, carefully turned around, and headed for home.

75   Five days later I was camped in the rain by the sea, marveling at the sight of moss, willows, mosquitoes. Two days after that, a small skiff motored into Thomas Bay and pulled up on the beach not far from my tent. The man introduced himself as Jim Freeman, a timber faller from Petersburg. It was his day off, he said, and he'd made the trip to show his family the glacier, and to look for bears. He asked me if I'd "been huntin' or what?"

"No," I replied sheepishly. "Actually I just climbed the Devils Thumb. I've 76 been over here 20 days."

Freeman kept fiddling with the cleat on the boat, and didn't say anything 77 for a while. Then he looked at me real hard and spat, "You wouldn't be givin' me double talk now, wouldja, friend?" Taken aback, I stammered out a denial. Freeman, it was obvious, didn't believe me for a minute. Nor did he seem wild about my snarled shoulder-length hair or the way I smelled. When I asked if he could give me a lift back to town, however, he offered a grudging, "I don't see why not."

The water was choppy, and the ride across Frederick Sound took two 78 hours. The more we talked, the more Freeman warmed up. He still didn't believe I'd climbed the Thumb, but by the time he steered the skiff into Wrangell Narrows he pretended to. When we got off the boat he insisted on buying me a cheeseburger. That night he even let me sleep in a derelict step-van parked in his backyard.

I lay down in the rear of the old truck for a while but couldn't sleep, so I 79 got up and walked to a bar called Kito's Kave. The euphoria, the overwhelming sense of relief, that had initially accompanied my return to Petersburg faded, and an unexpected melancholy took its place. The people I chatted with in Kito's didn't seem to doubt that I'd been to the top of the Thumb, they just didn't much care. As the night wore on, the place emptied except for me and an Indian at a back table. I drank alone, putting quarters in the jukebox, playing the same five songs over and over, until the barmaid yelled angrily, "Hey! Give it a fucking rest, kid!" I mumbled an apology, quickly headed for the door, and lurched back to [Freedman's] step-van. There, surrounded by the sweet scent of motor oil, I lay down on the floorboards next to a gutted transmission and passed out.

It is easy when you are young to believe that what you desire is no less 80 than what you deserve, to assume that if you want something badly enough it is your God-given right to have it. Less than a month after sitting on the summit of the Thumb I was back in Boulder, nailing up siding on the Spruce Street Townhouses, the same condos I'd been framing when I left for Alaska. I got a raise, to four dollars an hour, and at the end of the summer moved out of the job-site trailer to a studio apartment on West Pearl, but little else in my life seemed to change. Somehow, it didn't add up to the glorious transformation I'd imagined in April.

Climbing the Devils Thumb, however, had nudged me a little further away 81 from the obdurate innocence of childhood. It taught me something about what mountains can and can't do, about the limits of dreams. I didn't recognize it at the time, but I'm grateful for it now.

FOCUS ON ECOLOGY

1. In "The Devil's Thumb," Krakauer sets off for a solo adventure of mountain climbing. Unlike the pieces on mountain climbing that we looked at in

Chapter 3, however, Krakauer's adventure might be considered more than simple recreation. Why do you suppose some people engage in activities outdoors that put them at risk?

2. One of the overriding emotions conveyed in this essay is loneliness. Often those who are lost or stuck in the wilderness, fighting for survival, find that the loneliness they experience is overwhelming. In fact, even those who have been lost for only short times have talked about an unbearable loneliness while they were lost. What do you suppose triggers that loneliness?

3. Stories of survival, even those like Krakauer's in which he intentionally situates himself in a position that risks death, fascinate many of us because they tell of near-death experiences. Do you like to read stories like Krakauer's, ones in which the narrators risk their very lives for adventure? Why or why not?

FOCUS ON WRITING

1. Throughout this essay, Jon Krakauer uses terminology to describe the kinds of ice and rock face he climbs. Are you familiar with these terms? Why do you suppose climbers have different names for different kinds of ice? What effect does Krakauer gain by using these terms?

2. This narrative is not only about Krakauer's adventure but is, in many ways, about Krakauer himself. How is the narrative designed to let us get to know Krakauer at the same time we witness his adventure? Is there a difference between the adventure and the adventurer?

3. Do you like this story? Why or why not? Do you find it to be well written? What for you makes it good or bad writing?

FOR DISCUSSION

As I mentioned in the introduction to this chapter, many Americans are fascinated with stories of survival like Krakauer's. The closer people come to death in their adventures—or in some cases even if they are killed—the more fascinated we seem to be with the story. As a class, consider the source of this fascination.

WRITING IN RESPONSE

Countless stories of near-death experiences in nature are published each year. Select another adventure-in-nature story or book that addresses a survival aspect of nature. After you have read the piece, write a summary of it and then write a short critique. Is it interesting? Is it well written? What role does survival play in the narrative?

From *Minus 148°:*
The Winter Ascent of Mt. McKinley

Art Davidson

Art Davidson was born in 1943. When he was 24, Davidson and seven companions attempted to climb Mt. McKinley (now renamed Denali, which means "the High One"), North America's highest peak, in the winter. When Davidson and his companions made the climb in 1967, few climbers had attempted it, and none would dare do so in winter. Now, Denali sees more than a thousand climbers each year, but even today few dare a winter climb. His book, Minus 148°: The Winter Ascent of Mt. McKinley, *recounts all of the 1967 expedition.*

JOURNAL ASSIGNMENT

In this selection, Davidson and two friends become trapped in a storm near the summit of Mt. McKinley (Denali) in minus 148° wind chill. In addition to facing death-threatening weather and environmental conditions, they also risk starvation. In your journal, consider: does someone's death in a situation like this one—that was freely chosen—merit the same kind of response as a death from weather, environmental conditioning, or starvation, if these conditions were completely outside of a person's control?

March 1

The wind woke us. The wildly whipping parachute billowed and snapped with reports like those of a bullwhip or rifle. The wind blasted against the rocks we were nestled among with a deafening eruption of noise; crosscurrents in the storm fluctuated its pitch to a groan or a prolonged whine. A dull, aching pressure along my backside was the cold, pressed into me by the wind.

I twisted in my sleeping bag to grope for the loose section of parachute thrashing me from behind. The moment I caught it my hands were pierced with cold; groggy with sleep, I'd forgotten that the nylon, like everything else outside our sleeping bags, was about minus 40 degrees. The cold sank into my fingers while the parachute, jerking and cracking erratically, resisted my attempts to anchor it. As soon as I managed to gather the slack material under me, the weight of my body holding it down, I shot one hand under an armpit and the other into my crotch for warmth. I was out of breath from the effort.

Drawn tighter, the parachute made less noise, and I was able to relax for a few moments. My fingers, aching inside from being deeply chilled, began to gradually rewarm with strong tingling sensations. I pressed the length of my body against Dave to be warmer on that side, and I felt Dave shift inside his bag, trying to press against me. I snuggled close to him and lay quietly for a long time, hoping I'd fall asleep again, as if not thinking about the wind and cold would make them disappear.

I couldn't sleep, and the wind only grew more vicious. I tried to ignore the cold along my backside, away from Dave, but when the first shiver ran through my body I turned to check the sleeping bag where it touched my back. To my horror it was no thicker than its shell, two pieces of nylon. The wind had pushed the down away. I could hardly believe it possible that the parachute, designed to resist wind, was letting the wind eat through it and into my sleeping bag.

The parachute began cracking again. "Oh, hell," I mumbled. The cracking meant a portion of the parachute had broken loose again. Feeling I didn't have the strength for another attempt at anchoring it, I curled up in my bag, shivering occasionally, waiting for something to happen; I didn't know what. After what seemed like several minutes but was probably only a matter of seconds, I heard Pirate trying to tie down the parachute.

"Art." Pirate's voice sounded far off and unfamiliar. "Help me hold it."

Hearing his voice made me realize that the three of us had been awake for more than an hour before anyone had spoken. Burrowed into my sleeping bag, I didn't want to budge from its security, false as it was, for even a moment. While I was deciding whether to help Pirate or prolong my rest, I felt Dave get to his hands and knees and begin wrestling with the parachute, which was now pounding his head and back as it billowed and cracked back in rapid succession. Yanking and cursing, Dave managed to pull part of it around him again, only to have it whip off as soon as he settled down into his bag.

"Look, we gotta get outa here!" Dave yelled.

"Where? We'd never make it down!" I said, grabbing onto the piece of parachute that Pirate was clinging to. "Maybe it's a morning wind that'll die down."

"Morning wind?" Dave looked at me with disbelief. "It's a bloody hurricane, you fool! I'm checking the other side of the rocks."

"Awwghaaaaa. . . ," Pirate growled, staring up into the wind.

Instead of getting completely out of the bag, Dave tied the drawstring at the top tight around his middle. With his legs still in the sleeping bag and his arms free, he lurched toward the crest ten feet away. I was horribly apprehensive. If he lost his grip on the rocks he could easily get blown off the mountain. On the other side we'd never hear him again if he called for help. How far was he going? Maybe he'd be hidden behind a rock where we wouldn't be able to find him if we needed his strength. Besides the logic of my fear, I recoiled emotionally against Dave's leaving because it seemed to break our trust; it violated a fundamental law of survival—stay together.

"Dave," I cried. "Wait! I think it's safer here."

"Stay if you want!" he hollered back. "This wind's bad, and I'm gettin' out of it!"

"Where are you going?" Dave didn't hear me. "It's exposed over there!" He had disappeared over the crest.

Since my mittens were too bulky to grip the parachute, I pulled thick wool socks onto my hands; my fingers were nearly numb already. I was astonished as I looked up to see Pirate holding the parachute with his bare hands. Just as I yelled at him to get something over them, one of my socks started to slip off. Pulling it back on, I shifted position, and the wind seized the wind parka I had been sitting on. Inside its main pocket was the tape recorder I had been using for the physiological testing, but at that moment I was much more concerned about the loss of the half dozen cookies I'd stashed in the pocket. One moment the parka had been next to me, then I saw it whirling through the air, 50, 100 feet up, sailing in the direction of McKinley's summit.

With Dave gone, his loose end of the parachute caught the wind, and this threatened to rip the entire piece of nylon from our grip. We gave up trying to wrap the parachute around us; the pull on our arms wrenched our whole bodies as we clung to it to keep it from escaping. The parachute was our only shelter.

"My hands are bad!" Pirate's voice was weak, almost a whimper. His face was drawn up into a hideous, painful grin. Ice caked his beard.

"Bring them in!" I yelled, though his head was only inches from mine. His fingers felt like chunks of ice against my stomach.

"They're stiff!"

"Move them!" I reached for a better grip on the parachute. It slipped. I lunged. Pirate caught it as it whipped past him. He winced in pain.

"Aw, the hell with it!" Pirate sighed. As he let loose, the parachute twisted through the air. It snagged on a rock. I saw it starting to rip, then it was gone.

For the first time I noticed the sky. It was a blue wall, smashing into the mountain. Thin pieces of cloud shredding—everything grew blurred. My eyes were watering and stinging from squinting into the wind. Compared to anything I had ever experienced, this wind was like another element. It was as if gravity had shifted and, instead of holding us down, was pulling us across the landscape.

Pirate began digging his hands in under my parka. The top of my bag had fallen open to the wind. As I pulled it shut, I fell against Pirate. We grabbed each other.

"Hold onto me!"

"Art, let's get into one bag."

"How? There's no room. . . . Give me your hands." I felt his icy fingers grabbing the skin around my middle. My bag had opened again, and to keep the wind from getting to me Pirate pushed himself over the opening. I just leaned against him, trying to catch my breath. Shivering, teeth chattering, my whole body was shaking with cold.

"Pirate, it's no good!" Wind was coming into my bag. We were both losing our warmth. "Each in his own bag . . . it's better."

"I can't feel my fingers!"

"Put 'em between your legs!"

"I don't want to lose my hands!"

I remembered Dave. If it was less windy on the other side of the rocks, he would have come back to tell us. If it was just as windy, I thought he would have returned to be with us. Something must have happened to him. But maybe he had found a sheltered corner. How could he abandon us?

"Pirate, let's try the other side!"

"Naw . . . the wind's everywhere!"

We huddled together, hunched uptight in our sleeping bags, wedged tightly between two rocks. Whenever we relaxed the wind caught us, started us sliding along the ice which gradually sloped away, and forced us to push and fight our way back up into the rocks. Leaning against Pirate didn't make me any warmer, but it was comforting—I wasn't alone. We didn't talk. I could breath more easily with my head inside my bag. I wondered what the others were doing down in the cave. Shiro's cough, Gregg's foot, John's swollen ear— it was too frightening to think about.

Beneath me I felt the ice sliding. Slipping onto my side, I brought an arm out in time to grab Pirate's knee. I pulled myself back against the rocks. My arms trembled from exhaustion. Pirate stared blankly out of his bag. His head turned slowly toward me with a groggy nodding motion. Was he slipping into a stupor? I wondered whether I looked as awful.

"It's no use here," I sighed.

I could barely keep myself against the rocks. There was nothing I could do for Pirate. Maybe Dave had found a safe spot. I had to check the other side of the rocks, but that would be deserting Pirate. Yet there was no way I could help. How could I just leave him? I had to do something for myself.

"I'm going over." He didn't move. "Pirate," I yelled, "I'm going after Dave!"

His head shook from side to side as he half mumbled, half shouted, something I couldn't understand. I grabbed at the rock above me and pulled myself up the slope. Another rock; its sharp cold cut through the wool socks. Another pull. I reached the crest. To my tremendous relief I saw Dave crouched on the ice only about 15 feet away. His back was toward me.

"Dave!" He couldn't hear me. I worked a little closer to him. The wind threatened to throw me off the crest. Beyond lay bare glacier where I'd never catch anything to hold onto if I was blown from the rocks.

"Dave!" This time he turned and saw me. I was out of breath and must have been gasping as much as yelling. "Is it better where you are?"

"What? . . . It's the same. Go back!"

I didn't want to go back, and waiting here on the crest was impossible because it was completely exposed to the wind. Before I'd decided which way to go, a cross-current gust caught me. I grabbed for rocks. One came loose. I caught another one nearer Dave. Somehow the sock on my left hand had blown off. I shoved the bare hand into my sleeping bag. The other hand held onto a rock. The wind flung and tossed my body as though it were weightless.

My right hand ached with cold from gripping the rock, and my forearm began cramping from the strain. I couldn't go back into the wind, but neither could my right hand cling to the rock much longer. The only other rock I could reach was three feet to my left, near Dave. My numb right hand had become so dead that I couldn't feel the rock it held onto. My shivering body seemed on the verge of going into convulsions.

I tried to think. If I lost my grip, I'd be blown across the ice. My mind was racing. I had to grab for the rock near Dave with my left hand: it was bare, no mitten or sock. It would be frozen. I had to. Suddenly, my bare hand shot out to grab the rock. Slicing cold.

I saw Dave's face, the end of his nose raw, frostbitten. His mouth, distorted into an agonized mixture of compassion and anger, swore at me to get a glove on. I looked at my hand. It was white, frozen absolutely white.

I pulled my body onto the rock. Dave was only five or six feet away on the ledge he had chopped in the slightly sloping ice.

"Christ, Art." His voice cracked. "You froze your hands!"

I pushed off from the rock, letting the wind throw me against Dave. He flung his arms around me. All I could do was lie across him, wheezing and shaking, trying to catch my breath.

"Man," he said, "we gotta dig in!". . .

Dave cradled Pirate's feet against his belly and massaged them gently until they began to rewarm.

"Dave," I said, "you know you saved us out there." My words sort of hung in the air. They sounded hollow, and Dave bit at his lip self-consciously. I didn't say more, but my eyes followed Dave with admiration and a kind of love as he tucked Pirate in his bag and then reached for the stove.

For more than an hour I had clung to the ledge on the ice, feeling the frost-bite blisters swell on my hands and watching helplessly while Dave dug a cave in the ice. Just before he had completed it, Dave had collapsed from exhaustion; by then Pirate had pulled himself together, and despite his hands and feet, which were beginning to swell with frostbite blisters, he had somehow made it over the crest to finish hollowing out the cave. Dave had recovered enough strength to help me through the small hole in the ice which was the entrance to our new home.

Now inside our cave, Dave leaned on his elbows, and steadying the stove with one hand, he prepared some food with his free hand. In this cramped chamber under the ice cooking was more miserable than it had ever been in the last four weeks; Dave had quietly accepted the job because his were the only hands capable of working the stove. At least he had found some good food to fix—four pound-and-a-half cans of ham, bacon, and peas which had been cached by a previous expedition among the rocks we had bivouacked against. Since our pot had blown away, he heated the ham in its own can, then used the can to melt water in.

Flattened against the wall while Dave cooked in the middle, I realized how small our cave was. At the wide end there was barely enough room for our shoulders, and at the narrow end our feet in our sleeping bags were heaped on top of each other. Because of the rocks behind us, Dave and Pirate had been unable to make the cave long enough for us to stretch out completely. Over our feet the ceiling was about a foot and a half above the floor; toward the larger end there was just enough height to turn or lie on our sides with one shoulder touching the ice on the floor and the other touching the ice on the ceiling. We were quickly learning that our every movement bumped the next person. This cave certainly wasn't pleasant or comfortable by ordinary standards, but it kept us safe from the wind, and that was all that mattered, for the moment.

Dave looked for his journal and found it missing. We had lost too much to the wind—the use of four hands and two feet, an incalculable amount of body warmth, two packs with half our food in them, the parachute, my wind parka, and—perhaps our greatest loss—the foam pads which would have insulated us from the ice and helped to keep our bags dry. Yet we felt secure. We were supplied with enough gas to make water for another day, maybe two more days if we stretched it. With four lunches left, and three remaining cans of food, we needn't worry about starving.

That night ham and hot water were a feast, not filling, but delicious nonetheless; it was our first warm food since leaving the cave down at 17,200 feet more than 30 hours before. My hands had become so inflexible that Dave had to place each bite of ham—there were five of them—in my mouth, then tip the can to my lips to let me drink. Eating made us giddy with pleasure and al-most got us feeling warm.

We were actually exultant, not from any sense of conquering the wind, but rather from the simple companionship of huddling together in our little cave while outside in the darkness the storm raged through Denali Pass and on across the Alaska range.

We agreed that the wind coming out of the northwest was funneling through the pass at least 130 miles per hour. We remembered that a wind of such velocity, combined with the minus 30-, minus 40-degree air temperature outside our cave, created an equivalent wind-chill temperature somewhere off the end of the chart; the last figure on the chart was minus 148 degrees.

"148 degrees below zero."

It was frightening to say the least, but the worst was over, we thought. In the morning the wind should slack off; we would descend, greeting others at 17,200 feet with the news that we had made the summit; we could get off the mountain and go home. We wanted to believe the climb was over, that in a cou-ple of days everything would be warm and easy again. Yet the wind, howling and pounding the slope overhead, reminded us that we couldn't move until it died down. We talked of the cave as our refuge, but the suspicion that we were being held captive in the ice must have entered each of our minds as we fell asleep listening to the wind.

From Gregg's Diary, March 1: Those guys (trapped above) have only a bunch of lunch, one stove full of gas, a pot, and their sleeping bags. With these provi-sions and their personal reserves they can probably last two more days at the longest, but practically speaking they must make it down tonight or tommor-row at the latest. . . . What anguish we are all suffering for our friends' safety.

March 2

. . . Through the night I had slept restlessly, waking every time Dave's knees and shoulders pushed into me. Each time my mind started to clear, the thought that the wind might be down rushed up, but before I'd be fully awake the damnable roar would be running through my head. A shift of legs, or a roll to the other side—in any position the ice was too hard to be comfortable. Sleep made time pass, but the altitude caused a nervous wakefulness.

Staring at the ice, supposing the others were asleep, I looked forward to discussing a plan of action when they woke. Eventually their shifting to find a more comfortable position convinced me that they must already be awake. I asked, and they both said they had been lying silently for about an hour or more. I realized there was nothing to say. It was horribly simple. We would have to wait here until the wind stopped, at least until it died down. One sleepless hour after another we listened for the first lull.

During the morning the wind remained constant. The fluctuations in its monotonous tone were so slight that it reminded me of the perpetual roar inside a conch shell—only much, much louder. Later in the day, extraordinary blasts of wind hit the surface of the ice overhead with enough force to actually shake the roof of our cave, causing loose ice crystals to fall from the ceiling.

There was no joking, no idle conversation, hardly any talk at all. We retreated into ourselves, silent, waiting, staring at the ice on the ceiling, staring at the ice on the sides of the cave, staring into the darkness inside our sleeping bags. I tried to think constructively, develop a plan or project for the next summer, but it was useless. The altitude was heckling my mind—the same restless lightheadedness that was keeping me awake also prevented me from concentrating. Wandering thoughts always returned to the sound of the wind, and to the dreary question repeated continually—"When will it stop?"

The only event during the day which aroused my interest at all was our one meal, stretching from late afternoon till after dark. Dave, manning the stove again, thawed and melted more than he actually cooked. Patiently, he dropped chunks of snow and ice into the can, watched them melt, added more snow and ice, and finally—with what Pirate and I agreed was a stroke of genius—he dumped in a package of gorp. When the grog became hot the chocolate bits melted into a fascinating brew, filled with cashews and raisins. Flavored partly with my considerable thirst, it was undoubtedly the best drink I had ever tasted. However, when I had gotten my portion down, a curious, mildly unpleasant aftertaste remained.

About an hour after the hot drink, Dave served the rest of the ham. He heated it over the stove only long enough for it to thaw. Warming it would have meant wasting fuel, which we would need in case the wind held us here another day. Dave placed two pieces of ham, each about the size of an apricot, in my mouth, followed them with several slices of cheese and salami, and finished with three pieces of hard candy.

After another hour Dave melted enough snow and ice to fill the can with water. When it was warm he emptied a tiny can of chopped pork into the water to make a thin soup. Before I drank my portion I felt the need to relieve myself. Going outside was unthinkable.

"Dave," I asked, "isn't there a spare can or a plastic bag we can use for a pee bottle?"

"Nope, Art," he answered. "All we've got is the cooking can."

"Then what did you use?"

"Well," Dave started uncertainly, "I thought you wouldn't eat or drink if I told you, but I used the cooking can."

Now I recognized the scent or flavor that had remained as an aftertaste—urine. It didn't matter. I thought it should, but it just didn't.

After Dave poured the last soup into me, I prepared to use the can myself—inside my sleeping bag. This would be the first thing I had attempted to accomplish with my swollen fingers; it was a task that even under more normal conditions required considerable technique. An accident would not only be wretchedly unpleasant but disastrous as well, because the extra liquid in my bag would consolidate the down, thus ruining its insulation.

I listened anxiously as the can began to fill. The liquid level rapidly approached the rim, but in the nick of time I managed to maneuver out of what would have otherwise been a shameful and uncomfortable predicament and looked about for a place to empty the can. Not finding a suitable spot to my left and realizing Dave was guarding against my dumping it to my right, I raised the can precariously over my head and sloshed its contents against the ice behind me. Most of it melted in, but a little stream trickled under my bag. No matter, it would be frozen in seconds.

Dave calmly observed that my performance of holding the can was so skillful that I could damn well feed myself from now on.

I had heard Pirate's voice only two or three times throughout the day. Even though he lay along the opposite side of the cave, only four feet from me, I could barely hear his voice above the wind the few times he did speak. The altitude had cut off his exuberance and made him a slowed-down version of his old self. When I asked Dave whether Pirate was all right, he simply said that Pirate was worried about his feet, which had become worse than his hands. The swelling had leveled off, Dave told me, but most of his toes were insensitive to touch.

One particularly excruciating aspect of waiting was knowing that the longer we were held down the worse our frostbite would be. As our bodies began to dry up as a result of an inadequate liquid intake, they became more difficult to warm. Dave's toes were cold, but he didn't complain because he thought that was a good sign; better that they feel cold than numb. Only Dave and I had down booties, yet we had to frequently wiggle our toes to keep the circulation flowing through them. I considered lending my booties to Pirate, but the thought of my feet freezing while I slept discouraged me.

My main concern was my hands, which were swollen to nearly twice their normal size. To flex the tips of my fingers I had to painfully clench the muscles in my hand and forearm. I recalled the last time I had played my flute before leaving for McKinley. I had carefully watched my fingers run over the keys; I had wanted to appreciate them in case I lost them, and at the same time I had promised myself that I wouldn't lose them. I had begun to fear that was exactly what was happening every hour I lay in the cave. I caught myself wondering if I would still be able to play my flute with the first and second joints of my fingers missing.

Our stomachs hadn't really been full since we had left for the summit. An empty sort of craving had settled into my belly; I hoped it wouldn't develop into cramps which I had heard afflict people suffering from malnutrition. The others down below would be running short of food soon. Maybe they would have to retreat down the mountain. I asked Dave whether he thought the others had given up on us. He didn't answer; maybe he was asleep. Surely they'd come looking for us when the wind died down.

That night, long after it was dark, I found myself repeating the words of a Dylan Thomas poem: "Light breaks where no sun shines." Before I'd come on McKinley I had known the verses by heart; now I couldn't remember the first one past "Where no sea runs the waters of the heart push in their tides." Further on there was something about the things of light filing through the flesh. I couldn't remember. Just the first line—"Light breaks where no sun shines"—ran over and over in my mind.

I lay a long time in the dark, unable to sleep. The wind, a persistent, audible ache in our heads, had been with us for so long that its incessant sounds were like a silence that had settled over our lives. That silent, paralytic quality in the wind recalled images of unalterable bleakness; I remembered seeing the wind run through the broken windows of an abandoned cabin, the wind in the dried grass of a beach in November after the birds had migrated, the wind over the delta of a frozen river.

I couldn't remember what it was like not to hear the wind, but the three of us knew that if we heard it in the morning our situation would become critical. There appeared to be only enough gas to melt one more can of water.

Through more than 36 hours the wind had not even for a moment relinquished its hold on the mountain and on our lives. Surely, we reassured ourselves, the wind's force would be diminished by morning. . . .

From Gregg's Diary, March 2: The nightmare goes on. They didn't show up last night. I can't believe this is happening. While they are still strong they must make a break for it, all three slowly. It is windy and white-out this morning, very bad conditions. The irony of it: they are only one thousand feet above us, yet we can't help them. Lord I wish this nightmare would end. What a terrible ordeal they must be going through. I can't remember a more prolonged terror in my life. It is the damn quick changeable mountain weather that got us.

March 3

The infernal noise filled our heads.

The wind's vicious, I told myself. It's diabolical. Silently cursing it became a pastime. I tried to think of all the words that described its evil nature—fiendish, wicked, malicious. I called it a vampire sucking the life out of us.

But the wind didn't hear me, and I knew my words were irrelevant anyway. The wind wasn't malevolent; it wasn't out to get us; it had no evil intentions, nor any intentions at all. It was simply a chunk of sky moving about. It was a weather pattern, one pressure area moving into another. Still, it was more satisfying, somehow more comforting, to personify the wind, make it something I could hate or respect, something I could shout at. I wished I were an old Eskimo shaman, seeing devils and demons in the storm and understanding the evil spirits that lived in the mountain. I thought that a good shaman would know a chant that would chase away the wind. But I didn't know any magic, and I knew all my cursing was only an attempt to escape the simple facts; we had to descend, we couldn't descend in the wind, and the wind showed no sign of letting up.

We needed water most desperately. There was very little gas left in the stove; I wanted Dave to melt ice with it. I tried to think of the most pleasant ways of reminding him that we needed to drink, but whatever I said he growled at. I knew he felt the strain of having to do all the chores for Pirate and me. I felt too thankful, too dependent, almost too much at the mercy of Dave to pester him about the water. He told me that "later" he would melt some ice and thaw the bacon or peas, but gradually the day slipped by without our eating or drinking. Yet, if my hands had been all right, I would have put off the cooking the way Dave did because the altitude had cut away our motivation; it was so much easier to say "later" because, through we didn't really believe it, we always thought the wind might suddenly stop, letting us run down to the cave at 17,200 feet.

It was toward the middle of the afternoon when I heard Dave beginning to coax the stove back to life. He fiddled with it for several minutes without any luck, then decided to let it sit while he opened one of the large cans of bacon, ham, or peas.

It was the moment I had waited for all day.

"Which one do we want first?" he asked.

"Mix 'em all together," Pirate suggested.

Dave scraped the ice off the can of bacon with his knife, clearing the top so he could open it. I could already taste the bacon.

"Damn!" Dave swore in disgust. "Holes in the can! We can't eat the bacon! It's rotten!"

He reached for a can of peas.

It could certainly not happen again. Those holes had been an accident. Nevertheless, Pirate and I listened intently as Dave cleared the ice from the can of peas.

When only about half the ice was off, he swore again. More holes! Then he tried the ham, our last can. It was the same!

We sank back into a numb depression. For two days we had anticipated the flavor of the bacon. We had let ourselves dream of the juice of the peas in our mouths. Suddenly the food we had counted on was gone. The gnawing cramps in our stomachs weren't going to be quieted.

Immediately we were angry for being so cruelly cheated, but only after several minutes did we realize how the spoiled food had transformed our trial with hunger into a confrontation with starvation. We had almost nothing left to eat—three bags of gorp, a dozen slices of cheese, some hard candies, a little coffee, a three ounce can of chopped pork, and maybe a dozen cookies. The combined calorie count of our remaining food was probably adequate for one person for one day. Solemnly, Dave divided a little less than half of the remaining food into three equal portions.

Although Dave battled with the stove long after his fingers were insensitive from handling the cold metal, he failed to get it going. There was so little gas left that he couldn't build up enough pressure to vaporize it. At 30 below the gas was sluggish—he had to give up. Just like the punctured cans of food, our last drops of gas mocked us with their uselessness.

Our one hope was a gallon of gas Dave had cached on the far side of Denali Pass when he had climbed McKinley in the summer three years earlier. It might still be there; Dave had spotted the bottle of gas the first day we had tried for the summit. He thought we should take a look, but no one volunteered to go out. He said he had originally cached the gas only about 200 feet from where we lay. No one moved. Dave was the most fit to go out, and the most certain of the place it was cached, but the horror of entering the wind overcame the slightest inclination Dave might have had to go after it.

We tried to imagine what the others at 17,200 were doing. They had shelter, but only a limited supply of food. I remembered how a week or two before we had been concerned for the strength of John and George, about Shiro's cough and hemorrhoids, and about Gregg's uncontrollable emotions in a crisis. Now they were entirely dependent on their own resources; and the three of us who had once been the strongest might soon come to depend on their judgment and strength to be rescued.

We hoped the others would not attempt anything rash for our sake—that the strain of their fear for us wouldn't break them. We thought of the gallon of gas. We imagined how delicious a cup of water would taste. We shifted our hips and shoulders to relieve the hard cold beneath us.

We talked very little. The grayness inside the cave faded into darkness. . . .

From Gregg's Diary, March 3 [as Gregg and the four at 17,300 feet plan to descend]: It is nearly dark. Nasty weather all day. I hate splitting the party. If this weather lasts there will be no hope for those above. Please God don't let this happen. I must be dreaming.

March 4

I woke elated. The wind had stopped. I heard a helicopter.

Just outside the cave I heard the steady whir. Gregg must have gotten a rescue started. It sounded as if the copter had already landed. People must be searching the pass for us. I was afraid they wouldn't find our cave; it was such a small hole in the ice. Maybe they'd give up and leave.

"Dave!" I rolled toward him. "Dave, do you hear the helicopter? We'd better get outside right away."

"Go to sleep . . . it's the wind."

"No! It can't be. It's too steady, too constant. It's a copter. . . . Dave. . . ."

He didn't answer.

"It's a copter," I repeated to myself. "It's the steady whirl of a copter." I listened to be certain; but I wasn't certain. Maybe it was the wind; it couldn't be. I almost asked Dave to listen; but I knew he was right; yet I strained my ears for a voice, any sound that would let me believe there were rescuers outside.

There was only the wind.

After a long silence Dave admitted that he had been susceptible to my delusion; he had convinced himself for several minutes that the sound of the wind really was a rescue helicopter.

"But you know," Dave said, looking toward me, "it makes you feel kind of humble to know a helicopter couldn't possibly get to us."

Dave went on to explain how he felt good to know that no device of technology nor any effort on the part of our companions could conquer the storm, or even reach through it to help us. He said the three of us were alone in this sanctuary of the earth's wilderness, and that our only security lay in ourselves, in our individual abilities to endure, and in our combined capacities of willpower and judgment.

I said, "Dave, it may sound funny, but I feel closer to you than ever before."

Dave beamed and said, "Yeah, I know what you mean. If we can't fight our way out of this storm, at least we can stick together, and try to live in harmony with it."

I thought to myself how the storm itself was helping to protect us from its own fury. Ever since the McKinley massif had been thrust upward out of a flat land, the wind had been packing the snow and ice of Denali Pass into contours of least resistance. We were sheltered inside ice that conformed to the pattern of the wind. We had suffered and nearly succumbed to the storm that first morning when we had fought it head-on in the open, but now all the force of the wind only pounded more stability into the roof of our cave as it swept across the slope above us.

The altitude riddled our attention span into fragments of thoughts. Discomfort was the only thing on which my mind seemed able to concentrate. My lips were deeply cracked in several places. Moving my tongue along the roof of my mouth, I felt clumps of dried-up mucus; other experiences with dehydration had taught me that if I didn't get water soon, the rawest areas in my mouth would begin bleeding. The ligaments in my legs ached as they dried up. It was especially painful to stretch or change positions; unfortunately, the hardness of the ice made my hips and back sore whenever I remained still for more than a few minutes. I complained very little, not because I was naturally stoic, but because there was no one to complain to—each of us experienced the same discomforts; pain had become a natural condition of our life under the ice.

I was probably warmer than either Dave or Pirate because their sleeping bags were icing up faster than mine. Every time Dave had cooked, steam from the warm liquid had been absorbed into his bag, where it soon froze. As the down had matted together, its resilience had disappeared. It was particularly unsettling when Dave pointed out a number of lumps of ice mixed with the down. I didn't see how his bag could retain any warmth. Pirate's bag was a little better, but his down was fast becoming clogged with moisture from his breath because, against Dave's advice and mine, he persisted in burying his head in his bag, where his exhaled moisture had no escape. All of us sorely missed the foam pads. Without them, we were only able to place a spare wind parka or pair of wind pants under our buttocks and shoulders, leaving the rest of our sleeping bags on bare ice.

Pirate's hands were swollen, but he said he was worried most about his feet. He asked about my down booties. Though he didn't say it outright, I could tell he wanted to wear them. I tried to ignore him, acting as if I hadn't heard. My feet were cold with the booties; without them I thought they would surely freeze while I slept, or even while I lay awake. I avoided thinking about it, but that was exactly what was happening to Pirate's feet. He knew I didn't want to give them up, and didn't ask again. As he kicked his feet inside his bag to relieve their numbness, I knew he must be thinking of the warmth of my booties. Pretending to be asleep, I tried to forget about Pirate's feet.

I couldn't remember how many days we had been in the cave. The day we had gone to the summit, then that first day of the wind, the day we ate ham, then a day without water—it must have been the fourth day, but I was uncertain.

Sometime during the middle of the day Dave rationed us each a fig bar and two hard candies. Sucking on the candies brought a few minutes of relief to the rawness in my mouth. I put the fig bar aside. I wanted to save it for later in the afternoon as a break in the monotony of hunger. After about an hour I couldn't wait any longer. I had looked forward to saliva coming back into my mouth as I chewed the fig bar, but the crumbs only stuck to the gums and roof of my mouth. With some effort, I swallowed the sticky wad, feeling it tumble into my stomach, where it set off a series of cramps. The pain constructed a morbidly amusing picture of four or five hands in my stomach grabbing for the fig bar, fighting each other for it, tearing and ripping at it. After a few minutes the cramps died down and the usual steady ache returned.

Silently I cursed the punctured cans of food. Some careless climbers must have punched holes in them with their ice axes as they tried to chip away the ice that covered them. We all wished we had never seen the cans. Without them we might have been able to accept our hunger, but knowing that ham and peas, rotten as they were, lay within arm's reach while we were gradually starving was almost unbearable. The cruelest twist to the irony was the uncertainty; the canned food might still be good. Perhaps the food had remained frozen ever since it had been brought to Denali Pass. It was doubtful that there were any bacteria living at 18,200 feet. At least a portion of the ham, peas, and bacon might not be rancid, but to find out would be risking food poisoning.

Early in the afternoon it became obvious that we were going to spend another night in the cave. Even if the wind let up toward evening, we wouldn't have the time, nor perhaps the strength, to descend. We knew our dehydration was critical. We hadn't had a cup of liquid in over 36 hours. Because our circulation was down we were all chilly inside our bags with all our parkas and wind pants on. Occasionally, I would feel Dave's body tense and shake with shivers. We needed water, which meant we needed gas—which we didn't have.

The only possibility was the gas Dave had cached at Denali Pass three years before. If one of us went for the gallon of gas, he might not make it back through the wind to the cave. The gruesome reality of this possibility had kept us from retrieving the gas, but there was no longer any alternative. One of us had to go for the gas! Who? I couldn't go because of my hands, so I lay quietly in my bag, letting my silence ask someone else to go.

Dave resisted the thought of his going. He had dug the cave. He had cooked for us when there had been gas. He knew his efforts had kept Pirate and me alive. And we knew it.

It wasn't right that Dave go out into certain misery to possibly disappear in the wind. Yet, knowing Dave, I sensed he was struggling with his weariness and fear to find it in himself to go out. Since he was the only one of us who knew for certain where the gas should be, it was logical that he go. Neither Pirate nor I could ask him. Semiconscious from the altitude and the numbing hypnotism of the wind, we retained a sense of justice.

There was another reason we weren't anxious for Dave to go. He was our hands! We needed him to cook if we ever got some gas. We would need him to tie the rope around us and hold us on belay when we descended, whenever that might be.

Quietly—I don't remember hearing him say he would go—Pirate got out of his sleeping bag. When he started to pull on his boots, he found it difficult and painful to force his swollen feet into them. I offered him the use of my down booties. He took them and quickly had them tied on. Dave described the rocks among which the gas had been cached. Pirate pulled down his face mask.

The wind had become more erratic: there were gusts and then short—ten-to-30 second—lulls of comparative calm. Pirate lay on his stomach, facing the entrance, listening for the lull that sounded right to him. A resigned determination seemed to be all that was left of his former fierceness. Suddenly, he gave a short and not too loud "Arahhaa!" and began squirming out the entrance, uphill, through loose snow. Dave and I cheered, not loudly, but with all our remaining enthusiasm. For a moment we heard Pirate placing the pack across the entrance again. Then the lull ended abruptly, and all we heard was the wind.

For the longest time Dave and I listened without saying a word. Ten, 15 minutes passed. We knew Pirate should have returned, but we said nothing. He might call for help only 10 feet from the cave and we'd never hear him. . . . I couldn't help imagining what we'd have to do if he failed to return. Maybe Dave would make a try for the gas. Maybe the two of us would attempt to dash down from the pass. If Pirate didn't return within a few minutes there would be no reason to go looking for him. Maybe Dave and I would simply lie in the cave, waiting until Gregg, Shiro, George, and John could reach us, or until we passed into delirium.

We heard a movement at the entrance. Two immediate whoops of sheer joy expressed our relief. A flurry of snow, then a plastic jug shot into the cave, followed by an exhausted Pirate.

"Bad!" He was gasping. "I couldn't stand up, even in the lulls. Something's wrong with my balance." I had never heard Pirate say anything was rough or dangerous. "I crawled all the way, clawing into the ice with two ice axes. I can't feel my feet now."

We had gas! We could drink water!

With a merriment we'd forgotten ever existed Dave melted chunks of ice and piles of snow. The first can of water, especially, smelled and tasted sweet; we did not remember that the sweetness was the scent of urine. Dave heated can after can of water till they became hot. We drank, and drank, and always waited for yet another capful. For the first time in five days we went to sleep with full stomachs. That we were full of water mattered not at all—or so we thought.

My feet had become colder. I had to constantly wiggle my toes to keep them from becoming numb. Still, I was glad I had not asked Pirate to return my booties after his trip for the gas. . . .

From Gregg's Diary, March 4: Damn, we are still here . . . it is just too nasty out to move. It is harder to sit than to move at this point. The waiting is more terrible than moving. But to move now might complete the destruction of our party.

March 5

. . . The gusts and lulls of the wind sounded hopeful when we woke to another cold, gray morning under the ice. The ragged end of the storm seemed to be blowing itself out, and had we been strong we probably would have tried to dash down from the pass immediately. Unfortunately, we had become so weak that the wind would have to be completely gone before we could descend with any confidence. Yet, regardless of when the wind disappeared, this had to be our last day in the cave, because by the next morning there would be no food at all. For the three of us we had only a handful of gorp, four slices of cheese, and three little hard candies. When this food ran out the cold would take over our bodies unless we could make it down. We lay silent and brooding in our bags; cheerless as our situation was, I felt a curious sense of relief that it was so simple—without food, it was either descend or perish in this wretched cave.

Pirate refused to believe what the wind had done during the night. On going to sleep, he had fixed a rope to the pack which closed the cave's entrance, then tied that rope around his arm to keep the pack from being blown away if a gust dislodged it. He woke to find both the rope and the pack gone. As the wind had begun packing the entrance full of snow, some loose, fine-grained crystals has sifted into Pirate's sleeping bag; the bag had so little warmth that the snow lay in it without melting. Pirate stared at the snow for ten or 15 seconds, then mumbled hoarsely that he'd leave the snow in his bag because it might help insulate him. His reasoning sounded absurd. I thought of telling him to get the snow out of his bag as fast as he could, but it was easier to lie silent than begin talking. Then I began wondering whether Pirate might be right about the snow helping to insulate him—his bag and Dave's we're now little more than matted down and chucks of ice held together by the nylon shell.

Even after Pirate placed his boots and the gas bottle in the entrance to block the blowing snow from sealing us in, snow still blew through every time a gust of wind hit the slope above. Because the entrance wasn't tightly closed off from the storm, a steady draft circulated the minus 35-degree air through our cave. With the chill factor increased, I began shivering again. This wasn't particularly painful but it was unnerving to watch my body shake uncontrollably. What happens after you lose control of your body? I thought of asking Dave, but said nothing.

My thoughts wandered back to my childhood. I recalled my parents saying that when I was first learning to walk I enjoyed toddling around in the snow naked. I remembered the times when I was eight and nine and we'd run out into the spring windstorms that sweep across the plains of eastern Colorado; with bales of straw we built shelters from the driving wind and dust, and considered ourselves pioneers. In those days it had been great fun to run shouting from tree to tree in a thunderstorm or when the rain turned to hailstones the size of marbles and golf balls. How had those games in storms led to the desperate mess the three of us were trapped in? All I wanted now was to be free of the fear of freezing and being buried under the ice. I started imagining what we'd look like frozen solid. The feel of my mouth on Farine's cold lips came back. I saw his last expression frozen in his cheeks and eyelids. How much of a body could be frozen before the heart stopped? Was I acting cowardly to think this way? It wouldn't happen to us, not to me; yet, there was the cold in our hands and feet.

To get these thoughts out of my mind, I asked Dave if it seemed to him that the gusts were becoming less powerful and the periods of calm longer. He said, "Don't think about it." But I couldn't help being attentive to every fluctuation in the wind, even though I knew as well as Dave that it was only depressing to hear every lull end in a blast of wind.

Only food occupied our thoughts as much as the wind, especially the food in the punctured cans. Those cans haunted us. I felt the little holes staring at me whether the cans were in plain sight or hidden under a sleeping bag or out the entrance. After Dave had emptied the cans of their contents, he classified most of the food as definitely rotten, but there remained at least a pound of peas and a half pound of ham that he thought might be edible. He even thawed and heated some of the ham. It didn't smell or look bad; still, it had come from a partly spoiled can.

"Aw, I'm going to eat it," Pirate insisted.

But we wouldn't let him. There was no question in our minds that, as weak as we were, food poisoning would do us in. As long as we could just resist the canned food we had a chance; if we gave in and ate the doubtful ham and peas we might eliminate that chance. Of course, the food might be good, and it could easily provide the extra strength we might need to get down.

As our stomachs tightened with cramps and the deafening repetition of gusts and lulls whittled away our patience, each of us changed our minds about eating the canned food. One moment Pirate would declare he was going to eat the ham, and the next he would be restraining Dave or me from trying it. So far we had been able to check ourselves, but every moment of hunger increased the temptation.

We dreamed about feasts, banquets, exotic dishes, all our favorite foods. For what seemed like hours Dave and I listed every type of food we could think of. Sometimes we would be silent for ten or 15 minutes, as if the conversation had ended; then as soon as I'd mention something like "crab," Dave would say "Wow, oh honcho boncho! I'd forgotten crab!" Another ten minutes might pass before one of us would remember a forgotten delicacy.

Once Dave said, "Stuffed green peppers!"

"Yeah . . . with lots of raisins in the stuffing!" I answered.

We tantalized each other with difficult choices between different foods. "Dave," I asked, "would you prefer a mushroom pizza or a pepperoni pizza?"

"Mushroom, and if you could have one fruit, what would it be?"

"Awaarraghaa. . . . I want some bloody meat!" Pirate interrupted. There was enough gas to make as much water as we could drink; however, Dave had only enough motivation to make a minimal amount. As our dehydration continued, our frostbite became more severe. The swelling in my fingers had started to go down; I didn't know whether this was a sign of improvement or an indication that my body simply didn't have enough liquid to keep the swelling up. Much as I worried over the blisters, I realized they were my body's way of trying to save the tissue that had been frozen.

Dave couldn't feel the large toe on his right foot, nor parts of several other toes. There was so little he could do for his feet—rub them, wiggle the toes. He said they were becoming steadily colder. The scabby, frostbitten skin on the end of his nose was sickening to look at, but not nearly as frightening as the freezing that was beginning in his feet. The frostbite on his nose was isolated and had come about because he happened to have a long nose which protruded from his face mask, while the frostbite taking hold in his feet was not isolated; it was a sign that the cold was steadily creeping into his body. It was happening to each of us.

At times I was surprised that I wanted Pirate to continue wearing my booties, which I had previously guarded so selfishly. I knew I hadn't overcome my selfishness; Pirate was sort of included in it. Since his feet had suffered on his trip to get the gas, I had felt almost as protective toward his feet as toward my own. Later in the day Pirate passed one bootie back to me. Perhaps one bootie each would not be a practical way to halt the freezing in our feet, but, even if it was only a gesture, it was still the most touching thing I had ever seen Pirate do.

The one advantage of being dehydrated was that we rarely had to jeopardize ourselves by urinating into the can inside our sleeping bags. Likewise, our lack of food had saved us from the ordeal of a bowel movement in the wind. Nevertheless, our hour of reckoning came. We had postponed the moment until it appeared we wouldn't be safe another minute. To go outside would be risking the possibility of contracting a humiliating case of frostbite while our pants were down. By comparison, it was almost pleasant to contemplate attempting the feat inside our sleeping bags. Dave's ingenuity developed a technique which produced little packages, nicely wrapped in toilet paper. With some coaching from him I managed to get my bundles safely wrapped and out the cave's entrance. However, Pirate, who hadn't been very attentive, got himself into trouble. Soon after he had completely disappeared into his sleeping bag we heard him begin to mumble and swear. When the shape of his sleeping bag began shifting frantically, we offered him some advice.

"Oh, you had paper?" he moaned. "I didn't know you guys had used paper."

During the first days of the wind, sleep had been an effective way of waiting. Now it had become a continual twisting of hips and shoulders away from the hardness of the ice, a twisting away from the cold that seeped into our bags from the ice beneath. None of us had even a momentary respite from hunger cramps and the cramps and aches in our dried-up ligaments and muscles. Nevertheless, wakefulness continued to be a worse kind of half-consciousness; pain was felt more acutely by a more alert mind, and we realized that we weren't dreaming, that we were not going to wake up to find everything friendly and warm.

At times, I was unable to tell for certain whether I was awake or asleep. Dreams of Farine lying on the ice, of John calling from the bottom of that crevasse, of Shiro coughing, of our hands and feet turning black, filled my sleep and drifted over into the different levels of wakefulness that stretched through the day. Hours no longer existed. I once asked Dave how long we had been trapped under the ice; he said he didn't know.

In the afternoon, during one period of what I thought was clearsightedness it seemed as though the wind was finally dying. The lulls had become much longer, maybe as long as five or six minutes, and the gusts were less frequent and no longer hit with the force which had shaken our cave for so many days. I dozed fitfully, then woke in the dark to a strange sound. I was startled. To ears that had become unaccustomed to quietness, the silence sounded nearly as loud as the wind's roar had that first morning.

"Dave, the wind's gone! We can descend!"

"Yeah man, I'm cooking us up a farewell dinner to this awful hole," Dave said. In a moment his headlamp flicked on and several minutes later I heard the cheery purr of the stove. It was all over; we thought we had made it through. Our farewell dinner was a farewell to the very last of our food, to the cave, and, we hoped, to the wind. Dave passed the hot water and divided up the four slices of cheese.

From Gregg's Diary, March 5: The wind is still making noise like Niagra Falls. Time has become critical, and we just don't have the slightest hope for the three above. We don't discuss it. . . . This situation is a transition between life and death. It is so difficult to imagine somebody who was with you such a short time ago and who is now helpless and we can't help them.

March 6

. . . In the gray light and quietness we anxiously prepared to leave the cave, but it took us several hours to get ready. Dave melted ice. Pirate was a long time cramming his swollen feet into his boots. My feet and Dave's weren't swollen, but during the night we had both lost feeling in several toes. With my hands still mostly useless, I relied on Dave to stuff my feet into my boots, then lace them up.

Keyed-up by our departure, we felt more alert than we had at any time since the first day of the wind. When I decided to give the mental tests before we went down, Dave helped me with the stop-watch and the sheet of subtraction problems since my fingers were unable to hold them. Dave said he was thinking as clearly as he ever had; the test results did not agree. It took each of us twice as much time to answer a series of subtraction problems as we had needed to answer a similar series down on the Kahiltna. Although this was only a rough indication of one way in which our logical thought processes were impaired, I made a mental note to be damn careful if we had to make an important decision.

But we weren't really worried. There was no wind. After sticking out the storm we felt there was nothing we couldn't do. In a few hours we'd reach 17,300 feet; we might descend all the way to the 14,400-foot igloos before night. It was going to be great to walk in on the others; they had probably given up on us by now. A new excitement quickened our movements. We were going down, going home! Dave was the first outside. With one word he cut short all our excitement.

"Whiteout!"

"Whiteout." The word hung in the air. We had never considered the possibility of a whiteout after the wind. Dave could see only 20 to 30 feet. A mile of ice stretched between us and the 17,200-foot camp if we took a direct course; but on the slope below us there were four or five square miles of ice, in the basin below there were another four or five square miles of ice, and the basin fell away through 40 or 50 square miles of heavily crevassed glacier. Blinded by the whiteout, we might wander about the ice forever, or rather, until we collapsed, or walked off an edge, or fell into a crevasse.

We hoped the whiteout was merely a small passing cloud that would sift away in an hour or two. We dreaded to think of what would become of us if the whiteout proved to be the beginning of a week-long snowstorm.

I followed Pirate out of the cave only to see his hunched form stumble into Dave, who was also unable to straighten his back. For a moment I just watched the two lean against each other like drunks trying to maintain their balance. A mist of ice crystals crept silently over the rocks behind them.

With short, painful jerks of his head, Pirate twisted his face up to look Dave in the eye: "Dave," he said in hoarse whisper, "I think I'm too weak to go down."

For the first time since the night we had pulled Farine out of the crevasse, Dave's face went blank with shock. In an instant his confidence had been broken. It wasn't only Pirate's words that had shaken him. In the half-light of our cave we had been unable to see each other's features clearly, but now nothing was hidden. Pirate's appearance was the most appalling. It was as if he had emerged from the cave 20 years older; his voice was that of an old man; his face was furrowed with lines we had never seen before; his eyes were faded and glazed and sunk back into their sockets.

I felt shaky getting to my hands and knees and was unable to stand on my feet without Dave's help. I tumbled over with the first step I tried, hitting the ice with my shoulder to avoid falling onto my swollen hands. None of us had a sense of balance. Our legs were dried up and, along with our backs, were stiff from lying immobile for days. We practiced walking, but it took ten or 15 minutes of stretching and limbering up before we regained enough coordination to walk in a relatively straight line.

To be able to walk again was an achievement, but hardly a consolation, because even if the whiteout cleared, we didn't have nearly enough balance to climb down the hundreds of yards of steep ice that separated us from 17,200 feet. Yet waiting in the cave would be suicide, since one more day without food would certainly leave us without the strength to descend.

Dave grew nervous. Pirate leaned against a rock and mumbled to himself. Desperation made us begin to voice wild plans for escaping from the pass. We discussed the possibility of just Dave and I trying to make it out. Pirate said he'd wait by himself in the cave until we could get a rescue party to him; but of course assistance would not reach him for at least two days, and that would be too late. Once, feeling I was the strongest, I said I wanted to try it alone. I reasoned that if I made it down I could send in help, and if I didn't make it Dave and Pirate would still have a chance if the weather cleared.

How easy it might have been if I could have fully deceived myself. I knew my reasons for a solo descent were flimsily constructed excuses to conceal my desire to save Art Davidson above all else. I became afraid that my fear of our situation was stripping away my sentiments of loyalty to the others. I didn't want Dave or Pirate to see my ruthless self-centeredness. But then, wasn't this need to save myself a sense of self-preservation? And wasn't this healthy, even necessary?

As I began to feel panicky, my eyes glanced swiftly over the ice and rocks and at the whiteness all around us. Dave looked at me. Pirate appeared lost in his thoughts. I didn't know what to say. Despite the urgency of my desire to try it alone, that other sense of being unalterably bound to Dave and Pirate persisted. Maybe this inclination to stick it out with the others was only a reaction to loneliness, but perhaps it was a basic reaction I couldn't violate.

My fingers began to throb and my head felt light. I didn't seem to have control of my thoughts. I wanted to take off by myself, but I couldn't abandon Dave and Pirate. I had to save myself at any cost, but I wouldn't be alive now if it hadn't been for Dave and Pirate. What good was there in perishing together? If I had a better chance of making it alone, shouldn't I forget about Dave and Pirate and take off without them?

I felt I had to scream or run across the ice. To relieve my tension I looked at the clouds. I studied the different shades of grayness that walled us in. And it worked. My panic disappeared as quickly as it had rushed up.

Dave said we ought to hold off deciding what to do because the whiteout might clear. I nodded. Pirate looked at the hole in the ice that was our cave's entrance.

Clouds clung to the pass, filtering the sun's light into a bleak variety of flat grays and whites. An eerie quietness had settled over the mountain; soundless and still, it seemed impossible that this was the same pass the wind had stormed through. The sky that had been terrifyingly alive hung around us lifelessly. The entire range, which had seemed to be some sort of living being during the days the wind had howled, now was only a frozen waste of ice and rock.

Hiding under the ice from all the fury, I'd felt closed in, but this day, standing outside in the stillness of the whiteout, I began to feel brief moments of claustrophobia, as if I were being smothered along with the mountain and all the peaks around us. Standing on our patch of ice it seemed as if the whiteout had cut us off from the world. The sky was gone, and we had only our little island of light in this immense grayness.

Pirate said we had to do something. We continued to stare into the cloud, hoping it would break open to let us descend. *Hoping*—we had come to understand it so well that it had lost much of its meaning; but none of its appeal. I decided that to hope was to ignore the reality of our situation in favor of a wishful belief that some stroke of luck would befall us. No one could come for us through this whiteout. I berated myself for ever hoping, and warned myself never to hope again. Faith was what I lacked. I needed faith that this whiteout, like any stretch of foul weather, would eventually end; and faith that we'd have the presence of mind and stamina to take advantage of that moment when it came. I told Dave we'd be lost if we stopping believing in ourselves; he looked puzzled and said, "Huh?"

Several minutes later I realized I was once again staring at the clouds, hoping they'd part.

As we grew weary of waiting for the whiteout to clear we searched among the rocks for food—a cache someone else might have left behind or some of our own supplies that had been blown away—but found nothing. We stood at the edge of the pass, looking down toward the 17,200-foot camp. Through the grayness I tried to picture Gregg, Shiro, John, and George camped in the cave, waiting patiently for a chance to look for us. Then I remembered they would have run out of food by now. But surely they hadn't left us.

For many minutes no one spoke. All our mountaineering experience told us that we should not descend into the whiteout because we would almost certainly lose our way, or else, weak and without a sense of balance, we would fall. At the same time, we were certain of what would be in store for us if we waited in the cave.

Hours had slipped by since we had first crawled out of the cave. Although the lateness of the hour was beginning to force us to make up our minds, every alternative still appeared futile. It seemed absurd to choose. I thought that if we ever decided there was no chance at all of our getting down, I'd use my last energies to wander up toward McKinley's north summit.

I told myself that was another desperate thought that ought to be discouraged. Our situation demanded thoughtfulness which we weren't certain we were capable of. The most frustrating part of having our minds affected by the altitude was our inability to know to what extent we were affected. Probably the duller we became, the less we realized we were dull at all.

At length it became apparent that our greatest chance lay in trying to find our way down the ice wall, instead of waiting for the whiteout to clear. Besides, we were disgusted with the cave; Pirate said crawling back into it would be the same as crawling into our grave. By descending we would at least be active, be trying. Dave said we'd better get our crampons on. Pirate said O.K., and I didn't say anything.

Dave, with Pirate lagging behind, headed back up the 50 yards or so to the cave, where we had left our crampons. I waited near the edge of the pass because Dave had thoughtfully offered to bring down my crampons and gear after he was set himself. As Pirate passed the scattered ruins of a large cache, I called after him to ask if he had checked it for food. He said that he and Dave had looked all through it without finding anything edible. Nonetheless, Pirate plowed again through the rubble of a shredded tarp, pieces of wooden crates which must have been airdropped, torn clothes, silverware, all sorts of things we couldn't eat. I figured the cache was most likely one that Washburn had carefully prepared after one of his scientific expeditions, but 20 years of storms and curious climbers had left it a trash heap half buried in the ice. After a minute, Pirate stopped searching and looked at me without speaking. I asked if he had found anything.

"No." Very slowly he continued on up to get his crampons.

I stood in a daze, not wanting to do anything until someone came to take care of me. Staring at the cache, I remembered advice Shiro had once given me; since it was urging me to move, I tried to suppress the thought. Yet it nagged me: "When there is only one way to survive in the mountains, you must check every possibility to the very end in order to find the one that works." The cache was a possibility. Just possibly some food remained hidden toward the bottom of the rubbish; but the cache was 40 feet away, 40 feet uphill. I stood still, without the energy or desire to move. Shiro's words kept repeating themselves in my mind. I heard them in his soft accent: ". . . check every possibility to the very end." I resisted checking the cache; a waste of energy, I rationalized. Then, not realizing I had started, I was walking toward the cache. To get a grip on my ice axe I forced my fingers around the shaft, no longer caring whether my blisters broke—I was going to dig.

I whacked at the ice where it held the canvas tarp; my hands, revolting at the pain, dropped the axe. The tarp hadn't budged. I picked up the axe, and by the time I had swung a couple more times I was in a frenzy. I slashed and beat at the canvas frozen into the ice. I pried and yanked. Hitting with my axe as hard as I could, I must have struck a rock, because the axe's metal adze broke.

I became furious. I couldn't stop. I smashed at the pieces of wood, lashing out with my axe until I collapsed onto my knees. I was out of breath and dizzy, but as soon as my head began to clear I started swinging at the debris again. Still on my knees, I uncovered bits of rotten rope, pots, old socks, ladles, odd boots; and of all the absurd, useless luxuries there was even a colander.

I attacked the cache, driven by an obsession to reach the bottom of it. My hands throbbed with pain and my feet had become numb, but all that mattered was that I check every last inch of the trash. A rage drove me to see what was underneath. When I discovered another layer, I was careful not to destroy anything. I opened a box, but it was full of clothes.

I kicked some of the surface junk aside with my boots, then dug in again with my axe. Ice and splintered wood and strips of canvas were frozen around each other. I grabbed and yanked and kicked, and swung the axe, and eventually I reached another unopened box. I pried it open: more clothes on top, but underneath lay several cloth bags, small, white bags. Excited and exhausted, I felt my heart beating wildly as I fumbled to see what was in one of the bags. The drawstring came loose and as I looked into the bag I'm certain I would have cried, if my body had enough water to spare for tears.

Dried potatoes!

Farther inside the crate sat a box of raisins packaged in a wrapper that had gone out of style 15 years ago! I found two more bags of potatoes and even uncovered a can of ham with no holes in it!

We ate!

Dave enlarged the cave. Crouched on his knees the circulation to his legs was partly cut off. He mentioned that his feet were icy-cold below the arches, and mumbled about warming them on someone's stomach, but he didn't want to bother Pirate or me. I heard him ramble on to himself: "Oh, well, a couple of toenails lost, nothing new . . . It won't happen to you, Dave baby . . . don't sweat it. . . ."

Far into the night Dave brewed hot drinks and made quantities of raisin, ham, and potato stew. Life seemed easy again. Our cave was more comfortable and we had the security of knowing there would be something to eat the next day. We settled in, determined to hold out another week if necessary but hoping, as we had hoped for the last six nights, that we could descend in the morning.

Convinced the three above are dead, Gregg and three others descend.

From George's Journal, March 6: There is a flicker of hope—as anyone would have hope—but logically we reject the possibility that any of the three could come down alive. The more we think about it the more agonizing it becomes, so in conversation with one another we try to avoid the sentiments of death.

March 7

I dreamed that a kindly man cut off my feet every time they grew too large. There would be several minutes of relief each time he sliced them off and set them on a shelf, but always my feet, glowing a bright chartreuse, would swell again to the size of basketballs and ache as if about to burst until they were cut off. I was lying in a small, dark cellar, and before long the shelves that lined the walls were filled with huge, luminous, green feet.

Dave woke me to say that my tossing was keeping him awake. A sharp, pulsating ache made both my feet feel as if they were about to explode. They had become partly frozen while I had dug for the food. I wasn't sure whether they had thawed or frozen some more during the night. The only way to relieve the pain was to shift their position; sleeping, I had dreamed of each shift as a thoughtful slice of my friend's knife.

The wind was gone and the whiteout had disappeared. Soon we were all awake, eating, drinking, and wondering where we would meet Gregg, Shiro, and the others. Pirate tried to get us to laugh by saying they had probably scratched us off and flown on home. They must have descended to the 14,400-foot igloos for food, but I figured that they would be coming up to look for us and that we'd run into them on the wall below our cave or perhaps down at 17,200 feet. Dave, not quite so optimistic, said we wouldn't see them until we reached the igloos.

Two hours after waking we attempted to pull on our boots. Once I screamed out loud as Dave shoved and jammed my feet into my boots. Since Pirate's hands were as bad as mine, Dave had to help force his boots on too. When he got around to putting his own boots on, Dave had more trouble than he had with either Pirate or me. The ends of both his feet were swollen.

After crawling out of the cave, we bumped into each other and sprawled onto the ice as we tried to control the uncoordinated blocks of pain that were our feet. Every time one of our boots touched the ice a burning sensation shot up the calf. Pirate spotted a four-engine plane circling the summit. We were not just about to rush down onto the open ice toward 17,200 feet, where the plane could easily spot us. Before setting foot on the steep ice below the pass we had to learn to walk and climb on our injured feet. We stepped in place and practiced traversing a gentle slope. Unfortunately, walking downhill was the most painful and difficult because all our weight jarred onto our frozen and half-frozen toes. Dave strapped on my crampons, then helped Pirate tighten his. Because his were the only hands that hadn't been frozen Dave also took the important anchor position at the end of the rope when we finally decided we were ready to start down.

The ice wall fell away from the pass at an angle of 30 to 40 degrees. At sea level we could have almost played tag on ice no steeper than this; however, at 18,000 feet we had climbed this ice gingerly on the ascent, when our legs had been relatively strong and our balance keen. Now, as we wobbled on spindly, dried-up remnants of legs, each step was near the limit of our capability.

"Don't charge off, Pirate!" I felt I had to warn Pirate, who was leading, to go slowly even though he only crept out onto the ice wall. We tested each position of our feet before trusting our weight onto them.

Because the wind had stolen our packs we had our sleeping bags draped around our shoulders; they hung to our feet, sometimes snagging our crampons, but it was the only way we could carry the bags.

"Slower, Pirate!"

The only thing certain about each step was the pain it would send through our feet. Step after step Pirate led us across and down the ice. The rope tied us together with only a psychological protection; if one of us slipped, we would all peel off the wall. A belay was impossible. If we did come off there would be nothing we could do to arrest our fall until we crashed into the basin 600 feet below.

Pirate stopped.

"Oh, God!" I whispered to myself. One of his crampons had loosened. We were caught on the steepest section of ice. Dave and I chopped out small ledges to relieve some of the strain on our ankles. Pirate's fingers had been too stiff to tie his crampon laces when we had started, but now they had to bind his crampon to his boot.

Dave called anxiously at Pirate to hurry up. My ankles felt on the verge of buckling. Pirate grappled with the stiff straps, cursing at the cold cutting into his fingers—he had to handle the metal crampon with bare fingers. He knew everything depended on him. Should he lose his balance while tugging at the frozen bindings, all our efforts to hold out during the storm would be for nothing.

Pirate straightened; he grabbed his ice axe. I sighed with relief and turned to see Dave grinning behind me.

"All right, you guys. . . . We're goin' down!"

Tense with caution, we placed one foot in front of the other. Each step was carefully considered. The large military plane which Pirate had noticed earlier swung out over the Kahiltna. Even if the plane located us, there was no way it could help us now. We didn't see Gregg, John, Shiro, and George climbing up toward us. Their absence began to worry me because I knew they'd be here to help us down the ice if they could possibly manage it.

"Slow down, Pirate!"

With the steepest ice behind us, Pirate quickened his pace. Actually, he was taking a step only every two or three seconds, but that seemed dangerously fast to me.

"You're gettin' us down, Pirate—you crazy honcho!"

Pirate paused to turn and holler, "Aaahaaaa. . . ."

The rough but level ice of the basin began passing beneath us. "We did it, we did it," I repeated to myself.

However, as the ice rose ever so slightly toward the rocks, our feet became so heavy that we were soon stopping to rest every seven or eight steps. The rocks appeared unfamiliar. When Dave motioned for Pirate to turn right, I said I thought we had to head for the rocks on the left. After discussing the difference of opinion for a moment, we decided that none of us were certain which particular outcrop of rocks the cave was next to. Tired as we were, it was discouraging to think we might go 50 or 100 feet out of our way if we climbed toward the wrong rocks. We compromised by striking out in a line running directly between the two main rock outcroppings. Ten and then 20 yards of ice were covered; Pirate called out that he could see a bamboo pole sticking out of the ice. It looked to be about ten feet high. Since we had not brought a bamboo pole to this point, we figured a helicopter must have landed rescuers who left the pole behind. But where were they now? Maybe the others had had an accident. Anyway, the cave had to be near the pole.

Weary and growing apprehensive, we slowly approached the pole. One moment it was hundreds of feet away, then we suddenly realized it was only ten feet away and wasn't a bamboo pole at all. It was simply a willow wand. Our eyes had fooled us. Somehow the altitude or our dehydration or perhaps even our lack of food had affected our sense of depth perception. It was particularly startling because each of us had been deceived in the same way.

We passed by the willow wand and approached the cave. Just before we peered into it, I was seized with a sudden fear that we might see bodies. They could have been trapped here and could have never made it down for more food. We looked in; to my relief the cave was deserted. In one corner a small pile of food was stacked against a stove. They must have descended thinking we'd never come down; yet on the slight chance that we would they had left us the most favored delicacies—sausage, coconut balls Gregg's wife had made, and some of the fruitcake my grandmother had baked for us.

While we ate, the circling plane spotted us. Then Sheldon's silver Cessna 180 appeared and flew low over the basin. We waved. He swung around, came in lower yet, and dropped a bag. I retrieved it. Bits of a smashed orange were scattered on the ice. I picked up a carefully wrapped kit but couldn't figure out what it should be used for. Although it was tempting to leave it where it had fallen, I decided the others might be able to determine what it was. I felt somewhat foolish when Pirate immediately recognized it as a radio; the altitude was affecting me more than I wanted to admit. Either our minds were too fuzzy to operate the radio or else it had been damaged when dropped, because we couldn't get it to send or receive.

Filled with food and a little water, we continued the descent. With extreme caution we inched our way down among the rocks along the ridge. We were climbing several times more slowly than we had ever ascended this section of the route. Reaching the fixed ropes, we lowered our bags in front of us to free our arms for handling the ropes.

Our feet suffered a cutting pain every time our boots hit the ice. It became almost unbearable for Pirate and me to grip the rope with our frostbitten hands. Once I slipped, and as I grabbed the rope to halt my fall I could feel the skin and blisters tearing across my fingers.

Near the end of the ropes we entered a cloud. Despite the whiteout, there could be no thought of waiting because we had to avoid bivouacking for another night. Since Dave had climbed this part of the route more often than Pirate and I, he took the lead. We climbed down deeper into the cloud. The tops of the high ridges on either side disappeared. Somewhere ahead in the grayness were two igloos and our friends; beyond the igloos lay an ice fall of enormous crevasses. Should we pass by the igloos, we would walk blindly over the edge of a crevasse. The grayness grew so thick that from my position in the middle of the rope I could see neither Dave nor Pirate.

Dave stopped, then started again. My knees and ankles seemed on the verge of collapsing. Slack rope on the snow in front of me indicated that Dave had stopped again. We were lost.

Gray cloud and gray ice appeared the same; the glacier and the sky had become one wall of grayness. Since we couldn't see the slope where we set our feet, I began stumbling onto my hands with a crunching of stiff, swollen flesh.

I shouted into the grayness that I thought the igloos were to our right. The rope jerked me to a halt from behind; Pirate must have fallen onto the ice. I heard him yell that we should head more to the left. Dave said nothing. I lay flat on the ice myself, waiting for Pirate to pick himself up and retighten a loose crampon. After several minutes Dave called, "Let's go!"; with considerable effort I got to my feet, and we started staggering on through the whiteout. As we passed through the endless grayness, I began to think we had already gone beyond the igloos. I tried to pull my befuddled mind together to be ready to throw myself onto the ice in arrest position should Dave plunge into a crevasse. I still could not see him and the rope disappeared in the grayness about ten feet in front of me. We might have passed within ten feet of the camp without spotting it. As the snow became deeper, I began wondering whether the igloos would be buried. Dave plodded on.

Blind, and uncertain that my legs could manage another step, I let the rope running to Dave pull me on.

"Waahoooo. . . ." A call in front of me—unable to see Dave, I wasn't sure it had been his voice.

"Igloos!" It was Dave's voice.

With luck or an astonishing instinct he had led us straight to the igloos.

Dave waited for Pirate and me to appear out of the whiteout so the three of us could share that first moment of greeting the others. Nearly delirious with relief and joy we shoveled the entrance of the main igloo free of some drifted snow, then pulled back the tarp which closed the igloo from the weather. We peered inside.

Darkness! The igloo was empty. We found the other igloo also deserted and dark. There wasn't even a note. Were we alone on the mountain? Where were they? None of us felt like voicing our disappointment that the others were gone, that they must have given up on us.

We attacked the food left in the largest igloo. Mashed potatoes, rice, jello, gorp, freeze-dried meat—never had food been so satisfying, but never before had our appetites been really insatiable. Long after we were full we continued to stuff food into our mouths—we had a compulsion to devour everything that was edible. It seemed irreverent to leave any food uneaten.

Despite the excitement of our feast, we ate quietly because we were weary and apprehensive about the fate of the other four.

FOCUS ON ECOLOGY

1. Think about the conditions under which Dave, Pirate, and Art were crammed into the small ice cave. Think also about the struggle they had undergone just prior to Dave's work digging the cave. Imagine trying to survive under those conditions. What kind of energy and stamina must one summon to survive such a situation? How does one prepare mentally for such an event? What role does one's mental state and ability play in one's chances of surviving in such a situation?

2. At the beginning of the entry dated March 2, Davidson describes the uncomfortable conditions inside the ice cave and the difficulties in sleeping. One of the things he mentions is that "the altitude caused a nervous wakefulness." He also discusses the effect altitude had on his ability to think clearly and on Pirate's exuberance. Altitude has particular physical effects on the human body because of the change in ambient atmospheric pressure. (See Jimmy Carter's "Kilimanjaro" in Chapter 3 for another discussion of the effects of altitude on climbers.) In what ways do climbers have to account for altitude and changes in pressure when they plan climbs like the one Davidson describes? What kinds of training and knowledge must one have before engaging in such activities?

3. In addition to the environmental conditions, Dave, Art, and Pirate faced starvation. In many survival situations, starvation is as much a life-threatening issue as freezing or falling or any of the other environmental conditions that can kill a person. How might a person entering a wilderness survival situation eliminate starvation from the list of dangers in a wilderness survival scenario?

FOCUS ON WRITING

1. Just after Dave, Pirate, and Art huddle into the ice cave, Dave notices that his journal has been blown away by the wind. Likewise, the selection printed here is presented in the form of a remembered journal (a well-edited journal), broken into sections according to date. Why might keeping a journal be important to people who take on adventurous activities like climbing? Could Davidson have presented this same story in a style other than that of a journal? What does he gain or lose by using this style?

2. What role does distance play in this narrative?

3. How would you describe the pace of this narrative? Does the pace change at any point?

FOR DISCUSSION

As a class, discuss Dave, Art, and Pirate's predicament. How would various members of the class respond to such a situation? Individually, recount how and what you felt while reading about Dave, Art, and Pirate. Would you have survived? Why do you answer as you do?

WRITING IN RESPONSE

There are many stories of near-death climbs on Mt. McKinley (Denali). Doing a bit of research, find out how many people attempt to climb Denali each year and how many succeed in reaching the summit. After reading a few accounts of other climbs, write a short piece describing why so many people take on the climb up Denali.

"To Weave a World" from *Adrift: Seventy-Six Days Lost at Sea*

Steven Callahan

This selection, "To Weave a World," is taken from Steven Callahan's best-selling 1986 book Adrift: Seventy-Six Days Lost at Sea, *which recounts Callahan's time lost at sea aboard a five-foot inflatable (and leaking) life raft after his small sailboat sank in the mid-Atlantic in 1982. The story is true and told by Callahan through notes he took while aboard his small raft. Callahan, who was born in 1952 in Needham, Massachusetts, relies not only on his ability and equipment but also on the stability of his own mind in such a harrowing and physically demanding experience. As you read this selection, consider the role of Callahan's narrative voice, particularly remembering that he was isolated as the events he narrates occurs.*

JOURNAL ASSIGNMENT

Steven Callahan explains that he "must work harder and longer each day to weave a world in which I can live. Survival is the play and I want the leading role." In your journal, consider Callahan's words. What do you suppose he means?

The metal is hard and cold. After an hour of leaning over the bulwark, my elbows are in icy pain. I stand and thrust my hands deep into the wool coat the captain has brought me. "I'll bet you never thought you'd see this city again," he says, looking at me quizzically. I peruse the horizon. It is no longer flat and empty but is full of monolithic skyscrapers, gray smog. The noise of the city rises above even the rumble of reversed engines. Heavy, tattooed arms pull aboard hawsers as thick as thighs and whip them around the capstans. Slowly the ship is worked in to the dock. More and more lines are tossed and set. The water eddies around us. The behemoth is reeled in. No, I never thought I'd see New York again.

2   Then there is darkness and chaos. My head is struck with a club, cold, wet, and hard. The assaulter roars, rumbles, and rolls away into the night. I am on the dark side of the earth, a quarter world away from New York. The wind is up and so is the sea. *Rubber Ducky* lurches and crashes as if caught in a demolition derby. "Still here," I moan.

3   Each night, soft fabrics caress my skin, the smell of food fills my nostrils, and warm bodies surround me. Sometimes while wrapped in sleep I hear my conscious mind bark a warning: "Enjoy it while you can for you will soon awaken." I am used to the duality of it. Usually when I sail alone, the sounds of fluttering sails and waves, the motion of my boat rising and plunging, never leave me even as I hang in my bunk dreaming of faraway places. If a movement varies slightly or an unfamiliar noise slaps against my eardrum, I am immediately awakened. Yet last night's dream was almost too real. My life has become a composition of multilayered realities—daydreams, night dreams, and the seemingly endless physical struggle.

4   I keep trying to believe that all of these realities are equal. Perhaps they are, in some ultimate sense, but it becomes increasingly obvious that in the survival world my physical self and my instincts are the ringmasters that whip all of my realities into place and control their motions. My dreams and daydreams are filled with images of what my body requires and of how to escape from this physical hell. Since I have gotten the still to work and have learned how to fish more efficiently, there has been little to do but save energy, wait, and dream. Slowly, though, I find I am becoming more starved and desperate. My equipment is deteriorating.

5   I must work harder and longer each day to weave a world in which I can live. Survival is the play and I want the leading role. The script sounds simple enough: hang on, ration food and water, fish, and tend the still. But each little nuance of my role takes on profound significance. If I keep watch too closely, I will tire and be no good for fishing, tending the still, or other essential tasks. Yet every moment that I don't have my eyes on the horizon is a moment when a ship may pass me. If I use both stills now, I may be able to quench my thirst and keep myself in better shape for keeping watch and doing jobs, but if they both wear out I will die of thirst. My mind applauds some of my performances while my body boos, and vice versa. It is a constant struggle to keep control, self-discipline, to maintain a course of action that will best ensure survival, because I can't be sure what that course is. Is my command making the right decisions? Might immediate gratification sometimes be the best course to follow even in the long run? More often than not, all I can tell myself is, "You're doing the best you can."

6   I need more fish, and the constant nudging I feel through the floor of the raft tells me that the dorados are around in sufficient numbers to make fishing a reasonable expenditure of energy. After several misfires, I finally skewer a dorado by the tail, but it doesn't slow him down much. He yanks the raft all over the

place while I frantically try to hold on, wishing that I could train these fish to pull me in the direction I want to go. He pulls free before I can get him aboard. Oh well, try again. I start to reset the spear gun—but the power strap is gone, now sinking through three miles of seawater! This could be real trouble.

It's my first major gear failure; but I've dealt with a lot of jury rigs before so 7 I should be able to figure something out. It's always a challenge to try and repair an essential system with what one has at hand. In fact, I sometimes wonder if one of the major reasons for ocean racing and voyaging is to push one's self and one's boat just past the edge, watch things fail, and then somehow come up with a solution. In many ways, having a jury rig succeed is often more gratifying than making a pleasant and uneventful passage or even winning a race. Rising to the challenge is a common thread that runs through a vast wardrobe of sea stories. I've stuck back together masts, steering gear, boat hulls, and a host of smaller items. Although I don't have much to work with, repairing the spear should be relatively simple.

The important thing is to keep calm. The small details of the repair will de- 8 termine its success or failure. As always, I can only afford success. Don't hurry. Make it right. You can fish tomorrow. The arrow and the gun handle are still intact. It is only the source of power that is missing. I put the arrow on the shaft of the handle in the normal manner, but I pull the arrow out through the plastic loop on the end of the handle shaft in order to lengthen the weapon as much as possible. I wind two long lashings around the arrow and shaft. I use the heavy codline, which is better than synthetic line because it shrinks when it is wetted and then dried, thereby tightening the lashings. The smooth arrow still rotates, so I add a third lashing, then I add frappings to the lashings. These are turns of the line around the lashings at right angles. When pulled tight, the frappings cinch up the lashings and should keep them from spreading out haphazardly. There are notches in the butt of the arrow, which normally fit into the trigger mechanism in the handle. Through these notches and back through the trigger housing, I pass loops of line to keep the arrow from being pulled out forward by an escaping fish.

I am aware that my repaired spear is a flimsy rig for catching dorados . Nor- 9 mally a diver pulls on his spear gun arrow when retrieving a fish. I must drive my lance through the fish, putting the rig in compression rather than tension. When I pull a fish out of the water, it will put a large bending load on the arrow as well. However, my new lance feels pretty sturdy, and I'm ready to try it out. Patience is going to be the secret, and strength. Power was stored in the elastic power strap; now the improvised spear has to be thrust at a moment's notice with all the power I can muster if I'm to drive it through a thick dorado.

I lean my left elbow on the top tube of the raft to steady my aim, and I 10 lightly rest the arrow of the spear between my fingers. I pull the gun handle high up onto my cheek with my right arm, tensed and steady, awaiting the perfect shot. I can sight down the shaft, and rocking back and forth gives me a narrow field of fire. On the water's surface is an imaginary circle about a foot in diameter into which I can shoot without moving my steadying elbow off the raft tube. If I am not well braced, my shots will become wild. The effective range of the spear has been shortened from about six feet to three or four. I must wait until a fish swims directly under my point so that it will be in range and the problem of surface refraction—which makes the fish appear to be where it is not—will be minimized. This problem is extreme at oblique angles to the water. When I shoot, I must extend my range and power as much as possible. I thrust my arm out straight and lunge as hard as I can with my whole body, trying to hold my aim. The shot must be instantaneous, because the fish are so quick and agile, but it also must be perfectly controlled. Once I lift my left, steadying arm off of the tube, it becomes hopeless. I watch the fish swimming all over the place, but I must wait for one to swim within my field of fire. I remain poised for minutes that stretch into hours at a time. I feel like I'm becoming an ancient bronze statue of a bowless archer.

11   The doggies' nudging has become an advantage. I push my knees deeply into the floor just behind my arrow, luring them on. Bump, and a body slithers out, a little too far to starboard. Bump, a little too far to port. Head center! Do it! Splash! Strike! Ripping strong pull, white water, a cloud of blood. He's in the air. HUGE! A spray of blood. Ow! Feels like I'm being smashed by an oar as he slides down the spear toward me. Don't let go, get him in, quick! Fury flapping, blood flying. Watch the spear tip, the *tip, fool!* On the floor, onto him, now! The huge square-headed body lies still for a moment under my knee as I press my full weight down on him. His gills are puffing in rhythm with my gasps as I try to grasp the spear on both sides of his torso and give myself a moment's rest. A hole as big as my fist has been blasted out of his body, which stretches almost all the way across the floor. Globs of clotting blood swill about in the crater created by my other knee.

12   Whap, whap, whap! His thunderclapping tail smashes into action. I'm knocked over backward. He's escaped. The tip, watch the tip! He flops all round the raft, making for the exit. Pain in my wrist. Pain in my face. He's winning! I fumble for the tip of the spear as it whips about. Finally I tackle the fish, throw him down onto my sleeping bag and equipment sack, and bury the spear tip in the thick fabric. Both of us are panting. I can't reach my knife. His eye clicks around, calculating—little time left, and he knows it. Whap, whap, whap—he's off again. Look out! Fire shoots up my left arm. "Get down there, down!" Whap, whap, cracking around the raft like a bullwhip. Back on the bag again. Sprawled across him, pushing with my legs to get him pinned. Gills puffing. Get the knife. Push it in. Hits something hard—the spine. Twist it. Crack. Wait. He's still panting, slowly panting, stopped panting. Rest . . . I'll not do that again.

13   I can't believe that the raft hasn't been ripped. I examine the spear carefully; it is only slightly bent, and the lashings held. I listen but hear no hissing leaks. The tubes still feel hard. Blood and guts are spewed everywhere, some of it mine, no doubt. I'll try to stick to the smaller females in the future. Also from now on I will carefully arrange my equipment before beginning to fish. I'll stretch out the sailcloth across as much of the bottom as possible, put my cutting board down, and spread my sleeping bag over the tubes on the starboard

half of the raft above my equipment sack. I have overcome the first serious gear failure since I coaxed the solar still to work.

For hours I slice up my grand fish. First I hack it into four large chunks, [14] plus the head and tail. The I slice each chunk into four long pieces, one from each side of the back and one from each side of the belly. Finally I slice these into sticks which I hang on strings to dry, like dozens of fat fingers, delicious fat fingers. I write in my log that this is a strange prison in which I am slowly starved but occasionally thrown a twenty-pound filet mignon.

The first weeks of my unplanned raft voyage have gone well—as well as [15] can be expected. I escaped the immediate peril of *Solo*'s sinking, have adjusted to my equipment and the environment, and am now actually better stocked with food and water than when I began.

So much for the positive side. The negative is only too obvious. Lack of [16] starches, sugars, and vitamins has let my body wither. My gluteus maximus was the first to go. Where my plump ass once was, there was only hollows of flesh ridged by pelvic bones. I try to stand as often and as long as possible, but my legs have badly atrophied and hang from my hips like threads with little knots for knees. There was a time when three hands could not encircle my thighs; now two will do, and nicely at that. My chest and arms have thinned but remain fairly strong due to the exercise demanded by survival. How the body steals heat or food from one part to lend to another, how it compensates for deprivation by shutting down all but the essential systems, how it possibly can keep this wreck running in this demo-derby of flesh, is all beyond me, amazing, almost amusing. I write in my log, "No more fat on this honky!"

The cuts on my knees still have not healed. Other gashes have left thick [17] scars. Dozens of small slits on my hands, made by my knife or fish bones, never seem to mend. Scar tissue builds up around the wounds like little volcanoes, leaving raw craters inside. Though I'm meticulous about sponging up water and keeping *Ducky* dry, I've spent about half my time wet. The salt water sores begin as small infected boils that grow, burst open, and leave ulcers penetrating the skin. These continue to widen and deepen, as if a slow-burning acid were being dropped on the flesh. But so far my work at keeping dry has paid off. I have only a dozen or two open sores, about a quarter inch across, clustered on my hips and ankles. My cushion and sleeping bag, when dry, are encrusted with salt, which grinds into my wounds.

March 3
Day 27

It is sunrise of the twenty-seventh day since I began my voyage in *Rubber Ducky III*. [18] I roll and tie up the canopy's entry closure so its cold, wet skin won't lash across mine. I poke my head out, turn aft, and watch the rising sun as awestruck as a child witnessing it for the first time. I note its position relative to the raft.

Creases in *Ducky*'s soft tubes open and close like toothless black mouths, [19] munching on strings of glue and the white chalk markings of the raft inspectors.

Sometimes I wonder who made these marks and what they are doing now. I hope that they are well, for they have done a good job and I am grateful. I push the pump hose into the hard white valves and begin my work, a job as thankless and never-ending as washing dishes and as tiring as a marathon. Ringed treads on the pump have worn thick calluses into my thumbs. The bellows utters a short, high-pitched whimper each time I squeeze it, like those baby dolls that cry out and weep tears. Uuh, uuh, uuh, uuh, one, two, three, four . . . uuh, uuh, uuh, uuh, fifty-seven, fifty-eight, fifty-nine, sixty. I pause, panting, feel the tube—not quite as firm as a watermelon yet—and continue. Then the bottom tube. Noontime, sunset, midnight, and morning, I squeeze the crying pump. In the early days, I had to listen to only sixty whimpers each day; now I have to squeeze over three hundred from the hateful little beast.

20   The still is sagging. Each morning I blow it up, empty the salt water from the distillate, and prime it. Then I get up to take a look around. Tricky. On a ship's solid deck the waves' motions are averaged out. Here my legs fall and rise with every ripple. Tiny bubbles and gurgles tickle the bottoms of my soft feet. Their calluses washed off long ago. I hang lightly on to the canopy, conscious that a hard tug may collapse it and drop me into the sea. Standing up in my vessel is a little like walking on water.

21   The only companions in sight are a petrel and a graceful shearwater. The petrel looks as out of place as I, fluttering like a sea chickadee, teetering on the edge of flight, heading straight for a clumsy crash. In reality he is having no trouble. I've seen petrels in shrieking winds, flapping from one gigantic wave canyon to another. They weigh only a few ounces and you'd think that they'd be blown off the face of the world. The tiny petrels, even the much larger shearwaters, will make a very meager meal, but I'll still try to grab one if it ventures close enough. Neither has any need for my dangerous company. They are only curious enough to swoop by every now and then. Their minute black eyes flit over every detail of the raft as they pass. I can watch the flight of the shearwaters for hours. They rarely flap their wings, even when it is flat calm. Then they glide in a straight line close to the surface of the water in order to use the surface effect. In heavy airs they wheel about in large arcs and then dive down so close to the waves that you can't see any space between their feather tips and the water. To me, they are the gods of grace. The shearwaters make me feel very clumsy and remind me how ill suited I am to this domain.

22   Robertson's book includes tables of the sun's declination, which I use to fix my direction at sunrise. I can do the same at sunset. At night I can fix my heading from both the North Star and Southern Cross. The heavens have provided me with an unbreakable, immortal, fully guaranteed compass. To measure my speed, I time the passage of seaweed between *Rubber Ducky* and the man-overboard pole. Earlier I had calculated the distance to the pole to be about seventy feet, or $1/90$ of a nautical mile. If it takes one minute for a piece of weed or other flotsam to pass between *Ducky* and the pole, I am going $60/90$ of a mile each hour, or $2/3$ of a knot, which works out to 16 miles a day. I make up a table for times from 25 to 100 seconds, $9\frac{1}{2}$ to 38 miles a day. I never do see a 38-mile day.

Since my chart shows the entire Atlantic Ocean on one sheet, my snail's- 23
pace progress is hardly worth plotting on a daily basis, but every couple of
days I plot another eighth or quarter inch. I kid myself that I only have a little
ways left to travel—why, it's only about six inches on the map.

I am confident that we, that is *Ducky* and I, have reached the lanes and will 24
soon be picked up, but we may well have drifted beyond them. I have tried the
EPIRB again to no avail. The battery must be very low now. I must wait until I
see positive signs of land or air traffic before I try it again. As soon as we arrived at what I thought to be the edge of the lanes, the wind strengthened. Perhaps Zephyrus wants to push us through before we can be spotted. I'm not too
disappointed; it's a relief to be moving purposefully forward. There've been no
sharks. There has also been only one ship in six days—pretty empty ocean
highway.

Conditions are favorable for my tub. It's blowing hard enough to move us 25
well, but not so hard that the waves are blasted apart. Unless we are hit by a
rogue wave, *Ducky* will stay on her bottom. She slues down the slopes with
a speedy motion that is smooth, quiet, and peaceful, seemingly frictionless. I
get a vision in my head that I can't shake, one of a spaceship gliding in large
curving banks through the vastness of space. In my log I sketch *Rubber Ducky*
converted to a flyer saucer with a wide band around her perimeter, studded
with lights. I surround her with planets, stars, and fish.

Time for breakfast. I fall back on my cushion and lean up against the equip- 26
ment sack. I flip my sleeping bag over my legs, awaiting the warmth of the day.
The fish sticks that have been hanging for two days are semidried and slightly
chewy. Dorados begin their own daily routine, bumping my rear several times
before flipping off to hunt.

Eight hard-won pints of water are carefully stored in three unopened water 27
tins, two recapped and taped tins, two distillate plastic bags, and my working
water jug. The butcher shop is chock-a-block full of fish sticks. Wet fresh protein is digested with less water than cooked or dried meat, so I try to eat a lot of
my catch early on. As days pass and it gets chewier, I carefully ration the meat
and begin fishing again.

I've become worried about my digestive tract. Dougal Robertson points to 28
the case of one survivor who had no bowel movement for thirty days. By the
time the body is through digesting the miniscule amount of food taken in, there
simply is very little to move. I feel no urge to go but worry about a hemorrhoid
that has puffed out. Should my plumbing suddenly blast loose, I may be in for
a rupture and hemorrhage, which would be difficult to plug up and heal. I
begin modified yoga exercises—twisting, bending, arching, stretching—slowly
learning how to balance and compensate for the motion of my waterbed. On
the thirty-first day, the bloody bubble begins to subside and a small amount of
diarrhea relieves my apprehension.

Early morning, dusk, and night are the only times that I can coerce my 29
body to exercise. By noon the temperature has rocketed to ninety degrees or
more. It might as well be nine hundred. My body has no water to sweat. The

air trapped inside the raft is humid and stagnant. Staying conscious and tending the solar stills are major struggles. My spinning head coaxes me. Must get up, look around. Slow, easy now, to your knees. I gaze into the lively blue water. O.K. Wait now, maybe a few minutes. I try to get my eyes to focus, but they stumble about in my head, smash into the sides of my skull, and bounce back. Grab the can, careful not to drop it, already lost one. I dip it down with a gurgle, raise it above me, and let the water fall, massaging my neck and tangled hair with cool relief. Again I dip the can, again and again, imagining that I'm crawling into shaded tall wet grass under a billowing willow tree.

30   Slowly now, lift your head. Look right. Look left. O.K. Up on one leg, now the other. Stand. "Good boy," I say aloud as I sway about in semidelirium, hoping that I will cool off and my head will clear. The wind flash-dries the drops of seawater trickling down my body, escorting tiny streams of heat away. Sometimes the ritual works. I steady up and remain erect for several minutes. Other times my head feels as if it is being crushed by a heavy weight, my vision fills with swirling bluish haze, and I collapse, using the residue of my senses to guide my fall back into the raft. Yes, I am in much better shape than I thought I'd be by this time, but at high noon I am often "beyond the point of coherent action," as Robertson so dryly puts it. If I can just keep myself together, I can make it to the islands. But how much longer can I hang on like this?

31   Refiguring my position time and again, I put myself about a thousand miles away. Average speed, twenty-five miles a day. Total passage time, seventy days. If only I can guide myself to Guadeloupe. I've got the raft positioned with the canopy across the wind, and the line astern is just off center to guide *Rubber Ducky III* a little bit south of west just as fast as she can waddle.

32   From the Canaries I wrote to my parents and friends, "Expect me in Antigua around February 24." That was seven days ago. Yet I also warned them that the trade winds hadn't filled in yet, so I might arrive as late as March 10, seven days hence. If a search is made then, I will still be out of range, way too far out to sea. If only a ship will pick me up soon, those at home won't begin to worry.

33   I see a shark fin zigzagging in quick pumps across *Ducky*'s bow, about a hundred feet away. It's a small fin, but I'm still glad that he shows no interest in us. Instead, he slides off to the east against the wind and current to await food that is drifting or swimming with the North Equatorial stream.

34   Like most predators, sharks cannot afford to be seriously hurt because an injury or weakness can prevent them from hunting and may even invite an attack from their own kind. So most sharks bump their prey before attacking. If the prey puts up no defense, the shark will dig right in. They will eat anything; license plates and anchors have been found in their stomachs. I wonder about life rafts. I count on their bumping to give me a chance to drive them away. But I also think about *Jaws*. I have heard stories of two great white sharks caught since that film came out. Both of the real sharks were about the same size as the mechanical prop, twenty-five feet long, and weighed upward of four tons. Great whites are an unpredictable species. They are so big, ferocious, and powerful that they know no natural enemies and never worry about their prey putting

up a significant defense. They give no warning of their attacks and have been known to smash boats and even attack whales.

Then there are orcas, or killer whales, known to have blown large yachts 35 apart. I look at my little aluminum and plastic spear, weighing maybe a pound or two. The point might cause a small shark as much pain as I would feel from a mosquito bite. Even if a small shark forces a showdown at high noon, I'll be pathetically slow to the draw. I'd love the option to get out of this town.

With shivering nights and scorching days, only dusk and dawn offer a little 36 comfort. As the sun drops to the horizon, things begin to cool off. I lounge back again as I did in the morning, flip the sleeping bag over my legs, pump up *Ducky*'s sagging limbs, and watch the sky's grand finale through my picture window. The sharp white disk peeks out now and again from behind the puffy cumulus collected at the horizon. It is past noon in Antigua. If only I had a raft that could sail at a moderate three knots, I'd be snug in harbor already. I'll make it anyway . . . if only I can summon strength I never knew I had.

As the clouds mill about and wander into the sunset, I prepare my dinner, 37 choosing various pieces of fish for a balanced meal: a few chewy sticks, which I regard as sausages, an especially prized fatty belly steak, and a piece of back- bone bacon with thin strips of brown, crunchy flesh. I crack the backbone apart and drop gelatinous nuggets of fluid from between the vertebrae onto my board. A noodle runs down the spine, and I add it to the gelatin, making a chicken soup. An invisible Jewish mama coaxes me. "Eat, eat. Go ahead, my sick darling, you must eat your chicken soup to get well." Sumptuous tender- loin streaks come from the meaty back above the organ cavity. I choose a couple of fully dried sticks for toast, since they are overcooked and crunchy. The real treats are the organs, when I have them. Biting into the stomach and intestines is like chewing on a Uniroyal tire, so I don't bother with them, but all else I consume with delight, especially the liver, roe, heart, and eyes. The eyes are amazing, spherical fluid capsules an inch in diameter. Their thin, tough cover- ings are quite like polystyrene Ping-Pong balls. My teeth crush out a large squirt of fluid, a chewy dewdrop lens, and a papery thin, green-skinned cornea.

I spend an increasing amount of time thinking about food. Fantasies about 38 an inn-restaurant become very detailed. I know how the chairs will be arranged and what the menu will offer. Steaming sherried crab overflows flaky pie shells bedded on rice pilaf and toasted almonds. Fresh muffins puff out of pans. Melted butter drools down the sides of warm, broken bread. The aroma of bak- ing pies and brownies wafts through the air. Chilly mounds of ice cream stand firm in my mind's eye. I try to make the visions melt away, but hunger keeps me awake for hours at night. I am angry with the pain of hunger, but even as I eat it will not stop.

I save the bulk of my water ration for dessert. Since I have rebuilt my stock, 39 I can afford to drink a half pint during the day and three-quarters of a pint at dinner, and still have a couple of ounces for the night. I slowly roll a mouthful around on my tongue until the water is absorbed rather than swallowed. When I return, ice cream will be no more pleasurable.

40   In these moments of peace, deprivation seems a strange sort of gift. I find food in a couple hours of fishing each day, and I seek shelter in a rubber tent. How unnecessarily complicated my past life seems. For the first time, I clearly see a vast difference between human needs and human wants. Before this voyage, I always had what I needed—food, shelter, clothing, and companionship—yet was often dissatisfied when I didn't get everything I wanted, when people didn't meet my expectations, when a goal was thwarted, or when I couldn't acquire some material goody. My plight has given me a strange kind of wealth, the most important kind. I value each moment that is not spent in pain, desperation, hunger, thirst, or loneliness. Even here, there is richness all around me. As I look out of the raft, I see God's face in the smooth waves. His grace in the dorado's swim, feel His breath against my cheek as it sweeps down from the sky. I see that all of creation is made in His image. Yet despite His constant company, I need more. I need more than food and drink. I need to feel the company of other human spirits. I need to find more than a moment of tranquility, faith, and love. A ship. Yes, I still need a ship.

41   The sea has flattened. All is still. Inside of me I feel a symphony of excitement growing, like music that begins very low, almost inaudible, then grows stronger and stronger until the entire audience is swept up in it with a single synchronized, thumping heartbeat. I rise to scan the horizon. Blowing up from astern are gigantic clumps of cumulonimbus clouds. Rain bursts from their flat, black bottoms, above which thick, snowy fleece billows up to great heights, until it is blown off in anvil heads of feathery ice crystals. The clouds push bright blue sky ahead of their walls of gray rain streaking to earth. An invisible paintbrush suddenly splashes a full rainbow of sharply defined color from one horizon to the other. The top of its arc comes directly overhead, lost in turbulent white ten thousand feet up. The breeze caresses my face; the canopy of the raft snaps. The smooth, slate sea is broken with white tumbling cracks. The sun suddenly pops out between billowing sky sculptures far to the west and balances on the horizon. It sends warmth tracking to the east upon its path, heats my back, and sets the bright orange canopy aglow. Another invisible brush stroke paints another perfect rainbow inside and behind the first. Between their belts of color are walls of deep gray. The smaller rainbow is a cavernous mouth well lit on the rim, leading inward to a deeper, electric blue. I feel as if I am passing down the corridor of a heavenly vault of irreproducible grandeur and color. The dorados leap in very high arcs as if they are trying to reach the clouds, catching the setting sun on their sparkling skins. I stand comfortably, back to the sun, as cool rain splashes on my face, fills my cup, and washes me clean. Far away to the north and south the ends of the rainbows touch the sea. Four rainbow ends and no pots of gold, but the treasure is mine nonetheless. Perhaps until now I have always looked for the wrong kind of coin.

42   As the spectacle moves on, I empty the captured water into containers, pull the sleeping bag over me and close my eyes. My body is sore, but I am strangely at peace. For a short while I feel as if I've moved off of that seat in hell. The benign routine lasts three days. Sometimes for better, sometimes for worse, nothing lasts forever.

March 6
Day 30

By the night of March 6, it is blowing like hell again. All night I am thrown 43
about; it's like trying to sleep in a bumper car. The next day the gale reaches
forty knots. Combers crash down on *Rubber Ducky,* and I wonder if the strong
wind will pick us up and fly us to Antigua. Keeping watch is out of the question. The entrance is lashed down tight. Even tending the still is impossible. If
only I had windows, I could see what's going on outside before it leaps inside,
and maybe I would see a ship that could get me out of this mess.

Patiently waiting for the gale to blow over, I chew on a fish stick. Dorado 44
skin is much too tough to bite through, so I rake the meat off with my teeth. I
feel a hard, sharp object in my mouth, like a shard of bone. I fish it out and find
that it is plastic. Part of the cap that covers one of my front teeth has been
chipped off. When I was young, the cap came off a few times, and I have vivid
memories of the stabbing pain that ran down the exposed nerve of the uncapped
tooth stub and shot into my brain. I can feel that some of the cap remains over
the nerve, but it is loose and can't last much longer.

Water dribbles in constantly through the canopy. On March 8, *Ducky* is 45
knocked down again. I bail out the gallons of water and begin to wring out the
heavy lump that is supposed to be a sleeping bag. My cap is completely gone,
but amazingly the tooth doesn't hurt at all. The nerve must have died. Thank
heaven for small miracles. I haven't slept for two days. My skin is white, and
even my wrinkles have wrinkles. My hair sits dripping and tangled on my
head. Fish scales cling to me like ornamental slivers of nail polish. With a gap
in the middle of my smile, I must be quite a mess, a real hag. Well, we rafties
can't be at our charming best all of the time.

Two hours later *Ducky* is knocked down again. I sit among the floating de- 46
bris, exhausted, giving in, no longer able to keep cool. Beating my fists in a
splashing tantrum, I yell, "You god-damned son-of-a-bitch ocean!" For five
minutes I do nothing but curse the wind and sea. I break down sobbing: "Why
me? Why does it have to be me? I just want to go home, that's all. Why can't I
just go home?" Inside, a second voice scolds me to stop acting like a child. But
I'm beyond control. I yell back at myself. "I don't give one damn about being
reasonable! I'm hurt, hungry, tired, and scared. I want to cry." So I do.

What I do not know is that this same day, perhaps at this very moment, my 47
father is calling the U.S. Coast Guard to notify them that *Napoleon Solo* is over-
due. Sometime before, my mother had had a nightmare. She had seen me clawing through black waters, struggling to regain the surface. She awoke with a
start, sweating, shaking, and had been tense ever since, awaiting word from
me. None came.

After a few minutes, the fire inside me subsides. I set about the endless, 48
heavy work of bailing and wringing things out. Perhaps when I get back I will
have a picnic with friends and neighbors. Yes, I must return for that. There will
be laughter and children and fresh-cut grass, pine trees and trout ponds. I'll have
them at last. We will have a brontosaurus of a barbeque, trees of salads, and

hills of ice cream. People will ask me what it was like. I will tell them I hated it, all of it. There was not one slimy corner that did not stink. You can never love it. You can only do what you must. I hated the sea's snapping off shots of heavy rifle fire next to my ear, rolling heavy stones over me, ripping wounds open, beating me, winning. Weeks on end, no bells, no rounds, continued onslaught. I even hated the equipment that saved my life—the primitive raft that was an aimless, drifting pig of a boat, the wretched tent that turned clean water foul. I hated having to catch drinking water in the same box I had to defecate in. I hated having to haul aboard lovely creatures and tear into their flesh like a beast. I hated counting minutes for thirty-two days. I hated . . . I hated . . .

49   I did not know a man could have so much hatred and so much longing with in him. Yes, I will get home somehow. I must. Has the wind ceased a little or is it my imagination?

March 10
Day 34

50   No. For the next two days the gale continues and life is hellish. I have managed to catch another triggerfish, my third, and another dorado, my fourth. The dorado bent the spear again. I must ration the use of my equipment. Who knows how many dorados it will take to break my spear beyond repair? And how long must the spear last?

51   The distillate collection bag of the solar still was nearly full an hour ago. Now it hangs flaccid. A tiny, burred hole has been bitten from one edge of the bag. Friggin' triggerfish. I've lost over six ounces of water. That's a half day of life gone, old boy. Won't you feel like a jerk if you die just one half day before being picked up?

52   By March 11 things have calmed again, and I resume my more placid routine. I'm about halfway to the West Indies. Once again I have time to count my blessings. *Solo* stayed afloat long enough for me to salvage what I needed. My equipment is all working, and doing a fair job of it, too. Mountain climbing, camping, Boy Scouts, boat building, sailing, and design, and my family's continued encouragement to confront life head on have all given me enough skill to "seastead" on this tiny, floating island. I am getting there. So far it is a tale of miracles.

March 13
Day 37

53   On March 13, however, I am not feeling too chipper. Because of the bad weather, the last dorado that I caught never dried properly and turned pasty and rancid. I haven't eaten much, and I finally throw it out. I strain to do my yoga exercises, accomplishing in an hour and a half what usually takes only a half hour. Even in the calm of evening, I don't think I can last much longer.

54   Doing just enough to hang on will no longer do. I must keep myself in the best shape possible. I must eat more. I pull in the string farm trailing astern

and rake off the barnacles with the blade of my knife. I scrape some rust from the peanut and coffee cans into my drinking water in the hope of absorbing some iron and alleviating anemia.

I talk to the lazy vagrant in control of my body. I coax him to kneel by the entrance to await another dorado. At first my body is slow. A dorado swims out. I clumsily splash down. Miss. Another. Miss. But the pumping of blood helps to revive my other self, the physical part. On the third shot I ram my weapon through the fish's back. It pulls me down over the tube as it twists and jerks to get away. I play the fish as if he's on a light line, because I don't want to break or bend my lance. However, I must also retrieve it as quickly as possible, before it can escape. So I let it twist and jerk while I reach down and grab the shaft close to the body; then I lift it up without the risk of bending the shaft. I flip the fish inside, onto the sailcloth blanket that protects the floor. When I get the dorado pinned down with my knees, I slip the cutting board under its head just behind the gills, push my knife into the lateral line, and break the spine with a quick twist of the blade. Usually I completely clean the fish before eating, but now I'm very hungry. I simply gut it and place the rest aside.

By midafternoon I am eating the organs, and I feel as if I have had a transfusion. The dorado's stomach seems full of something. I cut it open. Five partially digested flying fish spill out onto the floor. I hesitate, take a small taste of a flyer, and almost vomit. I gather them up and toss them out. As soon as they are in the air I think, Fool! You should have washed them off and then tried them. Next time. But such a waste of five fish. I mop up the spilled stomach juices and finish cleaning the dorado. Sweat pours off of my head as I squat over my catch and labor in the heat to slice up the body. I stop twice to stretch out my legs and to relieve my cramped knees and back. The work is hard, but I move fast so that I can rest sooner. I always work that way—pushing myself as hard as I can so I can finish quickly and then find complete rest.

As I poke holes through the fish sticks in order to string them up, SLAM! *Rubber Ducky* crushes me between her tubes. Water dribbles in and she springs back to her normal shape as though nothing has happened. It takes me a moment to get my wind back and recover from the shock. The average wave height is only about three feet, but a monster leisurely rolls off ahead. I set to work again with a shrug. I am getting used to various levels of disaster striking with no warning.

The still lies lifeless, draped flat over the bow. It must have gotten smacked pretty hard. Air jets out of it almost as quickly as I can blow it in. The cloth across the bottom, which allows excess seawater to drain through and which is airtight when wet, now sports a hole. The cloth has deteriorated from the constant cycles of wetting and drying and from chafing against *Ducky*'s tubes. Less than thirty days of use, and the still is gonzo. I've never been able to coerce my remaining still to work. As we have drifted west, the number of light showers has increased, but I am lucky when I can trap six or eight ounces of water within a week. Another critical safety margin has disappeared. I'm in big trouble—not that I've been out of big trouble for quite a while now.

59   I must get the other still to work and keep it working, perhaps for longer than thirty days. I blow it up until it's thick as a tick. Just below the skirt through which the lanyard passes, a tiny mouth whistles a single-note tune until the balloon's lungs are emptied. The hole is in a tight corner and on a lumpy seam, which makes it impossible to effectively wedge a piece of repair tape into it. Making something watertight is difficult enough, even for a boat builder in an equipped shop. To make something airtight is an even taller order.

60   For hours I try to think of a way to seal the leaking still. Perhaps I can burn some pieces of plastic from the old still or its packaging and drip the melted globs over the hole. But I find that my matches are sodden and my lighter has been drained of fluid. So I wedge the tape in as firmly as I can and grouchily reinflate the still every half hour. Each time, the still begins to slump as soon as I stop pumping. Water begins to collect in the distillate bag, but it is salty. At this pace, I already feel like I have a case of lockjaw, and my mouth is very dry. I must find an effective solution. If only I had some silicone seal or other kind of goop.

March 16
Day 40

61   I have managed to last forty days, but my water stock is declining, and I have but a few hard pieces of fish dangling in the butcher shop. It is also a little disconcerting to realize that *Ducky* is guaranteed for forty days of use. If she fails me now, do you suppose I *can* get my money back?

62   Despite these problems, I have good reason to celebrate this milestone. I've lasted longer than I had dreamed possible in the beginning. I'm over halfway to the Caribbean. Each day, each hardship, each moment of suffering, has brought me another small step closer to salvation. The probability of rescue, as well as gear failure, continually increases. I imagine two stone-faced poker players throwing chips onto a pile. One player is named Rescue and the other is Death. The stakes keep getting bigger and bigger. The pile of chips now stands as tall as a man and as big around as a raft. Somebody is going to win soon.

63   The dorados begin their morning foray. They bang away at the bottom of the raft and sometimes run around the outside, cracking stiff shots against the raft with their tails. I grab my spear and wait. Sometimes I have a little trouble focusing. During the last gale I jabbed my eye with a piece of the polypropylene line I've rigged to keep the still in place. After a couple of days of oozing and swelling, my eye cleared up, but I was left with a spot in my vision, which I often take to be a glimpse of an airplane or the first hint of a fish shooting out before the tip of my spear. Dorados are so fast that my shot must be instantaneous, without thought, like a bolt of lightning. A head, a microsecond of hesitation, a splash, a strike, a hard pull on my arm, and an escape. On other days I've hit two or three morning and evening but most of the time come up with nothing. This morning I'm lucky and catch a nice fat female. Squatting over her for two hours on the rolling floor of the raft is hard work for my matchstick

legs. Finally the job is done and the fish hung up to dry. I begin to mop up the blood and scales, but my sponges have turned to useless little globs. Evidently the stomach juices that I swabbed up from the last dorado have digested them. Since my sleeping bag has proven its ability to soak up water, I take out some of the batting and bind this up with pieces of codline to use as sponges.

Each day now I set my priorities, based on my continuing analysis of raft 64 condition, body condition, food, and water. Each day at least one factor lags behind what I consider adequate. The dismal problem of collecting or distilling water is one I must find a solution to.

I take some of the black cloth wick from the first still, the one that I cut up 65 early in the game. I affix it across the hole of the still with the rotted bottom, letting the still's weight keep it in place. I now have one still aft and one forward, in the only positions available for frequent tending. Every ten minutes throughout the day, I am a human bellows at the service of one or the other still. In between inflations, I empty the distillate just in case salt water sneaks in to pollute it while I'm not watching. By nightfall I have collected a full two pints of fresh water. I am continually paying higher prices for my small successes. The work is demanding and boils off a lot of body fluid. I can't decide if my steaming cells gain anything from the exercise. There is little time to dream these days, barely enough time to live, but fruit mountains still stand in the panorama of my mind's eye.

The next day my debate over the value of operating both stills becomes 66 moot. The entire cloth bottom on the older still gives way. Throughout the day I keep one still working and try to devise a patch for the old. I painstakingly poke holes around the rim of the opening, using my awl, then thread through sail twine and sew on a new cloth bottom. I try to seal it with the bits of tape that I have left, but the patch remains an utter failure. The still lies dead no matter how hard and fast I try to resuscitate it.

Luckily I'm learning about the personality of the new still. The inside black 67 cloth wick is wetted by seawater dripping through a valve on the top of the still. The rate at which the inside wick is wetted is critical to production of fresh water. If it's too wet, it doesn't heat up efficiently. Instead, the excess, warm seawater just passes out through the bottom cloth. If the wick is too dry, there is less than the maximum amount of water available for evaporation. I must maximize the rates at which the water will evaporate, collect on the inside of the plastic balloon, condense, and finally drop into the distillate collection bag. It seems that the inside pressure of the still affects the rate of dripping through the valve. The still seems most efficient at a pressure that allows it to sag, but not so much that the wick hits the plastic balloon, because if that happens the salt water in the wick is drawn into the distillate. To keep her at just the right inflation requires constant attention.

To help prevent another failure of the bottom cloth, I make a diaper for the 68 still out of a square of sailcloth and add padding, using the cloth wicking from the cut-up still. I blanket the bottom of the still by tying the diaper up by its corners to the lanyard skirt, hoping the diaper will take the chafe from *Ducky* and will keep the bottom cloth constantly wet to delay rotting.

69   My rain collection systems also need improvement. At the first *thrrrap* of water droplets from the sky, I usually wedge the Tupperware box against the aft side of the still. It's held in place by the still bridle. The arrangement is simple and is quick to rig or empty, which is important in order to minimize salt water pollution from breaking waves and spray. However, I think that I can catch more water if I can find a way to mount the Tupperware box on top of the raft. I need to put a bridle around the box so that I have something to secure it with. The awl on my jackknife has a cutting edge, so I wind it into the plastic lip that runs around the box, boring a hole in each corner. Through these I string a collar made of sail twine. I secure the two ends of one bridle to *Ducky*'s tail, lead the middle of it to the top of the arch tube, and equip it with a quick-release metal clip that I've stolen from one of the stills. Forward, I tie a short lanyard to the canopy entrance and affix a second clip to the other end, which I also lead to the peak of the canopy. When I have to use the Tupperware for some other purpose, I leave the two clips hooked together, so that they are always ready. As soon as it begins to rain, I can quickly flip the clips onto the collar of the box, which keeps it pretty secure on the apex of the arch tube, angled more directly into the wind and higher away from the waves. Its biggest benefit is that it is no longer blanketed from rainfall by the canopy, which is now below it. In fact, it will prove twice as effective this way.

70   Finally I must tend to my steel knives. My Cub Scout jackknife with the awl is one that I found when I was twelve. The spring on its main blade has always been broken, so the blade flops about a little. It's a ball of rust now. I scrape it clean. I sharpen both it and my sheath knife frequently. Rubbing the steel hard against fish skin that has a tissue of fat attached produces a tiny drool of fat, which greases the blades until they shine. I treasure raw materials and basic tools; so much can be done with them. Paper, rope, and knives have always been my favorite human inventions. And now, all three are essential to my own sanity and survival.

March 18
Day 42

71   Each day seems longer. On my forty-second in the raft, the sea is as flat and hot as an equatorial tin roof in August. The sun in the sky is joined by hundreds that flash from water ripples. It is all I can do to try to move about in *Ducky*. We sit like a period in a book of blank pages.

72   I find that my sleeping bag helps to keep me cool as well as warm. I spread it out over the floor to dry in the sun. When I stick my legs under it, they are shaded and sandwiched between the wet bag and the cool, damp floor. It is not very good for my sores, but they are not too bad now and the relief from the heat is quite

noticeable. Without the bag covering, the black floor becomes very hot and the whole inside of *Ducky,* which is hot enough as is, becomes an unbearable oven.

Nothing to do but wait for the wind and try to score more food. Some good 73 fresh guts should help lift my spirits. Triggers, a school of them, flap up toward the side of the raft, then disappear under it, come up again, pirouette, dive, loop, and roll about each other in an amazing underwater ballet. They are very wary of me now and are becoming more difficult to catch than the dorados. They don't have the same sustained speed, but in quick little jerks they can dodge my spear deftly. They flirt just outside of my reach. Jab. Miss. I must two-arm a hit on a dorado, but maybe I can get a quick and penetrating one-arm shot on a trigger. Jab. Jab. Their waving fins taunt me. My arm snaps out straight; a trigger takes the spear in his belly. Inside the fish, I find large white sacs—must be the male organs—that I will soon treasure as much as the female's golden eggs.

Ducky, can't you please stop flopping about? You're bound to be sending 74 out a general invitation to every shark in the district. Maybe I should get more fish while things are so flat.

The sun sinks down to the horizon once again, and the dorados collect for 75 evening recess. They seem mesmerized by the calm conditions and glide about like phantoms, gently nudging us. The emerald elders still skirt the vicinity, keeping an eye on their school. I am coming to know individuals not only by their size, markings, and scars but also by their personalities. I am getting very attached to them. Some like to strike one side of the raft, while others prefer another. Some strike aggressively and quickly fly away, as if they are angry or are testing my strength. Others softly slide along the bottom and wiggle out . . . right . . . in . . . front. Fire! I hit too far aft, near the tail. She churns the surface and shakes loose. I rest.

Clouds sit like dirty fingerprints across a silver sun that reaches down to 76 touch the horizon. Bands of light, "Jesus rays," strike out across the heavens. On the eastern horizon, the sky has reached a deep blue, soon to be black and filled with twinkling stars. The soft, round waves remind me of long stretches of ripe wheat fields. Bending to a gentle breeze that marks where invisible heavens touch the earth, the heavy-headed stalks bow their heads and await the reaper's scythe. I haven't much time to fish. I take up my pose again.

A big form appears to my left. By now I'm used to awaiting the perfect shot, 77 but I may not get another this evening. What the hell. Without thinking, without fear of battle with another male, I roll to the right and jab the spear to the left. Humph! Solid hit. All is still.

Where is the fury? I'm grasping the gun tightly, leaning over the tubes, 78 frozen. In a second the battle will begin. But it doesn't. In his huge head the eye is glazed. His slightly opened mouth is paralyzed. His gills are glued shut. The tip of the spear rests in the stripe that runs down his side, which marks the position of the spine. The barb is still barely visible. The spear has not been driven straight through. I gently pull him toward me, grab the spear with my other hand, and ever so carefully begin to lift. It's like juggling a ball on the end of a stick. What a relief not to endure another dangerous battle. He is food for a week. The glassy surface bubbles up as his body begins to rise. Taking the weight now . . . Splash. I lunge to grab him. Too late. His smooth skin slips from my fumbling fingers.

79   The big, stiff body whirls downward like a bright dead leaf falling from a limb. His blank stare goes round and round as he sinks deeper and deeper. All of the other dorados have been watching. Like fingers reaching down to him, they descend. Deeper, still deeper. Finally their shapes converge like living petals blooming from the stamen of the dead fish. The tiny flower whirls even deeper, getting smaller and smaller, until it is no more. The sun is gone. The waters become black and empty. I stare into the depths.

FOCUS ON ECOLOGY

1. What does Callahan mean when he writes that "in the survival world my physical self and my instincts are the ringmasters that whip all of my realities into place and control their motions"?
2. What seems to be the role and the importance of performing tasks in survival situations? What tasks are important to Steven Callahan?
3. Callahan says that he has adjusted to his equipment and his environment after a few weeks lost at sea. In what ways does he exhibit those adjustments?

FOCUS ON WRITING

1. Why do you suppose Callahan writes during his time lost at sea? Why do you suppose he plots his estimated travel course on a chart? What does writing during a survival situation provide for the survivor?
2. Are you familiar with the animals (dorado, petrels, shearwaters) that Callahan tells us he encounters? Does knowing what these animals are affect how you read about their appearance in the narrative?
3. Why does Callahan reference the film *Jaws*? Why would someone stuck in this position think about *Jaws*? What does this reference suggest about the way *Jaws* has become a part of our cultural image of sharks? Likewise, in what ways does Callahan's text rely on another text—*Jaws*—in order to make its point?

FOR DISCUSSION

When *Rubber Ducky III*, Callahan's life raft, is knocked about by the strong winds, he spends some time cursing the ocean and the weather. For many, not just in survival situations but in everyday situations, cursing the weather, the environment, becomes a necessary part of confronting that weather, that environment. Why might someone who is challenged by the natural environment for survival curse that environment? What might doing so accomplish in terms of the person's survival? As a class, consider what it may mean to someone in a survival situation to become angry with and vocalize that anger toward the environment in which the individual struggles for survival.

WRITING IN RESPONSE

At several points in "To Weave a World," Steven Callahan describes and considers his emotions during his ordeal at sea. Emotions play an important role in one's ability to survive in wilderness situations. In a short essay, address how you imagine emotions would come into play in situations like the one Callahan was forced to endure. What emotions would work to one's benefit? To one's disadvantage? How might one control one's emotions during such trying times? How might one prepare emotionally for the possibility of such a challenge? How might one prepare emotionally for the possibility of one's death?

Film: *The Edge*

The film The Edge *was released by Twentieth-Century-Fox on September 26, 1997, and later on video on September 5, 2000. The film, written by David Mamet, stars Anthony Hopkins as Charles Morse, a billionaire; Alec Baldwin as Robert Green, assistant to Morse; and Elle McPherson as Micky Morse, Charles's model wife. At the beginning of the film, Morse accompanies his wife on a photo shoot in a cold, mountainous area. While scouting shoot locations, Morse, Robert Green, and another character are stranded after their plane crashes. The film addresses the male rivalry between Morse and Green—who is having an affair with Micky—the isolation they face, and their ultimate fight for survival in the wilderness. As you watch this film, consider the role knowledge plays in survival situations. Also, examine the ways the archetypal "man versus man" is depicted.*

JOURNAL ASSIGNMENT

Have you ever imagined what it might be like to survive a plane crash or a shipwreck and be stranded in the wilderness? In your journal, write about how (or whether) you would survive in a mountain wilderness if your plane crashed, leaving you the sole survivor.

FOCUS ON ECOLOGY

1. There are several important peripheral figures in this movie: the owner of the lodge, the bear, the Native American. How would you characterize the role of the bear in this film? The lodge owner? The Native American?
2. Why do you suppose this film was set in a mountain wilderness? Could this film have been made about a deserted island with the bear recast as a shark or another animal? Could it be set in a desert with the bear recast as a snake or scorpion? What is the relationship between the setting and the characters' survival?
3. In *The Edge,* Charles Morse tells us that most people who die in the woods die of shame. In the film, what is survival dependent on?

FOCUS ON WRITING

1. In the film, Morse reads a book about survival skills, What role does this book, play in his ultimate survival? Can the materials presented in books like this really help in such a situation? That is, what is the relationship between textual accounts of and guides for survival and hands–on experience and training?

2. Why did Mamet include the conflict between Charles Morse and Robert Green as part of the plot? Is that part of the plot necessary? Is the story about a group of plane crash survivors in the wilderness not an interesting enough story without adding tension between the two of them?
3. What does the carved paddle represent in this film? Is there a particular reason the message of the paddle is conveyed as a Native American text? What credence do we place culturally in Native American knowledge when it comes to issues of wilderness and survival ?

FOR DISCUSSION

One of the interesting things about *The Edge* is the mythology about bears it develops. Bear legends are an important part of wilderness lore, Native American culture, and other narratives. In fact, entire books have been devoted not just to the study of bears but to the telling of stories about bear attacks. As a class, consider how the bear is depicted in this film. What do you know about bears? What stories about bears have you heard? How would you characterize the role of bears in American culture? Is the bear in this film at all like Smokey the Bear, Winnie the Pooh, the Berenstein Bears, teddy bears, Baloo, and other bears with which we tend to be familiar? Are there stories of surviving bear attacks that are as famous as these bear images?

WRITING IN RESPONSE

Throughout *The Edge*, our attention is directed to a few specific pieces of equipment that make survival for Morse possible: the knife, the pin for the compass, the flare, the book, the watch pieces. If you were stuck in the woods as the characters of this film were, what would be the one piece of equipment (other than a radio, gun or other weapon, or transporter) you would want with you? Why? Describe what you would want to have with you and why in a short descriptive essay.

From *Their Eyes Were Watching God*

Zora Neale Hurston

Zora Neale Hurston was born in Eatonville, Florida, in 1891 and died in 1960 in Ft. Pierce, Florida. She attended Howard University from 1923 until 1924 and earned her B.A. from Barnard College in 1928. Hurston is one of the most important figures in twentieth-century African-American literature. Her work was critical to the Harlem Renaissance, and it influenced many other writers including Ralph Ellison, Alice Walker, and Toni Morrison. In his book Zora Neale Hurston: A Literary Biography, *Robert Hemenway describes Hurston as "flamboyant yet vulnerable, self-centered yet kind, a Republican conservative and an early black nationalist." Likewise, Henry Louis Gates, Jr., has explained that "part of Miss Hurston's received heritage . . . was the idea that racism had reduced black people to mere ciphers, to beings who react only to an omnipresent racial oppression, whose culture is 'deprived' where different, and whose psyches are in the main 'pathological.' . . . Miss Hurston thought this idea degrading, its propagation a trap. It was against this that she railed, at times brilliantly and systematically, at times vapidly and eclectically." The selection here is taken from her remarkable book* Their Eyes Were Watching God. *As you read this selection, note that the characters described in this piece struggle not only against forces of nature, but against social forces as well.*

JOURNAL ASSIGNMENT

What is a hurricane? In this selection from Zora Neale Hurston's *Their Eyes Were Watching God,* Hurston writes about enduring a hurricane. In your journal, write what you know about hurricanes. How much of what you know is based on the mythologies we have about hurricanes?

Since Tea Cake and Janie had friended with the Bahaman workers in the 'Glades, they, the "Saws," had been gradually drawn into the American crowd. They quit hiding out to hold their dances when they found that their American friends didn't laugh at them as they feared. Many of the Americans learned to jump and liked it as much as the "Saws." So they began to hold dances night after night in the quarters, usually behind Tea Cake's house. Often now, Tea Cake and Janie stayed up so late at the fire dances that Tea Cake would not let her go with him to the field. He wanted her to get her rest.

So she was home by herself one afternoon when she saw a band of Seminoles passing by. The men walking in front and the laden, stolid women following them like burros. She had seen Indians several times in the 'Glades, in twos and threes, but this was a large party. They were headed towards the Palm Beach road and kept moving steadily. About an hour later another party appeared and went the same way. Then another just before sundown. This time she asked where they were all going and at last one of the men answered her.

"Going to high ground. Saw-grass bloom. Hurricane coming."

Everybody was talking about it that night. But nobody was worried. The fire dance kept up till nearly dawn. The next day, more Indians moved east, unhurried but steady. Still a blue sky and fair weather. Beans running fine and prices good, so the Indians could be, *must* be, wrong. You couldn't have a hurricane when you're making seven and eight dollars a day picking beans. Indians are dumb anyhow, always were. Another night of Stew Beef making dynamic subtleties with his drum and living, sculptural, grotesques in the dance. Next day, no Indians passed at all. It was hot and sultry and Janie left the field and went home.

Morning came without motion. The winds, to the tiniest, lisping baby breath had left the earth. Even before the sun gave light, dead day was creeping from bush to bush watching man.

Some rabbits scurried through the quarters going east. Some possums slunk by and their route was definite. One or two at a time, then more. By the time the people left the fields the procession was constant. Snakes, rattlesnakes began to cross the quarters. The men killed a few, but they could not be missed from the crawling horde. People stayed indoors until daylight. Several times during the night Janie heard the snort of big animals like deer. Once the muted voice of a panther. Going east and east. That night the palm and banana trees began that long distance talk with rain. Several people took fright and picked up and went in to Palm Beach anyway. A thousand buzzards held a flying meet and then went above the clouds and stayed.

One of the Bahaman boys stopped by Tea Cake's house in a car and hollered. Tea Cake came out throwin' laughter over his shoulder into the house.

"Hello Tea Cake."

"Hello 'Lias. You leavin', ah see."

"Yeah man. You and Janie wanta go? Ah wouldn't give nobody else uh chawnce at uh seat till Ah found out if you all had anyway tuh go."

"Thank yuh ever so much, Lias. But we 'bout decided tuh stay."

"De crow gahn up, man."

"Dat ain't nothin'. You ain't seen de bossman go up, is yuh? Well all right now. Man, de money's too good on the muck. It's liable tuh fair off by tuhmorrer. Ah wouldn't leave if Ah wuz you."

"Mah uncle come for me. He say hurricane warning out in Palm Beach. Not so bad here, but man, dis muck is too low and dat big lake is liable tuh bust."

"Ah naw, man. Some boys in dere now talkin' 'bout it. Some of 'em been in de 'Glades fuh years. 'Tain't nothin' but uh lil blow. You'll lose de whole day tuhmorrer tryin' tuh git back out heah."

"De Indians gahn east, man. It's dangerous."

"Dey don't always know. Indians don't know much uh nothin', tuh tell de truth. Else dey'd own dis country still. De white folks ain't gone nowhere. Dey oughta know if it's dangerous. You better stay heah, man. Big jumpin' dance tuhnight right heah, when it fair off."

Lias hesitated and started to climb out, but his uncle wouldn't let him. "Dis time tuhmorrer you gointuh wish you follow crow," he snorted and drove off. Lias waved back to them gaily.

"If Ah never see you no mo' on earth, Ah'll meet you in Africa."

Others hurried east like the Indians and rabbits and snakes and coons. But the majority sat around laughing and waiting for the sun to get friendly again.

Several men collected at Tea Cake's house and sat around stuffing courage into each other's ears. Janie baked a big pan of beans and something she called sweet biscuits and they all managed to be happy enough.

Most of the great flame-throwers were there and naturally, handling Big John de Conquer and his works. How he had done everything big on earth, then went up tuh heben without dying atall. Went up there picking a guitar and got all de angels doing the ring-shout round and round de throne. Then everybody but God and Old Peter flew off on a flying race to Jericho and back and John de Conquer won the race; went on down to hell, beat the old devil and passed out ice water to everybody down there. Somebody tried to say that it was a mouth organ harp that John was playing, but the rest of them would not hear that. Don't care how good anybody could play a harp, God would rather to hear a guitar. That brought them back to Tea Cake. How come he couldn't hit that box a lick or two? Well, all right now, make us know it.

When it got good to everybody, Muck-Boy woke up and began to chant with the rhythm and everybody bore down on the last word of the line:

Yo' mama don't wear no *Draws*
Ah seen her when she took 'em *Off*
She soaked 'em in alco*Hol*
She sold 'em tuh de Santy *Claus*
He told her 'twas aginst de *Law*
To wear dem dirty *Draws*

Then Muck-Boy went crazy through the feet and danced himself and everybody else crazy. When he finished he sat back down on the floor and went to sleep again. Then they got to playing Florida flip and coon-can. Then it was dice. Not for money. This was a show-off game. Everybody posing his fancy shots. As always it broiled down to Tea Cake and Motor Boat. Tea Cake with his shy grin and Motor Boat with his face like a little black cherubim just from a church tower doing amazing things with anybody's dice. The others forgot the work and the weather watching them throw. It was art. A thousand dollars a throw in Madison Square Garden wouldn't have gotten any more breathless suspense. It would have just been more people holding in.

After a while somebody looked out and said, "It ain't gitting no fairer out dere. B'lieve Ah'll git on over tuh mah shack." Motor Boat and Tea Cake were still playing so everybody left them at it.

Sometime that night the winds came back. Everything in the world had a strong rattle, sharp and short like Stew Beef vibrating the drum head near the edge with his fingers. By morning Gabriel was playing the deep tones in the center of the drum. So when Janie looked out of her door she saw the drifting mists gathered in the west—that cloud field of the sky—to arm themselves with thunders and march forth against the world. Louder and higher and lower and wider the sound and motion spread, mounting, sinking, darking.

It woke up old Okechobee and the monster began to roll in his bed. Began to roll and complain like a peevish world on a grumble. The folks in the quarters and the people in the big house further around the shore heard the big lake and wondered. The people felt uncomfortable but safe because there were the seawalls to chain the senseless monster in his bed. The folks let the people do the thinking. If the castles thought themselves secure, the cabins needn't worry. Their decision was already made as always. Chink up your cracks, shiver in your wet beds and wait on the mercy of the Lord. The bossman might have the thing stopped before morning anyway. It is so easy to be hopeful in the day time when you can see the things you wish on. But it was night, it stayed night. Night was striding across nothingness with the whole round world in his hands.

A big burst of thunder and lightning that trampled over the roof of the house. So Tea Cake and Motor stopped playing. Motor looked up in his angel-looking way and said, "Big Massa draw him chair upstairs."

"Ah'm glad y'all stop dat crap-shootin' even if it wasn't for money," Janie said. "Ole Massa is doin' *His* work now. Us oughta keep quiet."

They huddled closer and stared at the door. They just didn't use another part of their bodies, and they didn't look at anything but the door. The time was past for asking the white folks what to look for through that door. Six eyes were questioning *God*.

Through the screaming wind they heard things crashing and things hurtling and dashing with unbelievable velocity. A baby rabbit, terror ridden, squirmed through a hole in the floor and squatted off there in the shadows against the wall, seeming to know that nobody wanted its flesh at such a time. And the lake got madder and madder with only its dikes between them and him.

In a little wind-lull, Tea Cake touched Janie and said, "Ah reckon you wish now you had of stayed in yo' big house 'way from such as dis, don't yuh?"

"Naw."

"Naw?"

"Yeah, naw. People don't die till dey time come nohow, don't keer where you at. Ah'm wid mah husband in uh storm, dat's all."

"Thanky, Ma'am. But 'sposing you wuz tuh die, now. You wouldn't git mad at me for draggin' yuh heah?"

"Naw. We been tuhgether round two years. If you kin see de light at daybreak, you don't keer if you die at dusk. It's so many people never seen de light at all. Ah wuz fumblin' round and God opened de door."

He dropped to the floor and put his head in her lap. "Well then, Janie, you meant whut you didn't say, 'cause Ah never *knowed* you wuz so satisfied wid me lak dat. Ah kinda thought—"

The wind came back with triple fury, and put out the light for the last time. They sat in company with the others in other shanties, their eyes straining against crude walls and their souls asking if He meant to measure their puny might against His. They seemed to be staring at the dark, but their eyes were watching God.

As soon as Tea Cake went out pushing wind in front of him, he saw that the wind and water had given life to lots of things that folks think of as dead and given death to so much that had been living things. Water everywhere. Stray fish swimming in the yard. Three inches more and the water would be in the house. Already in some. He decided to try to find a car to take them out of the 'Glades before worse things happened. He turned back to tell Janie about it so she could be ready to go.

"Git our insurance papers tuhgether, Janie. Ah'll tote mah box mahself and things lak dat."

"You got all de money out de dresser drawer, already?"

"Naw, git it quick and cut up piece off de table-cloth tuh wrap it up in. Us liable tuh git wet tuh our necks. Cut uh piece uh dat oilcloth quick fuh our papers. We got tuh go, if it ain't too late. De dish can't bear it out no longer."

He snatched the oilcloth off the table and took out his knife. Janie held it straight while he slashed off a strip.

"But Tea Cake, it's too awful out dere. Maybe it's better tuh stay heah in de wet than it is tuh try tuh—"

He stunned the argument with half a word. "Fix," he said and fought his way outside. He had seen more than Janie had.

Janie took a big needle and ran up a longish sack. Found some newspaper and wrapped up the paper money and papers and thrust them in and whipped over the open end with her needle. Before she could get it thoroughly hidden in the pocket of her overalls, Tea Cake burst in again.

"'Tain't no cars, Janie."

"Ah thought not! Whut we gointuh do now?"

"We got tuh walk."

"In all dis weather, Tea Cake? Ah don't b'lieve Ah could make it out de quarters."

"Oh yeah you kin. Me and you and Motor Boat kin all lock arms and hold one 'nother down. Eh, Motor?"

"He's sleep on de bed in yonder," Janie said. Tea Cake called without moving.

"Motor boat! You better git up from dere! Hell done broke loose in Georgy. Dis minute! How kin you sleep at uh time lak dis? Water knee deep in de yard."

They stepped out in water almost to their buttocks and managed to turn east. Tea Cake had to throw his box away, and Janie saw how it hurt him. Dodging flying missiles, floating dangers, avoiding stepping in holes and warmed on the wind now at their backs until they gained comparatively dry land. They had to fight to keep from being pushed the wrong way and to hold together. They saw other people like themselves struggling along. A house down, here and there, frightened cattle. But above all the drive of the wind and the water. And the lake. Under its multiplied roar could be heard a mighty sound of grinding rock and timber and a wail. They looked back. Saw people trying to run in raging waters and screaming when they found they couldn't. A huge barrier of the makings of the dike to which the cabins had been added was rolling and tumbling forward. Ten feet higher and as far as they could see the muttering wall advanced before the braced-up waters like a road crusher on a cosmic scale. The monstropolous beast had left his bed. The two hundred miles an hour wind had loosed his chains. He seized hold of his dikes and ran forward until he met the quarters; uprooted them like grass and rushed on after his supposed-to-be conquerors, rolling the dikes, rolling the houses, rolling the people in the houses along with other timbers. The sea was walking the earth with a heavy heel.

"De lake is comin'!" Tea Cake gasped.

"De lake!" In amazed horror from Motor Boat, "De lake!"

"It's comin' behind us!" Janie shuddered. "Us can't fly."

"But we still kin run," Tea Cake shouted and they ran. The gushing water ran faster. The great body was held back, but rivers spouted through fissures in the rolling wall and broke like day. The three fugitives ran past another line of shanties that topped a slight rise and gained a little. They cried out as best they could, "De lake is comin'!" and barred doors flew open and others joined them in flight crying the same as they went. "De lake is comin'!" and the pursuing waters growled and shouted ahead, "Yes, Ah'm comin'!", and those who could fled on.

They made it to a tall house on a hump of ground and Janie said, "Less stop heah. Ah can't make it no further. Ah'm done give out."

"All of us is done give out," Tea Cake corrected. "We'se goin' inside out dis weather, kill or cure." He knocked with the handle of his knife, while they leaned their faces and shoulders against the wall. He knocked once more then he and Motor Boat went round to the back and forced a door. Nobody there.

"Dese people had mo' sense than Ah did," Tea Cake said as they dropped to the floor and lay there panting. "Us oughta went on wid 'Lias lak he ast me."

"You didn't know," Janie contended. "And when yuh don't know, yuh just don't know. De storms might not of come sho nuff."

They went to sleep promptly but Janie woke up first. She heard the sound of rushing water and sat up.

"Tea Cake! Motor Boat! De lake is comin'!"

The lake *was* coming on. Slower and wider, but coming. It had trampled on most of its supporting wall and lowered its front by spreading. But it came muttering and grumbling onward like a tired mammoth just the same.

"Dis is uh high tall house. Maybe it won't reach heah at all," Janie counseled. "And if it do, maybe it won't reach tuh de upstairs part."

"Janie, Lake Okechobee is forty miles wide and sixty miles long. Dat's uh whole heap uh water. If dis wind is shovin' dat whole lake disa way, dis house ain't nothin' tuh swaller. Us better go. Motor Boat!"

"Whut you want, man?"

"De lake is comin'!"

"Aw, naw it 'tain't!"

"Yes, it is *so* comin'! Listen! You kin hear it way off."

"It kin jus' come on. Ah'll wait right here."

"Aw, get up, Motor Boat! Less make it tuh de Palm Beach road. Dat's on uh fill. We'se pretty safe dere."

"Ah'm safe here, man. Go ahead if yuh wants to. Ah'm sleepy."

"Whut you gointuh do if de lake reach heah?"

"Go upstairs."

"S'posing it come up dere?"

"Swim, man. Dat's all."

"Well, uh, Good bye, Motor Boat. Everything is pretty bad, yuh know. Us might git missed of one 'nother. You sho is a grand friend fuh uh man tuh have."

"Good bye, Tea Cake. Y'all oughta stay here and sleep, man. No use in goin' off and leavin' me lak dis."

"We don't wanta. Come on wid us. It might be night time when de water hem you up in heah. Dat's how come Ah won't stay. Come on, man."

"Tea Cake, Ah got tuh have mah sleep. Definitely."

"Good bye, then, Motor. Ah wish you all de luck. Goin' over tuh Nassau fuh dat visit widja when all dis is over."

"Definitely, Tea Cake. Mah mama's house is yours."

Tea Cake and Janie were some distance from the house before they struck serious water. Then they had to swim a distance, and Janie could not hold up more than a few strokes at a time, so Tea Cake bore her up till finally they hit a ridge that led on towards the fill. It seemed to him the wind was weakening a little so he kept looking for a place to rest and catch his breath. His wind was gone. Janie was tired and limping, but she had not had to do that hard swimming in the turbulent waters, so Tea Cake was much worse off. But they couldn't stop. Gaining the fill was something but it was no guarantee. The lake was coming. They had to reach the six-mile bridge. It was high and safe perhaps.

Everybody was walking the fill. Hurrying, dragging, falling, crying, calling out names hopefully and hopelessly. Wind and rain beating on old folks and beating on babies. Tea Cake stumbled once or twice in his weariness and Janie held him up. So they reached the bridge at Six Mile Bend and thought to rest.

But it was crowded. White people had preempted the point of elevation and there was no more room. They could climb up one of its high sides and down the other, that was all. Miles further on, still no rest.

They passed a dead man in a sitting position on a hummock, entirely surrounded by wild animals and snakes. Common danger made common friends. Nothing sought a conquest over the other.

Another man clung to a cypress tree on a tiny island. A tin roof of a building hung from the branches by electric wires and the wind swung it back and forth like a mighty ax. The man dared not move a step to his right lest this crushing blade split him open. He dared not step left for a large rattlesnake was stretched full length with his head in the wind. There was a strip of water between the island and the fill, and the man clung to a tree and cried for help.

"De snake won't bite yuh," Tea Cake yelled to him. "He skeered tuh go intuh uh coil. Skeered he'll be blowed away. Step round dat side and swim off!"

Soon after that Tea Cake felt he couldn't walk anymore. Not right away. So he stretched long side of the road to rest. Janie spread herself between him and the wind and he closed his eyes and let the tiredness seep out of his limbs. On each side of the fill was a great expanse of water like lakes—water full of things living and dead. Things that didn't belong in water. As far as the eye could reach, water and wind playing upon it in fury. A large piece of tar-paper roofing sailed through the air and scudded along the fill until it hung against a tree. Janie saw it with joy . That was the very thing to cover Tea Cake with. She could lean against it and hold it down. The wind wasn't quite so bad as it was anyway. The very thing. Poor Tea Cake!

She crept on hands and knees to the piece of roofing and caught hold of it by either side. Immediately the wind lifted both of them and she saw herself sailing off the fill to the right, out and out over lashing water. She screamed terribly and released the roofing which sailed away as she plunged downward into the water.

"Tea Cake!" He heard her and sprang up. Janie was trying to swim but fighting water too hard. He saw a cow swimming slowly towards the fill in an oblique line. A massive built dog was sitting on her shoulders and shivering and growling. The cow was approaching Janie. A few strokes would bring her there.

"Make it tuh de cow and grab hold of her tail! Don't use yo' feet. Jus' yo' hands is enough. Dat's right, come on!"

Janie achieved the tail of the cow and lifted her head up along the cow's rump, as far as she could above water. The cow sunk a little with the added load and thrashed a moment in terror. Thought she was being pulled down by a gator. Then she continued on. The dog stood up and growled like a lion, stiff-standing hackles, stiff muscles, teeth uncovered as he lashed up his fury for the charge. Tea Cake split the water like an otter, opening his knife as he dived. The dog raced down the backbone of the cow to the attack and Janie screamed and slipped far back on the tail of the cow, just out of reach of the dog's angry jaws. He wanted to plunge in after her but dreaded the water, somehow. Tea Cake rose out of the water at the cow's rump and seized the dog by the neck. But he was a powerful dog and Tea Cake was over-tired. So he didn't kill the dog with one stroke as he had intended. But the dog couldn't free himself either. They fought and somehow he managed to bite Tea Cake high up on his cheek-bone once. Then Tea Cake finished him and sent him to the bottom to stay there. The cow relieved of a great weight was landing on the fill with Janie before Tea Cake stroked in and crawled weakly upon the fill again.

Janie began to fuss around his face where the dog had bitten him but he said it didn't amount to anything. "He'd uh raised hell though if he had uh grabbed me uh inch higher and bit me in mah eye. Yuh can't buy eyes in de store, yuh know." He flopped to the edge of the fill as if the storm wasn't going on at all. "Lemme rest awhile, then us got tuh make it on intuh town somehow."

It was next day by the sun and the clock when they reached Palm Beach. It was years later by their bodies. Winters and winters of hardship and suffering. The wheel kept turning round and round. Hope, hopelessness and despair. But the storm blew itself out as they approached the city of refuge.

Havoc was there with her mouth wide open. Back in the Everglades the wind had romped among lakes and trees. In the city it had raged among houses and men. Tea Cake and Janie stood on the edge of things and looked over the desolation.

"How kin Ah find uh doctor fuh yo' face in all dis mess?" Janie wailed.

"Ain't got de damn doctor tuh study 'bout. Us needs uh place tuh rest."

A great deal of their money and perseverance and they found a place to sleep. It was just that. No place to live at all. Just sleep. Tea Cake looked all around and sat heavily on the side of the bed. "Well," he said humbly, "reckon you never 'spected tuh come tuh dis when you took up wid me, didja?"

"Once upon uh time, Ah never 'spected nothin', Tea Cake, but bein' dead from the standin' still and tryin' tuh laugh. But you come 'long and made somethin' outa me. So Ah'm thankful fuh anything we come through together."

"Thanky, Ma'am."

"You was twice noble tuh save me from dat dawg. Tea Cake, Ah don't speck you seen his eyes lak Ah did. He didn't aim tuh jus' bite me, Tea Cake. He aimed tuh kill me stone dead. Ah'm never tuh fuhgit dem eyes. He wuzn't nothin' all over but pure hate. Wonder where he come from?"

"Yeah, Ah did see 'im too. It wuz frightenin'. Ah didn't mean tuh take his hate neither. He had tuh die uh me one. Mah switch blade said it wuz him."

"Po' me, he'd tore me tuh pieces, if it wuzn't fuh you, honey."

"You don't have tuh say, if it wuzn't fuh me, baby, cause Ah'm *heah,* and then Ah want yuh tuh know it's uh man heah."

FOCUS ON ECOLOGY

1. At the beginning of this selection from *Their Eyes Were Watching God*, how are the Seminoles depicted? What role do they play in this selection? In general, what role does race play in this piece?
2. In this selection, what is the relationship between God, nature, and survival?

FOCUS ON WRITING

1. What role does the vernacular play in this piece? Why do you suppose Hurston chose to write the dialogue in this vernacular?
2. When the lake breaks free of its dikes, Hurston describes the lake as shouting "Yes, Ah'm comin'!" What does she accomplish in giving voice to the flood waters? Why do you suppose she chose to use this strategy?
3. How do you respond to Hurston's descriptions of the hurricane? What do you find effective and ineffective about these descriptions?

FOR DISCUSSION

Each year, countless coastal residents worry about hurricanes. In the United States, much of our coastal lands are inhabited by higher socioeconomic groups—that is, beach front property tends to be owned by the wealthy. However, on island communities like Puerto Rico, the wealthy tend to live inland and on higher parts of the islands. Consider the relationship between wealth and hurricanes (or any other "natural disaster" for that matter). Then, think about the ways that Hurston has depicted the relationships between the hurricane and the black characters and the hurricane and the whites. As a class, discuss how wealth, class status, and power affect how we survive natural events.

WRITING IN RESPONSE

In recent history, several major hurricanes have caused immense amounts of damage to the United States as well as to other coastal countries. Select a hurricane from recent history and learn what effect it had on the places it made landfall. Then, write an informative essay that reports the effects of the hurricane you have selected.

To Build a Fire

Jack London

John Griffith London was born in 1876 in San Francisco, California. London wrote numerous books, articles, short stories, and essays, in addition to more than 20 novels. Many of his books, such as White Fang, The Call of the Wild, *and* The Sea-Wolf, *were first printed as serials in different publications, including* The Saturday Evening Post, Century, *and* Outing. *His writing often addresses adventure in nature, and much of it was gleaned from his own experiences. During his life, London worked numerous jobs—as a patrol agent for the San Francisco Shore Police, a logger, a seal fisher, a mill worker, a salmon canner, a gold miner in the Yukon, a coal shoveler, and an oyster pirate, to name but a few. During one period he also joined a group of unemployed men, known as Coxey's Army, who marched from San Francisco to Washington, D.C. He was once arrested for vagrancy, and ran for mayor of Oakland, California, as a Socialist. As a reporter, he covered the Russo-Japanese War in 1904 and the Mexican Revolution for* Collier's *in 1914. His short story "To Build a Fire" is considered one of London's masterpieces and is one of the most frequently anthologized short stories in American literature. The story tells of a man and a dog walking*

back to their home camp on a dangerously cold day. As you read this short story,
consider how the man reacts to the cold and how such reactions affect his chance for
survival.

JOURNAL ASSIGNMENT

"To Build a Fire" is one of the countless fictional stories of wilderness survival
that have been written in America. In your journal, consider these questions:
Why might fiction be a good genre in which to write about survival? What
does fiction allow a writer to do with survival stories that nonfiction might not?

1   Day had broken cold and gray, exceedingly cold and gray, when the man
turned aside from the main Yukon trail and climbed the high earth bank, where
a dim and little-traveled trail led eastward through the fat spruce timberland.
It was a steep bank, and he paused for breath at the top, excusing the act to
himself by looking at his watch. It was nine o'clock. There was no sun nor hint
of sun, though there was not a cloud in the sky. It was a clear day, and yet there
seemed an intangible pall over the face of things, a subtle gloom that made the
day dark, and that was due to the absence of sun. This fact did not worry the
man. He was used to the lack of sun. It had been days since he had seen the sun,
and he knew that a few more days must pass before that cheerful orb, due
south, would just peep above the sky line and dip immediately from view.

2   The man flung a look back along the way he had come. The Yukon lay a
mile wide and hidden under three feet of ice. On top of this ice were as many
feet of snow. It was all pure white, rolling in gentle undulations where the ice
jams of the freeze-up had formed. North and south, as far as his eye could see,
it was unbroken white, save for a dark hairline that curved and twisted from
around the spruce-covered island to the south, and that curved and twisted
away into the north, where it disappeared behind another spruce-covered
island. This dark hairline was the trail—the main trail—that led south five hundred miles to the Chilkoot Pass, Dyea, and salt water; and that led north seventy miles to Dawson, and still on to the north a thousand miles to Nulato, and
finally to St. Michael, on Bering Sea, a thousand miles and half a thousand more.

3   But all this—the mysterious, far-reaching hairline trail, the absence of sun
from the sky, the tremendous cold, and the strangeness and weirdness of it
all—made no impression on the man. It was not because he was long used to
it. He was a newcomer in the land, a *chechaquo*, and this was his first winter.
The trouble with him was that he was without imagination. He was quick and
alert in the things of life, but only in the things, and not in the significance.
Fifty degrees below zero meant eighty-odd degrees of frost. Such fact impressed him as being cold and uncomfortable, and that was all. It did not lead

him to meditate upon his frailty as a creature of temperature, and upon man's frailty in general, able only to live within certain narrow limits of heat and cold; and from there on it did not lead him to the conjectural field of immortality and man's place in the universe. Fifty degrees below zero stood for a bite of frost that hurt and that must be guarded against by the use of mittens, ear flaps, warm moccasins, and thick socks. Fifty degrees below zero was to him just precisely fifty degrees below zero. That there should be anything more to it than that was a thought that never entered his head.

As he turned to go on, he spat speculatively. There was a sharp, explosive 4 crackle that startled him. He spat again. And again, in the air, before it could fall to the snow, the spittle crackled. He knew that at fifty below spittle crackled on the snow, but this spittle had crackled in the air. Undoubtedly it was colder than fifty below—how much colder he did not know. But the temperature did not matter. He was bound for the old claim on the left fork of Henderson Creek, where the boys were already. They had come over across the divide from the Indian Creek country, while he had come the roundabout way to take a look at the possibilities of getting out logs in the spring from the islands in the Yukon. He would be into camp by six o'clock; a bit after dark, it was true, but the boys would be there, a fire would be going, and a hot supper would be ready. As for lunch, he pressed his hand against the protruding bundle under his jacket. It was also under his shirt, wrapped up in a handkerchief and lying against the naked skin. It was the only way to keep the biscuits from freezing. He smiled agreeably to himself as he thought of those biscuits, each cut open and sopped in bacon grease, and each enclosing a generous slice of fried bacon.

He plunged in among the big spruce trees. The trail was faint. A foot of 5 snow had fallen since the last sled had passed over, and he was glad he was without a sled, traveling light. In fact, he carried nothing but the lunch wrapped in the handkerchief. He was surprised, however, at the cold. It certainly cold, he concluded, as he rubbed his numb nose and cheekbones with his mittened hand. He was a warm-whiskered man, but the hair on his face did not protect the high cheekbones and the eager nose that thrust itself aggressively into the frosty air.

At the man's heels trotted a dog, a big native husky, the proper wolf dog, 6 gray-coated and without any visible or temperamental difference from its brother the wild wolf. The animal was depressed by the tremendous cold. It knew that it was no time for traveling. Its instinct told it a truer tale than was told to the man by the man's judgment. In reality, it was not merely colder than fifty below zero; it was colder than sixty below, than seventy below. It was seventy-five below zero. Since the freezing point is thirty-two above zero, it meant that one hundred and seven degrees of frost obtained. The dog did not know anything about thermometers. Possibly in its brain there was no sharp consciousness of a condition of very cold such as was in the man's brain. But the brute had its instinct. It experienced a vague but menacing apprehension that subdued it and made it slink along at the man's heels, and that made it question eagerly every unwonted movement of the man as if expecting him to go into camp or to seek shelter somewhere and build a fire. The dog had learned fire, and it wanted fire, or else to burrow under the snow and cuddle its warmth away from the air.

7   The frozen moisture of its breathing had settled on its fur in a fine powder of frost, and especially were its jowls, muzzle, and eyelashes whitened by its crystaled breath. The man's red beard and mustache were likewise frosted, but more solidly, the deposit taking the form of ice and increasing with every warm, moist breath he exhaled. Also, the man was chewing tobacco, and the muzzle of ice held his lips so rigidly that he was unable to clear his chin when he expelled the juice. The result was that a crystal beard of the color and solidity of amber was increasing its length on his chin. If he fell down it would shatter itself, like glass, into brittle fragments. But he did not mind the appendage. It was the penalty all tobacco chewers paid in that country, and he had been out before in two cold snaps. They had not been as cold as this, he knew, but by the spirit thermometer at Sixty Mile he knew they had been registered at fifty below and at fifty-five.

8   He held on through the level stretch of woods for several miles, crossed a wide flat of nigger heads, and dropped down a bank to the frozen bed of a small stream. This was Henderson Creek, and he knew he was ten miles from the forks. He looked at his watch. It was ten o'clock. He was making four miles an hour, and he calculated that he would arrive at the forks at half-past twelve. He decided to celebrate that event by eating his lunch there.

9   The dog dropped in again at his heels, with a tail drooping discouragement, as the man swung along the creek bed. The furrow of the old sled trail was plainly visible, but a dozen inches of snow covered the marks of the last runners. In a month no man had come up or down that silent creek. The man held steadily on. He was not much given to thinking, and just then particularly he had nothing to think about save that he would eat lunch at the forks and that at six at o'clock he would be in camp with the boys. There was nobody to talk to; and, had there been, speech would have been impossible because of the ice muzzle on his mouth. So he continued monotonously to chew tobacco and to increase the length of his amber beard.

10   Once in a while the thought reiterated itself that it was very cold and that he had never experienced such cold. As he walked along he rubbed his cheekbones and nose with the back of his mittened hand. He did this automatically, now and again changing hands. But, rub as he would, the instant he stopped his cheekbones went numb, and the following instant the end of his nose went numb. He was sure to frost his cheeks; he knew that, and experienced a pang of regret that he had not devised a nose strap of the sort Bud wore in cold snaps. Such a strap passed across the cheeks, as well, and saved them. But it didn't matter much, after all. What were frosted cheeks? A bit painful, that was all; they were never serious.

Empty as the man's mind was of thoughts, he was keenly observant, and 11
he noticed the changes in the creek, the curves and bends and timber jams, and
always he sharply noted where he placed his feet. Once, coming around a bend,
he shied abruptly, like a startled horse, curved away from the place where he
had been walking, and retreated several paces back along the trail. The creek he
knew was frozen clear to the bottom—no creek could contain water in that arctic winter—but he knew also that there were springs that bubbled out from the
hillsides and ran along under the snow and on top of the ice of the creek. He
knew that the coldest snaps never froze these springs, and he knew likewise
their danger. They were traps. They hid pools of water under the snow that
might be three inches deep, or three feet. Sometimes a skin of ice half an inch
thick covered them, and in turn was covered by the snow. Sometimes there were
alternate layers of water and ice skin, so that when one broke through he kept
on breaking through for a while, sometimes wetting himself to the waist.

That was why he had shied in such panic. He had felt the give under his 12
feet and heard the crackle of a snow-hidden ice skin. And to get his feet wet in
such a temperature meant trouble and danger. At the very least it meant delay,
for he would be forced to stop and build a fire, and under its protection to bare
his feet while he dried his socks and moccasins. He stood and studied the creek
bed and its banks, and decided that the flow of water came from the right. He
reflected awhile, rubbing his nose and cheeks, then skirted to the left, stepping
gingerly and testing the footing for each step. Once clear of the danger, he took
a fresh chew of tobacco and swung along at his four-mile gait.

In the course of the next two hours he came upon several similar traps. 13
Usually the snow above the hidden pools had a sunken, candied appearance
that advertised the danger. Once again, however, he had a close call; and once,
suspecting danger, he compelled the dog to go on in front. The dog did not
want to go. It hung back until the man shoved it forward, and then it went
quickly across the white, unbroken surface. Suddenly it broke through, floundered to one side, and got away to firmer footing. It had wet its forefeet and
legs, and almost immediately the water that clung to it turned to ice. It made
quick efforts to lick the ice off its legs, then dropped down in the snow and
began to bite out the ice that had formed between the toes. This was a matter
of instinct. To permit the ice to remain would mean sore feet. It did not know
this. It merely obeyed the mysterious prompting that arose from the deep
crypts of its being. But the man knew, having achieved a judgment on the subject, and he removed the mitten from his right hand and helped tear out the ice
particles. He did not expose his fingers more than a minute, and was astonished at the swift numbness that smote them. It certainly was cold. He pulled
on the mitten hastily, and beat the hand savagely across his chest.

At twelve o'clock the day was at its brightest. Yet the sun was too far south 14
on its winter journey to clear the horizon. The bulge of the earth intervened between it and Henderson Creek, where the man walked under a clear sky at noon

and cast no shadow. At half-past twelve, to the minute, he arrived at the forks of the creek. He was pleased at the speed he had made. If he kept it up, he would certainly be with the boys by six. He unbuttoned his jacket and shirt and drew forth his lunch. The action consumed no more than a quarter of a minute, yet in that brief moment the numbness laid hold of the exposed fingers. He did not put the mitten on, but, instead, struck the fingers a dozen sharp smashes against his leg. Then he sat down on a snow-covered log to eat. The sting that followed upon the striking of his fingers against his leg ceased so quickly that he was startled. He had had no chance to take a bite of biscuit. He struck the fingers repeatedly and returned them to the mitten, baring the other hand for the purpose of eating. He tried to take a mouthful, but the ice muzzle prevented. He had forgotten to build a fire and thaw out. He chuckled at his foolishness, and as he chuckled he noted the numbness creeping into the exposed fingers. Also, he noted that the stinging which had first come to his toes when he sat down was already passing away. He wondered whether the toes were warm or numb. He moved them inside the moccasins and decided that they were numb.

15   He pulled the mitten on hurriedly and stood up. He was a bit frightened. He stamped up and down until the stinging returned into the feet. It certainly was cold, was his thought. That man from Sulphur Creek had spoken the truth when telling how cold it sometimes got in the country. And he had laughed at him at the time! That showed one must not be too sure of things. There was no mistake about it, it *was* cold. He strode up and down, stamping his feet and threshing his arms, until reassured by the returning warmth. Then he got out matches and proceeded to make a fire. From the undergrowth, where high water of the previous spring had lodged a supply of seasoned twigs, he got his firewood. Working carefully from a small beginning, he soon had a roaring fire, over which he thawed the ice from his face and in the protection of which he ate his biscuits. For the moment the cold of space was outwitted. The dog took satisfaction in the fire, stretching out close enough for warmth and far enough away to escape being singed.

16   When the man had finished, he filled his pipe and took his comfortable time over a smoke. Then he pulled on his mittens, settled the ear flaps of his cap firmly about his ears, and took the creek trail up the left fork. The dog was disappointed and yearned back toward the fire. This man did not know cold. Possibly all the generations of his ancestry had been ignorant of cold, of real cold, of cold one hundred and seven degrees below freezing point. But the dog knew; all its ancestry knew, and it had inherited the knowledge. And it knew that it was not good to walk abroad in such fearful cold. It was the time to lie snug in a hole in the snow and wait for a curtain of cloud to be drawn across the face of outer space whence this cold came. On the other hand, there was no keen intimacy between the dog and the man. The one was the toil slave of the other, and the only caresses it had ever received were the caresses of the whiplash and of harsh and menacing throat sounds that threatened the whiplash. So the dog

made no effort to communicate its apprehension to the man. It was not concerned in the welfare of the man; it was for its own sake that it yearned back toward the fire. But the man whistled, and spoke to it with the sound of whiplashes, and the dog swung in at the man's heels and followed after.

The man took a chew of tobacco and proceeded to start a new amber beard. 17 Also, his moist breath quickly powdered with white his mustache, eyebrows, and lashes. There did not seem to be so many springs on the left fork of the Henderson, and for half an hour the man saw no signs of any. And then it happened. At a place where there were no signs, where the soft, unbroken snow seemed to advertise solidity beneath, the man broke through. It was not deep. He wet himself halfway to the knees before he floundered out to the firm crust.

He was angry, and cursed his luck aloud. He had hoped to get into camp 18 with the boys at six o'clock, and this would delay him an hour, for he would have to build a fire and dry out his footgear. This was imperative at that low temperature—he knew that much; and he turned aside to the bank, which he climbed. On top, tangled in the underbrush about the trunks of several small spruce trees, was a high-water deposit of dry firewood—sticks and twigs, principally, but also larger portions of seasoned branches and fine, dry, last year's grasses. He threw down several large pieces on top of the snow. This served for a foundation and prevented the young flame from drowning itself in the snow it would otherwise melt. The flame he got by touching a match to a small shred of birch bark that he took from his pocket. This burned even more readily than paper. Placing it on the foundation, he fed the young flame with wisps of dry grass and with the tiniest dry twigs.

He worked slowly and carefully, keenly aware of his danger. Gradually, as 19 the flame grew stronger, he increased the size of the twigs with which he fed it. He squatted in the snow, pulling the twigs out from their entanglement in the brush and feeding directly to the flame. He knew there must be no failure. When it is seventy-five below zero, a man must not fail in his first attempt to build a fire—that is, if his feet are wet. If his feet are dry, and he fails, he can run along the trail for half a mile and restore his circulation. But the circulation of wet and freezing feet cannot be restored by running when it is seventy-five below. No matter how fast he runs, the wet feet will freeze the harder.

All this the man knew. The old-timer on Sulphur Creek had told him about 20 it the previous fall, and now he was appreciating the advice. Already all sensation had gone out of his feet. To build the fire he had been forced to remove his mitten, and the fingers had quickly gone numb. His pace of four miles an hour had kept his heart pumping blood to the surface of his body and to all the extremities. But the instant he stopped, the action of the pump eased down. The cold of space smote the unprotected tip of the planet, and he, being on that unprotected tip, received the full force of the blow. The blood of his body recoiled before it. The blood was alive, like the dog, and like the dog it wanted to hide away and cover itself up from the fearful cold. So long as he walked four miles an hour, he pumped that blood, willy-nilly, to the surface; but now it ebbed away and sank down into the recesses of his body. The extremities were the first to feel its absence. His wet feet froze the faster, and his exposed fingers numbed the faster, though they had not yet begun to freeze. Nose and cheeks were already freezing, while the skin of all his body chilled as it lost its blood.

21   But he was safe. Toes and nose and cheeks would be only touched by the frost, for the fire was beginning to burn with strength. He was feeding it with twigs the size of his finger. In another minute he would be able to feed it with branches the size of his wrist and then he could remove his wet footgear, and, while it dried, he could keep his naked feet warm by the fire, rubbing them at first, of course, with snow. The fire was a success. He was safe. He remembered the advice of the old-timer on Sulphur Creek, and smiled. The old-timer had been very serious in laying down the law that no man must travel alone in the Klondike after fifty below. Well, here he was; he had had an accident; he was alone; and he had saved himself. Those old-timers were rather womanish, some of them, he thought. All a man had to do was to keep his head, and he was all right. Any man who was a man could travel alone. But it was surprising, the rapidity with which his cheeks and nose were freezing. And he had not thought his fingers could go lifeless in so short a time. Lifeless they were, for he could scarcely make them move together to grip a twig, and they seemed remote from his body and from him. When he touched a twig, he had to look and see whether or not he had hold of it. The wires were pretty well down between him and his finger ends.

22   All of which counted for little. There was the fire, snapping and crackling and promising life with every dancing flame. He started to untie his moccasins. They were coated with ice; the thick German socks were like sheaths of iron halfway to the knees; and the moccasin strings were like rods of steel all twisted and knotted as by some conflagration. For a moment he tugged with his numb fingers, then, realizing the folly of it, he drew his sheath knife.

23   But before he could cut the strings, it happened. It was his own fault or, rather, his mistake. He should not have built the fire under the spruce tree. He should have built it out in the open. But it had been easier to pull the twigs from the brush and drop them directly on the fire. Now the tree under which he had done this carried a weight of snow on its boughs. No wind had blown for weeks, and each bough was fully freighted. Each time he had pulled a twig he had communicated a slight agitation to the tree—an imperceptible agitation, so far as he was concerned, but an agitation sufficient to bring about the disaster. High up in the tree one bough capsized its load of snow. This fell on the boughs beneath capsizing them. This process continued, spreading out and involving the whole tree. It grew like an avalanche, and it descended without warning upon the man and the fire, and the fire was blotted out! Where it had burned was a mantle of fresh and disordered snow.

24   The man was shocked. It was as though he had just heard his own sentence of death. For a moment he sat and stared at the spot where the fire had been.

Then he grew very calm. Perhaps the old-timer on Sulphur Creek was right. If he had only had a trail mate he would have been in no danger now. The trail mate could have built the fire. Well, it was up to him to build the fire over again, and this second time there must be no failure. Even if he succeeded, he would most likely lose some toes. His feet must be badly frozen by now, and there would be some time before the second fire was ready.

Such were his thoughts, but he did not sit and think them. He was busy all the time they were passing through his mind. He made a new foundation for a fire, this time in the open, where no treacherous tree could blot it out. Next he gathered dry grasses and tiny twigs from the high-water flotsam. He could not bring his fingers together to pull them out, but he was able to gather them by the handful. In this way he got many rotten twigs and bits of green moss that were undesirable, but it was the best he could do. He worked methodically, even collecting an armful of the larger branches to be used later when the fire gathered strength. And all the while the dog sat and watched him, a certain yearning wistfulness in its eyes, for it looked upon him as the fire provider, and the fire was slow in coming. 25

When all was ready, the man reached in his pocket for a second piece of birch bark. He knew the bark was there, and, though he could not feel it with his fingers, he could hear its crisp rustling as he fumbled for it. Try as he would, he could not clutch hold of it. And all the time, in his consciousness, was the knowledge that each instant his feet were freezing. This thought tended to put him in a panic, but he fought against it and kept calm. He pulled on his mittens with his teeth, and threshed his arms back and forth, beating his hands with all his might against his sides. He did this sitting down, and he stood up to do it; and all the while the dog sat in the snow, its wolf brush of a tail curled around warmly over its forefeet, its sharp wolf ears pricked forward intently as it watched the man. And the man, as he beat and threshed with his arms and hands, felt a great surge of envy as he regarded the creature that was warm and secure in its natural covering. 26

After a time he was aware of the first faraway signals of sensation in his beaten fingers. The faint tingling grew stronger till it evolved into a stinging ache that was excruciating, but which the man hailed with satisfaction. He stripped the mitten from his right hand and fetched forth the birch bark. The exposed fingers were quickly going numb again. Next he brought out his bunch of sulphur matches. But the tremendous cold had already driven the life out of his fingers. In his effort to separate one match from the others, the whole bunch fell in the snow. He tried to pick it out of the snow, but failed. The dead fingers could neither touch nor clutch. He was very careful. He drove the thought of his freezing feet, and nose, and cheeks, out of his mind, devoting his whole soul to the matches. He watched, using the sense of vision in place of that of touch, and when he saw his fingers on each side the bunch, he closed them—that is, he willed to close them, for the wires were down, and the fingers did not obey. He pulled the mitten on the right hand, and beat it fiercely against 27 his knee. Then, with both mittened hands, he scooped the bunch of matches, along with much snow, into his lap. Yet he was no better off.

28   After some manipulation, he managed to get the bunch between the heels of his mittened hands. In this fashion he carried it to his mouth. The ice crackled and snapped when by a violent effort he opened his mouth. He drew the lower jaw in, curled the upper lip out of the way, and scraped the bunch with his upper teeth in order to separate a match. He succeeded in getting one, which he dropped on his lap. He was no better off. He could not pick it up. Then he devised a way. He picked it up in his teeth and scratched it on his leg. Twenty times he scratched before he succeeded in lighting it. As it flamed he held it with his teeth to the birch bark. But the burning brimstone went up his nostrils and into his lungs, causing him to cough spasmodically. The match fell into the snow and went out.

29   The old-timer on Sulphur Creek was right, he thought in the moment of controlled despair that ensued: after fifty below, a man should travel with a partner. He beat his hands, but failed in exciting any sensation. Suddenly he bared both hands, removing the mittens with his teeth. He caught the whole bunch between the heels of his hands. His arm muscles not being frozen enabled him to press the hand heels tightly against the matches. Then he scratched the bunch along his leg. It flared into flame, seventy sulphur matches at once! There was no wind to blow them out. He kept his head to one side to escape the strangling fumes, and held the blazing bunch to the birch bark. As he so held it, he became aware of sensation in his hand. His flesh was burning. He could smell it. Deep down below the surface he could feel it. The sensation developed into pain that grew acute. And still he endured it, holding that flame of the matches clumsily to the bark that would not light readily because his own burning hands were in the way, absorbing most of the flame.

30   At last, when he could endure no more, he jerked his hands apart. The blazing matches fell sizzling into the snow, but the birch bark was alight. He began laying dry grasses and the tiniest twigs on the flame. He could not pick and choose, for he had to lift the fuel between the heels of his hands. Small pieces of rotten wood and green moss clung to the twigs and he bit them off as well as he could with his teeth. He cherished the flame carefully and awkwardly. It meant life, and it must not perish. The withdrawal of blood from the surface of his body now made him begin to shiver, and he grew more awkward. A large piece of green moss fell squarely on the little fire. He tried to poke it out with his fingers, but his shivering frame made him poke too far, and he disrupted the nucleus of the little fire, the burning grass and tiny twigs separating and scattering. He tried to poke them together again, but in spite of the tenseness of the effort, his shivering got away with him, and the twigs were hopelessly scattered. Each twig gushed a puff of smoke and went out. The fire provider had failed. As he looked apathetically about him, his eyes chanced on the dog, sitting across the ruins of the fire from him, in the snow, making restless, hunching

movements, slightly lifting one forefoot and then the other, shifting its weight back and forth on them with wistful eagerness.

The sight of the dog put a wild idea into his head. He remembered the tale 31 of the man, caught in a blizzard, who killed a steer and crawled inside the carcass, and so was saved. He would kill the dog and bury his hands in the warm body until the numbness went out of them. Then he could build another fire. He spoke to the dog, calling it to him; but in his voice was a strange note of fear that frightened the animal, who had never known the man to speak in such way before. Something was the matter, and its suspicious nature sensed danger—it knew not what danger, but somewhere, somehow, in its brain arose an apprehension of the man. It flattened its ears down at the sound of the man's voice, and its restless, hunching movements and the lifting and shifting of its forefeet became more pronounced; but it would not come to the man. He got on his hands and knees and crawled toward the dog. This unusual posture again excited suspicion, and the animal sidled mincingly away.

The man sat up in the snow for a moment and struggled for calmness. Then 32 he pulled on his mittens, by means of his teeth, and got upon his feet. He glanced down at first in order to assure himself that he was really standing up, for the absence of sensation in his feet left him unrelated to the earth. His erect position in itself started to drive the webs of suspicion from the dog's mind; and when he spoke peremptorily, with the sound of whiplashes in his voice, the dog rendered its customary allegiance and came to him. As it came within reaching distance, the man lost his control. His arms flashed out to the dog, and he experienced genuine surprise when he discovered that his hands could not clutch, that there was neither bend nor feeling in the fingers. He had forgotten for the moment that they were frozen and that they were freezing more and more. All this happened quickly, and before the animal could get away, he encircled its body with its arms. He sat down in the snow, and in this fashion held the dog, while it snarled and whined and struggled.

But it was all he could do, hold its body encircled in his arms and sit there. 33 He realized that he could not kill the dog. There was no way to do it. With his helpless hands he could neither draw nor hold his sheath knife nor throttle the animal. He released it, and it plunged wildly away, with tail between it's legs and still snarling. It halted forty feet away and surveyed him curiously, with ears sharply pricked forward.

The man looked down at his hands in order to locate them, and found them 34 hanging on the ends of his arms. It struck him as curious that one should have to use his eyes in order to find out where his hands were. He began threshing his arms back and forth, beating the mittened hands against his sides. He did this for five minutes, violently, and his heart pumped enough blood up to the surface to put a stop to his shivering. But no sensation was aroused in the hands. He had an impression that they hung like weights on the ends of his arms, but when he tried to run the impression down, he could not find it.

35   A certain fear of death, dull and oppressive, came to him. This fear quickly became poignant as he realized that it was no longer a mere matter of freezing his fingers and toes, or of losing his hands and feet, but that it was a matter of life and death with the chances against him. This threw him into a panic, and he turned and ran up the creek bed along the old, dim trail. The dog joined in behind and kept up with him. He ran blindly, without intention, in fear such as he had never known in his life. Slowly, as he plowed and floundered through the snow, he began to see things again—the banks of the creek, the old timber jams, the leafless aspens, and the sky. The running made him feel better. He did not shiver. Maybe, if he ran on, his feet would thaw out; and, anyway, if he ran far enough he would reach the camp and the boys. Without doubt he would lose some fingers and toes and some of his face; but the boys would take care of him, and save the rest of him when he got there. And at the same time there was another thought in his mind that said he would never get to the camp and the boys; that it was too many miles away, that the freezing had too great a start on him, and that he would soon be stiff and dead. This thought he kept in the background and refused to consider. Sometimes it pushed itself forward and demanded to be heard, but he thrust it back and strove to think of other things.

36   It struck him as curious that he could run at all on feet so frozen that he could not feel them when they struck the earth and took the weight of his body. He seemed to himself to skim along above the surface, and to have no connection with the earth. Somewhere he had once seen a winged Mercury, and he wondered if Mercury felt as he felt when skimming over the earth.

37   His theory of running until he reached camp and the boys had one flaw in it: he lacked the endurance. Several times he stumbled, and finally he tottered, crumpled up, and fell. When he tried to rise, he failed. He must sit and rest, he decided, and next time he would merely walk and keep on going. As he sat and regained his breath, he noted that he was feeling quite warm and comfortable. He was not shivering, and it even seemed that a warm glow had come to his chest and trunk. And yet, when he touched his nose or cheeks, there was no sensation. Running would not thaw them out. Nor would it thaw out his hands and feet. Then the thought came to him that the frozen portions of his body must be extending. He tried to keep this thought down, to forget it, to think of something else; he was aware of the panicky feeling that it caused, and he was afraid of the panic. But the thought asserted itself, and persisted, until it produced a vision of his body totally frozen. This was too much, and he made another wild run along the trail. Once he slowed down to a walk, but the thought of freezing extending itself made him run again.

38   And all the time the dog ran with him, at his heels. When he fell down a second time, it curled its tail over its forefeet and sat in front of him, facing him curiously eager and intent. The warmth and security of the animal angered him, and he cursed it till it flattened down its ears appeasingly. This time the shivering came more quickly upon the man. He was losing in his battle with the frost. It was creeping into his body from all sides. The thought of it drove

him on, but he ran no more than a hundred feet, when he staggered and pitched headlong. It was his last panic. When he had recovered his breath and control, he sat up and entertained in his mind the conception of meeting death with dignity. However, the conception did not come to him in such terms. His idea of it was that he had been making a fool of himself, running around like a chicken with its head cut off—such was the simile that occurred to him. Well, he was bound to freeze anyway, and he might as well take it decently. With this new-found peace of mind came the first glimmerings of drowsiness. A good idea, he thought, to sleep off to death. It was like taking an anesthetic. Freezing was not so bad as people thought. There were lots worse ways to die.

He pictured the boys finding his body next day. Suddenly he found himself 39 with them, coming along the trail and looking for himself. And, still with them, he came around a turn in the trail and found himself lying in the snow. He did not belong to himself any more, for even then he was out of himself, standing with the boys and looking at himself in the snow. It certainly was cold, was his thought. When he got back to the States he could tell the folks what real cold was. He drifted on from this to a vision of the old-timer on Sulphur Creek. He could see him quite clearly, warm and comfortable, and smoking a pipe.

"You were right, old hoss; you were right," the man mumbled to the old- 40 timer of Sulphur Creek.

Then the man drowsed off into what seemed to him the most comfortable 41 and satisfying sleep he had ever known. The dog sat facing him and waiting. The brief day drew to a close in a long, slow twilight. There were no signs of a fire to be made, and, besides, never in the dog's experience had it known a man to sit like that in the snow and make no fire. As the twilight drew on, its eager yearning for the fire mastered it, and with a great lifting and shifting of forefeet, it whined softly, then flattened its ears down in anticipation of being chidden by the man. But the man remained silent. Later the dog whined loudly. And still later it crept close to the man and caught the scent of death. This made the animal bristle and back away. A little longer it delayed, howling under the stars that leaped and danced and shone brightly in the cold sky. Then it turned and trotted up the trail in the direction of the camp it knew, where were the other food providers and fire providers.

FOCUS ON ECOLOGY

1. Where does this story take place? What do you know about the region? What does Jack London tell us about that region? Does the place where the story happens matter much to the story? Could this story have taken place in Siberia?
2. Notice that the main character of this story is a *chechaquo*, a newcomer to the region. What role do you suspect his being a novice plays in his ability to survive? What might Jack London be suggesting about regional knowledge?

FOCUS ON WRITING

1. Several of the selections found in this chapter (such as those by Steven Callahan, Art Davidson, and Jon Krakauer) are nonfictional accounts of survival—"real-life" stories. But Jack London's "To Build a Fire" is fictional. How do you respond to this fictional work compared to the nonfiction pieces you have read? Is a fictional survival story different from the "true" ones?
2. Why doesn't Jack London name the man? Would giving the man a name have affected the story?
3. Why do you suppose Jack London wrote "To Build a Fire" in the third person rather than in the first? How might you respond to a similar story told from the first-person perspective?

FOR DISCUSSION

At the end of this story we know that the man freezes to death and the dog survives. As a class, discuss why the dog survives and the man doesn't. Is the dog "naturally" better equipped to survive in such environmental conditions? Was the dog "smarter" about the situation than the man was?

WRITING IN RESPONSE

For this assignment, write a fictional account of a single individual lost in the wilderness. Be sure to account for how and why the person became lost. Explain how the person attempts to survive. Detail the environmental conditions of where the person is lost. Consider the mental condition and reactions of the individual. Consider how the person gathers food, prevents injury, or contends with starvation or injury.

Killer Wave Survivors

Pier Porrino

"Killer Wave Survivors" is taken from the November 29, 2001, edition of the San Francisco Examiner *online. Reported as a news story, it tells of two water-safety specialists who survive four consecutive monster waves. This story, though reported in a San Francisco newspaper, likely did not appear in most newspapers around the country. As you read this report, consider why this news was probably not circulated more widely than it was.*

JOURNAL ASSIGNMENT

In your journal, consider what might happen to a professional rescuer and a rescue student when they are confronted with a sudden survival situation. How might their training play a role in their reactions?

Big-wave season is on at Maverick's. But Shawn Alladio and Jonathan Cahill 1 already know that.

Alladio, 40, a water-safety specialist, and student Jonathan Cahill, 19, are still 2 recovering from getting caught in a massive series of waves that observers at the infamous Half Moon Bay big-wave spot say is the biggest they've ever seen.

The pair were three miles out at sea Nov. 21 as their version of "The Perfect 3 Storm" began to unfold. After a morning of solid, consistent surf, a crew of surfers returned to shore about 1:30 p.m. Thirty minutes later, Alladio and Cahill headed back out to the break in their Jetski-type watercraft.

"We wanted to experience the ocean as the swell peaked," Alladio said. 4 "Also, we didn't want to leave the break unguarded in case there were late arrivals, or tow-in surfers going back out."

But spectators on the cliff at nearby Pillar Point watched in shock, sensing 5 they were about to witness a horrific tragedy, as a wall of water estimated to be three miles long and 100 feet high moved across the horizon heading directly into the path of Alladio and Cahill.

Jeff Clark, the surfing legend who pioneered Maverick's in the mid-1970s 6 and has surfed the spot for more than 25 years, claimed it was "the biggest swell I have ever seen here."

Alladio has spent years around Maverick's gargantuan swells. But even 7 she was not prepared for what she was about to witness—and live through.

"I had been out on the water since daybreak, and my eyes were blurry from 8 all of the salt, Alladio said. "When I first saw the wave I blinked . . . rubbed my eyes, and blinked again. I simply could not process what I was seeing."

The rogue wave was moving at gazelle-like speed—and it was beginning 9 to feather. The channel (pipeline) had closed out, leaving no means of escape.

Their only chance of survival was to head up the face of the monster wave. 10

"It was a race for our lives—a survival ride," Alladio said, "I looked at JC, 11 and he was hanging tough and riding smart."

"It was like riding a dirt bike up a really steep hill, only the hill was mov- 12 ing," Cahill said. "I knew if we fell, or hesitated at all, we would die out there."

As their boats cleared the peak, they dropped 50 feet in the air, freefalling 13 and then impacting full-force into the ocean below. As they cleared the crest, they began to realize what the spectators on the cliff already knew—there were four more waves in this rogue set, and their size was building.

"When we cleared the final wave we stopped the WaveRunners and started 14 screaming, 'Oh, my God. Oh, my God,' over and over again," Alladio recalled.

15   The California Department of Boating and Waterways reports rogue waves are more common than one would think. Also referred to as "sneaker sets," they can appear with little or no warning and in seemingly moderate to calm sea conditions. Sneaker sets were witnessed previously at Pillar Point Harbor, as well as in Tomales Bay in Marin County, and Eureka in Humboldt County.

16   Last week's rogue set reverberated up and down the coast with such intensity that it moved cars in the parking lot at Rockaway Beach in Pacifica and tossed boulders and spectators off the jetty and into the water at Pillar Point Harbor.

17   For Alladio and Clark, big-wave enthusiasts who spend their lives chasing storm systems, last week's events were a clear indicator that the monster-wave season had arrived.

18   The Quiksilver/Maverick's Men who Ride Mountains contest kicks off officially on Dec. 8. On contest day, 20 competitors will vie for a total purse of $75,000 and a first-place prize of $30,000.

19   This year's event is dedicated to the memory of Jay Moriarity, a beloved Maverick's surfer from Santa Cruz who drowned in a free-diving accident in the Maldives in June while training for the upcoming big-wave season.

20   With a waiting period that runs through March 31, contest director Clark will be looking for the perfect day to hold the event—a day that combines the best of tide, wind and swell. Alladio will be working with Clark to provide water rescue for the elite cadre of big-wave surfers who will be competing at the event.

21   But Alladio won't soon forget the feeling she had after she cleared that final, deadly wave. "I was holding my head with both hands like my mind had been blown, because it had," she said.

FOCUS ON ECOLOGY

1. Why would 100-foot-high waves move cars parked a distance away from the impact zone? What is the effect of large waves hitting the shore?
2. How do you react to this story? Would you like to be racing to climb a 100-foot-high wave before it began to crash down?
3. Why do you suppose Alladio called their escape specifically "a survival ride"?

FOCUS ON WRITING

1. Why does Porrino make reference to *The Perfect Storm* when discussing rogue waves? To what does this refer? Does Porrino assume his readers will understand this reference?
2. Why is this piece written in such short paragraph form? How does this form affect the information conveyed?
3. Why would a story like this be printed in a newspaper? What does placing this story in a newspaper suggest about how we read and come to understand and think about an event like the one described here?

FOR DISCUSSION

Each year countless numbers of surfers, climbers, kayakers, and other adventurers (and nonadventurers) are rescued from survival situations by professional rescuers. What do you know about professional wilderness rescuers? As a class, discuss why people like Shawn Alladio and Jonathan Cahill become professional rescuers.

WRITING IN RESPONSE

Each year, newspapers around the country print stories of survival similar to the one reprinted here. Look through the last year of your local newspaper (searchable indices and data bases should make this easy) and find a story about someone surviving a natural event. Consider how it is written in comparison with Porrino's article. Does there seem to be a common rhetorical strategy for reporting survival stories in newspapers? In a short paper, compare and contrast the article you found with Porrino's article.

Come Quick!
I'm Being Eaten by a Bear

Cynthia Dusel-Bacon

In 1977, when Cynthia Dusel-Bacon was 31 and working as a field geologist in Alaska, she was attacked by a bear. The bear severed her right arm at the shoulder and her left arm just below the shoulder. She survived the attack, and she now says "I'm lucky to be alive." Fitted now with two prosthetic arms, Dusel-Bacon relies on several assistive devices such as light switches she steps on, straws for drinking, hair brushes and hair dryers mounted to the wall, and mouth sticks. The essay reprinted here was originally published in 1981 in the book Killer Bears *by Mike Cramond and reprinted in 1998 in the book* Attacked!, *edited by John Long. As you read this remarkable story, consider how Dusel-Bacon handled the attack and the language with which she describes such a frightening moment in her life.*

JOURNAL ASSIGNMENT

Like tales of sharks, stories of bear attacks have created a mythology of fear and respect for bears. In your journal, consider what you know about bears. How many kinds of bears are there? Where do they live? Why might a bear attack a person? Have you heard stories of bear attacks?

1   The summer of 1977 was my third summer in the Yukon-Tanana Upland of Alaska, doing geologic field mapping for the Alaskan Geology Branch of the U.S. Geological Survey. I began working for the USGS in the summer of 1975, making helicopter-assisted traverses in the highest terrain of the 6,000-square-mile Big Delta quadrangle.

2   The second summer, the project chief and I found it necessary to map the geology by backpacking, usually a week at a time, because our budget did not provide for helicopter expenses. Then, in 1977, we were again funded for helicopter transport, after an initial month of backpacking. All five geologists in our group, after being transported by air to the field area, usually mapped alone. Although I was concerned about the added risk brought about by working alone, I did enjoy the solitude and the opportunity to be by myself in a beautiful wilderness area.

3   Every summer in the upland area we saw bears. The first one I saw was walking slowly along on the far side of a small mountain meadow. I froze. It didn't see me and disappeared into the forest. Another time I was walking through a spruce forest and saw a black bear moving through the trees some distance away. Again, I apparently was not noticed. The second summer while I was backpacking, I encountered a small black bear coming along the trail toward me. I had been busy looking down at the ground for chips of rock when I heard a slight rustling sound. I looked up to see the bear about 40 feet in front of me. Startled, it turned around and ran off in the other direction, crashing through the brush as it left the trail. This particular experience reassured me that what I had heard about black bears being afraid of people was, in fact, true.

4   During the third summer, I saw my first grizzly, but only from the air. Although other members of our field party had seen them on the ground, I felt fortunate to have encountered only black bears. Grizzlies were generally considered to be more unpredictable and dangerous.

5   I had hiked through the bush unarmed each summer, because our project chief felt that guns would add more danger to an encounter than they might prevent. A wounded, angry bear would probably be more dangerous than a frightened one. Consequently, she had strongly discouraged us from carrying any kind of firearm. We all carried walkie-talkie radios to keep in constant touch with one another and with our base camp. Everyone was well aware of the dangers of surprising bears or getting between a mother and her cubs. Whenever I was doing field mapping, I always attempted to make noise as I walked, so that I would alert any bears within hearing distance and give them time to run away from me. For two summers this system worked perfectly.

In the summer of 1977 we were scheduled to complete the reconnaissance 6
mapping of the Big Delta quadrangle. Since it is such a large area, we needed
helicopter transportation to finish by mid-September. At about 8:30 A.M., August 13, 1977, Ed Spencer, our helicopter pilot, dropped me off near the top of a
rocky, brush-covered ridge approximately 60 miles southeast of Fairbanks. I
was dressed in khaki work pants and a cotton shirt. I wore sturdy hiking boots
and carried a rucksack. In the right outside pocket of my pack I carried a light
lunch of baked beans, canned fruit, fruit juice, and a few crackers. My walkie-
talkie was in the left outside pocket, complete with covering flap, strap, and
buckle. I was to take notes on the geology, collect samples with the geologist's
hammer I carried on my belt, record my location on the map, and stow the samples in my rucksack. Standard safety procedure called for me to make radio
contact with the other geologists and with our base camp several times during
the day at regular intervals. The radio in camp, about 80 miles south of the
mapping area, was being monitored by the wife of the helicopter pilot. I was to
be picked up by helicopter at the base of the four-mile-long ridge on a gravel
bar of the river at the end of the day.

After noticing, with unexpected pleasure, that I was going to be able to use 7
a narrow trail that had been bulldozed along the crest of the ridge, I started off
downhill easily, on the trail that passed through tangles of birch brush and over
rough, rocky slopes. The ridge was in one of the more accessible parts of the
quadrangle. There are a few small cabins about five to ten miles downstream
along the Salcha River, and a short landing strip for airplanes is about five miles
from the ridge. Fishermen sometimes venture this far up the river too, so bears
in the area probably have seen human beings on occasion. That particular morning I wasn't expecting to see bears at all; the hillside was so rocky and so dry
and tangled with brush that it just didn't seem like bear country. I felt that if I
were to see a bear at all that day, it would likely be at the end of the day, down
along the river bar and adjoining woods.

I descended the ridge slowly for several hundred yards, moving from one 8
outcrop of rock to another, breaking off samples and putting them in my pack.
I stopped at one large outcrop to break off an interesting piece and examine it.
A sudden loud crash in the undergrowth startled me and I looked around just
in time to see a black bear rise up out of the brush 10 feet away.

My first thought was, "Oh no! A bear. I'd better do the right thing." My next 9
thought was one of relief. "It's only a black bear, and a rather small one at that."
Nevertheless, I decided to get the upper hand immediately and scare it away.

I shouted at it, face to face, in my most commanding tone of voice. "Shoo! 10
Get out of here, bear! Go on! Get away!" The bear remained motionless and
glared back at me. I clapped my hands and yelled even louder. But even that
had no effect. Instead of turning and running away into the brush, the bear
began slowly walking, climbing toward my level, watching me steadily. I
waved my arms, clapped and yelled even more wildly. I began banging on the
outcrop with my hammer, making all the noise I could to intimidate the bear.

11   I took a step back, managing to elevate myself another foot or so in an attempt to reach a more dominant position. By this time the bear had reached the trail I was on and was slightly uphill from me. It slowly looked up the hill in the direction from which I had come and then stared back at me again. I knew that in this moment the bear was trying to decide whether it should retreat from me or attack. Suddenly the bear darted around behind the outcrop and behind me. My next sensation was that of being struck a staggering blow from behind. I felt myself being thrown forward, and I landed face down on the ground, with my arms outstretched.

12   I froze, not instinctively but deliberately, remembering that playing dead was supposed to cause an attacking bear to lose interest and go away. Instead of hearing the bear crashing off through the brush, though, I felt the sudden piercing pain of the bear's teeth biting deep into my right shoulder. I felt myself being shaken with tremendous, irresistible power by teeth deep in my shoulder. After playing dead for several minutes, I came to the horrible realization that the bear had no intention of abandoning its prey.

13   "I've got to get my radio in the pack. I've got to get a call out," I thought.

14   My left arm was free, so I tried to reach behind myself to the left outside pocket of my rucksack to get at the walkie-talkie. My heart sank as I discovered that the buckled flap on the pocket prevented me from getting out my radio. My movement caused the bear to start a new flurry of biting and tearing at the flesh of my upper right arm again. I was completely conscious of feeling my flesh torn, teeth against bone, but the sensation was more of numb horror at what was happening to me than of specific reaction to each bite. I remember thinking, "Now I'm never going to be able to call for help. I'm dead unless this bear decides to leave me alone."

15   The bear had no intention of leaving me alone. After chewing on my right shoulder, arm, and side repeatedly, the bear began to bite my head and tear at my scalp. As I heard the horrible crunching sound of the bear's teeth biting into my skull, I realized it was all too hopeless. I remember thinking, "This has got to be the worst way to go." I knew it would be a slow death because my vital signs were all still strong. My fate was to bleed to death. I thought, "Maybe I should just shake my head and get the bear to do me in quickly."

16   All of a sudden, the bear clamped its jaws into me and began dragging me by the right arm down the slope through the brush. I was dragged about 20 feet or so before the bear stopped to rest, panting in my ear. It began licking at the blood that was now running out of a large wound under my right arm. Again the bear pulled me along the ground, over rocks and through brush, stopping frequently to rest, and chewing at my arm. Finally it stopped, panting heavily. It had been dragging me and my 20-pound pack—a combined weight of about 150 pounds—for almost half an hour over rocks and through brush. Now it walked about four feet away and sat down to rest, still watching me intently.

17   Here, I thought, might be a chance to save myself yet—if only I could get at that radio. Slowly I moved my left arm, which was on the side away from the bear, and which was still undamaged, behind me to get at that pack buckle.

But this time the pocket, instead of being latched tight, was wide open—the buckle probably was torn off by the bear's clawing or from being dragged over the rocks. I managed to reach down into the pocket and pull out the radio. Since my right arm was now completely numb and useless, I used my left hand to stealthily snap on the radio switch, pull up two of the three segments of the antenna, and push in the button activating the transmitter. Holding the radio close to my mouth, I said as loudly as I dared, "Ed, this is Cynthia. Come quick, I'm being eaten by a bear." I said "eaten" because I was convinced that the bear wasn't just mauling me or playing with me, but was planning to consume me. I was its prey, and it had no intention of letting me escape.

I repeated my message and then started to call out some information. "Ed, [18] I'm just down the hill from where you left me off this morning . . ." but I got no further. By this time the bear had risen to its feet; it bounded quickly over to me and savagely attacked my left arm, knocking the radio out of my hand. I screamed in pain as I felt my good arm being torn and mangled by claws and teeth.

It was then I realized I had done all I could do to save my own life. I had [19] no way of knowing whether anyone had even heard my calls. I really doubted it, since no static or answering sound from anyone trying to call had come back over the receiver. I knew I hadn't taken time to extend the antenna completely. I knew I was down in a ravine, with many ridges between me and a receiving set. I knew there was really no chance for me. I was doomed. So I screamed as the bear tore at my arm, figuring that it was going to eat me anyway and there was no longer any reason to try to control my natural reactions. I remember that the bear then began sniffing around my body, down my calves, up my thighs. I could read the bear's mind as it tried to decide whether it should open new wounds or continue on the old ones.

I didn't dare look around at what was happening—my eyes were fixed [20] upon the dirt and leaves on the ground only inches below my face. Then I felt a tearing at the pack on my back, and heard the bear begin crunching cans in its teeth—cans I had brought for my lunch. This seemed to occupy its attention for a while; at least it left my arms alone and gave me a few moments to focus my mind on my predicament.

"Is this how I'm going to go?" I remember marveling at how clear my mind [21] was, how keen my senses were. All I could think of as I lay there on my stomach, with my face down in the dry grass and dirt and that merciless, bloodthirsty animal holding me down, was how much I wanted to live and how much I wanted to go back to Charlie, my husband of five months, and how tragic it would be to end it all three days before I turned thirty-one.

It was about ten minutes, I think, before I heard the faint sound of a heli- [22] copter in the distance. It came closer and then seemed to circle, as if making a pass, but not directly over me. Then I heard the helicopter going away, leaving me. What had gone wrong? Was it just a routine pass to transfer one of the other geologists to a different ridge, or to go to a gas cache to refuel and not an answer to my call for help? Had no one heard my call?

23   The bear had not been frightened by the sound of the helicopter. Having finished with the contents of my pack, it began to tear again at the flesh under my right arm. Then I heard the helicopter coming back, circling, getting closer. Being flat on my face, with both arms now completely without feeling, I kicked my legs to show whoever was up above me that I was still alive. This time, however, I was certain that I was to be rescued because the pilot hovered directly over me. But again I heard the helicopter suddenly start away over the ridge. In a few seconds all was silent; it was an agonizing silence. I couldn't believe it. For some reason they'd left me for the second time.

24   Suddenly I felt, or sensed, that the bear was not beside me. The sound of the chopper had frightened it away. Again—for about ten minutes—I waited in silence. Then I heard the helicopter coming over the ridge again, fast and directly toward me. In a few seconds the deafening, beautiful sound was right over me. I kicked my legs again and heard the helicopter move up toward the crest of the ridge for what I was now sure was a landing. Finally I heard the engine shut down, then voices, and people calling out. I yelled back to direct them to where I was lying. But the birch brush was thick, and with my khaki work pants and gray pack I was probably difficult to see lying on the ground among the rocks.

25   Ed was the first to spot me, and he called the two women geologists down the slope to help him. Together they managed to carry me up the hill and lift me up into the back seat of the helicopter. I remember the feeling of relief and thankfulness that swept over me when I found myself in that helicopter, going up and away over the mountain. I knew that my mind was clear and my breathing was good and my insides were all intact. All I had to do was keep cool and let the doctors fix me up. Deep down, though, I knew the extent of my injuries and knew that I had been too badly hurt for my body to ever be the same again.

26   They flew me to Fort Greeley army base in Delta Junction, about an hour's trip. There emergency measures were taken to stabilize my condition. I was given blood and probably some morphine to deaden the pain. An hour or so later I was flown up to the army hospital in Fairbanks and taken immediately into surgery. For the first time that day I lost consciousness—under the anesthesia.

27   My left arm had to be amputated above the elbow, about halfway between elbow and shoulder, because most of the flesh had been torn from my forearm and elbow. To try to save my right arm, which had not been so badly chewed, the doctors took a vein out of my left thigh and grafted it from underneath my badly damaged right arm, through the torn upper arm, and out to my lower arm. This vein became an artery to keep the blood circulating through my forearm and hand. Four surgeons continued working on me for about five hours, late into the evening. They also did some "debriding"—that is, removing hopelessly damaged tissue and cleaning the lacerated wounds of leaves, sticks, and dirt. I stayed at Fairbanks overnight and then was flown out at 3:00 P.M. Sunday for San Francisco.

By this time our branch chief had managed to notify Charlie, also a geolo- 28
gist for the U.S. Geological Survey, of my accident. Both were waiting for me
when I arrived at the San Francisco airport at 1:00 A.M. Monday. I was taken immediately by ambulance to Stanford Hospital and put in the intensive-care ward.

Then began the vain attempts to save my right arm. For more than a week 29
I held every hope that the vein graft was going to work. But a blood clot developed in the transplanted artery and circulation stopped. The pulse that had
been felt in my right wrist and the warmth in my fingers disappeared and the
whole arm became cold. Although another amputation was clearly going to be
necessary, the doctors felt they should wait until a clearer line between good
tissue and bad tissue became evident. Then they would amputate up to this
point and save the rest.

But before that line appeared, I began to run a very high temperature. Fear- 30
ing that the infected and dying arm was now endangering my life, the doctors
took me into the operating room, found the tissue in my arm to be dead almost
to the top of my shoulder, and removed the entire arm. Not even a stump of
that arm could be saved.

As if this was not trouble enough, my side underneath the right shoulder 31
had been opened up by the bear when it tore out and consumed the lymph
glands under my right arm. This area was raw and extremely susceptible to infection. It eventually would have to be covered by skin grafts, skin stripped
from my own body. But before the skin graft could be done, new tissue would
have to be regenerated in the wound to cover the exposed muscle and bone. I
stayed in the hospital for weeks, absorbing nourishing fluids and antibiotics
intravenously and eating high-protein meals of solid foods. Slowly, new flesh
grew back to fill the hole, and the plastic surgeon was able to graft strips of
skin taken from my right thigh to cover the raw flesh under my right shoulder.
The thigh skin was laid on in strips like rolls of sod, kept clean and open to the
air for many days, until it "took." These operations hospitalized me for a total
of six weeks.

I am determined to lead as normal a life as possible. I know that there are 32
certain limitations I can't get around, having to rely on artificial arms. But I'm
certainly going to do the best I can with all that I have left. And that's a lot.

FOCUS ON ECOLOGY

1. Why did Cynthia Dusel-Bacon assume she would see no bears the day she
   was attacked?
2. How does Cynthia Dusel-Bacon describe the bear that attacks her? Is she
   angry at the bear? Does she depict the bear as evil, intelligent, or malevolent?
3. Cynthia Dusel-Bacon writes, "I froze, not instinctively but deliberately, remembering that playing dead was supposed to cause an attacking bear to
   lose interest and go away." Was this the correct response? What else might
   Dusel-Bacon have done in this situation?

FOCUS ON WRITING

1. Why does Cynthia Dusel-Bacon begin her essay by telling readers of her previous bear encounters?
2. Which part of this essay do you find more disturbing: the section that describes the attack or the section that describes the results and aftermath of the attack? Why?
3. Could this story be told by a third-person narrator, by a voice other than Cynthia Dusel-Bacon's? Would it be as powerful if it were?

FOR DISCUSSION

In the case of the bear that attacked Cynthia Dusel-Bacon, after the bear is frightened away by the helicopter, there is little mention of what became of it. However, in many instances, animals that attack people are hunted and killed. As a class, consider this response to animal attacks. Should animals that attack humans be destroyed? Why or why not?

WRITING IN RESPONSE

Like shark attack stories, there are many famous bear attack stories. Locate another bear attack story and write a summary of that account. Then compare the events of that attack to the events of the Dusel-Bacon attack. Where did the attacks take place? How did the victims respond? How is the bear described? What happens to the bear after the attack? How does each story make you feel about bears?

DISCUSSING THE ISSUES

1. In several of the essays in this chapter, food becomes a crucial issue for survival. Food deprivation is often the most dangerous aspect of survival, not necessarily attack or injury. As a class, consider the role food plays in survival and how we tend to think about food in stories of survival.
2. Though each of the readings and films addresses survival differently, there do seem to be a few issues consistent throughout the chapter. Of these, the thought processes of the survivors seem to be prevalent in most of the selections. As a class, consider why mental acuity might be such an important part of how we see survival and how we read survival narratives.
3. Other than Cynthia Dusel-Bacon, Sara Corbett's article, and Shawn Alladio, there is little mention of women in these discussions of survival. Why might that be? Is this merely an editorial flaw on my behalf, or are survival stories more often seen as masculine stories? As a class, consider the role of gender in our attention to survival narratives.

WRITING ABOUT THE ISSUES

1. *Personal Experience:* Have you ever faced a survival scenario? Ever heard a good survival story from someone you know? In a personal narrative, tell a survival story that is familiar to you. Consider what makes a survival story worth telling.
2. *Local Context:* Chances are that someone has been forced into a survival scenario in your hometown or in local environments. Tornadoes, earthquakes, fires, or storms may have placed someone from your region in a survival scenarios. Someone may have been lost in local woods, desert, river, or mountains. Take some time to learn about local survival stories. Then, recount what you have learned about local environments and survival narratives.
3. *Research:* As I mentioned at the outset of this chapter, countless survival narratives are available to us in a variety of textual forms. Take some time to locate three or four survival narratives that address a similar survival scenario: lost at sea, lost in the woods, attacked by bears, and so on. Once you have read these accounts, write an essay that both compares and contrasts these texts and that examines the narratives for similarities as survival narratives.

RESEARCH PATHS

Cynthia Dusel-Bacon (www.fingertoes.theyeti.com/Cynthia.html)
Search and Rescue Dogs (sardog.org/index.asp)
Storm Stories (www.weather.com/newscenter/stormstories/)
Simply Survival (www.simplysurvival.com/surv_stories.html)
National Geographic Survival Forum (www.nationalgeographic.com/
    adventure/0111/forum_survival.html)
Men and Women against Nature (a bibliography) (library.ci.scottsdale.az.us/
    adult/againstnature.htm)

FURTHER READINGS

Gareth Wood, *South Pole: 900 Miles on Foot*
Jon Krakauer, *Into Thin Air*
Jon Krakauer, *Into the Wild*
Clint Willis, ed. *Epic: Stories of Survival from the World's Highest Peaks*
Art Davidson, *Minus 148°: The Winter Ascent of Mt. McKinley*
Bill Sherwonit, *The Top of Denali: Climbing Adventures on North America's
    Highest Peak*
R. J. Secor, *Denali Climbing Guide*
Film, *Cast Away*
Film, *The Perfect Storm*
Film, *Volcano*

Film, *Dante's Peak*
Film, *A Far Off Place*
William Golding, *Lord of the Flies*
Johann Wyss, *The Swiss Family Robinson*
John Long, *Attacked!*
Mike Cramond, *Killer Bears*
Louise Longo, *Let Me Survive: A True Story of Tragic Loss of Life at Sea*
Patrick Dillon, *Lost at Sea*
Spike Walker, *Nights of Ice: True Stories of Disaster and Survival on Alaska's High Seas*
Larry Kaniut, *Alaska Bear Tales*

CHAPTER **6**

Living With/In Nature

In the previous chapter, we examined how stories of survival pit human beings against forces of nature, and how reading and writing those stories affects how we think about our relationship to nature. In this chapter we are going to examine another facet of nature. We are going to ask what it means to live in and live with nature. That is, we are going to read and write about how humans live not in an antagonistic relationship with their surroundings but in a symbiotic relationship with them.

Just as American culture has a long history of narratives that situate humans struggling against nature, so too is there a tradition of addressing how humans can be a part of their environments. Writers like Henry David Thoreau (page 000), Rachel Carson (page 000), Edward Abbey (page 000), bell hooks (page 000), and Terry Tempest Williams (page 000) are only a few of the numerous writers who have produced texts that discuss nature as integral to how we live. What each of these writers posits is that the places in which we live have a direct effect on how we live, that being aware of and careful with the environments in which we live will improve our own quality of life.

As you read the selections found here, you should begin to think not only about the ways in which people venture into particular environments for recreational purposes (see Chapter 3) and then leave those places, or even how people are sometimes forced to survive against particular forces of nature (see Chapter 5), but instead how on a daily basis we all live *in* places, in environments, in nature. For many, there is a conscious decision to move away from urban areas to more rural, natural areas. For others, there is the recognition that all places, whether rural or urban, maintain elements of nature and require that we be aware of our environments. This chapter asks that we begin to think about how our daily lives require an acknowledgment of the places and environments we inhabit. Think, for instance, of the air you breathe, the food you eat, the water you drink. Think also about the organisms you encounter every day: ants, roaches, birds, dogs, cats, or other domesticated and nondomesticated animals. Think about the wood used to build buildings or the mined ore used to make the metals of cars, trains, and planes. Think, that is, about how our lives as human beings are inextricably linked to particular places, as well as the "resources" those places provide.

To facilitate our thinking about such issues, the selections found here address a variety of ways of thinking about living in and with nature. The readings ask you to think about

- making a conscious choice to live more closely connected with nature
- living within the means of what places, environments, and nature provide
- living in places normally considered "wilderness"
- retreating to a wilderness lifestyle to avoid the complexities of "civilized" life
- learning about our own lives through observation of places, environments, and nature
- how development affects the places in which we live and the cultures of those places
- how we "work" land and come to know that land through our work
- the ways in which nature is present even in city life
- the role of rivers in the history of African-Americans
- how the places in which we live affect how we see the world
- how we pollute the places in which we live
- how places, environment, and nature helped to comfort us after the terror of the September 11, 2001 attacks

"Where I Lived and What I Lived For" from *Walden*

Henry David Thoreau

Walden, *from which the reprinted selection "Where I Lived and What I Lived For" is taken, is one of the most important and influential works in American nature writing and* Henery David Thoreau *himself is known as one of America's greatest writers. During Thoreau's lifetime, however, he was not so widely acclaimed.* Walden *is an account of about two years that Thoreau spent living in his cabin in Concord, Massachusetts, the place of his birth in 1817. Thoreau, who vocally protested slavery during his time, has been noted as influencing the thinking and work of Mahatma Ghandi and Martin Luther King, Jr. During his lifetime, Thoreau was a close friend of Ralph Waldo Emerson (see Chapters 1 and 7). Through Emerson, Thoreau became involved with transcendentalism, a philosophy that is based on finding truth through spiritual intuition.* Walden *is generally considered one of the primary texts of the transcendentalist movement. As Thoreau explains: "If one listens to the faintest but constant suggestions of his genius, which are certainly true, he sees not to what extremes, or even insanity, it may lead him; and yet that way, as he grows more resolute and faithful, his road lies." He continues, "If the day and the night are such that you greet them with joy, and life emits a fragrance like flowers and sweet-scented herbs, is more elastic, more starry, more immortal,—that is your success. All nature is your congratulation, and you have cause momentarily to bless yourself." Thoreau died in 1862, and Emerson gave the eulogy at his funeral. The selection here discusses why Thoreau decided to live in Concord, and how he selected his home. In this piece, he makes clear that part of what he seeks is a relationship with the natural world. he lives. As you read, pay close attention to Thoreau's description of how living as he does affects the quality of his life.*

JOURNAL ASSIGNMENT

In this excerpt from *Walden*, Thoreau discusses wanting to live as enmeshed in nature as possible. At one point he writes, "Let us spend one day as deliberately as Nature." What do you suppose it means to live as "deliberately as Nature"? In your journal, consider two ideas: first, the desire to live close to nature and then, what it means to live as deliberately as nature.

At a certain season of our life we are accustomed to consider every spot as the possible site of a house. I have thus surveyed the country on every side within a dozen miles of where I live. In imagination I have bought all the farms in succession, for all were to be bought, and I knew their price. I walked over each farmer's premises, tasted his wild apples, discoursed on husbandry with him, took his farm at his price, at any price, mortgaging it to him in my mind; even put a higher price on it—took everything but a deed of it—took his word for his deed, for I dearly love to talk—cultivated it, and him too to some extent, I trust, and withdrew when I had enjoyed it long enough, leaving him to carry it on. This experience entitled me to be regarded as a sort of real-estate broker by my friends. Wherever I sat, there I might live, and the landscape radiated from me accordingly. What is a house but a *sedes*, a seat?—better if a country seat. I discovered many a site for a house not likely to be soon improved, which some might have thought too far from the village, but to my eyes the village was too far from it. Well, there I might live, I said; and there I did live, for an hour, a summer and a winter life; saw how I could let the years run off, buffet the winter through, and see the spring come in. The future inhabitants of this region, wherever they may place their houses, may be sure that they have been anticipated. An afternoon sufficed to lay out the land into orchard, wood-lot, and pasture, and to decide what fine oaks or pines should be left to stand before the door, and whence each blasted tree could be seen to the best advantage; and then I let it lie, fallow perchance, for a man is rich in proportion to the number of things which he can afford to let alone.

2   My imagination carried me so far that I even had the refusal of several farms—the refusal was all I wanted—but I never got my fingers burned by actual possession. The nearest that I came to actual possession was when I bought the Hollowell place, and had begun to sort my seeds, and collected materials with which to make a wheelbarrow to carry it on or off with; but before the owner gave me a deed of it, his wife—every man has such a wife—changed her mind and wished to keep it, and he offered me ten dollars to release him. Now, to speak the truth, I had but ten cents in the world, and it surpassed my arithmetic to tell, if I was that man who had ten cents, or who had a farm, or ten dollars, or all together. However, I let him keep the ten dollars and the farm too, for I had carried it far enough; or rather, to be generous, I sold him the farm for just what I gave for it, and, as he was not a rich man, made him a present of ten dollars, and still had my ten cents, and seeds, and materials for a wheelbarrow left. I found thus that I had been a rich man without any damage to my poverty. But I retained the landscape, and I have since annually carried off what it yielded without a wheelbarrow. With respect to landscapes,

> "I am monarch of all I *survey,*
> My right there is none to dispute."

3   I have frequently seen a poet withdraw, having enjoyed the most valuable part of a farm, while the crusty farmer supposed that he had got a few wild apples only. Why, the owner does not know it for many years when a poet has put his farm in rhyme, the most admirable kind of invisible fence, has fairly impounded it, milked it, skimmed it, and got all the cream, and left the farmer only the skimmed milk.

4   The real attractions of the Hollowell farm, to me, were: its complete retirement, being about two miles from the village, half a mile from the nearest neighbor, and separated from the highway by a broad field; its bounding on the river, which the owner said protected it by its fogs from frosts in the spring, though that was nothing to me; the gray color and ruinous state of the house and barn, and the dilapidated fences, which put such an interval between me and the last occupant; the hollow and lichen-covered apple trees, gnawed by rabbits, showing what kind of neighbors I should have; but above all, the recollection I had of it from my earliest voyages up the river, when the house was concealed behind

a dense grove of red maples, through which I heard the house-dog bark. I was in haste to buy it, before the proprietor finished getting out some rocks, cutting down the hollow apple trees, and grubbing up some young birches which had sprung up in the pasture, or, in short, had made any more of his improvements. To enjoy these advantages I was ready to carry it on; like Atlas, to take the world on my shoulders—I never heard what compensation he received for that—and do all those things which had no other motive or excuse but that I might pay for it and be unmolested in my possession of it; for I knew all the while that it would yield the most abundant crop of the kind I wanted, if I could only afford to let it alone. But it turned out as I have said.

All that I could say, then, with respect to farming on a large scale—I have 5 always cultivated a garden—was, that I had had my seeds ready. Many think that seeds improve with age. I have no doubt that time discriminates between the good and the bad; and when at last I shall plant, I shall be less likely to be disappointed. But I would say to my fellows, once for all, As long as possible live free and uncommitted. It makes but little difference whether you are committed to a farm or the county jail.

Old Cato, whose "De Re Rusticâ" is my "Cultivator," says—and the only 6 translation I have seen makes sheer nonsense of the passage—"When you think of getting a farm turn it thus in your mind, not to buy greedily; nor spare your pains to look at it, and do not think it enough to go round it once. The oftener you go there the more it will please you, if it is good." I think I shall not buy greedily, but go round and round it as long as I live, and be buried in it first, that it may please me the more at last.

The present was my next experiment of this kind, which I purpose to de- 7 scribe more at length, for convenience putting the experience of two years into one. As I have said, I do not propose to write an ode to dejection, but to brag as lustily as chanticleer in the morning, standing on his roost, if only to wake my neighbors up.

When first I took up my abode in the woods, that is, began to spend my 8 nights as well as days there, which, by accident, was on Independence Day, or the Fourth of July, 1845, my house was not finished for winter, but was merely a defense against the rain, without plastering or chimney, the walls being of rough, weather-stained boards, with wide chinks, which made it cool at night. The upright white hewn studs and freshly planed door and window casings gave it a clean and airy look, especially in the morning, when its timbers were saturated with dew, so that I fancied that by noon some sweet gum would exude from them. To my imagination it retained throughout the day more or less of this auroral character, reminding me of a certain house on a mountain which I had visited a year before. This was an airy and unplastered cabin, fit to entertain a travelling god, and where a goddess might trail her garments. The winds which passed over my dwelling were such as sweep over the ridges of mountains, bearing the broken strains, or celestial parts only, of terrestrial music. The morning wind forever blows, the poem of creation is uninterrupted; but few are the ears that hear it. Olympus is but the outside of the earth everywhere.

9   The only house I had been the owner of before, if I except a boat, was a tent, which I used occasionally when making excursions in the summer, and this is still rolled up in my garret; but the boat, after passing from hand to hand, has gone down the stream of time. With this more substantial shelter about me, I had made some progress toward settling in the world. This frame, so slightly clad, was a sort of crystallization around me, and reacted on the builder. It was suggestive somewhat as a picture in outlines. I did not need to go outdoors to take the air, for the atmosphere within had lost none of its freshness. It was not so much within-doors as behind a door where I sat, even in the rainiest weather. The Harivansa says, "An abode without birds is like a meat without season-ing." Such was not my abode, for I found myself suddenly neighbor to the birds; not by having imprisoned one, but having caged myself near them. I was not only nearer to some of those which commonly frequent the garden and the orchard, but to those wilder and more thrilling songsters of the forest which never, or rarely, serenade a villager—the wood thrush, the veery, the scarlet tanager, the field sparrow, the whip-poor-will, and many others.

10   I was seated by the shore of a small pond, about a mile and a half south of the village of Concord and somewhat higher than it, in the midst of an exten-sive wood between that town and Lincoln, and about two miles south of that our only field known to fame, Concord Battle Ground; but I was so low in the woods that the opposite shore, half a mile off, like the rest, covered with wood, was my most distant horizon. For the first week, whenever I looked out on the pond it impressed me like a tarn high up on the side of the mountain, its bot-tom far above the surface of other lakes, and, as the sun arose, I saw it throw-ing off its nightly clothing of mist, and here and there, by degrees, its soft ripples or its smooth reflecting surface was revealed, while the mists, like ghosts, were stealthily withdrawing in every direction into the woods, as at the breaking up of some nocturnal conventicle. The very dew seemed to hang upon the trees later into the day than usual, as on the sides of mountains.

11   This small lake was of most value as a neighbor in the intervals of a gentle rain-storm in August, when, both air and water being perfectly still, but the sky overcast, mid-afternoon had all the serenity of evening, and the wood thrush sang around, and was heard from shore to shore. A lake like this is never smoother than at such a time; and the clear portion of the air above it being shallow and darkened by clouds, the water, full of light and reflections, be-comes a lower heaven itself so much the more important. From a hill-top near by, where the wood had been recently cut off, there was a pleasing vista south-ward across the pond, through a wide indentation in the hills which form the shore there, where their opposite sides sloping toward each other suggested a stream flowing out in that direction through a wooded valley, but stream there was none. That way I looked between and over the near green hills to some

distant and higher ones in the horizon, tinged with blue. Indeed, by standing on tiptoe I could catch a glimpse of some of the peaks of the still bluer and more distant mountain ranges in the northwest, those true-blue coins from heaven's own mint, and also of some portion of the village. But in other directions, even from this point, I could not see over or beyond the woods which surrounded me. It is well to have some water in your neighborhood, to give buoyancy to and float the earth. One value even of the smallest well is, that when you look into it you see that earth is not continent but insular. This is as important as that it keeps butter cool. When I looked across the pond from this peak toward the Sudbury meadows, which in time of flood I distinguished elevated perhaps by a mirage in their seething valley, like a coin in a basin, all the earth beyond the pond appeared like a thin crust insulated and floated even by this small sheet of intervening water, and I was reminded that this on which I dwelt was but *dry land.*

    Though the view from my door was still more contracted, I did not feel 12 crowded or confined in the least. There was pasture enough for my imagination. The low shrub oak plateau to which the opposite shore arose stretched away toward the prairies of the West and the steppes of Tartary, affording ample room for all the roving families of men. "There are none happy in the world but beings who enjoy freely a vast horizon"—said Damodara, when his herds required new and larger pastures.

    Both place and time were changed, and I dwelt nearer to those parts of the 13 universe and to those eras in history which had most attracted me. Where I lived was as far off as many a region viewed nightly by astronomers. We are wont to imagine rare and delectable places in some remote and more celestial corner of the system, behind the constellation of Cassiopeia's Chair, far from noise and disturbance. I discovered that my house actually had its site in such a withdrawn, but forever new and unprofaned, part of the universe. If it were worth the while to settle in those parts near to the Pleiades or the Hyades, to Aldebaran or Altair, then I was really there, or at an equal remoteness from the life which I had left behind, dwindled and twinkling with as fine a ray to my nearest neighbor, and to be seen only in moonless nights by him. Such was that part of creation where I had squatted;

> "There was a shepherd that did live,
>   And held his thoughts as high
> As were the mounts whereon his flocks
>   Did hourly feed him by."

What should we think of the shepherd's life if his flocks always wandered to higher pastures than his thoughts?

    Every morning was a cheerful invitation to make my life of equal simplicity, 14 and I may say innocence, with Nature herself. I have been a sincere a worshipper

of Aurora as the Greeks. I got up early and bathed in the pond; that was a religious exercise, and one of the best things which I did. They say that characters
were engraven on the bathing tub of King Tching-thang to this effect: "Renew
thyself completely each day; do it again, and again, and forever again." I can
understand that. Morning brings back the heroic ages. I was as much affected
by the faint hum of a mosquito making its invisible and unimaginable tour
through my apartment at earliest dawn, when I was sitting with door and windows open, as I could be by any trumpet that ever sang of fame. It was Homer's
requiem; itself an Iliad and Odyssey in the air, singing its own wrath and wan-
derings. There was something cosmical about it; a standing advertisement, till
forbidden, of the everlasting vigor and fertility of the world. The morning,
which is the most memorable season of the day, is the awakening hour. Then
there is least somnolence in us; and for an hour, at least, some part of us awakes
which slumbers all the rest of the day and night. Little is to be expected of that
day, if it can be called a day, to which we are not awakened by our Genius, but
by the mechanical nudgings of some servitor, are not awakened by our newly
acquired force and aspirations from within, accompanied by the undulations
of celestial music, instead of factory bells, and a fragrance filling the air—to a
higher life than we fell asleep from; and thus the darkness bear its fruit, and
prove itself to be good, no less than the light. That man who does not believe
that each day contains an earlier, more sacred, and auroral hour than he has
yet profaned, has despaired of life and is pursuing a descending and darken-
ing way. After a partial cessation of his sensuous life, the soul of man, or its organs rather, are reinvigorated each day, and his Genius tries again what noble
life it can make. All memorable events, I should say, transpire in morning time
and in a morning atmosphere. The Vedas say, "All intelligences awake with the
morning." Poetry and art, the fairest and most memorable of the actions of men,
date from such an hour. All poets and heroes, like Memnon, are the children of
Aurora, and emit their music at sunrise. To him whose elastic and vigorous
thought keeps pace with the sun, the day is a perpetual morning. It matters not
what the clocks say or the attitudes and labors of men. Morning is when I am
awake and there is a dawn in me. Moral reform is the effort to throw off sleep.
Why is it that men give so poor an account of their day if they have not been
slumbering? They are not such poor calculators. If they had not been overcome
with drowsiness, they would have performed something. The millions are
awake enough for physical labor; but only one in a million is awake enough
for effective intellectual exertion, only one in a hundred millions to a poetic or
divine life. To be awake is to be alive. I have never yet met a man who was
quite awake. How could I have looked him in the face?

15   We must learn to reawaken and keep ourselves awake, not by mechanical
aids, but by an infinite expectation of the dawn, which does not forsake us in
our soundest sleep. I know of no more encouraging fact than the unquestion-
able ability of man to elevate his life by a conscious endeavor. It is something
to be able to paint a particular picture, or to carve a statue, and so to make a

few objects beautiful; but it is far more glorious to carve and paint the very atmosphere and medium through which we look, which morally we can do. To affect the quality of the day, that is the highest of arts. Every man is tasked to make his life, even in its details, worthy of the contemplation of his most elevated and critical hour. If we refused, or rather used up, such paltry information as we get, the oracles would distinctly inform us how this might be done.

I went to the woods because I wished to live deliberately, to front only the essential facts of life, and see if I could not learn what it had to teach, and not, when I came to die, discover that I had not lived. I did not wish to live what was not life, living is so dear; nor did I wish to practise resignation, unless it was quite necessary. I wanted to live deep and suck out all the marrow of life, to live so sturdily and Spartan-like as to put to rout all that was not life, to cut a broad swath and shave close, to drive life into a corner, and reduce it to its lowest terms, and, if it proved to be mean, why then to get the whole and genuine meanness of it, and publish its meanness to the world; or if it were sublime, to know it by experience, and be able to give a true account of it in my next excursion. For most men, it appears to me, are in a strange uncertainty about it, whether it is of the devil or of God, and have *somewhat hastily* concluded that it is the chief end of man here to "glorify God and enjoy him forever." 16

Still we live meanly, like ants; though the fable tells us that we were long ago changed into men; like pygmies we fight with cranes; it is error upon error, and clout upon clout, and our best virtue has for its occasion a superfluous and evitable wretchedness. Our life is frittered away by detail. An honest man has hardly the need to count more than his ten fingers, or in extreme cases he may add his ten toes, and lump the rest. Simplicity, simplicity, simplicity! I say, let your affairs be as two or three, and not a hundred or a thousand; instead of a million count half a dozen, and keep your accounts on your thumb-nail. In the midst of this chopping sea of civilized life, such are the clouds and storms and quicksands and thousand-and-one items to be allowed for, that a man has to live, if he would not founder and go to the bottom and not make his port at all, by dead reckoning, and he must be a great calculator indeed who succeeds. Simplify, simplify. Instead of three meals a day, if it be necessary eat but one; instead of a hundred dishes, five; and reduce other things in proportion. Our life is like a German Confederacy, made up of petty states, with its boundary forever fluctuating, so that even a German cannot tell you how it is bounded at any moment. The nation itself, with all its so-called internal improvements, which, by the way are all external and superficial, is just such an unwieldy and overgrown establishment, cluttered with furniture and tripped up by its own traps, ruined by luxury and heedless expense, by want of calculation and a worthy aim, as the million households in the land; and the only cure for it, as for them, is in a rigid economy, a stern and more than Spartan simplicity of life and elevation of purpose. It lives too fast. Men think that it is essential that the *Nation* have commerce, and export ice, and talk through a telegraph, and ride thirty miles an hour, without a doubt, whether *they* do or not; but whether we 17 should live like baboons or like men, is a little uncertain. If we do not get out sleepers, and forge rails, and devote days and nights to the work, but go to tinkering upon our *lives* to improve *them,* who will build railroads? And if railroads are not built, how shall we get to heaven in season? But if we stay at home and mind our business, who will want railroads? We do not ride on the railroad; it rides upon us. Did you ever think what those sleepers are that underlie the railroad? Each one is a man, an Irishman, or a Yankee man. The rails are laid on them, and they are covered with sand, and the cars run smoothly over them. They are sound sleepers, I assure you. And every few years a new lot is laid down and run over; so that, if some have the pleasure of riding on a rail, others have the misfortune to be ridden upon. And when they run over a man that is walking in his sleep, a supernumerary sleeper in the wrong position, and wake him up, they suddenly stop the cars, and make a hue and cry about it, as if this were an exception. I am glad to know that it takes a gang of men for every five miles to keep the sleepers down and level in their beds as it is, for this is a sign that they may sometime get up again.

18   Why should we live with such hurry and waste of life? We are determined to be starved before we are hungry. Men say that a stitch in time saves nine, and so they take a thousand stitches today to save nine tomorrow. As for *work,* we haven't any of any consequence. We have the Saint Vitus' dance, and cannot possibly keep our heads still. If I should only give a few pulls at the parish bell-rope, as for a fire, that is, without setting the bell, there is hardly a man on his farm in the outskirts of Concord, notwithstanding that press of engagements which was his excuse so many times this morning, nor a boy, nor a woman, I might almost say, but would forsake all and follow that sound, not mainly to save property from the flames, but, if we will confess the truth, much more to see it burn, since burn it must, and we, be it known, did not set it on fire—or to see it put out, and have a hand in it, if that is done as handsomely; yes, even if it were the parish church itself. Hardly a man takes a half-hour's nap after dinner, but when he wakes he holds up his head and asks, "What's the news?" as if the rest of mankind had stood his sentinels. Some give directions to be waked every half-hour, doubtless for no other purpose; and then, to pay for it, they tell what they have dreamed. After a night's sleep the news is as indispensable as the breakfast. "Pray tell me anything new that has happened to a man anywhere on this globe"—and he reads it over his coffee and rolls, that a man has had his eyes gouged out this morning on the Wachito River; never dreaming the while that he lives in the dark unfathomed mammoth cave of this world, and has but the rudiment of an eye himself.

19   For my part, I could easily do without the post-office. I think that there are very few important communications made through it. To speak critically, I never received more than one or two letters in my life—I wrote this some years ago—that were worth the postage. The penny-post is, commonly, an institution through which you seriously offer a man that penny for his thoughts which is so often safely offered in jest. And I am sure that I never read any memorable news in a newspaper. If we read of one man robbed, or murdered,

or killed by accident, or one house burned, or one vessel wrecked, or one steam-
boat blown up, or one cow run over on the Western Railroad, or one mad dog
killed, or one lot of grasshoppers in the winter—we never need read of another.
One is enough. If you are acquainted with the principle, what do you care for a
myriad instances and applications? To a philosopher all *news*, as it is called, is
gossip, and they who edit and read it are old women over their tea. Yet not a
few are greedy after this gossip. There was such a rush, as I hear, the other day
at one of the offices to learn the foreign news by the last arrival, that several
large squares of plate glass belonging to the establishment were broken by the
pressure—news which I seriously think a ready wit might write a twelve-
month, or twelve years, beforehand with sufficient accuracy. As for Spain, for
instance, if you know how to throw in Don Carlos and the Infanta, and Don
Pedro and Seville and Granada, from time to time in the right proportions—
they may have changed the names a little since I saw the papers—and serve up
a bull-fight when other entertainments fail, it will be true to the letter, and give
us as good an idea of the exact state or ruin of things in Spain as the most suc-
cinct and lucid reports under this head in the newspapers: and as for England,
almost the last significant scrap of news from that quarter was the revolution
of 1649; and if you have learned the history of her crops for an average year,
you never need attend to that thing again, unless your speculations are of a
merely pecuniary character. If one may judge who rarely looks into the newspapers, nothing new does ever happen in foreign parts, a French revolution
not excepted.

    What news! how much more important to know what that is which was   20
never old! "Kieou-he-yu (great dignitary of the state of Wei) sent a man to
Khoung-tseu to know his news. Khoung-tseu caused the messenger to be seated
near him, and questioned him in these terms: What is your master doing? The
messenger answered with respect. My master desires to diminish the number of
his faults, but he cannot come to the end of them. The messenger being gone, the
philosopher remarked: What a worthy messenger! What a worthy messenger!"
The preacher, instead of vexing the ears of drowsy farmers on their day of rest at
the end of the week—for Sunday is the fit conclusion of an ill-spent week, and
not the fresh and brave beginning of a new one—with this one other draggle-
tail of a sermon, should shout with thundering voice, "Pause! Avast! Why so
seeming fast, but deadly slow?"

    Shams and delusions are esteemed for soundest truths, while reality is fab-   21
ulous. If men would steadily observe realities only, and not allow themselves
to be deluded, life, to compare it with such things as we know, would be like a
fairy tale and the Arabian Nights' Entertainments. If we respected only what is
inevitable and has a right to be, music and poetry would resound along the
streets. When we are unhurried and wise, we perceive that only great and worthy things have any permanent and absolute existence, that petty fears and
petty pleasures are but the shadow of the reality. This is always exhilarating
and sublime. By closing the eyes and slumbering, and consenting to be deceived by shows, men establish and confirm their daily life of routine and habit

everywhere, which still is built on purely illusory foundations. Children, who play life, discern its true law and relations more clearly than men, who fail to live it worthily, but who think that they are wiser by experience, that is, by failure. I have read in a Hindoo book, that "there was a king's son, who, being expelled in infancy from his native city, was brought up by a forester, and, growing up to maturity in that state, imagined himself to belong to the barbarous race with which he lived. One of his father's ministers having discovered him, revealed to him what he was, and the misconception of his character was removed, and he knew himself to be a prince. So soul," continues the Hindoo philosopher, "from the circumstances in which it is placed, mistakes its own character, until the truth is revealed to it by some holy teacher, and then it knows itself to be *Brahme*." I perceive that we inhabitants of New England live this mean life that we do because our vision does not penetrate the surface of things. We think that that *is* which *appears* to be. If a man should walk through this town and see only the reality, where, think you, would the "Mill-dam" go to? If he should give us an account of the realities he beheld there, we should not recognize the place in his description. Look at a meeting-house, or a court-house, or a jail, or a shop, or a dwelling-house, and say what that thing really is before a true gaze, and they would all go to pieces in your account of them. Men esteem truth remote, in the outskirts of the system, behind the farthest star, before Adam and after the last man. In eternity there is indeed something true and sublime. But all these times and places and occasions are now and here. God himself culminates in the present moment, and will never be more divine in the lapse of all the ages. And we are enabled to apprehend at all what is sublime and noble only by the perpetual instilling and drenching of the reality that surrounds us. The universe constantly and obediently answers to our conceptions; whether we travel fast or slow, the track is laid for us. Let us spend our lives in conceiving then. The poet or the artist never yet had so fair and noble a design but some of his posterity at least could accomplish it.

22   Let us spend one day as deliberately as Nature, and not be thrown off the track by every nutshell and mosquito's wing that falls on the rails. Let us rise early and fast, or break fast, gently and without perturbation; let company come and let company go, let the bells ring and the children cry—determined to make a day of it. Why should we knock under and go with the stream? Let us not be upset and overwhelmed in that terrible rapid and whirlpool called a dinner, situated in the meridian shallows. Weather this danger and you are safe, for the rest of the way is down hill. With unrelaxed nerves, with morning vigor, sail by it, looking another way, tied to the mast like Ulysses. If the engine whistles, let it whistle till it is hoarse for its pains. If the bell rings, why should we run? We will consider what kind of music they are like. Let us settle ourselves, and work and wedge our feet downward through the mud and slush of opinion, and prejudice, and tradition, and delusion, and appearance, that alluvion which covers the globe, through Paris and London, through New York and Boston and Concord, through Church and State, through poetry and philosophy and

religion, till we come to a hard bottom and rocks in place, which we can call *reality*, and say, This is, and no mistake; and then begin, having a *point d'appui*, below freshet and frost and fire, a place where you might found a wall or a state, or set a lamp-post safely, or perhaps a gauge, not a Nilometer, but a Realometer, that future ages might know how deep a freshet of shams and appearances had gathered from time to time. If you stand right fronting and face to face to a fact, you will see the sun glimmer on both its surfaces, as if it were a cimeter, and feel its sweet edge dividing you through the heart and marrow, and so you will happily conclude your mortal career. Be it life or death, we crave only reality. If we are really dying, let us hear the rattle in our throats and feel cold in the extremities; if we are alive, let us go about our business.

Time is but the stream I go a-fishing in. I drink at it; but while I drink I see 23 the sandy bottom and detect how shallow it is. Its thin current slides away, but eternity remains. I would drink deeper; fish in the sky, whose bottom is pebbly with stars. I cannot count one. I know not the first letter of the alphabet. I have always been regretting that I was not as wise as the day I was born. The intellect is a cleaver; it discerns and rifts its way into the secret of things. I do not wish to be any more busy with my hands than is necessary. My head is hands and feet. I feel all my best faculties concentrated in it. My instinct tells me that my head is an organ for burrowing, as some creatures use their snout and fore paws, and with it I would mine and burrow my way through these hills. I think that the richest vein is somewhere hereabouts; so by the divining-rod and thin rising vapors I judge; and here I will begin to mine.

FOCUS ON ECOLOGY

1. In his quest for a home, for what kinds of characteristics does Thoreau seek to assure his closeness with nature? Are any of these characteristics reflected in the ways Americans now seek out homes? Think about the neighborhoods and homes in your community. Does proximity to nature play a role in their placement? Is nature made to fit near or in these homes?
2. What does Thoreau mean when he says that he "caged himself" near the birds? How do you respond to this concept?
3. What do you suppose Thoreau means when he says, "Every morning was a cheerful invitation to make my life of equal simplicity, and I may say innocence, with Nature herself"?

FOCUS ON WRITING

1. To what does Thoreau refer in these references: Atlas, Old Cato, Olympus, the Harivansa, Damodara, Pleiades, Hyades, Aldebaran, Altair, the Vedas, Memnon, Saint Vitus, and Ulysses? Why do you suppose he makes so many of these allusions and references?

2. Twice, Thoreau quotes lines of poetry in "Where I Lived and What I Lived For." Why do you suppose he makes these references? What is the source of these poems?
3. What does Thoreau mean by the last paragraph of this selection?

FOR DISCUSSION

Think about how your local community has been constructed in relationship to nature. As a class, discuss not only how the area's buildings have been constructed in relationship to nature, but how nature has also been interjected into that scheme. Think, for instance, about the placement of parks, trees that are planted along sidewalks, planters at malls and other shopping areas, the animals that inhabit your community (squirrels, birds, rodents, cats, dogs, and so on), the view of the sky, how snow and rain are dealt with, how irrigation and water supplies are managed, where the sun penetrates windows, and so on.

WRITING IN RESPONSE

For many Americans, residences are established out of convenience: proximity to work or school, cost efficiency, availability, and so on. Yet others choose to live where they do because of what those places mean to them. If you could live anywhere, where would you live? Why would you live there? In an essay about your own philosophies of place and living, describe your ideal place of residence. Don't get hung up writing about the material conditions of the home—things like 12 bedrooms, a 10-car garage, and gilded window frames aren't important. Think specifically about where the home would be. What can you see from the windows? Are there windows?

Film: *Jeremiah Johnson*

The 1972 film Jeremiah Johnson *is set in the mid-1800s. Filmed entirely in Utah during the winter, the film tells the story of Jeremiah Johnson, played by Robert Redford, and his decision to become a mountain man. He seeks the solitude of the mountain wilderness, never questioning the purity or beauty of that wilderness. Directed by Sydney Pollack and based on Vardis Fisher's novel* Mountain Man, *this film is a spectacular tale of human relationships with the wilderness. As you watch this film, pay close attention not only to the ways that Johnson's relationship with the wilderness develops, but notice also how the other characters express their relationships with the mountain wilderness.*

JOURNAL ASSIGNMENT

Why might someone leave civilization for a solitary life in the mountains? In your journal write about why someone might make such a decision and consider whether you would want to do so.

FOCUS ON ECOLOGY

1. One of the promotional blurbs provided for *Jeremiah Johnson* says that this film "captures the epic scale of an unconquered Nature and the small struggles of a loner trying to start a fire during a blizzard, cross a meadow knee-deep in snow or catch something—anything—to eat. *Jeremiah Johnson* 'gets back to Nature' in a way no film has before or since." Think about these claims for a moment. What might be meant by "unconquered Nature"? How does this film "get back to Nature"?
2. What is the relationship between Native Americans and the white people in this film? Why does one chief speak French? How is the Native American philosophy toward land and wilderness expressed in this film?
3. Before meeting Bear Claw Chris Lapp, Johnson faces possible starvation and freezing. Bear Claw Chris Lapp, however, takes Johnson in and teaches him how to survive in the wilderness. What kinds of things does Bear Claw teach Johnson? Why couldn't Jeremiah learn these skills on his own?

FOCUS ON WRITING

1. What war did Johnson fight in prior to heading into the mountains? How do you know? That is, how does this film contextualize itself historically for viewers?
2. At the point when the troop of men arrive to ask Jeremiah Johnson to help them rescue the wagon train of settlers, Johnson laughs and says, "It's been a long time since I've had so much of the English language spoke at me." What is Johnson's relationship with and need for language throughout this film?
3. This movie was filmed entirely in Utah. What connections does Robert Redford have with Utah?

FOR DISCUSSION

The film depicts several different approaches to living in the wilderness: Johnson as a novice, the old trapper's experience, the Indian hunters' and warriors' view of trespassing, Del Gue's relationships with the Indians, and Johnson's wife Sawn's simple approach to the wilderness, and the rescue party's indifference. As a class consider how the different characters view nature and their approaches to living in the wilderness. Which approach do you most agree with? Why?

WRITING IN RESPONSE

In the brief moments that we see Jeremiah Johnson in contact with other white people (in the town at the beginning of the film and when the rescue party comes to ask his help), Johnson's solitude and desire to be alone in the mountains is seen as a bit eccentric but not as outlandish behavior. How might such a character be viewed now? If *Jeremiah Johnson* were to be remade featuring a soldier fleeing societal constraints after the year 2004, how might that character be received? In a short narrative, describe the reaction we might have to a person in contemporary times taking off to live in the mountains. Would there be wildernesses large enough for such a person to live in? How would other people respond to him or her? How would he or she live?

"The First Morning"
from *Desert Solitaire*

Edward Abbey

Edward Abbey introduced the idea of eco-terrorism to the American public. His hard-hitting 1975 novel The Monkeywrench Gang *made popular the characters of Hayduke and his friends who attempt to protect the environment through such acts as blowing up the Glen Canyon Dam on the Colorado River. Abbey, adamant in all of his writing about protecting environments throughout Arizona, Utah, and Colorado, identified with the goals of the Monkeywrench Gang. Born in 1927, Abbey spent a good deal of his adult life as a park ranger and fire lookout for the National Park Service. His book* Desert Solitaire, *from which the selection "The First Morning" is taken, recounts a year of his time as a park ranger spent alone in a remote part of Arches National Monument. As you read this selection, think about the ways Abbey writes about luxury and necessity in terms of what is needed to live in a wilderness.*

JOURNAL ASSIGNMENT

In your journal, consider what it might be like to work in a national park, to spend your summer in a protected wilderness area. For those of you who have had this kind of experience, write in your journal about what you learned from your time working in the park.

This is the most beautiful place on earth.   1

There are many such places. Every man, every woman, carries in heart and   2
mind the image of the ideal place, the right place, the one true home, known or

unknown, actual or visionary. A houseboat in Kashmir, a view down Atlantic Avenue in Brooklyn, a gray gothic farmhouse two stories high at the end of a red dog road in the Allegheny Mountains, a cabin on the shore of a blue lake in spruce and fir country, a greasy alley near the Hoboken waterfront, or even, possibly, for those of a less demanding sensibility, the world to be seen from a comfortable apartment high in the tender, velvety smog of Manhattan, Chicago, Paris, Tokyo, Rio or Rome—there's no limit to the human capacity for the homing sentiment. Theologians, sky pilots, astronauts have even felt the appeal of home calling to them from up above, in the cold black outback of interstellar space.

3   For myself I'll take Moab, Utah. I don't mean the town itself, of course, but the country which surrounds it—the canyonlands. The slickrock desert. The red dust and the blunt cliffs and the lonely sky—all that which lies beyond the end of the roads.

4   The choice became apparent to me this morning when I stepped out of a Park Service housetrailer—my caravan—to watch for the first time in my life the sun come up over the hoodoo stone of Arches National Monument.

5   I wasn't able to see much of it last night. After driving all day from Albuquerque—450 miles—I reached Moab after dark in cold, windy, clouded weather. At park headquarters north of town I met the superintendent and the chief ranger, the only permanent employees, except for one maintenance man, in this particular unit of America's national park system. After coffee they gave me a key to the housetrailer and directions on how to reach it; I am required to live and work not at headquarters but at this one-man station some twenty miles back in the interior, on my own. The way I wanted it, naturally, or I'd never have asked for the job.

6   Leaving the headquarters area and the lights of Moab, I drove twenty miles farther north on the highway until I came to a dirt road on the right, where a small wooden sign pointed the way: Arches National Monument Eight Miles. I left the pavement, turned east into the howling wilderness. Wind roaring out of the northwest, black clouds across the stars—all I could see were clumps of brush and scattered junipers along the roadside. Then another modest signboard:

> WARNING: QUICKSAND
> DO NOT CROSS WASH
> WHEN WATER IS RUNNING

7   The wash looked perfectly dry in my headlights. I drove down, across, up the other side and on into the night. Glimpses of weird lumps of pale rock on either side, like petrified elephants, dinosaurs, stone-age hobgoblins. Now and then something alive scurried across the road: kangaroo mice, a jackrabbit, an animal that looked like a cross between a raccoon and a squirrel—the ringtail cat. Farther on a pair of mule deer started from the brush and bounded obliquely through the beams of my lights, raising puffs of dust which the wind, moving faster than my pickup truck, caught and carried ahead of me out of sight into the dark. The road, narrow and rocky, twisted sharply left and right,

dipped in and out of tight ravines, climbing by degrees toward a summit which I would see only in the light of the coming day.

Snow was swirling through the air when I crossed the unfenced line and passed the boundary marker of the park. A quarter-mile beyond I found the ranger station—a wide place in the road, an informational display under a lean-to shelter, and fifty yards away the little tin government housetrailer where I would be living for the next six months. 8

A cold night, a cold wind, the snow falling like confetti. In the lights of the truck I unlocked the housetrailer, got out bedroll and baggage and moved in. By flashlight I found the bed, unrolled my sleeping bag, pulled off my boots and crawled in and went to sleep at once. The last I knew was the shaking of the trailer in the wind and the sound, from inside, of hungry mice scampering around with the good news that their long lean lonesome winter was over— their friend and provider had finally arrived. 9

This morning I awake before sunrise, stick my head out of the sack, peer through a frosty window at a scene dim and vague with flowing mists, dark fantastic shapes looming beyond. An unlikely landscape. 10

I get up, moving about in long underwear and socks, stooping carefully under the low ceiling and lower doorways of the housetrailer, a machine for living built so efficiently and compactly there's hardly room for a man to breathe. An iron lung it is, with windows and venetian blinds. 11

The mice are silent, watching me from their hiding places, but the wind is still blowing and outside the ground is covered with snow. Cold as a tomb, a jail, a cave; I lie down on the dusty floor, on the cold linoleum sprinkled with mouse turds, and light the pilot on the butane heater. Once this thing gets going the place warms up fast, in a dense unhealthy way, with a layer of heat under the ceiling where my head is and nothing but frigid air from the knees down. But we've got all the indispensable conveniences: gas cookstove, gas refrigerator, hot water heater, sink with running water (if the pipes aren't frozen), storage cabinets and shelves, everything within arm's reach of everything else. The gas comes from two steel bottles in a shed outside; the water comes by gravity flow from a tank buried in a hill close by. Quite luxurious for the wilds. There's even a shower stall and a flush toilet with a dead rat in the bowl. Pretty soft. My poor mother raised five children without any of these luxuries and might be doing without them yet if it hadn't been for Hitler, war and general prosperity. 12

Time to get dressed, get out and have a look at the lay of the land, fix a breakfast. I try to pull on my boots but they're stiff as iron from the cold. I light a burner on the stove and hold the boots upside down above the flame until they are malleable enough to force my feet into. I put on a coat and step outside. Into the center of the world, God's navel, Abbey's country, the red wasteland. 13

The sun is not yet in sight but signs of the advent are plain to see. Lavender clouds sail like a fleet of ships across the pale green dawn; each cloud, planed flat on the wind, has a base of fiery gold. Southeast, twenty miles by line of sight, stand the peaks of the Sierra La Sal, twelve to thirteen thousand feet above sea level, all covered with snow and rosy in the morning sunlight. The air is dry 14 and clear as well as cold; the last fogbanks left over from last night's storm are scudding away like ghosts, fading into nothing before the wind and the sunrise.

15   The view is open and perfect in all directions except to the west where the ground rises and the skyline is only a few hundred yards away. Looking toward the mountains I can see the dark gorge of the Colorado River five or six miles away, carved through the sandstone mesa, though nothing of the river itself down inside the gorge. Southward, on the far side of the river, lies the Moab valley between thousand-foot walls of rock, with the town of Moab somewhere on the valley floor, too small to be seen from here. Beyond the Moab valley is more canyon and tableland stretching away to the Blue Mountains fifty miles south. On the north and northwest I see the Roan Cliffs and the Book Cliffs, the two-level face of the Uinta Plateau. Along the foot of those cliffs, maybe thirty miles off, invisible from where I stand, runs U.S. 6–50, a major east-west artery of commerce, traffic and rubbish, and the main line of the Denver–Rio Grande Railroad. To the east, under the spreading sunrise, are more mesas, more canyons, league on league of red cliffs and arid tablelands, extending through purple haze over the bulging curve of the planet to the ranges of Colorado—a sea of desert.

16   Within this vast perimeter, in the middle ground and foreground of the picture, a rather personal demesne, are the 33,000 acres of Arches National Monument of which I am now sole inhabitant, usufructuary, observer and custodian.

17   What are the Arches? From my place in the front of the housetrailer I can see several of the hundred or more of them which have been discovered in the park. These are natural arches, holes in the rock, windows in stone, no two alike, as varied in form as in dimension. They range in size from holes just big enough to walk through to openings large enough to contain the dome of the Capitol building in Washington, D.C. Some resemble jug handles or flying buttresses, other natural bridges but with this technical distinction: a natural bridge spans a watercourse—a natural arch does not. The arches were formed through hundreds of thousands of years by the weathering of the huge sandstone walls, or fins, in which they are found. Not the work of a cosmic hand, nor sculptured by sand-bearing winds, as many people prefer to believe, the arches came into being and continue to come into being through the modest wedging action of rainwater, melting snow, frost, and ice, aided by gravity. In color they shade from off-white through buff, pink, brown and red, tones which also change with the time of day and the moods of the light, the weather, the sky.

18   Standing there, gaping at this monstrous and inhuman spectacle of rock and cloud and sky and space, I feel a ridiculous greed and possessiveness come over me. I want to know it all, possess it all, embrace the entire scene intimately, deeply, totally, as a man desires a beautiful woman. An insane wish? Perhaps not—at least there's nothing else, no one human, to dispute possession with me.

19   The snow-covered ground glimmers with a dull blue light, reflecting the sky and the approaching sunrise. Leading away from me the narrow dirt road, an alluring and primitive track into nowhere, meanders down the slope and toward the heart of the labyrinth of naked stone. Near the first group of arches, looming over a bend in the road, is a balanced rock about fifty feet high,

mounted on a pedestal of equal height; it looks like a head from Easter Island, a stone god or a petrified ogre.

Like a god, like an ogre? The personification of the natural is exactly the tendency I wish to suppress in myself, to eliminate for good. I am here not only to evade for a while the clamor and filth and confusion of the cultural apparatus but also to confront, immediately and directly if it's possible, the bare bones of existence, the elemental and fundamental, the bedrock which sustains us. I want to be able to look at and into a juniper tree, a piece of quartz, a vulture, a spider, and see it as it is in itself, devoid of all humanly ascribed qualities, anti-Kantian, even the categories of scientific description. To meet God or Medusa face to face, even if it means risking everything human in myself. I dream of a hard and brutal mysticism in which the naked self merges with a nonhuman world and yet somehow survives still intact, individual, separate. Paradox and bedrock. 20

Well—the sun will be up in a few minutes and I haven't even begun to make coffee. I take more baggage from my pickup, the grub box and cooking gear, go back in the trailer and start breakfast. Simply breathing, in a place like this, arouses the appetite. The orange juice is frozen, the milk slushy with ice. Still chilly enough inside the trailer to turn my breath to vapor. When the first rays of the sun strike the cliffs I fill a mug with steaming coffee and sit in the doorway facing the sunrise, hungry for the warmth. 21

Suddenly it comes, the flaming globe, blazing on the pinnacles and minarets and balanced rocks, on the canyon walls and through the windows in the sandstone fins. We greet each other, sun and I, across the black void of ninety-three million miles. The snow glitters between us, acres of diamonds almost painful to look at. Within an hour all the snow exposed to the sunlight will be gone and the rock will be damp and steaming. Within minutes, even as I watch, melting snow begins to drip from the branches of a juniper nearby; drops of water streak slowly down the side of the trailerhouse. 22

I am not alone after all. Three ravens are wheeling near the balanced rock, squawking at each other and at the dawn. I'm sure they're as delighted by the return of the sun as I am and I wish I knew the language. I'd sooner exchange ideas with the birds on earth than learn to carry on intergalactic communications with some obscure race of humanoids on a satellite planet from the world of Betelgeuse. First things first. The ravens cry out in husky voices, blue-black wings flapping against the golden sky. Over my shoulder comes the sizzle and smell of frying bacon. 23

That's the way it was this morning. 24

FOCUS ON ECOLOGY

1. What might Abbey mean when he writes, "I feel a ridiculous greed and possessiveness come over me. I want to know it all, possess it all, embrace the entire scene intimately, deeply, totally"? Have you ever felt this way about a place you have seen? Describe that place.

2. When Abbey says of his job, "I am required to live and work not at head-quarters but at this one-man station some twenty miles back in the interior, on my own," why does he also add "The way I wanted it, naturally, or else I'd never have asked for the job"?

3. Why does Abbey say, "The personification of the natural is exactly the tendency I wish to suppress in myself, to eliminate for good"?

FOCUS ON WRITING

1. When writing about the luxuries of his trailer, Abbey explains that his mother "raised five children without any of these luxuries and might be doing without them yet if it hadn't been for Hitler, war and general prosperity." What might he mean by the latter part of this statement? How do you read this statement in terms of Abbey's overall argument?

2. What role does description play in this piece?

3. To what does Abbey refer when he says he wants to look at trees and rocks "anti-Kantian"? Are you familiar with his reference? Do readers need to be?

FOR DISCUSSION

For many, the living conditions that Abbey describes in his trailer might be less than ideal. Yet he explains that for him they are luxurious. As a class, consider why Abbey considered such accommodations "luxurious" and whether they might be suitable for different class members should they be given a similar job. Why would one's living conditions affect how one experiences a place like Arches National Park?

WRITING IN RESPONSE

At the beginning of this selection Abbey writes, "This is the most beautiful place on earth." He continues by observing that everyone has a place that he or she finds to be the perfect place for home. For Abbey it is the area of Arches National Monument. Yet, as we read this selection, we find that this is his first day at the site. The location of his trailer must have had an enormous effect on him for him to make the adamant and emotional claim he does. Have you ever been some place that had such an effect on you? Perhaps you have been some place that you knew immediately you never wanted to revisit. If so, describe that place and explain why it made such an impression on you. If you have never had such an experience, write an essay describing the kind of place that might affect you in such a way.

From *Winter: Notes from Montana*

Rick Bass

Rick Bass *was born in 1958 in Fort Worth, Texas, but now makes his home on an isolated ranch in Montana in an area known as the Yaak Valley. His writing, often a synthesis of personal narrative and environmental concern, is most frequently about environmental protection. His* The Book of the Yaak *makes a strong plea for protecting the unique ecosystems of the Yaak Valley. In addition to his activism, Bass writes of his relationships with the places he lives. His first book,* The Deer Pasture, *recounts his childhood in Texas and what he learned hunting with his family on their land. Likewise,* Winter: Notes from Montana *describes his first winter in the Yaak Valley. The selection here, taken from* Winter: Notes from Montana, *describes his first days getting settled into his winter home before the full onset of winter. As you read this selection, think specifically about how Bass begins to establish relationships between himself and his home and himself and others.*

JOURNAL ASSIGNMENT

Winter: Notes from Montana recounts what it was like for Bass to experience his first winter in the Yaak Valley. Before reading this selection, consider why a person might want to keep a journal about his or her first season living in a new place. Record your thoughts in your own journal.

SEPTEMBER 13

The first overcast day. Wonderful and gray and cold and heavy with moisture 1
when I first got up, but finally, by mid-morning, the sun labors, burning a hole through the mist, spreading blue into the valley. I'm eager to see how rain falls here, but know I'll get my chance. It's very quiet and still. You can hear sounds from a long way off: the dogs chewing and gnawing like bears on some deer legs they found near one of the old butchering cabins; birds whose names I don't know, birds back in the woods; a truck passing. Out over the valley it is blue, but up here on the side of Lost Horse Mountain there is a hard silence, and the sun burns through the damp clouds, then is shrouded over. I keep forgetting that I am to eat spaghetti with Dave Pruder and his girlfriend tonight.

When it starts to snow, I'm going to write in the greenhouse. There's a 2
wood stove, and I'll keep warm that way. Two sticks of wood should equal one page, if I'm lucky. I've built a little gym up in the loft of the greenhouse, and

will be able to do dips, curls, bench presses, and triceps extensions in a jungle of green, sweating while I look out at winter, when it gets here.

3 I bought a bottle of wine to take over to Dave Pruder's this evening. Dave is tall and friendly, a horseman, and owns the two horses in Holger's (our) pasture, in addition to the Dirty Shame Saloon. His girlfriend, Suzie, used to be a card dealer in Las Vegas. She's small, red-haired, high-cheekboned, beautiful. I hope that she and Elizabeth will get to be good friends. Dave is boyish, and his eyes have lots of excitement. He's been up here eight years, and you could watch him and believe, easily, that each year is his first.

SEPTEMBER 15

4 A writer in a valley of workers. Perhaps the novelty of it will allow them to tolerate me. No one asks if I'm going to be staying for the winter; instead, the way they phrase it is, "So, are you going to try to winter here?"

5   Then I will be a resident—if I last the season. After I've wintered, I will be able to move around the valley with more ease. I will see more things, hear more things, more things will be told to me.

6   Truman Zinn, Dave's friend, was saying how nice winter is. "A truck might go by your house only once a week, and it will be a real treat. You'll hear it coming from a long way off."

7   That's what they talk about most when they talk about winter: the silence. Jim Kelly, a retired forest cruiser—wild-looking, handsome, long straight black hair, Indian cheekbones, dark river-stone eyes—says he gets so crazy in winter that he just throws on his snowshoes and runs into the woods, up Hensley Face Mountain and back, a ten-mile trip, just for something to do. He says mountain lions follow him. He crosses their tracks in the snow sometimes, deep in the woods. On his return trip home, he finds their tracks on top of his, shadowing him.

8   Later on today I am going to bait Homer by saying, "Where is Elizabeth?" He hasn't heard me say her name in over two weeks. It will be interesting to see if he remembers, and then, too, at the train station.

9   I have a two-week beard. The train station will be fun.

10 Can't get enough wood! Ran back to the house to use the bathroom—cold and windy, blustery and damp—and when I went out to the greenhouse again, the aspen logs smelled good, popping in the wood stove: good warm dry heat on a nasty day. I'm lucky.

11   I hope Elizabeth likes cabbage. It's all over the place outside in the garden. I see it when I'm sitting at the desk; looking out my window, which still has beads of rain on it from last night. The lettuce stands bright and green from the rain too. I'm not much on vegetables. I should open the garden gate and let all the deer in, a Christmas surprise in mid-September.

12 One old woman, whom everyone calls Grandma, has lived up here all her life. Eighty years in the Yaak. Think of all the things she has missed. But think of all

the things she has seen that the rest of the world has missed. No one can get it all no matter where they are.

I don't know how to write about this country in an orderly fashion, because 13
I'm just finding out about it. If a path develops, I'll be glad to see it—as with math, chemistry, genetics, and electricity, things with rules and borders—but for now it is all loose events, great mystery, random lives.

    If I see a good piece of wood by the side of the road, I stop and pick it up. 14

    I'm waiting for the propane truck to drive up. I'm going to buy 900 gallons 15
of propane for the stove and generator (69.9 cents per gallon). For the family that lived here before me—husband, wife, two babies—that would have been three or four months' worth. I am going to make it last five or six months.

Later in the afternoon. I just returned from Yaak, where I made a call at one of 16
the twin pay phones, talked to Dick McGary for quite a while (it was warm inside his store), and bought ten chances for the Yaak Volunteer Ambulance's quilt raffle. The quilt hangs from the rafters in the store, scorching white in the sun that comes through the high windows. A dollar a raffle, and the quilt is the color of snow, of winter.

    I went and picked up a truckload of wood: such good wood. Thick stumps, 17
already cut, and long lodgepole pieces, dozed up into towering slash piles like toothpicks, where the logging has gone on—clearcuts, usually. Too damn much logging, slash piles everywhere, and wood going to waste, wood that was too small to use but got in the way. Here and there in the slash piles I'll find some larch, which is the driest of woods up here and burns hot; it's everyone's favorite.

    Didn't see anyone up on Hensley Face. Didn't want to see anyone. The dogs 18
played on top of the slash pile, leaping from lodgepole to lodgepole, burrowing down into the piles after the scent of who knows what. Their fur is getting thicker.

    Driving back afterward with a beer from the Dirty Shame, I met Truman 19
and Dave, who were fixing to go into town proper, Libby. They asked if I needed anything; this made me feel good. When I crossed the south fork of the Yaak and saw our pasture, Dave's old line-backed dun, Buck, was lying curled up, resting, and the sorrel, Fuel, was standing with his hind legs tucked slightly.

    They say Tom and Nancy Orr's cabin has polished elkhorn handles on the 20
drawers, cabinets, and doors. Nancy cross-country skis all winter long, and finds the antlers in the woods.

    The wind is lifting and creaking the shingles and rafters over my head. Inside the greenhouse it smells like smoke, like meat, along with the heroic, leftover, holdout smell of spring, of things still growing. 21

    Homer, crazy Homer, is eating tomatoes off the bush, standing knee-deep 22
in flowers to reach them. Ann is napping in a patch of sun. My clothes smell like wood smoke.

    Dick McGary said they had done an estimate and found out that it would 23
take $80,000 to run an electrical line out here. Good, I said. Wonderful.

    This light, this bronzed tintype light, the light of late summer, Indian 24
summer—it seems to be saying something. This light is everywhere. It's not

wavering, not brightening, nor is it dulling: it's just shiny, frozen, existing in itself.

25   Thinking now about the old woman who's lived here eighty years.

26   More talk about winter. McGary says they got a foot and a half of snow last Halloween night.

SEPTEMBER 17

27 Nancy Orr, who came to dinner over at the Dirty Shame, was telling us about her dream hoops. She weaves wreaths out of cane and then braids them with feathers from all the birds in the valley. She covers the entire wreath, leaving a small opening in the center. According to Indian lore, you hang the dream hoop over your head at night, and as you sleep, any nightmares and fears that come to you will get tangled up in the feathers. Only good dreams are able to pass, through the small hole in the center.

28   It's so spooky, and so sure of its own logic—so fantastic—that you know it must work. Dave and Suzie, as well as Nancy, swear that it does.

29   A good dinner. All the spaghetti in the world, and beyond. Long, lazy days. Fish jumping out on the river across the road from the saloon. Elizabeth arrives at the train station tomorrow.

SEPTEMBER 19

30 I picked Elizabeth up at the train station before daylight yesterday morning. Everybody should get to do this at least once: wait like that, in the darkness. I could hear geese flying over the mountains, going south. It's a wonderful thing, just waiting, with the train running late—it was due in at four-thirty A.M.—but knowing that it is coming, and then seeing the light.

31   All the rest of our old life fell away into the past when I saw that light far down the tracks. The station in Libby is an old one. No one else was waiting for the train at that hour of the morning, and nobody else got off the train, just Elizabeth.

32   I feel fractured, filled with luck. I gathered her up—she was grinning as if she were fifteen, sixteen years old—and we put the bags in the truck, and she hugged the dogs too.

33   We stopped and got coffee at the all-night café and then started up the narrow cliff road to Yaak Valley. It was intoxicating to have nothing behind us anymore, and to have everything ahead of us. Deer ran back and forth across the road, passing through our headlights. A month is a long time when your life is new.

34   We reached the ranch, drove up the long drive, went inside—the smell of logs—and went upstairs. It was still dark and cold in the cabin, cold outside.

35   When we woke up, the sky was blue and Elizabeth could see that the leaves had started changing already. The wind was still blowing, and it was from the north.

SEPTEMBER 20

We got four loads of wood yesterday, about one cord. It's hard getting used to 36
talking and listening to someone else. I'm delighted to have her here, but am
surprised at the adjustment I need to make.

    We've been having hard frosts every night, twenty-five, twenty-six degrees; 37
but we're in shirtsleeves and barefoot again during the day.

    The dogs keep finding more bones. Things seem to die all the time around here. 38

    Things to do: Clean chimney trap. Clean chicken coop and convert it to 39
winter dog residence. Shovel ashes out of fireplace, wood stoves. Git wood.

Good things to know if you are a logger: wear high boots, of course, to protect 40
your ankles against spike limbs, but also wear high-cuffed pants that are open
around the cuffs, not unlike bell-bottoms. You want them stopping up high,
around the ankle, so that when you are climbing around in a pile of slash, every
little branch and limb doesn't go up your leg and trip you. You want baggy,
flaring pants, so that if a branch does run up your cuff, then it won't wedge in
there and trip you; you can just step out of it. Truman told me this over beers a
few nights ago, and I'd forgotten it until yesterday, when I fell. Everyone's so
helpful.

    I introduced Elizabeth to the McGarys yesterday, up at the mercantile. Dick 41
was talking about how wonderful winter can be; how it got down to eighty
below (windchill) their first year up here; how on a cold, clear day in the heart
of winter, with no one around, you can look up and see the sky swirling and
sparkling with flashing ice crystals—above you the whole sky, crystals falling
out of blue air, even though there is no wind.

    Check the antifreeze. This is a simple, stupid thing that someone from easy 42
times, from the warm, simple growth of Mississippi, might easily forget.

    Everyone back east wants me to send them pictures, but very few of them 43
sound serious about wanting to visit. This is fine with me. I will send them pictures.

    A few nights ago, while getting wood, I saw some grouse. They are big, 44
muscular, quail-chicken birds, runners and scooters, and they taste wonderful.

    Haven't seen Tom and Nancy since Elizabeth got in. I think about Nancy a 45
good bit. I want to ask both of them questions all day long, all winter—about
dream hoops, about ravens, about trapping.

    The consensus, unanimously so, is that this is going to be a fierce winter: 46
fuzzy deer already, men's breads growing faster, old people feeling it in their
bones, their hearts; the way stars flash and glimmer at night; the way trees
stand dark against the sky. Driving back from the Shame late at night, I've already seen snowshoe hares turned completely white. They've staked their lives
on the fact, or feeling, that it's going to be an early winter, and a hard one.

    Great huge fat white rabbits, like magicians, rabbits the size of large cats, 47
hide out in the darkness of the woods, waiting for the snow that will save them.
Evolving all these thousands of years, tens of thousands: the foolish ones were
long ago weeded out, the willy-nilly, turn-white-for-no-reason rabbits; those

that turned white when there really wasn't any snow coming, or those that turned white too early, had nowhere to hide, and so were quickly consumed, visible prey to wolves, coyotes, hawks, owls, bobcats, lions, everything. And the hares that stayed brown, the ones that did not feel the hard winter coming and did not prepare for it, they got theirs.

48   So I figure these rabbits know. What a remarkable thing, to bet your life each year, twice a year actually, because they must know when to turn brown again. This year I have been seeing rabbits come out of hiding after the sun goes down, white rabbits hopping across the logging roads as I come down off the mountain with a load of wood—trying, with the windows rolled down, to listen and feel for myself, and to learn rather than always having to be told. I think that I can learn.

49   There are cars and trucks parked outside the Dirty Shame when I go past— mostly trucks—and it looks warm and inviting, a glow in the night woods. But I've got my window rolled down, I can feel it, feel what I *should* be feeling. What it tells me is that I have gotten up here late to this little valley, maybe too late; but once I'm home, unloading the wood from the truck, smelling the fresh cut of it and feeling the silence of the woods all around me, what I feel, like the rab- bits, is this: surely better late than never. With a flashlight, after eleven o'clock, I go back into the night again, driving past the Dirty Shame once more and up onto the mountain for more wood, trying to beat what, like everyone else up here, I now know, rather than think, is coming.

50   What I feel is that I had better not stop, that I have lost time to make up for.

51 Hard dreams, of the line-backed dun across the road, his face iced over with snow and sleet, his back to the wind, staring straight ahead as if seeing some- thing far out in front of him; as if watching, through a looking glass, spring and its thaw, its greenness. Dreams of heavy axes hitting frozen wood, of steaming coffee from a thermos, of sitting inside the Dirty Shame, the whole valley—thirty or forty of us trapped by a blizzard—cheering at the football game on the little TV screen, yelling and making bets as to who will win.

52   What Edward Hoagland has called the courage of turtles, I can see now as the wisdom of rabbits. There is so much to learn. Everything I have learned so far has been wrong. I'm having to start all over. I want to find Nancy today and ask her one more time about those dream hoops, ask her again how they work, ask if there are life hoops as well, though already I know she will tell me that yes, there are.

53   It can be so wonderful, finding out you were wrong, that you are ignorant, that you know nothing, not squat. You get to start over. It's like snow falling that first time each year. It doesn't make any sound, but it's the strongest force you know of. Trees will crack and pop and split open later in the winter. Things opening up, learning. Learning the way it really is.

54   All through the forest, they say, you can hear the trees on the coldest of nights: cracking and popping like firecrackers, like cannons, like a parade, while rabbits, burrowed in the snow beneath them, sit quietly, warm and white, saved, having learned—having made the right bet.

Nancy, in the Shame, was telling me about how she hurt her wrist skiing one 55 year. It wouldn't heal and it was all drawn up and forever cramping; a guy told her to stop drinking coffee, and she did, and two days later the wrist was supple again, strong.

I had bad dreams and a recurring headache all night, dreams of dying, mur- 56 der, cancer, fires, traffic jams. I need a dream hoop.

Evening. I'm writing again, and throwing wood into the stove. Little wrist-size 57 pieces, they burn almost as fast as you can look at them. Energy. Can't have too much wood. It makes the valley smell good. Of course, there are only thirty of us in the valley. This is the proper number. The Dirty Thirty. Next March I will be thirty. If everyone in the world burned as much wood as I am going to this winter, the planet would be obscured, one great wood-smoke cloud. I don't know what to think about that. We're all dirty, but we're all sweet!

I recycle my aluminum! I don't litter! I try to pee on the rocks, not on the 58 soil, to keep from killing things with too much nitrogen.

I remember now how my father pronounces the word "moron" when aim- 59 ing it at me: "mo-ron." Maybe I am a mo-ron for using wood for fuel rather than the similarly priced propane (though I get my wood for free, with the saw, the ax, the biceps, the deltoids).

We all have dirt in us. Wood is better than coal, but not as good as gas.   60

No, that's hypocritical, rationalizing. Wood is bad, inefficient, dirty, but it 61 smells good. It's fun to chop, and I like to watch the flames, watch the erratic, pulsating heat it gives, and I like the snaps and pops, and when I'm dead and gone, I'll be glad I used it.

"Mo-ron," the children of the centuries after me will cry. But there will be 62 jealousy as well as anger in their cries (and we are all the same, always have been), and there is wood lying all around, wood everywhere, and it is free, and I have a life to live. Me first, it feels like I am saying. It is my turn, and you may not even get yours.

You should hear my father say it—in traffic, or watching a baseball game, 63 when the manager makes a bad move: "mo-ron." It's like a wave at sea, rolling high on the "mo" and cresting, rolling down into the curl and lick and wave of "ron," sliding softly to shore. The word of the nineties, I'm afraid, is environ-mental mo-ron, mo-ron, mo-ron . . .

I know I should be burning gas, not wood. I know I should.   64

FOCUS ON ECOLOGY

1. What is the relationship between the time one stays in the valley, according to Bass, and one's acceptance by the other residents of the valley?
2. How does Bass describe the Yaak, the place where he lives? How do you re-spond to the living conditions as he describes them? Would you want to live in the Yaak? Why or why not?

3. What do you suppose Bass means when he writes, "Everyone back east wants me to send them pictures, but very few of them sound serious about wanting to visit. This is fine with me. I will send them pictures"?

FOCUS ON WRITING

1. What does Rick Bass seem to convey when he writes early in this selection, "When it starts to snow, I'm going to write in the greenhouse. There's a wood stove, and I'll keep warm that way. Two sticks of wood should equal one page, if I'm lucky." What might Bass be suggesting about his writing and its relationship with nature?
2. What does Bass mean when he writes, "I don't know how to write about this country in an orderly fashion, because I'm just finding out about it"? What does this suggest about the kinds of knowledge one must have of a place to write about it in an "orderly fashion"?
3. How would you characterize Bass's writing style in this piece?

FOR DISCUSSION

Consider the ways Bass describes the Yaak Valley. As a class, discuss the ways his writing conveys a sense of place. What do we as readers come to learn about the place where Bass lives both directly and indirectly from his writing?

WRITING IN RESPONSE

As you have seen from the journal assignments in *Saving Place*, keeping a journal is often a good way to sort out how we think about our daily interactions with the environments where we live. Bass's book *Winter: Notes from Montana* serves as an effective way for Bass, and ultimately for us as readers, to come to terms with his new home. For this assignment, keep a journal of your daily living for the next week. Focus not on your daily actions, but on the ways the place where you live affects how you live. Then, once you have written in the journal for a week, revise the prose so that the journal might be read by an audience other than yourself.

The Negro Speaks of Rivers

Langston Hughes

Langston Hughes was born in Joplin, Missouri, in 1902. He earned a reputation as a writer during the 1920s in a period known as the "Harlem Renaissance," when many new young black authors were gaining attention. Early in his career, Hughes gained acclaim for his poetry, nonfiction, and fiction, but also gained much criticism from black critics for the ways he depicted black life in America. Despite the criticism, Hughes continued to gain attention for his writing, particularly for his fiction and his weekly column "From Here to Yonder," which appeared in the Chicago Defender *and the* New York Post. *Hughs wrote more than 15 books of poetry. This poem, "The Negro Speaks of Rivers," addresses the role rivers have played in the lives and histories of African-Americans.*

JOURNAL ASSIGNMENT

"The Negro Speaks of Rivers" is about the relationship between African-American history and the history of some important rivers. In your journal, speculate as to why the history of a particular group of people, such as African-Americans, might be strongly tied to the history of rivers or other natural formations like mountains, oceans, or plains.

I've known rivers:
I've known rivers ancient as the world and older than the
          flow of human blood in the human veins.

My soul has grown deep like the rivers.

I bathed in the Euphrates when dawns were young.
I built my hut near the Congo and it lulled me to sleep.
I looked upon the Nile and raised the pyramids above it.
I heard the singing of the Mississippi when Abe Lincoln
          went down to New Orleans, and I've seen its muddy
          bosom turn all golden in the sunset.

I've known rivers:
Ancient, dusky, rivers.

My soul has grown deep like the rivers.

FOCUS ON ECOLOGY

1. Hughes identifies four rivers specifically in this poem: the Euphrates, the Congo, the Nile, and the Mississippi, and to each of these rivers he links a historical moment important in the history of African-Americans. First, identify the location of each of these rivers. Second, identify why each of these rivers plays an important historical part in the narrative of this poem.
2. What is a river? How do you define it scientifically? How is it different from other bodies of water like creeks, streams, lakes, or ponds?
3. Are there other rivers to which Hughes might have referred in this poem that would have the same effect? If so, which ones and why? If not, why not?

FOCUS ON WRITING

1. Who is the "I" who narrates this poem?
2. Is there any significance to the shape of the poem on the page? What effect does the variation in line length have?
3. Why does "Abe Lincoln" appear in the poem?

FOR DISCUSSSION

"The Negro Speaks of Rivers" describes a historical, long-term relationship with rivers. As a class, consider why this poem is presented here in a chapter discussion about living in and with nature.

WRITING IN RESPONSE

It is likely that there is a river near your home that has had an impact historically in your community and the surrounding area. Take some time to learn more about the history of a local river. Find out about the river's natural history. Where are its headwaters? To where does it flow? When did it form? Has its course changed? Has its course been manipulated through human intervention? What animals inhabit it? Then, learn about its human history. Through what towns and cities does it flow? Was it used for transportation? What cargo shipped on it? Who has claimed ownership of the river? What pollutants are dumped in it? Who cares for it? Do you or your family have a relationship with that river? Once you have learned about the river, write a historical account of that river, detailing all that you have learned. It might help, also, if you could visit the river to see the thing you are writing about, to experience its history. If you do not live near a river (which, I must say, is doubtful), select a river you've heard or read about and write a history of that river.

From *From Sand Creek:*
Rising in This Heart
Which Is Our America

Simon J. Ortiz

Simon J. Ortiz *is a native speaker of the Acoma Pueblo language, but he writes in English, a language he did not learn until he was in school. His poetry and short stories have made him one of today's best Native American writers. Ortiz is critically aware of the role of language in his writing, and his work is characterized by careful consideration of the words he chooses. His writing adopts the sound of traditional Native American oral storytelling, and his work generally addresses issues of Native American life. Throughout his life, Ortiz has recognized that as a Native American he is forced to live and function in a system unlike his Acoma culture. He has been clear to himself and to his readers, in works like* Fight Back: For the People, for the Land, *that in order to defend his Acoma heritage he must learn to operate in the larger system; hence, he writes in English because that is the language of publication in this country, the language that reaches audiences. Throughout his work, the recurring theme of connectedness appears, and issues of human relationships with nature are prevalent. The poem reprinted here is taken from his book* From Sand Creek: Rising in This Heart Which Is Our America, *a series of poems set in a Colorado veterans hospital just after the Vietnam War. In this book, Ortiz parallels the 1864 Sand Creek Massacre, where 133 Indian women and children were killed, with the massacres of the Vietnam war. In the poem reprinted here, Ortiz comments on how American farming has disappeared and how bars have flourished, leaving little room for natural living. As you read this poem, think about your own community and the numbers of bars there are compared with places that sell and grow food.*

JOURNAL ASSIGNMENT

In your journal, consider the relationship between farming and alcohol in Native American life. Why might Ortiz be linking these issues?

Even the farmer has become a loser; in small Kansas, Iowa, Nebraska towns, there are more bars than churches or food stores.

    Dreams
    thinned

and split
can only produce
these bones.

      The last outpost
known,
the rusted plowshare.

Talked to a farmer
about Arapaho schemes.
They knew things
were too good to last,
said he.

      In Denver,
I could drink them under
the table anytime.

All they remembered
was open plain and mountains.
They wouldn't even/couldn't even
consider Denver anyway.

Me,
I think as far as California,
I do.

FOCUS ON ECOLOGY

1. What is this poem about?
2. What does Ortiz mean when he writes, "even the farmer has become a loser"?
3. To what do these lines refer: "All they remembered / was open plain and mountains"? Why couldn't they "even / consider Denver anyway"?

FOCUS ON WRITING

1. Who are the characters identified in this poem?
2. What is meant by "Arapaho schemes"?
3. Why do you suppose Simon J. Ortiz begins this poem with the short explanation about the farmers, churches, and bars? (Note: in the book *From Sand Creek,* from which this poem is excerpted, Ortiz begins each poem with a similar, short explanation.)

FOR DISCUSSION

In the first of the Focus on Ecology questions I asked "what is this poem about?" As a class, return to this question and try to come to some consensus as to what Simon Ortiz is saying are in this poem.

WRITING IN RESPONSE

Many Native American narratives have been written about Native American cultures being removed from contact with land and nature through the influence of North American colonizers. Simon J. Ortiz's poem discusses how both the reduction of farm lands in the United States and the influx of alcohol in Native American cultures has affected how we all live in relation to nature. In an essay, explore how both farming and Native American cultures have affected America's overall way of life in relationship with nature. You will need to do a bit of reading to explore the history of farming and the changes in that history. Similarly, you will need to research the changes that have been inflicted upon Native American ways of life.

This Land Is Your Land:
Turning to Nature in a Time of Crisis

William Cronon

William Cronon, who was born in New Haven, Connecticut, in 1954, has become one of the most renowned contemporary writers and speakers. Cronon's first book, Changes in the Land, *addresses the destruction of New England's natural habitats by colonists' farming methods, exploitation of natural resources, and the near elimination of Native Americans in the region by diseases brought from Europe. "This Land Is Your Land: Turning to Nature in a Time of Crisis" first appeared in* Audubon, *a publication of the Audubon Society, in its January/February 2002 edition. It was one of several pieces in a special section of the magazine dedicated to how Americans turned to nature following the attacks on the World Trade Center and the Pentagon on September 11, 2001. The piece is powerful in its message that nature provides us with a place to find comfort in times of fear and sadness. As you read this piece, think back to your own reactions to the September 11 attacks and ask yourself in what ways nature did or didn't give you comfort during those frightening times.*

JOURNAL ASSIGNMENT

In your journal, address why wild places might have been important to Americans following the 9/11 attacks.

1   Stand on this familiar ground, gazing out across the lake in the city that is my home, with the buildings of the University of Wisconsin and the dome of the State Capitol rising from the water on the horizon. Today I've sought out what may seem a rather humble refuge: a mile-long strip of land, often no more than a few dozen yards across, stretching far out into Madison's Lake Mendota. It is called Picnic Point, a homely sort of name from a time when what Americans sought from such places was "pleasuring grounds" for genteel retreat.

2   On this particular autumn day, I linger for a time beside a small swamp half-way down the peninsula. Yellow leaves drift downward as I watch, alighting on the water to become miniature boats afloat on their own bright reflections, miracles of fall color mingled with the dark hues of approaching winter. It is a blessedly commonplace scene, evoking the wheel of the seasons and the cycles of life and death. I stand in its presence as only the most recent of a long line of other human beings who have also sought solace in retreats like this one.

3   Then I turn back to gaze at the city on the horizon. Ordinarily, I might find in this view a welcome reminder that even in the midst of "civilization," nature is omnipresent, if only we care to see it. But today my thoughts are elsewhere. I see two towers burning in the sky, orange flames pouring from their ruptured sides, dark clouds churning toward the heavens, tiny figures gazing helplessly from windows above the fires, and then, in what seems to be but is not slow motion, the long terrible descent as everything dissolves and crumples to the earth below. Try as I might to escape it, this nightmare vision inscribes itself on the clear air before my eyes. The familiar buildings framed by the colors of autumn on the far side of this lake are where I live and work. Usually they seem so calm, so normal, that one might reasonably expect to take them for granted. But now, in the looming shadow of those vanished towers, it suddenly seems clear not only that one cannot take such things for granted but that one *must* not. They are too precious.

4   This pilgrimage I have made to Picnic Point is hardly mine alone. I'm quite certain that most of us have made similar journeys in the days since September 11. In doing so, I think we're recalling one of the oldest reasons we humans have for turning to the natural world in our search for meaning. We, of course, protect wild places for many reasons. In recent years we've come to think of them as preserves of biological diversity, places where life can go about its evolutionary business with less interference from us than it might encounter elsewhere. But wild places—whether they be domesticated patches like Picnic Point or great wilderness areas like the Arctic National Wildlife Refuge—have carried many other historical meanings as well. They've served as symbolic reminders

of what the landscape looked like before we threatened to turn all of nature into either a source of commodities or a playground for recreation. They've recalled for us the frontier conditions under which pioneers once lived as they seized this land from its earlier inhabitants and made homes for themselves in the wilderness. They've provided patriotic monuments to American nationalism, such as Yosemite and Grand Canyon, extraordinary parks whose grandeur can compete with anything that Europe might have to offer. And they've stood as icons of a romantic godhead sublimely immanent in all of creation.

But people have also turned to nature for solace of a much more personal 5 sort, never more so than in times of crisis and turmoil. The young men who endured the bloodshed of the Civil War also discovered that their months of living in the open air would call to them for the rest of their lives, leading them to seek outdoor retreats like no prior generation of Americans, and producing the first great wilderness parks in the United States, at places like Yellowstone and the Adirondacks. There they could reenact the vivid moments of their youth where, as Walt Whitman wrote,

> *The numerous camp-fires scatter'd near and far, some away up on the mountain / The* 6 *shadowy forms of men and horses, looming, large-sized, flickering / And over all the sky— the sky! Far, far out of reach, studded, breaking out, the eternal stars.*

A century later the movement to give legal protection to wild places in the 7 United States would culminate in the great Wilderness Act of 1964. The dreams of visionaries like John Muir and Bob Marshall and Aldo Leopold finally came to fruition at the height of the Cold War, two years after the Cuban Missile Crisis and less than a year after John Kennedy's assassination. The timing was no accident. It was a moment when the most potent symbol of terror was not a pair of burning skyscrapers but a mushroom cloud. "We learn to live with horrors," wrote the poet Nancy Newhall in the Sierra Club's *This Is the American Earth,* "evils as old as man, suddenly expanded into new until they hang worldwide, sky-high, above our lives." Nuclear war was the backdrop against which the preciousness of wild nature was cast into stark relief. "In the decades to come," Wallace Stegner wrote, "it will not be only the buffalo and the trumpeter swan who need sanctuaries. Our own species is going to need them too. It needs them now."

As Stegner well knew, it is not species that feel this need; it is individual 8 human beings who seek harbor in times of storm. So I stand on this narrow strip of wild land, searching not just the world around me but my own heart. These falling leaves, the light dancing on this water, this gray sky, the pungent smell of this damp soil as the life around me returns to the earth that nurtures it. Although all these are ever changing, they also stand apart from the terrible human drama that now engulfs us. They bear witness, as Wendell Berry once remarked, to "wild things who do not tax their lives with forethought of grief." Picnic Point, humble though it may be, offers sanctuary: a place consecrated by the truths it helps us recollect, a refuge to which we can retreat in time of need, a place we go looking to find ourselves.

9   Retreat, of course, does not mean escape. One of the things I love about this peninsula is that it carries me into nature even as I remain in the heart of my city, for, of course, we are never outside the natural world, no matter where we live or what we do. The great challenge of modernity is to *remember,* in the face of all that tempts us to forget, just how interconnected the world is. That is even true of those blazing towers, which remind us of the immense natural forces implied by a very large object moving very quickly with many tons of jet fuel on board, a Faustian bargain we have made with kinetic energy in the service of our own freedom. Nature is there, too.

10   It is likewise present in those minute spores we have so recently learned to dread, wafting invisibly through the air in search of dark damp locations where they can enlist macrophages in the work of manufacturing still more spores. We suddenly remember where our oil comes from. We suddenly remember what can be done with enriched uranium. We suddenly remember what can happen when we ignore the pain and hatred of those who might wish the world different from what it is. The nature we change and use for our own purposes needs remembering as much as the nature we preserve as wild sanctuaries, if we are truly to understand our place in the world—and if we are to save both it and ourselves.

11   There is fear in such remembering, of course, but there is also hope. Recognizing vulnerability is itself an act of strength. The journey back to nature is also necessarily a journey into ourselves to remember who we are and what we believe. For how else are we to change the world, how else are we to take responsibility for it, than by reminding ourselves that the choices we make and the lives we lead have consequences for which we can and should hold ourselves accountable? We go to sanctuaries to remember the things we hold most dear, the things we cherish and love. And then—the great challenge—we return home seeking to enact this wisdom as best we can in our daily lives.

FOCUS ON ECOLOGY

1. Cronon claims that in making pilgrimages to wild places away from the cities and towns in which we live, Americans recall . . . "one of the oldest reasons we humans have for turning to the natural world in our search for meaning." First, what is that reason, as Cronon explains it? Second, do you agree with his assessment?
2. Are there natural landmarks that you consider to be patriotic? How does patriotism get to be associated with a particular place?
3. How do you respond to Cronon's parallels between the history of national parks American tragedies?

FOCUS ON WRITING

1. Why do you suppose Audubon published this essay and others about the role of nature after the 9/11 attacks?

2. Why does Cronon include the excerpt from Walt Whitman's poem in this essay? From where is this poem taken? What effect does it have on the essay?
3. What does Cronon mean when he writes, "Retreat, of course, does not mean escape"?

FOR DISCUSSION

How do you respond to Cronon's essay? As a class, discuss the role America's parks and wilderness areas played in the aftermath of the 9/11 attacks. Did you make a retreat into the wilderness to search for comfort or meaning? If so, why did this become an outlet for you? If not, did you consider doing so? And if not, why do you suppose doing so did not cross your mind?

WRITING IN RESPONSE

Take some time to think about how the parks and natural recreation areas in your region were used after the 9/11 tragedies. Contact local park officials and ask them if park use increased in the months following 9/11. Then, in a short narrative, discuss the ways your local wilderness areas and parks might have been a retreat for people searching for meaning after the 9/11 attacks.

DISCUSSING THE ISSUES

1. Living in and with nature takes into account many of the subjects of other chapters in *Saving Place:* how we define nature, how we consume nature, how we recreate in nature, how we survive in nature, and how we develop relationships with the environments in which we live. After having examined a number of the essays in this chapter, discuss with your class all of the things we might want to consider when establishing a home for ourselves. What should we know about the place where we want to live? How do we gather such information? Do we really need to consider our relationship to that place?
2. The title of this chapter, "Living in and with Nature," asks us to consider how our lives interact with nature, and more specifically, how we live both *in* and *with* nature. As a class, consider the distinctions between living with nature and living in nature. Then, discuss how each of us lives both with and in nature on a daily basis.

WRITING ABOUT THE ISSUES

1. *Personal Experience:* Assuming you could live anywhere on the planet, where would you most want to live? What kinds of things would you need to live a safe and comfortable life there? In a personal narrative, write about what things you would need to know to live in that ideal place.

2. *Local Context:* The writers in this chapter have offered many directions for thinking about how we live in and with nature. Many of the questions forwarded by these writers might be (and probably should be) considered in terms of where we each now live. Looking back at any one of the selections found in this chapter, consider how the issues raised in that selection might be applied to where you live. Then, using that selection as a starting point, write about your home in the same context as the selection you have chosen.

3. *Research:* For most of us, it should be a straightforward task to think about how our local communities now address issues of nature in terms of daily living. However, we may also want to consider how nature was thought of during earlier moments of our region's history. Take some time to learn about an earlier period in your community's history (and by this I specifically mean its history of human inhabitation, not its natural history) and about how nature was addressed by earlier residents of the area. Then, in a research paper describe how those historical approaches to nature have or have not changed.

RESEARCH PATHS

Mofro (www.fogworld.com/mofro/)
Arches National Park (www.infowest.com/Utah/canyonlands/arches.html)
Arches National Park (www.americanparknetwork.com/parkinfo/ar/)
Wildlands Project (www.twp.org/)
Sheryl St. Germain (www.public.iastate.edu/~sgermain/)
Superfund (www.epa.gov/superfund/)

FURTHER READINGS

Edward Abbey, *Desert Solitaire*
Edward Abbey, *The Monkeywrench Gang*
Edward Abbey, *Hayduke Lives!*
Edward Abbey, *The Journey Home: Some Words in Defense of the American West*
Robert Bullard, *Dumping in Dixie*
Derrick Jensen, *Listening to the Land*
Alicia Bay Laurel, *Living on the Earth*

CHAPTER 7

Our Future in/with/of Nature

So, where do we go from here? This final chapter of *Saving Place* asks that you not allow these final readings to end your own inquiry into how your life interacts with, is affected by, and affects the world in which you live. It asks that you continue to develop your awareness of environments, places, and nature and the roles reading and writing play in developing those relationships. The readings in this chapter look toward the future, toward thinking about the kinds of actions and thinking that might affect the future of environments, places, and nature.

In many ways, the readings in this chapter as well as the questions I ask you and the writing prompts I provide do not work toward a conclusion, as one might expect in the final chapter of a book. Rather, these readings open new doors, offer avenues of inquiry we have not yet considered. In the Introduction to *Saving Place*, I commented that this book is about writing, particularly about how writing affects and is affected by places, environments, and nature. This final chapter extends your exploration of these relationships by examining how writers look toward possible futures.

The readings here cover a range of subjects, including

- ways we think about our relationships with places, nature, and environments
- what we might do to protect our forests
- how we might think about environmentalism in the future
- how we might re-think our positions in the world
- ways we might be "loving" our resources away
- ways we might re-think our political boundaries based on ecological systems
- what options we might have in terms of chemical pollutants
- how we might protect endangered species of animals

- how we might be more efficient in our use of resources

- how we might re-conceptualize change in terms of nature, place, and environment

- how we might protect particular water systems

A Shark in the Mind of One Contemplating Wilderness

Terry Tempest Williams

Terry Tempest Williams's writing walks an interesting line between faith and feminism. Brought up in the Mormon faith, Williams has also been deeply influenced by French feminists, particularly Helene Cixous. Facing a life marked by deaths in her family from cancers caused by nuclear testing in the Great Salt Lake area, Williams's writing explores the relationships between the slow decay of feminine bodies and the environmental destruction that inflicted cancers on the bodies of her family. Paralleling her commentary on nuclear testing and the effect on her family with a detailed study of the decline of bird life around the same area, Williams makes remarkable links between thinking about environmental destruction and individual lives. The problematics of family and place resound throughout her work. One of her most important books, Refuge: an Unnatural History of Family and Place, *adresses the place of the Great Salt Lake and the death of her mother. For Williams, making such connections between environment and human life is crucial because, as she has explained in the* Blooms-bury Review, *"That's the premise of Refuge—that an intimacy with the natural world initiates an intimacy with death, because life and death are engaged in an endless, inseparable dance." As you read this selection, consider how Williams has organized the piece and how she asks us to think about wilderness.*

JOURNAL ASSIGNMENT

In "A Shark in the Mind of One Contemplating Wilderness," Williams discusses how wilderness is designated and seen in the same ways that art is designated and viewed. Consider for a moment how wilderness and art might be seen as similar (or different). In your journal write about how you see wilderness and art being related

A shark swims past me in a kelp forest that sways back and forth with the current. It is deliberate and focused. I watch the shark's sleek body dart left and right as its caudal fin propels it forward. Its eyes seem to slice through the water in a blood gaze as the gills open and close, open and close. Around and around, I watch the shark maneuver through schools of fish. It must not be hungry. The only thing separating me from the shark is a tall glass pane at the Monterey Sea Aquarium. Everything is in motion. I press my hands on the glass waiting for the shark to pass by again and when it does, I feel my own heart beating against the mind of this creature that kills.

•　•　•

In the enormous blue room of the American Museum of Natural History, I stare at the tiger shark mounted on the wall of the second floor. Its surface shines with the light of taxidermy, creating the illusion of having just left the sea, now our own natural-history trophy. I see how out of proportion its mouth is to the rest of its body and wonder how many teeth hung from its gums during its lifetime, the rows of teeth, five to twenty of them, biting and tearing, thrashing and chomping on flesh, the teeth constantly being replaced by something akin to a conveyor-belt system. Somewhere in my mind I hold the fact that a shark may go through 20,000 teeth in a life span of ten years. I imagine the shark sensing the electrical field of a seal, swimming toward the diving black body now rising to the surface, delivering with great speed its deadly blow, the jaws that dislocate and protrude out of its mouth, the strong muscles that open, then close, the razor teeth that clamp down on the prey with such force that skin, cartilage and bone are reduced to one clean round bite, sustained over and over again. The blue water now bloody screams to the surface. Even in death, I see this shark in motion.

•　•　•

Sensation. I enter the Brooklyn Museum of Art to confront another tiger shark, this the most harrowing of all the requiem sharks I have encountered in a weeklong period. Requiem sharks. They say the name is derived from the observation that once these large sharks of the order *Carcharhinid* attack a victim, the only task remaining is to hold a requiem, a mass for the dead. *Galeocerdo cuvieri.* It is neither dead nor alive, but rather a body floating in space, a shark suspended in solution. Formaldehyde. To preserve. What do we choose to preserve? I note the worn, used sense of its mouth, shriveled and receding, looking more manly than fish. The side view creates a triptych of head, dorsal fin and tail, through the three panels of glass in the frame of white painted steel.

I walk around the shark and feel the charge of the front view, a turquoise night-mare of terror that spills into daylight. Sensation. Damien Hirst is the creator of The Physical Impossibility of Death in the Mind of Someone Living (1991).

I do not think about the shark. I think about myself.

● ● ●

> *I like the idea of a thing to describe a feeling. A shark is frightening, bigger than you are, in an environment unknown to you. It looks alive when it's dead and dead when it's alive. . . . I like ideas of trying to understand the world by taking things out of the world. . . . You ex-pect [the shark] to look back at you.*
>
> (Damien Hirst)

As a naturalist who has worked in a museum of natural history for more than fifteen years, how I am to think about a shark in the context of art, not science? How is my imagination so quickly rearranged to see the suspension of a shark, pickled in formaldehyde, as the stopped power of motion in the jaws of death, an image of my own mortality?

My mind becomes wild in the presence of creation, the artist's creation. I learn that the box in which the shark floats was built by the same company that con-structs the aquariums of Brighton Sea World. I think about the killer whales kept in tanks for the amusement of humans, the killer whales that jump through hoops, carry humans on their backs as they circle and circle and circle the tank, day after day after week after month, how they go mad, the sea of insanity churning inside them, inside me as I feel my own captivity within a culture—any culture—that would thwart creativity: We are stopped cold, our spirits sus-pended, controlled, controlled sensation.

Tiger shark, glass, steel, 5 percent formaldehyde solution.

Damien Hirst calls the shark suspended in formaldehyde a sculpture. If it were in a museum of natural history, it would be called an exhibit, an exhibit in which the organism is featured as the animal it is. Call it art or call it biology, what is the true essence of shark?

How is the focus of our perceptions decided?

Art. Artifact. Art by designation.

Thomas McEvilley, art critic and author of *Art & Otherness*, states,

> The fact that we designate something as art means that it is art for us, but says noth-ing about what it is in itself or for other people. Once we realize that the quest for

essences is an archaic religious quest, there is no reason why something should be art for one person or culture and non-art for another.

Wild. Wilderness. Wilderness by designation. What is the solution to preserving that which is wild?

I remember standing next to an old rancher in Escalante, Utah, during a contentious political debate over wilderness in the canyon country of southern Utah. He kicked the front tire of his pickup truck with his cowboy boot.

"What's this?" he asked me.

"A Chevy truck," I responded.

"Right, and everybody knows it."

He then took his hand and swept the horizon. "And what's all that?" he asked with the same matter-of-fact tone.

"Wilderness," he answered before I could speak. "And everybody knows it, so why the hell do you have to go have Congress tell us what it is?"

Damien Hirst's conceptual art, be it his shark or his installation called A Thousand Years (1990)—where the eye of a severed cow's head looks upward as black flies crawl over it and lay eggs in the flesh that metamorphose into maggots that mature into flies that gather in the pool of blood to drink, leaving tiny red footprints on the glass installation, while some flies are destined to die as a life-stopping buzz in the electric fly-killing machine—all his conceptual pieces of art, his installations, make me think about the concept and designation of wilderness.

Why not designate wilderness as an installation of art? Conceptual art? A true sensation that moves and breathes and changes over time with a myriad of creatures that formulate an instinctual framework of interspecies dialogues; call them predator-prey relations or symbiotic relations, niches and ecotones, never before seen as art, as dance, as a painting in motion, but imagined only through the calculations of biologists, their facts now metamorphosed into designs, spontaneously choreographed moment to moment among the living. Can we not watch the habits of animals, the adaptations of plants, and call them performance art within the conceptual framework of wilderness?

To those who offer the critique that wilderness is merely a received idea, one that might be "conceptually incoherent" and entranced by the myth of the pristine," why not answer with a resounding yes, yes, wilderness is our received idea as artists, as human beings, a grand piece of performance art that can embody and inspire *The Physical Impossibility of Death in the Mind of Someone Living or Isolated Elements Swimming in the Same Direction for the Purpose of Understanding* (1991).

Call it a cabinet of fish preserved in salt solution to honor the diversity of species, where nothing is random. Or call it a piece of art to celebrate color and form found in the bodies of fishes. Squint your eyes: *Imagine a world of spots. Colored dots in the wilderness. They're all connected.* Damien Hirst paints spots.

"Art's about life and it can't really be about anything else. There isn't anything else." Tell us again, Damien Hirst, with your cabinet of wonders; we are addicted to wonders, bottles of drugs lined up, shelf after shelf, waiting to be opened, minds opened, veins opened, nerves opened. Wilderness is a cabinet of pharmaceuticals waiting to be discovered.

Just as we designate art, we designate wilderness, large and small, as much as we can, hoping it begins a dialogue with our highest and basest selves. We are animals, in search of a home, in relationship to Other, an expanding community with a mosaic of habitats, domestic and wild; there is nothing precious or nostalgic about it. We designate wilderness as an installation of essences, open for individual interpretation, full of controversy and conversation.

"I always believe in contradiction, compromise . . . it's unavoidable. In life it can be positive or negative, like saying, 'I can't live without you.'" Damien Hirst speaks again.

I cannot live without art. I cannot live without wilderness. Call it *Brilliant Love* (1994-95). Thank the imagination that some people are brave enough, sanely crazy enough, to designate both. *"Art is dangerous because it doesn't have a definable function. I think that is what people are afraid of."*

Yes, Damien, exactly, you bad boy of British art who dares to slice up the bodies of cows, from the head to the anus, and mix them all up to where nothing makes sense and who allows us to walk through with no order in mind, twelve cross-sections of cow, so we have to take note of the meat that we eat without thinking about the topography of the body, the cow's body, our body; we confront the wonder of the organism as is, not as a continuum but as a design, the sheer beauty and texture of functional design. We see the black-and-white hide; there is no place to hide inside the guts of a cow sliced and stretched through space like an accordion between your very large hands. You ask us to find *Some Comfort Gained from the Acceptance of the Inherent Lies in Everything* (1996).

We have been trying to explain, justify, codify, give biological and ecological credence as to why we want to preserve what is wild, like art, much more than a specimen behind glass. But what if we were to say, Sorry, you are right, wilderness has no definable function. Can we let it be, designate it as art, *art of the wild*, just in case one such definition should arise in the mind of one standing in the tall grass prairies of middle America or the sliding slope of sandstone in the erosional landscape of Utah?

Wilderness as an aesthetic.

Freeze. Damien Hirst brought together a community of artists and displayed their work in a warehouse in England, these Neo-Conceptualists who set out to explore the big things like death and sex and the meaning of life. Wilderness designation is not so dissimilar. In your tracks, *freeze,* and watch the performance art of a grizzly walking through the gold meadows of the Hayden Valley in Yellowstone. In your tracks, *freeze,* a constellation of monarch butterflies has gathered in the mountains of Mexico. No definable function except to say, wilderness exists like art, look for an idea with four legs, with six legs and wings that resemble fire, and recognize this feeling called survival, in this received idea of wilderness, our twentieth-century installation as Neo-Conservationists.

A shark in a box.

Wilderness as a box.

Wilderness as *A Thousand Years* with flies and maggots celebrating inside the corpse of things.

Q: What is in the boxes?
A: Maggots.

Q: So you're going to put maggots in the white boxes, and then they hatch and then they fly around . . .
A: And then they get killed by the fly-killer, and maybe lay eggs in the cow heads.

Q: It's a bit disgusting.
A: A bit. I don't think it is. I like it.

Q: Do you think anyone will buy it?
A: I hope so.

(*Damien Hirst interview with Liam Gillick*, Modern Medicine, 1990)

Do I think anyone will buy the concept of wilderness as conceptual art? It is easier to create a sensation over art than a sensation over the bald, red-faced sale and development of open lands, wild lands, in the United States of America.

I would like to bring Damien Hirst out to the American West, let him bring along his chain saw, *Cutting Ahead* (1994), only to find out somebody has beat him to it, creating clear-cut sculptures out of negative space, eroding space, topsoil running like blood down the mountainsides as mud. Mud as material. He would have plenty of material.

The art of the wild is flourishing.

How are we to see through the lens of our own creative destruction?

A shark in a box.

Wilderness as an installation.

A human being suspended in formaldehyde.

My body floats between contrary equilibriums. (Federico García Lorca)

When I leaned over the balcony of the great blue room in the American Museum of Natural History, I looked up at the body of the Blue Whale, the largest living mammal on earth, suspended from the ceiling. I recalled being a docent, how we brought the schoolchildren to this room to lie on their backs, thrilled beyond words as they looked up at this magnificent leviathan who, if alive, with one quick swoosh of its tail would be halfway across Central Park.

I only then noticed that the open spaces below where the children used to lie on their backs in awe was now a food court filled with plastic tables and chairs. The tables were crowded with visitors chatting away, eating, drinking, oblivious to the creatures surrounding them. How had I missed the theater lights, newly installed on the balcony, pointing down to illuminate the refrigerators humming inside the showcases with a loud display of fast foods advertising yogurt, roast beef sandwiches, apples and oranges?

The Blue Whale, the Tiger Shark, Sunfish, Tunas, Eels and Manta Rays, the Walrus, the Elephant Seals, the Orca with its head poking through the diorama of ice in Antarctica, are no longer the natural histories of creatures associated with the sea but simply decoration.

Everything feels upside down these days, created for our environment. Requiem days. The natural world is becoming invisible, appearing only as a backdrop for our own human dramas and catastrophes; hurricanes, tornadoes, earthquakes and floods. Perhaps if we bring art to the discussion of the wild we can create a sensation where people will pay attention to the shock of what has always been here *Away from the Flock* (1994).

Wild Beauty in the Minds of the Living.

FOCUS ON ECOLOGY

1. To what does Terry Tempest Williams refer when discussing the tiger shark in the formaldehyde and when she asks "what do we choose to preserve?"
2. What, according to Williams, is the connection between art and wilderness? Do you agree with her?
3. How do you respond to Williams's idea of "wilderness as an aesthetic"?

FOCUS ON WRITING

1. Why do you suppose Terry Tempest Williams relies so heavily on the ideas of Damien Hirst in "A Shark in the Mind of One Contemplating Wilderness"? What effect does her references to his work have on the overall agenda of this essay?
2. Toward the end of this essay, Williams uses some interesting rhetorical choices in her writing: for example, the refrain of "freeze," and the short sentences and single-sentence paragraphs. What effect do these choices have on the essay?
3. Why do you suppose Williams capitalizes her final sentence as though it were a title?

FOR DISCUSSION

Williams writes, "just as we designate art, we designate wilderness." As a class consider what Williams means by this statement and address the implications of equating the designation of wilderness with the designation of art.

WRITING IN RESPONSE

Most communities and many campuses have museums that contain images of or preserved bodies of animals. Visit a museum near you and look at the ways that animals are depicted. Then, consider a particular exhibit both in its artistic presentation and for what it conveys about the animals it depicts. Consider where in the museum the exhibit is located, the text (if any) that accompanies it. Write a paper that describes what you observed and then argue as to whether the exhibit is displayed for aesthetic reasons or for environmental educational reasons.

"Second Coming" from *Ecology of a Cracker Childhood*

Janisse Ray

Janisse Ray was born in 1962 in Appling County, Georgia, a place about which she writes in her magnificent book Ecology of a Cracker Childhood. *Ray, who grew up in a junkyard, has become one of the South's most vocal and important environmental activists. She is a founding board member of the Altamaha Riverkeepers. In addition to* Ecology of a Cracker Childhood, *which in 2000 won both the Southern Environmental Law Center Award for Outstanding Writing on the Southern Environment and the Southern Book Critics Circle Award, Ray's writing has appeared in numerous venues, including* Wild Earth, Hope, Tallahassee Democrat, Alaska Quarterly Review, Missoula Independent, Natural History, Orion, Orion Afield, Florida Wildlife, Florida Living and Georgia Wildlife, The Woods Stretched for Miles, Wild Heart of Florida: Writers on Florida's Wildlands, *and* American Nature Writing 2000. *As you read the selection here, consider Ray's use of description.*

JOURNAL ASSIGNMENT

In "Second Coming," Ray compares the junkyard in which she grew up with wilderness and compares the restoration of the wilderness that was torn down to make room for the junkyard with the restoration of an old car. In what ways might the restoration of an old car be seen like the restoration of a pine forest wilderness? In your journal, consider this question and write about any similarities or differences you see.

> Through the acres of wrecks she came
> With a wrench in her hand,
>
> Through dust where the blacksnake dies
> Of boredom, and the beetle knows
> The compost has no more life.
>
> —James Dickey, "Cherrylog Road"

When my father bought a ten-acre lowland out U.S. 1 north on the outskirts of   1
Baxley, Georgia, intending to use it as a junkyard, it had already been logged.
So the unhitching of the first junker wasn't so much a travesty as it was a mon-
ument to my deepest regret.

Birding in the junkyard now, one finds nothing very unusual: cardinals,   2
brown thrashers, red-winged blackbirds, crows. They eat the ripe elderberries
and the mosquitoes that rise from the environs of foundered vehicles. Although
I did not as a child know their name, Carolina wrens nest in the old cars, from
which anoles and snakes come crawling. Field mice birth pink babies into
shredded foam under back seats.

But where are the eastern bluebirds, winter chickadees, yellow-rumped   3
warblers, white-eyed vireos? Where are tree swallows and savanna sparrows?
Where is yellow colic root and swamp coreopsis? Where is bird's-foot violet
and blue-eyed grass? Where are meadowlarks? River swamp frogs and sweet
bay magnolias should be there, an alligator or two. What happened to the
cougar and the red wolf?

Sometimes I dream of restoring the junkyard to the ecosystem it was when   4
Hernando de Soto sauntered into Georgia, looking for wealth but unable to
recognize it. Because it is a lowland, perhaps transitional to a bog, slash pine
would have dominated. Slash pines still grow here and there, as well as other
flora native to a wet pinewood: hatpins, sundews, gallberry. I dream about it
the way my brother dreams of restoring the '58 Studebaker, a fender at a time.

Eighty to 95 percent of the metals of vehicles of that era are recyclable, but   5
what do you do with the gas tanks? What about heavy metal accumulations in
the soil, lead contamination, battery acid leaks, the veins of spilled oil and gasoline? The topsoil would have to be scraped away: where would it go? What about
the rubber, plastic, and broken glass? Would we haul it all to the county dump?

It might take a lifetime, one spent undoing. It might require even my son's   6
lifetime. And where would we find all the replacement parts for this piece of
wasted earth? Yet, might they not come, slowly, very slowly?

A junkyard is a wilderness. Both are devotees of decay. The nature of both is   7
random order, the odd occurrence and juxtaposition of miscellany, backed by a
semblance of method. Walk through a junkyard and you'll see some of the
schemes a wilderness takes—Fords in one section, Dodges in another, or older
models farthest from the house—so a brief logic of ecology can be found.

In the same way, an ecosystem makes sense: the canebreaks, the cypress   8
domes. Pine trees regenerate in an indeterminate fashion, randomly here and
there where seeds have fallen, but also with some predictability. Sunlight and
moisture must be sufficient for germination, as where a fallen tree has made a
hole in the canopy, after a rain. This, too, is order.

Without fail in a junkyard you encounter the unexpected—a doll's head,   9
bodyless; a bike with no handlebars; a cache of wheat pennies; thirty feet of
copper pipe; a boxy '58 Edsel. Likewise, in the middle of Tate's Hell Swamp

you might look unexpectedly into the brown eyes of a barred owl ten feet away or come upon a purple stretch of carnivorous bladderworts in bloom, their BB-sized bladders full of aquatic microorganisms.

10   In the junkyard as in wilderness there is danger: shards of glass, leaning jacks, weak chains; or rattlesnakes, avalanches, polar bears. In one as in the other you expect the creativity of the random, how the twisted metal protrudes like limbs, the cars dumped at acute, right, and obtuse angles, how the driveways are creeks and rivers.

11   This from my brother Dell:

> There is a place in the old junkyard that, when I encounter it, turns magical. I become a future savage, half-naked, silently creeping through the dense canopy of trees and scrub. A feeling of dread increases with each step but curiosity draws me on. My footsteps falter but never completely stop. Suddenly I see mammoth beasts, eyes staring sightless forward. I see huge shining teeth in these monsters. As I move my hand gently among their flanks, I realize that I am in a graveyard speckled with dead prehistoric creatures. I am filled with awe. I can only speculate about their lives, imagine them roaring about and shudder at what they fed on. I know that this is hallowed ground and I remember that this place was spoken of in soft mutterings of the old ones, long dead, around the fires at night. But hunger pangs drive me on, for beyond this place are the animals that clothe and feed me. As I grope the haft of the spear and prepare to leave, I wonder if the pangs are from hunger or from a sense of loss.

12   Pine lilies don't grow in the junkyard anymore, nor showy orchids, and I've never seen a Bachman's sparrow flitting amid the junk. I'd like to. I have a dream for my homeland. I dream we can bring back the longleaf pine forests, along with the sandhills and the savannas, starting now and that we can bring back all the herbs and trees and wild animals, the ones not irretrievably lost, which deserve an existence apart from slavery to our own.

FOCUS ON ECOLOGY

1. What do you suppose Ray means by "an existence apart from slavery to our own"?
2. What do you think Ray mean by saying that "a junkyard is a wilderness"? Do you agree with her? Why or why not?

FOCUS ON WRITING

1. Why does Ray include the quote from her brother? What is its purpose in this piece?
2. What role does naming play in this reading? What kind of names does Ray offer readers and why?
3. Who was Hernando de Soto? Why is he important to the piece?

FOR DISCUSSION

One of the interesting things about Ray's "Second Coming" is the way she describes the animals and plants living in the junkyard. These descriptions indicate that nature lives in and around our junk and our other artifacts. What kinds of plants and animals live among the artifacts of your campus? As a class, develop a list of plants and animals that live in or near your classroom building. Are some of these placed there intentionally (landscaping, for instance)? Do people try to eliminate or control the presence of others (insects, rodents, weeds)?

WRITING IN RESPONSE

Consider places you see every day in your community: grocery stores, parking lots, schools, banks, streets, and so on. What wilderness existed on those locations before they were plowed over to make room for development? In a descriptive essay, pick a familiar location in your community and write about what that place might have been like before human intervention. Describe what it would take to return that place to its earlier, natural state. Would you want to make such a change? Why or why not?

Coming into the Watershed

Gary Snyder

Gary Snyder is the author of many poems, articles, and books including Turtle Island *(1975),* The Practice of the Wild *(1990), and* Coming into the Watershed *(1994). He is considered one of the most important contemporary nature writers, and his poetry is often associated with beat poetry, focusing on mystical and environmental themes. Snyder has worked both as a seaman and as a forester. He has spent many years in Japan studying Buddhism. In the essay reprinted here, Snyder argues for a unique way of reconceiving how we demarcate places based on ecological/environmental divisions rather than political divisions. As you read this essay, think about how and why your home regions have been divided.*

JOURNAL ASSIGNMENT

"Coming into the Watershed" argues that we should reconsider how we divide places. Think for a moment about how the area you live in is divided in terms of both political boundaries (towns, counties, cities, states, countries) and regions (valleys, mountain ranges, flood plains, and so on). Reflect in writing on the different kinds of division.

1   I had been too long in the calm Sierra pine groves and wanted to hear surf and the cries of seabirds. My son Gen and I took off one February day to visit friends on the north coast. We drove out of the Yuba River canyon, and went north from Marysville—entering that soulful winter depth of pearly tule fog—running alongside the Feather River and then crossing the Sacramento River at Red Bluff. From Red Bluff north the fog began to shred, and by Redding we had left it behind. As we crossed the mountains westward from Redding on Highway 299, we paid special attention to the transformations of the landscape and trees, watching to see where the zones would change and the natural boundaries could be roughly determined. From the Great Valley with its tules, grasses, valley oak, and blue oak, we swiftly climbed into the steep and dissected Klamath range with its ponderosa pine, black oak, and manzanita fields. Somewhere past Burnt Ranch we were in the redwood and Douglas fir forests—soon it was the coastal range. Then we were descending past Blue Lake to come out at Arcata.

2   We drove on north. Just ten or fifteen miles from Arcata, around Trinidad Head, the feel of the landscape subtly changed again—much the same trees, but no open meadows, and a different light. At Crescent City we asked friends just what the change between Arcata and Crescent City was. They both said (to distill a long discussion), "You leave 'California.' Right around Trinidad Head you cross into the maritime Pacific Northwest." But the Oregon border (where we are expected to think "the Northwest" begins) is still many miles farther on.

3   So we had gone in that one afternoon's drive from the Mediterranean-type Sacramento Valley and its many plant alliances with the Mexican south, over the interior range with its dry pine-forest hills, into a uniquely Californian set of redwood forests, and on into the maritime Pacific Northwest: the edges of four major areas. These boundaries are not hard and clear, though. They are porous, permeable, arguable. They are boundaries of climates, plant communities, soil types, styles of life. They change over the millennia, moving a few hundred miles this way or that. A thin line drawn on a map would not do them justice. Yet these are the markers of the natural nations of our planet, and they establish real territories with real differences to which our economies and our clothing must adapt.

4   On the way back we stopped at Trinidad Head for a hike and little birding. Although we knew they wouldn't be there until April, we walked out to take a look at the cliffs on the head, where tufted puffins nest. For tufted puffins, this is virtually the southernmost end of their range. Their more usual nesting ground is from southeastern Alaska through the Bering Sea and down to northern Japan. In winter they are far out in the open seas of the North Pacific. At

this spot, Trinidad, we could not help but feel that we touched on the life realm of the whole North Pacific and Alaska. We spent that whole weekend enjoying "liminality," dancing on the brink of the continent.

I have taken to watching the subtle changes of plants and climates as 5 I travel over the West. We can all tell stories, I know, of the drastic changes we have noticed as we raged over this or that freeway. This vast area called "California" is large enough to be beyond any one individual's ability (not to mention time) to travel over and to take it all into the imagination and hold it clearly enough in mind to see the whole picture. Michael Barbour, a botanist and lead author of *California's Changing Landscapes*, writes of the complexity of California: "Of the world's ten major soils, California has all ten. . . . As many as 375 distinctive natural communities have been recognized in the state. . . . California has more than five thousand kinds of native ferns, conifers, and flowering plants. Japan has far fewer species with a similar area. Even with four times California's area, Alaska does not match California's plant diversity, and neither does all of the central and northeastern United States and adjacent Canada combined. Moreover, about 30 percent of California's native plants are found nowhere else in the world."

But all this talk of the diversity of California is a trifle misleading. Of what 6 place are we speaking? What is "California"? It is, after all, a recent human invention with hasty straight-line boundaries that were drawn with a ruler on a map and rushed off to an office in D.C. This is another illustration of Robert Frost's lines, "The land was ours before we were the land's." The political boundaries of the western states were established in haste and ignorance. Landscapes have their own shapes and structures, centers and edges, which must be respected. If a relationship to a place is like a marriage, then the Yankee establishment of a jurisdiction called California was like a shotgun wedding with six sisters taken as one wife.

California is made up of what I take to be about six regions. They are of respectable size and native beauty, each with its own makeup, its own mix of birdcalls and plant smells. Each of these proposes a slightly different lifestyle to the human beings who live there. Each led to different sorts of rural economies, for the regional differences translate into things like raisin grapes, wet rice, timber, cattle pasture, and so forth.

The central coast with its little river valleys, beach dunes and marshes, and 8 oak-grass-pine mountains is one region. The great Central Valley is a second, once dominated by swamps and wide shallow lakes and sweeps of valley oaks following the streams. The long mountain ranges of the Sierra Nevada are a third. From a sort of Sonoran chaparral they rise to arctic tundra. In the middle elevations they have some of the finest mixed conifer forests in the world. The Modoc plateau and volcano country—with its sagebrush and juniper—makes a fourth. Some of the Sacramento waters rise here. The fifth is the northern coast with its deep interior mountains—the Klamath region—reaching (on the coast) as far north as Trinidad Head. The sixth (of these six sisters) consists of the coastal valleys and mountains south of the Tehachapis, with natural connections on into Baja. Although today this region supports a huge population with water drawn from the Colorado River, the Owens Valley, and the great Central Valley, it was originally almost a desert.

9   One might ask, What about the rest? Where are the White Mountains, the Mojave Desert, the Warner Range? They are splendid places, but they do not belong with California. Their watersheds and biological communities belong to the Great Basin or the lower Colorado drainage, and we should let them return to their own families. Almost all of core California has a summer-dry Mediterranean climate, with (usually) a fairly abundant winter rain. More than anything else, this rather special type of climate is what gives our place its fragrance of oily aromatic herbs, its olive-green drought-resistant shrubs, and its patterns of rolling grass and dark forest.

10   I am not arguing that we should instantly redraw the boundaries of the social construction called California, although that could happen some far day. But we are becoming aware of certain long-range realities, and this thinking leads toward the next step in the evolution of human citizenship on the North American continent. The usual focus of attention for most Americans is the human society itself with its problems and its successes, it icons and symbols. With the exception of most Native Americans and a few non-natives who have given their hearts to the place, the land we all live on is simply taken for granted—and proper relation to it is not considered a part of "citizenship." But after two centuries of national history, people are beginning to wake up and notice that the United States is located on a landscape with a severe, spectacular, spacy, wildly demanding, and ecstatic narrative to be learned. Its natural communities are each unique, and each of us, whether we like it or not—in the city or countryside—lives in one of them.

11   Those who work in resource management are accustomed to looking at many different maps of the landscape. Each addresses its own set of meanings. If we look at land ownership categories, we get (in addition to private land) the Bureau of Land Management, national forest, national park, state park, military reserves, and a host of other public holdings. This is the public domain, a practice coming down from the historic institution of the commons in Europe. These lands, particularly in the arid West, hold much of the water, forest, and wildlife that are left in America. Although they are in the care of all the people, they have too often been managed with a bent toward the mining or logging interests and toward short-term profits.

12   Conservationists have been working since the 1930s for sustainable forestry practices and the preservation of key blocks of public land as wilderness. They have had some splendid success in this effort, and we are all indebted to the single-minded dedication of the people who are behind every present-day wilderness area that we and our children walk into. Our growing understanding of how natural systems work brought us the realization that an exclusive emphasis on disparate parcels of land ignored the insouciant freeness of wild creatures. Although individual islands of wild land serving as biological refuges are invaluable, they cannot by themselves guarantee the maintenance of natural variety. As biologists, public land managers, and the involved public

have all agreed, we need to know more about how the larger-scale natural systems work, and we need to find "on-the-ground" ways to connect wild zone to wild zone wherever possible. We have now developed the notion of biological corridors or connectors. The Greater Yellowstone Ecosystem concept came out of this sort of recognition. Our understanding of nature has been radically altered by systems theory as applied to ecology, and in particular to the very cogent subdisciplines called island biogeography theory and landscape ecology.

No single group or agency could keep track of grizzly bears, which do not 13 care about park or ranch boundaries and have necessary, ancient territories of their own that range from late-summer alpine huckleberry fields to lower-elevation grasslands. Habitat flows across both private and public land. We must find a way to work with wild ecosystems that respects both the rights of landowners and the rights of bears. The idea of ecosystem management, all the talk now in land management circles, seems to go in the right direction. Successfully managing for the ecosystem will require as much finesse in dealing with miners, ranchers, and motel owners as it does with wild animals or bark beetles.

A "greater ecosystem" has its own functional and structural coherence. It 14 often might contain or be within a watershed system. It would usually be larger than a county, but smaller than a western U.S. state. One of the names for such a space is "bioregion."

A group of California-based federal and state land managers who are try- 15 ing to work together on biodiversity problems recently realized that their work could be better accomplished in a framework of natural regions. Their interagency "memorandum of understanding" calls for us to "move beyond existing efforts focused on the conservation of individual sites, species, and resources . . . to also protect and manage ecosystems, biological communities, and landscapes." The memorandum goes on to say that "public agencies and private groups must coordinate resource management and environmental protection activities, emphasizing regional solutions to regional issues and needs."

The group identified eleven or so such working regions within California, 16 making the San Francisco Bay and delta into one, and dividing both the Sierra and the valley into northern and southern portions. (In landscapes as in taxonomy, there are lumpers and splitters.) Since almost 50 percent of California is public domain, it is logical that the chiefs of the BLM, the Forest Service, California Department of Fish and Game, California Department of Forestry, State Parks, the federal Fish and Wildlife Service, and such should take these issues on, but that they came together in so timely a manner and signed onto such a far-reaching plan is admirable.

Hearing of this agreement, some county government people, elected offi- 17 cials, and timber and business interests in the mountain counties went into a severe paranoid spasm, fearing—they said—new regulations and more centralized government. So later in the fall, an anonymous circular made its way around towns and campuses in northern California under the title "Biodiversity or New Paganism?" It says that "California Resource Secretary Doug Wheeler and his self-appointed bioregional soldiers are out to devalue human life by placing greater emphasis on rocks, trees, fish, plants, and wildlife." It quotes me as having written that "those of us who are now promoting a biore-gional consciousness would, as an ultimate and long-range goal, like to see this continent more sensitively redefined, and the natural regions of North America—Turtle Island—gradually begin to shape the political entities within which we work. It would be a small step toward the deconstruction of America as a superpower into seven or eight natural nations—none of which have a budget big enough to support missiles." I'm pleased to say I did write that. I'd think it was clear that my statement is not promoting more centralized govern-ment, which seems to be a major fear, but these gents want both their small-town autonomy and the military-industrial state at the same time. Many a would-be westerner is a rugged individualist in rhetoric only, and will scream up a storm if taken too far from the government tit. As Marc Reisner makes clear in *The Cadillac Desert*, much of the agriculture and ranching of the West exists by virtue of a complicated and very expensive sort of government welfare: big dams and water plans. The real intent of the circular (it urges people to write the state governor) seems to be to resist policies that favor long-range sustain-ability and the support of biodiversity, and to hold out for maximum resource extraction right now.

18   As far as I can see, the intelligent but so far toothless California "biore-gional proposal" is simply a basis for further thinking and some degree of co-operation among agencies. The most original part is the call for the formation of "bioregional councils" that would have some stake in decision making. Who would be on the bioregional councils is not spelled out. Even closer to the roots, the memorandum that started all this furor suggests that "watershed councils" would be formed, which, being based on stream-by-stream communities, would be truly local bodies that could help design agreements working for the preservation of natural variety. Like, let's say, helping to preserve the spawn-ing grounds for the wild salmon that still come (amazingly) into the lower Yuba River gravel wastelands. This would be an effort that would have to involve a number of groups and agencies, and it would have to include the blessing of the usually development-minded Yuba County Water Agency.

19   The term *bioregion* was adopted by the signers to the Memorandum on Bio-logical Diversity as a technical term from the field of biogeography. It's not likely that that they would have known that there were already groups of people around the United States and Canada who were talking in terms of bioregion-ally oriented societies. I doubt they would have heard about the first North American Bioregional Congress held in Kansas in the late eighties. They had no idea that for twenty years communitarian ecology-minded dwellers-in-the-land have been living in places they call "Ish" (Puget Sound and lower British Columbia) or "Columbiana" (upper Columbia River), or "Mesechabe" (lower Mississippi), or "Shasta" (northern California), and all of them have produced newsletters, taken field trips, organized gatherings, and at the same time par-ticipated in local politics.

20   That "bioregion" was an idea already in circulation was the bad, or good, luck of the biodiversity agreement people, depending on how you look at it.

As it happens, the bioregional people are also finding "watershed councils" to be the building blocks of a long-range strategy for social and environmental sustainability.

A watershed is a marvelous thing to consider: this process of rain falling, 21 streams flowing, and oceans evaporating causes every molecule of water on earth to make the complete trip once every two million years. The surface is carved into watersheds—a kind of familial branching, a chart of relationship, and a definition of place. The watershed is the first and last nation whose boundaries, though subtly shifting, are unarguable. Races of birds, subspecies of trees, and types of hats or rain gear often go by the watershed. For the watershed, cities and dams are ephemeral and of no more account than a boulder that falls in the river or a landslide that temporarily alters the channel. The water will always be there, and it will always find its way down. As constrained and polluted as the Los Angeles River is at the moment, it can also be said that in the larger picture that river is alive and well under the city streets, running in giant culverts. It may be amused by such diversions. But we who live in terms of centuries rather than millions of years must hold the watershed and its communities together, so our children might enjoy the clear water and fresh life of this landscape we have chosen. From the tiniest rivulet at the crest of a ridge to the main trunk of a river approaching the lowlands, the river is all one place and all one land.

The water cycle includes our springs and wells, our Sierra snowpack, our 22 irrigation canals, our car wash, and the spring salmon run. It's the spring peeper in the pond and the acorn woodpecker chattering in a snag. The watershed is beyond the dichotomies of orderly/disorderly, for its forms are free, but somehow inevitable. The life that comes to flourish within it constitutes the first kind of community.

The agenda of a watershed council starts in a modest way: like saying, 23 "Let's try and rehabilitate our river to the point that wild salmon can successfully spawn here again." In pursuit of this local agenda, a community might find itself combating clear-cut timber sales upstream, waterselling grabs downstream, Taiwanese drift-net practices out in the North Pacific, and a host of other national and international threats to the health of salmon.

If a wide range of people will join in on this effort—people from timber 24 and tourism, settled ranchers and farmers, fly-fishing retirees, the businesses and the forest-dwelling new settlers—something might come of it. But if this joint agreement were to be implemented as a top-down prescription, it would go nowhere. Only a grass-roots engagement with long-term land issues can provide the political and social stability it will take to keep the biological richness of California's regions intact.

All public land ownership is ultimately written in sand. The boundaries and 25 the management categories were created by Congress, and Congress can take them away. The only "jurisdiction" that will last in the world of nature is the watershed, and even that changes slightly over time. If public lands come under greater and greater pressure to be opened for exploitation and use in the twenty-first century, it will be the local people, the watershed people, who will prove to be the last and possibly most effective line of defense. Let us hope it never comes to that.

26   The mandate of the public land managers and the Fish and Wildlife people inevitably directs them to resource concerns. They are proposing to do what could be called "ecological bioregionalism." The other movement, coming out of the local communities, could be called "cultural bioregionalism." I would like to turn my attention now to cultural bioregionalism and to what practical promise these ideas hold for fin-de-millennium America.

27   Living in a place—the notion has been around for decades and has usually been dismissed as provincial, backward, dull, and possibly reactionary. But new dynamics are at work. The mobility that has characterized American life is coming to a close. As Americans begin to stay put, it may give us the first opening in over a century to give participatory democracy another try.

28   Daniel Kemmis, the mayor of Missoula, Montana, has written a fine little book called *Community and the Politics of Place* (Norman: University of Oklahoma Press, 1990). Mr. Kemmis points out that in the eighteenth century the word *republican* meant a politics of community engagement. Early republican thought was set against the federalist theories that would govern by balancing competing interests, devise sets of legalistic procedures, maintain checks and balances (leading to hearings held before putative experts) in place of direct discussion between adversarial parties.

29   Kemmis quotes Rouseau: "Keeping citizens apart has become the first maxim of modern politics." So what organizing principle will get citizens back together? There are many, and each in its way has its use. People have organized themselves by ethnic background, religion, race, class, employment, gender, language, and age. In a highly mobile society where few people stay put, thematic organizing is entirely understandable. But place, that oldest of organizing principles (next to kinship), is a novel development in the United States.

30   "What holds people together long enough to discover their power as citizens is their common inhabiting of a single place," Kemmis argues. Being so placed, people will volunteer for community projects, join school boards, and accept nominations and appointments. Good minds, which are often forced by company or agency policy to keep moving, will make notable contributions to the neighborhood if allowed to stay put. And since local elections deal with immediate issues, a lot more people will turn out to vote. There will be a return of civic life.

31   This will not be "nationalism" with all its danger, as long as sense of place is not entirely conflated with the idea of a nation. Bioregional concerns go beyond those of any ephemeral (and often brutal and dangerous) politically designated space. They give us the imagination of "citizenship" in a place called (for example) the great Central Valley, which has valley oaks and migratory waterfowl as well as humans among its members. A place (with a climate, with bugs), as Kemmis says, "develops practices, creates culture."

Another fruit of the enlarged sense of nature that systems ecology and biore- 32
gional thought have given us is the realization that cities and suburbs are all
part of the system. Unlike the ecological bioregionalists, the cultural bioregionalists absolutely must include the cities in their thinking. The practice of urban
bioregionalism ("green cities") has made a good start in San Francisco. One can
learn and live deeply with regard to wild systems in any sort of neighborhood—
from the urban to a big sugar-beet farm. The birds are migrating, the wild
plants are looking for a way to slip in, the insects in any case live an untrammeled life, the raccoons are padding through the crosswalks at 2:00 A.M., and
the nursery trees are trying to figure out who they are. These are exciting, convivial, and somewhat radical knowledges.

An economics of scale can be seen in the watershed/bioregion/city-state 33
model. Imagine a Renaissance-style city-state facing out on the Pacific with its
bioregional hinterland reaching to the headwaters of all the streams that flow
through its bay. The San Francisco/valley rivers/Shasta headwaters bio-city-
region! I take some ideas along these lines from Jane Jacob's tantalizing book,
Cities and the Wealth of Nations (New York: Random House, 1984), in which she
argues that the city, not the nation-state, is the proper locus of an economy, and
then that the city is always to be understood as being one with the hinterland.

Such a non-nationalistic idea of community, in which commitment to pure 34
place is paramount, cannot be ethnic or racist. Here is perhaps the most delicious turn that comes out of thinking about politics from the standpoint of
place: anyone of any race, language, religion, or origin is welcome, as long as
they live well on the land. The great Central Valley region does not prefer English over Spanish or Japanese or Hmong. If it had any preferences at all, it
might best like the languages it heard for thousands of years, such as Maidu or
Miwok, simply because it's used to them. Mythically speaking, it will welcome
whoever chooses to observe the etiquette, express the gratitude, grasp the tools,
and learn the songs that it takes to live there.

This sort of future culture is available to whoever makes the choice, regard- 35
less of background. It need not require that a person drop his or her Buddhist,
Jewish, Christian, animist, atheist, or Muslim beliefs but simply add to that faith
or philosophy a sincere nod in the direction of the deep value of the natural
world and the subjecthood of nonhuman beings. A culture of place will be created that will include the "United States," and go beyond that to an affirmation
of the continent, the land itself, Turtle Island. We could be showing Southeast
Asian and South American newcomers the patterns of the rivers, the distant
hills, saying, "It is not only that you are now living in the United States. You are
living in this great landscape. Please get to know these rivers and mountains,
and be welcome here." Euro-Americans, Asian Americans, African Americans
can—if they wish—become "born-again" natives of Turtle Island. In doing so
we also might even (eventually) win some respect from our Native American
predecessors, who are still here and still trying to teach us where we are.

Watershed consciousness and bioregionalism is not just environmentalism, 36
not just a means toward resolution of social and economic problems, but a move

toward resolving both nature and society with the practice of a profound citizen-ship in both the natural and the social worlds. If the ground can be our common ground, we can begin to talk to each other (human and nonhuman) once again.

> California is gold-tan grasses, silver-gray tule fog,
> olive-green redwood, blue-gray chaparral,
> silver-hue serpentine hills.
> Blinding white granite,
> Blue-black rock sea cliffs.
> —Blue summer sky, chestnut brown slough water,
> steep purple city streets—hot cream towns.
> Many colors of the land, many colors of the skin.

FOCUS ON ECOLOGY

1. What do you suppose Gary Snyder means when he writes, "these are the markers of the natural nations of our planet, and they establish real territories with real differences to which our economies and our clothing must adapt"?
2. What, according to Snyder, is the effect of land division on animal populations?
3. What is a watershed? Why might we, according to Snyder, want to recon-ceive of regions in terms of watersheds?

FOCUS ON WRITING

1. How do you feel about the renaming of areas based on bioregional divisions rather than on the political geographies by which we now name areas? What effect might such a renaming have?
2. Why do you suppose Snyder concludes this essay with a poem?

FOR DISCUSSION

Snyder suggests that the idea of "citizenship" ought to include more than just the human inhabitants of a place, that plants and animals are also citizens of a place. As a class, consider the implications of such a statement, Discuss what you understand citizenship to be, how plants and animals might participate in that citizenry, and how human citizens should consider those other citizens.

WRITING IN RESPONSE

How do you respond to Gary Snyder's idea of redefining boundaries in terms of bioregions? In an argumentative essay, take a stand in response to Snyder's ideas.

The Other Road

Rachel Carson

Rachel Carson was born in Springfield, Pennsylvania, in 1907. She taught at the University of Maryland and Johns Hopkins University and also worked with the U.S. Bureau of Fisheries (now the Fish and Wildlife Service), but Carson's fame grew from her writing. During her career, she wrote 13 books. Of these, her two most famous and most influential works were The Sea Around Us, *which won the National Book Award in 1951 and* Silent Spring, *from which "The Other Road" is taken.* The Sea Around Us *is a magnificent book about the complexities and dynamics of the world's oceans. The book took Carson more than two years to write because of the amount of research involved in its writing.* Silent Spring, *it could be said, is one of the most environmentally influential books ever published, if not the most controversial.* Silent Spring, *which sold more than a half a million hardcover copies, examines the use of poisonous chemical fertilizers by the agriculture industry and the dangerous and deadly effects such chemical fertilizers have on humans, animals, and birds. The book, which was hailed by environmentalists and criticized as one-sided by others, indicts the agriculture industry for its use of chemical fertilizers. As you read this selection from* Silent Spring, *consider the ways Carson turns to science to further her argument.*

JOURNAL ASSIGNMENT

Carson explains in *Silent Spring* that pesticide and fertilizer use has far-reaching consequence beyond the farms where they are applied. In your journal, consider how first the pesticides might affect environments beyond the farms where they are used, then address what other options there may be.

We stand now where two roads diverge. But unlike the roads in Robert Frost's 1
familiar poem, they are not equally fair. The road we have long been traveling
is deceptively easy, a smooth superhighway on which we progress with great
speed, but at its end lies disaster. The other fork of the road—the one "less traveled by"—offers our last, our only chance to reach a destination that assures
the preservation of our earth.

   The choice, after all, is ours to make. If, having endured much, we have at 2
last asserted our "right to know," and if, knowing, we have concluded that we

are being asked to take senseless and frightening risks, then we should no longer accept the counsel of those who tell us that we must fill our world with poisonous chemicals; we should look about and see what other course is open to us.

3   A truly extraordinary variety of alternatives to the chemical control of insects is available. Some are already in use and have achieved brilliant success. Others are in the stage of laboratory testing. Still others are little more than ideas in the minds of imaginative scientists, waiting for the opportunity to put them to the test. All have this in common: they are *biological* solutions, based on understanding of the living organisms they seek to control, and of the whole fabric of life to which these organisms belong. Specialists representing various areas of the vast field of biology are contributing—entomologists, pathologists, geneticists, physiologists, biochemists, ecologists—all pouring their knowledge and their creative inspirations into the formation of a new science of biotic controls.

4   "Any science may be likened to a river," says a Johns Hopkins biologist, Professor Carl P. Swanson. "It has its obscure and unpretentious beginning; its quiet stretches as well as its rapids; its periods of drought as well as of fullness. It gathers momentum with the work of many investigators and as it is fed by other streams of thought; it is deepened and broadened by the concepts and generalizations that are gradually evolved."

5   So it is with the science of biological control in its modern sense. In America it had its obscure beginnings a century ago with the first attempts to introduce natural enemies of insects that were proving troublesome to farmers, an effort that sometimes moved slowly or not at all, but now and again gathered speed and momentum under the impetus of an outstanding success. It had its period of drought when workers in applied entomology, dazzled by the spectacular new insecticides of the 1940's, turned their backs on all biological methods and set foot on "the treadmill of chemical control." But the goal of an insect-free world continued to recede. Now at last, as it has become apparent that the heedless and unrestrained use of chemicals is a greater menace to ourselves than to the targets, the river which is the science of biotic control flows again, fed by new streams of thought.

6   Some of the most fascinating of the new methods are those that seek to turn the strength of a species against itself—to use the drive of an insect's life forces to destroy it. The most spectacular of these approaches is the "male sterilization" technique developed by the chief of the United States Department of Agriculture's Entomology Research Branch, Dr. Edward Knipling, and his associates.

7   About a quarter of a century ago Dr. Knipling startled his colleagues by proposing a unique method of insect control. If it were possible to sterilize and release large numbers of insects, he theorized, the sterilized males would, under certain conditions, compete with the normal wild males so successfully that, after repeated releases, only infertile eggs would be produced and the population would die out.

8   The proposal was met with bureaucratic inertia and with skepticism from scientists, but the idea persisted in Dr. Knipling's mind. One major problem remained to be solved before it could be put to the test—a practical method of

insect sterilization had to be found. Academically, the fact that insects could be sterilized by exposure to X-ray had been known since 1916, when an entomologist by the name of G. A. Runner reported such sterilization of cigarette beetles. Hermann Muller's pioneering work on the production of mutations by X-ray opened up vast new areas of thought in the late 1920's, and by the middle of the century, various workers had reported the sterilization by X-rays or gamma rays of at least a dozen species of insects.

But these were laboratory experiments, still a long way from practical application. About 1950, Dr. Knipling launched a serious effort to turn insect sterilization into a weapon that would wipe out a major insect enemy of livestock in the South, the screw-worm fly. The females of this species lay their eggs in any open wound of a warm-blooded animal. The hatching larvae are parasitic, feeding on the flesh of the host. A full-grown steer may succumb to a heavy infestation in 10 days, and livestock losses in the United States have been estimated at $40,000,000 a year. The toll of wildlife is harder to measure, but it must be great. Scarcity of deer in some areas of Texas is attributed to the screw-worm. This is a tropical or subtropical insect, inhabiting South and Central America and Mexico, and in the United States normally restricted to the Southwest. About 1933, however, it was accidentally introduced into Florida, where the climate allowed it to survive over winter and to establish populations. It even pushed into southern Alabama and Georgia, and soon the livestock industry of the southeastern states was faced with annual losses running to $20,000,000.

A vast amount of information on the biology of the screw-worm had been accumulated over the years by Agriculture Department scientists in Texas. By 1954, after some preliminary field trials on Florida islands, Dr. Knipling was ready for a full-scale test of his theory. For this, by arrangement with the Dutch Government, he went to the island of Curaçao in the Caribbean, cut off from the mainland by at least 50 miles of sea.

Beginning in August 1954, screw-worms reared and sterilized in an Agriculture Department laboratory in Florida were flown to Curaçao and released from airplanes at the rate of about 400 per square mile per week. Almost at once the number of egg masses deposited on experimental goats began to decrease, as did their fertility. Only seven weeks after the releases were started, all eggs were infertile. Soon it was impossible to find a single egg mass, sterile or otherwise. The screw-worm had indeed been eradicated on Curaçao.

The resounding success of the Curaçao experiment whetted the appetites of Florida livestock raisers for a similar feat that would relieve them of the scourge of screw-worms. Although the difficulties here were relatively enormous—an area 300 times as large as the small Caribbean island—in 1957 the United States Department of Agriculture and the State of Florida joined in providing funds for an eradication effort. The project involved the weekly production of about 50 million screw-worms at a specially constructed "fly factory," the use of 20 light airplanes to fly pre-arranged flight patterns, five to six hours daily, each plane carrying a thousand paper cartons, each carton containing 200 to 400 irradiated flies.

13   The cold winter of 1957–58, when freezing temperatures gripped northern Florida, gave an unexpected opportunity to start the program while the screw-worm populations were reduced and confined to a small area. By the time the program was considered complete at the end of 17 months, $3\frac{1}{2}$ billion artificially reared, sterilized flies had been released over Florida and sections of Georgia and Alabama. The last-known animal wound infestation that could be attributed to screw-worms occurred in February 1959. In the next few weeks several adults were taken in traps. Thereafter no trace of the screw-worm could be discovered. Its extinction in the Southeast had been accomplished—a triumphant demonstration of the worth of scientific creativity, aided by thorough basic research, persistence, and determination.

14   Now a quarantine barrier in Mississippi seeks to prevent the re-entrance of the screw-worm from the Southwest, where it is firmly entrenched. Eradication there would be a formidable undertaking, considering the vast areas involved and the probability of re-invasion from Mexico. Nevertheless, the stakes are high and the thinking in the Department seems to be that some sort of program designed at least to hold the screw-worm population at very low levels, may soon be attempted in Texas and other infested areas of the Southwest.

15   The brilliant success of the screw-worm campaign has stimulated tremendous interest in applying the same methods to other insects. Not all, of course, are suitable subjects for this technique, much depending on details of the life history, population density, and reactions to radiation.

16   Experiments have been undertaken by the British in the hope that the method could be used against the tsetse fly in Rhodesia. This insect infests about a third of Africa, posing a menace to human health and preventing the keeping of livestock in an area of some $4\frac{1}{2}$ million square miles of wooded grasslands. The habits of the tsetse differ considerably from those of the screw-worm fly, and although it can be sterilized by radiation some technical difficulties remain to be worked out before the method can be applied.

17   The British have already tested a large number of other species for susceptibility to radiation. United States scientists have had some encouraging early results with the melon fly and the oriental and Mediterranean fruit flies in laboratory tests in Hawaii and field tests on the remote island of Rota. The corn borer and the sugarcane borer are also being tested. There are possibilities, too, that insects of medical importance might be controlled by sterilization. A Chilean scientist has pointed out that malaria-carrying mosquitoes persist in his country in spite of insecticide treatment; the release of sterile males might then provide the final blow needed to eliminate this population.

18   The obvious difficulties of sterilizing by radiation have led to search for an easier method of accomplishing similar results, and there is now a strongly running tide of interest in chemical sterilants.

19   Scientists at the Department of Agriculture laboratory in Orlando, Florida, are now sterilizing the housefly in laboratory experiments and even in some field trials, using chemicals incorporated in suitable foods. In a test on an island

in the Florida Keys in 1961, a population of flies was nearly wiped out within a period of only five weeks. Repopulation of course followed from nearby islands, but as a pilot project the test was successful. The Department's excitement about the promise of this method is easily understood. In the first place, as we have seen, the housefly has now become virtually uncontrollable by insecticides. A completely new method of control is undoubtedly needed. One of the problems of sterilization by radiation is that this requires not only artificial rearing but the release of sterile males in larger number than are present in the wild population. This could be done with the screw-worm, which is actually not an abundant insect. With the housefly, however, more than doubling the population through releases could be highly objectionable, even though the increase would be only temporary. A chemical sterilant, on the other hand, could be combined with a bait substance and introduced into the natural environment of the fly; insects feeding on it would become sterile and in the course of time the sterile flies would predominate and the insects would breed themselves out of existence.

The testing of chemicals for a sterilizing effect is much more difficult than [20] the testing of chemical poisons. It takes 30 days to evaluate one chemical— although, of course, a number of tests can be run concurrently. Yet between April 1958 and December 1961 several hundred chemicals were screened at the Orlando laboratory for a possible sterilizing effect. The Department of Agriculture seems happy to have found among these even a handful of chemicals that show promise.

Now other laboratories of the Department are taking up the problem, testing [21] chemicals against stable flies, mosquitoes, boll weevils, and an assortment of fruit flies. All this is presently experimental but in the few years since work began on chemosterilants the project has grown enormously. In theory it has many attractive features. Dr. Knipling has pointed out that effective chemical insect sterilization "might easily outdo some of the best of known insecticides." Take an imaginary situation in which a population of a million insects is multiplying five times in each generation. An insecticide might kill 90 per cent of each generation, leaving 125,000 insects alive after the third generation. In contrast, a chemical that would produce 90 per cent sterility would leave only 125 insects alive.

On the other side of the coin is the fact that some extremely potent chemi- [22] cals are involved. It is fortunate that at least during these early stages most of the men working with chemosterilants seem mindful of the need to find safe chemicals and safe methods of application. Nonetheless, suggestions are heard here and there that these sterilizing chemicals might be applied as aerial sprays—for example, to coat the foliage chewed by gypsy moth larvae. To attempt any such procedure without thorough advance research on the hazards involved would be the height of irresponsibility. If the potential hazards of the chemosterilants are not constantly borne in mind we could easily find ourselves in even worse trouble than that now created by the insecticides.

The sterilants currently tested fall generally into two groups, both of which [23] are extremely interesting in their mode of action. The first are intimately related to the life processes, or metabolism, of the cell; i.e., they so closely resemble a substance the cell or tissue needs that the organism "mistakes" them for the true metabolite and tries to incorporate them in its normal building processes. But the fit is wrong in some detail and the process comes to a halt. Such chemicals are called anti-metabolites.

24   The second group consists of chemicals that act on the chromosomes, probably affecting the gene chemicals and causing the chromosomes to break up. The chemosterilants of this group are alkylating agents, which are extremely reactive chemicals, capable of intense cell destruction, damage to chromosomes, and production of mutations. It is the view of Dr. Peter Alexander of the Chester Beatty Research Institute in London that "any alkylating agent which is effective in sterilizing insects would also be a powerful mutagen and carcinogen." Dr. Alexander feels that any conceivable use of such chemicals in insect control would be "open to the most severe objections." It is to be hoped, therefore, that the present experiments will lead not to actual use of these particular chemicals but to the discovery of others that will be safe and also highly specific in their action on the target insect.

25   Some of the most interesting of the recent work is concerned with still other ways of forging weapons from the insect's own life processes. Insects produce a variety of venoms, attractants, repellants. What is the chemical nature of these secretions? Could we make use of them as, perhaps, very selective insecticides? Scientists at Cornell University and elsewhere are trying to find answers to some of these questions, studying the defense mechanisms by which many insects protect themselves from attack by predators, working out the chemical structure of insect secretions. Other scientists are working on the so-called "juvenile hormone," a powerful substance which prevents metamorphosis of the larval insect until the proper stage of growth has been reached.

26   Perhaps the most immediately useful result of this exploration of insect secretion is the development of lures, or attractants. Here again, nature has pointed the way. The gypsy moth is an especially intriguing example. The female moth is too heavy-bodied to fly. She lives on or near the ground, fluttering about among low vegetation or creeping up tree trunks. The male, on the contrary, is a strong flier and is attracted even from considerable distances by a scent released by the female from special glands. Entomologists have taken advantage of this fact for a good many years, laboriously preparing this sex attractant from the bodies of the female moths. It was then used in traps set for the males in census operations along the fringe of the insect's range. But this was an extremely expensive procedure. Despite the much publicized infestations in the northeastern states, there were not enough gypsy moths to provide the material, and hand-collected female pupae had to be imported from Europe, sometimes at a cost of half a dollar per tip. It was a tremendous breakthrough, therefore, when, after years of effort, chemists of the Agriculture Department recently succeeded in isolating the attractant. Following upon this discovery was the successful preparation of a closely related synthetic material

from a constituent of castor oil; this not only deceives the male moths but is apparently fully as attractive as the natural substance. As little as one microgram (1/1,000,000 gram) in a trap is an effective lure.

All this is of much more than academic interest, for the new and economical "gyplure" might be used not merely in census operations but in control work. Several of the more attractive possibilities are now being tested. In what might be termed an experiment in psychological warfare, the attractant is combined with a granular material and distributed by planes. The aim is to confuse the male moth and alter the normal behavior so that, in the welter of attractive scents, he cannot find the true scent trail leading to the female. This line of attack is being carried even further in experiments aimed at deceiving the male into attempting to mate with a spurious female. In the laboratory, male gypsy moths have attempted copulation with chips of wood, vermiculite, and other small, inanimate objects, so long as they were suitably impregnated with gyplure. Whether such diversion of the mating instinct into nonproductive channels would actually serve to reduce the population remains to be tested but it is an interesting possibility.

The gypsy moth lure was the first insect sex attractant to be synthesized, but probably there will soon be others. A number of agricultural insects are being studied for possible attractants that man could imitate. Encouraging results have been ordained with the Hessian fly and the tobacco hornworm.

Combinations of attractants and poisons are being tried against several insect species. Government scientists have developed an attractant called methyl-eugenol, which males of the oriental fruit fly and the melon fly find irresistible. This has been combined with a poison in tests in the Bonin Islands 450 miles south of Japan. Small pieces of fiberboard were impregnated with the two chemicals and were distributed by air over the entire island chain to attract and kill the male flies. This program of "male annihilation" was begun in 1960: a year later the Agriculture Department estimated that more than 99 per cent of the population had been eliminated. The method as here applied seems to have marked advantages over the conventional broadcasting of insecticides. The poison, an organic phosphorus chemical, is confined to squares of fiberboard which are unlikely to be eaten by wildlife; its residues, moreover, are quickly dissipated and so are not potential contaminants of soil or water.

But not all communication in the insect world is by scents that lure or repel. Sound also may be a warning or an attraction. The constant stream of ultrasonic sound that issues from a bat in flight (serving as a radar system to guide it through darkness) is heard by certain moths enabling them to avoid capture. The wing sounds of approaching parasitic flies warn the larvae of some sawflies to herd together for protection. On the other hand, the sounds made by certain wood-boring insects enable their parasites to find them, and to the male mosquito the wingbeat of the female is a siren song.

What use, if any, can be made of this ability of the insect to detect and react to sound? As yet in the experimental stage, but nonetheless interesting, is the initial success in attracting male mosquitoes to playback recordings of the flight sound of the female. The males were lured to a charged grid and so killed. The repellant effect of bursts of ultrasonic sound is being tested in Canada against corn borer and cutworm moths. Two authorities on animal sound, Professors Hubert and Mable Frings of the University of Hawaii, believe that a field method of influencing the behavior of insects with sound only awaits discovery of the proper key to unlock and apply the vast existing knowledge of insect sound production and reception. Repellant sounds may offer greater possibilities than attractants. The Fringses are known for their discovery that starlings scatter in alarm before a recording of the distress cry of one of their fellows; perhaps somewhere in this fact is a central truth that may be applied to insects. To practical men of industry the possibilities seem real enough so that at least one major electronic corporation is preparing to set up a laboratory to test them.

32   Sound is also being tested as an agent of direct destruction. Ultrasonic sound will kill all mosquito larvae in a laboratory tank; however, it kills other aquatic organisms as well. In other experiments, blowflies, mealworms, and yellow fever mosquitoes have been killed by airborne ultrasonic sound in a matter of seconds. All such experiments are first steps toward wholly new concepts of insect control which the miracles of electronics may some day make a reality.

33   The new biotic control of insects is not wholly a matter of electronics and gamma radiation and other products of man's inventive mind. Some of its methods have ancient roots, based on the knowledge that, like ourselves, insects are subject to disease. Bacterial infections sweep through their populations like the plagues of old; under the onset of a virus their hordes sicken and die. The occurrence of disease in insects was known before the time of Aristotle; the maladies of the silkworm were celebrated in medieval poetry; and through study of the diseases of this same insect the first understanding of the principles of infectious disease came to Pasteur.

34   Insects are beset not only by viruses and bacteria but also by fungi, protozoa, microscopic worms, and other beings from all that unseen world of minute life that, by and large, befriends mankind. For the microbes include not only disease organisms but those that destroy waste matter, make soils fertile, and enter into countless biological processes like fermentation and nitrification. Why should they not also aid us in the control of insects.

35   One of the first to envision such use of microorganisms was the 19th-century zoologist Elie Metchnikoff. During the concluding decades of the 19th and the first half of the 20th centuries the idea of microbial control was slowly taking form. The first conclusive proof that an insect could be brought under control by introducing a disease into its environment came in the late 1930's with the discovery and use of milky disease for the Japanese beetle, which is caused by the spores of a bacterium belonging to the genus *Bacillus*. This classic example of bacterial control has a long history of use in the eastern part of the United States, as I have pointed out in Chapter 7.

36   High hopes now attend tests of another bacterium of this genus—*Bacillus thuringiensis*—originally discovered in Germany in 1911 in the province of

Thuringia, where it was found to cause a fatal septicemia in the larvae of the flour moth. This bacterium actually kills by poisoning rather than by disease. Within its vegetative rods there are formed, along with spores, peculiar crystals composed of a protein substance highly toxic to certain insects, especially to the larvae of the mothlike lepidopteras. Shortly after eating foliage coated with this toxin the larva the suffers paralysis, stops feeding, and soon dies. For practical purposes, the fact that feeding is interrupted promptly is of course an enormous advantage, for crop damage stops almost as soon as the pathogen is applied. Compounds containing spores of *Bacillus thuringiensis* are now being manufactured by several firms in the United States under various trade names. Field tests are being made in several countries: in France and Germany against larvae of the cabbage butterfly, in Yugoslavia against the fall webworm, in the Soviet Union against a tent caterpillar. In Panama, where tests were begun in 1961, this bacterial insecticide may be the answer to one or more of the serious problems confronting banana growers. There the root borer is a serious pest of the banana, so weakening its roots that the trees are easily toppled by wind. Dieldrin has been the only chemical effective against the borer, but it has now set in motion a chain of disaster. The borers are becoming resistant. The chemical has also destroyed some important insect predators and so has caused an increase in tortricids— small, stout-bodied moths whose larvae scar the surface of the bananas. There is reason to hope the new microbial insecticide will eliminate both the tortricids and the borers and that it will do so without upsetting natural controls.

In eastern forests of Canada and the United States bacterial insecticides 37 may be one important answer to the problems of such forest insects as the budworms and the gypsy moth. In 1960 both countries began field tests with a commercial preparation of *Bacillus thuringiensis*. Some of the early results have been encouraging. In Vermont, for example, the end results of bacterial control were as good as those obtained with DDT. The main technical problem now is to find a carrying solution that will stick the bacterial spores to the needles of the evergreens. On crops this is not a problem—even a dust can be used. Bacterial insecticides have already been tried on a wide variety of vegetables, especially in California.

Meanwhile, other perhaps less spectacular work is concerned with viruses. 38 Here and there in California fields of young alfalfa are being sprayed with a substance as deadly as any insecticide for the destructive alfalfa caterpillar—a solution containing a virus obtained from the bodies of caterpillars that have died because of infection with this exceedingly virulent disease. The bodies of only five diseased caterpillars provide enough virus to treat an acre of alfalfa. In some Canadian forests a virus that affects pine sawflies has proved so effective in control that it has replaced insecticides.

Scientists in Czechoslovakia are experimenting with protozoa against web- 39 worms and other insect pests, and in the United States a protozoan parasite has been found to reduce the egg-laying potential of the corn borer.

To some the term microbial insecticide may conjure up pictures of bacterial 40 warfare that would endanger other forms of life. This is not true. In contrast to chemicals, insect pathogens are harmless to all but their intended targets. Dr. Edward Steinhaus, an outstanding authority on insect pathology, has stated emphatically that there is "no authenticated recorded instance of a true insect pathogen having caused an infectious disease in a vertebrate animal either experimentally or in nature." The insect pathogens are so specific that they infect only a small group of insects—sometimes a single species. Biologically they do not belong to the type of organisms that cause disease in higher animals or in plants. Also, as Dr. Steinhaus points out, outbreaks of insect disease in nature always remain confined to insects, affecting neither the host plants nor animals feeding on them.

41   Insects have many natural enemies—not only microbes of many kinds but other insects. The first suggestion that an insect might be controlled by encouraging its enemies is generally credited to Erasmus Darwin about 1800. Probably because it was the first generally practiced method of biological control, this setting of one insect against another is widely but erroneously thought to be the only alternative to chemicals.

42   In the United States the true beginnings of conventional biological control date from 1888 when Albert Koebele, the first of a growing army of entomologist explorers, went to Australia to search for natural enemies of the cottony cushion scale that threatened the California citrus industry with destruction. As we have seen in Chapter 15, the mission was crowned with spectacular success, and in the century that followed the world has been combed for natural enemies to control the insects that have come uninvited to our shores. In all, about 100 species of imported predators and parasites have become established. Besides the vedalia beetles brought in by Koebele, other importations have been highly successful. A wasp imported from Japan established complete control of an insect attacking eastern apple orchards. Several natural enemies of the spotted alfalfa aphid, an accidental import from the Middle East, are credited with saving the California alfalfa industry. Parasites and predators of the gypsy moth achieved good control, as did the *Tiphia* wasp against the Japanese beetle. Biological control of scales and mealy bugs is estimated to save California several millions of dollars a year—indeed, one of the leading entomologists of that state, Dr. Paul DeBach, has estimated that for an investment of $4,000,000 in biological control work California has received a return of $100,000,000.

43   Examples of successful biological control of serious pests by importing their natural enemies are to be found in some 40 countries distributed over much of the world. The advantages of such control over chemicals are obvious: it is relatively inexpensive, it is permanent, it leaves no poisonous residues. Yet biological control has suffered from lack of support. California is virtually alone among the states in having a formal program in biological control, and many states have not even one entomologist who devotes full time to it. Perhaps for want of support biological control through insect enemies has not always been carried out with the scientific thoroughness it requires—exacting studies of its impact on the populations of insect prey have seldom been made, and releases

have not always been made with the precision that might spell the difference between success and failure.

The predator and the preyed upon exist not alone, but as part of a vast web 44 of life, all of which needs to be taken into account. Perhaps the opportunities for the more conventional types of biological control are greatest in the forests. The farmlands of modern agriculture are highly artificial, unlike anything nature ever conceived. But the forests are a different world, much closer to natural environments. Here, with a minimum of help and a maximum of noninterference from man, Nature can have her way, setting up all that wonderful and intricate system of checks and balances that protects the forest from undue damage by insects.

In the United States our foresters seem to have thought of biological con- 45 trol chiefly in terms of introducing insect parasites and predators. The Canadians take a broader view, and some of the Europeans have gone farthest of all to develop the science of "forest hygiene" to an amazing extent. Birds, ants, forest spiders, and soil bacteria are as much a part of a forest as the trees, in the view of European foresters, who take care to inoculate a new forest with these protective factors. The encouragement of birds is one of the first steps. In the modern era of intensive forestry the old hollow trees are gone and with them homes for woodpeckers and other tree-nesting birds. This lack is met by nesting boxes, which draw the birds back into the forest. Other boxes are specially designed for owls and for bats, so that these creatures may take over in the dark hours the work of insect hunting performed in daylight by the small birds.

But this is only the beginning. Some of the most fascinating control work in 46 European forests employs the forest red ant as an aggressive insect predator—a species which, unfortunately, does not occur in North America. About 25 years ago Professor Karl Gösswald of the University of Würzberg developed a method of cultivating this ant and establishing colonies. Under his direction more than 10,000 colonies of the red ant have been established in about 90 test areas in the German Federal Republic. Dr. Gösswald's method has been adopted in Italy and other countries, where ant farms have been established to supply colonies for distribution in the forests. In the Apennines, for example, several hundred nests have been set out to protect reforested areas.

"Where you can obtain in your forest a combination of birds' and ants' pro- 47 tection together with some bats and owls, the biological equilibrium has already been essentially improved," says Dr. Heinz Ruppertshofen, a forestry officer in Mölln, Germany, who believes that a single introduced predator or parasite is less effective than an array of the "natural companions" of the trees.

New ant colonies in the forests at Mölln are protected from woodpeckers 48 by wire netting to reduce the toll. In this way the woodpeckers, which have increased by 400 per cent in 10 years in some of the test areas, do not seriously reduce the ant colonies, and pay handsomely for what they take by picking harmful caterpillars off the trees. Much of the work of caring for the ant colonies (and the birds' nesting boxes as well) is assumed by a youth corps from the local school, children 10 to 14 years old. The costs are exceedingly low; the benefits amount to permanent protection of the forests.

49   Another extremely interesting feature of Dr. Ruppertshofen's work is his use of spiders, in which he appears to be a pioneer. Although there is a large literature on the classification and natural history of spiders, it is scattered and fragmentary and deals not at all with their value as an agent of biological control. Of the 22,000 known kinds of spiders, 760 are native to Germany (and about 2000 to the United States). Twenty-nine families of spiders inhabit German forests.

50   To a forester the most important fact about a spider is the kind of net it builds. The wheel-net spiders are most important, for the webs of some of them are so narrow-meshed that they can catch all flying insects. A large web (16 inches in diameter) of the cross spider bears some 120,000 adhesive nodules on its strands. A single spider may destroy in her life of 18 months an average of 2000 insects. A biologically sound forest has 50 to 150 spiders to the square meter (a little more than a square yard). Where there are fewer, the deficiency may be remedied by collecting and distributing the baglike cocoons containing the eggs. "Three cocoons of the wasp spider [which occurs also in America] yield a thousand spiders, which can catch 200,000 flying insects," says Dr. Ruppertshofen. The tiny and delicate young of the wheel-net spiders that emerge in the spring are especially important, he says, "as they spin in a teamwork a net umbrella above the top shoots of the trees and thus protect the young shoots against flying insects." As the spiders molt and grow, the net is enlarged.

51   Canadian biologists have pursued rather similar lines of investigation, although with differences dictated by the fact that North American forests are largely natural rather than planted, and that the species available as aids in maintaining a healthy forest are somewhat different. The emphasis in Canada is on small mammals, which are amazingly effective in the control of certain insects, especially those that live within the spongy soil of the forest floor. Among such insects are the sawflies, so-called because the female has a saw-shaped ovipositor with which she slits open the needles of evergreen trees in order to deposit her eggs. The larvae eventually drop to the ground and form cocoons in the peat of tamarack bogs or the duff under spruce or pines. But beneath the forest floor is a world honeycombed with the tunnels and runways of small mammals—whitefooted mice, voles, and shrews of various species. Of all these small burrowers, the voracious shrews find and consume the largest number of sawfly cocoons. They feed by placing a forefoot on the cocoon and biting off the end, showing an extraordinary ability to discriminate between sound and empty cocoons. And for their insatiable appetite the shrews have no rivals. Whereas a vole can consume about 200 cocoons a day, a shrew, depending on the species, may devour up to 800! This may result, according to laboratory tests, in destruction of 75 to 98 per cent of the cocoons present.

52   It is not surprising that the island of Newfoundland, which has no native shrews but is beset with sawflies, so eagerly desired some of these small, efficient

mammals that in 1958 the introduction of the masked shrew—the most efficient sawfly predator—was attempted. Canadian officials report in 1962 that the attempt has been successful. The shrews are multiplying and are spreading out over the island, some marked individuals having been recovered as much as ten miles from the point of release.

There is, then, a whole battery of armaments available to the forester who 53 is willing to look for permanent solutions that preserve and strengthen the natural relations in the forest. Chemical pest control in the forest is at best a stop-gap measure bringing no real solution, at worst killing the fishes in the forest streams, bringing on plagues of insects, and destroying the natural controls and those we may be trying to introduce. By such violent measures, says Dr. Ruppertshofen, "the partnership for life of the forest is entirely being unbalanced, and the catastrophes caused by parasites repeat in shorter and shorter periods . . . We, therefore, have to put an end to these unnatural manipulations brought into the most important and almost last natural living space which has been left for us."

Through all these new, imaginative, and creative approaches to the prob- 54 lem of sharing our earth with other creatures there runs a constant theme, the awareness that we are dealing with life—with living populations and all their pressures and counter-pressures, their surges and recessions. Only by taking account of such life forces and by cautiously seeking to guide them into channels favorable to ourselves can we hope to achieve a reasonable accommodation between the insect hordes and ourselves.

The current vogue for poisons has failed utterly to take into account these 55 most fundamental considerations. As crude a weapon as the cave man's club, the chemical barrage has been hurled against the fabric of life—a fabric on the one hand delicate and destructible, on the other miraculously tough and resilient, and capable of striking back in unexpected ways. These extraordinary capacities of life have been ignored by the practitioners of chemical control who have brought to their task no "high-minded orientation," no humility before the vast forces with which they tamper.

The "control of nature" is a phrase conceived in arrogance, born of the Ne- 56 anderthal age of biology and philosophy, when it was supposed that nature exists for the convenience of man. The concepts and practices of applied entomology for the most part date from that Stone Age of science. It is our alarming misfortune that so primitive a science has armed itself with the most modern and terrible weapons, and that in turning them against the insects it has also turned them against the earth.

FOCUS ON ECOLOGY

1. What are the relationships between consumption and the insect control issues Carson discusses?

2. How does Carson depict the relationship between science and the future of the environment?
3. What are some of the methods for pest control other than chemical pesticides? How do you evaluate the possibilities of their uses?

FOCUS ON WRITING

1. Are you familiar with the poem Carson refers to at the beginning of her essay? What is that poem about? Why does she cite it?
2. What role does research play in this selection? That is, could Rachel Carson have written this piece based solely on personal experience and observation? Why or why not?
3. How do you respond to Carson's conclusion?

FOR DISCUSSION

One of the interesting things that Carson leads us to think about is how we perceive insects. For many people, insects are seen as pests, not as a part of nature that should be protected. Stepping on an ant or swatting a mosquito usually doesn't receive the same kind of response from people as does killing a whale or a seal. Why do you suppose that is? Why isn't there outcry against programs to find ways to kill off entire populations of insects—like the one Dr. Knipling is working on involving sterilization? Look back at Carson's essay and reread the discussion of Dr. Knipling's project, only replace the word *insects* with the word *lions*. As a class, discuss how Americans tend to characterize insects. don't we think of insects in the same ways do other animals? Why are there few (if any) organizations with environmental agendas of "save the cockroach"? Each year we use pesticides to kill millions of insects, yet there is little outcry for the lives of the insects (though there often is outcry regarding the other effects of the pesticides, primarily effects on humans). Imagine if we were to hear of a spray designed to rid an area of bears, squirrels, or other animals: "Raid. Kills Chimpanzees Dead."

WRITING IN RESPONSE

Since the publication of Rachel Carson's *Silent Spring* in 1962, many other alternatives to chemical pesticides have been developed, some with positive results, others as destructive or more destructive than their chemical predecessors. Take some time to learn about new alternatives to chemical pesticides. Then, in a short expository essay, report about how the alternative method you investigated was developed, how it works, its successes and failures, and its potential for the future.

Nature as Measure

Wendell Berry

Wendell Berry is a farmer, a teacher, and a writer. Born in 1934 in Henry County, Kentucky, Berry has written more than 25 books of poetry, 20 collections of essays, 6 novels, and 3 collections of short stories. Berry's writing most frequently addresses the relationship between humans and nature, and his message, as Contemporary Authors *reports it, is always clear: "Humans must learn to live in harmony with the natural rhythms of the earth or perish." Berry has said that "We must support what supports local life, which means community, family, household life—the moral capital our larger institutions have to come to rest upon. If the larger institutions undermine the local life, they destroy that moral capital just exactly as the industrial economy has destroyed the natural capital of localities—soil fertility and so on. Essential wisdom accumulates in the community much as fertility builds in the soil." As you read the essay here, think about how Berry defines things that are good and things that are bad. Do you agree with him?*

JOURNAL ASSIGNMENT

Berry's "Nature as Measure" argues that American farming has been destroyed by economic demands and that America itself is being destroyed due to the loss of traditional farming. In your journal, explore what you know about farming in the United States.

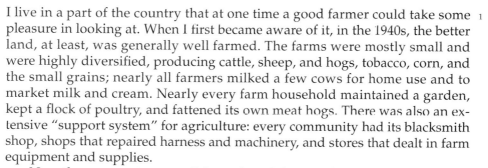

I live in a part of the country that at one time a good farmer could take some   1
pleasure in looking at. When I first became aware of it, in the 1940s, the better land, at least, was generally well farmed. The farms were mostly small and were highly diversified, producing cattle, sheep, and hogs, tobacco, corn, and the small grains; nearly all farmers milked a few cows for home use and to market milk and cream. Nearly every farm household maintained a garden, kept a flock of poultry, and fattened its own meat hogs. There was also an extensive "support system" for agriculture: every community had its blacksmith shop, shops that repaired harness and machinery, and stores that dealt in farm equipment and supplies.

Now the country is not well farmed, and driving through it has become a   2
depressing experience. Some good small farmers remain, and their farms stand out in the landscape like jewels. But they are few and far between, and they are getting fewer every year. The buildings and other improvements of the old

farming are everywhere in decay or have vanished altogether. The produce of the country is increasingly specialized. The small dairies are gone. Most of the sheep flocks are gone, and so are most of the enterprises of the old household economy. There is less livestock and more cash-grain farming. When cash-grain farming comes in, the fences go, the livestock goes, erosion increases, and the fields become weedy.

3   Like the farm land, the farm communities are declining and eroding. The farmers who are still farming do not farm with as much skill as they did forty years ago, and there are not nearly so many farmers farming as there were forty years ago. As the old have died, they have not been replaced; as the young come of age, they leave farming or leave the community. And as the land and the people deteriorate, so necessarily must the support system. None of the small rural towns is thriving as it did forty years ago. The proprietors of small businesses give up or die and are not replaced. As the farm trade declines, farm equipment franchises are revoked. The remaining farmers must drive longer and longer distances for machines and parts and repairs.

4   Looking at the country now, one cannot escape the conclusion that there are no longer enough people on the land to farm it well and to take proper care of it. A further and more ominous conclusion is that there is no longer a considerable number of people knowledgeable enough to look at the country and see that it is not properly cared for—though the face of the country is now everywhere marked by the agony of our enterprise of self-destruction.

5   And suddenly in this wasting countryside there is talk of raising production quotas on Burley tobacco by twenty-four percent, and tobacco growers are coming under pressure from the manufacturers to decrease their use of chemicals. Everyone I have talked to is doubtful that we have enough people left in farming to meet the increased demand for either quantity or quality, and doubtful that we still have the barnroom to house the increased acreage. In other word, the demand going up has met the culture coming down. No one can be optimistic about the results.

6   Tobacco, I know, is not a food, but it comes from the same resources of land and people that food comes from, and this emerging dilemma in the production of tobacco can only foreshadow a similar dilemma in the production of food. At every point in our food economy, present conditions remaining, we must expect to come to a time when demand (for quantity or quality) going up will meet the culture coming down. The fact is that we have nearly destroyed American farming, and in the process have nearly destroyed our country.

7   How has this happened? It has happened because of the application to farming of far too simple a standard. For many years, as a nation, we have asked our land only to produce, and we have asked our farmers only to produce. We have believed that this single economic standard not only guaranteed good performance but also preserved the ultimate truth and rightness of our aims. We have bought unconditionally the economists' line that competition and innovation would solve all problems, and that we would finally accomplish a technological end-run around biological reality and the human condition.

Competition and innovation have indeed solved, for the time being, the 8 problem of production. But the solution has been extravagant, thoughtless, and far too expensive. We have been winning, to our inestimable loss, a competition against our own land and our own people. At present, what we have to show for this "victory" is a surplus of food. But this is a surplus achieved by the ruin of its sources, and it has been used, by apologists for our present economy, to disguise the damage by which it was produced. Food, clearly, is the most important economic product—except when there is a surplus. When there is a surplus, according to our present economic assumptions, food is the *least* important product. The surplus becomes famous as evidence to consumers that they have nothing to worry about, that there is no problem, that present economic assumptions are correct.

But our present economic assumptions are failing in agriculture, and to 9 those having eyes to see the evidence is everywhere, in the cities as well as in the countryside. The singular demand for production has been unable to acknowledge the importance of the sources of production in nature and in human culture. Of course agriculture must be productive; that is a requirement as urgent as it is obvious. But urgent as it is, it is not the *first* requirement; there are two more requirements equally important and equally urgent. One is that if agriculture is to remain productive, it must preserve the land, and the fertility and ecological health of the land; the land, that is, must be used *well*. A further requirement, therefore, is that if the land is to be used well, the people who use it must know it well, must be highly motivated to use it well, must know how to use it well, must have time to use it well, and must be able to afford to use it well. Nothing that has happened in the agricultural revolution of the last fifty years had disapproved or invalidated these requirements, though everything that has happened has ignored or defied them.

In light of the necessity that the farm land and the farm people should thrive 10 while producing, we can see that the single standard of productivity has failed.

Now we must learn to replace that standard by one that is more compre- 11 hensive: the standard of nature. The effort to do this is not new. It was begun early in this century by Liberty Hyde Bailey of the Cornell University College of Agriculture, by F. H. King of the University of Wisconsin College of Agriculture and the United States Department of Agriculture, by J. Russell Smith, professor of economic geography at Columbia University, by the British agricultural scientist Sir Albert Howard, and by others; and it has continued into our own time in the work of such scientists as John Todd, Wes Jackson, and others. The standard of nature is not so simple or so easy a standard as the standard of productivity. The term "nature" is not so definite or stable a concept as the weights and measures of productivity. But we know what we mean when we say that the first settlers in any American place recognized that place's agricultural potential "by its nature"—that is, by the depth and quality of its soil, the kind and quality of its native vegetation, and so on. And we know what we mean when we say that all too often we have proceeded to ignore the nature of our places in farming them. By returning to "the nature of the place" as standard, we acknowledge the necessary limits of our own intentions. Farming cannot take place except in nature; therefore, if nature does not thrive, farming cannot thrive. But we know too that nature includes us. It is not a place into which we reach from some safe standpoint outside it. We are in it and are a part of it while we use it. If it does not thrive, we cannot thrive. The appropriate measure of farming then is the world's health and our health, and this is inescapably *one* measure.

12   But the oneness of this measure is far different from the singularity of the standard of productivity that we have been using; it is far more complex. One of its concerns, one of the inevitable natural measures, is productivity; but it is also concerned for the health of all the creatures belonging to a given place, from the creatures of the soil and water to the humans and other creatures of the land surface to the birds of the air. The use of nature as measure proposes an atonement between ourselves and our world, between economy and ecology, between the domestic and the wild. Or it proposes a conscious and careful recognition of the interdependence between ourselves and nature that in fact has always existed and, if we are to live, must always exist.

13   Industrial agriculture, built according to the single standard of productivity, has dealt with nature, including human nature, in the manner of a monologist or an orator. It has not asked for anything, or waited to hear any response. It has told nature what it wanted, and in various clever ways has taken what it wanted. And since it proposed no limit on its wants, exhaustion has been its inevitable and foreseeable result. This, clearly, is a dictatorial or totalitarian form of behavior, and it is as totalitarian in its use of people as it is in its use of nature. Its connections to the world and to humans and the other creatures become more and more abstract, as its economy, its authority, and its power become more and more centralized.

14   On the other hand, an agriculture using nature, including human nature, as its measure would approach the world in the manner of a conversationalist. It would not impose its vision and its demands upon a world that it conceives of as a stockpile of raw material, inert and indifferent to any use that may be made of it. It would not proceed directly or soon to some supposedly ideal state of things. It *would* proceed directly and soon to serious thought about our condition and our predicament. On all farms, farmers would undertake to know responsibly where they are and to "consult the genius of the place." They would ask what nature would be doing there if no one were farming there. They would ask what nature would permit them to do there, and what they could do there with the least harm to the place and to their natural and human neighbors. And they would ask what nature would *help* them to do there. And after each asking, knowing that nature will respond, they would attend carefully to her response. The use of the place would necessarily change, and the response of the place to that use would necessarily change the user. The conversation itself would thus assume a kind of creaturely life, binding the place and its inhabitants together, changing and growing to no end, no final accomplishment, that can be conceived or foreseen.

Farming in this way, though it certainly would proceed by desire, is not vi- 15 sionary in the political or utopian sense. In a conversation, you always expect a reply. And if you honor the other party to the conversation, if you honor the *otherness* of the other party, you understand that you must not expect always to receive a reply that you foresee or a reply that you will like. A conversation is immitigably two-sided and always to some degree mysterious; it requires faith.

For a long time now we have understood ourselves as traveling toward 16 some sort of industrial paradise, some new Eden conceived and constructed entirely by human ingenuity. And we have thought ourselves free to use and abuse nature in any way that might further this enterprise. Now we face overwhelming evidence that we are not smart enough to recover Eden by assault, and that nature does not tolerate or excuse our abuses. If, in spite of the evidence against us, we are finding it hard to relinquish our old ambition, we are also seeing more clearly every day how that ambition has reduced and enslaved us. We see how everything—the whole world—is belittled by the idea that all creation is moving or ought to move toward an end that some body, some human body, has thought up. To be free of that end and that ambition would be a delightful and precious thing. Once free of it, we might again go about our work and our lives with a seriousness and pleasure denied to us when we merely submit to a fate already determined by gigantic politics, economics, and technology.

Such freedom is implicit in the adoption of nature as the measure of eco- 17 nomic life. The reunion of nature and economy proposes a necessary democracy, for neither economy nor nature can be abstract in practice. When we adopt nature as a measure, we require practice that is locally knowledgeable. The particular farm, that is, must not be treated as any farm. And the particular knowledge of particular places is beyond the competence of any centralized power or authority. Farming by the measure of nature, which is to say the nature of the particular place, means that farmers must tend farms that they know and love, farms small enough to know and love, using tools and methods that they know and love, in the company of neighbors that they know and love.

In recent years, our society has been required to think again of the issues of 18 the use and abuse of human beings. We understand, for instance, that the inability to distinguish between a particular woman and any woman is a condition predisposing to abuse. It is time that we learn to apply the same understanding to our country. The inability to distinguish between a farm and any farm is a condition predisposing to abuse, and abuse has been the result. Rape, indeed, has been the result, and we have seen that we are not exempt from the damage we have inflicted. Now we must think of marriage.

1989

FOCUS ON ECOLOGY

1. In "Nature as Measure," Berry relies on an underlying assumption that the old ways of farming are better, that old farm life was a better life. How do

you respond to this assumption, particularly when Berry claims, "The fact is that we have nearly destroyed American farming, and in the process have nearly destroyed our country"?

2. What, according to Berry, is the relationship between economic production and the fall of American agriculture? Do you agree with his assessment? Why or why not?

3. What does Berry mean when he writes, "Farming cannot take place except in nature"?

FOCUS ON WRITING

1. Why does Berry explain that the effort to live by the "standard of nature" had been attempted by people at universities and in the United States Department of Agriculture? What credence is given to these people by listing their professional affiliations?

2. Berry writes "After each asking, knowing that nature will respond, they would attend carefully to her response." Why do you suppose Berry refers to nature with the feminine pronoun *her*?

3. To whom do you suppose Berry is addressing "Nature as Measure"? What leads you to your conclusion?

FOR DISCUSSION

In "Nature as Measure," Berry claims that "The reunion of nature and economy proposes a necessary democracy, for neither economy nor nature can be abstract in practice." As a class, consider this statement, particularly in light of what Berry has argued in this selection. Discuss the relationship between economy and nature, democracy and nature.

WRITING IN RESPONSE

Every state in the United States is home to some kind of farming. Both small farms and large commercial farms operate in your home state. Take some time to learn about farming in your state. If you grew up on a farm or live in a farming community, take some time to consider what other types of farming are done beyond what you are familiar with. Learn about where farms are located, what kinds of crops are grown, what kinds of animals and animal-based products (like milk and eggs) are produced. Find out how many farms operate in your state. How many of those are small farms like the ones about which Wendell Berry writes?

"Sifting through the Embers"
from *Last Chance to See*

Douglas Adams

Douglas Adams was born in Cambridge, England, in 1952. Adams gained a good deal of recognition as a writer in the late 1970s and 1980s through the publication of his science fiction books in the Hitchhiker's Guide to the Galaxy *series:* The Hitchhiker's Guide to the Galaxy; The Restaurant at the End of the Universe; Life, the Universe, and Everything; So Long, and Thanks for All the Fish; *and* Mostly Harmless. *In 1978, Adams began working for the BBC producing and scriptwriting the* Hitchhiker's Guide to the Galaxy *radio and television shows. He was also a script editor for the television series,* Dr. Who. *In the late 1980s the BBC paired Adams with zoologist Mark Carwardine to travel around the world filming and discussing endangered species. In 1990, Adams published* Last Chance to See, *a book based on his travels with Carwardine to Indonesia, Zaire, New Zealand, China, and Mauritius. The selection here is taken from that book. Adams died unexpectedly in 2001; he was just 49.*

JOURNAL ASSIGNMENT

"Sifting through the Embers" is the final chapter of *Last Chance to See,* in which Adams recounts his adventures in traveling around the world to see the most endangered species of animals on the planet. In the Chapter, Adams recounts the story of the Sybilline books, books that contain all of the knowledge of the world, and one town's refusal to pay for the books, even as they are being destroyed. In essence, Adams relates a parable that he equates with the destruction of the world's environments. Do you recall any fairy tales or parables that seem appropriately fitting to how you see the ecological and environmental problems the world faces? In your journal, retell that story.

There's a story I heard when I was young that bothered me because I couldn't understand it. It was many years before I discovered it to be the story of the Sybilline books. By that time all the details of the story had rewritten themselves in my mind, but the essentials were still the same. After a year of exploring some of the endangered environments of the world, I think I finally understand it.

It concerns an ancient city—it doesn't matter where it was or what it was called. It was a thriving, prosperous city set in the middle of a large plain. One summer, while the people of the city were busy thriving and prospering away, a strange old beggar woman arrived at the gates carrying twelve large books, which she offered to sell to them. She said that the books contained all the knowledge and all the wisdom of the world, and that she would let the city have all twelve of them in return for a single sack of gold.

The people of the city thought this was a very funny idea. They said she obviously had no conception of the value of gold and that probably the best thing was for her to go away again.

This she agreed to do, but first she said she was going to destroy half of the books in front of them. She built a small bonfire, burnt six of the books of all knowledge and all wisdom in the sight of the people of the city, and then went on her way.

Winter came and went, a hard winter, but the city just about managed to flourish through it and then, the following summer, the old woman was back.

"Oh, you again," said the people of the city. "How's the knowledge and wisdom going?"

"Six books," she said, "just six left. Half of all the knowledge and wisdom in the world. Once again I am offering to sell them to you."

"Oh yes?" sniggered the people of the city.

"Only the price has changed."

"Not surprised."

"Two sacks of gold."

"What?"

"Two sacks of gold for the six remaining books of knowledge and wisdom. Take it or leave it."

"It seems to us," said the people of the city, "that you can't be very wise or knowledgeable yourself or you would realize that you can't just go around quadrupling an already outrageous price in a buyer's market. If that's the sort of knowledge and wisdom you're peddling, then, frankly, you can keep it at any price."

"Do you want them or not."

"No."

"Very well. I will trouble you for a little firewood."

She built another bonfire and burnt three of the remaining books in front of them and then set off back across the plain.

That night one or two curious people from the city sneaked out and sifted through the embers to see if they could salvage the odd page or two, but the fire had burnt very thoroughly and the old woman had raked the ashes. There was nothing.

Another hard winter took its toll on the city and they had a little trouble with famine and disease, but the trade was good and they were in reasonably good shape again by the following summer when, once again, the old woman appeared.

"You're early this year," they said to her.

"Less to carry," she explained, showing them the three books she was still carrying. "A quarter of all the knowledge and wisdom in the world. Do you want it?"

"What's the price?"

"Four sacks of gold."

"You're completely mad, old woman. Apart from anything else, our economy's going through a bit of a sticky patch at the moment. Sacks of gold are completely out of the question."

"Firewood, please."

"Now wait a minute," said the people of the city, "this isn't doing anybody any good. We've been thinking about all this and we've put together a small committee to have a look at these books of yours. Let us evaluate them for a few months, see if they're worth anything to us, and when you come back next year, perhaps we can put in some kind of reasonable offer. We are not talking sacks of gold here, though."

The old woman shook her head. "No," she said. "Bring me the firewood."

"It'll cost you."

"No matter," said the woman, with a shrug. "The books will burn quite well by themselves."

So saying, she set about shredding two of the books into pieces which then burnt easily. She set off swiftly across the plain and left the people of the city to face another year.

She was back in the late spring.

"Just the one left," she said, putting it down on the ground in front of her. "So I was able to bring my own firewood."

"How much?" said the people of the city.

"Sixteen sacks of gold."

"We'd only budgeted for eight."

"Take it or leave it."

"Wait here."

The people of the city went off into a huddle and returned half an hour later.

"Sixteen sacks is all we've got left," they pleaded, "times are hard. You must leave us with something."

The old woman just hummed to herself as she started to pile the kindling together.

"All right!" they cried at last, opened up the gates of the city, and led out two ox carts, each laden with eight sacks of gold. "But it had better be good."

"Thank you," said the old woman, "it is. And you should have seen the rest of it."

She led the two ox carts away across the plain with her, and left the people of the city to survive as best they could with the one remaining twelfth of all the knowledge and wisdom that had been in the world.

FOCUS ON ECOLOGY

1. What is Adams suggesting in connecting the story of the Sybilline books with endangered environments of the world?
2. What is the relationship between knowledge and money in the story Adams tells? Why is this significant?
3. What does Adams seem to be suggesting about our future?

FOCUS ON WRITING

1. Why do you suppose Adams decided to tell the story of the Sybilline books to make his point? Could he have made his argument more directly? Would it have been more effective or less effective? Why?
2. Are you familiar with the story of the Sybilline books? Where is the story from?
3. What does Adams mean by the title of this chapter? Why do you suppose he has chosen this title?

FOR DISCUSSION

What might have happened had the town purchased the books? What might happen if a town had all of the world's knowledge? As a class, consider the relationship between knowledge and environmental destruction. Do we know all we need to know? Have we passed up opportunities for gaining more knowledge or knowingly ignored certain knowledge?

WRITING IN RESPONSE

Adams's telling of the story of the Sybilline books ends with the town in possession of one book of knowledge and the old woman in possession of sixteen sacks of gold. What does the town do with the book? What knowledge does it contain? Of what knowledge have the townspeople deprived themselves by not buying all of the books earlier? In your own narrative, continue the story. Write about the year that follows their acquiring the single book. Does the old woman return again a year later? What happens with the book, with the town?

"Eden Changes" from *A Naturalist in Florida: A Celebration of Eden*

Archie Carr

From 1938 until 1987, Archie Carr taught biology at the University of Florida. But to say that Carr was just a teacher would be to severely understate his accomplishments. Author of 13 books, Carr was noted as one of the world's foremost naturalists. Renowned as the leading authority on sea turtles, Carr, by way of his book The Windward Road: Adventures of a Naturalist on Remote Caribbean Shores, *initiated a worldwide interest in protecting sea turtles.* The Windward Road *is often considered one of the landmark books in conservationism. Carr wrote and published more than a hundred papers, and in 1994, seven years after his death, Carr's wife Marjorie Harris Carr published many of his best-loved essays in* A Naturalist in Florida: A Celebration of Eden, *from where the selection "Eden Changes" is taken. As you read this essay, note how Carr defines correlations between humans and wildlife destruction.*

JOURNAL ASSIGNMENT

"Eden Changes" address the ways humans have ruined a good deal of natural Florida. Yet Carr is optimistic for the future of Florida, citing not only examples of destruction, but how particular transgressions have begun to be righted. Think about and explain in your journal some of the ways your home region has suffered at the hands of humans. Then consider some of the ways that people, either individually or as a community, have attempted to protect those regions for the future.

The history of man and nature in Florida has not been a wholly happy one. 1 Very recently it became possible to balance some of the violence we have done to the natural world with a few signs of goodwill; but the change was slow in coming, and the delay has cost us heavily.

The irony of this is that, more than almost anywhere else in America, it was 2 nature that drew people to Florida to start with. Partly the early violations were a sign of the times. To our forebears, cleared land was better than forests, and killing nonhuman creatures was only natural. Besides that there was from the beginning an obsession with the goodness of population growth. From the outset the natives saw profit in visitors who could be overcharged for a side of bacon or a mule, or guided to good shooting in a heron rookery. This helped generate the heady magic of growth and made the word synonymous with progress.

3   The history of Florida has been a desperate sort of striving for growth and development. The result of this has been the most protracted crowding in of outsiders that any state has had. Inevitably, this has dimmed or destroyed much of the natural charm that originally drew people here. There is no way that the favors of wild nature can be infinitely shared about, like loaves and fishes. The climate has not so far been materially hurt, but all other ecologic assets have to some extent been changed, and some have been forever lost. But it is no longer a walkaway for the fast-money chaps, and though they still have a lot to learn, they seem to be learning it.

4   When a naturalist whose delight is wild creatures and unworn country sets out to write about Florida, it is hard to refrain from bemoaning lost wilderness, as John Small did in *From Eden to Sahara* or Thomas Barbour did in *That Vanishing Eden*. Actually, if you look around for them, there are pleasant things to be told. And there are things to be thankful for. The return of the manatees to the limestone springs, for instance. Thirty years ago it was next to impossible to see a manatee in the primordial wintertime habitat of the species—the big springs of the central peninsula. Manatees are good to eat, and they were hunted out of the springs long ago. Those not killed for meat were idly shot by duck hunters or by kids with .22s. Today the poachers and irresponsible gun-toters are fewer; and manatees, though still an endangered species, are back, in some of the springs at least. And that is a blessing because manatees are neat, very neat.

5   It is somewhat the same with alligators. When Bartram was here, there were alligators galore. By the late 1800s, however, hide hunting and recreational slaughter were going on everywhere, and alligators has disappeared from much of their natural range. Populations declined drastically, even in Florida, and tourists could count on seeing alligators only in the alligator farms. A few years ago the alligator was declared an endangered species. Under protection it has proved surprisingly resilient. In a few parts of its original range the species is obviously no longer endangered. A visitor who looks around can now usually see wild alligators in natural habitat; and in some suburban bodies of water they have even become a nuisance. The existence of these localized sites of abundant, brash alligators generated the retrogressive scheme to reopen a hunting season. The potential for harm in this proposal is complex, and one can only hope that nothing comes of it. Meantime, having visible wild alligators in the landscape is a thing to be thankful for.

6   Besides that, there are otters. During the first half of this century otters were heavily trapped and shot, and seeing one became a rare occurrence. Today hunting pressure has relaxed, and the main enemy of otters is the highway. Otters are very bright, but for some reason their brain copes poorly with automobiles; they are often found dead on any stretch of paved highway through marsh country. Away from the fast cars, though, they are much more numerous now that they were in the 1940s, and their return is cause for celebration.

So is the return of the beavers. Beavers probably never entirely disappeared 7
from the Panhandle of Florida, but as far as most Floridians could tell they
might as well have been completely gone. Now they are increasing their range
and abundance in the state. A few single-minded entrepreneurs have even
begun to cry out for beaver control on the grounds that timberland is being
flooded by their work. But most people probably would figure beavers in
Florida are worth a few drowned planted pines.

Another pleasant change—one more conspicuous to the casual visitor than 8
the return of sea cows, alligators, otters, and beavers—is the spread of long-
legged wading birds. A part of the new look that these produce is contributed by
the cattle egret, an Old World species that for some wholly unknown reason
began crossing the ocean three decades ago and is now a common sight standing
with cows in pasture lands. But these new immigrant white egrets being here
should not obscure the important fact that other water birds too have returned
as a regular feature of the landscape, in the roadside ditches and out on the wet
prairies. It took many years for them to recover from the plume-hunting massacres that were finally stopped by the Audubon Society wardens in the early
1900s. But herons are again decorating the wet places. Even roseate spoonbills
can be seen with little searching, and this was undreamed of only a while ago.

There has been another pleasing change in the look of much of the land- 9
scape of interior Florida. Open country free of people and agriculture is more
lush and comforting to the eye than it used to be. This change has come about
because of the decline of the Cracker habit of letting wildfire loose in any patch
of woods anytime it would burn. Planned, monitored burning of pinelands is a
useful tool for keeping out hardwood seedlings that would turn pine woods
into hammock. In fact, it is altogether essential to the maintenance of pine flatwoods and of other pineland as well. But unless the burning is done with skill it
makes a shocking mess of the land. The old Floridians burned heedlessly, aim-
ing only to be rid of debris from timbering or to stimulate the growth of new
grass that would rescue their cattle from a winter diet of palmetto fans. Or, if
they had no cows, they burned to kill ticks and rattlesnakes or to flush out game.

Some people just don't like the look of flatwoods anyway. Jacob Rhett 10
Motte, an army surgeon of Charleston, South Carolina, who arrived in Florida
during the Second Seminole War, was appalled by the appearance of the
pinelands around the Georgia-Florida line. They seemed to him a "dull, insipid pine barren, where the listlessness of blank vacuity hung upon the flag-
ging spirits." Motte was probably just prejudiced. Most naturalists would give
a lot for a chance to see what those pinelands looked like before they were cut
down. But later on the flatwoods were cut over, most of them more than once,
and the Crackers burned them into blackened, bare-floored semidesert, devoid
of animal life except for razorback hogs that plowed up the bayheads and thin
sooty cattle that stood around in the road or wandered through the unfenced
country foraging morosely for scattered sprigs of wire grass.

Now the ritual burning has stopped. In some cases the protection is over- 11
done, but a new and pleasantly lush look has come over the land. It is not a

wholly natural look. Even before the Crackers and Seminoles came to Florida the woods used to burn over, in natural fires, and the present fire-free regimen will make hardwood hammock of much of what once was pineland. Meantime, however, what you see from a traveling car is far greener and more opulent country than what they used to see from the Model T Fords.

12   So there are bright spots in our relationship with natural Florida. When you think of the abuse much of our heritage has suffered, however, it is not easy to stay cheerful. Take the decline of the big springs, for instance—the biological communities in the limestone springs of the state. The ecological degradation of these incomparable springs is one of the major losses the state has suffered and one that clearly illustrates the problem of saving the diverse values of natural landscapes.

13   Florida is underlain by soluble limestone. Where this lies near the surface, solution has formed caves, chimneys, and sinkholes, and much of the drainage of the region goes into subterranean streams rather than running over the surface to the sea. Rivers disappear into the ground and emerge a mile or more away; lakes gurgle out overnight through newly opened holes in their bottoms. Such terrain is known as karst topography, after a region in Hungary. There are numerous karst regions in the world, but nowhere are big river-making springs as abundant as they are in Florida.

14   And nowhere in the Florida landscape is natural beauty distilled to its essence as it is in the big springs—wherever their natural biologic organization has been spared. There is a dreamlike quality to the appeal of these places. It is a stirring thing to come upon a line of them unexpectedly, whether you walk in overland and find it suddenly glowing in shadows of live oaks and magnolias or you paddle up a cypress-bordered run, wondering where the run comes from, and then all at once see the trees open in a circle and live water surging up like a liquid blue crystal. When William Bartram wrote of his journeys through the limestone country in the late 1700s the springs evoked some of his most rhapsodic prose. Three hundred years before that, it was surely rumors of the supernatural beauty of the springs that generated tales of the Fountain of Youth.

15   Each spring is different from all the others; but in the intensity of its grace and color each is a little ecologic jewel in which geology and biology have created a masterwork of natural art. In all of them the water wells up in shades of blue and silver that vary with depth and the slant of your view. In the unviolated basins there are submarine beds of water plants of half a dozen kinds, each a different shade of red-brown and green waving slowly in the current or spreading over quiet bottom like patchwork quilts of velvet. Where the flow is too fast for plants to hold, the bare sand of the bottom shows white, and in some of the springs white chips of fossil shell or flakes of marl swirl up like snow with the roiling newborn water.

16   It would be hard to find a better example than these springs to show the kinds of troubles that hinder the preservation of biological landscape. The springs are still there, most of them. Fountains still surge up out of rock caverns and make sudden streams that give a strange look to the contour map.

But all of them are distressingly fragile treasures that have without exception suffered damage, in some cases irretrievably.

One of the magnificent springs of the Gulf drainage of Florida is Manatee 17 Springs, which makes a tributary to the Suwannee River in Dixie County. It was once an old haunt of mine. I used to go there, partly because two species of freshwater turtles I was interested in lived thereabouts, but also simply because it was a lonely, magic bit of landscape. I first saw it in 1935. There was little animal life of any kind within the spring itself except for occasional roving schools of mullet; a trio or pair of needlefish here and there; a few red-eyed Suwannee bass; itinerant small gangs of bluegills, redbreasts, punkinseeds, and stumpknockers; a few shy Suwannee chicken cooters, one of the turtles I used to go there after; and great numbers of big-headed stinkjims, known less colloquially as loggerhead musk turtles.

That was long before the spring had become a state park. The road out 18 there from Old Town was a long sand-track through the flatwoods. The place was so hard to get to that hardly anybody ever went there except to make moonshine or to dynamite fish. The sparseness of the fauna of those days was no doubt mainly the work of the dynamiters—the cut-bait fishermen, as they are euphemistically called.

And I knew one of the best of all the cut-bait fishermen. His name was John 19 Henry. He used to bring his mule to help Tom Barbour and Ted White dig out fossils at the Thomas Farm over in Gilchrist County northwest of Bell. The Thomas Farm dig had just become known to paleontologists and was being called the best deposit of Miocene fossils east of the Mississippi—or of the Rockies, I forget which. Anyway, Dr. Barbour bought the place for Harvard and the University of Florida and used to come down once in a while to help Ted work it. My wife and I used to go out there with them. They would work away with a grapefruit knife for several days, scratching the clay away from the skulls of horses or camels or dier-wolves that died 30 million years ago, and then, when everything the grapefruit knife could reach was out and safely shrouded in plaster, John Henry would bring over his mule and mule-shovel and scrape off the overburden until more pay dirt lay within reach of the grapefruit knives. There were two other local fellows who came out into the worn-out turkey-oak farm to help with the digging, but they weren't cut-bait men. One was called Uncle Leonard, and he was a solid, quiet man. The other was known to me only as Uncle Goo; I don't remember why. It could have been because his teeth were all gone on one side of his lower jaw, and snuff juice kept running out that side of his mouth and down his chin. He never bothered to wipe it away. Anyway, I can't help but take a moment to tell about the time they were all out there watching Ted tease away the final scraps of clay matrix from around the skull of a giant Miocene carnivore of some kind—a bear-dog, Ted called it, a creature of the line from which all the bears and dogs of today have come from, and with canine teeth more frightening than you ever saw. The three local men had been at work for a couple of seasons and had grown fairly familiar with the fauna of the dig. They gave their own homely names to the fossil bones that appeared, as well as to the animals the bones suggested to their minds. A femur of a giant peccary was a "hambone of the boar-hog," for example; and they had a long list of other terms relating the bones of animals nowadays to those of species no longer prevalent in Gilchrist County. One lazy afternoon, while waiting around for Ted to get the bear-dog out of the clay, they idly fell to wondering about the times when such giants were in the land, and Uncle Leonard said, "You reckon there was any folks around here in them days?"

20   "Shore," John Henry said. "There's always been folks around these parts."

21   Ted was used to the way his colleagues telescoped time in order to make sense of the incredible beasts they dug out of the dig, so he just kept on scraping out clay from around the emerging great jaw and said nothing. Leonard pondered the faraway times for a while, and then he said, "Well, what kind a rig you reckon they had to handle a critter like this-yer-un?"

22   John Henry faced him and scornfully spit snuff juice against a clod of blue clay. "Great God-a-mighty," he said. "What you reckon they had them long roffles fer?"

23   Leonard nodded thoughtfully and said, "Shore," and Goo said shore, too.

24   That digression had nothing to do with my subject, except that besides knowing answers like that, John Henry was the champion cut-bait fisherman between Bell and Branford. He knew how to drop a weighted half-stick of "powder," as he called dynamite, and turn a single good channel-cat belly-up twenty feet down in a spring. He could fix up a charge with just the proper fuse and weight, drop it down into a dark eddy of the Suwannee and get out with enough fish for a church fish fry long before the game warden came sneaking down the river to where he had heard the deep bump of the explosion that meant cut-bait fishermen were at work. The best test of John Henry's skill was cut-baiting for mullet. He would take a little chunk of powder, a quarter or an eighth of a stick, and put on a cap and fuse so short that lighting it seemed like suicide; and he could get that out into a nervous school of big, cruising mullet in an arc so well-timed that it would go off as it hit and blow the fish out of the water before they could shy at the splash.

25   John Henry was proud of his skill with dynamite. He kept some of it on him most of the time. According to Goo, he had some on him one time when they put him in jail for fighting. They overlooked it in his pocket, and John Henry blew a wall out of the jail and went away. Nothing ever came of it, either, Goo said. What John Henry said at the time was that somebody else blasted the wall from the outside.

26   Although my digression got out of hand, it has a relevant point, really, which is that the cut-bait fishermen, the dynamiters of fish, used to be dismally prevalent in Florida, and they undoubtedly routed great quantities of fish out of many a spring.

27   At Jody's Spring, near Silver Glen in the Ocala National Forest, there is a charming bit of the world, described by Marjorie Kinnan Rawlings in the opening chapter of her book *The Yearling*. It is a place where you can sit for a while in the dim cool of a scrap of hammock surrounded by sand-pine scrub and marvel over a superb small gem of the natural landscape.

Jody's Spring is unique. There is no one big, river-making outpouring but 28
instead a scattering of gentle little geysers of crystal water and snowy sand
bubbling in the bottom of a shallow pool surrounded by evergreen hammock.
Each sand-boil makes a lively snow-white pit in the leaf-strewn bottom. Some
of the boils are no bigger than your fist, some are the size of a washtub. Killifish
cruise about among them, and wherever one is big enough to hold him, a young
bass or half-grown redbreast bream is usually ensconced, working his gill flaps
and eyeing any visitor through the air-clear water. Thin conical snails creep
across the brown leaves on the bottom of the pool; and dragonflies course above
it or bask on twig-tips in splashes of sunlight. Where the outlet leaves there are
patches of cress and lizard's tail, and neverwets spread velvet leaves about the
banks, their flowers glowing gold in the gloom. The pool feeds a stream that
wanders away through the woods to join Silver Glen Run a short way off. In
any setting Jody's Spring would be an enchanted place. Set out there in the heart
of the vast hot scrub, with little bubbling boils gleaming white and silver in their
quiet patch of deep, cool shade, a marvelously unreal aura is generated.

There are ecologic lessons to be learned at Jody's Spring. The hammock is 29
a striking variant of the scrub community where, because of the presence of
the springs, the sand-pine forest gives way to a moist woods of broadleafed
trees. There is an abrupt transition, a narrow ecozone, where tall cabbage palms
can be seen standing almost side by side with the closely related dwarf-sabals
that grow only in scrub. And yet if you go there and sit in the cool quiet for a
while, the important thing you will see is a work of art.

As you sit there admiring it, however, as likely as not a car will come tear- 30
ing up and stop out on the road. Doors will slam and people will charge down
through the hammock, thrash out into the pool, and enter into a raucous competition to see who can sink down deepest into the heaving sand of the little
springs. To a quiet watcher on the bank the invasion seems a violent assault.
The worst of it is, to the people engaged in the assault it is harmless horseplay
and a lot of fun—an offbeat and stimulating thing to do. So the predicament of
Florida's springs clearly exemplifies the intractability of wilderness preservation when both aesthetic values and opportunities for physical recreation are
involved—which they almost always are.

This dilemma hinders most efforts to save wild places to which the public 31
is admitted. In the case of the springs, their unique value is a fragile loveliness
that depends on their integrity as biologic landscape. They are all attractive for
other reasons, too; and many of the people drawn by these other qualities often
miss the real point completely.

Long before Florida settled up so badly, the springs had begun to suffer. 32
Those located in farmland were used for irrigation. The moonshiners liked the
water for their stills. Springs near towns made superb swimming holes, and
some of them became popular spas, to which people from other parts of the
South came every summer to take the waters. So the wear and tear began long
ago, but more recently it became much worse. Madmen in outboard-powered
boats have raced round and round in the boils, making deserts of the basins.
And into the deepest and most enchanted the scuba divers have gone. They

come from everywhere, by the hundreds, to test their skills in enchanted caves and fountains, and by the mere passing of their countless bodies and the bubbling of their regulators scour and scare to lifelessness some of the best of the spring communities.

33   With most of the Florida rheocrene springs already damaged and some utterly wrecked, any that remain in anything like natural ecological diversity and organization ought to be made inviolate sanctuaries, kept perpetually free of contact with either boats or human bodies. That is tough, because a part of the artistic appreciation of springs is getting into them, putting on a face mask and going down and looking through the airlike water at nuances of light, life, and color never thought of back on the bank. One human quietly flippering about in a spring or spring run does no harm to speak of. But as viewers multiply, even reverent ones, the place begins to wear. So there is really a cruel dilemma to be faced, if even the handful of unspoiled springs is to be saved. And while the trouble reaches a peak in the special case of the springs, it is much the same wherever the complex organized interplay of animals, plants, and their living space is the treasure to be preserved.

34   In listing some reasons for optimism over the state of nature and man in Florida, on favorable development outweighs all the rest. It is not another species on the mend or a new park or preserve or sanctuary established. It is rather a change in the heart of the people. Although original Florida is still undergoing degradation, an assessment of the trends would show the rate of loss being overtaken by the growth of a system of ecologic ethics, by a new public consciousness and conscience. There was a time when "preservationism" was a dirty word, a name for visionary folk whose aim was to keep the world the way the Indians had it. But now the farsighted kinds of people who saved the white birds in 1913 and three decades later generated the Everglades National Park, have multiplied and are influencing the whole political climate for conservation and preservation. In 1972, by a 65 percent majority, Floridians voted to tax themselves for an endangered lands program, set up to purchase outright wild land threatened by development. These changes in the public mood are reflected in government policies as well.

35   The rise of this new stewardship gives heart to opponents of ecologic ruin everywhere and brings promise of better times for man and nature in Florida.

FOCUS ON ECOLOGY

1. How do you respond to Carr's explanation for why manatees should be protected: "because manatees are neat, very neat"? Does the "neatness" of a manatee warrant protection? What reasons might you provide for protecting manatees (or any other species for that matter) other than seeing the animal as "very neat"?

2. Specifically, how does Carr detail the causal relationship between humans and the destruction (or changing) of Florida's wild environments? What role

does recreation play in this relationship? Are there parallels between what Carr says people have done in Florida and what people have done in your region (if you live some place other than Florida)? Explain.

3. What hope does Carr see for Florida? Do you agree with him? Why or why not? Do you see hope in your region? If so, what examples might you offer? If not, why not?

FOCUS ON WRITING

1. What is the relationship between the words *progress* and *growth*? How do you understand the definitions of each of those words? How are those words used in context of one another in conversations about the region in which you live?
2. Who is "Bartram," to whom Carr refers?
3. Why does Carr digress into the story about John Henry and Uncle Goo? What purpose does this digression serve in "Eden Changes"?

FOR DISCUSSION

As a class, consider some of the specific ways that Carr identifies humans as having had an effect on Florida's natural environment. Take some time to consider the possible motivations for such actions. Could some of the damage that was done to Carr's Florida have been avoided? If so, how? If not, why not?

WRITING IN RESPONSE

If Archie Carr had written this essay about your region (assuming that you don't live in Florida), what kinds of things would he address? What animals would he discuss? What geographical characteristics would he describe? If you were to write a similar essay, would you call it "Eden Changes"? Could your region have been described as Eden? In an essay, detail some of the ways that human relationships with that area have altered your own Eden.

DISCUSSING THE ISSUES

1. The readings in this chapter ask us to consider our future in and with nature and the future of nature and environments. For many of the authors in this chapter, issues as far-ranging as economics, science, ethics, and emotions play into how potential futures might unfold. Looking specifically at these four categories—economics, science, ethics, and emotions—address the impact each has on how we think about, plan for, and offer prophecies of what the future might hold for natural environments, for places, for other organisms. After you address as a class how these four categories affect our thinking, select a place in your community and apply these four categories to how

you might think about that place's future. What impact will economics have on the future of that place? How will science affect that place? What ethical considerations must be or might be applied to thinking about the future of that place and whose ethics will likely affect that place's future? And what role will our feelings toward a place play in its future?

2. Does it matter if we consider the future in terms of environment and place, or will environment and place go on, no matter how humans act? That is, does it matter what role we as humans play in the future of this planet, or is our participation in the planet a natural part of its future?

WRITING ABOUT THE ISSUES

Because this is the final series of questions in *Saving Place*, and because in many ways this chapter asks you to consider many of the subjects we have explored in this book, I am not going to offer the same series of three questions I have asked in each previous chapter. Instead, I'm going to ask that you combine the idea of *Research, Personal Experience*, and *Local Context* in a single writing project. I'm going to ask that you take some time to learn about a place that is important to you and to become active part in working to save that place.

No matter where you live in the United States, you will find that some place near you—a park, a beach, an empty lot, a field, a river—is being discussed as a site for change, whether that change be for restoration or development, for growth or protection. Spend some time learning about local issues that call into question the future of a specific place, preferably a place in which you are invested, a place that means something to you, or at minimum, a place with which you are familiar. Learn about this place, its past, its future. What changes have been proposed and why? Who initiated these discussions? Do the proposed changes, in your view, benefit the protection of that place? As you become even more familiar with that place, with the politics of that place, with the discussions of that place's future, write what you have learned about that place. Then, as you develop your own position about the proposed changes, take what you have written and write how you feel about those changes. Use your writing to enter into the public conversations of that place. Get involved. Write an editorial for the local newspaper; help others become aware. Go to public meetings about the future of the place; become vocal and active. If the place is being discussed in terms with which you agree, voice your support. Take sides. Be a part of the places in which you live.

I recognize that in many ways what I'm asking you to do here is hard. But that's OK. Sometimes the things we find hardest to do have the greatest value to us in the long run. I'm asking you to take risks in your writing, to take the chance of being a public voice. That can be scary, even dangerous. But without each of us taking such steps, decisions may be made without the benefit of our voices. To me, that is even more frightening.

Credits

Edward Abbey. "Eco-Defense" from *One Life at a Time, Please* by Edward Abbey. Copyright © 1988 by Edward Abbey. Reprinted by permission of Henry Holt and Company, LLC.

Edward Abbey. "The First Morning" from *Desert Solitaire: A Season in the Wilderness* by Edward Abbey. Reprinted by permission of Don Congdon Associates, Inc. Copyright © 1968 by Edward Abbey, renewed 1996 by Clarke Abbey.

Douglas Adams. "Sifting Through the Embers." From *Last Chance to See* by Douglas Adams and Mark Carwardine. Copyright © 1990 by Serious Productions Ltd. and Mark Carwardine. Illustration copyright © 1991 by Dean Bornstein. Used by permission of Harmony Books, a division of Random House, Inc., and Macmillan, London, UK.

Joe Balaz. "Anyting you kill, You Gada Eat," *Hawaii Review*, 1988. Reprinted by permission of the author.

Rick Bass. "Why I Hunt." Reprinted with permission from the July/August 2001 issue of *Sierra* magazine. © Rick Bass.

Rick Bass. Excerpts from *Winter: Notes from Montana* by Rick Bass. Copyright © 1991 by Rick Bass. Reprinted by permission of Houghton Mifflin Company. All rights reserved.

Wendell Berry. "The Pleasures of Eating" and "Nature as Measure" from *What Are People For?* by Wendell Berry. Copyright © 1990 by Wendell Berry. Reprinted by permission of North Point Press, a division of Farrar, Straus and Giroux, LLC.

Steven Callahan. "To Weave a World." From *Adrift* by Steven Callahan. Copyright © 1986 by Steven Callahan. Reprinted by permission of Houghton Mifflin Company. All rights reserved.

James Campbell. © 2001, "Paddling a Watery Wilderness," by James Campbell. First published in *Audubon* magazine, July–August 2001. Reprinted by permission.

Fritjof Capra. "Ecological Literacy." From *The Web of Life* by Fritjof Capra. Copyright © 1996 by Fritjof Capra. Used by permission of Doubleday, a division of Random House, Inc.

Archie Carr. "Eden Changes" from *A Naturalist in Florida: A Celebration of Eden*, edited by Marjorie Harris Carr. New Haven, CT: Yale University Press, 1994. Reprinted by permission of David Carr, Executor of the Estate of Archie Carr. This essay first appeared in *Born of the Sun: The Official Florida Bicentennial Commemorative Book* (1975).

Rachel Carson. "The Other Road," from *Silent Spring* by Rachel Carson. Copyright © 1962 by Rachel L. Carson, renewed 1990 by Roger Christie. Reprinted by permission of Houghton Mifflin Company. All rights reserved.

Jimmy Carter. "Kilimanjaro" from *An Outdoor Journal: Adventures and Reflections* by Jimmy Carter. Reprinted by permission of the University of Arkansas Press. Copyright © 1994 by Jimmy Carter.

William Cronon. "The Trouble with Wilderness; or, Getting Back to the Wrong Nature" by William Cronon, from *Uncommon Ground*, edited by William Cronon. Copyright © 1995 by William Cronon. Used by permission of W. W. Norton & Company, Inc.

William Cronon. "This Land Is Your Land: Turning to Nature in a Time of Crisis," by William Cronon. © 2002. First published in *Audubon* magazine, January–February 2002. Reprinted by permission.

Art Davidson. From *Minus 148°: The First Winter Ascent of Mt. McKinley* by Art Davidson. Seattle, WA: The Mountaineers Books, 1999. Reprinted by permission of the author. Copyright © 1969, 1986 by Art Davidson.

Annie Dillard. "The Deer at Providencia" from *Teaching a Stone to Talk: Expeditions and Encounters* by Annie Dillard. Copyright © 1982 by Annie Dillard. Reprinted by permission of HarperCollins Publishers Inc.

Daniel Duane. Excerpt from *Caught Inside* by Daniel Duane. Copyright © 1996 by Daniel Duane. Reprinted by permission of North Point Press, a division of Farrar, Straus and Giroux, LLC.

Alan Thein Durning. "The Conundrum of Consumption" from *How Much Is Enough?: The Consumer Society and the Future of the Earth* by Alan Durning. Copyright © 1992 by Worldwatch Institute. Used by permission of W. W. Norton & Company, Inc.

Cynthia Dusel-Bacon. "Come Quick! I'm Being Eaten by a Bear" from *Killer Bears* by Mike Cramond. Copyright © 1981 by Mike Cramond. Reprinted by permission of The Lyons Press, an imprint of Globe Pequot.

Paul R. Ehrlich and Anne H. Ehrlich. "Food: The Ultimate Resource" from *The Population Explosion* by Paul R. Ehrlich and Anne H. Ehrlich. Copyright © 1990 by Paul R. Ehrlich and Anne H. Ehrlich. Reprinted by permission of William Morris Agency, Inc. on behalf of the Authors.

Mark Foo. "Occurrence at Waimea Bay." Copyright © Sharlyn Foo, from *The Big Drop!*, edited by John Long and Hai-Van K. Sponholz. Falcon Books, 1999. Used by permission of Falcon Books, a division of Globe Pequot Press. First appeared in *Surfing*, 1985.

Stephen Gorman. © 2001, "Trekking Tropical Trails," by Stephen Gorman. First published in *Audubon* magazine, July–August 2001. Reprinted by permission.

Lorian Hemingway. "The Young Woman and the Sea" from *Uncommon Waters: Women Write about Fishing*, edited by Holly Morris. Seal Press, 1991.